W9-BKD-355

Human Resource
Selection

Robert D. Gatewood
University of Georgia

Hubert S. Feild
Auburn University

THE DRYDEN PRESS
Chicago   New York   Philadelphia   San Francisco   Montreal   Toronto   London   Sydney
Tokyo   Mexico City   Rio de Janeiro   Madrid

Acquisitions Editor: Joan Resler
Project Editor: Jan Doty
Design Director: Alan Wendt
Production Supervisor: Diane Tenzi
Director of Editing, Design, and Production: Jane Perkins

Text and Cover Designer: Margery Dole
Copy Editor: Charlene Posner
Compositor: Donnelley Rocappi
Text Type: 10½/12 Goudy Old Style

Library of Congress Cataloging-in-Publication Data

Gatewood, Robert D.
    Human resource selection.

    Includes index.
    1. Employee selection. I. Feild, Hubert S.
II. Title.
HF5549.5.S38G37   1987   658.3'112   86-2661
ISBN 0-03-063962-X

Printed in the United States of America
789-038-98765432

Copyright 1987 CBS COLLEGE PUBLISHING
All rights reserved

Address orders:
383 Madison Avenue
New York, NY 10017

Address editorial correspondence:
One Salt Creek Lane
Hinsdale, IL 60521

CBS COLLEGE PUBLISHING
The Dryden Press
Holt, Rinehart and Winston
Saunders College Publishing

Dedication

Each night before we go to bed, our reader,
We whisper a little prayer for you, our reader,
And tell all the stars above
"This book is dedicated to the ones we love. . . ."

The Duke of Earl, and
especially *our families*
Betsy, Jennifer, and Nat Gatewood
Claire and Taylor Feild

The Dryden Press
Series in Management

Arthur G. Bedeian, Consulting Editor

Albanese and Van Fleet
**Organizational Behavior:
A Managerial Viewpoint**

Bedeian
Management

Bedeian
**Organizations: Theory and Analysis,
Text and Cases**
Second Edition

Boone and Kurtz
Contemporary Business
Fifth Edition

Bowman and Branchaw
**Business Communication:
From Process to Product**

Bowman and Branchaw
Business Report Writing

Chen and McGarrah
**Productivity Management:
Text and Cases**

Compaine and Litro
Business: An Introduction

Cullinan
**Business English for Industry
and the Professions**

Gaither
**Production and Operations
Management: A Problem-Solving and
Decision-Making Approach**
Third Edition

Gatewood and Feild
Human Resource Selection

Greenhaus
Career Management

Higgins
**Strategy: Formulation,
Implementation, and Control**

Higgins and Vincze
**Strategic Management and
Organizational Policy: Text and Cases**
Third Edition

Hills
Compensation Decision Making

Hodgetts
Modern Human Relations at Work
Third Edition

Holley and Jennings
**Personnel/Human Resource
Management: Contributions
and Activities**
Second Edition

Holley and Jennings
The Labor Relations Process
Second Edition

Huseman, Lahiff, Penrose, and Hatfield
**Business Communication:
Strategies and Skills**
Second Edition

Huseman, Lahiff, and Penrose
**Readings and Applications in
Business Communication**
Second Edition

Jauch, Coltrin, Bedeian, and Glueck
**The Managerial Experience: Cases,
Exercises, and Readings**
Fourth Edition

Kuehl and Lambing
**Small Business: Planning
and Management**

Lee
Introduction to Management Science

Miner
Theories of Organizational Behavior

Miner
**Theories of Organizational
Structure and Process**

Paine and Anderson
Strategic Management

Paine and Naumes
**Organizational Strategy and Policy:
Text and Cases**
Third Edition

Ray and Eison
Supervision

Robinson
**International Business Management:
A Guide to Decision Making**
Second Edition

Robinson
**The Internationalization of Business:
An Introduction**

Smith
**Management Systems: Analyses
and Applications**

Stone
Understanding Personnel Management

Tombari
**Business and Society: Strategies for the
Environment and Public Policy**

Varner
Contemporary Business Report Writing

Weekly and Aggarwal
**International Business: Operating in
the Global Economy**

Zikmund
Business Research Methods

P R E F A C E

All of us have been involved in the selection program of an organization at one time or another. We have either been an applicant to a school or a business; or we have been on the other side, one of the organization members making decisions about applicants. From either perspective, a common reaction to selection is uneasiness and uncertainty. How many times have we heard an applicant say something like, "I wonder what he was looking for?" or an organization decision maker mutter, "How can I tell the difference among these people? I hope I made the right choice."

The procedure of selection is familiar to most of us. We all know that it is necessary to collect information from applicants about themselves. Such devices as applications, interviews, and various kinds of tests are used for this purpose. We also know that this information is then used to make comparisons among applicants in the hopes of identifying strong future performers. Even so, the question often arises, "If selection procedures are so commonly known, why do uneasiness and uncertainty still occur?"

We think there are two reasons: (a) there are some inherent features of selection in evaluating applicants and predicting future performance that cannot be totally controlled, and (b) even though selection procedures are well known, the more important parts of selection, such as what characteristics of applicants should be examined, which devices should be used to gather information, and how information should be combined to identify desirable applicants, are not well understood. Understanding the variables in each of these aspects is critical to building an effective selection program and, to a lesser extent, being comfortable with its operation. We think of these aspects as the technical components of selection—technical in the sense that psychometric procedures, statistical analyses, the conceptual framework of selection, the findings of previous empirical research, and the various legal constraints all contribute to a scientific understanding of the field.

It is the purpose of this book to present this technical information in a manner that will be useful and, we hope, interesting to those who are or will be involved in the development and implementation of a selection program for an organization. In our writing, we summarized the most important research in selection with an emphasis on the conclusions and only minimal attention to the research steps and procedures. We then incorporated these results into recommendations for the actual development of a selection program. The book, therefore, is intended to be both generally informative and directly useful to those working in selection. The text is divided into the following six sections which systematically present the technical aspects of selection.

Part I: *An Overview of Human Resource Selection.* This section presents the nature of selection programs and their legal context. Chapter 1 describes the purpose of selection—the identification of high-performing individuals—and outlines the major steps that must be taken to develop an effective selection program, concluding with the limitations that must be addressed in these programs. Chapter 2 presents the legal constraints that must be considered in selection by discussing laws, federal guidelines, court cases, and methods used to determine discrimination.

Part II: *Foundations of Measurement for Human Resource Selection.* These chapters treat the psychometric measurement concepts that are basic to selection. Chapter 3 introduces the topic of measurement and discusses its definition and nature. Chapter 4 is devoted entirely to the importance of reliability and methods of estimating reliability. Chapter 5 discusses types of validity and focuses on the interpretation and meaning of empirical validation.

Part III: *Job Analysis in Human Resource Selection.* This section describes the first steps in developing a selection program. Chapter 6 gives an overview of job analysis in selection and the implementation of a job analysis program in an organization. Chapter 7 thoroughly describes the most common job analysis methods and how they are used. Chapter 8 discusses the identification of worker knowledge, skills, abilities, and other employee specifications using the various job analysis methods. The emphasis is on how these data are translated into selection instruments.

Part IV: *Predictors of Job Performance.* This section, composed of six chapters, is the longest. Each chapter discusses a different major selection instrument. The discussion reviews the research about the validity of the instrument and treats its appropriate construction and use.

Part V: *Criteria Measures.* This section presents only one topic. Chapter 15 is an overview of the essential characteristics and methods of measuring work performance for use as criterion data in validation. This is a critical component in developing a complete selection program.

Part VI: *Summary.* Chapter 16 presents the major points that should be addressed in developing a selection program or evaluating an existing one. These points are put in the form of checklist questions that should be answered about the selection program of interest. The questions are keyed to information presented in the previous chapters.

ACKNOWLEDGMENTS

One of the nicest aspects of writing a book is that it presents a formal opportunity for the authors to thank individuals who have had positive influences on both them and their text.

Robert Gatewood would like to thank two couples for long-term contributions. Maurice and Sophie Gatewood, my parents, have, of course, guided me from the start. However, their actions during my teens and early twenties were especially necessary. Robert and Evelyn Perloff directed most of my graduate and early professional activities. From them I learned not only technical knowledge but also professional and ethical behavior that has been even more lasting.

Hubert Feild would like to thank Hubert and Bernice Feild, my parents. Their love, support, and sacrifice will always be remembered. Bob Teare and Bill Owens served as important role models early in my career. Their work with me will always be appreciated. Finally, I am indebted to Art Bedeian, Bill Giles, Bill Holley, and Kevin Mossholder for their encouragement, and to Achilles Armenakis for his support and our "miles of therapy" through the cemetery. All of these individuals have meant so much to me.

Several people have been instrumental in the writing of this text. James Breaugh and Lyle Schoenfeldt carefully read early versions of the manuscript and provided detailed comments that shaped the final product. Jerald Greenberg, Marvin Katzman, Mary Lewis, Betty Jo Licata, Stephan Schuster, and Brian Steffy were also kind enough to review the manuscript, sometimes suffering through nonsequential chapters. Their frank and direct remarks helped us to correct some of the inconsistencies and omissions that were present in early stages. Melanie Barber, Billie Najour, Nancy Parks, and Karen Turner had the patience and skill to prepare the manuscript and many of the figures. They managed to take several rough drafts and transform them into a polished document. Neal Shirley and Macon Lee of the Academic Information Systems division of IBM provided equipment on which much of the manuscript was written. Their assistance is most appreciated.

The people at The Dryden Press were, of course, the main force behind this effort. Art Bedeian got us started on the project and provided useful advice throughout the time-consuming process. Joan Resler, Teresa Chartos, Jan Doty, and Charlene Posner were unlucky enough to be involved in the day-to-day drudgery and administration of review, revision, and production. Their professional competence and humor made our work much, much easier. To all of the above individuals, we simply say "Thank you."

Robert D. Gatewood
Athens, Georgia

Hubert S. Feild
Auburn, Alabama

September 1986

Robert D. Gatewood

Robert Gatewood received his Ph.D. in industrial psychology from Purdue University and is currently an Associate Professor of Management at the University of Georgia. Before that he worked for IBM, the American Institutes for Research, and the University of Pittsburgh. In addition he has served as the Visiting Professor of Business at the Netherlands School of Business in Breukelen, the Netherlands. His major areas of professional interest are in human resource selection and psychometric measurement. He has presented papers at the national meetings of the Academy of Management and the American Psychological Association and has published articles in the *Journal of Applied Psychology, Personnel Psychology, Human Resource Planning, The Personnel Administrator,* and the *Personnel Journal.*

He is currently serving as a co-principal investigator on a two-year NSF funded grant entitled "Impact of Human Resource Management on Productivity and Minority Employment." The major thrust of the grant is to develop a forecasting simulation model useful for human resource managers.

Professor Gatewood has done consulting for several organizations, including PPG Industries, Westinghouse, Gulf Power Company, the Department of Transportation, and the Savings and Loan Institute.

Hubert S. Feild

Hubert S. Feild is Alumni Professor of Management in the Department of Management at Auburn University. He has published numerous journal articles covering topics such as performance appraisal, personnel research methods, and legal issues in personnel management. Recently, he published the book *Jurors: A Study in Psychology and Law.* He has served as a reviewer for such journals as *Personnel Psychology, Journal of Personality and Social Psychology, Law and Human Behavior, Journal of Management,* and *Human Relations.* In addition, he has served as a reviewer of research proposals for the National Science Foundation and the National Institutes of Mental Health.

His consulting activities have involved more than 30 profit and not-for-profit organizations, including PPG Industries, West Point Pepperell, SONY, U.S. Commission on Civil Rights, and the Merit Systems Protection Board.

Professor Feild received his B.S. degree in management and M.S. in economics from Mississippi State University. He received his Ph.D. in industrial psychology from the University of Georgia where he worked as a research associate for the Institute of Behavioral Research and the Paraprofessional Utilization Project. Most recently, he served as Research Fellow with the Southeastern Center for Electrical Engineering Education (St. Cloud, Florida). For the Department of Management at Auburn, he also serves as Director of Graduate Programs in Management.

CONTENTS

■ PART ONE
An Overview
of Human
Resource
Selection
1

CHAPTER 1
An Overview of Selection   3

Selection As Part of P/HRM   5
Selection and Training   5
Selection and Recruitment   5
Steps in the Selection Process   9
Selection Program Development Steps   11
Steps to Process Applicants   14
Issues in the Development of Selection
   Programs   17
Small Sample of Applicant Behavior   18
*Measurement of Jobs, Individuals, and Work
   Performance*   18
Other Factors Affecting Work Performance   20
Plan of This Book   20

CHAPTER 2
Legal Issues in Selection   23

Federal Regulation   24
Regulatory Model   24
EEO Laws and Executive Orders   26
Discrimination: Definition and Evidence   30
Discrimination Defined   30

xi

Measurement   32
The Uniform Guidelines on Employee
  Selection Procedures   35
Selection Court Cases   38
EEO Considerations in Selection   46
Basis of Discrimination   46
Evidence of Discrimination   46
Options of the Organization   47

■ PART TWO   **CHAPTER 3**
Foundations   **Human Resource Measurement in**
of   **Selection**   51
Measurement
for Human   Fundamentals of Measurement: An Overview   51
Resource   *The Role of Measurement in Human Resource*
Selection   *Selection*   51
49   *Measures Used in Human Resource Selection*   64
                    Finding and Constructing Selection Measures   68
                    Locating Existing Selection Measures   70
                    Constructing New Selection Measures   74
                    Interpreting Scores on Selection Measures   81
                    Using Norms   81
                    Using Percentiles and Standard Scores   82

                    CHAPTER 4
                    Reliability of Selection Measures   87

                    What Is Meant by Reliability?   87
                    A Definition of Reliability   89
                    Errors of Measurement   89
                    Methods of Estimating Reliability   94
                    Test-Retest Reliability Estimates   96
                    Parallel or Equivalent Forms of Reliability
                      Estimates   100
                    Internal Consistency Reliability Estimates   102
                    Interpreting Reliability Coefficients   107
                    What Does a Reliability Coefficient Mean?   107
                    How High Should a Reliability Coefficient Be? 110
                    Factors Influencing the Reliability of a Measure 111
                    Standard Error of Measurement   114
                    Evaluating Reliability Coefficients   116

                    CHAPTER 5
                    Validity of Selection Measures   119

                    An Overview of Validity   119
                    Validity: A Definition   119
                    The Relation Between Reliability and Validity 120
                    Types of Validity Strategies   121

Criterion-Related Validity Strategies   121
Concurrent Validity   121
Predictive Validity   126
Content Validity Strategy   128
Major Characteristics of a Content Valid
    Measure   129
Some Examples of Content Validation   131
Inappropriateness of Content Validation   135
Content Versus Criterion-Related Validity: Some
    Requirements   137
Construct Validity Strategy   139
Empirical Considerations in Criterion-Related
    Validity Strategies   140
Correlation   140
Prediction   144
Factors Affecting the Size of Validity Coefficients   151
Minimum Validity of a Selection Measure   158
Selection Measure Utility   161
Broader Perspectives of Validity   161
Synthetic Validity   162
Validity Generalization   164

■ PART
THREE
Job Analysis
in Human
Resource
Selection
169

CHAPTER 6
Preparing for Job Analysis: An Overview   171

Role of Job Analysis in Human Resource
    Selection   171
A Definition and Model   171
Growth in Job Analysis   172
Legal Issues in Job Analysis   174
Summary   176
Implementation of a Job Analysis   177
Organizing for a Job Analysis   177
Choosing Jobs to Be Studied   179
Reviewing the Relevant Literature   182
Selecting Job Agents   183

CHAPTER 7
Applying Job Analysis Techniques   191

Collecting Job Information   191
A Categorization of Job Analysis Methods   193
A Survey of Job Analysis Methods   193
The Job Analysis Interview   194
Description   194
An Example   196
Guidelines for Use   199
Limitations of the Job Analysis Interview   201
The Job Analysis Questionnaire   202
Description   202

The Task Analysis Inventory   202
The Position Analysis Questionnaire (PAQ)   209
Description   209
Application   211
Advantages and Disadvantages   212
Supplementary Methods for Collecting Job
    Information   214
Collection of Job Information: A Comparison
    of Methods   215
Potential Usefulness of Methods   216
Use of Multiple Job Analysis Methods   221

APPENDIX TO CHAPTER 7
Some Additional Job Analysis Techniques   225

CHAPTER 8
Incorporating Job Analysis Results in
Selection Measures   247

Identification of Employee Specifications   248
Determination of Employee Specifications: Task-
    Analysis Approach   249
Determination of Employee Specifications: PAQ
    Approach   263
Incorporation of Employee Specifications in
    Selection Instruments   265
Development of a Selection Plan: Task-Analysis
    Approach   266
Development of a Selection Plan: PAQ Approach   270

CHAPTER 9
Application Forms and Reference Checks   277

Application Forms   277
Nature and Role of Application Forms in
    Selection   277
Legal Implications of Application Forms   278
Selecting Application Form Content   280
Developing and Revising Application Forms   289
Accuracy of Application Form Data   291
Using Application Forms in Human Resource
    Selection   292
Reference Checks   298
The Role of Reference Checks in Selection   298
Types of Reference Information Collected   298
Methods of Collecting Reference Data   299
Usefulness of Reference Data   303
Legal Issues in Using Reference Checks   305

■ **PART FOUR**
Predictors of
Job
Performance
275

CHAPTER 10
Weighted Application Blanks and Biographical Data   313

Weighted Application Blanks   313
*The Need for Systematic Scoring of Application
  Forms*   313
The Nature of the Weighted Application Blank   314
*The Development of Weighted Application
  Blanks*   315
Using WABs in Human Resource Selection   322
Biographical Data   326
What Are Biographical Data?   326
The Development of a Biodata Questionnaire   331
*The Validity of Biodata in Human Resource
  Selection*   337

CHAPTER 11
The Selection Interview   347

Uses of the Interview in Selection   348
Selling the Applicant on the Job   348
Measuring Applicant KSAs   350
Selection Evaluation by an Organization Member   351
Interviewer Decision Making   353
Explanations of Interviewer Decision Making   356
Pre-interview Factors   356
Ongoing Interview Factors   358
Attempts to Improve the Interview   359
Training   359
Interview Panels   363
Discrimination and the Interview   363
Court Cases   363
Some Common Practices   365
Recommendations for Interview Use   366
Narrow the Scope of the Interview   366
Limit Use of Pre-Interview Data   369
The Semi-Structured Format   370
Use Job-Related Questions   371
Multiple Questions for Each KSA   375
The Formal Scoring Format   376
Use An Interview Panel   377
Training the Interviewer   379

CHAPTER 12
Ability Tests   383

History of Ability Tests in Selection   383
Definition of Ability Test   384

Mental Ability Tests 385
History 386
What is Measured 387
The Wonderlic Personnel Test 387
The Wechsler Adult Intelligence Scale 389
Verbal Subtests 389
Performance Subtests 390
General Comments About Mental Ability Tests 391
Mechanical Ability Tests 391
Bennett Mechanical Comprehension Test 392
MacQuarrie Test for Mechanical Ability 393
Clerical Ability 394
The Minnesota Clerical Test 395
Sensory Abilities 396
Vision 396
Hearing 397
Honesty Testing 397
Polygraph Testing 398
Paper-and-Pencil Honesty Tests 400
The Validity of Ability Tests 401
The Validity of Occupational Aptitude Tests 401
Validity Generalization Studies 404
Ability Tests and Discrimination 406
Differential Validity 407
Adverse Impact 408
Conclusions 411
Using Ability Tests in Selection 412
Review Reliability Data 413
Review Validity Data 414
CHAPTER 13
Personality Assessment 419

Definition and Use of Personality in
  Selection 420
Arguments for Use in Selection 420
Evidence against Use in Selection 421
Personality Traits 422
Interaction of Personality Traits and Situations 425
Personality Measurement Methods 427
Inventories in Personality Measurement 427
The Interview in Personality Measurement 437
*Behavioral Assessment in Personality
  Measurement* 442
Factors in the Appropriate Use of Personality
  Data 444
Personality Traits in Terms of Job Behaviors 444
Importance of Situational Factors 446
Appropriate Measuring Device 447

CHAPTER 14
Performance Tests and Assessment
Centers   **451**

Performance Tests   451
Differences from Other Selection Devices   451
Limitations   453
Consistency of Behavior   454
Examples of Performance Tests   455
Development of Performance Tests   458
An Example of Developmental Steps   466
The Effectiveness of Performance Tests   469
Assessment Centers   471
The History of Assessment Centers   471
Assessment Centers in Industry   472
Assessment Center Exercises   473
The Training of Assessors   479
The Effectiveness of Assessment Centers   484

■ **PART FIVE**   **CHAPTER 15**
Criteria   **Measurement of Worker Performance**   **491**
Measures
489   Types of Job Performance Measures   492
                         Production Data   492
                         Personnel Data   494
                         Training Proficiency   498
                         Judgmental Data   500
                         Characteristics of Selection Criteria Measures 506
                         Individualization   506
                         Controllability   507
                         Relevance   508
                         Measurability   508
                         Reliability   509
                         Differentiation   509
                         Practicality   510
                         No Contamination   510
                         Specificity for Selection   510
                         Concluding Comments   511
                         Single vs. Multiple Criteria   511
                         When to Use Each   512
                         Forming the Single Measure   513
                         Work Measurement and EEO Issues   514
                         Uniform Guidelines   514
                         Court Decisions   516

■ **PART SIX**   **CHAPTER 16**
Summary   **The Human Resource Selection Audit**   **523**
521

■ **INDEX**
532

PART ONE

An Overview of

Human Resource

Selection

Recent management practices have emphasized the effective use of the employees in an organization. We are all familiar with programs that are intended to allow employees to use their talents fully in their work. Central to this approach is the assumption that employees and jobs are suitably matched. If they are not well matched, practices that highlight employees' activities will be less successful than desired. Selection is critical to a suitable match because it is the process that initially assigns individuals to specific jobs. Optimally, this placement is done on the basis of similarity between the individual's talents and the job's demands. The basic viewpoint of this book is that a properly designed selection program will considerably increase the probability of achieving a good match. To do this properly requires the use of specialized information by those involved. As you probably have guessed, the purpose of this book is to present this information.

Unless this is the first book you have read, you have also probably guessed that this first section will present a general treatment of selection. (The word *Overview* in the section title also might have given a hint.) We know it's not nice to disappoint readers early in a book (that usually happens later), so a general treatment is what is coming. After reading the two chapters in this section you should understand these four specific topics:

1. The interaction of selection with other human resource functions, especially recruitment and training.

2. The steps to be taken in developing a useful selection program.

3. The inherent difficulties and constraints of selection that must be addressed in developing a program.

4. The specific legal demands upon selection. These take the form of laws, executive orders, court decisions, and guidelines for selection practices.

C H A P T E R

1

An Overview

of Selection

Definition of Selection

Human resource selection is one area within the field of Personnel/Human Resource Management (P/HRM). Selection is critical for the management of organizations because it "provides the very essence of organizations — their human resources."[1] The definition of human resource selection that we use in this text reflects the many factors that operate in this area.

> **Selection** is the process of collecting and evaluating information about an individual in order to extend an offer of employment. Such employment could be either a first position for a new employee or a different position for an existing employee. The selection process is performed under legal and environmental constraints to protect the future interests of the organization and the individual.

This definition of selection is more inclusive than traditional ones that typically have been phrased as the process of choosing qualified individuals to fill positions in the organization. We will now amplify the basic parts of this definition.

From the perspective of personnel specialists much work must take place before an individual can be selected from a pool of applicants. Actually the "choosing" is the last step in the selection process. The steps that take place before this decision focus on gathering useful information about the nature of the job under consideration, the major aspects of performance on the job, the worker's knowledge/skills/abilities (KSAs) necessary to do the job, and how these KSAs might be identified in people before they actually work on the job. As in other management decisions, the better the information used in making the selection decision the greater are the chances that the decision will be correct.

Selection V. Hiring   We do not include all hiring practices that occur in organizations in the term selection, as used in this book. The first sentence of our definition mentions ". . . collecting and evaluating information about an individual." Both actions are important to selection. They refer to obtaining information primarily about the skills/abilities of the applicant and then comparing this information to the requirements for performing the job successfully. If the comparison is favorable, usually an employment offer follows. For various reasons, employment offers are at times extended by an organization without completing these two actions. We refer to this as **hiring** rather than selection.

Hiring often occurs, for example, when an organization desperately needs individuals to fill unskilled or semiskilled positions. This has most commonly happened in manufacturing, textile, food processing, and some service organizations with high turnover and many positions. For one reason or another, the organization has a need to fill positions within a very short period of time. As a result little or no evaluation is done of the applicant's skills/abilities. Availability is the critical variable. Another form of hiring occurs when a job offer is made because of the applicant's connection to the organization. The applicant is either a relative or a friend of an organization member or client and consequently no evaluation of other characteristics is completed. Obviously the assumption made is that being affiliated with the organization is adequate for successful job performance. This is not consistent with our concept of selection.

Factors Affecting Selection   From an organization's viewpoint, the selection decision is ideally made in circumstances in which the organization has a great deal of influence or control over the number of applicants that seek the job, the information that can be gathered from these applicants, and the decision rules used by the organization in evaluating this information. However, as for so much else, the world is not perfect for selection. For example, there are great fluctuations in the number of applicants, frequently due to general economic or educational conditions over which the organization has little control. There are also numerous federal and state laws and administrative rulings that restrict the information that can be gathered from applicants and the way this information can be evaluated. Equal Employment Opportunity laws and guidelines regarding discrimination in selection are a good example.

There is also a growing realization that the usefulness of the selection decision should be viewed in terms of effects over time. One factor frequently mentioned in this connection is the match of the individual's talents and needs with the organization's talent demands and job characteristics.[2] It is generally recognized that the interests of both parties must be treated in the selection process or the result will be less than optimal. Rapid and costly turnover, lower performance levels, and friction between an employee and the organization are among the results of a mismatch of interests.[3]

Now that you have a better understanding of what is meant by selection our next task is to provide a clear overview of the various parts of this subject. To do this the first chapter of a textbook frequently follows one of two patterns: it either traces the history of the subject matter back to the Greeks, Romans, and Egyptians; or it elaborates on how the subject relates to all that is important and how the subject must be treated for the correct ordering of the universe. We could only trace selection back to the Chinese, somewhere around 200 B.C. That reached only the Romans. Falling short of the Greeks and Egyptians, we had to adopt the second pattern for this chapter. Therefore, the following sections will describe how selection relates to other P/HRM activities, what personnel specialists must do to develop an effective selection program, and, finally, what problems inhere in the selection process that the specialist must deal with. We know you will be amazed. We hope you will gain a better understanding of the complexity of this field and the technical knowledge it requires. In the meantime, we will dig farther into history. Plato's *Republic* seems like a good prospect.

Selection as Part of P/HRM

Selection and Training

Selection, as we have described it, has a major interaction with the other P/HRM areas, as is shown in Exhibit 1.1. The work skills and other personal characteristics of those who are hired obviously interact with training, compensation, and career movement systems. For example, training is designed to teach necessary job skills and abilities to those individuals who have accepted a job offer as a result of the selection process. The content, length, and nature of training are affected by the level of skills and abilities of the individuals selected. If these skills and abilities are well developed for the job, then minimal training should suffice. If necessary job skills and abilities are low, then training should be more extensive. Career development and movement systems are similarly related to selection. Compensation interacts in the level and method of payment offered to the selected individual.

Selection and Recruitment

Selection, however, is more closely related to recruitment than it is to these other P/HRM areas. The reason is that recruitment and selection are both

6

Exhibit 1.1 Major Human Resource Management Systems in Organizations

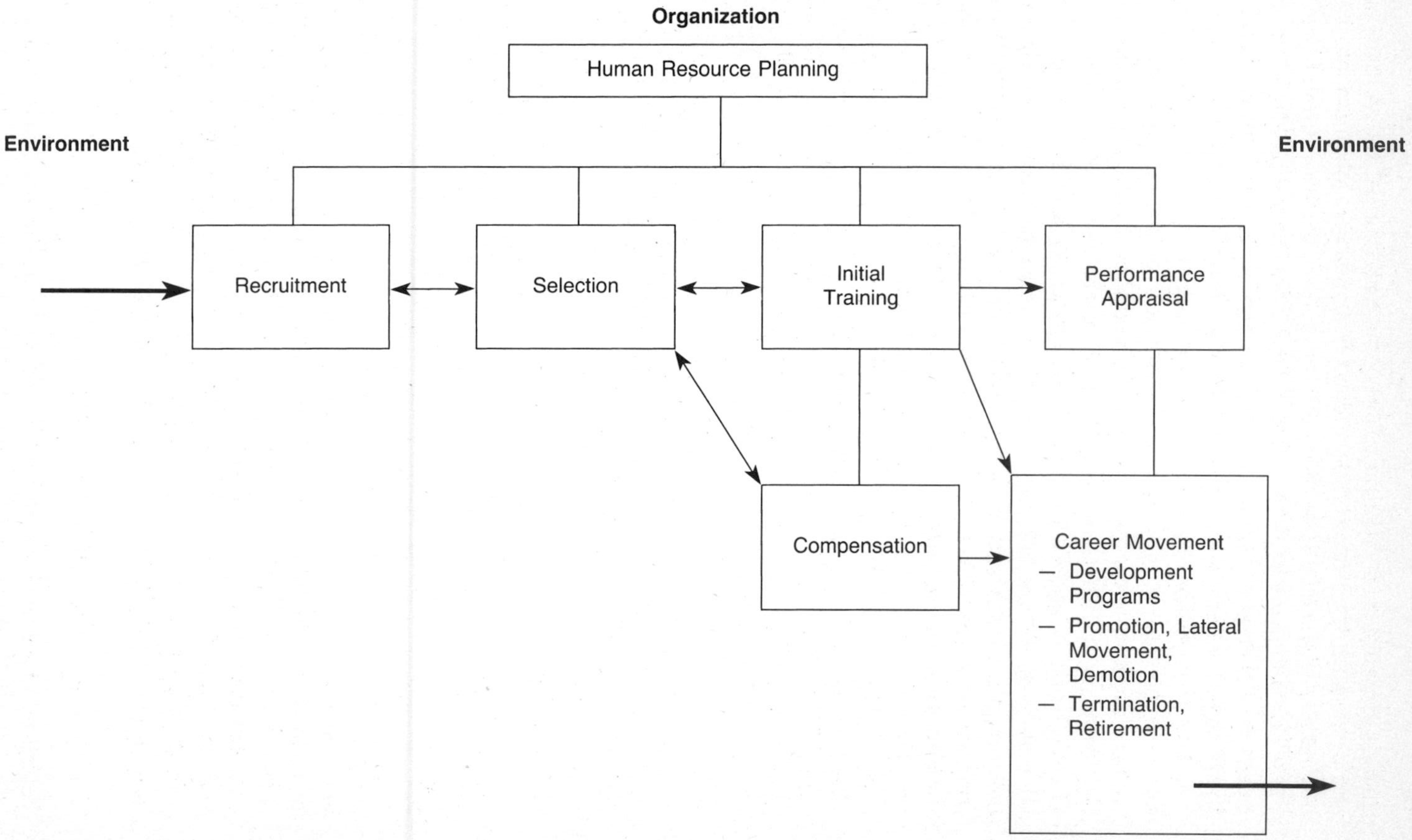

Organization

Environment

Environment

Human Resource Planning

Recruitment

Selection

Initial Training

Performance Appraisal

Compensation

Career Movement

- Development Programs
- Promotion, Lateral Movement, Demotion
- Termination, Retirement

concerned with processing individuals to place them in jobs. Other P/HRM areas treat individuals after they have been placed. Recruitment is the P/HRM area that seeks and obtains potential job candidates in sufficient numbers and quality that the organization can select the most appropriate people to fill its job needs.[4] Although a complete treatment of recruitment is beyond the scope of this book, we will summarize some of its major characteristics to indicate its critical importance to selection.

There are two general forms of recruitment, external and internal. As the terms imply, *external recruitment* is of potential workers who are currently not members of the organization, and *internal recruitment* is of those who are current members. Selection for entry level positions depends upon external recruitment. Selection for higher positions often involves candidates from both types of recruitment. However, it is fairly common for organizations to state that selection for higher level positions should, if possible, be made only from internal applicants. This is thought to motivate employees and provide career mobility for all organization members.

External Recruitment   External recruitment is one of the main ways of bringing into the organization individuals who have new skills/abilities and different ways of approaching job tasks. Of course, the negative side of this policy is that these individuals are unfamiliar with the organization's policies, work methods, and performance standards. Because applicants produced by external recruiting methods are new to the organization, little or nothing is known of their job related skills/abilities. The selection program must elicit all such information. The major methods of external recruitment are:

College and Secondary Recruiting—the organization sends professional recruiters to campuses.

Advertising—brief messages of job openings are placed in selected media.

Walk-ins—unsolicited individuals initiate the contact with the organization.

Employment Agencies—names are sought from public and private organizations that maintain lists of individuals seeking jobs. Usually these agencies have records of the general employment skills/abilities of applicants.

Associations and Unions—many occupations have state, regional, or national associations that hold meetings and represent the interest of the occupation. Such associations frequently have job placement units.

Employee Referral Programs—a word of mouth recruitment technique in which present employees let it be known to friends and acquaintances that positions are open. A formal program provides to the current employees both written information about the job and also evaluations of the individuals whom they recommended.

Internal Recruitment   Internal recruitment, in contrast, uses only two methods: job posting and review of internal personnel records. Job posting is a formal method of notifying members of the organization about job openings and the proper method of applying for these openings. Most often information about the job such as title, job activities, and necessary characteristics of applicants are printed and posted on bulletin boards or published in flyers and company newsletters. Employees who feel they are qualified are encouraged to apply for the position. Such applicants are then processed through the selection program.

Review of internal personnel records is the process in which an organization tries to identify a few employees who are thought to be qualified for another job. Data banks called "talent banks" or "succession banks" are kept for this purpose. These are data files in which information such as performance evaluation, academic and training programs completed, or assessment center evaluations for each employee are kept.

Purposes of Recruitment   In terms of human resource selection, recruitment has three major purposes:

1. To increase the pool of job applicants with minimum cost

2. To meet the organization's legal and social obligations regarding the demographic composition of its workforce

3. To help increase the success rate of the selection process by reducing the number of applicants who are either poorly qualified or have the wrong skills

Concerning increasing the pool of job applicants, it has been demonstrated that the value of selection to the organization increases as the pool of qualified applicants grows. Essentially a larger pool means that there are more very well qualified applicants for the same number of positions. An effective selection program can identify these well-qualified individuals and use them to fill the openings. If the recruitment program produces a small number of applicants relative to the number of available positions, the situation approaches what we have referred to as hiring rather than selection.

We will elaborate in the next chapter the various laws and directives that focus on eliminating discrimination that is due to non–job related worker characteristics. As we shall see, an organization's compliance with such laws and directives is often determined by the demographic characteristics of those selected. However, the demographic characteristics of those hired are directly related to the characteristics of the applicant pool. If the recruitment program does not provide a mixed set of applicants, it is unlikely that the selection program will produce a demographically balanced set of hirees.

The third purpose of recruitment refers to the costs of selection. Processing applicants can be very expensive. Even the initial steps of the selection program require staff time, materials, and physical facilities. If the recruitment program produces applicants who do not match the requirements of the open positions, the result can be disastrous. The money spent on evaluating unsuitable candidates is totally wasted. Moreover, the extra time needed for looking further is an extra cost to the organization. There is simply no justification for sloppy recruiting given the methodology available today.

Realistic Recruitment   A related problem is recruiting individuals in such a way as to communicate an unrealistic concept of the job and the organization. This frequently happens to some degree in most recruitment. Traditionally, emphasis is given to the most favorable parts of employment. Experts now think that it is unproductive to create false expectations in the applicant.[5] Once selected, some individuals find the differences between their expectations and the actual job are unpleasantly large. Such discrepancies can cause a lack of commitment to the organization and rapid job turnover.[6] Obviously, in such cases the whole cost of selection must be repeated as other applicants are processed. In place of such recruitment activities, John Wanous recommends "Realistic Job Preview (RJP)."[7] In realistic recruitment activities the potential hires are shown the negative aspects of the job as well as the positive. For example, Southern New England Telephone made a film for potential operators that made clear that the work was closely supervised, repetitive, and sometimes required dealing with rude or unpleasant behavior from customers. Such information led to a self-selection process whereby those candidates who regarded these job aspects negatively removed themselves from further consideration by the organization. Those that remained made up a recruitment pool of individuals for selection with fairly accurate expectations of job demands and characteristics.[8] This use of realistic recruitment clearly underscores the close link between recruitment and selection and how the manner in which applicants are attracted to and informed about the organization can have a direct effect on the selection system.

Steps in the Selection Process

We have referred to the steps in the selection system or process. The question that naturally arises is "What specifically are these steps?" We will discuss them from two points of view: (a) Those steps that are implemented by the organization to process applicants, i.e., the procedures used to gather the information about applicants that is used in deciding to whom to offer a job, and (b) those steps necessary to develop the programs that collect information from the applicants (see Exhibit 1.2). These latter steps are the activities that personnel specialists undertake to gather the data about jobs, job performance, and workers' KSAs that we previously said was essential for

Exhibit 1.2 *Steps in the Development of Selection Programs*

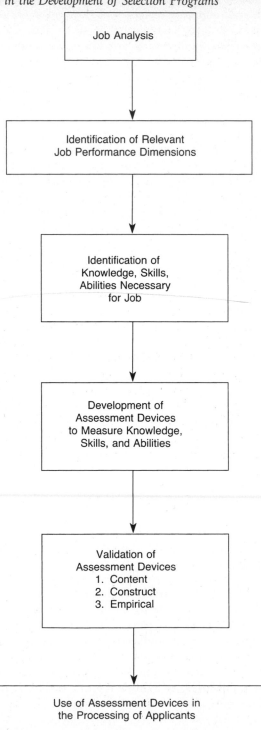

making the selection decision. This book will concentrate mainly on the steps necessary to develop the selection process, presenting issues and methods that are useful for the work of personnel specialists. We will also address the steps for processing applicants through a discussion of the nature and use of the instruments that are most often used by organizations to gather information about applicants. The next sections will briefly discuss each of these two parts of the selection process.

Selection Program Development Steps

We have mentioned that a good deal of work must be completed by organization members, especially personnel specialists, before the selection process is implemented. We contend that the adequacy of these developmental steps strongly influences the adequacy of the selection process. If little attention and effort is devoted to the development of the selection program, then its usefulness will be limited. If these developmental steps are seriously addressed, the usefulness of the selection process improves. Another way of viewing this issue is that a selection process itself can be implemented quite easily. An application form can quite easily be printed or purchased; interviews can be conducted without too much prior work; employment tests (with names that sound like they should produce useful information for selection) can be purchased and administered to applicants. The crucial issue, however, is not whether an organization can collect information from applicants and then decide which are to be given employment offers. Obviously this is possible. Rather the issue is whether the organization can collect information from applicants about individual characteristics that are closely related to job performance and effectively use these data to identify the best applicants for employment offers. Many who study human resource selection think that it is the developmental steps of the selection program that provide a better match between applicant and job.[9] The following paragraphs will briefly describe these steps.

Job Analysis Information   If the purpose of the selection program is to identify the best individuals to perform a job within the organization, then information about the job would be the logical starting point in the development of this program. *Job analysis* is the gathering of information about a job in an organization. This information should be descriptive of the tasks or activities, the results (products or services), the equipment, material, and individuals, and the environment (working conditions, hazards, work schedule, etc.) that characterize the job. Such information is, of course, essential to all P/HRM activities: selection, compensation programs, training, performance appraisal, career development, etc. For selection it serves two main purposes. The first is to convey to potential applicants information about the nature and demands of the job. This helps minimize inappropriate expectations and provides information so that the applicants can go through a self-screening process, that is, remove themselves from the application for jobs that they feel are inappropriate. The second purpose is actually the more critical for the development of selection programs. The job analysis information provides a database for the other steps in the developmental process.

Identification of Relevant Job Performance Measures   One of the major purposes of selection programs is to identify those applicants that will be successful on the job that is under consideration. We assume that actual differences among workers can be measured on aspects of the job that are important to the performance of that job. In other words, there is some way that the organization can tell how successful the workers are on the job. At first this may seem relatively easy to do: find out how much work an employee finishes and how well it is done. However, there are a number of factors in present organizations that make this measurement of job performance difficult: many jobs do not produce tangible products; jobs are interdependent so that it is difficult to determine how much any one individual has contributed; jobs are paced by machines or assembly lines with little opportunity for an employee to do more or less. Under such circumstances, it is the immediate superior's judgment of job performance that is gathered. In other cases variables such as being on time for work duties, or consistently coming to work, or completing an extensive training program might be indicants of job success. Frequently, more than one variable is identified as important in job performance. In any case, the information provided by the job analysis should help measure job performance.

Inference of Worker Characteristics   Using both the job analysis information and the job performance data, the personnel specialist must identify the KSAs and other employee characteristics that a worker should possess in order to perform the job successfully. These KSAs become the basic pool of characteristics to be evaluated in applicants. This identification is an extremely difficult task. As will be discussed in Chapter 8, there are a few methods that attempt to identify these KSAs in terms of a limited number of predetermined variables. In most cases, however, personnel specialists rely on their judgment. Work requirements, worker attributes, worker characteristics, or job requirements are all terms that are frequently used in the same context that we have used the term KSAs.

Identification of Assessment Devices   After the KSAs of primary interest have been identified, it becomes necessary either to find or construct the appropriate selection devices for collecting information from applicants. These devices are in fact the instruments that will be discussed in the next section, *Steps To Process Applicants.* These instruments can be classified into the following groups: application blanks, biodata forms, and references; the selection interview; mental ability and special abilities tests; personality assessment instruments; and simulation and performance measures. There are two basic principles for choosing the selection device(s) to be used. The first is that the device must be representative of the KSAs identified previously. This might appear to be relatively simple but in fact is frequently quite complex and difficult. There are numerous interview schedules, personality inventories, leadership questionnaires, etc., that are available from various organizations. Deciding among these must be done by considering both test construction principles and the similarity between KSAs measured by the device and those necessary for the job.

The second principle is that the assessment device should be able to differentiate among applicants. The assumption in selection is that applicants possess *different amounts of the KSAs necessary for job performance.* The purpose of the assessment device is to measure these differences (usually by means of differences in numerical scores). It is in this way that promising applicants can be distinguished from unpromising. If all, or nearly all, applicants performed about the same on these assessment devices, the selection decisions would be very difficult. The applicants would appear to be equal. Obviously there would be difficulty in choosing a few applicants from a larger group of equals. The problem of lack of differentiation occurs in the use of interviews that emphasize general questions about career goals and self-assessment of strengths and weaknesses, personality inventories that are transparent in purpose (for example, scales that measure the amount of social interaction preferred or attitudes toward stealing or dishonesty), and simple math or clerical tests. Knowledge of how tests are constructed and information from job analysis and job performance analysis will help the professional get around this problem.

Let us briefly summarize the steps completed at this point. Information has been collected describing important aspects of both job activities and outcomes. This information has been used to identify a set of KSAs that a worker needs to succeed on the job. A set of selection instruments has been identified that will measure the amount of the KSAs in applicants. If these steps are performed with care, we should reasonably expect to obtain the information needed to choose the right applicants. Frequently, however, the developmental work of the selection program stops at this point. If this happens, the difficulty is that there is very little evidence to verify the accuracy of the steps taken. Robert Guion likens these first steps to the development of hypotheses.[10] That is, the human resources specialist has formulated testable statements as to the worker characteristics that should be related to successful job performance. The last steps in the development of a selection program can be viewed as a testing of these hypotheses. Technically referred to as *validation,* these steps focus on the collection and evaluation of information to determine whether the worker characteristics thought to be important are, in fact, related to successful job performance. If they are, then the selection program should be useful to the organization. If, on the other hand, it turns out that the identified worker characteristics are not related to job performance, it is better to learn this as early as possible so that alternatives can be developed.

Validation Procedures   There are several ways to validate the selection process. In *empirical validation,* for example, two types of data are collected: (a) the scores on the selection devices of a representative sample of individuals, and (b) measures of how well each of these individuals is performing on important parts of the job. The purpose of validation is to provide evidence that data from the selection instruments are related to job performance. Statistical data analysis, usually correlational analysis, is the most straightforward manner of producing this evidence. Since empirical validation involves calculating correlation coefficients between scores on the selection instruments and scores on the job performance measure, this information can be used to assess the usefulness of the selection program.

In addition to empirical validation, other validation procedures, such as *content* and *construct,* can be used. No matter which type is employed it is really only after the validation phase has been completed that one has evidence that the information collected by the selection devices is indicative of job performance and, therefore, is useful in choosing among applicants. It is these steps from job analysis to validation that we referred to previously in stating that much developmental work must precede the installation of the selection process. If all these steps have not been completed then, in Guion's terms, the organization is using a set of selection instruments that are thought to be useful for the identification of potentially successful workers, but there is no real evidence to support this.

If the instruments are not related to job performance, their use can be costly in two different ways. One is that less than a preferred group of workers is being selected for employment. This obviously could have serious economic effects on the organization. For example, it has been estimated that the use of a specific, validated computer programming test for one year could provide a net productivity gain to the federal government of $97.2 million, depending on current selection conditions.[11] Similar large financial returns have been estimated for private sector organizations. The second consequence is that if nonvalidated selection devices are used and major demographic imbalances in selection patterns result, the organization is vulnerable to charges of discrimination in the courts.

The development of selection programs is not new. Early descriptions of selection contain procedures similar to those enumerated here.[12] Frequently, however, these steps are not fully carried out in organizations. Less time-consuming and less rigorous procedures are adopted.[13] In such cases long-term consequences and costs are downplayed or ignored.

Steps to Process Applicants

The number and nature of selection instruments used varies among organizations. Similarly, there are differences in how the data from these selection instruments are used. Exhibit 1.3 depicts how typical selection devices can be used in what is called a *multiple-hurdle* selection program. In this commonly used program, the applicant pool is reduced after the use of each selection device. Generally, less expensive devices are used first and more expensive ones later, when fewer applicants are left. All instruments, whenever they are used, should be valid. We will discuss the steps in this type of selection program to illustrate what the product of the work of a selection specialist may look like.

Preliminary Screening   The preliminary screening interview is frequently used by organizations that continually receive inquiries from those interested in working for them. These might be individuals who walk into the employment office of a manufacturing or sales organization, or college students signing up for on-campus interviews with college recruiters. The purpose of this interview is both to provide some basic information about the organization and its jobs to the applicant and also to screen these applicants on some fundamental characteristics related to job performance. Those who are interested in the organization and thought to have valued characteristics are given an application form to complete. Others are removed from further consideration.

The application blank is a form the applicants are asked to complete that asks further information about their backgrounds. Among the questions asked are usually ones about previous work experience, education, activities, and interests that may utilize skills necessary for the job, and the applicant's work or location preferences. This information is reviewed and frequently used in connection with the employment interview. Those applicants whose qualifications indicate necessary KSAs for the job are asked to participate in an employment interview. Others are dropped from further consideration. It is at this step that environmental factors sometime affect the decision as to who should be given an employment interview and who should not. A difficult decision has to be made in cases where there are more seemingly qualified applicants than positions open or time for staff to administer employment interviews. In instances such as these, government directives concerning the processing of applicants become important to the decision of whom to process further and whom to terminate.

Selection Interview   The selection interview is longer than the pre-employment interview because it is necessary to collect more specific information from the applicant. The interviewer asks a series of questions that should be related to the KSAs necessary for the job. These questions are frequently quite involved and may present hypothetical situations or focus on specific knowledge necessary for job performance. Once again, those applicants who are thought to have the necessary KSAs are advanced to the next step; the remainder are dropped from further consideration. In many cases the next steps are the gathering of additional information through employment tests, communicating with personal or professional associates of the applicant,

Exhibit 1.3 Representative Steps in the Processing of Applicants in Selection

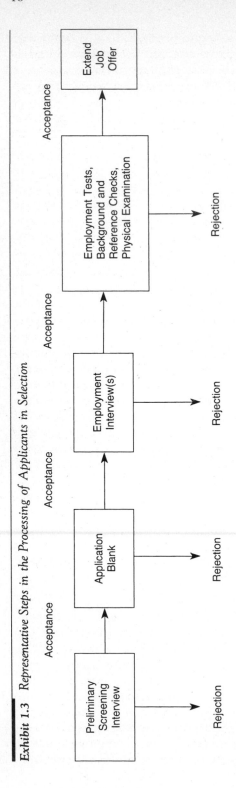

and/or having the applicant undergo a physical examination to determine physical capability or insurability. In other cases, especially in smaller organizations, no further information is gathered from applicants and job offers are extended based on information gathered during the employment interview.

Employment Tests   Employment tests can be either written tests or simulation exercises. Reading comprehension, mathematical knowledge, and specific job skills are the subjects of some of the written tests that have been used in selection programs. Simulation exercises are performance instruments which require the applicant to actually do something relevant to the job. Delivering speeches or presentations, typing, welding, or participating with a group of other applicants to reach a business decision are all examples of simulation tests. Employment tests are usually given only to the relatively small number of applicants that are still being seriously considered after the employment interview. These tests provide another way of selecting from among a group of relatively well-qualified individuals.

Personal Data Instruments   Background checks and letters of reference are used for the same purpose. Information gathered from these sources, however, is not very useful.[14] Usually references supplied by the applicant are selected because they have a favorable opinion of the applicant or because they might have something to gain by the employment of the applicant (like a solution to their own problem of what to do with the person). This usually means that these references are not impartial reporters, and they frequently provide only positive comments. At times this prompts rather dubious behaviors — selection decision-makers may try to interpret the significance of characteristics of the applicant that are not mentioned in the reference.

Physical examinations are used to identify those who are physically unable to perform the job or a critical part of it, to provide basic information for the organization's medical records, or to prevent the hiring of those with serious or communicable diseases. Tests may be used to determine the presence of alcohol or drug abuse.

For those applicants that continue through all the steps of the selection process, the data are gathered and analyzed. The result is, of course, an employment offer or a rejection because of either a lack of suitability for the job or the availability of an even more qualified applicant. In either case the applicant and organization have each gone through a costly and time-consuming process of providing, gathering, and evaluating information.

Issues in the Development of Selection Programs

If we assume that the primary purpose of a selection program is to choose from among a number of applicants those that have a high possibility of performing well on the job, the essence of selection is *prediction* or forecasting. Specifically, a major concern is using the information gathered from the selection devices to determine differences among applicants on job-related KSAs and on the basis of this information to choose those applicants that will do well on the job under consideration. In human resource selection, as in medicine, stock market analysis, meteorology, and economics, prediction is an uncertain activity.[15] Even with a well-developed selection program, not all of the predictions about future job performance are going to be correct. There are a number of factors that greatly affect the selection process and must be considered by P/HRM specialists.

Small Sample of Applicant Behavior

The quality of selection decisions, as in other areas of managerial decision-making, depends in part on the accuracy and completeness of the data gathered from the applicants. In general, the greater the amount of accurate data obtained, the more complete the assessment of the applicants' characteristics. However, in selection the extensiveness of the data collected is often severely limited by the cost of obtaining the data. The organization incurs cost for such items as materials and facilities, staff time, travel expenses for staff and applicants, and data storage and analysis. These costs usually limit the amount of data collected, especially early in the processing of applicants. For example, a college campus interviewer frequently spends only 30 minutes with each applicant and part of this time is devoted to the presentation of information about the organization. In other cases either application forms and/or resumés are extensively used as major screening devices for many positions. However, in both cases the selection devices used can obtain only limited, basic information about applicants. Especially where there is a large number of applicants for a few positions, difficult decisions about the acceptability of applicants must be made from limited information. Such constraints affect the accuracy of the decisions.

Measurement of Jobs, Individuals, and Work Performance

A basic assumption of this book is that the development of a selection program requires the measurement of characteristics of jobs, individuals, and work performance. By **measurement** we mean quantitative description, that is the use of numbers.[16] Numbers are used to represent such information as the amount of time spent in a certain job activity, or the level of mathematical knowledge needed to perform a certain task, or the score of an applicant on a verbal skill test, or the quality of a worker's performance in preparing an advertisement. Numbers are necessary because they facilitate comparison of jobs or people; they transmit information more succinctly than words; and they permit statistical manipulation which provides even more information about the selection program. For example, assume that there are 12 applicants for an entry level position in the loan department of a bank. All are interviewed and complete a brief test of financial terms and financial analysis.

Quantifying the performance of each candidate on each of the two selection instruments is the most practical way of comparing the twelve. If scores are not developed, the selection specialist is placed in an extremely complex situation; differences must be determined among the 12 using descriptive information such as "He seemed able to express himself pretty well," or "She knew most of the financial terms but did not seem comfortable judging the risk of the loan." Obviously, when there are such statements about a number of individuals, the difficulty in identifying the most promising of the applicants is enormous.

The problem of measurement for the personnel specialist, however, is to insure that the numbers generated are actually accurate descriptions of the characteristic of the applicant, the job, or the job performance under study. We will address specific measurement issues throughout this text, especially in Chapters 3–5. For now we will discuss two basic measurement issues that must be addressed by the personnel specialist in the measurement of job characteristics, worker traits, and work performance dimensions.

Defining What Is To Be Measured   The more important issue is the *definition* of the attribute to be measured. For example, in constructing a selection device it might be decided that "verbal ability" is an important worker trait for the job of public relations officer in a utility company. The question then is what exactly is meant by the term "verbal ability." Do we mean the ability to convey technical product information to consumers, to deliver prepared public relations documents to the media, or to respond to unanticipated questions or demands from government regulatory offices? Each would be considered a verbal ability; however, there are differences among them and their measurement would not yield interchangeable information concerning the evaluation of applicants. Therefore, the personnel specialist must be as precise as possible in defining the attribute to be measured.

Measurement Operations   The second important measurement issue is the way operations are used to gather data about the defined attribute. By *operations* we mean the procedures and devices that are used to collect data.[17] Suppose that we had decided that "the ability to convey technical product information to consumers" is the appropriate definition of verbal ability that we wish to measure in applicants prior to making a selection decision. Various operations measure this ability. The personnel specialist could use a multiple choice or essay test that presents a consumer problem and asks the applicant to identify the appropriate product information to answer the problem and the means to present this information to consumers. Another operation would be to have an interviewer pose questions to the applicant and have the applicant orally respond with the interviewer grading the response. A third operation might be to bring the applicant together with a small group of consumers, have the applicant orally respond to a predetermined set of questions, and measure the consumers' increase in knowledge as a measure of the applicant's ability to convey technical product information.

It is probable that an applicant would not perform the same on each of these three operations. The implication is that each of the three operations would yield different measurement information about the applicant being considered. We can see, then, that the personnel specialist must make difficult choices at a number of points in the measurement process, two of the most critical being the definition of the attribute to be measured and the choosing of measurement operations. The quality of these decisions helps determine the appropriateness and the usefulness of the data gathered.

Other Factors Affecting Work Performance

A third issue to keep in mind regarding selection programs is that many factors affect work performance. The purpose of selection is to enhance the probability of making correct hiring decisions — extending offers to those who will perform well in the organization and not extending job offers to those who will not do as well. Typically any evaluation of the adequacy of the selection program should be made in terms of job performance.

However, it is apparent that the KSAs of those hired are not the sole determiners of job performance. Practitioners and researchers have identified numerous other factors in an organization that affect individual performance. Among these organizational factors are training programs for employees, appraisal and feedback methods, goal-setting procedures, financial compensation systems, work design strategies, supervisory methods, organizational structure, decision-making techniques, work schedules, and socio-technical work systems design.[18]

The implication of these findings for the evaluation of selection programs is clear. A selection program focuses on a few of the many variables that influence performance. Often it is difficult to assess adequately the effectiveness of a selection program. At times a thoughtfully developed program might seem to have only a minimal measurable relationship to performance. It is possible in such cases that one or more of these other variables is adversely affecting performance levels and negating the contribution of the selection program. The conclusion is that it is advisable in judging selection programs to examine several other organizational systems before an accurate diagnosis of deficiencies can be made.

Plan of This Book

The major purpose of this book is to discuss each of the steps necessary in the development of selection programs within organizations. We will concentrate on the characteristics of the data that should be gathered and the types of decisions the personnel specialist should make at each step. We will try to incorporate recent research about selection and discuss its implications for the development of human resource selection programs. One thing that should be clearly understood is that there is not one blueprint for the development of selection programs and we do not wish to give that impression. The steps we refer to are different stages in the accumulation and processing of information about jobs, individuals, and job performance. At each step the personnel specialist must make a number of decisions about the kind of data that are needed and what must be done to these data. The particular selection needs of the organization will dictate the appropriate actions; we hope this book will provide information necessary for evaluating options at each stage.

The book is divided into sections. The first two chapters convey an overview of the selection program and its legal environment. These two chapters should provide a framework within which to organize the rest of the subject. Chapters 3–5 are devoted to the major measurement issues in selection. These chapters provide the basic information necessary to quantify characteristics of applicants, jobs, and job performance. The next three chapters, 6–8, explain job analysis and the identification of KSAs and other important employee characteristics. This information is the basis of selection. Chapters 9–14 discuss in detail the various selection instruments. They present common forms of each instrument, indicate measurement concerns, and suggest the most appropriate use for each instrument. Chapter 15 summarizes the methods of measuring job performance for use in selection programs. The last chapter serves as a summary of all the material in the book. It takes the form of what we have called a selection audit. It consists of a series of questions and answers that address the major aspects of developing and using a selection program.

References for Chapter 1

[1] Michael R. Carrell and Frank E. Kuzmits, *Personnel Management of Human Resources* (Columbus, Ohio: Charles E. Merrill Publishing, 1982), p. 203.

[2] John P. Wanous, "Effects of a Realistic Job Preview on Job Acceptance, Job Attitudes, and Job Survival," *Journal of Applied Psychology* 58 (1973): 327–332.

[3] John P. Kotter, "The Psychological Contract: Managing the Joining Up Process," *California Management Review* 15 (1973): 91–99.

[4] Randall S. Schuler, *Personnel and Human Resource Management*, 2d ed. (St. Paul, Minn.: West Publishing Co., 1984), p. 123.

[5] John P. Wanous, *Organizational Entry: Recruitment, Selection, and Socialization of Newcomers* (Reading, Mass.: Addison-Wesley Publishing Co., 1980), p. 34.

[6] William F. Glueck, *Personnel: A Diagnostic Approach*, 3d ed. (Plano, Tex.: Business Publications, Inc., 1982), p. 246.

[7] John P. Wanous, *Organization Entry*, p. 42.

[8] John P. Wanous, "Effects of a Realistic Job Preview," p. 329.

[9] Robert M. Guion, "Recruitment, Selection, and Job Placement," in *Handbook of Industrial and Organizational Psychology*, Marvin D. Dunnette, ed. (Chicago: Rand McNally College Publishing Co., 1976), pp. 777–828; Wayne F. Cascio, *Applied Psychology in Personnel Management*, 2d ed. (Reston, Va.: Reston Publishing Co., 1982), p. 206.

[10] Robert M. Guion, "Recruitment, Selection, and Job Placement," p. 778.

[11] Frank L. Schmidt, John E. Hunter, Robert C. McKenzie and Tressie W. Moldrow, "Impact of Valid Selection Procedures on Work-Force Productivity," *Journal of Applied Psychology* 64 (1979): 609–626.

[12] M. Freyd, "Measurement in Vocational Selection: An Outline of Research Procedure," *Journal of Personnel Research* 2 (1923): 215–249, 268–284, 377–385; Hugo Munsterberg, *Business Psychology* (Chicago: La Salle Extension University, 1917).

[13] Robert M. Guion, "Recruitment, Selection, and Job Placement," p. 784.

[14] James Mosel and Howard Goheen, "Validity of Employment Recommendation Questionnaire in Personnel Selection," *Personnel Psychology* (Winter 1958): 481–490.

[15] J. Scott Armstrong, *Long-Range Forecasting* (New York: John Wiley & Sons, 1978).

[16] Edwin E. Ghiselli, John P. Campbell, and Sheldon Zedeck, *Measurement Theory for the Behavioral Sciences* (San Francisco: W. H. Freeman and Company, 1981), p. 2.

[17] Ibid., p. 19.

[18] Raymond A. Katzell and Richard A. Guzzo, "Psychological Approaches to Productivity Improvement," *American Psychologist* 38 (1983): 468–472.

2

Legal Issues

in Selection

As was discussed in Chapter 1, the development of a selection program is a formidable task even when one deals only with the measurement issues. It becomes even more complex when one adds the legal policies that must be considered. Some contend that legal policies currently are the most significant aspect of human resource management in general[1] and of selection in particular.[2] These legal policies influence the records that must be kept on all employment decisions, the determination of fair treatment of all applicants, and the methods for identifying the job-relatedness of selection devices.

Legal policies significantly affect the work of personnel specialists in the development and use of selection programs. If these legal policies are not respected, the organization will be vulnerable to charges of discrimination. A court judgment against the organization in such a case can be extremely costly. Courts have ordered organizations to make back pay settlements to individuals they had not hired, to change selection devices and decision rules, and to maintain specified percentages of women and minority group members in future hiring patterns. It is imperative that personnel specialists have a thorough understanding of the legal guidelines for selection decisions. As a result, every selection program should have two major objectives: (a) to maximize the probability of making accurate selection decisions about applicants, and (b) to insure that these selection decisions are carried out in such a manner as to minimize the chance of a judgment of discrimination being brought against the organization. The two are not mutually exclusive objectives and actually overlap considerably in necessary procedures and data. The preceding chapter presented the major considerations important for meeting the first objective. This chapter will do the same for the second objective by discussing the following:

1. The basic principles of federal regulation of personnel activities

2. An overview of the specific laws and executive orders appropriate to selection

3. The types of data that are used in deciding when discrimination has occurred

4. The major court cases in selection

5. The most important legal issues to consider in a selection program

Federal Regulation

Many personnel specialists incorrectly think that federal laws and directives designed to regulate the actions of organizations are a recent phenomenon in American business. Such regulation can actually be traced back to the creation of the Interstate Commerce Commission (ICC) in 1887. For many years coping with government regulation has been a part of business activities. What is different in recent years is the nature of that regulation. Traditionally, regulation was confined to a given industry. For example, the ICC regulates the railroad and trucking industries and the Federal Communications Commission (FCC) regulates the radio, telephone, and television industry. For the most part these traditional agencies act to increase competition and to prevent a monopoly from developing. One of their major purposes is to promote the well-being of the industry by preventing domination by a few members. In this sense industry companies are actually the constituents of the regulatory agency because the agency works on their behalf.

Regulatory Model

Newer regulatory agencies have a very different approach. James Ledvinka has developed a regulatory model of this approach which is represented in Exhibit 2.1. Understanding this model is useful to personnel specialists, enabling them to explain and even anticipate actions of newer regulatory agencies.

The thrust of federal regulation for personnel activities is equal employment opportunity (EEO). The major characteristic that differentiates regulation in this area from traditional regulation is that it is not specific to one industry but, rather, is applied to many. Rather than being directed to the well-being of a particular industry, as in the past, regulation is now addressed to social and economic problems, as shown in the left column of Exhibit 2.1. It is important to recognize that EEO regulation is directed to the solution of

Exhibit 2.1 *Regulatory Model of EEO*

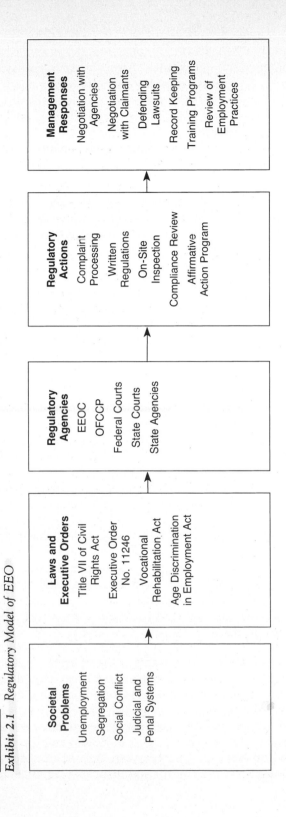

Societal Problems	Laws and Executive Orders	Regulatory Agencies	Regulatory Actions	Management Responses
Unemployment	Title VII of Civil Rights Act	EEOC	Complaint Processing	Negotiation with Agencies
Segregation	Executive Order No. 11246	OFCCP	Written Regulations	Negotiation with Claimants
Social Conflict	Vocational Rehabilitation Act	Federal Courts	On-Site Inspection	Defending Lawsuits
Judicial and Penal Systems	Age Discrimination in Employment Act	State Courts	Compliance Review	Record Keeping
		State Agencies	Affirmative Action Program	Training Programs
				Review of Employment Practices

Source: Adapted from James Ledvinka, *Federal Regulation of Personnel and Human Resource Management* (Boston: Kent Publishing Co., 1982), p. 23

national issues, such as employment inequalities. Also the constituents of EEO regulatory agencies are not business organizations but rather political and social groups devoted to the solution of employment problems. Realizing this is key to understanding the changes in emphasis in regulation as well as the apparent disregard of business interests.

The various components of this regulation process are depicted in Exhibit 2.1. As Ledvinka explains the model:

> The most succinct way . . . is to say that (1) regulation begins with the social political problems, which cause lawmakers to pass laws; (2) those laws empower agencies to take the regulatory actions that trigger management responses; and (3) the courts oversee this process by settling disputes between the parties to it.[3]

To fully understand EEO regulation it is necessary, therefore, to be familiar with two factors: (a) the laws and executive orders that state general principles and empower regulatory agencies, and (b) court decisions that interpret these general principles in specific situations. We will treat both of these topics, starting with the laws and directives and discussing the court cases later in the chapter.

EEO Laws and Executive Orders

EEO laws are federal laws whose purpose is the elimination of discrimination in human resource management decisions. EEO executive orders are statements made by the executive branch of the government intended for the same purpose but aimed at organizations that do business directly with the government. The scope of both EEO laws and executive orders is broader than selection decisions, although selection decisions have received a great deal of publicity, especially early in the history of the enforcement of EEO laws.

Ledvinka lists 21 separate federal laws and executive orders that taken together would be considered EEO laws.[4] Most of these contain directives for several areas of human resource employment decisions. In this book we will examine four major laws and one order and focus on their regulation of selection while acknowledging that they have broader impact on human resource management. Table 2.1 lists the laws and the order with a brief summary of the major provisions of each.

Title VII Civil Rights Act of 1964   Under this law employers, unions, employment agencies, and joint labor-management committees that direct apprenticeship and training programs are prohibited from discriminating on the basis of *sex, race, color, religion,* or *national origin.* This law has been amended twice. In 1972 enforcement powers were strengthened and coverage was expanded to include governmental and educational system employers as well as private employers with more than 15 employees. A 1978 amendment prohibited discrimination based on pregnancy, childbirth, or related condi-

Table 2.1   Major EEO Laws and Executive Orders for Selection

Law or Regulation	Major Provisions for Selection
Title VII Civil Rights Act of 1964	Discrimination based on race, color, religion, sex, or national origin
Executive Order 11246	Discrimination based on race, color, religion, sex, or national origin
Age Discrimination in Employment Act of 1967	Age discrimination against those between the ages of 40 and 70
The Rehabilitation Act of 1973	Discrimination based on physical or mental handicaps
Vietnam Era Veterans Readjustment Act of 1974	Discrimination against disabled and Vietnam era veterans

tions. The only major employers not yet covered by Title VII are the U.S. Congress, the military, private clubs, and religious organizations.

The Equal Employment Opportunity Commission (EEOC) is the enforcement agency for Title VII. Basically it acts in response to a charge of discrimination filed by one of the EEOC commissioners, by an aggrieved person, or by someone acting on the behalf of an aggrieved person. In most cases the charge of discrimination must be filed within 180 days of the alleged act. After the EEOC has assumed jurisdiction, the first step is the no-fault settlement attempt, an invitation to the accused to settle the case without an admission of guilt. If this option is not accepted, the case will be taken to the second step, that of investigation. During this period the employer is prohibited from destroying any records related to the charge, and is invited to submit a position paper regarding the charge which becomes part of the investigatory data. At the completion of this phase the district director of EEOC issues a statement of "probable cause" or "no probable cause." In the case of a "probable cause" decision, an attempt is made at conciliation between the two parties. This usually involves some major concessions on the part of the employer regarding the employment practice under question. If it fails to obtain a conciliation agreement, the EEOC can either undertake litigation itself or issue a right-to-sue notice to the charging party, informing this party that he/she may bring his/her own action in federal court.

Executive Order 11246   This order is directed toward contractors doing business with the federal government. Originally enacted in 1965 and amended in 1968, it prohibits the same discriminatory acts as Title VII. In addition, it requires contractors to develop *affirmative action plans*. These are formal, specific personnel programs that are designed to increase the participation of protected groups. An affirmative action program is not a requirement of Title VII.

Enforcement of executive orders is the responsibility of the Department of Labor, specifically the Office of Federal Contract Compliance Programs

(OFCCP). Investigations by the OFCCP are not dependent on charges of discrimination being filed but, instead, are a product of the OFCCP's administrative review of contractors. The review usually begins with a request to the contractor to forward the affirmative action plan. When this is received an office review and an on-site visit are conducted. If deficiencies are found, the contractor is usually informed of them by the OFCCP and an attempt is made to adjust them. If the attempt fails, a formal deficiency letter is drawn up and formal conciliation attempts are undertaken. If these fail, the OFCCP issues a show-cause letter that formally states that the contractor is not in compliance with the executive order. Noncompliance can adversely affect the contractor's participation in government business. If the deficiencies are not corrected at this time, an administrative hearing procedure before an administrative-law judge can be initiated. The whole procedure can take several years. The government's position is that during this time it can deny the contractor any two contracts, regardless of total size.

Age Discrimination in Employment Act of 1967 This act, amended in 1978, protects both employees and applicants who are *at least 40* but less than 70 years of age. It prohibits discrimination against these people by employers, labor organizations, employment agencies, and both federal and state governments. The act reads very similarly to Title VII. However, there are important differences between the two. The Age Discrimination in Employment Act (ADEA) addresses only the 40–70-year age bracket; it does not address itself to hiring or other employment decisions that relate to younger workers. It also forbids an organization from forcing employees to retire before the age of 70. The only exceptions are employees who are entitled to at least $26,000 in pension benefits.

Enforcement of the ADEA resides in the EEOC and is usually initiated by the filing of a charge of discrimination. However, the EEOC has the authority to review organizations when there is no charge. The Act also provides for trial by jury. This is thought to be potentially beneficial to the person bringing suit in that the plaintiff's age and other personal characteristics may elicit a sympathetic reaction from the jury.[5]

The Rehabilitation Act of 1973 This Act requires both nondiscrimination in employment practices and also affirmative action toward the handicapped. The Act has been difficult for employers to respond to because of ambiguity in the term "handicapped." The Department of Labor (OFCCP), which enforces the Act, defines a handicapped individual to be one with any mental or physical impairment that "substantially limits one or more major life functions," or who has a record of such an impairment, or is regarded by others as having such an impairment. In addition to visible handicaps, such conditions as diabetes, heart disease, epilepsy, obesity, and mental problems such as retardation and emotional disorders are covered.[6] OFCCP considers a person handicapped if this limitation applies to only one job. The term "substantially limits" means in essence that the handicap affects employability. "Major life activities" includes activities such as communication, ambulation, and transportation.

Employer obligations, according to OFCCP guidelines, are defined as follows:

> A contractor must make a reasonable accommodation to the physical and mental limitation of an employee or an applicant unless the contractor can demonstrate that such an accommodation would impose an undue hardship on the conduct of the contractor's business. In determining the extent of a contractor's accommodations, the following factors among others may be considered: (1) business necessity and (2) financial cost.[7]

No exact definition is given of the meanings of "reasonable accommodation" and "undue hardship." Consequently, no one is sure of the scope of the terms. The Rehabilitation Act itself says nothing about the obligation to make reasonable accommodation, nor does the executive order that gives enforcement power to the Department of Labor mention such a requirement.

Charges of discrimination under this act against government contractors are first referred by the OFCCP back to the contractor if that organization has an internal grievance procedure. If no such procedure exists, the OFCCP can press charges. The usual vehicle is an administrative hearing which can bring administrative sanctions, termination of contract, or withholding of progress payments.

The Vietnam Era Veterans Readjustment Act of 1974   This Act, also under the direction of the Department of Labor (OFCCP), relates only to government contractors. Veterans covered are either those who served during the Vietnam War (not necessarily in Vietnam, however), defined as the period between August 5, 1964, and May 7, 1975, or those who have a compensable disability rated at 30 percent or more by the Veterans Administration.

A contractor is required under the Act to list all employment openings at the local office of the state employment agency. These listings must be made before, or at least at the same time as, others being released through any other recruitment mechanism. Compliance reviews may be made by the OFCCP even without the filing of a charge. Enforcement can be through court ruling or administrative sanctions, which can include such penalties as termination of or debarment from contracts, or the withholding of progress payments.

This brief review of the important EEO laws highlights the major points of the regulatory model. These laws are clearly addressed to societal problems; they focus on safeguarding the fair treatment in employment of groups that traditionally have not had access to the American dream of success. These laws created agencies designed to monitor the compliance of organizations in various industries and to represent the claims of individuals who feel they were unfairly treated. Such actions require the employment practices of organizations to be evaluated. In most cases the well-being of the organization itself is not of major concern.

Discrimination: Definition and Evidence

The previously cited laws and orders clearly prohibit discrimination in selection and other human resource management actions. The difficulty for members of organizations is to identify when discrimination is present. As we have said, laws state principles. Putting these principles into operation is another step. As the regulatory model indicates, this step is based on court decisions in discrimination cases and on the *Uniform Guidelines on Employee Selection Procedures* published in 1978 by the EEOC. The court decisions set legal precedent and yield specific comments about the treatment of evidence of alleged discrimination in specific situations. These legal precedents serve as benchmarks for subsequent legal interpretation. The *Uniform Guidelines,* while being neither law nor court decisions, are important because they represent the joint statement of the agencies empowered by law to enforce the EEO laws. The *Uniform Guidelines* describe what evidence will be considered in judging discrimination and how an employer may defend a selection program. In addition, the guidelines are given "great deference" by the courts when considering discrimination cases. The next sections of this chapter will discuss the definition and evidence of discrimination in human resource management policies, summarize the major points of the *Uniform Guidelines,* and review the major court cases. The purpose is to familiarize the reader with the technical operation of EEO law and to develop a set of basic ideas that should be incorporated into the development of selection programs to minimize the possibility of a court's finding a pattern of discrimination in selection practices.

Discrimination Defined

Intentional Prejudice   The most basic definition of discrimination is *intentional prejudice.* By this is meant those situations in which certain groups are treated negatively because of a personal characteristic stated in one of the EEO laws. Examples of this would be employment notices indicating "Males Only" or "Blacks need not apply." This is obviously the most blatant form of discrimination and is seen very infrequently in recent times.

Unequal Treatment The second form of discrimination is *unequal treatment*. This describes those situations in which different standards are applied to various groups of individuals even though there may not be an explicit statement of intentional prejudice. Examples are such practices as not hiring women with young children while hiring men with such children, or hiring minority group members to fill cleaning jobs in a restaurant while similarly qualified white hirees are made cashiers or waiters. The effect of such decisions, even though they may be prompted by the employer's idea of good business practice, is to subject a specific group to negative treatment because of a personal characteristic.

Adverse Impact The third form of discrimination is that of *adverse impact*. In this form organizational selection standards are applied uniformly to all groups of applicants, but the net result of these standards is to produce differences in the selection of various groups. Two classic examples of such discrimination are the requirement of a high school diploma, which had been used extensively for entry level positions, and of height minimums, for example 5'6", which have been used for police and some manual labor positions. Both standards are usually applied to all individual applicants consistently, and, therefore, at first might not seem to be discriminatory.

The problem is that such standards have been demonstrated to have the effect of disqualifying from employment a much larger percentage of some groups then others. For example, traditionally, more whites have high school diplomas than do most minority groups. Therefore, the requirement of a diploma would automatically limit the percentage of minority applicants in comparison to white applicants. Similarly, a minimum height requirement usually limits the number of women, Orientals, and Hispanics who would be eligible to apply even though they otherwise could be found to be acceptable for employment. Table 2.2 lists selection requirements and instruments that have been identified in court decisions as having adverse impact. That is, the use of each of these has been linked to the disqualification of a high percentage of at least one demographic group of applicants.

These are the three forms that discrimination may take. The development of these forms can be best understood in terms of the regulatory model. Defining discrimination only in terms of intentional prejudice really was not

---

Table 2.2 Selection Requirements Having Adverse Impact

Arrest Records	Interviews
Type of Military Discharge	Financial Status
Minimum Height and Weight	Educational Degrees
Paper and Pencil Tests	Relationship to Organization Employees

effective in correcting employment imbalances for which the laws were intended. Such behavior could easily be masked by organizations. Unequal
treatment was more effective but still limited because many traditional selection requirements such as those listed in Table 2.2 could be applied equally,
but still perpetuate employment imbalance. When the EEO agencies and the
courts used adverse impact as the definition, discrimination was judged directly in terms of the employment imbalances that were the causes of the
EEO laws. As will be described in the next paragraphs, this definition also
provided a method of measuring discrimination through the monitoring by
regulatory agencies of the selection results of organizations. In such cases
some type of statistical analysis of employment data is usually used.

Measurement

Four-Fifths Rule   According to the EEOC's *Uniform Selection Guidelines,* a
common rule of thumb for determining discrimination is to compare the
following ratio:

$$\frac{\text{number of a minority group hired}}{\text{number of minority group applicants}} : \frac{\text{number of nonminority hired}}{\text{number of nonminority applicants}}$$

The ratio of any group must be at least 80 percent of the ratio of the most
favorably treated group. For example, if 60 percent of white applicants are
hired, then the selection proportion of any minority group should be at least
48% (.80 × .60). Let us say that there are numerous entry level retail clerk
positions to be filled for a large department store. Through recruiting, 120
white applicants are processed and 72 (60%) are hired. Through the same
recruiting process, 50 blacks apply for the positions. If blacks were hired at
the same rate as the whites, we would expect that 30 black applicants would
be hired (50 × .60). However, according to this guideline exact parity is not
expected. The minimum number of black hirees would be expected to be 24
(30 × .80), which is 80% of the 60% hire rate of whites. This guideline is
referred to as the "four-fifths rule." If the ratio is smaller, the *initial* conclusion is that discrimination in selection has occurred.

Standard Deviation Rule   Another analysis that has been utilized is the
standard deviation analysis formula. This formula is:

$$\sqrt{\frac{\text{total minority applicants}}{\text{total applicants}} \times \frac{\text{total nonminority applicants}}{\text{total applicants}} \times \text{total persons selected}}$$

For example, let us assume that 200 individuals were selected from an applicant pool of 500. Of these 500 applicants, 200 were black and 300 were white. Applying these data to the formula yields the following:

$$\text{S.D.} = \sqrt{\frac{200}{500} \times \frac{300}{500} \times 200}$$
$$= \sqrt{.4 \times .6 \times 200}$$
$$= \sqrt{48}$$
$$= 6.93$$

If blacks were selected in the same proportion as they were represented in the applicant pool, one would expect that 80 blacks would have been selected (200 hirees $\times$ .40 of applicants). The standard deviation rule provides a rule of thumb to judge whether or not the number of blacks actually hired is roughly representative of their proportion in the applicant pool. The general rule is that the number selected should be within a range defined by $\pm$ 2 standard deviation units from the expected number selected. In this case the expected number hired is 80 and one standard deviation is 6.93. Two standard deviations would be approximately 14. The acceptable selection range would therefore be 80 $\pm$ 14, or the range of from 66 to 94 blacks selected. Obviously, in most cases the lower boundary of the range is given the most importance. According to this type of analysis, if fewer than 66 blacks were in the group of 200 selected, evidence of discrimination would exist.

Labor Market Analysis   As has been demonstrated in the previous examples, in many cases the data used are those illustrating impact on applicants. In other cases the applicant pool may not be representative of labor market characteristics because of recruiting techniques or company image. In these cases different information is used. Courts have used data that illustrate impact on *potential* rather than actual applicants and have analyzed the representativeness of the employer's work force in comparison to the *relevant labor market*. For example, in one court case the percentage in the whole state of a minority group with a high school degree was compared to the percentage of the majority group in the state holding a high school degree.[8] In another example, the percentage of a minority group at a certain job level of an organization would be compared with the percentage of the minority in the labor market thought to possess appropriate skills and abilities for that job level. For example, in Company A, 10 of 150 (.07) middle level managers are black. The percentage is compared with the percentage of blacks in the relevant labor market. If statistical analysis indicates that the difference between the two percentages is larger than is permissable, evidence of discrimination is present.

The comparison with the relevant labor market is always difficult and at times uncertain. Both the physical boundaries of the labor market and the measurement of skills to determine appropriate applicant pools within the market are very unsure and open to much interpretation. For this reason, in many cases in which discrimination has been charged, a major portion of the litigation is devoted to a definition of the relevant labor market. This could make a significant difference in large metropolitan areas that have a large minority population in certain sections.

Importance of Selection Patterns In summary, the possibility of illegal discrimination in selection is raised when unequal hiring decisions concerning one or more of the groups specified in the EEO laws has taken place. This possible discrimination can be attributed to either intentional prejudice, unequal treatment, or adverse impact. In most cases statistical analyses of employment data are necessary to indicate possible discrimination. These analyses reveal the general effect of selection requirements on groups of individuals. It is important for personnel specialists to realize that discrimination is not usually judged in terms of a single selection decision, but rather on a pattern of such decisions. In those cases in which a single selection decision is the basis for possible discrimination, the Supreme Court has indicated the following as a foundation for such a charge:

> The complainant in a Title VII trial must carry the initial burden under the statute of establishing a *prima facie* case of racial discrimination. This may be done by showing: (i) that he belongs to a racial minority; (ii) that he applied and was qualified for a job for which the employer was seeking applicants; (iii) that, despite his qualifications, he was rejected, and (iv) that, after his rejection, the position remained open and the employer continued to seek applicants from persons of the complainant's qualifications.[9]

Although this statement is written in terms of racial discrimination, the same standards are, presumably, appropriate for other types of discrimination. The essence is that a *qualified* individual is not hired and that further processing of applicants takes place for that position. The implication is that the qualified candidate was rejected because of a specific characteristic protected by EEO law.

The preceding paragraphs used the words "possible" discrimination because the issues addressed do not conclusively "prove" that discrimination has occurred, but only indicate that on the surface there is evidence to support the claim that selection decisions not in compliance with EEO laws may have taken place. In such circumstances the organization is asked to provide evidence to support the proposition that even though such selection decisions have occurred, they are defensible in terms of the provisions of EEO law. This is in fact possible to do. The most complete statement of what data an organization should produce to support its selection practices is contained in the EEOC's *1978 Uniform Guidelines on Employee Selection Procedures.*

The Uniform Guidelines on Employee Selection Procedures

The *Uniform Guidelines* represent a joint statement of the Equal Employment Opportunity Commission, the Civil Service Commission, the Department of Labor, and the Department of Justice as to the characteristics of acceptable selection procedures. As such, these guidelines are not themselves legally binding. However, because they represent the viewpoints of the federal agencies charged with the enforcement of EEO laws, the guidelines serve as a primary reference for court decisions and have been cited in various cases. The most important aspects of the *Uniform Guidelines* are summarized in this section.

Determination of Adverse Impact   The *Uniform Guidelines* clearly state that the central issue in judging discrimination in selection is the use of any selection procedure that has adverse impact. However, it must be noted that in certain cases the *Uniform Guidelines* provide exceptions to this. When large numbers of applicants are being selected, discrimination could be indicated even if comparison proportions of applicants are within the four-fifths rates. Statistically significant differences in selection rates could be determined because of the large sample sizes. In addition enforcement agencies would naturally be quite concerned with differences in which large numbers of individuals are affected. Conversely, in cases in which very small numbers of applicants are processed, the four-fifths rule may not always be accepted as determining discrimination. With small samples, differences in decisions about one or two applicants could greatly change the comparison ratios. This factor is thus taken into account and differences greater than the four-fifths ratio allows may not be viewed negatively.

Selection Methods   The *Uniform Guidelines* also state that *any* method of selection that results in a decision is covered. Many individuals have incorrectly assumed that only scored selection tests are addressed in the guidelines. This is clearly incorrect as the following indicates:

> When an informal or unscored selection procedure which has an adverse impact is utilized, the user should eliminate the adverse impact or modify the procedure to one which is a formal, scored or quantified measure.[10]

Defense of Adverse Impact   The *Uniform Guidelines* are not concerned, except with respect to record keeping, with selection programs that do not demonstrate adverse impact. For those selection programs that do have adverse impact, the options of the organization are specified. First, the organization may cease use of the selection device(s) under question and adopt other procedures that do not result in adverse impact. If this is not acceptable, the organization may defend its practices by producing evidence to indicate that the selection program is based on job-related information and the adverse impact merely reflects differences in worker attributes necessary for job performance. This defense may take one of three forms: *validation, business necessity,* or *bona fide occupational qualifications* (BFOQ). We have already discussed validation. Business necessity occurs when the employer can clearly demonstrate (a) that there is a strong relationship between the selection test and performance, and (b) that without this method of selection, the employer's training expenses and failure rate of persons trained would make operating costs prohibitive.

A BFOQ defense means that *no* person of a particular sex, age, religion, or national origin can adequately perform a given job. The defense mainly relates to sex discrimination and may be applied to jobs like restroom attendant. In reality both business necessity and BFOQ defenses are very difficult to use. Validation is the more common defense. If validation evidence is used, it should specifically address the use of the selection instrument with all groups for whom the test is to be used. At a minimum this means that statistical validation should include a representative number of women and minorities. In content validation the steps should address the issue of "test fairness" or the comparative performance of various groups on the test. A large portion of the *Uniform Guidelines* are in fact devoted to the steps, data, and procedures of validation strategies. If such validation evidence is accepted, the *Uniform Guidelines* indicate that the resultant adverse impact should be legally permissible. There is an added provision, however, that the organization should demonstrate that there are no other alternative selection programs that are both valid and have less adverse impact. This requirement, however, has not been tested in court.

Employment Requirements   There are several other aspects of selection programs that are specifically addressed. Skills and abilities easily learned during a brief training program are not acceptable as selection requirements. Requirements drawn from higher level jobs are permissible only if it can be documented that a majority of individuals move to the higher level job within a reasonable time period. This time period is not precisely defined but the *Uniform Guidelines* state "a reasonable period of time will vary for different jobs and employment situations but will seldom be more than five years." The various forms of selection cut-off scores are also discussed. The least stringent cut-off is a score above which all applicants are judged equally acceptable. Scores on selection devices may also be grouped according to the magnitude of the score with the first applicants considered for selection to be those with scores in the highest group. Selection proceeds down score groups until all open positions are filled. This could result in selection being completed before some score groups are even considered. An even more severe version of this is to individually rank all applicants and proceed down this list of individuals. The *Uniform Guidelines* indicate when these latter two forms of cut-off scores are used, and if adverse impact results, the organization must not only demonstrate the validity of the selection devices but also justify the contention that scores above a minimum are indicative of higher job performance.

Job Performance Measures   In a discussion of measures of job performance that are useful in the demonstration of validity, the *Uniform Guidelines* allow a variety of such measures, e.g., production quantity or quality, supervisors' ratings, turnover, and absenteeism records. Whatever ones are used, however, they must represent important work behaviors or work outcomes that are free from factors that would unfairly alter the scores of any particular groups. We will discuss performance measures in Chapter 15 to fully develop this issue. The *Uniform Guidelines* also permit validation evidence to be gathered by means of a multiunit study or evidence borrowed from other companies, as long as data are produced indicating the similarity of the job being considered. The necessary procedures of such job analysis will be discussed in Chapter 8.

Record Keeping   Another major requirement of the *Uniform Guidelines* is record-keeping. All organizations are required to keep information about the demographic characteristics of applicants and hirees and to produce such information if requested. This requirement applies only to the groups that constitute at least two percent of the relevant labor market. All organizations are technically required to record such data; however, if adverse impact is not characteristic of the selection program, the probability of a request by an enforcement agency for this documentation is remote. Organizations with fewer than 100 employees should record by sex, race, and national origin, the number of persons hired, promoted, and terminated for each job level. Data are also necessary indicating the number of applicants for both entry level positions and promotion. These data should also be categorized by sex, race, and national origin. Finally selection procedures should be described. Organizations with more than 100 employees must develop records indicating whether the total selection process for each job, or any part of that selection process, has had adverse impact on any group that constitutes at least two percent of the relevant labor market. In cases in which there is an insufficient number of selections to determine whether there is an adverse impact, the organization should continue to collect, maintain, and have available the information on individual components of the selection process until the information is sufficient to determine if adverse impact has occurred or until the job changes substantially. In the latter case, presumably a new round of record keeping would begin.

In summary, the *Uniform Guidelines on Employee Selection* direct personnel specialists as to appropriate selection program procedures and records. The determination of adverse impact as indicated by the four-fifths rule is of primary importance. If such impact is determined, using required organizational records, the company must either cease the selection procedure and adopt a nondiscriminatory one or produce evidence of the job-relatedness of the selection program with the adverse impact. However, even with these directives, to fully understand the impact of EEO law on selection development and practices it is necessary to be familiar with the major court cases on the subject because these judicial opinions and decisions, in essence, operationalize acceptable procedures.

Selection Court Cases

Griggs v. Duke Power (1971)   The first landmark case decided by the Supreme Court under Title VII was *Griggs v. Duke Power*.[11] The case began in 1967 when 13 black employees filed a class action suit against Duke Power, charging discriminatory employment practices. The suit centered on recently developed selection requirements for the company's operations units. The plaintiffs charged that the requirements were arbitrary and screened out a much higher proportion of blacks than whites. The requirements, which were implemented in 1965, included a high school diploma, passage of a mechanical aptitude test, and a general intelligence test. When the requirements were initiated, they were not retrospective and so did not apply to current employees in the company's operations units. There was no attempt made by the company to determine the job-relatedness of these requirements.

A lower district court found in favor of the company on the grounds that any former discriminatory practices had ended and there was no evidence of discriminatory intent in the new requirements. An appellate court agreed with the finding of no discriminatory intent and in the absence of such intent the requirements were permissible.

The Supreme Court, in a unanimous decision, reversed the previous decisions. The court ruled that lack of discriminatory intent was not a sufficient defense against the use of employment devices which exclude on the basis of race. In North Carolina at that time 34 percent of the white males had high school degrees whereas only 12 percent of the black males did. The court acknowledged that tests and other measuring devices could be used, but held that they must be related to job performance. Duke Power had contended that their two test requirements were permissible because Title VII allowed the use of "professionally developed tests" as selection devices.

Because there were employees already working in the operational units of the company who did not have a high school diploma or had not taken the tests and were performing their duties in a satisfactory manner, Duke Power had no evidence relating the requirements to job performance. The court stated that if "an employment practice that operates to exclude Negroes cannot be shown to be related to job performance, it is prohibited."[12]

Two important precedents were set by the *Griggs* case, both of which are related to burdens of proof. The applicant carries the burden of proving the adverse impact of a particular selection device. Once adverse impact has been determined, the burden shifts to the employer to prove the validity or job-relatedness of the device. The court said the *EEOC Guidelines* were entitled to deference for proving validity.

United States v. Georgia Power (1973)   While the Supreme Court held in the *Griggs* decision that employment tests must be job related, attention was directed in later cases to the question of just what an employer must do to demonstrate job-relatedness, and the extent to which the *Guidelines* define that. For example, in February 1973, the 5th Circuit Court of Appeals upheld the 1970 *EEOC Guidelines* in *United States v. Georgia Power.*[13]

In 1969 the Attorney General brought suit against the Georgia Power Company for discrimination against blacks. Evidence was presented that at that time only 543 of the company's 7,515 employees were black (7.2%) despite the existence of a large pool of black applicants. Moreover, while blacks were classified exclusively as janitors, porters, maids, and laborers, almost all white employees occupied higher positions.

Beginning in 1960, in order to qualify for employment, all new employees were required to have a high school diploma or evidence of equivalent educational accomplishment. Then in 1963, all new employees were required also to pass a battery of tests developed by the Psychological Corporation. This requirement was instituted less than one month after the discontinuance of formal job segregation. In 1964 the company imposed the diploma requirement on all incumbent employees who wanted to transfer from the position of janitor, porter, or maid, but did not add that requirement for transferring from elsewhere in the company's structure. No study of these tests to determine job-relatedness had been conducted prior to the filing of the suit.

Recognizing its obligation under *Griggs* to provide proof of the job-relatedness of its test battery, the company began a validation study after the initiation of the suit. An official of the company conducted a validity study using an all white sample. The study collected supervisors' ratings on employees who had earlier been hired on the basis of the tests to be validated, and then compared those ratings with the test scores. This sample was admittedly small and excluded the 50% of the applicants who failed the test. Nevertheless, statistical evidence was produced by Georgia Power that supported the relationship of their selection test scores to the job performance ratings of supervisors, thereby demonstrating job-relatedness.

The court, however, held that the validation study did not meet the minimum standards recommended for validation strategy by the *EEOC Guidelines*. One failure was the absence of blacks from the validation study. With an applicant population that was one-third black, the court concluded that such a study could at least have been attempted. The court also held that there were black employees in three of the company's job classifications in numbers as large as some of the all white samples used by Georgia Power; therefore, the company could have attempted separate validation studies and, even though the studies would have been conducted on different job categories, some data could have been generated indicating whether the tests treated both races equally.

The *EEOC Guidelines* also required that the sample of subjects be representative of the normal applicant group for the job or jobs in question. Since there was an absence of blacks in the sample, the court ruled that this requirement had not been fulfilled. Also, according to the *Guidelines*, tests must be administered under controlled and standardized conditions. In this case, the court found that testing of new applicants was uniform, but that testing of incumbents was not.

Finally, the court held that even without regard to the *Guidelines*, the validation study was not a proper way of determining whether these tests predicted job success because it did not validate the acutal testing procedure used by the company. The company required a preset passing score on each of three tests by any applicant before he/she would be considered for employment. However, the Georgia Power study evaluated the three-test battery by weighting the numerical test scores twice as high as the verbal and calculating a composite score on the battery. Therefore, the court concluded that not only did the study not meet the minimum requirements of the *Guidelines*, but also that the study was irrelevant because it was not conducted on the actual practice followed by the company in administering its testing program. Also, in accordance with the *Griggs* decision, the court struck down the company's use of diploma requirements on the grounds that there was no evidence relating the possession of a diploma to job performance.

Albemarle Paper Company v. Moody (1975)   The issue of job-relatedness was addressed again by the Supreme Court in 1975 with the landmark case of *Albemarle Paper Company v. Moody*.[14] In 1966 four black employees filed a class action suit against the Albemarle Paper Company, charging discriminatory hiring practices. The requirements for employment at the company were that applicants had to pass three professionally developed tests. The hiring scores for these tests were based on published national norms. No validation of these tests had been conducted.

Four months before the Albemarle case went to trial the Supreme Court ruled on the *Griggs* case, making it clear that tests had to be shown to be job related. The Albemarle Paper Company had no such evidence. So, in the four months before the trial date the company attempted to do a validation study on its tests. The company hired an industrial psychologist who spent half a day at the plant and designed a validation study which company officials conducted without his supervision.[15] The sample size for the study was 105, all but four of whom were white. Thirty jobs were selected and categorized into ten job groupings based on their closeness in terms of advancement, not on the basis of any skills required to do the jobs. Within each of the ten job groupings, employees' test scores were correlated with the average of independent ratings made by two employees' supervisors. Results showed that both tests correlated significantly with only two job groupings even though both tests were required for all jobs, including jobs which were not a part of the study. The court called these findings "an odd patchwork of results" and held that partial evidence of job-relatedness was insufficient.

Also, the court criticized the company for not meeting the *Guideline*'s standards regarding the use of subjective ratings as criteria in validity studies, stating that the company could have been more careful in conducting that part of the study. The court objected to the fact that instructions to the supervisors were vague and that the supervisors had not had a standardized set of criteria upon which to base their ratings.

Another objection was that tests used for lower level positions were validated on upper level positions. According to the *Guidelines*, this is only permissible if it can be shown that new employees will most likely be promoted after a reasonable amount of time. Albemarle could not meet this requirement.

Also, the court pointed out that the sample used in the study was not representative of the applicant pool. The sample was composed of job-experienced white workers, while applicants had a large proportion of inexperienced nonwhites.

The Supreme Court made two significant rulings in this case. One, it reaffirmed that the *Guidelines* were "entitled to great deference." The other ruling concerned the awarding of back pay as penalty for violation of Title VII. The court stated that back pay should be awarded to victims of discrimination regardless of whether an employer had acted in "good faith."

Washington v. Davis (1975)   A case that was decided at about the same time as *Albemarle, Washington v. Davis* upheld the use of selection tests where adverse impact was shown.[16] A class action suit was brought against the police department by a group of blacks who had failed a verbal skills test that the department was using as a selection device. The suit charged that with a black failure rate four times the rate of whites, the test screened out blacks disproportionately, so was therefore discriminatory. The department claimed that because the scores on the test related statistically with results of the police academy training program, the test was shown to be job related.

A district court upheld the department's claim of validity. The court of appeals reversed the lower court decision on the grounds that success in a training program could not be used as a criterion for proving job-related validity. When the Supreme Court ruled on the case, it upheld the original district court decision.

The court ruled that performance in a training program could be used as a measure of job performance if the training had a content relationship to actual job duties. The court pointed out that there was no single method for appropriately validating employment tests for their relationship to job performance.

EEOC v. Detroit Edison (1975)   *EEOC v. Detroit Edison* affirmed the broad application of Title VII beyond objective tests to interviews and other subjective devices.[17] The case began when three black employees of Detroit Edison filed a class action suit charging the company with a variety of discriminatory employment policies involving both selection and promotion. These practices included the use of unrelated employment tests and of interview procedures which excluded blacks for non-job-related reasons.

The case went first to a district court which found in favor of the employees. The court held that the evidence established a case of deliberate discrimination and ordered the payment of punitive damages to the three plaintiffs, who had also filed suit individually. The U.S. Court of Appeals for the Sixth Circuit upheld the lower court's ruling with some modifications. The appellate court agreed with the finding that Detroit Edison had a history of discriminatory employment practices which had an adverse impact on minorities. The policies which the court ruled discriminatory included the practice of relying on referrals rather than using the marketplace for recruitment of applications. The court also ruled against Detroit Edison's heavy reliance on subjective interview judgments. In reviewing the interview procedures, the court observed that interviewers and supervisory personnel in high level positions made the final decision regarding selection. None of the individuals was black or had personal contact with blacks. In the selection interview, the interviewer made extremely subjective judgments about an applicant's personality, appearance, dress, and speech. There was no structured or written format for questions to be asked or how information was to be interpreted. Another complication was the fact that a sizable proportion of white applicants either were relatives or friends of current Detroit Edison employees.

The appellate court agreed with the district court's finding of discriminatory employment practices, but it overruled the district court's awarding of punitive damages to the original three plaintiffs. Although the appellate court ruled that discrimination under Title VII did not warrant the awarding of damages, all black employees of Detroit Edison would be eligible for consideration for back pay awards. Detroit Edison claimed that after the suit was filed it had come under new management and had stopped discriminatory practices. The court held that the company still had responsibility for its past actions and that the court must still prescribe remedial provisions, such as the allowance for payment of back pay.

Spurlock v. United Airlines (1972)   The case of *Spurlock v. United Airlines* involved a demonstration of the job-relatedness of selection instruments other than tests.[18] In this case, Spurlock filed suit against United Airlines after his application for the job of flight officer had been rejected. Spurlock charged the airline with discrimination against blacks and offered as evidence the fact that only 9 flight officers out of 5,900 were black. In the suit, Spurlock challenged two of the requirements for the job: a college degree and a minimum of 500 hours of flight time.

United contended that both these selection requirements were job related. Using statistics, United showed that applicants with a greater number of flight hours are more likely to succeed in the rigorous training program which flight officers must complete after being hired. Statistics also showed that 500 hours was a reasonable minimum requirement. In addition, United contended that, because of the high cost of the training program, it was important that those who begin the training program eventually become flight officers.

United officials also testified that the possession of a college degree indicated that the applicant had the ability to function in a classroom atmosphere. This ability is important because of the initial training program and because flight officers are required to attend intensive refresher courses every six months.

The court accepted the evidence presented by United as proof of the job-relatedness of the requirements and, in a significant ruling, stated that when a job requires a small amount of skill and training and the consequences of hiring an unqualified applicant are insignificant, the courts should closely examine selection instruments which are discriminatory. On the other hand, when the job requires a high degree of skill and the economic and human risks involved are great, the employer bears a lighter burden to show that selection instruments are job-related.

Connecticut v. Teal (1982)   The central issue in the case of *Connecticut v. Teal* was whether discrimination occurred in a multi-step selection program even though the total program did not demonstrate adverse impact.[19] Four black employees of the Department of Income Maintenance of the State of Connecticut were provisionally promoted to Welfare Eligibility Supervisor and served in that capacity for almost two years. According to departmental policy, to permanently gain the position an individual had to participate successfully in a multi-step selection process. The first step was a passing score on a written examination. This exam was administered to 48 black and 259 white applicants. Of these, 26 blacks (54%) and 206 whites (80%) passed. The four black individuals serving as provisional supervisors did not pass.

Even though the rate of passing for blacks was below the recommended four-fifths ratio, the remaining parts of the selection program were conducted in such a way as to insure nondiscrimination in the final selection. Forty-six persons in total were promoted, 11 of whom were black and 35 of whom were white. This meant that 23% of the black applicants were promoted and 14% of the whites. The Department argued that, as a consequence, no discrimination against blacks in selection was demonstrated.

The court disagreed with this position, pointing out the adverse impact of the written test. The decision stated that Title VII prohibits employment practices that deprive "any individual of employment opportunities." Therefore, the focus of the statute is on the individual, not the minority group as a whole. Title VII does not permit the victims of discriminatory policy to be told they have not been wronged because other persons of their race or sex were hired. The Department, therefore, had to insure that each part of the selection program was nondiscriminatory.

Personnel Administrator of Massachusetts v. Feeney (1979)[20]   This case reviewed an apparent conflict between a state's veterans' preference employment policy and women's rights. For a certain type of state position, Massachusetts had long used a statute that stated that all veterans who qualify for state civil service positions must be considered for appointment ahead of any qualifying nonveterans. Because there were many more male than female veterans in the state, the statute adversely affected female applicants.

During 12 years as a public employee, the plaintiff had taken and passed a number of open, competitive examinations. For example, she received the second highest score on an examination for a job with the Board of Dental Examiners. However, because of veteran preference, she was ranked sixth on the selection list and a lower scoring male was appointed. She also achieved the third highest score on a test for an Administrative Assistant, but was placed 13th, behind 12 male veterans, 11 of whom had lower scores.

The court agreed that the statute discriminated against women, but sustained it. In its decision the court said that preference in hiring veterans represents an awkward exception to the idea that merit should prevail in government employment. Such laws are commonly passed after wars to reward veterans for the sacrifice of military service, to ease the transition from military to civilian life, to encourage patriotic service, and to attract loyal people to civil service occupations. This may not be good employment policy but the statute was not illegal by its nature.

The major points of each of these cases are summarized in Table 2.3. We can see that the result of the various court decisions is to identify selection practices that in the presence of adverse impact are either acceptable or unacceptable. Unfortunately for selection specialists, most decisions identify unacceptable actions. We, therefore, know more about what *not* to do than what we can do. This is somewhat unsettling. It would be more convenient if the courts could assemble a description of acceptable selection practices. From all that has been said in this chapter, however, you should realize that such an action by the courts is not possible. Selection practices are too varied

Table 2.3   Key Issues in Major Selection Court Cases

Case	Selection Policy Addressed
Griggs v. Duke Power (1971)	1. Lack of discriminatory intent not sufficient defense 2. Selection test must be job related if adverse impact results 3. Employer bears burden of proof in face of apparent adverse impact
United States v. Georgia Power (1973)	1. Validation strategy must comply with EEOC guidelines 2. Validation must include minority members 3. Validation must reflect selection decision practices 4. Testing must occur under standardized conditions
Albemarle Paper Company v. Moody (1975)	1. Supervisors' ratings of performance used in validation were vague and not standardized 2. Tests used for selection for lower level positions were reflective of higher positions 3. Validation sample not reflective of applicant sample in terms of job experience
Washington v. Davis (1975)	1. Performance in a training program could be used as measure of job performance if related to job duties 2. Adverse impact could be justified on such a basis
EEOC v. Detroit Edison (1975)	1. Use of referrals for recruitment not acceptable if adverse impact results 2. No black interviewers used 3. Interview not standardized 4. Use of subjective interviewer selection decisions not permitted
Spurlock v. United Airlines (1972)	1. College degree and experience requirements can be shown to be job related 2. Company's burden of proof against adverse impact diminishes as human risks increase
Connecticut v. Teal (1982)	1. Company must insure that all parts of a multiple step-selection program have no adverse impact
Personnel Administrator of Massachusetts v. Feeney (1979)	1. Veterans' preference in selection is permitted

and too interrelated. In terms of the regulatory model, the main responsibility of the courts and agencies is to stop organizations from perpetuating the societal problems which prompted the EEO laws. It is the responsibility of those who design selection programs to develop the various parts of their programs so that they comply with the the the laws. Government regulation is a major reason why, as we said at the beginning of Chapter 1, selection has increasingly become such a complex activity.

EEO Considerations in Selection

This chapter has presented the major EEO laws and discussed their impact on human resource selection programs. This last section will summarize the major legal concepts regarding discrimination that personnel specialists need to be aware of in either reviewing an existing selection program or developing a new one.

Basis of Discrimination

Charges of discrimination in selection practices must be linked to one of the personal characteristics specified in EEO law. The federal laws and directives identify race, color, religion, sex, national origin, age (between 40 and 70), physical or mental handicaps, and Vietnam era veteran status as the covered characteristics. Although this is indeed a long list, it clearly means that, unless there is a state or local law, many of the charges of discrimination that are threatened against organizations (e.g., discrimination based on homosexuality, hair or clothing style, school affiliation, etc.) are not feasible according to EEO law unless the charge can be linked to one of the specified characteristics. The specification of the characteristics also defines the groups that personnel specialists should consider when reviewing the vulnerability of a selection program to discrimination charges. An analysis of possible discrimination can be conducted on those groups with characteristics that are both specified in EEO law and constitute at least two percent of the relevant labor market. Although this will constitute a lengthy list, it has the advantage of defining the scope of compliance to EEO law.

Evidence of Discrimination

A charge of discrimination can be brought against an organization with little substantiating evidence other than the fact that an individual was not selected for a position. In many cases such a charge constitutes a public embarrassment for an organization. Also, many times organizations do not wish to bear the cost of legal action, especially if such action may be prolonged. The result is that the organization frequently will negotiate a settlement to the charge. Although this may be a pragmatic solution to a particular occurrence, it does little to resolve a potentially recurrent problem. It is important for personnel specialists to realize that judicial rulings about discrimination in selection practices generally have been based on patterns of selection decisions over a period of time rather than on an isolated instance. A particular selection decision means that one (or a few) individual(s) has been hired from a pool of applicants. The others have been denied employment. Perhaps several of these rejected applicants differ from the one who was selected on a personal characteristic specified in EEO law, e.g., color, race, or religion. This difference and the denial of employment could serve as an *indicator* of discrimination in selection. Courts have generally recognized, however, that each individual selection is favorable to some applicants and unfavorable to others. The crucial data are the pattern that is evident when one views the overall result of a series of decisions. If such data indicate that one group, e.g., white males, are selected in more cases than one would expect to find, given the relevant labor market's demographic characteristics, then the usual judgment has been that the questioned selection decision is, in fact, discriminatory. However, if the review of this series of selection decisions indicates that over time the demographic pattern of those selected is similar to the demographic profile of the relevant labor market, the usual judgment is that the questioned selection decision is not an indicant of discrimination and that the consequences of a particular selection decision are a natural and nondiscriminatory by-product of the selection process.

Options of the Organization

If, after reviewing selection patterns for specific jobs and applying the appropriate statistical analysis (e.g., the four-fifths rule or the standard deviation test) to the demographic groups specified in EEO law, the personnel specialist notes large selection differences, the organization has two options for reducing its vulnerability. The first is to discontinue the current procedures and develop alternative ones that would result in small differences in selection among the various demographic groups. At first this may seem a formidable task, but there are many situations in which such a change is actually fairly straightforward. We previously discussed the interaction between recruitment and selection. Some organizations have found that, especially for entry level positions, a broadening of recruitment activities to systematically include women and minorities has provided a sufficiently qualified applicant pool to substantially change selection patterns. Other cases would require the reevaluation of selection requirements, such as the number of years of experience and the education degrees, to determine their necessity for job performance. Such requirements, especially if they are used stringently at an early stage of the processing of applicants, can have a large effect on the applicant pool. The second alternative, if large selection differences exist, is to conduct a validation study to support the organization's contention that the selection instruments are job related. As the *Uniform Guidelines* indicate, such studies must conform to common methodological procedures to be maximally useful. Chapter 5 of this text presents the steps in the most common of these validation methods.

A final important point to keep in mind is that there is not a legal requirement either to demonstrate the job-relatedness of all selection devices or to hire unqualified applicants in order to increase the "numbers" of specific groups. As has been pointed out previously, proof of job-relatedness becomes necessary only if discrimination is evidenced. Looked at another way, if an organization is willing to live with the consequences of selection decisions based on applicant information that is not demonstrated to be related to job performance, then the organization ought to share this risk among all relevant demographic groups. However, if an organization goes through the process of building job-relatedness into the data that are used for selection decisions, the organization is not obligated to ignore such work and hire only because the applicant belongs to a certain demographic group. This is a point often overlooked and frequently results in hiring decisions made primarily to increase the employment of certain groups. If these individuals are not qualified for the jobs into which they are hired, their selection is not a service to either themselves or the organization.

References for Chapter 2

[1] William F. Glueck, *Personnel: A Diagnostic Approach,* 3d ed. (Plano, Tex.: Business Publications, Inc., 1982), p. 201.

[2] Kenneth J. McCulloch, *Selecting Employees Safely Under The Law* (Englewood Cliffs, N.J.: Prentice-Hall, Inc., 1981), p. 3.

[3] James Ledvinka, *Federal Regulation of Personnel and Human Resource Management* (Boston: Kent Publishing Co., 1982), p. 11.

[4] Ibid., pp. 24–26.

[5] Kenneth J. McCulloch, *Selecting Employees Safely Under the Law,* p. 16.

[6] Leslie B. Milk, "The Key to Job Accommodations," *Personnel Administrator* 24 (1979): 31–33, 38.

[7] 41 Code of Federal Regulations §60.741 (1981).

[8] *Griggs v. Duke Power Co.,* 401 U.S. 424 (1971).

[9] *McDonnell Douglas v. Green,* 411 U.S. 792 (1973).

[10] Equal Employment Opportunity Commission, Civil Service Commission, Department of Labor, and Department of Justice, *Adoption of Four Agencies of Uniform Guidelines on Employee Selection Procedures,* 43 Federal Register 38, 290–38, 315 (Aug. 25, 1978).

[11] *Griggs v. Duke Power Co.,* 401 U.S. 424 (1971).

[12] Ibid.

[13] *United States v. Georgia Power,* 474 F. 2d 906 (1973).

[14] *Albemarle Paper Company v. Moody,* 422 U.S. 405 (1975).

[15] Thaddeus Holt, "A View From Albemarle," *Personnel Psychology* 30 (1977): 65–80.

[16] *Washington v. Davis,* 426 U.S. 229 (1975).

[17] *EEOC v. Detroit Edison,* 515 F. 2d 301 (1975).

[18] *Spurlock v. United Airlines,* 475 F. 2d 216 (10th Cir. 1972).

[19] *Connecticut v. Teal,* 457 U.S. 440 (1982).

[20] *Personnel Administrator of Massachusetts v. Feeney,* 422 U.S. 256 (1979).

PART TWO

Foundations of

Measurement for

Human Resource

Selection

The collection of information on job candidates through selection measures is central to any human resource selection system. Information is the basis for all decisions concerning the selection of job applicants. Sometimes, however, personnel selection decisions turn out to be wrong. Perhaps individuals who were predicted to be outstanding performers actually contribute very little to an organization. Others who were forecast to stay with an organization for a lengthy period of time leave after only several months. And, in cases that are not verifiable, persons who were thought to be very poor employees for a firm and not hired would have been valuable contributors had they been employed. In each of these situations, we would conclude some inappropriate selection decisions had been made. Yet, when we analyze the situation, it may not be the decisions themselves that were wrong, but the data on which they were based that were faulty. Thus, it is imperative that managers have sound data on which to base selection decisions. What do we mean by "sound data?" The three chapters in this section address this question. Specifically, the objectives of this section are as follows:

1. To explore the role of human resource "measurement" in selection decision making.

2. To examine the concepts of "reliability" and "validity" of selection data as well as their role in choosing useful selection measures and making effective selection decisions.

3

Human Resource
Measurement
in Selection

Fundamentals of Measurement: An Overview

An important assumption in selection decision making is that information is available with which selection decisions can be made. But, what types of information can be used? Where does this information come from? What characteristics should this information have in order to be most useful for selection purposes? These are only a few of the questions addressed in the present chapter on human resource measurement. Specifically, the focus is on (a) the basics of psychological measurement as they apply to human resource selection and (b) the locating, developing, and interpreting of measures commonly used in human resource selection.

The Role of Measurement in Human Resource Selection

If you have watched competent carpenters build a house or a piece of furniture, you cannot help being impressed by how well the various pieces fit together. For example, when a door is hung in place, the door will have a snug fit with its frame. Or, perhaps, you have watched a rocket lift off for space. It is amazing that we can launch a craft from Cape Canaveral, send it thousands of miles into space, have it orbit Earth numerous times, and then days later have the craft land at a precise time and place. Although there are many things that contribute to the success of a carpenter installing a door and a scientist launching a rocket, one of the factors common to the success of both is their ability to employ "measurement." How could a door be made to fit if a carpenter could not determine the exact dimensions of the opening the door was designed to fit? How could a rocket be launched and safely returned to a specified location if a scientist could not measure factors such as time, distance, and speed? Measurement is the answer, and, as we will see, measurement is also essential to the successful implementation and administration of a human resource selection program.

The Nature of Measurement   Let's imagine for a moment that we are in charge of hiring personnel for a large company. We have position openings for the job of sales representative. Because of current economic conditions and the nature of the job, many people are interested in applying for the position. As we sit in our office, we see numerous applicants coming in to be screened for employment. Each person completes an application, takes a test, and is interviewed by us. After several days of assessing applicants, we can draw at least one obvious conclusion: *people are different.* As we think about the applicants that enter our office, we notice that some are tall, some are short; some pleasant and agreeable, others serious and even unpleasant. Still other applicants seem intelligent and others rather dull; some seem assertive and outgoing, while others appear very shy and withdrawn. Although our usual system of classifying individuals in these extreme categories may be useful for *describing* people in a gross way, it may not be very useful for choosing among applicants. In a personnel selection context, we will probably find that few people really fall at these extreme points. For example, only a few of our applicants will be extremely bright and only a few extremely dull. For the many others, we will need a means for making finer distinctions among them for the various characteristics (intelligence, assertiveness, etc.) which are of interest to us. We will need to use "measurement" to make these discriminations and to study in detail the relations between applicant characteristics and employee performance on the job.

A *Definition*   But, what is measurement? Numerous writings have been directed toward the topic; some have emphasized its meaning, others have addressed methods involved in its application. From the perspective of human resource selection, we can offer one definition. Simply put, *measurement involves the application of rules for assigning numbers to objects to represent quantities of attributes.*[1] Let's explore this definition. As Jum Nunnally points out, *rules* suggest that the basis for assigning numbers is clearly specified. For any measure that we might use in selection, say a test, it is important that if different users employ the measure they will obtain similar results. Thus, if job applicants take a test, differences among applicants' scores should be due to individual differences in their test performance and not to the way in which different scorers scored the tests. Rules for assigning numbers to our selection measures help to standardize the application of these measures.

A second point in our definition involves the concept of an *attribute*. In reality, when we measure an object, we do not measure the object per se, rather we assess an attribute or property of the object. When we measure *physical* attributes of people, many of these attributes (for example, sex) can be assessed through direct observation. However, when we are interested in assessing *psychological* characteristics, some attributes of people are not so easily observable. Psychological characteristics (such as, aggressiveness, intelligence, job knowledge, mathematical and verbal abilities) must be inferred from *indicants* of these objects. An indicant simply represents something that points toward something else.[2] A score on a mathematics test is an indicant of a job applicant's mathematical ability. With our test, we are not measuring the applicant but the mathematical ability of the applicant. Notice in our description we have not talked about how well we measure an attribute. Obviously, if we want to measure mathematical ability, we want an indicant (a test, for example) that is a good measure of this ability. But, our obtaining a good measure of such elusive but nevertheless critical attributes (such as various knowledge, skills, abilities, personality, and other traits) is not always easy. To measure an applicant's physical characteristics is one thing. However, to measure the psychological characteristics of an applicant is a different problem. Yet, in contrast to physical characteristics, it is psychological attributes that will typically be identified as important indicators of how well an applicant can perform a job.

When we use measures (such as tests or interviews) of psychological attributes, we have to draw inferences from these measures. Because inferences are involved, however, we are on much shakier ground than when we can directly observe an attribute. An interviewer conducting a selection interview might believe that the extent of an applicant's eye contact with the interviewer reflects the applicant's interest in the company. Or, the firmness of a handshake reflects the interviewee's self-confidence. But, are these inferences warranted? This is an important question to answer if we are to use in a meaningful way indicants of important psychological attributes in selection decision making. We will see shortly what characteristics we might look for in obtaining a good measure of any attribute important in selecting human resources.

A third and final point in our definition of measurement is that *numbers* represent quantities of attributes. Numbers play a very useful role in summarizing and communicating the degree or amount of an assessed attribute. Thus, as a form of label, numbers can provide a convenient means for characterizing and differentiating among job applicants. Numbers generally play an important role in the current use of selection techniques.[3]

Criteria and Predictors in Selection Research   A fundamental problem in personnel selection is to choose from a large group of job applicants, a smaller group to be employed. The goal of personnel selection is to designate the individuals who should be hired. These individuals are chosen because the selection techniques predict that they can best perform the job in question. When the term "predict" is used, it is assumed that a selection manager has the information on which to base these predictions. Where does this information come from? Basically, the information is derived from an analysis of the job. A job analysis is designed to identify the attributes needed by incumbents to perform the job successfully. Once the attributes of employee success are known, we can name employee specifications required for the job. We can measure applicants with respect to these specifications and make our predictions accordingly.

Measurement plays a vital role in helping the selection manager make accurate predictions. Predicting who should be hired generally requires the identification and measurement of two types of variables. The first of these is called the *criterion* (or *criteria* when more than one criterion is being considered). A criterion usually serves as a measure or definition of what is meant by employee success on the job. It is the dependent variable to be predicted. Criteria are defined by thoroughly studying the job(s) for which a selection system is being developed. A wide array of variables might serve as criteria. Some criteria deal with employee behaviors. For example, absenteeism, tardiness, number of goods produced, dollar sales, amount of scrap produced in manufacturing tasks, and speed of performance are a small sampling of criteria that depict what some workers *do*. On the other hand, some criteria may be equally important but involve affective reactions to a job as reported by an incumbent, rather than specific behaviors. These reactions are usually recorded on a self-report questionnaire. Job satisfaction, employee morale, and intention to stay with an organization are but a few examples of such criteria. Further, supervisory ratings of employee behavior, such as employee productivity, are also often used.

There are numerous types of criteria that can be predicted. Nevertheless, criteria should not be chosen or measured in a cavalier, unsystematic, or haphazard manner. They *must* be important to the job, and they *must* be appropriately measured. Since criteria are the basis for characterizing employee success, the utility of a selection system will depend to a significant degree on their selection, definition, and measurement.

A second type of variable required in predicting applicants' job success is called *predictor* variables. Predictors represent the *indicants* of those attributes identified through a job analysis as being important for job success. Thus, predictors are used to predict our criteria. This book discusses a wide variety of selection measures that have been found to be useful in predicting employee performance. Tests, interviews, biographical data questionnaires, application blanks, and assessment centers are just some of the types of predictors you will read about. But, like criteria, there are two important requirements in developing and using predictors: (a) they *must* be important to the job and (b) they *must* be appropriate measures of attributes identified as critical to job success.

Measurement and Individual Differences   Earlier in this chapter, we noted a basic law of psychology applicable to human resource selection: people are different. Furthermore, we said that one goal of selection is to predict which individuals should be hired for a job. Measurement of individual differences with our predictors and criteria helps us to meet our goal. Suppose, for instance, you were charged with the responsibility for hiring workers who could produce high quantities of work output. The workers individually manufacture wire baskets. After looking at some recent production records, you plot graphically the quantity of output for a large number of workers. Exhibit 3.1 shows the results of your plot. This "bell-shaped" or "normal" curve is a typical distribution for a variety of human characteristics such as intelligence, motivation, height, and weight, when sufficiently large numbers of observations are available.

Our plot suggests several things. First, because there is variability in productivity scores, there must be individual differences among employees in their levels of productivity. Second, relatively few produce a very large or very small number of baskets. Many, however, fall between these two extremes. If we can assume that our quantity of productivity measure is a suitable criterion, our objective is to obtain a predictor that will detect the individual differences or variance in productivity. If our predictor is a good one, scores on the predictor will be related with individuals' productivity scores.

The above example highlights the important role of measurement in selection research. Numbers assigned to predictor and criterion attributes enable us to make the necessary fine distinctions among individuals. Subsequent analyses of these numbers help us meet one of our roles: prediction of job performance. Without measurement, we would probably be left with our intuition and personal best guesses. Perhaps, for a very small number of us, these judgments will work. For most of us, however, "deciding by the seat of our pants" will simply not suffice.

Scales of Measurement   Use of predictors and criteria in selection research requires that these variables be measured. Measurement is prerequisite to any statistical analysis to be performed in a selection study. However, the refinement of our distinctions among people is determined by the precision with which we measure the variables. In addition, the level of precision will dictate what statistical analyses can be done with the numbers obtained from measurement.

In the context of selection research, a *scale of measurement* is simply a means by which individuals can be distinguished from one another on a variable of interest. Because we use a variety of scales, our research variables tend to differ rather dramatically in terms of precision. For example, suppose we were developing a selection program for bank management trainees. One criterion we want to predict is "trainability," that is, trainee success in a management training program. We could measure trainability in several ways. On one hand, we could simply classify individuals in terms of who did and who did not graduate from the training program. (Graduation, for example, may be based on trainees' ability to pass a test on banking principles and regulations.) Our criterion would be a dichotomous category, that is, unsuc-

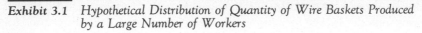

Exhibit 3.1   *Hypothetical Distribution of Quantity of Wire Baskets Produced by a Large Number of Workers*

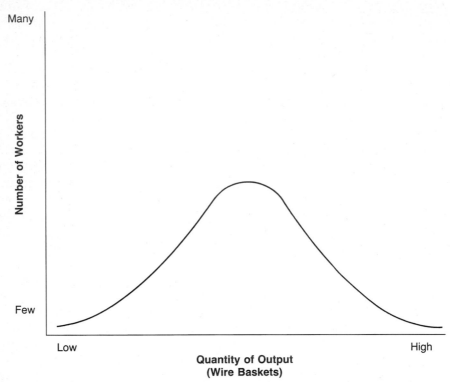

cessful and successful. Thus, our predictor variable would be used to differentiate between those applicants who could and those who could not successfully complete their training.

On the other hand, we could evaluate trainability by the *degree* of trainee success as measured by training performance test scores. Again, our test might be used to assess how much trainees know at the end of their training program. But, notice that in this case our criterion is not a categorical measure (that is, success or failure) but rather a measure of degree.

Exhibit 3.2 shows the distributions of trainees' scores for the two methods of measuring trainability. Notice that our simple *classification* of success criterion is not as precise a measure as our *degree* of success criterion. Greater individual differences in trainability can be mapped by the latter criterion measure than by the former one. The variable "trainability" is the same in both of the above examples. But, the two examples differ with respect to the level of measurement involved. *It is the manner in which the variable is measured and not the variable itself that determines level of measurement.* As such, we can draw more precise conclusions with one measure than we can with the other.

There are four types of scales or levels of measurement: (a) nominal, (b)

Exhibit 3.2   *Hypothetical Distributions of Trainees for Two Criteria of Trainee Success*

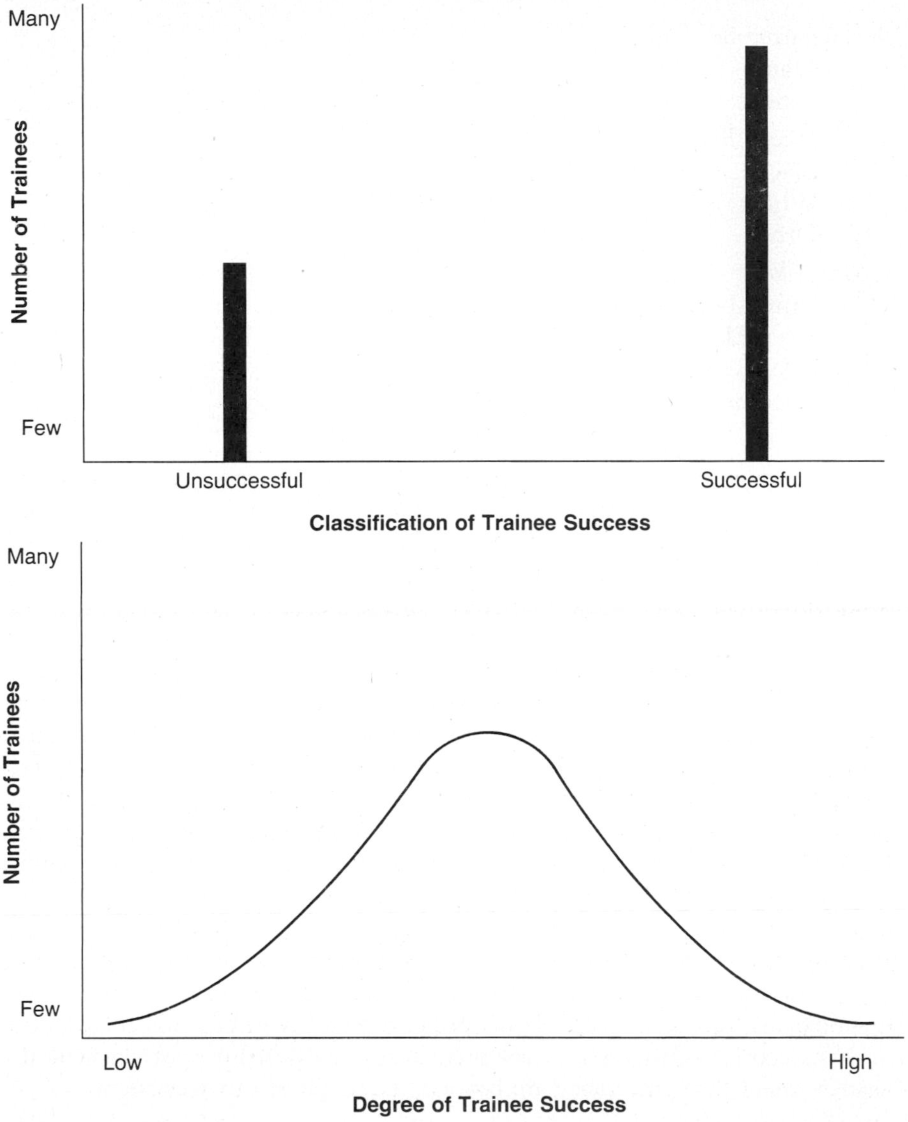

Classification of Trainee Success

Degree of Trainee Success

ordinal, (c) interval, and (d) ratio. The degree of precision with which we can measure differences among people increases as we move from nominal to ratio scales. Increased precision provides us with more detailed information about people on the variables being studied. More powerful statistical analyses can then be performed with our data. These analyses, in turn, can help us develop more accurate human resource selection methods.

Nominal Scale   A nominal scale is one composed of two or more mutually exclusive categories. Examples of nominal scale measurement for the variables of applicant sex, applicant race, and job class include the following:

A. *Applicant Sex*
   1. Male
   2. Female

B. *Applicant Race*
   1. Black
   2. White
   3. Other

C. *Job Class*
   1. Sales Manager
   2. Sales Clerk
   3. Sales Representative
   4. Salesperson
   5. Other

In nominal scale measurement, all individuals having a common characteristic are assigned to the same category or class. Members in the category are regarded as being equivalent. Persons possessing a different characteristic are assigned to a different category. Since the categories are mutually exclusive, individuals can belong to only one of the classes. Numbers can be given to individuals assigned to the scale categories, however, the numbers serve merely as labels. They carry no numerical meaning. Thus, if we are using the variable "applicant sex" in a study, we could assign a code of "1" to all male applicants and a code of "2" to all females. Numerical codes provide a convenient form for distinguishing between categories of "applicant sex." We could use other numbers as well (such as 0 and 1) to identify males and females. Both scoring schemes have the same meaning. The number codes themselves do not indicate how males and females differ. The only information we have through our numerical codes is an applicant's sex. Because we cannot state *how* members assigned to nominal scale categories differ, this type of scale is the simplest form of measurement.

Some statistical analyses can be performed with nominal scale data. For example, we can count and obtain percentages of members assigned to our scale categories. Other statistical procedures are possible, but we will not discuss them here since they are beyond the scope of our treatment.

Ordinal Scale   An ordinal scale is one that ranks objects, such as individuals, from "high" to "low" on some variable of interest. Ordinal scales can be found rather frequently in selection research. In developing criteria measures, for instance, supervisors are sometimes asked to rank their subordinates with respect to some attribute. One example of a completed rank-order scale used by supervisors to evaluate their subordinates is shown in Exhibit 3.3.

Exhibit 3.3   *Example of an Ordinal Scale of Measurement*

Ranking of Employees

Below are listed the names of your 10 subordinates. Read over the list and then rank the individuals in terms of their *quality of work completed* on their jobs. By "Quality of Work Completed," it is meant a *minimum* amount of re-work necessary to correct employee mistakes. You should give the subordinate you believe is *highest* in quality of work performed a rank of "1," the employee *next* highest in quality of work a "2," the next a "3," and so on until a "10" is given to the employee who is *lowest* in quality of work completed.

Note:

> 1 = Highest Quality
> .
> .
> .
> 10 = Lowest Quality

Employee	Rank on Quality of Work Completed
A. A. Armenakis	4
A. G. Bedeian	2
W. F. Giles	1
W. H. Holley	7
R. E. Niebuhr	9
D. R. Norris	5
W. B. Boyles	3
P. A. Pinto	6
C. M. Pushinni	8
L. F. Schoenfeldt	10

The ordinal scale provides us with more information than does a nominal scale. Individuals are not only assigned a number representative of a category, as on a nominal scale, but differences between the numbers assigned yield additional information. Numerical differences indicate the relative position of individuals for the variable on which they are ranked. For example, in Exhibit 3.3, we know that the individual ranked 1 was highest in quality of work completed. Furthermore, we know that each individual down the scale produces better quality work than the following individual. However, an ordinal scale does not provide information on the *magnitude* of the differences among the ranks. In our personnel ranking example, the employee ranked 1 may be only marginally more productive in quality of work than the employee ranked 2. However, the employee ranked 2 may be considerably better than the employee ranked 3.

Another example of an ordinal scale often encountered in selection involves test scores. Percentiles are sometimes used to interpret the results of a test. A percentile represents the proportion of persons taking a test who make below a given score. If we know that a job applicant scored at the 76th percentile, we know that 76 percent of the individuals who took the test scored lower and 24 percent scored higher. As in our previous example, we do not know how much better or worse the next individual performed in terms of a specific test scored.

From the two examples above, we see we can only draw "greater than" or "less than" conclusions with ordinal data; we do not know the amount of difference that separates individuals or objects being ranked. Information relative to magnitude differences is provided by our next two scales.

Interval Scale   With an interval scale, differences between numbers take on meaning. In addition to rank-order information, it is also known how different objects being measured are with respect to an attribute.

The interval scale has an arbitrary but not an absolute zero point. Although an object being measured may be given a score of zero, the score of zero is set by convention. Let's look at an example to clarify the point. Assume we have given a mathematics ability test to a group of job applicants. The test consists of 100 math problems, each item counting one point. Possible test scores can range from 0 to 100 (no items missed). A difference between scores of 40 and 60 would not represent the same difference *in applicants' mathematical abilities* as the difference between 60 and 80. If individuals scored 0, we could not say they did not have any mathematical ability. Such a conclusion would imply that our test covered *all* possible items of mathematical ability; in fact, our test is only a *sample* of these items. Obviously, we cannot make this statement since zero is only set by convention for our specific test. Also, because of the absence of an absolute zero, we cannot state that an individual who scores 80 on our test has twice as much ability as one who scores 40.

Rating scales are frequently used as criterion measures in selection studies. For example, many job performance measures consist of performance appraisal ratings. Most rating scales used in this manner are Likert-type scales such as that shown in Exhibit 3.4. When these ratings are treated as an interval scale, it is assumed that the magnitude of the difference between rating points is the same. Thus, raters are expected to view the difference between points 1 and 2 on the scale the same as the difference between points 4 and 5.

Variables measured by interval scales tap the differences, order, and equality of the magnitude of the differences in the data. These scales are more powerful than the nominal and ordinal scales; therefore, more powerful statistical methods can be employed. Interval data can be analyzed by many of the procedures important in personnel research. For example, means, standard deviations, and various correlational procedures can be employed.[4]

Exhibit 3.4 *Example of an Interval Scale Used in Rating Employee Job Performance*

Rating Factors				Ratings

1. Quality of Work—The extent to which the employee actually completes job assignments.

1	2	3	4	5
Almost always makes errors, has very low accuracy	Quite often makes errors	Makes errors but equals job standards	Makes few errors, has high accuracy	Almost never makes errors, has very high accuracy

Comments: _____ _____

2. Quantity of Work—The extent to which the employee produces a volume of work consistent with established standards for the job.

1	2	3	4	5
Almost never meets standards	Quite often does not meet standards	Volume of work is satisfactory, equals job standards	Quite often produces more than required	Almost always exceeds standards, exceptionally productive

Comments: _____ _____

3. Attendance/Punctuality—The extent to which the employee adheres to work schedule.

1	2	3	4	5
Excessively absent or tardy	Too frequently absent or tardy	Occasionally absent or tardy	Infrequently absent or tardy	Almost never absent or tardy

Comments: _____ _____

4. Relationship With Co-Workers—The extent to which the employee establishes and maintains good relations with co-workers.

1	2	3	4	5
Does not get along well with co-workers; definitely hinders effectiveness	Has difficulty in getting along with co-workers	Gets along with co-workers adequately; average skills in human relations	Above average skills in human relations	Excellent skills in human relations; increases effectiveness

Comments: _____ _____

5. Use of Work Time—The extent to which the employee uses time to effectively and efficiently accomplish job tasks.

1	2	3	4	5
Quite often wastes time	Too frequently wastes time	Makes adequate use of time	Utilizes time wisely	Exceptionally effective in use of time

Comments: _____ _____

These procedures are essential for developing the models to be used in selection decision making.

Ratio scale   As on the interval scale, differences between numerical values on a ratio scale have meaning. In contrast, though, a ratio scale has an absolute zero point. The presence of an absolute zero point permits statements to be made about the ratio of one individual's scores to another based on the amount of the attribute being measured. Thus, if one worker produces 100 wire baskets in an hour while another produces 50, we can then state that the second worker produces only half as much as the first.

The numerical operations that can be performed with the data suggest the origin of the name "ratio" scale. Numerical values on a ratio scale can be added, subtracted, multiplied, and divided. Ratios of scale numbers can be used, and the meaning of the scale will be preserved.

Most scales involving physical measurements (such as, height, weight, eyesight, hearing, and physical strength) or counting (such as, amount of pay, number of times absent from work, months of job tenure, number of promotions received, and number of goods produced) are ratio scales. There is at least one situation in selection where frequencies are not ratio scales. For instance, if we score a test by the number of items correct and want to draw conclusions with respect to this number, then we have a ratio scale. However, if we want to draw conclusions in terms of the ability or some other trait measured by the test, then we no longer have a ratio scale. In the first case, we have an absolute zero point (with respect to the number of items correct). In the other case, we do not have an absolute zero point; we have an arbitrary one (in terms of the trait measured).

In the field of human resource selection, we simply do not have as many ratio scales available to us as we might like. As we discussed earlier, many of our measures are psychological rather than physical in nature; they do not lend themselves to ratio measurement.

From the above discussion, you can probably surmise that interval and ratio scales are the most desirable. Because of the precision of the scales and the statistical manipulations they permit, interval and ratio scales are to be preferred. A number of writers have raised questions about the scale of measurement that many of our selection measures (for example, tests) have. Several earlier writers argued that many of these measures have underlying ordinal scales. But, to treat these measures as ordinal scales would limit our use of many powerful statistical methods. More recently researchers have suggested that to treat many of our psychological measures as if they approximate interval scale data does not do an injustice to the data. Thus, they recommend the use of interval scale statistical methods with those measures that approach interval scale quality. They further recommend that a researcher following this strategy should be constantly alert to the possibility of gross inequalities in measurement intervals (as might occur when a manager is asked to rank subordinates according to some criterion).[5] Table 3.1

Table 3.1   *General Characteristics of the Four Scales of Measurement*

Type of Scale[a]	Scale Characteristics				Example Operation in Selection Research
	Classification	Order	Equality of Difference	Absolute Zero	
Nominal	Yes	No	No	No	Classifying applicants by their sex
Ordinal	Yes	Yes	No	No	Supervisory ranking of subordinates
Interval	Yes	Yes	Yes	No	Supervisory rating of subordinates
Ratio	Yes	Yes	Yes	Yes	Counting employee absences from work

[a]This portion of the table was based in part on Uma Sekaran, *Research Methods for Managers* (New York: John Wiley, 1984), p. 134.

summarizes the general characteristics of the four types of scales of measurement.

Measures Used in Human Resource Selection

One of the principal roles of a manager involved in human resource selection is deciding whether applicants should or should not be employed. Predictor and criterion variables that we defined earlier in the chapter are used by a manager in selection decision making. Predictors are measures (such as a test) that are employed in deciding whether to accept or reject applicants for a specific job. Criteria (such as supervisory ratings of job performance) are employed as part of a research study designed to determine if the predictors are really measuring those aspects of job success that the predictors were designed to predict. This type of research study is known as a "validation study." We will have more to say about validity and validation studies in Chapter 5. But, for now, you should understand that criterion measures really help serve as a standard for evaluating how well predictors do the job they were intended to do. Predictors have a *direct* impact on the decisions reached by a manager involved in human resource selection decisions. A manager actually reviews an applicant's scores for a predictor and uses this information in deciding whether to accept or reject the applicant. Criteria play an *indirect* role in that they are employed in determining which predictors should actually be incorporated in the selection decision-making process.

We began this chapter by reviewing the impact that scales of measurement have on the application and interpretation of data collected by predictors and criteria. The emphasis of the rest of the chapter will be on discussing additional measurement principles that apply to the use of these two types of variables. These principles are very important for understanding the application of the selection techniques and issues you will encounter in the remaining chapters. However, before we can continue our discussion in any meaningful way, it might be helpful to give you a brief overview of the various types of predictors and criteria employed in research involving human resource selection. Later chapters will go into greater detail about specific measures. As you read, you should remember that when we talk about "selection measures," we mean *both* predictors and criteria. Now, let's look at some of the more common types of predictors and criteria in use.

Types of Selection Measures   When we refer to *measurement methods* in the context of human resource selection, we mean *a systematic instrument, technique, or procedure for measuring a sample of behavior.* A measurement method may provide data on a variable that serves as either a predictor or a criterion; a method may involve any one of our four scales of measurement. A procedure is "systematic" in the following three ways:

1. *Content* — All persons being assessed are measured by the same information or content

2. *Administration* — Information is collected in the same way each time the selection measure is applied.

3. *Scoring* — Rules for scoring are specified in advance of administration of the measure and are applied the same way with each application.[6]

Predictors   There are numerous types of predictors that have been used to forecast employee performance. In general, the major types tend to fall roughly into three categories. These categories are described below. Keep in mind as you read these descriptions, our intention is not to give a complete account of each type of predictor. We simply want to acquaint you with the variety of predictors currently in use in selection. Subsequent chapters will provide a more detailed review of many of these measures.

1. *Background information* — Application forms, reference checks, and biographical data questionnaires are generally used to collect information on job applicants and their backgrounds. *Application forms* typically consist of a form asking job applicants to describe themselves and their previous work histories. Questions are usually asked about current address, previous education, past employment, and the like. *Reference checks* are made by the prospective employer's contacting individuals who can accurately comment on the applicant's characteristics and background. These checks are often used to verify information obtained from the application form as well as to provide additional data on the applicant. *Biographical data questionnaires* consist of questions about the applicant's past life history. The assumption is that past life experiences are good indicators of future work behaviors.

2. *Interviews* — Selection interviews are also used to collect information about the applicant. The selection interview principally consists of questions asked by a job interviewer. Responses are used for assessing an applicant's suitability for a job.

3. *Tests* — There are literally hundreds of tests that have been used for selection purposes. A variety of schemes have been offered for classifying these measures. We will not review any one system for describing the types of tests that are available, but we can use some of the descriptive labels that have been assigned to give you a feeling for the range of options available. *Aptitude* tests, for example, are used to measure the potential of an individual for doing a job. Abilities measured by aptitude tests include intellectual, mechanical, spatial, perceptual, and motor. *Achievement* tests are employed to assess an individual's proficiency at the time of testing (for example, job proficiency or knowledge). (For the purposes of this book, you will see in Chapter 12 that we have combined aptitude and achievement tests into the general category "ability" tests.) *Personality* tests in the context of selection are used on the assumption that knowing a person's motivation or the manner in which an individual responds to a variety of situations can help predict success in a job.[7]

Most of the tests you will encounter will probably fall into one of the above categories. You should keep in mind, though, that you will find some differences among tests within each of these categories. Some may require an individual to respond with a paper and pencil; others may require the manipulation of physical objects. Some will have a time limit; others will not. Some can be administered in a group setting while others can only be given to one applicant at a time.

Criteria   Measurement methods oriented toward criteria can generally be clustered in terms of the type of data they provide.[8] These categories include:

1. *Objective production data* — These data tend to be physical measures of work or as Robert Guion states "simply a count of the results of work."[9] Number of goods produced, amount of scrap left, and dollar sales are examples of objective production data.

2. *Personnel data* — Personnel records and files frequently contain information on workers that can serve as important criterion measures. Absenteeism, tardiness, accident rates, salary history, promotions, and special awards are examples of such measures.

3. *Judgmental data* — Performance appraisals or ratings often serve as criteria in selection research. They most often involve a supervisor's rating of a subordinate on a series of behaviors or characteristics found to be important to job success. Supervisor or rater judgments play a predominant role in defining this type of criterion data.

4. *Job or work sample data* — These data are obtained from a measure developed to resemble the actual job. Basically, a job sample represents the job in miniature. Measurements (for example, quantity and error rate) are taken on individual performance of these job tasks, and these measures serve as criteria.

5. *Training proficiency data* — These criteria measures focus on how well employees respond to job training activities. Often, such criteria are labeled "trainability" measures. Error rates on the job during a training period, scores on training performance tests administered during training sessions are just some examples of training proficiency data.

Use of Predictors and Criteria   We have mentioned various types of predictors and criteria likely to be encountered in selection research. But, to what extent do organizations use these measurement methods? A recent survey conducted by the Bureau of National Affairs (BNA) of 437 personnel executives who were members of the American Society for Personnel Administration gives us some idea.[10] Table 3.2 summarizes the percentage of firms that employed various types of predictors and criteria. For predictors, the BNA researchers found:

1. Reference checks, interviews, and skill performance tests were the procedures most likely to be used in hiring. Assessment centers, physical abilities tests, and polygraph tests were the least likely to be employed.

Table 3.2   *Percentage of Employers Using Various Predictors*
                and Criteria in Selection Research

Predictors	Percentage of Companies[a,b]	Criteria	Percentage of Companies[a,c]
Background Information		**Objective Production Data**	
Reference/record checks	97%	Production rate	18%
Weighted application blanks	11		
Investigation by outside agency	26	**Personnel Data**	
		Length of service	21
Interviews		Absence/tardiness record	16
Unstructured	81	Success in training	16
Structured	47	Pay increases/promotions earned	9
Ability Testing		**Judgmental data**	
Skill performance		Actual performance evaluation	
test/work sample	75	record	37
Mental ability test	20	Research performance evaluation	31
Job knowledge test	22		
Physical abilities test	6		
Assessment center	6		
Other Predictors			
Medical examination	52		
Polygraph test	6		
Personality test	9		
Other	3		

[a]Percentages will sum to more than 100 percent since companies used multiple measures.
[b]These percentages are based on 437 companies that had validated any of their selection
procedures according to the *Uniform Guidelines*.
[c]These percentages are based on 68 companies that had validated any of their selection procedures
according to the *Uniform Guidelines*.

Source: Based on the Bureau of National Affairs, ASPA-BNA *Survey No. 45 Employee Selection
Procedures* (Washington, D.C.: Bureau of National Affairs, May 5, 1983), pp. 2, 8.

2. Generally the same selection methods were used (in roughly the same
proportions) regardless of the skill level of the job, type of industry, or size
of organization.

3. Approximately one-third (132) of the organizations used commercially
available tests. Of these, 80 percent used standard tests for office/clerical
positions; 30 percent used existing tests for professional or technical
applicants.

For criteria used in selection or validation research studies (which we
will discuss later), it was noted:

1. Judgmental criteria (supervisory ratings) were most often employed.

2. Objective criteria (pay increases, promotion rates, work samples) were
less frequently used.

Earlier studies have documented results similar to some of those reported in the BNA survey.[11] These studies do not necessarily represent what
should or should not be done but only what appears to be common practice.

Thus, in sum, interviews and skill tests (as predictors) and supervisory ratings (as criteria) are likely to be the most common measurement methods used in human resource selection research.

Criteria for Evaluating Selection Measures   Now that we have provided an overview of some of the measurement methods used in selection, let's assume that you have already conducted a thorough analysis of the job in question to identify those worker characteristics thought to lead to job success. (In Chapters 6, 7, and 8, we will provide some details on the job analysis process.) At this point, you are interested in choosing some measures to be employed as predictors and criteria indicative of job success. One of several questions you are likely to have is "What characteristics should I look for in selecting a predictor or a criterion?"

There are a number of characteristics or qualities you should consider in choosing or developing a selection measure. Although it is not an exhaustive list, a number of characteristics that you should carefully examine are listed in question form in Table 3.3. Some are more critical to predictors, some more essential for criteria, and some important for both types of measures. As you read these characteristics, you might think of them as a checklist to be reviewed for each measure you are considering. Unless you can be sure that a measure meets these standards, you *may* not have the best measure you need for your selection research. In that case, you have at least two options: (a) determine if there are adjustments you can make in your data or with the calculation of the measure itself so it will meet each measurement evaluation criterion or (b) if this option is not viable, find or develop another, more suitable measure.

Each of the characteristics is not of equal importance. Issues concerning reliability, validity, and freedom from bias are obviously more critical than some of the administrative concerns such as acceptability to management. Other characteristics will vary in importance depending upon the specific selection situation. Regardless, the wise selection manager will give serious consideration to each one.

Finding and Constructing Selection Measures

The process of identifying selection measures to be used in a human resource selection research study should not be taken lightly. Identification of measures is not made by "seat-of-the-pants" decision making. It is not made simply by one's "gut instincts" and personal whims about what measures are best in a specific situation. As we will see in our later chapters on job analysis, systematic research is conducted to identify what types of measures should be used. Thorough analyses of jobs are made to identify the necessary knowledge, skills, abilities, and other characteristics necessary for successful job performance. Then, once we know the qualifications needed to perform the job, we are ready to begin the process of identifying and implementing our selection measures. Obviously, the identification of selection measures is

Table 3.3   *Criteria to Consider in Choosing or Developing Measures*
for Use in Selection Research

For Predictors:

1. *Does the predictor appear appropriate for the group or problem for which it is to be used?*
   Predictors have been used that are entirely inappropriate for the group or the problem
   to be addressed. A careful review of the predictor should be made to determine if it is
   appropriate.
2. *Is the cost of the predictor in dollars or cents or human values less than the cost of making an*
   inaccurate decision?
   Cost in purchasing or developing a predictor, scoring, and conducting validation studies
   should be considered. In a validation study, predictor content should be reviewed for
   offensiveness to applicants or employees.
3. *Has the predictor been "standardized"?*
   Administration and scoring procedures should be the same whenever a predictor is
   given. Data should also be available on how relevant groups of individuals have scored
   on the measure so that comparative data are available for interpreting the results.
4. *Does the predictor require highly-trained persons for administration and scoring?*
   A predictor that can be administered and scored by persons not having high levels of
   training is less expensive than one requiring high levels.
5. *Can the predictor be administered to a group rather than just to an individual?*
   Group predictors are more economical than individual predictors. Group predictors can
   be given to individuals, but many individual predictors cannot be given to groups.

For Criteria:

6. *Is the criterion realistic and representative of the job for which it is chosen to measure success?*
   All important aspects of the job under study should be covered by the criterion.
7. *Is the criterion acceptable to management?*
   Unless management accepts the criterion to be predicted there will be very little support
   for a system that may predict that which is considered to be meaningless.
8. *Is situation change likely to alter the criterion?*
   Jobs and situations change. Thus, measures of success today may be inappropriate a year
   later. Criteria should be periodically reviewed for their relevancy.
9. *Is the criterion uncontaminated and free of bias so that meaningful comparisons among*
   individuals can be made?
   Unless jobs and work environments are identical, comparisons among individuals will be
   biased. Opportunity bias occurs when factors are beyond the control of the employee.
   Examples include: differences between sales territories, differences in tools and
   equipment, differences in work shift, differences in physical conditions of the job. Group
   bias occurs when a group characteristic is related to employee performance. Examples
   include: age and job tenure which can be related to performance. Rating bias can occur
   because of many factors that can influence supervisory ratings given to subordinates.
10. *Will the criterion detect differences among individuals if differences actually exist? Are there*
    meaningful differences among individuals actually scored on the criterion?
    If variance or individual differences in criterion scores cannot be obtained, then no
    predictor can be found to predict it.

For Predictors and Criteria:

11. *Does the measure unfairly discriminate against sex, race, age, or other protected groups?*
    Significant differences among protected groups on a measure do not necessarily mean
    discrimination. However, any group differences found should be carefully examined for
    bias or unfairness.
12. *Does the measure lend itself to quantification?*
    For purposes of personnel selection, quantitative data are more desirable than are
    qualitative data. Measures on an interval or ratio scale are most preferred.
13. *Is the measure objective?*
    Specific rules and procedures should be available for scoring individuals on the measure.
    Different scorers of an individual's performance should obtain the same score.

(continued)

Table 3.3   (*continued*)

14. *How dependable are the data provided by the measure? Will different results be obtained with each administration of the measure?*
    A measure should provide information that is dependable and accurate. Consistency of measurement is desirable. Thus, repeated application of a measure (if the context of measurement is the same with each application) should yield the same scores.
15. *How well does the measure predict that which it is designed to predict?*
    Measures chosen should assess what they are supposed to measure.

Sources: Based, in part, on Lewis E. Albright, J. R. Glennon, and Wallace J. Smith, *The Use of Psychological Tests in Industry* (Cleveland: Howard Allen Publishers, 1963), pp. 34–35, 41–47; Charles H. Lawshe and Michael J. Balma, *Principles of Personnel Testing* (New York: McGraw-Hill, 1966), pp. 35–37; Milton L. Blum and James C. Naylor, *Industrial Psychology: Its Theoretical and Social Foundations* (New York: Harper and Row, 1968), pp. 180–182; G. C. Helmstadter, *Principles of Psychological Measurement* (Englewood Cliffs, N.J.: Prentice-Hall, 1964), pp. 34–35.

an important one. It is also one where a consultant, usually an industrial psychologist, may be needed. However, whether selection measures are identified by a consultant or by personnel staff within an organization, you need to be familiar with the basic approach to be taken. In identifying these measures, we have two choices: (a) we can locate and choose from existing selection measures, or (b) we can develop our own. In all likelihood, we will probably need to take both options.

Locating Existing Selection Measures

There are several advantages to finding and using existing selection measures. Some of these advantages include the following:

1. Use of existing measures is usually less expensive and less time-consuming than developing new ones.

2. If previous research has been conducted, we will have some idea about the reliability, validity, and other characteristics of the measures.

3. Existing measures *may* be superior to what could be developed in-house.

In searching for suitable selection measures, you will find that there are many types of measures available. The vast majority of these are intended to be used as predictors, such as tests. A variety of predictors are commercially available, for example, intelligence, aptitude, ability, interest, and personality inventories. Other predictors such as application blanks, biographical data questionnaires, reference check forms, interview schedules, and work sample measures will probably have to be developed. Published criteria measures are generally not available and will probably have to be constructed by a user. Sometimes variables other than predictors and criteria are employed in a selection study to describe a sample of employees or to help interpret the data available. For instance, job analysis measures are included in most selection research investigations. Existing job analysis measures can be obtained, and they can usually be found in the research literature. (Some of the more prominent job analysis measures will be mentioned later.)

Information Sources for Existing Measures There are several sources for obtaining information on existing measures that can be used in personnel selection studies. Although most of these sources will not present the measures themselves, they will provide descriptive information on various options to be considered. Each of these sources is described below.

Text and Reference Books Several books are available that provide excellent reviews of predictors and other measures that have been used in hiring for a variety of jobs. Some of the books are organized around the types of jobs in which various measures have been used, while others are centered around types of selection measures. Still others are organized around the technical aspects of the human resource selection process. Many of the relevant books on personnel selection are cited in this book.

In addition, the *Annual Review of Psychology,* published yearly, should also be consulted. On occasion, reviews of current selection research are published. These reviews offer an excellent, up-to-date look at research on measures and other issues relevant to personnel selection.

Buros's **Mental Measurements Yearbooks** The *Mental Measurements Yearbook* has been the most important source for information on paper-and-pencil tests. Historically, a new edition of the *Yearbook* has been published every six years with the most recent edition being the *Ninth Mental Measurements Yearbook* (1985).[12] Previously, Oscar Buros was editor of the *Yearbook,* but following his death, his institute was moved to the University of Nebraska. His work is now being carried on by the Buros Institute of Mental Measurements at that university.

The *Yearbook* consists of critical reviews by test experts and bibliographies of virtually every test printed in English. In addition, Buros has published several supplementary books containing additional bibliographies and reviews. These references include *Tests in Print III,*[13] *Reading Tests and Reviews II,*[14] and *Personality Tests and Reviews II.*[15] The latter two volumes also contain master indexes of tests reviewed in the *Yearbook.* Unquestionably, the Buros publications represent some of the most valuable sources for identifying existing tests to be considered for personnel selection applications.

Bibliographic Retrieval Service For those persons interested in continuous access to the latest reviews of tests, the Bibliographic Retrieval Service (BRS) can be accessed. The BRS is a computer retrieval service which is available through most major university and other libraries. It contains factual information, critical reviews, and reliability/validity information on all 1,184 English language tests covered in the *Mental Measurements Yearbook.* In addition, very recent tests published after the *Yearbook* are included as regular updates to the database.

Journals Several journals are also suitable sources for information on selection measures. In particular, the *Journal of Applied Psychology* (*JAP*) and *Per-*

sonnel *Psychology* are most relevant. *JAP* has a long history as a major journal in the field of industrial psychology. In general, it is technical and focuses on empirical research in applied psychology. Articles on various predictors, criteria, and other issues related to personnel selection can be found. Any search for measures should definitely include *JAP* as a source.

Personnel Psychology also has a long history of publishing articles concerned with personnel selection and related topics. From 1954 to 1965, *Personnel Psychology* included a special feature called the "Validity Information Exchange." In order to encourage the publication of validation studies completed in the context of human resource selection, the Exchange offered an outlet requiring minimal time and effort to prepare a validity study for publication. Although the studies reported in the Exchange are dated, they offer a source for possible ideas concerning selection measures. Since 1965, articles have appeared periodically dealing with measures involved in selection.

Other journals such as the *Journal of Occupational Psychology, The Industrial Psychologist (TIP), Educational and Psychological Measurement,* and *Applied Psychological Measurement* will have articles from time to time dealing with the application of selection measures. At times, reviews of specific tests that may be relevant to industrial personnel selection can also be found in the *Journal of Educational Measurement* and the *Journal of Counseling Psychology.* In order to have a thorough search, these journals should be reviewed for possible ideas. *Psychological Abstracts* and *Personnel Management Abstracts* as well as the computerized literature searches offered through many libraries and the American Psychological Association can also be employed to identify potential selection measures.

Test Publishers   A number of organizations publish tests that are used in human resource selection. Catalogs describing the various tests offered can be obtained from each publisher. A comprehensive list of test publishers and addresses can be found in Buros's *Mental Measurements Yearbook.*

Catalogs obtained from these publishers will present information on the most current tests that are available. Once a test is located that may appear to meet a specific need, a test manual and specimen set can be ordered by qualified users. The test manual will provide information on the administration, scoring, and interpretation of results. In addition, reliability and validity data will also be presented. These materials will help users decide if a test is appropriate prior to actually adopting it.

However, just because a test is identified for use does not mean that anyone may purchase it. Some test publishers use a scheme (originally developed by the American Psychological Association but later dropped from the association's 1985 revision of its testing standards) for classifying their tests and for determining to whom tests can be sold. There are three levels of classification:

1. *Level A* — This level consists of those tests that require very little formal training to administer, score, and interpret the results. Most personnel

practitioners may purchase tests at this level. A typing test is representative of tests in this classification.

2. *Level B*—Tests classified in this category require some formal training and knowledge of psychological testing concepts to properly score and interpret. Aptitude tests that are designed to forecast individuals' potential to perform are of this type. Individuals wishing to purchase Level B tests must be able to document their qualifications to correctly use such tests. These qualifications usually include evidence of formal education in tests and measurement as well as psychological statistics.

3. *Level C*—These tests require the most extensive preparation on the part of the test administrator. In general, personality inventories and projective techniques make up this category. A Ph.D. in psychology and documentation of training, such as courses taken on the use of a particular test, are required. Tests in this category tend to be less frequently used in industrial personnel selection contexts than tests in levels A and B.

A more complex approach to describing appropriate test selection practices than the classification scheme described above can be found in the *Standards for Educational and Psychological Testing,* published by the American Psychological Association (APA).[16] Although it is not a source of selection measures per se, APA's *Test Standards* provide an excellent treatment of the considerations in selecting and using tests.

Professional Associations   Various professional associations may also be a source of selection measures. For example, the American Banking Association has supported research to develop selection measures for use in hiring clerical personnel in banking. The American Petroleum Institute has sponsored research to review the use of tests in selection of clerical personnel. Other trade and professional associations should be contacted as possible sources for selection measures or research on such measures.

Certain management associations may also be able to provide guidance in locating possible selection measures for specific situations. The American Society for Personnel Administration (ASPA) and the International Personnel Management Association (IPMA) are two potential sources of information.

Sourcebooks   Several sourcebooks have been published that provide information on little known instruments. Not all of the instruments cited in these references are suitable in the context of personnel selection, but it may be worthwhile to consult them. A *Sourcebook for Mental Health Measures*[17] contains over 1,000 abstracts describing tests, questionnaires, rating scales, and other measures used to evaluate both aptitude and personality variables. *Measures for Psychological Assessment*[18] contains references and bibliographies on 3,000 measures cited in 26 measurement-oriented journals published between 1960 and 1970.

Constructing New Selection Measures

There are obvious advantages to using existing selection measures, and when suitable measures can be found, they certainly should be used. But, sometimes, selection researchers may not be able to find the precise measure that they need for their purposes. At this point, they have no choice but to develop their own. In this section, we plan to outline the major steps that should be taken in developing any selection measure.

Before proceeding, we need to note some questions for consideration. Some legitimate concerns that might be raised by human resource professionals are whether it is reasonable to expect practitioners to develop selection measures, particularly in light of the technical and legal ramifications associated with them and whether an organization would have the resources in time and expertise to develop such measures. In addition, one might ask, "Can't a little knowledge be dangerous? That is, won't some well-meaning practitioners be encouraged to attempt to develop and use measures that 'appear' to be 'good' but really are worthless?"

Our intention is not to prepare readers nor even encourage them to go out to develop selection measures themselves but to enable them to work productively with a specialist or expert. The development of such measures is a complex, resource-consuming process where expert advice is usually required. The risks associated with the process can be quite high. Most human resource managers will simply not have the resources nor, perhaps, the skills necessary to engage in selection measure development. Thus, consultants will likely be needed.[19] Given that consultants are employed, the material presented in this and related chapters is intended to serve as a means by which the work of a consultant can be monitored and evaluated as well as the literature describing selection measures studied and reviewed. In addition, if consultants are hired, knowledge of the basic issues involved in selection measure development, validation, and application can help bridge any possible "communications gap" between the organization and the consultant.

Steps in Developing Selection Measures   Although the details may vary somewhat depending upon the specific selection measure being developed, there are eight major steps typically taken. These general steps include the following:

1. Analyzing the job for which a measure is being developed
2. Selecting the method of measurement to be used
3. Developing the specifications or plan of the measure
4. Constructing the preliminary form of the measure
5. Administering and analyzing the preliminary form
6. Preparing a revised form
7. Determining the reliability and validity of the revised form for the jobs studied

8. Implementing and monitoring the measure in the human resource selection system

Now, let's examine each of these steps.

Analyzing the Job   The first step in the instrument development process is perhaps the most crucial. If this step is inappropriately carried out, then all subsequent steps will be flawed. It is for this reason that we have devoted three chapters of this text (Chapters 6, 7, and 8) to the role of job analysis in personnel selection. The role of job analysis in the context of selection is to determine the knowledge, skills, abilities, and other characteristics necessary to adequately perform a job. From knowledge of these requisite characteristics as well as the activities and conditions under which these activities are performed, the developer of a selection measure gains insights and forms hypotheses as to what types of measures may be appropriate. Whether a measure is being developed or whether existing measures are being considered, job analysis *must* be performed as an initial step.

In addition to its role in developing and selecting selection measures, job analysis also provides the foundation for developing criteria measures of job proficiency. We cannot do systematic research on the selection of personnel until we know which of the applicants we have selected have become successful employees. Intimate knowledge of the job gained through job analysis will help us to identify or develop measures of job success. Ultimately, through validation research we will determine the extent to which our selection measures can actually predict these criteria.

As you will see in later chapters, there are many approaches to job analysis. In the context of selection, these can be classified into basically two categories: (a) work-oriented methods and (b) worker-oriented methods. Under the work-oriented method, the researcher principally addresses the activities and functions performed on the job. Measures are sought that reproduce these features of the job. Thus, if typing activities are a central function of a clerk's position, a typing test based on materials like those encountered on the job might be developed. In determining whether adequate coverage of the job has been taken, the job analyst may ask: "If tasks A, B, C, . . ., Z are required on the job, do I have a measure or can I develop one that will require a worker to perform similar tasks?"

Notice that under the work-oriented approach the focus is on the *functions* of the job rather than the human attributes necessary to perform it. Under our second general method of job analysis, the worker-oriented approach, the focus is on the *qualities* of the job incumbent needed to perform it rather than characteristics of the job itself. Under this approach, the analyst may ask what special attributes, such as, physical requirements, sensory and perceptual requirements, intellectual functioning, specific knowledge and skills, etc., are needed to perform this job? Using this approach, an analysis of a clerk's job may show that perceptual accuracy is necessary to complete the task of checking long lists of numbers for correctness.

No one job analysis method is necessarily more correct than the other. In practice, both approaches or combinations of both are involved. A skilled analyst will attempt to use the best approach for the situation at hand. In general, the more a researcher knows about a specific job, the more likely his or her hypotheses and ideas about selection measures will have predictive utility for that job. Therefore, the researcher will choose the method of analysis he or she believes will yield the most useful information about a job.

Selecting the Measurement Method   Once we have identified the important job activities and necessary characteristics of personnel to adequately perform a job, we are ready to consider the approach we will use in selection. There are a host of methods available, including paper-and-pencil tests, job or work sample tests, interviews, and biographical data questionnaires to name only a few. The specific nature of the job (such as, tasks performed, level of responsibility), the skill of the individual(s) responsible for administering, scoring, and interpreting selection measures, the number and types of applicants making application (such as level of reading and writing skills, presence of physical handicaps), the costs of testing, and the resources (such as, time and dollars) available for test development are just some of the variables that will impact on the selection of a measurement medium. If large numbers of applicants are making application for the job, paper-and-pencil measures will be carefully considered. If applicant appearance (both physical and interpersonal) is critical, then some form of a behavioral exercise might be proposed. If manipulative skills appear to be critical to job success, then tests involving the manipulation of a physical apparatus may be necessary to measure respondents' motor responses. The method chosen will ultimately depend on the job and organizational context in which the job is performed.

Exhibit 3.5 presents an example of a checklist that was used to identify selection methods to be developed for selecting industrial electricians. The listing under "Job Requirements" consists of elements of the job identified through job analysis that were found to be critical to the job success of a company's industrial electricians. The requirements are the knowledge, skills, and individual attributes that a newly hired electrician must have upon entry into the job. The listing under "Selection Methods" represents the possible means by which the essential job requirements can be assessed. After studying the job and the organization, the selection researcher decided that certain methods would be suitable for assessing some requirements while other measures would be appropriate for other job requirements. The suitable methods for specific job requirements are indicated by a check mark. For example, it was decided that a paper-and-pencil test was most suitable for determining applicants' knowledge of the principles of electrical wiring, whereas a work sample test was chosen to determine applicants' ability to solder electrical connections.

Developing Specifications for the Selection Measure   After a job has been analyzed and some tentative methods considered for assessing the important

Exhibit 3.5   *Checklist Used to Match Selection Methods with Job Requirements for the Job of Industrial Electrician*

Selection Method

Job Requirements	Work sample test	Paper-and-pencil test	Selection interview	Biographical data form	Reference check	Application form
1. Knowledge of principles of electrical wiring		✓				
2. Ability to solder electrical connections	✓					
3. Ability to troubleshoot electrical wiring problems using a voltmeter		✓				
4. Care and repair of electrical equipment		✓				
⋮	⋮			⋮		
N. Previous work experience in hazardous work environments			✓		✓	✓

aspects of the job, the selection researcher probably has some vague mental picture of what each method may be like. In this step, the researcher attempts to clarify the nature and details of each selection measure by developing specifications for their construction. For each measure considered, the specifications developed should include the following:

1. The functions the measure is intended to serve

2. Operational definitions of each variable to be measured

3. The number and examples of each type of item, question, etc., to be included in the measure

4. The nature of the population for which the measure is to be designed

5. The time limits for completing the measure

6. The statistical procedures to be used in selecting and editing items, questions, etc., on the measure[20]

Referring again to our electrician's job, we can see how job content might be translated into some of the specifications for a paper-and-pencil test. In preparing the test, the first step is to examine the principal content of the job by preparing a topical outline. From discussions with incumbents and supervisors as well as additional job analysis information, the job of industrial electrician is broken down into several components as is shown in Exhibit 3.6. Although the outline is informative, it is not immediately clear what test items could be prepared on each of these topics. The outline in Exhibit 3.7 takes us a step further by showing what a worker needs to know to perform the principal components of the job. Breaking down what a worker needs to know in an outline similar to that in Exhibit 3.7 makes it easier to prepare appropriate questions. Finally, in Exhibit 3.8, the two topical outlines are merged. The chart shown helps us to specify the test item budget, that is, the specific number of items to be prepared for measuring the components of the job. Theoretically, at least one item could be developed for each cell in the chart shown in Exhibit 3.8. Our test, however, is only a *sampling* of behavior; we cannot ask all possible questions covering all possible elements of information. By using the chart in collaboration with knowledgeable and competent personnel involved with the job, we can specify a reasonable number of test items for each cell to be included in the test. Test items may now be constructed in proportion to the number identified in the cells of the chart.

Constructing the Preliminary Form of the Measure   Now that the specifications for a measure have been determined, we are ready to prepare an initial version of our measure. The items, questions, etc., chosen to compose

---

Exhibit 3.6   *Outline of Major Components of the Industrial Electrician's Job*

I. **Using Electrical Equipment**

    A. Motors
    B. Fixtures, switches, junction boxes
    C. Appliances (refrigerators, air conditioners, fans)
    D. Communication devices (intercom, telephone)

II. **Using Electrical Instruments**

    A. Ohmmeter
    B. Voltmeter
    C. Ammeter
    D. RPM meter
    E. Oscilloscope

III. **Working with Hand and Power Tools**

    A. Drills (1/2″ and 1/4″)
    B. Socket wrenches
    C. Soldering iron
    D. Wire cutters
    E. Screw drivers

IV. **Using Electrical Components and Materials**

    A. Coaxial cable
    B. Electrical wiring (#6 to #22)
    C. Solder

Exhibit 3.7   *What An Industrial Electrician Needs to Know to Perform the Job*

I. **Technical Skills**
   A. Reading schematic drawings
   B. Calculating electrical units of measurement
   C. Understanding fundamental operations
   D. Knowledge of principles of electricity

II. **Knowledge of Trade Terms**
   A. Electrical components
   B. Electrical wiring
   C. Tools

III. **Knowledge of Care and Use of Tools**
   A. Selection for appropriate tasks
   B. Correct procedures
   C. Care and maintenance
   D. Purchasing tools

IV. **Safety Information**
   A. Prevention of injury to self
   B. Prevention of injury to others

V. **Information About Electrical Supplies**
   A. Specifications for choosing supplies
   B. Purchasing supplies

---

the contents of the preliminary form should be developed in concert with the specifications laid out in the previous step.

Administering the Preliminary Form   Following development, the initial form should be pilot-tested. The measure should be administered to a sample of people from the same population for which the measure is being developed. In order to provide data suitable for analyzing the contents of the measure, the measure should be given to a rather sizable sample. For example, if a test is being developed where item analyses are to be performed, a sample of at least 100, preferably several hundred, may be needed.

Preparing the Revised Form   Based on the data collected in the previous step, analyses are performed on the preliminary data. The objective is to revise the proposed measure by correcting any weaknesses and deficiencies noted. For example, if a test is being developed, item analyses are used to choose the content of the test so that it will discriminate between those who know and those who do not know the information covered.

Determining Reliability and Validity of the Measure   At this point, we have a revised measure that we hypothesize will predict some aspect(s) of job success. Thus, we are ready to conduct reliability and validity studies to test our hypothesis. We will examine in the next two chapters how reliability and validation research may be conducted. Essentially, we want to answer from this research: "Are the scores on our selection measure dependable for selec-

Exhibit 3.8   Form Used to Determine the Item Budget for the Industrial Electrician Test

	Topic	Technical Skills	Information Knowledge of Trade Terms	Knowledge of Care and Use of Tools	Safety Information	Information About Electrical Supplies	TOTAL ITEMS
Electrical Equipment	Motors						
	Fixtures, switches, junction boxes						
	Appliances						
	Communication devices						
Electrical Instruments	Ohmmeter						
	Voltmeter						
	Ammeter						
	RPM meter						
	Oscilloscope						
Tools	Drills						
	Socket wrenches						
	Soldering iron						
	Wire cutters						
	Screw drivers						
Electrical Components	Coaxial cable						
	Electrical wiring						
	Solder						

tion decision-making purposes" and "Is the selection measure predictive of job success?"

Implementing the Selection Measure   After we have obtained the necessary reliability and validity evidence, we can then implement our measure. Cut-off or passing scores will need to be developed. Norms or standards for interpreting how various groups (in terms of sex, race, level of education, etc.) score on the measure may also be needed to help interpret the results. Once implemented, we will continue to monitor the performance of the selection measure to insure that it is performing the function for which it is intended.

As you can see, there is a great deal of technical work involved in the development of a selection measure. Shortcuts are seldom warranted and, in fact, are to be discouraged. In addition, there are significant costs associated with the development of selection measures. The technical ramifications and the associated costs in developing selection measures are two principal reasons why selection researchers frequently use suitable, existing measures rather than developing their own.

Interpreting Scores on Selection Measures

Using Norms

If you took a test, had it scored, and then were told that you made a 69, how would you feel? Probably not very good! But a moment after receiving your score, you would probably ask how this score compared to what others made. Your question underscores one of the basic principles of interpreting the results of selection measurement procedures. That is, in order to interpret the results of measurement intelligently we need two essential kinds of information: (a) information on how others scored on the measure and (b) information on the validity of the measure.[21]

Let's return to your test score of 69 for a moment. Suppose you were told that the top score was 73. All of a sudden you might feel a lot better than you felt a few moments ago. However, you are also told that everyone else who took the test scored 73. Now, how do you feel? Without information on how relevant others scored, any score is practically meaningless. In order to attach any meaning to a score, we need to compare it to relevant others' scores, where others may be similar in terms of characteristics such as age, level of education, type of job applied for, sex, race, etc. Thus, a score may take on different meanings depending upon how it stands relative to others' scores in particular groups. In some groups, such as those based on age, a score of 69 may be high. In other groups, such as level of education, the score may be very low. Our interpretation just depends on the score's relative standing in these other groups.

These scores of relevant others in groups that we use for score interpretation are called *norms*. They are used to show how well an individual performs with respect to a specified group of people. For example, standardized norms reported in test manuals are designed to rank-order examinees from high to low on the attribute that is being assessed. The purpose is to determine how much of the measured attribute a person has in relation to others on whom the same test information is available. The *Wonderlic Personnel Test*, for instance, reports norms based on groups defined by the following variables: age of applicant, educational attainment, sex, position applied for, type of industry, and geographical region.

Normative data can be useful in understanding and evaluating scores on selection measures. However, there are several points that should be kept in mind when using norms to interpret scores. First, the norm group selected should be *relevant* for the purpose it is being used. Norms will be meaningless or even misleading if they are not based upon groups with whom it is sensible to compare individuals being considered for employment. For example, suppose individuals applying for the job of an experienced electrician took the *Purdue Test for Electricians*. Let's assume that normative data were available for trade school graduates who had taken the test as well as the employer's experienced electricians. If the company is trying to hire experienced electricians, the relevant norm group would be the company's experienced electricians rather than the norm group representing trade school graduates. Clearly, the former is more relevant to company needs for experienced personnel. If the norm group consisting of inexperienced personnel had been used, very misleading results, perhaps some with serious consequences, could have occurred. There can be many norm groups reported in selection manuals. Care must be exercised to insure the appropriate group is chosen when interpreting scores on measures.

Second, rather than using norms based upon national data, an employer should accumulate and use *local* norms. A local norm is one based upon selection measures administered to individuals making application for employment with a particular employer. Initially, when a test is implemented, appropriate norms published in a test manual may have to be used, but local norms should be developed as soon as 100 or more scores in a particular group have been accumulated. Passing test scores should then be established on the basis of these local data rather than just taken from published manuals.[22]

A third point to consider is that norms are *transitory*. That is, they are specific to the point in time when they were collected. Norms may, and probably do, change over time. If the attribute being assessed is not likely to change, then older norms are likely to be more or less relevant. However, the more likely the attribute may change over time, the more current the normative data should be.

There is no prescribed period of time for publishers of selection measures to collect new normative data. Some may collect such information every four or five years; others may collect normative data every ten years. The point is that norms which appear to be dated should be interpreted very cautiously. Where feasible, normative data should be continuously collected by the user of selection measures.

Using Percentiles and Standard Scores

The most frequently used statistic in reporting normative data is the *percentile*. Since the purpose of a norm is to show relative standing in a group, percentile scores are derived to show *the percentage of persons in a norm group who fall below a given score on a measure*. Thus, if an individual makes a 75 on a test and this score corresponds to the 50th percentile, then that individual would have scored better than 50 percent of the people in a particular group who took the test. Exhibit 3.9 illustrates how normative percentile data are typically reported in test manuals.

Percentile scores are very useful in interpreting test scores; however, they are subject to misuse. As Charles Lawshe and Michael Balma point out, there is a tendency for some users to want to interpret these percentile scores as if they were on a ratio scale.[23] Thus, if Susan Shadow, an applicant for a job, scores 5 percentile points higher on a selection test than Jack Nackis, another job applicant, some may want to conclude that Susan is 5 percent better than Jack for the job. However, such use of percentile scores cannot be made for at least two reasons.

First, a difference of five percentile points may not indicate a real difference in people; the difference may be nothing but chance resulting from unreliability of the test. (In the next chapter, you will see how the standard error of measurement can be used to make such a determination.) Second, percentile scores are based upon an *ordinal* scale of measurement, not a ratio scale. Thus, we can make greater than or less than statements in comparing scores, but we cannot say how much higher or how much lower one percentile score is from another. For instance, a percentile score of 60 is not twice as good as a percentile score of 30.

There is another limitation of percentile scores that should also be noted. Because percentile scores are on an ordinal scale, they cannot be legitimately added, subtracted, divided, or multiplied. Statistical manipulations are not possible with percentiles. For this and other reasons, test scores are also frequently expressed as *standard* scores. There are many different types of standard scores that may be reported in manuals accompanying commercially available tests to be used in selection. We will not go into the statistical derivation of standard scores since that is beyond our present treatment. We do need to make a few comments about their role in interpreting scores on selection measures, however. Standard scores represent adjustments to raw scores so that it is possible to determine the proportion of individuals who fall at various standard score levels. More importantly, these scores are on a

---

Exhibit 3.9   *Hypothetical Illustration of How Percentile Norms Are Frequently Reported in Test Manuals*

Test Raw Score	z Score	Percentile
50	3.0	99.9
45	2.0	97.7
40	1.0	84.1
35	0.0	50.0
30	−1.0	16.0
25	−2.0	2.0
20	−3.0	1.0

scale so that score differences have equal intervals and, therefore, can be added, subtracted, multiplied, and divided.

In addition, standard scores permit the relative comparison between individuals' scores on selection measures as well as comparison of an individual's performance on different measures.[24] For example, Exhibit 3.10 shows the scores of our two job applicants, Jack Nackis and Susan Shadow, on three selection measures they took when applying for the job of computer programmer. Also shown in the figure are the means and standard deviations of the scores of 100 male and 100 female applicants who took these same measures when applying for a programming job with the company. The information of concern to us now is the z score data shown. Looking at this information, we can see that Jack scored one standard deviation above the mean for male applicants on the programming test and two standard deviations above the male means for the selection interview and biographical data questionnaire. In contrast, Susan scored one standard deviation above the women's mean scores for the programming test and the interview. On the biographical data questionnaire, she scored one-half standard deviation above the mean. A z score of 0.5 (one-half standard deviations above the mean) corresponds to a score higher than approximately 67 percent of persons on whom comparable data are available; a z score of 1.0 corresponds to approximately 84 percent of the cases, and two standard deviations corresponds to about 99 percent of the cases. Which of our two applicants appears to be the better bet based on their selection measure scores? From the information shown in Exhibit 3.10, it would appear that both Jack and Susan may be good bets; however, other things being equal and relative to their normative group, Jack appears to be the better applicant.

Exhibit 3.10 *Hypothetical Scores for Two Applicants Applying for the Job of Computer Programmer*

	Current Job Applicants				Previous Job Applicants			
	Jack Nackis		Susan Shadow		All Males		All Females	
Selection Measures	Raw Score	z Score	Raw Score	z Score	Mean	Standard Deviation	Mean	Standard Deviation
Computer Programming Test	70	1.0	40	1.0	65	5	35	5
Interview	50	2.0	75	1.0	40	5	70	5
Biographical Data Questionnaire	75	2.0	60	0.5	55	10	50	10

Note: the formula for determining the z score is: an individual's raw score on a measure minus previous applicants' (by sex) mean score on the measure divided by previous applicants' (by sex) standard deviation. Thus, the z score for Jack Nackis on the Computer Programming Test was determined as follows: $70 - 65 / 5 = 1.0$.

   The biggest problem with the use of standard scores is that they are subject to misinterpretation. For this reason, percentiles are the most common metric presented by publishers of selection measures.

   Although normative data are helpful in interpreting scores on selection measures, what we really want to know is how well a selection measure predicts future job performance? Norms do not tell us what a score means in terms of important job behaviors or criteria of job performance. Sometimes, users will assume that a relationship exists between selection measures and these criteria, but without reliability and validity evidence, we do not know if this assumption is warranted. In the next two chapters, we will review methods for determining the reliability of selection measures as well as methods for examining the link between predictors and job success.

References for Chapter 3

[1] Jum C. Nunnally, *Introduction to Psychological Measurement* (New York: McGraw-Hill, 1970), p. 7.

[2] Fred N. Kerlinger, *Foundations of Behavioral Research* (New York: Holt, Rinehart, and Winston, 1973), p. 432.

[3] Edwin E. Ghiselli, *Theory of Psychological Measurement* (New York: McGraw-Hill, 1964), pp. 9–35.

[4] The "mean" is the average score of a group of persons on a variable such as a test. The "standard deviation" is a number that represents the spread of scores for a group of persons around the group's average score on a variable. As the standard deviation increases, the spread or differences among individuals' scores becomes larger. "Correlations" show the degree of relationship between variables. Chapter 5 will give a more thorough description of correlational procedures used in selection research.

[5] See Kerlinger, *Foundations of Behavioral Research*, pp. 438–441; J. P. Guilford, *Psychometric Theory* (New York: McGraw-Hill, 1954), pp. 15–16.

[6] Wayne Cascio, *Applied Psychology in Personnel Management* (Reston, Va.: Reston Publishing Company, 1982), p. 127.

[7] Frank J. Landy and Donald A. Trumbo, *Psychology of Work Behavior* (Homewood, Ill.: Dorsey Press, 1980), p. 81.

[8] C. H. Lawshe and Michael J. Balma, *Principles of Personnel Testing* (New York: McGraw-Hill, 1966), pp. 35–42.

[9] Robert Guion, *Personnel Testing* (New York: McGraw-Hill, 1965), p. 91.

[10] Bureau of National Affairs, *ASPA-BNA Survey No. 45 — Employee Selection Procedures* (Washington, D.C.: The Bureau of National Affairs, May 5, 1983), pp. 1–12.

[11] *Personnel Management: Policies and Practices — Report No. 22* (Englewood Cliffs, N.J.: Prentice-Hall, April 2, 1975). See also Carlyn J. Monahan and Paul M. Muchinsky, "Three Decades of Personnel Selection Research: A State-of-the-Art Analysis and Evaluation," *Journal of Occupational Psychology* 56 (1983): 215–225; R. H. Lent, H. A. Aurbach, and L. S. Levin, "Research Design and Validity Assessment," *Personnel Psychology* 24 (1971): 247–274; R. H. Lent, H. A. Aurbach, and L. S. Levin, "Predictors, Criteria, and Significant Results," *Personnel Psychology* 24 (1971): 519–533.

[12] James V. Mitchell, *Ninth Mental Measurements Yearbook* (Lincoln, Neb.: Buros Institute of Mental Measurements, University of Nebraska, University of Nebraska Press, 1985).

[13] Oscar K. Buros, *Tests in Print III* (Highland Park, N.J.: Gryphon Press, 1975).

[14] Oscar K. Buros, *Reading Tests and Reviews II* (Highland Park, N.J.: Gryphon Press, 1975).

[15] Oscar K. Buros, *Personality Tests and Reviews II* (Highland Park, N.J.: Gryphon Press, 1975).

[16] American Psychological Association, *Standards for Educational and Psychological Testing* (Washington, D.C.: American Psychological Association, 1985).

[17] A. L. Comrey, T. E. Backer, and E. M. Glaser, *A Sourcebook for Mental Health Measures* (Los Angeles: Human Interaction Research Institute, 1973).

[18] Ki-Taek Chun, Sidney Cobb, and J. R. P. French, *Measures for Psychological Assessment* (Ann Arbor, Mich.: Institute for Social Research, The University of Michigan, 1976).

[19] In several places throughout the book, we suggest that a consultant may be necessary to perform certain tasks or to accomplish specific selection objectives. Ideally, these tasks and objectives could be accomplished *within* the organization. However, access to needed organizational resources is not always possible. External consultants may be required. When should outside advice be sought? Basically, whether a selection consultant is or is not used depends on the answer to the following question: *Does the organization have the expertise, time, and other resources to adequately solve the selection problem?* If the answer is "no," then a consultant is necessary.

Assuming a selection consultant is needed, we might ask "What qualities should be sought in a consultant?" Many criteria can be listed, but, *at a minimum*, a selection consultant should:

1. hold a Ph.D. in industrial/organizational psychology with training in psychological measurement, statistics, and selection-related content areas, such as, job analysis, test construction, performance evaluation;
2. have conducted selection, test validation, and job analysis research projects in other organizations; and
3. provide references from client organizations where selection research projects have been completed.

In addition to these criteria, a selection consultant will likely have published books or selection-oriented articles in the industrial-organizational psychology and personnel management literature.

Other factors are also important in choosing a consultant. For a discussion of these considerations and the roles and values of a consultant, see Achilles A. Armenakis and Henry B. Burdg, "Consultation Research: Contributions to Practice and Directions for Improvement," unpublished paper, Department of Management, Auburn University, 1985.

[20] Robert L. Thorndike, *Personnel Selection* (New York: John Wiley, 1949), p. 50.

[21] Cascio, *Applied Psychology in Personnel Management*, p. 141.

[22] Harold G. Seashore and James H. Ricks, *Norms Must Be Relevant* (Test Service Bulletin No. 39) (New York: The Psychological Corporation, May 1950), p. 19.

[23] Lawshe and Balma, *Principles of Personnel Testing*, p. 75.

[24] Cascio, *Applied Psychology in Personnel Management*, p. 143.

4

Reliability of

Selection Measures

What Is Meant by Reliability?

Have you ever shot a rifle? If you have, you can probably appreciate the workmanship that goes into producing a quality firearm. But, suppose you shot a rifle that one day would shoot just high of a target and the next day just below it? Even though you knew you had your sights on the target in exactly the same way each day you shot, for some strange reason, the rifle would sometimes shoot high and at other times shoot low. Perhaps, the quality of manufacture of the rifle left something to be desired. Whatever the reason, you would probably say you do not have a dependable, accurate rifle.

As in our rifle example, we have similar concerns with measures commonly used in human resource selection. That is, we want to be sure we have measures that will produce dependable, consistent, and accurate results when we use them. If we are going to be using data to make predictions concerning the hiring of people, we need to be sure that these decisions are based upon data that are reliable and accurate. We do not want to use measures that give one type of information at one time and on another occasion produce a completely different set of data. Obviously, we need accurate data to identify and hire the best people available. We also need accurate information for moral and legal reasons as well. Let's look at another example involving the dependability of information, but in this case, in the context of selection.

Taylor Spottswood, personnel manager at Datasources, Inc., had just finished scoring a computer programming aptitude test that had been admin-

istered to ten individuals making application for a job as a computer programmer. Since it was around 5:00 p.m. and he had some errands to run, he
decided to carry the tests home and review them that night. While on his
way home, Taylor stopped by a store to pick up some office supplies. Without thinking, Taylor inadvertently left his briefcase containing the ten tests
on the front seat of his car. When he returned, the briefcase was missing.
After filing a report with the police, Taylor went home, wondering what he
was going to do. The next day, Taylor decided that all he could do was locate
the applicants and have them return again for testing. After a day of calling
and explaining the lost test scores, arrangements were made for the ten applicants to come in and retake the programming aptitude test. Two days later all
ten applicants arrived and, once again, took the same test. Wouldn't you
know it though; the day after readministering the tests, Taylor received a
visit from the police with his briefcase and its contents intact. Taylor removed the ten tests and set them beside the stack of ten tests just taken. He
muttered to himself, "What a waste of time." Out of curiosity, Taylor scored
the new set of exams just to see how the applicants had done on the retest.
He carefully recorded the two sets of scores. His recorded results are shown
in Table 4.1.

After reviewing the data, Taylor thought "What a perplexing set of
results!" The scores on the original tests had changed, and changed rather
dramatically. Taylor pondered the results for a moment. He had expected the
applicants' test scores to be the same from one testing to the next. They were
not. Each of the ten persons had a different score for the two tests. "Now
why did that happen? Which of the two sets of scores represents these
applicants' programming aptitudes?" he mused.

The situation we've just described is similar to that represented by our
rifle illustration. Taylor, too, needs dependable, accurate, consistent data for
selection decision making. Yet, from our selection example, we can see that

---

Table 4.1   Summary of Hypothetical Test and Retest Results for Ten
Applicants Taking the Programming Aptitude Test

Applicant	First Test	Second Test
D. C. Zymski	35	40
S. B. Green	57	69
G. T. Johnson	39	49
C. A. Snyder	68	50
J. A. Fukai	74	69
K. W. Mossholder	68	66
C. A. Cronen	54	38
A. A. Armenakis	71	78
J. R. Parrish	41	52
K. R. Davis	44	59

his test scores are different for no apparent reason. Thus, it appears he does not have the consistent, dependable data he needs. These characteristics of data that we have mentioned, that is, "consistency," "dependability," "stability," are all meant when we refer to the concept of *reliability*.

A Definition of Reliability

Reliability is a characteristic of selection measures that is necessary for effective human resource selection. In our example above, the computer programming aptitude test was apparently an unreliable measure, and it is this unreliability that may have contributed to the large differences in test scores that Taylor found.

There are a host of definitions that have been given for the term "reliability." In our discussion, we will touch upon several of these. But, for now, we want to consider a fundamental definition of the concept. In the context of human resource selection, when we refer to reliability, we simply mean *the degree of dependability, consistency, or stability of measurement of a measure (either predictors, criteria, or other variables) used in selection research.* Thus, in our earlier selection example, we would have expected the programming aptitude test to have yielded very similar results from one testing period to the next *if* the test produced reliable data. Since similar results were not obtained, we would probably conclude there were errors in measurement with the test. Thus, a careful study of the reliability of the test should be made.

Errors of Measurement

It is important to keep in mind that reliability deals with *errors of measurement*. In this sense, when a measure is perfectly reliable, it is free of errors. Relative to measures of psychological characteristics, most measures of physical attributes have high degrees of measurement reliability. However, many of our selection measures that are designed to assess important job-related characteristics such as knowledge, skills, and abilities do not have the same preciseness of measurement as measures of physical characteristics. By examining Exhibit 4.1, you can see that reliability tends to be higher for the physical characteristics at the top of the figure than for the psychological attributes at the bottom. This is not to say that our measurement reliability of important selection characteristics is poor. But, because selection measures do not have perfect reliability, they contain some degree of measurement error. In general, the greater the amount of measurement error, the lower the reliability of a selection measure; the less the error, the higher the reliability will be. Thus, if errors of measurement can be assessed, a measure's reliability can be determined. What, then, are "errors of measurement?"

As we have seen, when we use selection devices such as tests, we obtain numerical scores on the measures. These scores serve as a basis for selection decision making. Since we are using scores as a basis for our decisions, we want to know the "true" scores of applicants for each characteristic being

Exhibit 4.1   *Relative Reliability of Measurement of Various Human
Attributes*

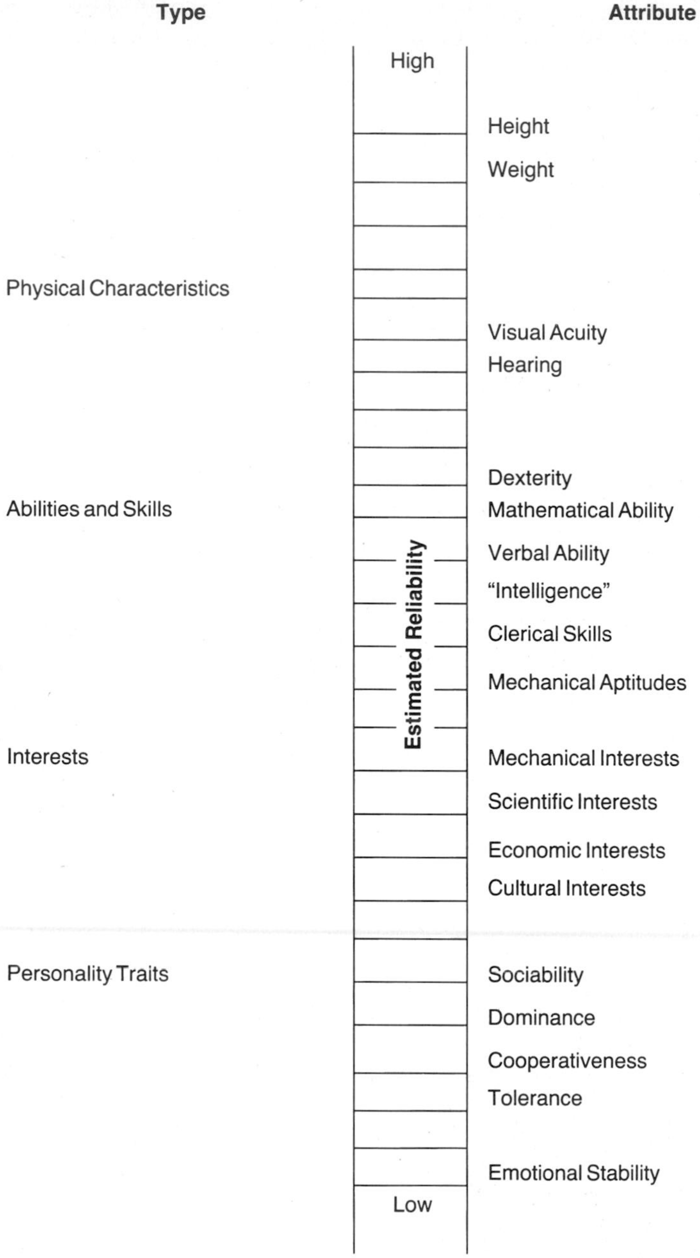

Type	Estimated Reliability	Attribute
	High	
		Height
		Weight
Physical Characteristics		
		Visual Acuity
		Hearing
		Dexterity
Abilities and Skills		Mathematical Ability
		Verbal Ability
		"Intelligence"
		Clerical Skills
		Mechanical Aptitudes
Interests		Mechanical Interests
		Scientific Interests
		Economic Interests
		Cultural Interests
Personality Traits		Sociability
		Dominance
		Cooperativeness
		Tolerance
		Emotional Stability
	Low	

Source: Based on Lewis E. Albright, J. R. Glennon, and Wallace J. Smith, *The Use of Psychological Tests in Industry.* (Cleveland: Howard Allen, 1963), p. 40.

measured. For example, if we administer a mathematics ability test, we want to know the "true" math ability of each testee. But, unless our measure is perfectly reliable, we will encounter some difficulties in knowing these true scores. In fact, we may get mathematics ability scores for individuals that are quite different from their true abilities. Let's see why.

The score obtained on a measure, that is the *obtained score*, consists of two parts: a *true* component and an *error* component. Thus, the components of any obtained score (X) can be summarized by the following equation:

$$X_{obtained} = X_{true} + X_{error}$$

where

$X_{obtained}$ = obtained score for a person on a measure,

X_{true} = true score for a person on the measure, i.e., actual amount of the attribute measured that a person really possesses, and

X_{error} = error score for a person on the measure, i.e., amount that a person's score was influenced by chance factors present at the time of measurement.

This notion of a score being composed of error and true parts is a basic axiom of measurement theory.[1]

True Score   The true score is really an ideal conception. It is the score individuals would obtain if external and internal conditions to the test were perfect. For example, in our mathematics ability test, an ideal or true score would be one where the following conditions existed:

1. Individuals answered correctly the same percentage of problems on the test that they would have if *all possible* problems had been given, and

2. Individuals answered correctly the problems they actually knew without being affected by any external factors, such as lighting or temperature of the room in which the testing took place, their emotional state, or their physical health.

Another way of thinking about a true score is to imagine that an individual takes a test measuring a specific ability many different times. With each testing, his scores will differ somewhat; after a large number of testings, the scores will take the form of a normal distribution. The differences in scores are treated as if due to errors of measurement. But, the average of all test scores best approximates his true ability. Therefore, we might think of a true score as being *the mean or average score made by an individual on many different administrations of a test.*

This idealized situation does not exist. The notion of a true score, however, helps to define the idea that there is a specific score that would be obtained *if* measurement conditions were perfect.

Error Score　A second part of the obtained score is the error score. This score represents errors of measurement. Errors of measurement are *those factors that affect obtained scores but are not related to the characteristic, trait, or attribute being measured.*

Exhibit 4.2 shows the relationship between reliability and errors of measurement for three levels of reliability of a selection measure. Hypothetical obtained and true scores are given for each of the reliability levels. Errors of measurement are shown by the shaded area of each bar. With *decreasing* errors of measurement, reliability of the measure *increases*. Notice that with increasing reliability, more precise estimates of an individual's true score on the measure can be made. That is, there is not as much error present. For example, suppose an individual's true score on the measure is 50. For a measure that has low reliability, a wide discrepancy between the obtained scores (40 to 60) and the true score (50) is possible. In contrast, in a measure with high reliability the possible obtained scores (45 to 55) yield a closer estimate of the true score (50).

In general, there are two types of errors: (a) random and (b) constant errors. *Random* errors are chance factors present at the time of measurement that distort respondents' scores either over or under what they would have been in an ideal context. These errors are not systematic or constant; they do not occur in the same way each time measurement takes place. They are random errors whose presence will vary from time to time and from situation to situation. For example, a loud noise that occurs while an individual is taking a test and that affects his or her answers is one form of random error.

Constant errors are factors that occur consistently over repeated measurement and affect individuals' scores. They may be found in the selection measure itself or even within the person responding to the measure. For instance, suppose the written directions on a test are wrong. Individuals' scores on the test will be affected. Error will occur because we are not correctly assessing individuals' true scores on the measure. The error is constant because it occurs with each administration of the test.

An example of constant error associated with an individual would be, for instance, if a person had difficulty reading a test because he or she needed glasses. The applicant's true ability would not be measured by the test because of the inability to correctly read the questions. The error is constant because it will be present each time the test is taken without glasses. Constant errors occurring within the individual are particularly important since they affect individuals to different degrees.

If scores on a selection measure contain too much error variance, we should be concerned. Regardless of whether this variation results from the measure, the respondent, or the conditions under which measurement takes place, we will not have much confidence in a selection device as a measure of an attribute if excessive error variation in scores is present. Table 4.2 summarizes some of the sources of error that could affect an individual's responses to a selection measure.

Exhibit 4.2 Relationship between Errors of Measurement and Reliability of a Selection Measure for Hypothetical Obtained and True Scores

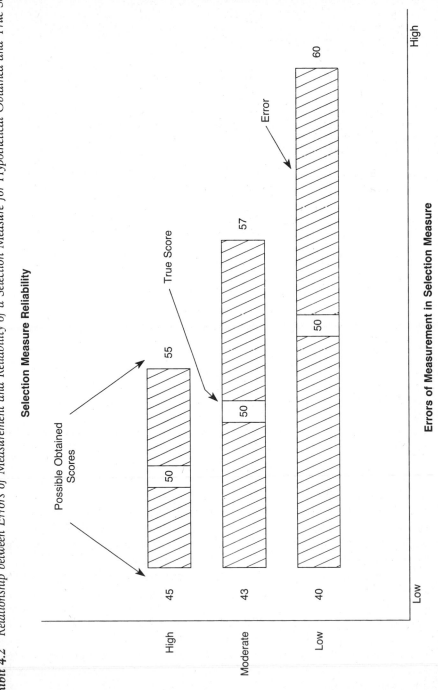

Table 4.2   *Sources of Error of Measurement Contributing to Variations in a Respondent's Answers to a Selection Measure*

  I. Factors That Are Temporary But Affect Responses to a Selection Measure, For Example, a Respondent's:
     A. Physical health
     B. Fatigue
     C. Level of motivation
     D. Emotional stress
     E. General "test-wiseness" in how to answer or respond to a measure
     F. Readiness to complete a measure
     G. Physical conditions (heating, cooling, lighting, etc.) under which the measure is administered
 II. Factors That Are Temporary and Apply to a Specific Measure
     A. Factors that apply to the measure as a whole
        1. Respondent's understanding of the instructions for a measure
        2. Respondent's knowledge of specific tricks or techniques in responding to a measure
        3. Amount of practice available to a respondent for specific tasks required in responding to a measure
     B. Factors that apply to particular questions on a measure
        1. Lapses of memory
        2. Fluctuations in respondent's attention
III. Other Factors
     A. Variations due to "guessing" or random answering
     B. "Chance" element associated with specific items chosen for a measure

---

Source: Based, in part, on Robert L. Thorndike, *Personnel Selection* (New York: John Wiley, 1949), p. 73.

Methods of Estimating Reliability

Reliability is generally determined by examining the relationship between two sets of measures measuring the same thing.[2] Where the two sets of measures yield *similar* scores, reliability will be *raised*. If scores from the measures tend to be *dissimilar*, reliability will be *lowered*. Referring again to our earlier example involving Taylor, personnel manager of Datasources, we saw that he had two sets of programming aptitude test scores. In Taylor's case, the two sets of test scores were completely different from each other. Because the two sets of scores were different, they suggested that the stability of measurement of programming aptitude was low.

Where scores are generally consistent for people across two sets of measures, reliability of a measure will be enhanced. For example, if a person's math ability score remains the same for two different administrations of a test, it will add to the reliability of the test. However, if factors (such as fatigue) cause differential *changes* in people across both sets of measures, the factors will contribute to *unreliability*. These factors are then considered as sources of error in measurement because they are chance factors influencing responses to a measure.

Since reliability theory is only an idealized concept of what does or does not contribute to reliability, we cannot measure reliability per se. We can only *estimate* it. Thus, we should not think of *the* reliability of a measure, but rather an *estimate* of reliability. We will see that alternative procedures can be used to provide different estimates of reliability. One of the principal ways in which these procedures differ is in terms of how they treat the various factors (see Table 4.2) that may alter measurements of people. Some procedures will consider some of these factors to be error while others will not. Obviously, you might ask: "Which method should be used?" There is not one best way. The choice will depend upon each specific situation for which a reliability estimate is desired.

Statistical procedures are commonly used to calculate what are called "reliability coefficients." Most often, techniques involving the *Pearson product-moment correlation coefficient* are utilized to derive reliability coefficients. We will not go into the statistical details of the correlation coefficient here; those will be discussed in the next chapter. But, we need to describe briefly how the coefficient is obtained. Specifics concerning the interpretation of the coefficient in terms of reliability will be given in the next section.

A reliability coefficient is simply an index of relationship. It summarizes the relation between two sets of measures for which a reliability estimate is being made. The calculated index typically varies from .00 to 1.00. The *higher* the index or coefficient, the less the measurement error, and the *higher* the reliability estimate. Conversely, as the coefficient approaches .00, error of measurement increases and reliability correspondingly decreases. Of course, we want to employ selection measures having high reliability coefficients. With high reliability, we can be more confident that a particular measure is giving a dependable picture of an individual's true score for whatever the attribute being measured.

There are many ways to estimate reliability. We will discuss the three principal ones most often employed or reported in selection research studies. These procedures are (a) test-retest, (b) parallel or equivalent forms, and (c) internal consistency estimates. As Milton Blum and James Naylor point out, an important characteristic that differentiates among these procedures is what each method considers to be error of measurement. One method may treat a factor as error while another may treat the same factor as meaningful information. The method chosen will depend upon what factors a researcher may want to treat as error as well as which of the following questions are to be addressed by reliability procedures.

1. How dependably can people be assessed with a measure at a given moment?

2. How dependably will data collected by a measure today be representative of the same people at a future point in time?

3. How accurately will scores on a measure represent the true ability of people on the trait being sampled by a measure?[3]

Test-Retest Reliability Estimates

One obvious way for assessing the reliability of scores obtained on a selection measure is to administer the measure twice and then correlate the two sets of scores. This method is referred to as test-retest reliability. It is called test-retest reliability because the *same* measure is used to collect data at two *different* points in time. Because a correlation coefficient is calculated between the two sets of scores over time, the obtained reliability coefficient represents a *coefficient of stability.* Thus, the coefficient will indicate how well scores on a measure can be generalized over the two time periods.

An example of test-retest reliability might be as follows.[4] Assume that we wanted to know the reliability of our mathematics ability test. First, we administer the test to a representative group of individuals. After a period of time, say three months or so, we readminister and score the same test for the same individuals.

In order to estimate test-retest reliability, we simply correlate the two sets of scores (test scores at time 1 correlated with scores at time 2) using the Pearson product-moment correlation. In graphical form in Exhibit 4.3, scores on the initial testing are represented by the circle labeled *Test-Time 1* while scores on the retest are labeled *Test-Time 2*. The true score component (that is, the degree to which the two sets of scores are identical) is the overlap of the two circles representing the two sets of scores. Error is represented by

Exhibit 4.3   *Representation of Test-Retest Reliability (Correlation) of Math Ability Test Scores over Time 1 and Time 2*

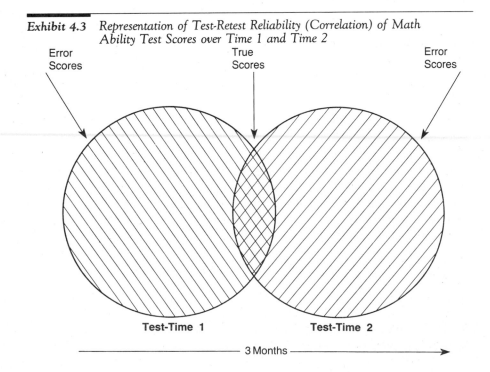

those portions of the circles that do *not* overlap (that is, the amount by which the two sets of scores are different). The correlation or reliability coefficient is also depicted by the overlap between the two circles.

The higher the test-retest reliability coefficient, the greater the true score, and the less error that is present. Thus, with increasing reliability, the overlap between the two circles will increase. If reliability were equal to 1.00, the circles would be superimposed one on top of the other and no error would exist in the scores; true scores would be perfectly represented by the scores on the test. A coefficient this high would imply that scores on the measure are not subject to changes in the respondents or the conditions of administration. If reliability were equal to .00, the circles would be completely separate with no intersection present. A test-retest reliability coefficient this low would suggest that obtained scores on the test are nothing more than error, and no level of math ability is represented by the test scores. Correlations of 1.00 and .00 are shown pictorially in Exhibit 4.4.

As we saw in Table 4.2, there are many sources of error that can change scores over time, and hence, lower test-retest reliability. Some of these errors will be associated with differences within individuals occurring from day to day (such as illness on one day of testing) while others will be associated with administration of a measure from one time to the next (such as distracting noises occurring during an administration). Further, there are two additional factors that may also affect test-retest reliability. These factors are (a) *memory* and (b) *learning.*

Recall that earlier we said *any* factor that causes scores to change over time will decrease test-retest reliability. Similarly, *any* factor that causes scores to remain the same over time will increase the reliability estimate. If respondents on a selection measure remember their previous answers to an initial administration of a measure and then on the retest respond according to their memory, the reliability coefficient will increase. How much it will increase will depend upon how well they remember their previous answers.

The effect of memory, however, will be to make the reliability coefficient artificially high — an *overestimate* of the true reliability of scores obtained on the measure. Rather than reflecting stability of a measure's scores over time, a test-retest reliability coefficient may tend to reflect the accuracy of respondents' memories. In general, when considering reliability we are not interested in measuring the stability or accuracy of respondents' memories. But, we are interested in evaluating the stability of the scores produced by the measure.

One way of lessening the impact of memory on test-retest reliability coefficients is to increase the interval of time between the two administrations. As the length of time increases, respondents are less likely to recall their responses. Thus, with increasing time intervals, test-retest reliability coefficients will generally decrease.

You can probably see that there could be many different test-retest reliability estimates depending upon when the two administrations take place.

Exhibit 4.4 *Representation of Test-Retest Reliability of Math Ability Test Scores When Reliability = 1.00 and .00.*

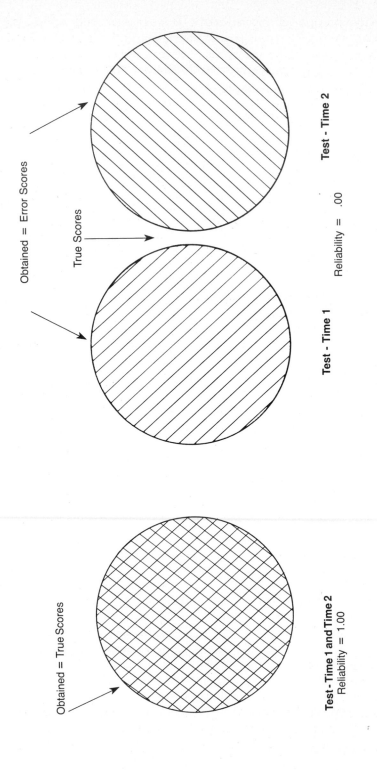

Obtained = Error Scores

True Scores

Test - Time 1

Test - Time 2

Reliability = .00

Obtained = True Scores

Test - Time 1 and Time 2
Reliability = 1.00

Theoretically speaking, the number of estimates could be infinite. How long a period should be used? There is no one best interval, but probably from several weeks up to six months is reasonable depending upon the measure and the specific situation.

Although a lengthy interval between two administrations would appear to be a viable alternative for countering the effects of memory, too long a period opens up another source of error — *learning.* If respondents between the two time intervals of testing learn in such a way that their responses to a measure are different on the second administration of a measure than they were on the first, then test-retest reliability will be lowered. For instance, if respondents recall items asked on an initial administration of a test and then learn answers so that their responses are different on the second administration, learning will have changed their scores. Or, in another instance, respondents may have been exposed to information (such as a training program) that will cause them to alter their answers the second time a test is administered. Whatever the source, when individual differences in learning take place so that responses are differentially affected, reliability will be lowered.

Notice that because of learning, we may have a selection measure with scores that are not stable over time. Yet, their unreliability is not really due to the errors of measurement we have been discussing. In fact, systematic, but different rates of change among respondents through learning may account for what would appear to be unreliability. Nevertheless, actual calculation of a test-retest reliability coefficient will treat such changes as error, thus contributing to unreliability. Therefore, with a long time interval between administrations of a measure, test-retest reliability may *underestimate* reliability because learning could have caused scores to change.

In addition, selection measures that involve traits of personality, attitudes, or interests are usually not considered to be static but in a state of change. Here again, it may be inappropriate to use test-retest reliability with measures of these attributes because any changes found will be treated as error.

Given some of the potential problems with test-retest reliability, when should it be used? There are no hard and fast rules, but some general guidelines can be offered. These guidelines include the following:

1. Test-retest reliability is appropriate when the length of time between the two administrations is long enough to offset the effects of memory or practice.[5]

2. When there is little reason to believe that memory will affect responses to a measure, test-retest reliability may be employed. A situation where memory may have minimal effects may be one where (a) there is a large number of items on the measure, (b) the items are too complex to remember (for example, items involving detailed drawings, complex shapes, or detailed questions), and (c) retesting occurs after at least eight weeks.[6]

3. Test-retest reliability may be necessary if resources are not available to develop alternative or parallel forms for the measure.

4. If interest is solely in the stability of a specific measure over time rather than the stability of a sample of questions chosen to represent the attribute being measured, then test-retest reliability may be appropriate.

Robert Guion further notes that the method is useful for certain types of measures such as those involving sensory discrimination and psychomotor abilities.[7] However, he cautions that careful consideration should be given before using the procedure with performance rating data. (As we indicated earlier, performance ratings are frequently used as criterion measures.) Many different factors can influence the stability of ratings. Changes in performance or day-to-day incidents can occur within relatively brief periods and may affect the stability of rating data. Then, too, there is the question of whether the technique is measuring the stability of ratees' performance or stability of raters' ratings.

Parallel or Equivalent Forms Reliability Estimates

In order to control the effects of memory on test-retest reliability (which can produce an overestimate of reliability), one strategy is to use, not the same measure twice, but equivalent versions of the measure. Each version of the measure has different items, but the questions assess the same attribute being measured in precisely the same way. One form of the measure would be administered to respondents followed by a second administration of the other form. Like our test-retest procedure, a Pearson correlation would be computed between the two sets of scores (Form A correlated with Form B scores) to develop a reliability estimate. Estimates computed in this manner are referred to as *parallel or equivalent forms reliability* estimates. The reliability coefficient itself is often called a *coefficient of equivalence* because it represents the consistency with which an attribute is measured from one version of a measure to another. As the coefficient approaches 1.00, the *set* of measures is viewed as equivalent or the same for the attribute measured.

To have a parallel forms reliability estimate, at least two equal versions of a measure must exist. Looking again at the math ability test that we referred to earlier, we can review the basic requirements of equivalent forms of a measure. The basic process in developing parallel forms is outlined in Exhibit 4.5.

Initially, a universe of possible math ability items is identified. Items that represent the specific topics and types of math abilities important to us compose what is called the "universe of possible math items." This universe of math ability item content is also referred to as the "content domain" of the test. From the content domain, two samples of items are drawn, say, two random samples of 100 items each. Sample 1 items compose Form A of our math ability test while Sample 2 items make up Form B. If our defining and sampling of math ability item content has been correctly conducted, we should have two equivalent forms of our math ability test. Among the various statistical criteria used to define form equivalency are the following:

Exhibit 4.5   *Basic Measurement Procedures and Requirements for Developing*
Equivalent Forms (A and B) of a Math Ability Test

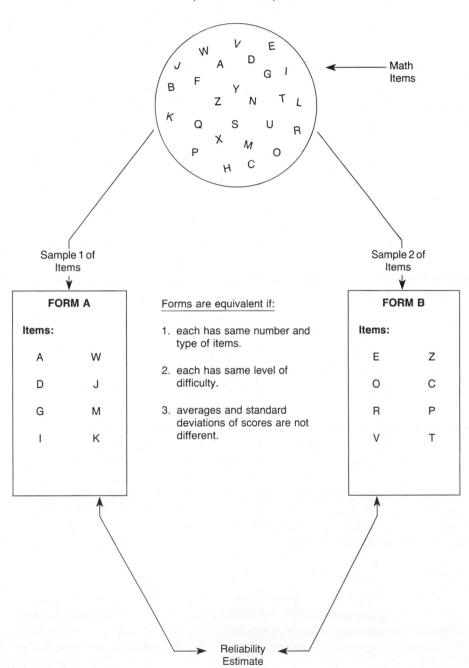

Universe of Possible Math Items
(Content Domain)

Math Items

Sample 1 of Items

Sample 2 of Items

FORM A

Items:

A	W
D	J
G	M
I	K

Forms are equivalent if:

1. each has same number and type of items.

2. each has same level of difficulty.

3. averages and standard deviations of scores are not different.

FORM B

Items:

E	Z
O	C
R	P
V	T

Reliability Estimate

1. The forms should contain the same number and type of items.
2. Each form should have the same level of difficulty.
3. Averages and standard deviations of the scores obtained by respondents to the forms should be the same.

Once created, one form is administered after the other form has been given. The time interval between the two administrations can be brief, within a day or so, or long, for instance, two weeks. In this manner, a reliability estimate can be obtained rather quickly without concern for the effects of memory on responses. However, short-term effects of changes in administration of the measure or in respondents cannot be completely controlled. If a longer time interval exists between the two administrations, the coefficient of equivalency takes on the characteristics of a coefficient of stability as well. But, like test-retest reliability estimates, parallel forms estimates cannot control random sources of error occurring over time nor some of the effects of learning.

In practice, equivalency of forms is not easy to achieve. Chance or random effects of the ways in which samples of items are selected can produce item differences in the forms. As a consequence, the forms will be different, thus curtailing reliability. For example, item differences on the two forms of our math ability test could result in one form being more difficult than the other. Form-to-form differences will cause individuals to have changes in their scores from one administration to the next, and reliability of test scores will be lowered.

For some selection measures, such as math, spelling, and vocabulary tests, it may be possible to obtain reasonably equivalent forms. Equivalent forms of these and other aptitude measures are commercially available. However, the construction of equivalent forms of a biographical data or personality inventory would require considerable effort, time, skills, and other resources.

Because genuine or true equivalent forms are difficult to obtain and because differences may exist from one administration to another, reliability coefficients computed between parallel forms tend to be conservative estimates. Yet, where equivalent forms can be obtained, this estimate of reliability is almost always preferable to test-retest reliability. If a high parallel-forms reliability estimate is obtained, the coefficient suggests that individuals' scores on the measure would be very similar if they had taken an equivalent test on a different occasion.

Internal Consistency Reliability Estimates

Guion has noted that one important characteristic of a reliable measure is that the various parts of a total measure should be so interrelated that they can be interpreted as measuring the same thing. An index of a measure's similarity of content is an *internal consistency reliability* estimate. Basically, an internal consistency reliability estimate shows the extent to which all parts of a measure (for example, items or questions) are similar in what they measure.[8] Thus, the estimate tends to indicate the degree of homogeneity (that is, similarity) of measurement by all parts of a measure. A high estimate suggests that a respondent's answers to one part are similar to his or her responses to other parts of the measure.

Internal consistency estimates tend to be among the most popular procedures used. In general, the following two procedures are used most often: (a) split-half reliability and (b) Kuder-Richardson (or coefficient alpha) reliability.

Split-half Reliability Estimates   So far, we have discussed reliability in the context of *two* administrations of a measure. But, what if we want to control the effects of memory on responses and do not have the time to wait for memory to be diminished before administering a retest? Or, what if an equivalent form of a selection measure does not exist? There are options available to handle those situations where retests or equivalent forms are not feasible.

One of these options is referred to as *split-half* or *subdivided test reliability* estimates. Split-half reliability involves a *single* administration of a selection measure. Then, *for scoring purposes,* the measure is divided or split into two halves so that scores for each part can be obtained for each individual. To assess split-half reliability, the first problem is how to split the measure to obtain the most comparable halves? The most common method for creating these two halves of a measure is to score all *even*-numbered items as a test and all *odd*-numbered items as a test. When split in this manner, the distribution of the items into the two parts approximates a random assignment of items. Then, as in our previous estimates, the Pearson correlation is used to obtain the extent of relation between the two part scores. The resulting correlation coefficient is the reliability estimate.[9] Strictly speaking, a split-half reliability estimate is not a pure measure of internal consistency.[10] Like the parallel forms reliability coefficient, the obtained coefficient primarily represents a coefficient of equivalence. Thus, the coefficient tends to show similarity of responses from one form to an equivalent one.

Exhibit 4.6 illustrates how two parts of a measure may be developed and split-half reliability determined. However, the example shown is a bit different from some of our earlier illustrations. Previously, we employed *predictors* in our examples, but in Exhibit 4.6 we are using a *criterion* measure. As we specified earlier in the chapter, reliability estimates are important for *all* variables being studied.

Let's assume that we wanted to know the reliability of an employee productivity measure that was serving as a criterion in a selection research study involving bicycle assemblers. Basically, the measure is the total number of bicycles assembled by each employee during a 28-day period. For purposes of brevity, we have shown in Exhibit 4.6 the total number of bicycles assembled by three employees during an abbreviated 28-day period.

Exhibit 4.6   *Representation of Odd-Even (Day) Split-Half Reliability Computed for a Job Performance Criterion Measure*

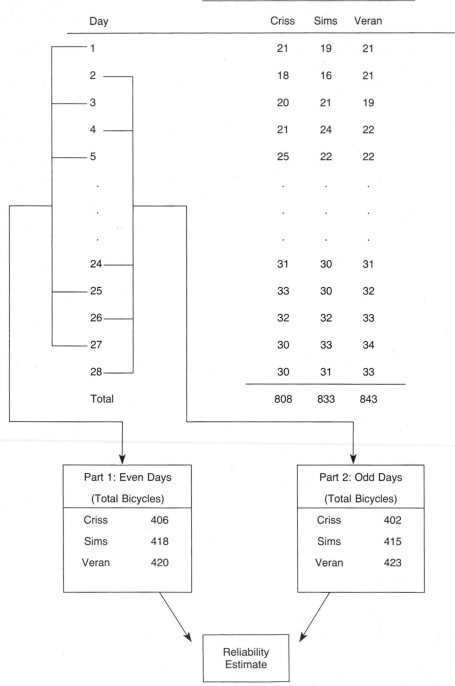

Employee Productivity (Bicycles Assembled)

Day	Criss	Sims	Veran
1	21	19	21
2	18	16	21
3	20	21	19
4	21	24	22
5	25	22	22
.	.	.	.
.	.	.	.
24	31	30	31
25	33	30	32
26	32	32	33
27	30	33	34
28	30	31	33
Total	808	833	843

Part 1: Even Days
(Total Bicycles)

Criss	406
Sims	418
Veran	420

Part 2: Odd Days
(Total Bicycles)

Criss	402
Sims	415
Veran	423

Reliability Estimate

Once we have complete data for our employees on each of the 28 days, we can subdivide our measure into two parts. The odd-numbered days (day 1, 3, 5, . . ., 25, 27) and the associated production for each employee compose Part 1 while the even-numbered days (day 2, 4, . . ., 24, 26, 28) and their associated employee productivity data are assigned to Part 2. Total scores or total productivity is obtained for each part by summing the respective daily production rates. Next, a correlation is computed between the employees' production rates (Part 1 correlated with Part 2) to obtain a reliability estimate of the employee productivity measure. This same procedure could be applied to a predictor, such as a test, as well. Rather than having odd- and even-numbered days, odd- and even-numbered items on the measure would be used. Identical procedures as outlined in Exhibit 4.6 would then be applied.

The obtained reliability coefficient developed on the two halves of a measure is not a very precise estimate. Other things being equal, reliability increases with increasing length of a measure. Our split-half reliability estimate, however, is based upon a correlation obtained between scores on only half of the measure, thus, it *underestimates* actual reliability. The length of the measure was reduced when we split it into two halves, an odd-numbered and an even-numbered part. Therefore, a correction is needed to determine the reliability of the full or complete measure. A special formula, the Spearman-Brown prophecy formula, is used to make the correction. We will not go into the statistical details here since they can be obtained elsewhere.[11] But, essentially the formula shows what the reliability estimate would have been if the correlation had been based on the full rather than part measures.

Because it is computed from a one-time only administration of a measure, split-half reliability does not detect any of the errors in measurement that can occur over time, such as changes in individual respondents or changes in administration of a measure. Therefore, this procedure will tend to result in a liberal estimate of reliability.

This method of reliability estimation is *not* appropriate for any measure that has a time limit associated with its completion. In many cases, for example, timed tests have rather easy questions and scores are a function of how many items are completed. If questions are very simple, then individuals are likely to get correct nearly all that are attempted. As a result, individuals are likely to differ only in terms of how many questions they complete. Odd and even scores will be very similar up until the point time has expired because most items will be answered correctly. Beyond that point, responses will also be very similar because they were not answered. As a consequence, a split-half reliability estimate computed on a test with a time limit will be spuriously high and meaningless.

Kuder-Richardson (Coefficient Alpha) Reliability Estimates   Another method for determining internal consistency reliability is the Kuder-Richardson procedure. (There are several different types of Kuder-Richardson formulas. The most popular and the one on which this discussion is based is called K-R 20.) It, too, involves the single administration of a measure. The procedure is used for determining the consistency of respondents' answers to items within a measure. Whereas the split-half method examines consistency of response *between* parts or halves of a measure, the Kuder-Richardson method assesses *interitem* consistency of response. The resulting coefficient estimates the average of the reliability coefficients that would result from all possible ways of subdividing a measure.[12] Because it represents an average of all possible splits, Kuder-Richardson reliability estimates are usually lower than those obtained from split-half estimates.

In general, the more similar or homogeneous the content of a measure, the more likely respondents' answers will be similar. As the content of a selection measure becomes more similar, Kuder-Richardson reliability coefficients will increase. Thus, large reliability coefficients will reflect high interitem consistency and, therefore, high homogeneity or similarity of content. A high coefficient suggests that items on the measure "hang together" and have a lot in common. For example, if one arithmetic ability test contains only items dealing with division while another arithmetic test contains items dealing with division, multiplication, addition, and subtraction, the first test will demonstrate more interitem consistency than the latter one.[13] The first test addresses only one aspect of arithmetic ability while the other test assesses four. In addition, scores on the first test will be less ambiguous than scores on the second test. For instance, on the first test a score of 20 can only be arrived at by some knowledge of division. However, for the second test, a score of 20 could be arrived at in a variety of ways. Various combinations of items correct for each of the four arithmetic operations could result in a score of 20. Thus, our understanding of what a score represents on the first test will be clearer than for the second test.

The Kuder-Richardson procedure can be applied to any measure that has items scored in only two categories. For example, questions on an achievement test are typically scored as either "right" or "wrong." Sometimes, however, items or questions on selection measures are not scored as a dichotomy. Instead, a continuum or range of response options representing an interval scale is given for an item. In Exhibit 3.4, for instance, we presented an example of an employee performance appraisal rating form where total scores on the form could be used as a criterion in a selection research study. Returning again to the form, suppose that we wanted to determine the consistency of raters' ratings among the items that are added together to obtain a total performance score. Kuder-Richardson reliability would not be appropriate since each item involves more than two response categories. In those cases in which we are interested in knowing the internal consistency of responses to a measure but in which responses are based on an interval scale, we have to use another technique. In these situations, Cronbach's *coefficient alpha* (α) can be employed and the results interpreted like Kuder-Richardson reliability.[14] Table 4.3 (on pages 108 and 109) provides a descriptive summary of the methods we have discussed for estimating the reliability of selection measures.

Interpreting Reliability Coefficients

The chief purpose behind the use of measures in human resource selection research is to permit us to arrive at sound judgments concerning people to whom these measures are applied. For these judgments to have any value, they must be based upon dependable data. When data are not dependable, any decisions based on this information are of dubious worth. Thus, one goal of selection managers is to utilize measures that will provide dependable information.

Reliability analyses help us to determine the dependability of data we will use in selection decision making. Through reliability we can estimate the amount of error included in scores on any measure we choose to study. Knowing reliability, we can estimate how precisely or loosely a score for a measure can be interpreted. But, how do we go about interpreting a reliability coefficient? What exactly does a coefficient mean? How high or low must a coefficient be for a particular measure to be used? These are but a few of the questions that can be asked in interpreting a reliability coefficient. Below, we will examine some of the issues that will bear upon the interpretation of reliability.

What Does a Reliability Coefficient Mean?

As we said earlier in the chapter, calculation of reliability estimates results in an index or a coefficient ranging from .00 to 1.00. A variety of symbols are used to indicate reliability; typically, reliability is represented by an r followed by two identical subscripts. For example, the following would be the reliability symbols for the four measures of X, Y, 1, and 2: r_{xx}, r_{yy}, r_{11}, and r_{22}.

After the symbol, a numerical coefficient is reported. Again, the values will range from .00 indicating no reliability (a measure composed entirely of error) to 1.00 or perfect reliability (no error present in the measure). Without going through too many of the technical details, let's see what the coefficient means. Harold Gulliksen has shown that the reliability coefficient is equivalent to the squared correlation between true and obtained scores for a measure and can be directly interpreted as the coefficient of determination.[15] Or,

$$r_{xx} = r^2_{tx}$$

where

r_{xx} = reliability coefficient

r^2_{tx} = squared correlation between true and obtained scores

x = obtained scores

t = true scores

Therefore, the reliability coefficient can be interpreted as *the extent (in percentage terms) to which individual differences in scores on a measure are due to "true"*

Table 4.3 *Descriptive Summary of Major Methods for Estimating Reliability of Selection Measures*

Reliability Method	Question Addressed	Number of Forms	Number of Administrations	Description	Assumptions	Sources of Error That Lower Reliability
Test-Retest	Are the scores on a measure consistent over time?	1	2	1 version of a measure is given to same respondents during 2 sessions with a time interval in between.	• Respondents do not let answers on first administration affect those on second administration. • Respondents do not "change" (for example, through learning) from one administration to the other.	• Any changes in respondents and differences in answers for test and retest due to changes occurring over time.
Parallel Forms (immediate administration)	Are the 2 forms of a measure equivalent?	2	1	2 versions of a measure are given to same respondents during 1 session.	• The 2 forms are parallel. • Respondents do not let completion of first version affect completion of second.	• Any differences in similarity of content between the 2 forms.
Parallel Forms (long-term administration)	• Is the attribute assessed by a measure stable over time? • Are the 2 forms of a measure equivalent?	2	2	2 versions of a measure are given to same respondents during 2 sessions with a time interval in between.	• The 2 forms are parallel. • Respondents do not let completion of first version affect completion of second.	

Method	Question		Procedure	Conditions	Possible Errors
					• Respondents do not "change" (for example, through learning) from one administration to the other.
Split-Half (Odd-Even)	Are respondents' answers on one half (odd items) of a measure similar to answers given on the other half (even items)?	1	1 version of a measure is given to respondents during 1 session.	• Splitting a measure into 2 halves produces 2 equivalent halves. • Measure is not speeded (answers are not based on a time limit).	• Any differences in similarity of content in one half of the measure versus the other half.
Kuder-Richardson and Coefficient Alpha	• To what degree do items on the measure seem to be measuring the same attribute? • How well do items on a measure "hang together"?	1	1 version of a measure is given to respondents during 1 session.	• Only 1 attribute is measured. • Measure is not speeded (answers are not based on a time limit). • K-R 20 is suitable for dichotomous items. • Coefficient alpha is suitable for items on a continuum.	• Any differences in similarity of item content. • More than 1 attribute assessed by a measure.

differences in the attribute measured and the extent to which they are due to chance errors. For example, if we have a test called "X," and the reliability of Test X equals .90 (that is $r_{xx} = .90$), then 90 percent of the differences in test scores is due to true variance and only 10 percent due to error. The reliability coefficient provides an indication of the proportion of total differences in scores that is attributable to true differences rather than error.

As Alexander Wesman has concluded, reliability coefficients can serve two basic purposes: (a) to estimate the precision of a specific measure and (b) to estimate the consistency of respondents' performance on the measure.[16] As our discussion has shown, these purposes are served by the methods used to estimate reliability. The second purpose, however, actually includes the first. It is important to recognize that it is possible to have unreliable performance by a respondent on a reliable measure, but reliable performance on an unreliable measure is impossible.

How High Should a Reliability Coefficient Be?

This question has been asked many times. Different opinions exist. Unfortunately, there is no clear-cut, generally agreed upon value that can be given above which reliability is acceptable and below which it is unacceptable. Obviously, we want the coefficient to be as high as possible; however, how low a coefficient can be and still be used will depend on the purpose for which the measure is to be used. The following principle will generally apply: *The more critical the decision to be made, the greater the need for confidence in the precision of the measure and the higher the required reliability coefficient.*[17]

From the perspective of job applicants, highly reliable selection measures are a necessity. In many selection situations, there are more applicants than job openings available. Competition can be keen for the available openings. Thus, a difference of a few points in some applicants' scores can determine whether they do or do not get hired. Any measurement error in a selection measure could seriously affect, in a negative and unfair way, some applicants' employment possibilities. You might be asking, but isn't it possible this same measurement error could produce higher scores for some applicants than might be expected, thus helping them obtain employment? Yes, it is possible for some scores to be inflated through error; here again, these scores could be unfair to the applicants "benefited" by error of measurement. Because of misleading scores, organizations may be hiring such individuals and placing them in job situations they may not be able to handle. Job requirements may be too high relative to their true abilities. Although they may get the job, they may not be able to cope with it, leading to frustration and dissatisfaction for both employee and employer.

From the perspective of the organization attempting to hire executives or other key personnel (whose decisions may affect the success of the entire organization), reliable evidence of applicants' qualifications is also a necessity. The cost of being wrong in the assessment of key managerial personnel can be very high. Imprecise selection measures can have long-term consequences for an organization. Dependable measures are important to accurately evaluating these key personnel.

Several writers have offered some rough guidelines regarding desirable magnitudes of reliability coefficients for selection measures. On the whole, their thoughts are directed toward predictors rather than criteria or other variables that might be present in selection situations. Jum Nunnally has suggested that in applied settings when important decisions are being made with respect to test scores, a reliability of .90 is the absolute minimum that should be accepted.[18] Lewis Aiken thinks that if a procedure is being used to compare one individual with another, a reliability of .85 or higher is necessary.[19] His suggested reliability coefficient is somewhat lower than Kelly's recommended minimum of .94 to evaluate the level of individual accomplishment.[20] All in all, where both predictors and criteria are concerned, we generally feel that a reliability coefficient no lower than .85 (and preferably .90 or higher) should be the absolute minimum in most selection situations. However, our conclusion needs to be tempered somewhat since a number of factors can influence the size of an obtained reliability coefficient. Through the impact of factors, such as the range of talent in the respondent group for the attribute being assessed, it is possible for a reliability coefficient lower than .85 to be fully as good as one substantially higher. Reliability is specific to the group on which it is calculated. It can be higher in one situation than another because of situational circumstances that may or may not affect the preciseness (reliability) of measurement. To clarify how these can influence reliability in a context involving selection measures, let's briefly examine several of these factors.

Factors Influencing the Reliability of a Measure

As we have discussed, a reliability coefficient is an estimate. Many factors can have an effect on the actual magnitude of a coefficient. Here, we will mention four important factors that can affect estimated reliability: (a) method of estimating reliability, (b) individual differences among respondents, (c) length of a measure, and (d) construction/administration of a measure.

Method of Estimating Reliability   We have seen that different procedures for computing reliability treat errors of measurement in different ways. One result is that different reliability estimates will be obtained on a measure simply from the choice of procedure used to calculate the estimate. Some methods will tend to give more liberal (upper-bound or higher) estimates while others will tend to be more conservative (lower-bound or lower) in their estimates of the true reliability of a measure. Therefore, it is important for any individual evaluating a particular selection procedure to know which procedure was used and to know what methods tend to give liberal and conservative estimates.

Exhibit 4.7 presents a very rough characterization of relative reliability in terms of whether methods tend to give upper- or lower-bound estimates of a

Exhibit 4.7   *Rough Characterization of Reliability Methods in Terms of Generally Providing Upper- or Lower-Bound Estimates*

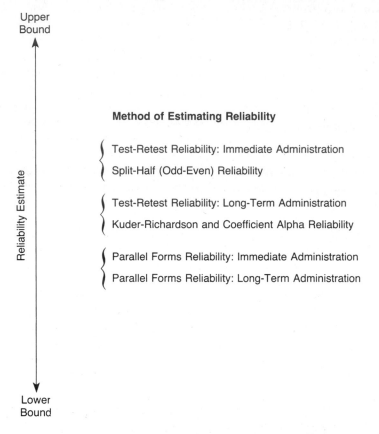

measure's true reliability, *other things being equal.* We will discuss a few of these "other things" — factors that can affect reliability — in this section. It is important to emphasize the fact that the hierarchy in Exhibit 4.7 is based upon general results reported for selected measures. In any one specific situation, it is possible that the rank-order of methods may vary; a method characterized as usually providing lower-bound reliability may in fact give a higher estimate than one generally ranked above it.

Parallel test reliability generally provides a lower estimate than other techniques because of changes occurring over time and from one form to another. These changes contribute to error of measurement. If a test is measuring more than one attribute, Kuder-Richardson or coefficient alpha reliability will tend to underestimate true reliability; if a measure has a time limit, reliability will be overestimated by the procedure. Because of memory, test-retest reliability will likely be high, but as the time interval between administrations lengthens, memory will have less impact and estimated reliability will fall. The effect on reliability of lengthening the time interval between administrations will be similar for parallel forms reliability as well.

Frank Womer has suggested several informal guidelines for judging reliability coefficients estimated by various methods.[21] For split-half reliability (odd-even split, Kuder-Richardson, and coefficient alpha), he feels that one should be skeptical of reliability coefficients lower than .85. For parallel form reliability, estimates can be somewhat lower, say around .80, and still be acceptable. Of course, these guidelines are one person's opinion. Some may think they are too stringent and others that they are not stringent enough.

Individual Differences among Respondents   Another factor influencing a reliability estimate is the range of individual differences or variability among respondents on the attribute being measured. Generally speaking, the greater the variability or individual differences on the characteristic being measured, the higher the reliability. In part, this finding is based on the conception of reliability and its calculation by means of a correlation coefficient. Change or variation *within* a person, such as changing a response from one administration to another, detracts from reliability; we have already discussed this issue as error of measurement. On the other hand, differences *among* people are considered to be true differences. Such true variation contributes to reliability. Therefore, if variability or individual differences increase among respondents while variation within individuals remains the same, reliability will increase. Because individual differences can vary a great deal for various groups, such as those based on educational level, age, and ethnic group status, it is imperative for a user of selection measures to review reliability data for relevant subgroups of respondents. Developers and publishers of commercially available predictors should report separate reliability coefficients for such subgroups of respondents.

Length of a Measure   In general, as the length of a measure increases, its reliability will also increase. One way of thinking about this relationship is to look out of a window for a second or two and then try to describe in detail what you saw. As you increase the number of times you look out of the window in one to two second intervals, you will probably find that the accuracy and details of your description increase. Thus, with increasing measurement, that is, observation out of the window, your description begins to approximate the true situation outside the window. A similar effect occurs when a selection measure is lengthened. Only a sample of possible items is used on a given measure. If all possible questions could be used, a person's score on the measure would very closely approximate his or her true score. Thus, as we add more and more relevant items to our measure, we get a more precise and reliable assessment of the individual's true score on the attribute measured.

Construction/Administration of a Measure   As we have noted, various factors we have called errors of measurement can have a bearing on the reliability of a measure. For example, emotional and physical states of respondents, lack of rapport with the administrator of a measure, and inadequate knowledge of how to complete a measure can contribute to errors of measurement. Where errors of measurement are present, reliability will be lowered.

Standard Error of Measurement

We have just seen that reliability coefficients are useful for describing the general stability or homogeneity of a measure. The coefficient gives us some degree of assurance of the dependability of *most* respondents' scores on a measure. However, the various methods of computing reliabilities that we have discussed do not give us an idea of the error to be expected in a particular *individual's* score on the measure. Reliability is a group-based statistic.

In order to obtain an estimate of the error for an individual, we can use another statistic called the *standard error of measurement*. The statistic is simply a number in the same units as the measure for which it is being calculated. The *higher* the standard error, the *more* error present in the measure, and the *lower* its reliability. Thus, the standard error of measurement is not another approach to estimating reliability; it is just another way of expressing it. The formula for calculating the standard error is as follows:

$$\sigma_{meas} = \sigma_x \sqrt{1 - r_{xx}}$$

where

σ_{meas} = standard error of measurement for measure X

σ_x = standard deviation of obtained scores on measure X

r_{xx} = reliability of measure X.

For example, let's assume that the mathematics ability test that we referred to earlier has a reliability of .90 and a standard deviation of 10. The standard error of measurement for a mathematics ability score on this test would be calculated as follows:

$$10\sqrt{1 - .90} = 10\sqrt{.10} = 10(.316) = 3.16.$$

To illustrate how the standard error of measurement can be applied, let's look at an example. Suppose we had an applicant come into our employment office, take our math ability test, and make a score of 50. We could use the standard error to estimate the degree his/her test score would vary if he/she were retested with the test on another day. By adding and subtracting the standard error from the math test score (50 ± 3.16), we would obtain a range of math ability scores (46.84 to 53.16). One possible interpretation of this range might be that the chances are two to one that the applicant's true math ability lies somewhere between 46.8 and 53.2. Alternatively, we could say if he/she were given the test 100 times, we would expect that roughly two-thirds (68 percent) of the time the math ability scores would fall within the range of 46.8 to 53.2.

The standard error of measurement possesses several unique advantages.[22] First, unlike the reliability coefficient, the standard error of measurement is not affected by variability within the group of respondents to whom a measure has been administered. Further, the measure is useful in that it forces us to think of scores on a measure not as exact points but instead as a band or range of scores. Importantly, it can also be used to determine whether scores for individuals differ significantly from one another. For instance, imagine that we had two job applicants who had taken our math ability test. Jacob Farrar scored 50 while Alicia Tatum scored 47. Can we conclude that Jacob is the better applicant solely in terms of math ability as measured by the test? The standard error of measurement can help us decide. If our standard error of measurement is 3.16 and the difference between our two applicants' scores is 3, then it is entirely possible that the difference in scores is due to chance. On retesting, Alicia may score higher than Jacob.

With respect to interpreting differences in individuals' scores, Lewis Aiken has offered the following guidelines:

1. The difference between two individuals' scores should not be considered significant unless the difference is at least twice the standard error of measurement of the measure.

2. The difference between scores of the same individual on two different measures should be greater than twice the standard error of measurement of either measure before the difference should be treated as significant.[23]

Another use of the standard error of measurement is in establishing how confident we may be in individual scores obtained from different groups of respondents. For example, suppose we had administered a test to 100 male and 100 female job applicants. For the male applicants, reliability for the test was .85 (standard deviation = 26) while for the female applicants, it was .70 (standard deviation = 10). On the face of reliability information alone, it would appear that we might have more confidence in individual scores obtained for men than in those for women. However, when we use the reliability data *and* standard deviation information to compute the standard error, we find that the standard error of measurement for men is 10.1, and for women it is 5.5. Therefore, we should have greater confidence in a female applicant's test score than we should in a male applicant's score. This example highlights an important conclusion: *Without considering the variability of the group on the attribute measured (the standard deviation), reliability information alone will not permit us to compare relative confidence in scores for individuals in different groups.* Because the standard error is not affected by group variability, the statistic can enable us to make this important comparison.

The standard error of measurement is a statistic you will likely come across in reading and studying various commercially available predictors (in particular, tests) to be used in selection. Because of its importance, the statistic should be routinely reported with each reliability coefficient computed for a measure. In practice, if you want to compare the reliability of different measures, the reliability coefficient should be used. However, to help interpret individual scores on a measure, the standard error of measurement is appropriate.

Evaluating Reliability Coefficients

From our discussion of reliability, you probably recognize that there are many issues to be considered in evaluating a reliability coefficient. To help you, we have summarized some of these in Table 4.4. All of these have been

Table 4.4   *Questions to Consider in Evaluating Reliability Coefficients*

Question	Comment
1. Does the coefficient reflect the precision of a measure by indicating how well items "hang together" in measuring an attribute?	If interest is in determining the degree to which items on a measure are assessing the same content, an internal consistency estimate is appropriate.
2. Does the coefficient reflect the constancy or stability of an attribute as assessed by a specific measure over time?	If stability of performance is of interest, some form of test-retest reliability should be reported.
A. Is the interval between test and retest so short that memory could have an effect?	Depending upon the situation, the interval should not be shorter than several weeks.
B. Is the interval between test and retest so long that learning or other changes in respondents could have occurred?	Depending upon the situation, the interval should not be longer than six months or so.
C. Is the coefficient based upon parallel forms of a measure administered over time?	If so, are data available to indicate that the forms are indeed parallel?
D. Is a test-retest coefficient computed for a measure that can be expected to change because of the nature of the attribute being measured?	Some measures can be expected to change over time because of their nature. Examples might include performance ratings and attitudinal measures.
3. Do scores on the measure for which the coefficient is computed depend on how quickly respondents can respond to the measure? Is a time limit involved?	If a time limit for completing a measure is involved, the coefficient should not be based on an internal consistency estimate.
4. Is the coefficient based upon respondents like those for which a measure is being considered?	A coefficient is more meaningful if it is based on a group like the one to which the measure will be administered. For example, if a measure is going to be given to job applicants, a coefficient should be available for similar job applicants.
5. Is the coefficient based upon a large enough number of people that confidence can be placed on the magnitude of the coefficient?	The larger the sample size on which the coefficient is based, the more dependable the estimate of reliability.
6. Is information provided on the range of ability for the attribute measured of the group on which the coefficient is based?	Standard deviations and ranges of scores should be given for each group on which a coefficient is reported.
7. Is a standard error of measurement provided for the reliability coefficient?	An index of the standard error of measurement should be given for each coefficient.
Once these questions have been addressed, then a user may ask:	
8. Is the coefficient high enough to warrant use of the measure?	The more important the selection decision to be based on a specific measure, the higher the required reliability coefficient.

Source: Questions 3, 4, 5, and 7 were based in part on Alexander G. Wesman, *Reliability and Confidence* (Test Service Bulletin No. 44) (New York: The Psychological Corporation, May 1952), p. 7.

addressed in this chapter. When examining reliability coefficients of selection measures, the checklist can serve as a useful means for reviewing the major considerations involved in reliability interpretation.

References for Chapter 4

[1] Our treatment of reliability is based upon *classical* reliability theory. More recent developments have offered alternative approaches to the study of reliability theory (see, for example, Lee J. Cronbach, Goldine C. Gleser, Harinder Nanda, and Nageswari Rajaratnam, *The Dependability of Behavioral Measurements: Theory of Generalizability for Scores and Profiles* (New York: John Wiley, 1972); however, for the beginning student, our approach will suffice.

[2] Robert M. Guion, *Personnel Testing* (New York: McGraw-Hill, 1965), p. 37.

[3] Milton Blum and James Naylor, *Industrial Psychology: Its Social and Theoretical Foundations* (New York: Harper and Row, 1968), p. 41.

[4] This example was adapted from G. C. Helmstadter, *Principles of Psychological Measurement* (New York: Prentice-Hall, 1964), p. 63.

[5] Wayne Cascio, *Applied Psychology in Personnel Management* (Reston, Va.: Reston Publishing, 1982), pp. 134–135.

[6] Jum C. Nunnally, *Introduction to Psychological Measurement* (New York: McGraw-Hill, 1970), p. 123.

[7] Guion, *Personnel Testing*, p. 40.

[8] Walter Dick and Nancy Hagerty, *Topics in Measurement* (New York: McGraw-Hill, 1971), pp. 23–24.

[9] In practice, the coefficient needs to be "corrected" by use of the Spearman-Brown prophecy formula. For further information, see note 11.

[10] Guion, *Personnel Testing*, p. 42.

[11] David Magnusson, *Test Theory* (Reading, Mass.: Addison-Wesley, 1966), pp. 73–74. The Spearman-Brown prophecy formula to be applied to a split-half reliability coefficient is as follows:

$$r_{ttc} = \frac{2r_{tt}}{1 + r_{tt}}$$

where

r_{ttc} = corrected reliability coefficient

r_{tt} = split-half reliability coefficient.

[12] Anne Anastasi, *Psychological Testing* (New York: Macmillan Publishing Company, 1976), p. 116.

[13] Anastasi, *Psychological Testing*, p. 116.

[14] Jum C. Nunnally, *Psychometric Theory* (New York: McGraw-Hill, 1967), pp. 196–197; 210–211.

[15] Harold Gulliksen, *Theory of Mental Tests* (New York: John Wiley, 1950).

[16] Alexander G. Wesman, *Reliability and Confidence* (Test Service Bulletin No. 44) (New York: The Psychological Corporation, May 1952), p. 2.

[17] Wesman, *Reliability and Confidence*, p. 3.

[18] Nunnally, *Psychometric Theory*, p. 226.

[19] Lewis R. Aiken, *Psychological Testing and Assessment* (Boston: Allyn and Bacon, 1979).

[20] T. Kelly, *Interpretation of Educational Measurements* (Yonkers, N.Y.: World Book, 1927).

[21] Frank B. Womer, *Basic Concepts in Testing* (Boston: Houghton Mifflin, 1968), p. 41.

[22] Cascio, *Applied Psychology in Personnel Management*, p. 140; see also Magnusson, *Test Theory*, p. 82.

[23] Aiken, *Psychological Testing and Assessment*, p. 61.

5

Validity of

Selection Measures

An Overview of Validity

In the last chapter we pointed out that one important characteristic we need to have in any test, interview, or other selection measure we may use is *reliability*. So far, we have examined in some detail various issues regarding the reliability of measures. Here, we want to focus on the topic of *validity*, its relation to reliability, and the principal analytic strategies available for determining the validity of measures.

Validity: A Definition

When we are concerned with the judgments or inferences we can make from scores on a selection measure, then we are interested in its *validity*. In this sense, validity refers to "the degree to which inferences from scores on tests or assessments are justified by the evidence."[1] In the context of human resource selection, we want to know how well a measure is related to criteria important to us. If a measure is correlated with job-relevant criteria, then we can draw inferences from scores on the measure about individuals' job performance in terms of these criteria. For example, if we have a test that is related to job performance, then scores on the test can be used to infer a job candidate's ability to perform the job in question. Because test scores are related to job performance, we can be assured that, on the average, applicants who score high on the test will do well on the job. Therefore, we can use test scores as one basis for employing job candidates.

Historically, people have tended to think of *the* validity of a measurement device. Actually, it is not the measure that is valid, but the inferences that can be made from the scores on the measure. There is not just one validity; there can be many. The number will depend on the number of *inferences* to be made. Validity is not an inherent property of a selection measure but is a relationship between the selection measure and some aspect of the job. In some cases, validity may be expressed quantitatively or in other cases, judgmentally. Whatever the form, there may be many different validities for any one measure. These validities will simply depend on those criteria found or judged to be related to the measure and the inferences to be drawn from these relations.

The process that we go through in discovering what and how well a device measures is called *validation*. The results of this process tell us what types of inferences may be made from scores obtained on the measurement device. For instance, let's suppose that a manager believes that a master's degree is essential for satisfactory performance in a job involving technical sales. The manager is inferring that possession of the degree leads to adequate job performance while absence of the degree results in unacceptable job performance. In validating the use of the educational credential as a selection standard, he is attempting to verify the inference that the degree is a useful predictor of future job success. He is not validating the educational selection standard per se, but rather the inferences made from it. Therefore, there can be as many validities related to the standard as there are inferences about the scores on the standard.[2] Thus, validation involves the research processes we go through in testing the appropriateness of our inferences.

The Relation Between Reliability and Validity

When we discussed the concept of reliability, we used terms such as "dependability," "consistency," and "precision" of measurement. Although these are important characteristics of any measurement device, it is possible to have a measure that is very reliable but does not measure what we want. For example, suppose we have a device that will measure job applicants' eye color in a very precise and dependable manner. Now, suppose we use the device to try and predict applicants' job performance. Subsequent research, however, shows that color of applicants' eyes has no relation to how well they perform their job. Thus, our results show that our highly reliable measure is quite worthless for meeting our objective of predicting subsequent job performance. As you can see, the question of *what* is being measured by a device is as critical as the question of *how dependable* is the measure.

Rather than existing as two distinct concepts, reliability and validity go hand-in-hand. Let's see how they are interrelated. With respect to our eye color measure, we may have a highly reliable tool that has no validity in human resource selection. However, we *cannot* have high validity if we do not have high reliability. If a measure cannot correlate with itself, then we should not expect it to correlate with some criterion external to the measure. High reliability is a necessary but not a sufficient condition for high validity.

Statisticians have also demonstrated the intimate quantitative interrelationship between validity and reliability. It has been shown that:

$$r_{xy} \leq \sqrt{r_{xx}}$$

where

r_{xy} = correlation between measure X and criterion Y (the validity coefficient) and

r_{xx} = reliability coefficient of measure X.

For example, if the reliability of a test is .64, then its *maximum possible* validity is .80. If the reliability falls to only .49, then the maximum possible validity of the test is .70. Thus, from the formula above, it can be seen that the reliability or unreliability of a measure limits its *possible* validity.[3]

Types of Validity Strategies

There are many different types of validity strategies which have been discussed by a number of writers. For our purposes there are four methods or strategies of validation which have been recognized as appropriate for validating measures that may be used in personnel decision making: criterion-related or empirical validity consisting of both *concurrent* and *predictive* validation strategies, *content* validity, and *construct* validity.

Criterion-Related Validity Strategies

Criterion-related validity involves the statistical examination of the relationship between a predictor and a criterion. There are two basic criterion-related approaches: (a) concurrent validity and (b) predictive validity.

Concurrent Validity

In a concurrent validation strategy, sometimes referred to as the "present-employee method," information is obtained on both a measure (a predictor or independent variable such as an employment test) and a criterion (for example, some measure of job success) for a *current* group of employees. Because predictor and criterion data are collected roughly at the same time, this approach has been labeled "concurrent validity." Once the two sets of data (predictor and criterion information) have been collected, they are statistically correlated. The validity of the inference to be drawn from the measure is signified by a relationship found between the predictor and measure of job success.

An Example   As an example of a concurrent validation study, let's imagine we want to determine if some ability tests might be valid predictors of successful job performance of industrial electricians working in a firm. First, a thorough analysis of the job of industrial electrician is undertaken. Drawing on job analysis methods and techniques such as those described in Chapters 7 and 8, we would attempt to uncover the critical tasks, elements, or functions actually performed on the job. From these identified tasks, we would then infer the requisite knowledge, skills, abilities (KSAs), and other characteristics required for successful job performance. Exhibit 5.1 summarizes three hypothetical tasks and two relevant KSAs that were found to be important in our industrial electrician's job. (Keep in mind, we are providing only three example tasks and KSAs; there could be more in an actual job setting.) Two of the three example KSAs were found to be critical in performing the three job tasks: (a) Knowledge of Electrical Equipment and (b) Ability to Design/Modify Mechanical Equipment for New Purposes. A third KSA, Ability to Follow Oral Directions, was judged to be of less importance in successfully performing the job and was not used as a basis for choosing our selection tests.

After the requisite KSAs have been identified, the next step is to select or develop those tests that appear to measure the relevant attributes found necessary for job success. As shown in Exhibit 5.1, three commercially available tests were chosen as experimental predictors of electricians' job success. These three tests were (a) *Bennett Mechanical Comprehension Test* (Form AA), (b) *Purdue Test for Electricians,* and (c) *Purdue "Can You Read a Working Drawing?"* test. How were these three tests selected? The tests were chosen based upon our knowledge of what KSAs were required on the job and our knowledge of those existing tests which seemed to tap these KSAs. As we will explain in Chapter 7, usually this process of inferring what devices might be used to measure the derived KSAs involves some form of subjective judgment. Expert advice can play an important role in choosing the most appropriate measures. For this reason, experienced selection consultants are often employed in choosing and developing selection measures.

Next, our three tests are administered to industrial electricians currently working in the firm. They are told that their participation is voluntary; the tests are being given for research purposes only; and their test scores will not affect how they are evaluated or their relationship with the company.

Shortly after, or while the tests are being administered, another step in the validation process is undertaken. In this step, criterion information representing measures of electricians' job performance is collected. Performance appraisal ratings or more objective measures such as accident rates or errors in equipment repair might serve as criteria. Whatever the criteria, it is critical that the measures chosen are relevant indicators of performance as identified by the job analysis.

At this point, both predictor and criterion data have been collected. As

Exhibit 5.1   *Selection of Experimental Ability Tests to Predict Important KSAs for the Job of Industrial Electrician*

	Linking of KSAs to Critical Job Tasks (10 = High Relation; 1 = Low Relation)			
		KSAs		
Critical Job Tasks	**1. Knowledge of Electrical Equipment**	**2. Ability to Design/Modify Mechanical Equipment for New Purposes**	**· · ·**	**8. Ability to Follow Oral Directions**
1. Maintains and repairs lighting circuits and electrical equipment such as motors and hand tools	10	3	· · ·	1
	· · ·	· · ·		· · ·
5. Installs equipment according to written specifications and working drawings	10	3	· · ·	2
	· · ·	· · ·		· · ·
10. Independently constructs basic electrical/mechanical devices	7	9	· · ·	1

	Does Test Appear Suitable For Assessing KSA?			
Selected Tests	**KSA 1**	**KSA 2**	**· · ·**	**KSA 8**
A. Bennett Mechanical Comprehension Test (Form AA)	No	Yes	· · ·	N.A.
B. Purdue Test for Electricians	Yes	No	· · ·	N.A.
C. Purdue "Can You Read A Working Drawing?" Test	Yes	Yes	· · ·	N.A.

Note: The numbers shown are mean ratings given by subject matter experts used in the analysis of the industrial electrician's job. High ratings indicate that a particular KSA is relevant to the successful performance of a critical job task. "Yes" indicates that a test appears to be useful in assessing a particular KSA.

depicted in Exhibit 5.2, the final step is to analyze the results using statistical procedures. A common practice is to statistically correlate the sets of predictor and criterion data. Tests are considered to be valid predictors of performance if statistically significant relationships with criteria exist. If one or more of our try-out tests is found to be significantly correlated with a criterion, we will give serious consideration to incorporating the measure(s) in our selection program. In summary, Table 5.1 outlines the basic steps taken in a concurrent validation study.

Strengths and Weaknesses　　If it can be assumed that the necessary requirements for conducting an empirical concurrent validation study are met, there is a positive argument for using this method. With a concurrent validity approach, an investigator has almost immediate information on the utility of a selection device. However, there are three principal factors that can affect

Exhibit 5.2　*Representation of Relating Predictor Scores with Criterion Data to Test for Validity*

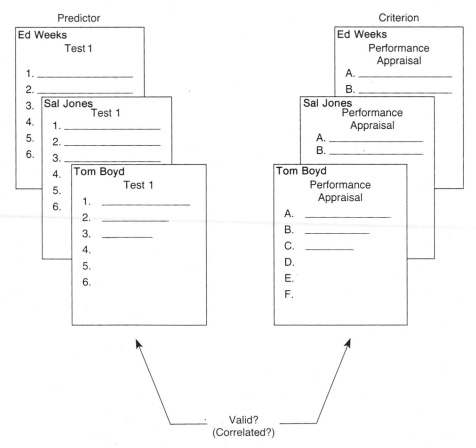

Table 5.1   *Summary of Major Steps Undertaken in Conducting Concurrent and Predictive Validation Studies*

Concurrent Validation	Predictive Validation
1. Conduct analyses of the job	1. Conduct analyses of the job
2. Determine relevant KSAs and other characteristics required to successfully perform the job	2. Determine relevant KSAs and other characteristics required to successfully perform the job
3. Choose the experimental predictors of these KSAs	3. Choose the experimental predictors of these KSAs
4. Select criteria of job success	4. Select criteria of job success
5. Administer predictors to *current employees* and collect criterion data	5. Administer predictors to *job applicants* and file results
6. Analyze predictor and criterion data relationships	6. *After passage of a suitable period of time,* collect criterion data
	7. Analyze predictor and criterion data relationships

the usefulness of a concurrent validation study: (a) differences in tenure of employment of the employees who participate in the study, (b) the representativeness (or unrepresentativeness) of present *employees* to job *applicants,* and (c) the motivation of employees to participate in the study.

If job experience is related to performance on the job, then any predictor/criterion relationship may be adversely affected by an irrelevant variable — job tenure. Since most people learn as they perform their jobs, it is entirely feasible that job experience may indeed influence their scores on either a predictor or criterion measure.

Second, if a concurrent validation study is being undertaken for a selection measure, another problem may arise. We want to use the predictor or selection device whose validity is based on current *employees* to predict subsequent job success of job *applicants.* If applicants are characteristically different from job incumbents (for example, younger, with less job experience, less education), then the generalizability of the results of our study based on incumbents may not apply to applicants. Because of employee turnover or dismissal, our current employee group may be highly select and not at all representative of applicants.

Finally, since we are basing our study on employees who have a job rather than applicants who do not, our participants may not have a high level of motivation to properly respond to our experimental selection measure. As a consequence, our concurrent validation study may be significantly limited.

Although job tenure and use of employees rather than applicants are legitimate concerns, recent research has suggested that some of the limitations associated with concurrent validation may not apply to cognitive ability tests. Gerald Barrett, James Phillips, and Ralph Alexander's review of validity estimates of ability tests showed there were no significant differences in validity estimates for concurrent and predictive validity methods.[4] Their results suggest that a concurrent validation approach may be just as viable as a predictive validation approach. However, their review applies to only one class of predictors — cognitive ability tests. Data are not available on how the two methods compare for other types of predictors.

Anne Anastasi has noted that the use of concurrent validation is aimed at the description of the existing status of people.[5] If the inference to be tested addresses the question of the validity of a measure at the present time, concurrent validation is appropriate. For example, if we want to study the validity of a performance appraisal rating form, we might adopt a concurrent validation approach to answer our question. However, if we are interested in the prediction of *future* behavior, such as, inferring future job success of job applicants, then we may want to employ another empirical validation strategy, that is, predictive validity.

Predictive Validity

Rather than collecting predictor and criterion data at one point in time (like our concurrent validity approach), predictive validity involves the collection of data *over* time. In the context of human resource selection, job applicants rather than job incumbents are used as the source of data. For this reason, it is sometimes known as the "future-employee" or "follow-up" method. The basic steps are also summarized in Table 5.1.

An Example   To illustrate the predictive validation method, let's return to the industrial electrician example. The steps involving job analysis and the selection of tests we want to try out are identical to those under the concurrent validation approach. The really significant difference between the two methods occurs at the next step — *test administration.* Here, our tests are administered to job *applicants* rather than current employees. Once administered, the measures are then filed and applicants hired on the basis of other available selection data (such as other tests, interviews, etc.). Answers to our experimental measures are *not* used in making hiring decisions. After our electrician applicants have been hired, trained, placed in their jobs, and have had time to learn their jobs adequately (perhaps as long as six months or more), criterion data representing job success are collected on the applicants. Then, after criterion data have been assembled, the two sets of scores (scores on our experimental predictors and criterion) are statistically correlated and examined for any possible relationships.

Strengths and Weaknesses   There are several important differences between predictive and concurrent validity. Under predictive validity, there is a time interval between the collection of predictor and criterion data. Applicants rather than incumbents serve as the data source and, as such, may have a higher, more realistic level of motivation when they complete the predictor measure. Differences with respect to job tenure are not a problem since the same level of job experience applies to all study participants. Under the predictive validity approach, the inference tested or question answered is: Can the predictor predict future behavior as measured by criterion data?

Because of the inference tested by predictive validity, the method is most appropriate for measures used in human resource selection. The method addresses itself to the basic selection issue as it normally occurs in the employment context, that is, how well will job applicants *be able* to perform on the job. The biggest weakness, of course, with the predictive validity model is the time interval required to determine the validity of the measure being examined. If relatively few people a month are being hired by an organization, it may take months to obtain a sufficient sample size for a predictive validity study. Moreover, it can be very difficult to explain to managers the importance of filing selection measure information *before* using the data for human resource selection purposes.

From our discussion of concurrent and predictive validity strategies, it may seem there is only one way in which each of these validity designs may be carried out. In practice, however, there may be several different ways for conducting concurrent and predictive validity studies. Robert Guion and C. J. Cranny, for instance, have summarized five different ways in which a predictive study might be conducted.[6] These are illustrated in Exhibit 5.3.

Exhibit 5.3 *Examples of Different Predictive Validity Designs*

Type of Predictive Validity Design	Description of Procedure
1. Follow up — Random Selection	Applicants are tested and selection is random; predictor scores are correlated with subsequently collected criterion data.
2. Follow up — Present System	Applicants are tested and selection is based on whatever selection procedures are already in use; predictor scores are correlated with subsequently collected criterion data.
3. Select By Predictor	Applicants are tested and selected on the basis of their predictor scores; predictor scores are correlated with subsequently collected criterion data.
4. Hire and Then Test	Applicants are hired and placed on the payroll; they are subsequently tested (e.g., during a training period) and predictor scores are correlated with criteria collected at a later time.
5. Shelf Research	Applicants are hired and their personnel records contain references to test scores or other information that might serve as predictors. At a later date, criterion data are collected. The records are searched for information that might have been used and validated had it occurred to anyone earlier to do so.

Source: Based on Robert M. Guion and C. J. Cranny, "A Note on Concurrent and Predictive Validity Designs: A Critical Reanalysis," *Journal of Applied Psychology* 67 (1982): p. 240; and Frank J. Landy, *Psychology of Work Behavior* (Homewood, Ill: The Dorsey Press, 1985), p. 65.

In a similar fashion, different versions of the concurrent validity strategy also exist. These different ways of conducting a criterion-related validity study serve to show that in practice, a variety of approaches might be used.

At times the particular criterion-related design employed might not fit neatly into our categories of predictive and concurrent validity. For instance, suppose a personnel manager hypothesizes that college grade point average (GPA) is related to job performance of sales personnel. GPA was *not* used in making hiring decisions but is only available for *current employees*. To test her hypothesis, she correlates GPA with first-year sales and finds a relationship between the two variables. Is this a predictive validity study (it was *not* really done with applicants)? Is this a concurrent validity strategy (the data were gathered over time)? As you can see, our study design has elements of both predictive and concurrent validity strategies; it does not fall cleanly into either category. Whatever the design employed, the critical issue is not so much the criterion-related validity category to which it belongs. As we have seen, some designs such as that of our college grades and sales performance example may be difficult to classify. Rather the real question to be answered is "What inferences will the design of a criterion-related validity study permit?"[7]

Content Validity Strategy

Within the last five years or so, content validation has been receiving increasing attention by practitioners involved in selection. Because of this increased interest, we want to spend some time reviewing this method.

Basically, a selection measure has content validity when it can be shown that its content (items, questions, etc.) representatively samples the content of the job for which the measure will be used.[8] In content validity terminology, "content of the job" is often called the *job content domain.* The content domain of the job is the knowledge, skills, and abilities that are necessary for effective job performance. Thus, if the measure under concern is a content valid predictor, then the knowledge, skills, and abilities (KSAs) it assesses should match the KSAs required for effective performance on the job. If we want to infer the extent to which an applicant possesses a skill or knowledge that is necessary to perform a job at the present time (present job competence), then a content validity strategy is appropriate.[9]

Content validity differs from predictive and concurrent validity in two important ways. First, the prime emphasis in content validity is on *construction* of a *new* measure rather than validation of an *existing* one. The procedures employed are designed to help insure that the measure being constructed representatively samples what is to be measured, such as the KSAs required on a job. Second, the method principally involves the role of expert judgment in determining the validity of a measure rather than the application of quantitative techniques. Thus, this approach is applicable when concurrent and predictive strategies are not feasible. *Judgments* are used to describe the degree to which the content of a measure represents what is being measured. For this reason, content validity has been called a form of "descriptive" validity.[10] With its emphasis on *description,* content validity contrasts sharply with concurrent and predictive validities, where the emphasis is on *prediction.*

Sometimes, *face* validity is confused with the concept of *content* validity. Whereas content validity deals with the representative sampling of the content domain of a job by a selection measure, *face* validity concerns the *appearance* of whether a measure is measuring what is intended. A selection test has face validity if it appears to job applicants taking the test that it is related to the job. However, just because a test appears to have face validity does not mean it has content or criterion-related validity — it may or may not. Hence, face validity is not a form of validity in a technical sense. But, face validity can be important. If a test appears to test takers to be related to the job, then they are likely to have a more positive attitude toward the organization and its selection procedures. Positive attitudes toward selection measures may yield very positive benefits for an organization. For example, applicants who believe selection procedures are face valid indicators of their ability to perform a job may be more motivated to perform their best on these procedures. Also, if rejected for a job, applicants may perceive the selection procedures to be less biased than if measures without face validity were used. In this situation, rejected applicants from protected groups may be less likely to file a discrimination charge against an organization that uses face valid selection measures than an organization that does not. From this perspective, face validity may be thought of as a "comfort factor." Since some job candidates and some managers may be very resistant to the use of selection measures such as tests, they need to "feel" that a measure is fair and appropriate. Face validity of a measure helps to provide this comfort factor.

Major Characteristics of a Content Valid Measure

A selection measure that is content valid generally has three important characteristics:

1. The job for which a measure is going to be used has been thoroughly analyzed to determine those tasks necessary for successful job performance.

2. The KSAs necessary to successfully perform these tasks have been determined.

3. Statements, questions, or other content of the selection measure have been developed so that they are representative of the KSAs identified as critical to job success.

Each of these characteristics is briefly discussed.

Job Analysis   Job analysis is the heart of any validation study. In particular, job analysis is the essential ingredient to the successful conduct of a content validation study. The results of the job analysis serve to define the job content domain; by matching the job domain to the content of the selection procedure, content validity is established.

A number of court cases have affirmed the necessity for analyzing the content and nature of the job for which a selection procedure is used.[11] For example, the Supreme Court ruled in *Albemarle Paper Co. v. Moody* that job analysis must play an integral role in any validation study.[12] With respect to content validation studies per se, the *Uniform Guidelines* specify that a job analysis should result in the following products:

1. A description of the tasks performed on the job
2. Measures of the criticality and/or importance of the tasks
3. Specification of KSAs required to perform these tasks
4. KSAs which include
   a. an operational definition of each KSA
   b. a description of the relationship between each KSA and each job task
   c. a description of the complexity/difficulty of obtaining each KSA
   d. an indication of whether each KSA is necessary for successful performance on the job[13]

Specification of KSAs   Each important job task identified in the job analysis will likely require some minimal KSA for successful task performance. Here, the KSAs required to perform these tasks are specified. Most often, these KSAs are identified by working with subject matter experts who have considerable knowledge of the job and the necessary KSAs needed to perform it. This step typically involves subjective judgment on the part of participants in identifying the important KSAs. Because inferences are involved, the emphasis in this step should be on defining *specific* KSAs for *specific* job tasks. By focusing on specific definitions of tasks and KSAs, the judgments involved in determining what KSAs are needed to perform which tasks are less likely to be subject to human error.

Specification of Selection Measure Content   Once the KSAs have been appropriately identified, the items, questions, or other content to compose the measure are specified. This phase of content validation is often referred to as *domain sampling*. That is, the items or questions chosen to compose the selection measure are selected so that they represent the KSAs found essential to job task performance. Further, the proportion of items or content included is in proportion to the relative importance of the KSAs identified. Subject matter experts who are familiar with the job in question review the content of the measure and judge it as to its suitability for the job in question. Final determination of selection measure content depends upon these experts' judgments.

Some Examples of Content Validation

Since the content validity approach can have wide applicability in the selection of individuals for jobs requiring generally accepted skills (such as reading, mathematics, ability to read drawings, etc.), we will present three examples of content validation to illustrate the breadth of the method.

Lyle Schoenfeldt and his colleagues were interested in developing an industrial reading test for entry-level personnel of a large chemical corporation. Job analysis was used to determine *what* materials entry-level personnel needed to be able to read upon job entry as well as the *importance* of these materials to job performance. These analyses showed that entry-level employees read four basic types of materials: (a) safety (signs, work rules, safety manuals), (b) operating procedures (instruction bulletins, checklists), (c) day-to-day operations (log books, labels, schedules), and (d) other (memos, work agreements, application materials). The safety and operating procedures materials were judged most important, as they accounted for roughly 80 percent of the materials read while performing the job. The test was then constructed so that approximately 80 percent of the test items reflected these two types of materials. The test items themselves were developed from the content of *actual* materials current employees had to read upon job entry.[14]

In our second example, imagine we want to build content valid measures for use in selecting typist-clerks in an office setting. Again, based on the job analysis procedures discussed previously, it is found that incumbents need specific KSAs to perform specific tasks. From the example tasks and KSAs shown in Exhibit 5.4, two specific job performance domains or areas are identified that we want to be able to predict: (a) typing performance and (b) calculating performance. For our measures to have content validity, we need to build them in such a way that their content representatively samples the content of each of these domains. Where should the measures' contents come from? For the contents to be most representative, they should be derived from what incumbents actually do on the job. For example, we might develop a performance measure that would ask an applicant to format an actual business letter in a specific style and then type it within a prescribed period of time. Similarly, we might ask applicants to use a ten-key adding machine to compute and check some actual, reported business expenses. Further, in computing scores, the measures might be weighted so that each reflects its relative importance in performing the job. In our example, typing correspondence accounts for approximately 75 percent of the job while 15 percent involves calculating expense claims. (The remaining 10 percent consists of other tasks.) Thus, our typing measure should be weighted 75 percent to reflect its relative importance to calculating. As you can tell from our example task statements, KSAs, and measures, we are attempting to develop selection measures whose content representatively maps the actual content of the job itself. To the extent we are successful, content validity of the measures can be supported.

Exhibit 5.4   *Example Tasks, KSAs, and Selection Measures for Assessing KSAs of Typist-Clerks*

Example KSAs of Typist-Clerk	Example Job Tasks of Typist-Clerk		Measures of KSAs
	1. Types and proofreads business correspondence, reports, and proposals upon written instruction	••• 5. Checks and computes travel claims and expenses using a ten-key adding machine	
1. Ability to type reports and correspondence at a minimum of 50 words per minute	✓		Typing test of example of business correspondence
2. Ability to read at 12th grade reading level	✓		Reading test involving reports, correspondence, and proposals at 12th grade reading level
3. Ability to use basic business styles for typing of business correspondence	✓		Typing test of example of business correspondence
4. Knowledge of arithmetic at 10th grade level including addition, subtraction, division, and multiplication		✓	Arithmetic test requiring arithmetic calculations on business expense data using ten-key adding machine
• • •	• • •	• • •	• • •
9. Ability to operate a ten-key adding machine		✓	Arithmetic test requiring arithmetic calculations on business expense data using ten-key adding machine
Percent (%) of time performed	75%	••• 15%	

Note: A check mark indicates that a KSA is required to perform a specific job task. Measures of KSAs are those developed to assess particular KSAs.

   Job incumbents serving as subject matter experts play an important role in establishing the content validity of our measures. These experts are used to identify the important tasks performed on the job and the relevant KSAs needed to perform these tasks successfully. They may also serve in judging the appropriateness of content for the measures. All of these judgments taken in sum represent the foundation for determining content validity of the selection measures being developed for our typist-clerk position.

   Our first two examples involved the *development* of a content valid measure. In our third case, let's assume we have an *existing* selection measure. Let's assume further that a content validation study of this measure is going to be undertaken. In this situation, a social services agency has been using an educational degree, specifically the Master of Social Work or MSW degree, as a basis for employing social workers in the agency. Individuals without the degree have been excluded from employment while those possessing the degree have been given further employment consideration. The assumption the agency has made is that individuals possessing the degree have the necessary KSAs to successfully perform the social worker's job whereas applicants without the degree do not. However, the administrator of the agency has been wondering about the validity of this inference. She has asked if possession of the degree is associated with successful performance on the job. Of course, criterion-related validation methods might be employed; but, in many cases, suitable criteria are not readily available for evaluating social service workers' job performance. Therefore, at least as a first step, a content validation research study can be implemented.

   In performing a content validity study for an educational credential used as a selection measure, a variety of steps would be involved. However, for our purposes, we have summarized these into three major analytic components. These components are depicted in Exhibit 5.5.

   As in our previous example, the first component would involve an analysis of the social worker job to identify the tasks involved in performing the job. From these tasks, relevant KSAs necessary for successful job performance would then be derived. The second component would involve an analysis of the educational courses and experiences of students achieving the MSW degree. These educational courses and experiences would define the curriculum content domain. From this domain, the KSAs obtained by students pursuing the MSW educational credential would be specified. Finally, once the job and curriculum domains as well as their associated KSAs have been specified, subject matter experts would be used to determine the match between the two sets of KSAs. This third component, that is, determination of the match between the job and the educational sets of KSAs, would represent the content validity of the MSW degree in predicting job success of social workers in the agency. Where the match is high, it indicates that the KSAs acquired by a student achieving an MSW degree are linked to the KSAs needed to successfully perform the job of social worker. In this context then, the evidence suggests that the MSW educational credential is a content valid selection measure.[15]

Exhibit 5.5   *Example Depiction of Content Validation of the Master of Social Work (MSW) Degree used as a Selection Credential for the Job of Social Worker*

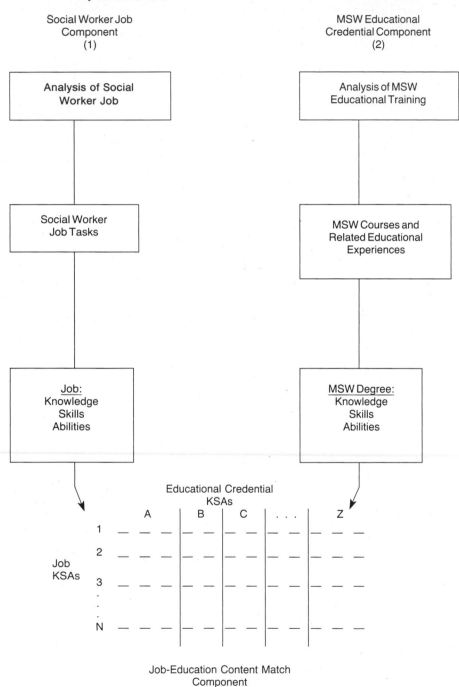

Inappropriateness of Content Validation

As we have seen, content validity provides evidence that a selection measure representatively samples the universe of job content. This evidence is based principally on expert judgment. As long as a selection measure assesses *observable* job behaviors, for example, a driving test used to measure a truck driver applicant's ability to drive a truck, the inferential leap in judging between what a selection device measures and the content of the job is likely to be rather small. However, the more abstract the nature of a job and the KSAs necessary to perform it (for example, the skill of a manager to provide leadership, the possession of emotional stability), the greater the inferential leap required in judging the link between the content of these job requirements and a selection measure. Where inferential leaps are large, human error is more likely to be present. Therefore, it is much more difficult to accurately establish content validity for those jobs characterized by more abstract functions and KSAs than for jobs whose functions and KSAs are more observable.

What is central to the concept of content validity is that the selection measure appropriately samples the domain of job content. Whenever there is a difference in the specific content of the measure and the KSAs required to perform the tasks of a job, then an inferential leap or judgment is necessary for determining if the measure appropriately samples the job. Exhibit 5.6 descriptively summarizes the inference points required in establishing the content validity of a measure. The first inference point (1) is from the job itself to the tasks identified as composing it. Where careful and thorough job analysis techniques are undertaken, the judgments necessary for determining whether the tasks accurately represent the job will probably have minimal error. The next inference point (2) is from the tasks of the job to identified KSAs required for successful job performance. Here again, complete, thorough job analyses can minimize possible error. The final point (3) in judgment is from the KSAs on the task side to the KSAs assessed by the selection device. It is at this point that final judgments of content validity of the selection standard are made. As long as the inferential leaps are acceptably small, that is, the selection measure is composed of content that clearly resembles job tasks and KSAs, arguments for content validity are plausible. For jobs involving activities and processes that are *directly observable* (such as for the job of a typist), only a *small inference* may be required in judging the relation between what is done on the job and what personal characteristics are necessary to do the job. For jobs whose activities and work processes are *less visible* and more abstract (such as those of an executive), a greater inference must be made between job activities and applicant requirements for successful performance. *The greater the inferential leap in specifying job requirements, the more likely errors will exist in job specifications.* Because of the possibility of error, content validity is a more appropriate validation strategy for those jobs involving observable job activities, such as trade and craft jobs.

Exhibit 5.6 *Depiction of the Inference Points from Job Content to Selection Measure Content in Content Validation*

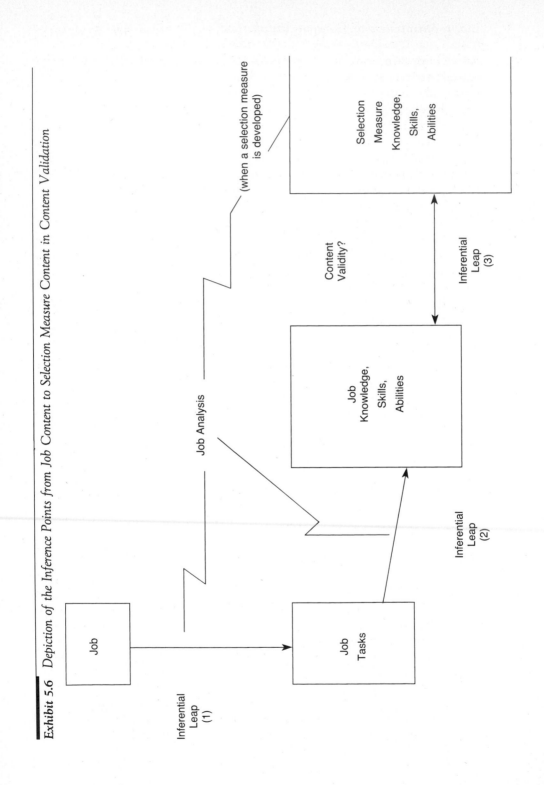

The *Uniform Guidelines* recognize the limits of content validation and specify some situations where content validation alone is not appropriate; other validation methods also have to be used. These situations include the following:

1. When job applicants are ranked (from high to low) on the basis of scores on the selection measure[16]

2. When the match of the KSAs assessed by the measure and the KSAs required on the job uses subjective judgements.[17]

3. When mental processes, psychological constructs, or personality traits (such as judgment, integrity, dependability, motivation) are not directly observable but inferred from the selection device[18]

4. When the the selection procedure involves KSAs which an employee is expected to learn on the job[19]

5. When the content of the selection device does not resemble a work behavior; when the setting and administration of the selection procedure does not resemble the work setting[20]

From our discussion, it should be evident that, as a validation method, content validity differs from criterion-related techniques in the following ways: (a) in content validity, the focus is on the predictor or measure itself, while in the others, the focus is on an external variable, (b) criterion-related validity is narrowly based on a specific set of data, whereas content validity is based on a broader base of data and inference, and (c) a statement of criterion-related validity is couched in terms of precise quantitative indices (prediction) while content validity is generally characterized using broader, more judgmental descriptors (description).[21]

Because content validation emphasizes judgmental rather than statistical techniques for assessing the link between the selection standard and indicators of the job, some writers question its use. The main criticism is that content validity is primarily concerned with inferences about the *construction* of content of the selection procedure rather than with predictor scores. Thus, since validity of selection standards concerns the accuracy of inferences from predictors, that which is "content validity" is not really validity at all.[22]

Content Versus Criterion-Related Validity: Some Requirements

So far, we have discussed three approaches to validation. The choice of a validation strategy implies that certain requirements must first be evaluated and met. Each of the validation strategies discussed to this point has a particular set of requirements. These requirements must be met for a specific strategy to be viable. A review of these requirements serves as a means for determining the feasibility of a particular validation methodology. We have prepared a summary of requirements where human resource selection issues are in question. Drawing principally from the *Uniform Guidelines*, the *Principles*,[23] and other sources in the literature, the major feasibility requirements for conducting criterion-related (concurrent and predictive) and content validation methods have been identified. These requirements are listed in Table 5.2. The requirements shown are not meant to be exhaustive, only illustrations of major considerations where human resource selection is involved. Also, the requirements serve as considerations for deciding upon the feasibility of a particular validation approach; they are *not* complete technical requirements.

Table 5.2   *Basic Considerations for Determining the Feasibility of Criterion-Related and Content Validation Strategies*

Criterion-Related Validation[a]	Content Validation
1. Must be able to assume the job is reasonably stable and not undergoing change or evolution	1. Must be able to obtain a complete analysis of each of the jobs for which the validation study is being conducted. Used to identify the content domain of the job under study
2. Must be able to obtain a relevant, reliable, and uncontaminated measure of job performance (that is, a criterion)	2. Applicable when a selection device purports to measure existing job skills, knowledge, or behavior. Inference is that content of the selection device measures content of the job
3. Should be based as much as possible on a sample which is representative of the people and jobs to which the results are to be generalized	3. Although not necessarily required, should be able to show that a criterion-related methodology is not feasible
4. Should have adequate statistical power in order to identify a predictor-criterion relationship if one exists. To do so, must have: a. adequate sample size b. variance or individual differences in scores on the selection measure and criterion	4. Inferential leap from the selection device to job content should be a small one
5. Must be able to obtain a complete analysis of each of the jobs for which the validation study is being conducted. Used to justify the predictors and criteria being studied	5. Most likely to be viewed as suitable when skills and knowledge for doing a job are being measured
6. Must be able to make the inference that performance on the selection measure can predict future job performance	6. Not suitable when abstract mental processes, constructs, or traits are being measured or inferred
7. Must have ample resources in terms of time, staff, and money	7. Most likely will not provide sufficient validation evidence when applicants are being ranked

[a]Criterion-related validity includes both concurrent and predictive validity.

Sources: American Psychological Association, Division of Industrial and Organizational Psychology, *Principles for the Validation and Use of Personnel Selection Procedures* 2d ed. (Berkeley, Calif.: 1980), p. 7; Equal Employment Opportunity Commission, Civil Service Commission, Department of Labor, and Department of Justice, *Adoption of Four Agencies of Uniform Guidelines on Employee Selection Procedures*, 43 Federal Register 38,295, 38,300-38,301, 38,303 (Aug. 25, 1978); Robert M. Guion, *Personnel Testing* (New York: McGraw-Hill, 1965).

Construct Validity Strategy

The last type of validity strategy we want to mention is construct validity. In many ways the method is, perhaps, more difficult to comprehend than the previous ones we have discussed. Fewer construct validation studies are performed than studies involving any one of the other validation methods. Yet, construct validity is central to truly understanding what a measure is actually measuring.

When psychologists use the term "construct" of a measure, they are generally referring to the concept, attribute, or quality being assessed by a measure. When a measure is developed and used in selection research, it is believed that the measure assesses "something." That something is what is known as a *construct*.[24] Most often, when we use a measure in a research study, we have some idea about what construct is being measured. But, does our measure really assess the construct that we think it does? For instance, if we develop a performance appraisal rating form, we create the measure to evaluate employees' job performance. We hypothesize that it does; but does it? Construct validation helps us answer the question.

Although you may find a single predictive or concurrent validation study that purports to establish the validity of a measure to predict some future behavior, one single study does not establish construct validity.[25] In general, construct validity is only established after an accumulation of evidence that a measure does indeed assess what is intended. A series of research investigations is used to produce a body of evidence on what is being measured. Based on this body of evidence, judgments are used to determine what is being measured. For a new rating measure of job performance, for instance, we might hypothesize that if it is measuring performance, then scores on our new measure should correlate with scores on other, known measures of job performance. To the extent such correlations are found, we can argue that our measure is indeed tapping the construct of job performance; hence, we have some evidence to support the idea of our measure's construct validity.

We might also hypothesize that not only should our new measure relate to known, existing measures of job performance, but it should also correlate with other variables found to be related to job performance. For instance, suppose the literature showed that job performance was related to the following variables in the following ways: negative correlation with job turnover, negative correlation with absenteeism, negative correlation with accident rates, and positive correlation with quality of goods produced. We might conduct a study using our new appraisal measure to determine if it exhibited the same, consistent patterns as found with other performance measures. If our data collected from a series of research investigations produced empirical evidence of these hypothesized correlations, then we would have additional evidence of construct validity. You can probably surmise from our illustration that construct validity is a continuous process of accumulating supporting empirical evidence of what a measure measures. The more evidence we collect, the more assurance we have in our judgments that a measure is really doing what was intended. As such, construct validation represents a much broader definition of validity than we might find in a single criterion-related or content validation study. Through accumulated evidence, the emphasis in a construct validity strategy is on what (the construct) and how well a selection measure assesses what it measures.

Empirical Considerations in Criterion-Related Validity Strategies

Even if we have conducted content or construct validation studies on a selection measure, at some point, we will want to answer two important questions:

1. Is there a relationship between applicants' responses to our selection measure and their performance on the job?
2. If so, is the relationship strong enough to warrant the measure's use in employment decision making?

Questions such as these imply the need for statistical or empirical methods for determining validity, that is, criterion-related validity. Because of their importance, we will review some of the empirical methods and issues most commonly encountered in conducting criterion-related validation research.

Correlation

Computing Validity Coefficients   One of the most frequent terms you will see in reading selection research studies is the term *validity coefficient*. Basically speaking, a validity coefficient is simply an index that summarizes the degree of relationship between a predictor and criterion. Where does the validity coefficient come from? What does it mean? To answer these questions, let's refer to an example. Consider for a moment that a predictive validity study is being conducted. We want to know if a psychological test is useful in predicting the job performance of operative workers. During a one-week employment period, we administered the test to 50 job applicants. No employment decisions were based on the test scores. Six months later, we can identify 20 individuals who were hired and are still employed.[26] (In practice, we would want to have more than just 20 people in our validation study. Ideally, we would have several hundred people on whom both predictor and criterion data are available. Due to space considerations, we have used a small sample to *illustrate* the data in the accompanying tables and exhibits.) As a measure of job performance, we ask their supervisor to judge their performance using a performance appraisal rating form. Total scores on the appraisal form are calculated, and they represent employee job performance. Thus, for each employee we have a pair of scores: (a) scores on their job application test and (b) their six-month performance appraisal. These example data are shown in Table 5.3.

A scattergram or scatterplot is initially made of data like those in Table 5.3 for visual inspection of any possible relationships between predictor and criterion variables. An example scattergram of our data is shown in Exhibit 5.7. Each point in the graph represents a plot of the *pair* of scores for a single employee. For instance, employee Q has a test score of 79 and a performance rating of 91. Although a scattergram is useful for estimating the existence and direction of a relationship, it really does not help us specify the *degree* of relationship between our selection measure and job performance. For this purpose, a more precise approach is to calculate an index that will summarize the degree of any relationship that might exist. Most often, the Pearson product-moment or simple correlation coefficient (r) is used to provide that index. The correlation coefficient, or in the context of personnel selection the "validity coefficient," summarizes the relationship between our predictor and criterion. Often, the validity coefficient is represented as r_{xy} where r represents the degree of relationship between X (the predictor) and Y (the criterion). Other types of correlation coefficients (such as, phi and biserial) may serve as validity coefficients, but the Pearson is the most common.

Table 5.3   *Test Score and Performance Rating Data Collected on 20 Operative Employees*

Employee ID	Test Score	Performance Rating
A	86	74
B	97	91
C	51	67
D	41	31
E	60	52
F	70	70
G	73	74
H	79	59
I	46	44
J	67	61
K	71	52
L	88	75
M	81	92
N	40	22
O	53	74
P	77	74
Q	79	91
R	84	83
S	91	91
T	90	72

Note: Test Score = Number of items correct on a 100-item test taken at time of employment. Performance Rating = Supervisory rating given after six months employment, where 1 = poor performance and 100 = outstanding performance.

Exhibit 5.7   *Scattergram of Test Scores and Job Performance Ratings for 20 Operative Workers*

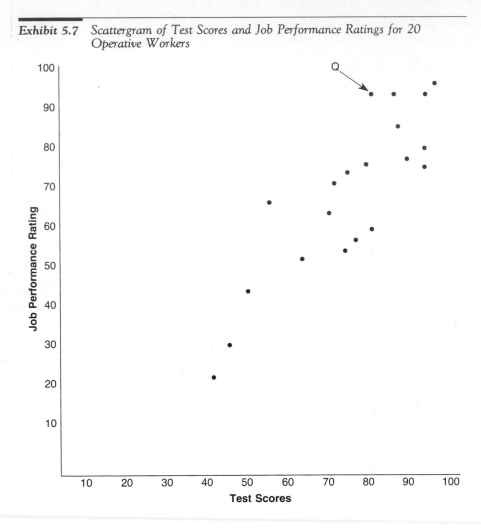

There are two important elements to a validity coefficient: (a) its sign and (b) its magnitude. The sign (either + or −) indicates the *direction* of a relationship while its magnitude indicates the *strength* of association between a predictor and criterion. The coefficient itself can range from −1.00 to .00 to +1.00. As the coefficient approaches +1.00, there is a *positive* relationship between performance on a selection measure and a criterion. That is, high scores on a selection measure are associated with high scores on a criterion and low scores on the measure are related with low criterion scores. As the coefficient moves toward −1.00, however, there is a *negative* or inverse relation-tion between scores on the predictor and criterion. But, as the index moves toward .00, then any relationship between the two variables falls. When the validity coefficient is not statistically significant or is equal to .00, then no relationship exists between a predictor and criterion. If a validity coefficient is not statistically significant, then the selection measure is not a valid predictor of a criterion. These predictor/criterion relations are summarized in Exhibit 5.8.

Using simple correlation, suppose we find that the validity coefficient for our example data in Exhibit 5.7 is .80. Next, after consulting the appropriate statistical table (usually found in psychological measurement or statistics books), we test the coefficient to see if there is a true or statistically significant relationship between our test and job performance or if the correlation arose simply because of chance. Our significance test will help us determine the probability that the relationship identified for our *sample* of 20 job applicants can be expected to be found only by chance in the *population* of job applicants from which our sample came. Usually, if the probability is equal to or less than .05, it is concluded that there is a statistically significant relationship between a predictor and criterion. That is, a true relationship exists between the predictor and criterion for the population of job applicants. In our example, assume we find that our validity coefficient of .80 is statistically significant (usually written as "$r = .80, p \leq .05$"). A significant result suggests that if we conducted our study in the same manner 100 times, in 95 of these we would find a similar relation between our predictor and criterion. In only five cases, we would not. Thus, we are reasonably confident that the relation did not arise because of chance, and a dependable relationship exists. We can now conclude that our test is valid for predicting job performance.

Exhibit 5.8 *Descriptive Predictor/Criterion Relationships of a Validity Coefficient*

Predictor/Criterion Relationships

Validity Coefficient			
Strong Positive Relation	+1.00	High Predictor Scores Low Predictor Scores ⟶	High Criterion Scores Low Criterion Scores
No Relation	.00	High Predictor Scores Low Predictor Scores ⟶	??? Criterion Scores ??? Criterion Scores
Strong Negative Relation	−1.00	High Predictor Scores Low Predictor Scores ⟶	Low Criterion Scores High Criterion Scores

Interpreting Validity Coefficients   Once we have found a statistically significant validity coefficient, we might well ask what precisely does the coefficient mean. There are several approaches (such as the calculation of a coefficient of determination or preparation of an expectancy table or chart) we can take to answer this question.

When we look at the distribution of our criterion scores shown in Table 5.3, one fact is evident. Some employees perform better than others; some do very well, others not so well. If our predictor is useful, it should help in explaining some of these differences in performance. By squaring the validity coefficient, we can obtain an index that indicates our test's ability to account for these individual performance differences. This index, called the *coefficient of determination,* represents the percentage of variance in the criterion that can be explained by variance associated with the predictor. In our case, the coefficient of determination is .64 (.80²), indicating that 64 percent of the differences (or variance) in individuals' job performance can be explained by their differences in test scores. Relatively speaking, our validity coefficient of .80 (or coefficient of determination of .64) for this sample of 20 employees is high. Only on rare occasions do validity coefficients exceed .50; a more common size of coefficient is in the range of .30 to .50. Thus, coefficients of determination for many validity coefficients will range from roughly .10 to .25.

In addition to a coefficient of determination, we can take an additional step to aid our interpretation of a validity coefficient. This step involves the construction of an *expectancy table* or *chart.* Since expectancy tables are also used in making selection decisions, we will discuss them in the next section.

Prediction

A statistically significant validity coefficient is helpful in showing that for a *group* of persons a test is related to job success. However, the coefficient itself does not help us in predicting the job success of *individuals.* Yet, the prediction of an individual's likelihood of job success is precisely what an employment manager may want. For individual prediction purposes, we can turn to the use of linear regression and expectancy charts to aid us in selection decision making. In using these methods, a practitioner is simply taking predictor information, such as test scores, and predicting individuals' job success, such as rated job performance, from this information. For each method, one key assumption is that we are utilizing information collected on a past or present group of employees and making predictions for a *future* group of employees.

Linear Regression   Basically, linear regression involves the determination of how changes in criterion scores are functionally related to changes in predictor scores. A regression equation is developed that mathematically describes the functional relationship between the predictor and criterion. Once the regression equation is known, criterion scores can then be predicted from predictor information. In general, there are two common types of linear regression you are likely to come across, simple and multiple regression.

In simple regression, there is only one predictor. To illustrate, let's refer back to Exhibit 5.7 which depicted the relationship between an employment test and job performance for 20 operative workers. In Exhibit 5.9, we show the same scattergram except that we have also fitted a special line to the plotted scores. This line is called the *regression line*. It summarizes the relationship between the test and the job performance ratings. The line has been fitted statistically so that it is at a minimum distance from each of the data points in the figure. Thus, the regression line represents the line of "best fit."

In addition to depicting the fit of the regression line graphically, we can also describe it mathematically in the form of an equation called the *regression*

Exhibit 5.9 *Plot of the Regression Line for Test Scores and Job Performance Ratings for 20 Operative Workers*

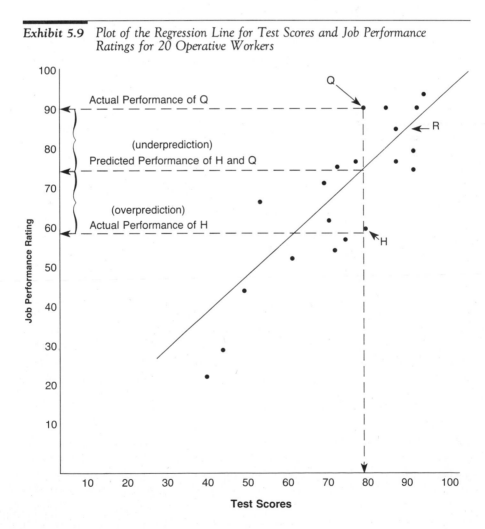

or prediction equation. This equation takes the form of the algebraic expression for a straight line, that is,

$$\hat{Y} = a + bX$$

where

$\hat{Y}$ = predicted score of the criterion variable

a = intercept value of the regression line

b = slope of the regression line or regression weight

X = score of the predictor variable.

The data points around the regression line and the validity coefficient are closely related. The validity coefficient represents how well the regression line fits the data. As the validity coefficient approaches + or −1.00, the data points move closer to the line. If a validity coefficient equals + or −1.00, then the data points will fall exactly on the regression line itself, prediction will be perfect. However, as the coefficient moves away from + or −1.00 (toward .00), the points will be distributed farther from the regression line, and more error will exist in our predictions.

To illustrate the role of the regression line and regression equation in prediction, let's look further at our example. The regression line in Exhibit 5.9 is represented by the equation: $\hat{Y} = 3.02 + .91(X)$ where, $\hat{Y}$ is predicted job performance (our criterion) and X is a score on our selection test administered to applicants for the operative job. The intercept (3.02) is the value where the regression line crosses the Y-axis. It represents an applicant's predicted job performance if his or her test score were zero. Finally, the slope of the line is represented by .91. The slope is often called a *regression weight or regression coefficient* because it is multiplied times the score on the predictor (our selection test). The slope or regression weight represents the amount of change in the criterion variable per one unit change in the predictor. Thus, for every one unit increase in applicants' test scores, we would expect a .91 increase in job performance. A positive validity coefficient indicates a positive slope of the regression line and, hence, a positive regression weight. A negative validity coefficient means a negative slope and negative regression weight.

Once we have our regression line, we can use it to predict our criterion scores. For example, if an applicant applying for our operative job is given the test, we would locate the score on the X-axis, move upward to the regression line, and then move across to the Y-axis to find his or her predicted job performance score. As you can see in Exhibit 5.9, individual R who has a test score of 84 is predicted to have a job performance rating of approximately 80. Since individual R actually has a performance rating of 83, our prediction is close. As there is not a perfect 1.00 correlation between the test and job performance, there will be some error in prediction. For instance, persons H and Q both scored 79 on the test, but notice our predictions have error. For person H, we would *overpredict* performance. With a test score of 79, performance is predicted to be 73, but it is actually only 59. Conversely, for person Q, performance would be *underpredicted*. With the same test score (79), predicted performance is 73 but actual performance is 91. Even though errors in prediction are made and even though some may appear rather large, they will be smaller for the *group* of persons than if the predictor information and regression line is not used and only random guesses are made.

Rather than using the regression line, we can use our regression equation to predict job performance. By substituting a person's test score for X in our regression equation, multiplying the test score times the regression coefficient, and then adding it to the constant value, we can derive a predicted job performance score. Thus, for our test score of 86, we would predict subsequent rated job performance to be equal to 81. Our calculation would be as follows:

$$\hat{Y} = 3.02 + .91(X)$$
$$\hat{Y} = 3.02 + .91(86)$$
$$\hat{Y} = 3.02 + 78.26$$
$$\hat{Y} = 81.28 \text{ or } 81.$$

As we saw in our above example, because our test is not perfectly related to job performance, we will have some error in our predictions. Only if all of our data points fall precisely on the regression line ($r_{xy} = +$ or -1.00) will error not be present. In making employment decisions, we must take this degree of error into account. The *standard error of estimate* is a useful index for summarizing the degree of error in prediction.[27] It is determined from the following equation:

$$sd_{y \cdot x} = sd_y \sqrt{1 - r_{xy}^2}$$

where

$sd_{y \cdot x}$ = standard error of estimate

sd_y = standard deviation of criterion scores

r_{xy} = validity coefficient for predictor X and criterion Y.

The standard error of estimate can be interpreted as the standard deviation of the errors made in predicting a criterion from a selection measure. It is expected that, on the average, 68 percent of *actual* criterion scores will fall within ±1 standard error of *predicted* criterion scores and 95 percent of actual criterion scores will fall within ±1.96 standard errors of predicted criterion scores. For example, assume the standard deviation of our job performance ratings is 7.5. Also, assume that the validity of our test designed to predict these ratings is .80. The standard error of estimate would be computed as follows:

$$sd_{y \cdot x} = 7.5 \sqrt{1 - .80^2}$$

$$sd_{y \cdot x} = 7.5 \sqrt{.36}$$

$$sd_{y \cdot x} = 4.50.$$

Now, assume that a person scores 86 on the test. Using the regression equation we discussed in the previous section, we calculate that all persons scoring 86 on the test would be predicted to have a job performance rating of 81. Notice that we have a *predicted* level of job success, but how confident can we be that individuals' *actual* job success will approximate the predicted level? The standard error of estimate can help us. Basically, it enables us to establish a range of predicted criterion scores within which we would expect a percentage of actual criterion scores to fall. For applicants with a predicted performance rating of 81, we would expect, on the average, 68 percent of them to have *actual* performance ratings between 77 and 86 (81 ± 4.50). For this same performance level, we would also expect 95 percent of the applicants' actual job performance ratings to fall between 72 and 90 [81 ± (1.96 × 4.50)].

In addition to simple regression, *multiple* regression can also be used to predict criterion scores for job applicants. Whereas the simple regression model assumes only *one* predictor, multiple regression assumes *two or more* predictors are being used to predict a criterion. If the additional predictors explain more of the individual differences among job applicants' job performance than would have been explained by a single predictor alone, our ability to predict a criterion will be enhanced. As our ability to predict improves (that is, validity increases), fewer errors will be made in prediction of applicants' subsequent job performance.

The general model for multiple regression is as follows:

$$\hat{Y} = a + b_1X_1 + b_2X_2 + \ldots + b_nX_n$$

where

$\hat{Y}$ = predicted criterion scores

a = intercept value of the regression line

b_1, b_2, b_n = regression weights for predictors X_1, X_2, and X_n

X_1, X_2, X_n = scores on predictors X_1, X_2, and X_n.

If, for example, we had administered a psychological test and a biographical data questionnaire and if the two predictors are related to our job performance measure, we could derive a regression equation just as we did with simple regression. However, in this case, our equation would have two regression weights rather than one. Suppose our multiple regression equation looked as follows:

$$\hat{Y} = 3.18 + .77X_1 + .53X_2$$

where

$\hat{Y}$ = predicted criterion scores (job performance measure)

3.18 = intercept value of the regression line (*a*)

.77 = weight of the psychological test

.53 = weight of the biographical data questionnaire

X_1 = score on psychological test

X_2 = score on biographical data questionnaire.

In order to obtain a predicted job performance score, we would simply substitute an individual's two predictor scores in the equation, multiply the two scores times their weights, sum the products, and add the intercept value to obtain predicted performance. For instance, suppose an individual scored 84 on the test and 30 on the biographical data questionnaire. The predicted job performance score would be obtained as follows:

$$\hat{Y} = 3.18 + .77(84) + .53(30)$$
$$\hat{Y} = 3.18 + 64.68 + 15.90$$
$$\hat{Y} = 83.76 \text{ or } 84$$

The multiple regression approach has also been called a *compensatory* model. It is called compensatory because different combinations of predictor scores can be combined to yield the same predicted criterion score. Thus, if an applicant were to do rather poorly on one measure, he/she could compensate for his/her low score by performing better on the other measure. Examples of compensatory selection models include those frequently used as a basis for making admission decisions in some professional graduate schools.

Cross-Validation   Whenever simple or multiple regression equations are used, they are developed to optimally predict the criterion for an existing group of persons. But, when the equations are applied to a new group, the predictive accuracy of the equations will most always fall. This "shrinkage" in predictive accuracy is because the new group is not identical to the one on which the equations were developed. Because of the possibility of error, it is important that the equations be tested for shrinkage *prior* to their implementation in selection decision making. This check-out process is called *cross-validation*. There are two general methods of cross-validation: (a) *empirical* and (b) *formula* estimation. With *empirical* cross-validation, there are several approaches that can be taken. In general, a regression equation developed on one sample of individuals is applied to another sample of persons. If the regression equation developed on one sample can predict scores in the other sample, then the regression equation is "cross-validated." One common procedure of empirical cross-validation involves the following steps:

1. A group of persons on whom predictor and criterion data are available is randomly divided into two groups.

2. A regression equation is developed on one of the groups (called the "weighting group").

3. Next, the equation developed on the weighting group is used to predict the criterion for the other group (called the "holdout group").

4. Predicted criterion scores are obtained for each individual in the holdout group.

5. For persons in the holdout group, *predicted* criterion scores are then correlated with their *actual* criterion scores. A high statistically significant correlation coefficient indicates that the regression equation is useful for individuals other than those on whom the equation was developed.

As an alternative to empirical cross-validation, *formula* cross-validation can be used. Under this procedure, only one sample of persons is used. Special formulas are employed to predict the amount of shrinkage that would occur if a regression equation were applied to a similar sample of persons. With knowledge of (a) the number of predictors, (b) the original multiple correlation coefficient, and (c) the number of people on which the original multiple correlation was based, the *predicted* multiple correlation coefficient can be derived. This predicted multiple correlation coefficient represents the coefficient that would be obtained if the predictors were administered to a new but similar sample of persons and the multiple correlation statistically computed. The obvious advantage to these formulas is that a new sample of persons does not have to be taken. Philippe Cattin has summarized these formulas and the circumstances when they are appropriate.[28] In addition, Kevin Murphy has provided additional evidence on the accuracy of such formulas.[29] In general, he has concluded that formula cross-validation is more efficient, simpler to use, and no less accurate than empirical cross-validation.

Whatever the approach, cross-validation is *essential.* It should be routinely implemented whenever regression equations are used in prediction.

Expectancy Tables and Charts   An expectancy *table* is simply a table of numbers that shows the probability that a person with a particular predictor score will achieve a defined level of success. An expectancy *chart* presents essentially the same data except that it provides a visual summarization of the relationship between a predictor and criterion.[30] As we suggested earlier, expectancy tables and charts are useful for communicating the meaning of a validity coefficient. In addition, they are helpful as an aid in predicting the probability of success of job applicants. As outlined by Lawshe and Bolda, the construction of expectancy tables and charts is basically a five-step process. These steps include the following:

1. Individuals on whom criterion data are available are divided into two groups, Superior Performers and Others. Roughly, half of the individuals are in each group.

2. For each predictor score, frequencies of the numbers of employees in the Superior and Other groups are determined.

3. The predictor score distribution is divided into fifths.

4. The number and percentage of individuals in the Superior group and Other group is determined.

5. An expectancy chart is then prepared.[31]

To illustrate the development of an expectancy table and chart, let's go through a brief example. First, let's assume that we have the test scores from 65 machinists who took the Machinist Aptitude Test, as well as their most recent performance appraisal ratings. For our purposes, assume we have determined that individuals with a performance rating of 9 or more are Superior performers while those with scores of 8 or less are classified in the Other group. A Pearson product-moment correlation between the sets of test scores and appraisal data for our 65 machinists indicates there is a statistically significant validity coefficient of .45 between the test scores and performance ratings. Exhibit 5.10 shows the scattergram of the test scores plotted against performance ratings. The horizontal lines represent roughly equal fifths of the distribution of predictor scores. Table 5.4 is the expectancy table developed from the plotted data. Basically, it shows the chances out of 100 of an individual's being rated superior on the job, given a range of Machinist Aptitude Test scores. For example, persons scoring between 30 and 34 have roughly an 85 percent chance of being rated superior while those scoring between 1 and 6 have only a 33 percent chance. The individual expectancy chart, Exhibit 5.11, summarizes these same results in a graphic fashion.

As you can see in Exhibits 5.11 and 5.12, there are two types of expectancy charts: (a) individual and (b) institutional. The *individual* chart shows the probability that a person will achieve a particular level of performance given his or her score on the test. Thus, the individual chart permits individual prediction.

The *institutional* chart indicates what will happen within an organization if all applicants above a particular *minimum* score are hired. For example, in our study of machinists, 77 percent of the applicants with a minimum score of 23 on the Machinist Aptitude Test will be superior, while only 64 percent of those with a minimum score of 7 will be rated superior. By using the institutional chart, one can estimate what will happen in the organization if various passing or cut-off scores are used for a selection measure.

Factors Affecting the Size of Validity Coefficients

Robert Guion has pointed out that the size of a validity coefficient is dependent upon a variety of factors.[32] Any number of factors may have an effect,

Exhibit 5.10 *Scattergram of Scores by 65 Machinists on the Machinist Aptitude Test Plotted against Performance Ratings*

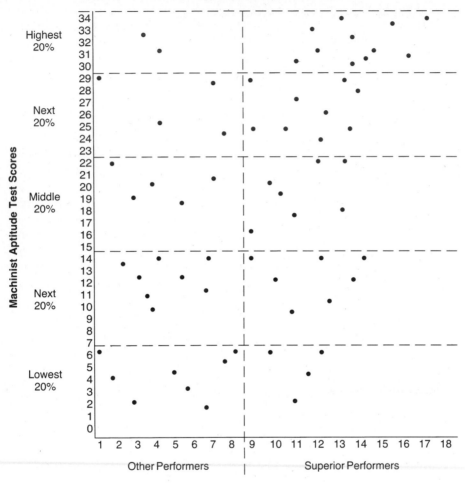

Job Performance Rating

but four seem to be predominant in determining the magnitude of a validity coefficient.

Reliability of Criterion and Predictor   Earlier we described the intimate interrelationship between reliability and validity. There is no need to repeat our discussion here. The point we want to make is that to the extent a predictor or criterion has error, it will be unreliable. The more error present, the more unreliable these variables will be. Any unreliability in *either* the criterion or predictor will lower the correlation or validity coefficient computed between the two. If *both* predictor and criterion variables have measurement error, error is compounded and the validity coefficient will be low-

Table 5.4   *Percentage of Machinists Rated As Superior*
for Various Machinist Aptitude Test Score Ranges

Machinist Aptitude Test Score Range	Other Performers	Superior Performers	Total	% Superior Performers
Top 20%:				
30-34	2	11	13	85
Next 20%:				
23-29	4	9	13	69
Middle 20%:				
15-22	5	7	12	58
Next 20%:				
7-14	8	7	15	47
Low 20%:				
1-6	8	4	12	33
Total	27	38	65	

ered even further. Because of the negative effect of lowered reliability on validity, we should strive for high reliability of both the predictor and criterion to get an accurate assessment of what true validity may be.

Restriction of Range   One of the important assumptions in calculating a validity coefficient is that there is variance in individuals' scores on the criterion and predictor. By variance, we simply mean that people have different scores on these measures, that is, individual differences. When we calculate a validity coefficient, we are asking do these predictor and criterion score differences move together? That is, are systematic differences among people on the criterion associated with differences on the predictor? If there is little variance or range in individuals' scores for one or both variables, then the magnitude of the validity coefficient will be lowered. "Restriction in range" is the term used to describe situations with little variance in the measures. How can restriction in range of scores occur? Range restriction can result in any number of ways. For instance, many of us will probably agree that there are great differences among professors in their teaching ability. Yet, in many schools where professors' teaching performance is evaluated for promotion, tenure, and compensation decisions, it is not unusual to find relatively few differences in their teaching evaluation ratings. Even though we may "know" there are large differences among professors, the measurement device used to evaluate teaching may not be sensitive enough to pick up these differences. Consequently, teaching evaluation scores of the professors will be restricted.

Let's take another example more specific to selection. In a predictive

Exhibit 5.11 *Individual Expectancy Chart Showing Chances in 100 of Being Rated Superior on the Job of Machinist for Various Score Ranges on the Machinist Aptitude Test*

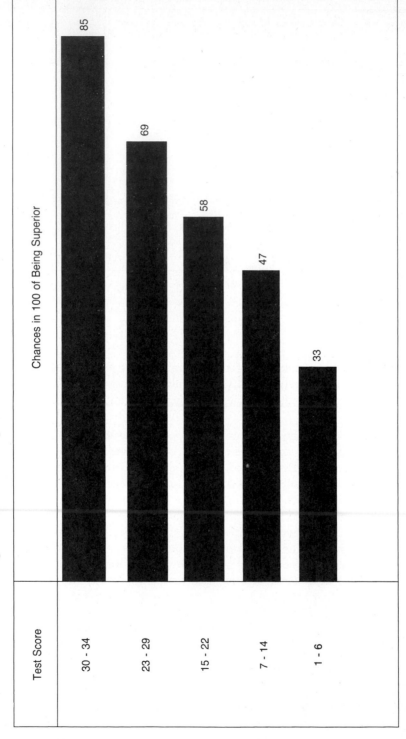

Exhibit 5.12 *Institutional Expectancy Chart Showing Percentage of Persons Above Various Minimum Score Categories on Machinist Aptitude Test Who Can Be Expected to be Considered Superior in the Job of Machinist*

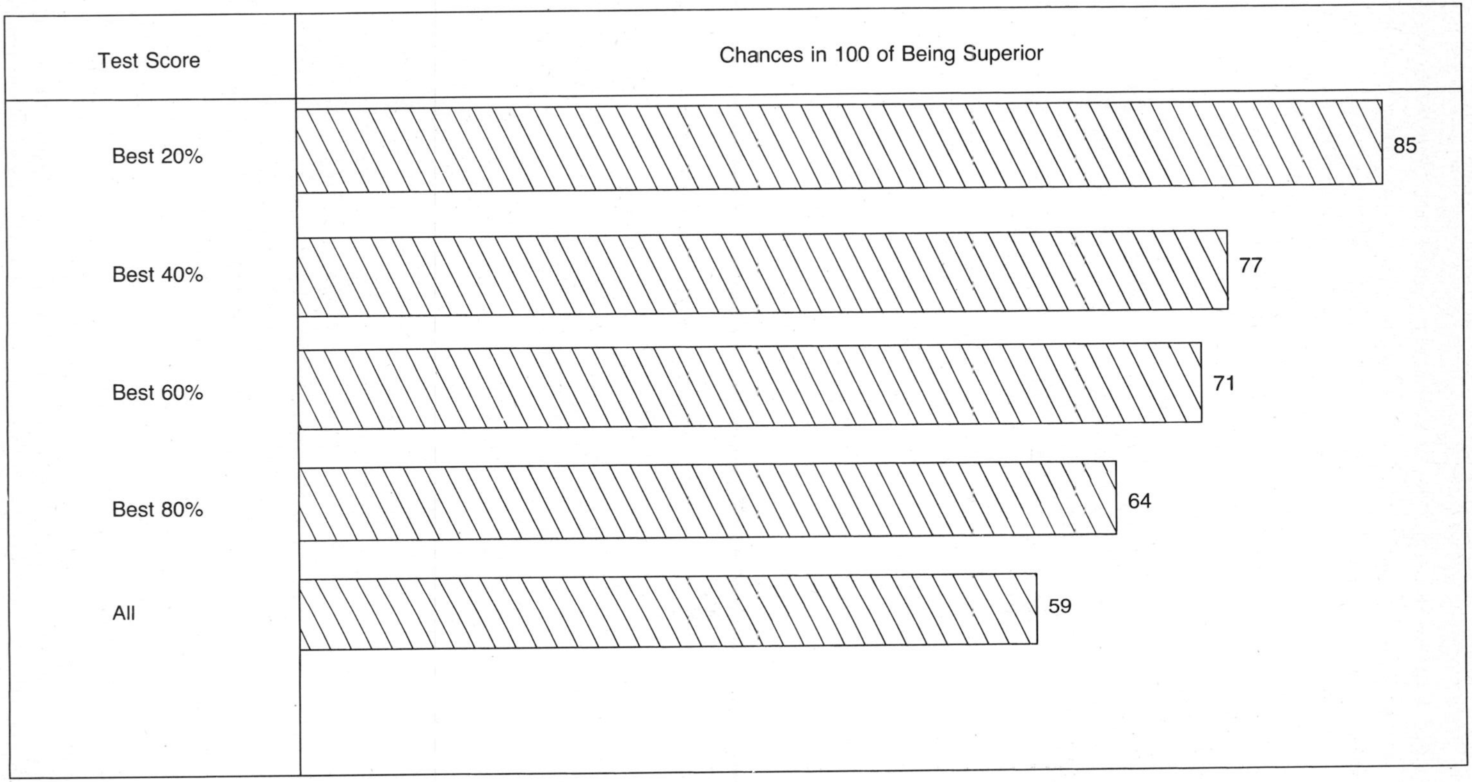

Test Score	Chances in 100 of Being Superior
Best 20%	85
Best 40%	77
Best 60%	71
Best 80%	64
All	59

validation study, suppose an employer uses a test being validated as a basis for selection decision making. The range of test scores will be restricted because low scorers do not get employed. When the test scores are then correlated with a criterion, the validity coefficient will be curtailed because of the restriction of range in the predictor scores. In turn, criterion scores may also be restricted. Restriction of criterion scores may occur because turnover, transfer, or termination of employees has taken place prior to the collection of criterion data.

From our examples, it can be seen that restriction in the range of scores may occur for either predictor or criterion variables. Either predictor or criterion restriction will lower a validity coefficient. When restriction is a problem, restriction can be statistically corrected to obtain a better estimate of true validity (that is, the validity of the predictor if scores had not been restricted). Robert Thorndike has provided formulas that can be used to correct a validity coefficient affected by range restriction problems. When the degree of range restriction in either the predictor or criterion can be estimated, these formulas can be applied.[33]

Criterion Contamination   If scores on a criterion are influenced by variables other than the predictor, then criterion scores may be contaminated. The effect of contamination is to alter the magnitude of the validity coefficient. For instance, one criterion frequently used in validation studies is a performance evaluation rating. We may want to know if performance on a selection measure is associated with performance on the job. However, performance ratings are sometimes subject to being contaminated or biased by extraneous variables such as sex and race of ratees or raters or by the job tenure of persons being rated. If criterion ratings are influenced by variables that have nothing to do with actual job performance, then our obtained validity coefficient will be affected.

Consider another example. One of the authors was recently engaged in a validation study of a selection measure for bank proof machine operators. A proof machine is used by operators to encode magnetic numbers on the bottom of checks so they can be processed by computer. The bank kept meticulous records of the number of checks processed by operators within specific time periods. Thus, it appeared that a sound, behavioral measure of performance was available that could be used as a criterion in the validation study. However, further analysis showed that even though the proof machines looked the same externally, some of the machines had different internal components. These different components permitted faster check processing. Our apparently good criterion measure was contaminated. Rather than solely measuring differences in operators' performance, the productivity measure was also tapping differences in equipment. Without proper adjustments, the measure would be useless as a criterion.

Where contaminating effects are known, they should be controlled either by statistical procedures such as partial correlation or by the research design of the validation study itself. Again, the reason for controlling contaminating variables is to obtain a more accurate reading of the true relationship between a predictor and a criterion.

Violation of Statistical Assumptions   Among others, one important assumption of a Pearson correlation is that there is a *linear* relationship between a predictor and a criterion. If the relationship is nonlinear, the validity coefficient will give an underestimate of the true relationship between the two variables. For example, in Exhibit 5.13, four scattergrams summarizing

Exhibit 5.13 *Appropriateness of Pearson* r *for Various Selection Measure-Criterion Relationships*

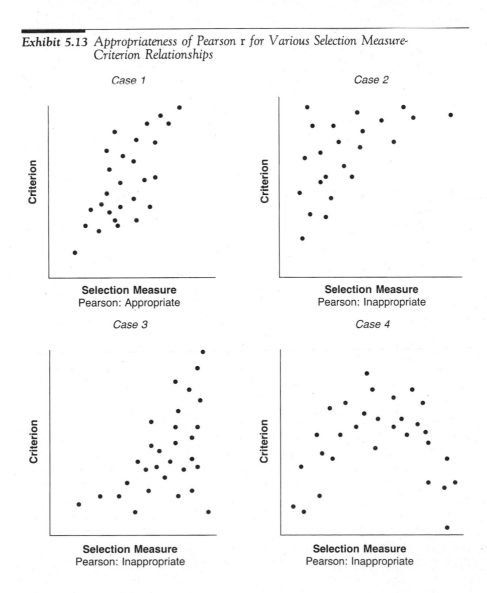

various relations between a selection measure and criterion are shown. Case 1 shows a situation in which there is a linear or straight-line relationship. A Pearson correlation coefficient would be appropriate for representing the relationship. However, the other three cases show nonlinear associations; in these, the Pearson would be inappropriate. In Case 4, for instance, if a Pearson correlation were calculated on these data, the correlation would be equal to .00. Yet, we can see that there is a relationship. Low as well as high test performance are associated with low criterion scores, whereas moderate test performance is associated with high criterion scores. We know that a relation exists in Case 4, but our Pearson statistic will not detect it; other analyses are called for. If we had simply computed the correlation without studying the scattergram, we could have drawn an incorrect conclusion. Nonlinear predictor/criterion relationships such as those depicted in Cases 2 through 4 are not often found in practice. Nevertheless, prior to computing a validity coefficient, a scattergram should *always* be plotted and studied for the possibility of nonlinear association.

Minimum Validity of a Selection Measure

Invariably, the question comes up "How low can the validity coefficient of a selection measure be and the measure still be useful in selection?" The answer to the question is a bit more complicated than may first appear. However, in brief, as long as the validity coefficient is statistically significant (that is, significant at $p \leq .05$), use of the measure will be better than random selection without the measure.[34] But, how much better? There are several factors that will affect the relative functional value of a selection measure. Depending upon their relative values, these factors will determine how useful a measure will be in selection. These include the following: (a) validity of the measure, (b) the selection ratio, and (c) the percentage of employees successful on the job *without* use of the selection measure, that is, the base rate. We have already discussed validity. Now, we want to turn our attention to the selection ratio and base rate to see their impact on the relative value of a selection measure.

Selection Ratio   The selection ratio is the ratio of the number of persons hired to the number of applicants available. If a firm hires everyone who applies for a job, then the firm's selection ratio is 1.0. Conversely, if only one of every 10 applicants is employed, then the selection ratio is .10. As the selection ratio increases or moves toward 1.0, it becomes more unfavorable for the organization. As the selection ratio decreases toward .00, the selection ratio becomes more favorable for the organization. With a low selection ratio, a firm can be much more selective in who is hired. Thus, a higher cut-off or passing score on a selection measure can be set. If there is a significant positive relationship between a selection measure and a criterion, then a higher cut-off score will, on the average, yield more effective employees.

Errors in prediction can be reduced by having a low selection ratio and by increasing the cut-off score. In this sense, a low selection ratio can compensate for low validity of a selection measure.

Base rate   The base rate refers to the proportion of employees successful on the job without use of the selection measure.[35] For a measure to be useful, the proportion of successful employees selected *with* the measure should be greater than the proportion of successful employees selected *without* use of the selection measure. Let's examine how the base rate might affect the value of a test.

Thinking back to our Machinist Aptitude Test for a minute, imagine that we have obtained additional test and performance appraisal data on 100 machinists. A scattergram is plotted, and a validity coefficient of .80 is obtained. In Exhibit 5.14, we have plotted the scattergram. Notice in this figure, we have drawn an ellipse to represent the general pattern of relationship between the pairs of scores. In addition, there are two other lines shown. The horizontal line shows the minimum acceptable job performance. Employees with rating scores above the line were judged as acceptable while individuals with scores below the line were considered unsatisfactory. The vertical line represents the passing or cut-off score to be used on the test in selecting machinists in the future. Applicants scoring above the cut-off score (to the right of the line) would be accepted while those scoring below the cut-off point (to the left) would be rejected.

Now, when we plot our scores (the ellipse), minimum acceptable performance (the horizontal line), and cut-off score (the vertical line), we end up with four sections or quadrants. These quadrants represent the outcomes of prediction when we use our test to predict job performance of machinists. In our diagram, these quadrants consist of the following:

1. Quadrant A—This section represents the proportion of individuals (35 percent) predicted to be successful who were successful (*true positive*).

2. Quadrant B—This quadrant represents the proportion of individuals (15 percent) predicted to be successful who were not (*false positive*).

3. Quadrant C—This portion represents the proportion of individuals (35 percent) predicted to be unsuccessful who were unsuccessful (*true negative*).

4. Quadrant D—This section represents the percentage of individuals (15 percent) predicted to be unsuccessful but who were successful (*false negative*).

In looking at this figure, we can answer several questions. For example, we can obtain the base rate by the following formula:

$$\frac{A + D}{A + B + C + D} \quad \text{or} \quad \frac{.15 + .35}{.35 + .15 + .35 + .15} = .50$$

Exhibit 5.14 *Base Rates and Selection Decision Outcomes When Using a Valid Test*

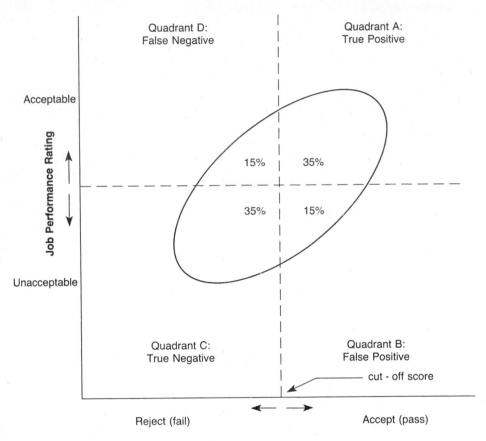

Machinist Aptitude Test Score

A base rate of .50 would indicate that 50 percent of the applicants would have been successful if the test had *not* been used in selection. If we want to know how well the test actually predicted job performance, we would use the following formula:

$$\frac{A + C}{A + B + C + D} \text{ or } \frac{.35 + .35}{.35 + .15 + .35 + .15} = .70$$

Our value of .70 would indicate that 70 percent of the predictions using our test score as a basis were correct. Thus, the gain of 20 percent in predictive accuracy in using our test versus not using the test (70 to 50 percent) indicates the marginal value of test information in prediction.

If there is a low base rate, it suggests that with the current selection system, there is difficulty in identifying satisfactory employees. Other things being equal, the use of a *valid* test in selection should improve the identification of satisfactory employees. If there is a high base rate, a new selection measure may have little to offer in identifying satisfactory employees since the existing system is already identifying a high proportion of successful employees. In general, the lower the base rate, the greater the gain in identifying satisfactory employees that may be anticipated in using a valid test.

We have mentioned three important factors that affect the value of a test in selection. Different values and combinations of these factors can have dramatic effects on the proportion of people who will be satisfactory on the job. Taylor and Russell have compiled tables that predict the effects of selection measure validity, the base rate, and selection ratio on the percentage of employees who will be satisfactory when using a selection measure.[36]

Selection Measure Utility

In recent years, there has been a renewed interest in determining the *utility* of selection procedures. When the term "utility" has been used, it has generally meant the degree to which a selection procedure improves the quality of individuals selected over that without use of the measure.[37] In the previous section, we reviewed one model of utility, the Taylor-Russell model. Other models such as the Naylor-Shine model[38] and Cronbach-Gleser model[39] have also been proposed. In general, the emphasis of these models has been on developing a meaningful definition of "quality of the work" of individuals.

One important thrust in selection measure utility research has been on defining quality in terms of the dollar payoff resulting from use of a selection procedure. For example, Schmidt and Hunter examined the dollar payoff of using a valid test in selecting computer programmers in the federal government.[40] Results of their analyses showed that under the worst possible selection conditions (selection ratio = .80; validity of previous selection procedure = .50), estimated productivity increase for one year's use of the test was *$5.6 million.* Under the best possible selection conditions (selection ratio = .05; validity of previous selection procedure = .00), estimated productivity increase was *$97.2 million.* Other researchers have also attempted to translate selection procedure utility into dollar payoffs.[41]

In the future, the use of test utility in terms of dollar payoffs will likely increase. As Wayne Cascio points out, rising costs of personnel programs will result in more demands for accountability.[42] Utility-based selection systems appear to be one effective means to meet these challenges.

Broader Perspectives of Validity

Concurrent, predictive, content, and construct validity are generally recognized as being the principal methods employed in validation studies. However, two other approaches have been offered that take a broader perspective of validity. Rather than studying predictor and criterion data collected on employees in *one* job and *one* organization, these methods attempt to incorporate information obtained on jobs and incumbents across a *number* of situations. These methods are called *synthetic validity* and *validity generalization*.

Synthetic Validity

One of the real dilemmas in conducting criterion-related validation research is the need for having a relatively large number of people on whom both predictor and criterion data are available. Because of the statistical procedures commonly employed, substantial amounts of data are required in order to detect any dependable relationships that might exist between predictors and criteria, that is, criterion-related validity. Except for relatively few lower-level or operative types of jobs, many organizations may not have jobs that have large numbers of applicants or incumbents on whom validation research can be conducted. Small organizations have rather obvious problems in terms of numbers of people available for participation. In addition, since many upper-level jobs are becoming more specialized, limiting even further the number of research participants available, the opportunities for conducting criterion-related validation studies on such jobs may also be very limited. As Robert Guion points out, when a small organization of 50 or so people may be hiring only one or two people a year, ordinary empirical validation cannot be performed.[43] Thus, the organization has three options: (a) to use tests or other measures without validation, (b) to rely on subjective judgments of whom to hire, or (c) to not use any selection measures at all. If a firm wants to use tests, some form of validation is essential. To use tests without supporting validity evidence is to ask for problems. Yet, if only small sample sizes are available, what can an organization do?

As one means for dealing with the problem of small validation sample sizes, *synthetic validity* has been suggested.[44] Basically, synthetic validity is an approach that involves the following:

1. The conducting of job analyses for a number of different jobs

2. The identifying of dimensions of work common to the jobs for all jobs analyzed

3. The validating of selection measures for the common job dimensions by using employees on these jobs

As a simple example, suppose an organization wants to validate some tests for three different jobs. After using a job analysis questionnaire, it is found that even though the job titles are different, some of the jobs require identical types of tasks. Exhibit 5.15 illustrates three jobs and the task dimensions that are common to each. As you can see, the three jobs and their number of incumbents are as follows: (a) Typist (n = 60), (b) Clerk (n = 50), and (c) Receptionist (n = 40). Three example job dimensions characterizing these jobs include (a) Following Directions, (b) Typing, and (c) Dealing with the Public. The Xs in the matrix represent the job dimensions common

Exhibit 5.15 *Illustration of Test Validation Using Synthetic Validity*

		Job Dimension		
Job	Number of Employees	Following Directions I	Typing II	Dealing with the Public III
Typist	60	X	X	
Clerk	50	X		X
Receptionist	40		X	X
Total employees in combined jobs		110	100	90

	Job Dimension		
Tests	I	II	III
Oral Directions Test	**		
Typing Test		**	
Public Relations Test			**
Total number of employees available for test validation	110	100	90

Note: An "X" represents job dimensions characteristic of a job. Jobs sharing an "X" for the same job dimension require the same job function. A "**" indicates the selection measure chosen for predicting success on a particular job dimension.

to each job. For instance, Following Directions and Typing characterize the job of Typist while Typing and Dealing with the Public are most descriptive of the Receptionist job.

In the lower half of Exhibit 5.15, the measures that were developed or chosen from commercially available ones to assess each of the job dimensions are listed. For example, the Oral Directions Test was selected to determine if it could predict the job dimension "Following Directions." Criterion measures (such as performance ratings) are developed for each job dimension. Jobs sharing a common dimension are combined for validating the selection measure. For instance, for the job dimension "Following Directions," the Typist and Clerk jobs are combined (combined sample size = 110); for the job dimension "Typing," the Typist and Receptionist jobs are grouped together (combined sample size = 100); and, finally, for the job dimension "Dealing with the Public," the jobs of Clerk and Receptionist are combined (combined sample size = 90). Notice that by combining jobs that require the same work activity, we are able to increase our sample sizes substantially over those which would have been available if any one job had been used. We can collapse jobs together because we are studying a common work activity. In this sense, validity is "synthetic"; we are not creating validity per se but rather creating a situation that will permit a better estimate of validity. The major advantage is that selection measures are validated across several jobs in an organization rather than for only one job.

Once the jobs have been combined on common job dimensions, criterion measures have been collected on each employee performing the job dimensions, and selection measures have been administered, test and criterion data are then correlated. Statistically significant relationships indicate a valid selection measure. As you can see, rather than validating a measure for a whole job, we have broken jobs down into component job dimensions and validated our selection measure against each of these components. Because our sample sizes are larger than they would have been for any one job, we can obtain a more reliable estimate of validity.

For the small firm or for jobs in which there are relatively few incumbents, synthetic validity may offer one solution to the thorny problem of small sample size. The principal assumption in employing a synthetic validity approach is that our analyses of jobs will identify job dimensions common to those jobs studied. For lower-level, clerical, or operative types of jobs, it seems that synthetic validity may be a viable option. However, the applicability of the method to higher-level positions, where work functions may be more diverse and more difficult to measure, is still open to question.

Validity Generalization

In the past, it has generally been assumed that the results of many validation studies are specific to the situation or job for which the validation study was completed. Although a few published synthetic validity studies suggested a broader interpretation of validity, many industrial psychologists have generally assumed that the results of validity studies are situation specific. That is, a test that is valid for a job in one situation may not be valid for the same job in different situations. This assumption was based largely on various research findings that different validities for the same selection measures were found from one study to another even when the jobs were practically identical. Thus, the myth has developed that a test which is valid in one job or employment situation may not be valid in a different job or employment situation.[45] Past adherents to this idea believed that a validity study needed to be conducted for each situation in which a test was going to be used. For example, supporters reported that it was not uncommon to find that a test might have one validity in one organization and a completely different validity in another. Validity differences were attributed to dissimilarities in the nature of the specific employment situation or job in which a study was conducted, for example, type of criteria used, nature of the organization, insensitivity of a job analysis to identifying "real" job differences. Therefore, it was recommended that in each unique situation in which a measure is employed, it should be revalidated. However, Frank Schmidt, John Hunter, and their colleagues have argued that much of a measure's validity differences found *across* validation studies are not due to situation specificity but rather to statistical *artifacts* (such as, sampling error, restriction in the range of scores on the measures used, reliability of the test and criteria, and differences in sample sizes of study participants).[46] They concluded from their analyses that there were no real differences in the validities of a measure from one situation to another. Their findings suggest that validity results are more generalizable than had been previously thought. Thus, from the evidence of Schmidt, Hunter, and others, the idea that validity is situation specific appears to be more of a myth than a reality.

The numerous studies that have addressed the assumption above suggest an important conclusion: the validity of a test is more generalizable across *similar* situations and *similar* jobs than has been previously thought. This conclusion should not be interpreted as meaning that a test which is valid in one job *will* be valid for any other job. However, validity information on one job *may* be generalizable to other, very *similar* jobs. This implies that if validity generalization evidence for a test is available, a manager may not need to actually carry out a validity study. Instead, the manager may be able to use previous validation research to support the utility of the test. However, the manager must be able to provide the following:

1. Current evidence of a measure's validity for similar jobs in other situations

2. Data showing similarity between jobs for which the validity evidence is reported and the job under study (a comprehensive job analysis is mandatory)

3. Data showing similarity between the research samples and measures in other studies comprising the validity evidence and those samples or measures under study[47]

If validity generalization evidence can be provided and *if* it is accepted by the courts, validity generalization will play an extremely important role in future validation efforts. A new validation research study may not have to be conducted for every job or new employment situation that may arise. A thorough, well-documented job analysis that can show that a job is similar to a class of jobs about which validity of a measure is known may be all that is necessary. An obvious advantage to validity generalization is that time and resource savings could be considerable. In addition, our fundamental understanding of what contributes to job performance and success may also be enhanced. However, some writers have cautioned that it is premature, at this point, to accept the far-reaching conclusions of Schmidt and his colleagues as fact.[48] Further research on the validity generalization model, future versions of federal guidelines on human resource selection, and future decisions in employment discrimination cases will together inform us when validity generalization has matured as a validation technique.

References for Chapter 5

[1] American Psychological Association, Division of Industrial and Organizational Psychology, *Principles for the Validation and Use of Personnel Selection Procedures* 2d ed. (Berkeley, Calif.: American Psychological Association, 1980), p. 2.

[2] C. H. Lawshe, "Inferences From Personnel Tests and Their Validity," *Journal of Applied Psychology* 70 (1985): 237–238; Marvin D. Dunnette and Walter C. Borman, *Annual Review of Psychology* 30 (1979): 477–525. For an example of a published validation study, see John Arnold, J. Rauschenberger, W. Soubel, and Robert Guion, "Validation and Utility of a Strength Test for Selecting Steelworkers," *Journal of Applied Psychology* 67 (1982): 588–604.

[3] Edwin E. Ghiselli, John P. Campbell, and Sheldon Zedeck, *Measurement Theory for the Behavioral Sciences* (San Francisco: Freeman, 1981).

[4] Gerald V. Barrett, James S. Phillips, and Ralph A. Alexander, "Concurrent and Predictive Validity Designs: A Critical Reanalysis," *Journal of Applied Psychology* 66 (1981): 1–6. A review of validity studies published over a 19-year period also reported no important differences between concurrent and predictive validity coefficients — see Neal Schmitt, Richard Z. Gooding, Raymond A. Noe, and Michael Kirsch, "Metaanalyses of Validity Studies Published Between 1964–1982 and the Investigation of Study Characteristics," *Personnel Psychology* 37 (1984): 407–422.

[5] Anne Anastasi, *Psychological Testing* (New York: Macmillan, 1982).

[6] Robert M. Guion and C. J. Cranny, "A Note on Concurrent and Predictive Validity Designs: A Critical Reanalysis," *Journal of Applied Psychology* 67 (1982): 239–244.

[7] Frank J. Landy, *Psychology of Work Behavior* (Homewood, Ill.: The Dorsey Press, 1985), p. 65.

[8] American Psychological Association, Division of Industrial/Organizational Psychology, *Principles for the Validation and Use of Personnel Selection Procedures* (Washington: American Psychological Association, 1979). An interesting example of the content validity of a biographical data questionnaire developed to predict test performance of electrician job applicants can be found in Ronald D. Pannone, "Predicting Test Performance: A Content Valid Approach to Screening Applicants," *Personnel Psychology* 37 (1984): 507–514.

[9] Lawshe, "Inferences From Personnel Tests and Their Validity," p. 237.

[10] Lawshe has shown that a form of quantitative analysis may be applied in content validity — see C. H. Lawshe, "A Quantitative Approach to Content Validity," *Personnel Psychology* 28 (1975): 563–575. For an example of a study using Lawshe's quantitative content validity approach, see M. K. Distefano, Margaret W. Pryer, and Robert C. Erffmeyer, "Application of Content Validity Methods to the Development of a Job-Related Performance Rating Criterion," *Personnel Psychology* 36 (1983): 621–632.

[11] Larry S. Kleiman and Robert H. Faley, "Assessing Content Validity: Standards Set By the Court," *Personnel Psychology* 31 (1978): 701–713.

[12] *Albemarle Paper Company v. Moody,* 422 U.S. 405 (1975).

[13] Equal Employment Opportunity Commission, Civil Service Commission, Department of Labor, and Department of Justice, *Adoption of Four Agencies of Uniform Guidelines on Employee Selection Procedures,* 43 Federal Register 38,305 (Aug. 25, 1978).

[14] Lyle F. Schoenfeldt, Barbara B. Schoenfeldt, Stanley R. Acker, and Michael R. Perlson, "Content Validity Revisited: The Development of a Content-Oriented Test of Industrial Reading," *Journal of Applied Psychology* 61 (1976): 581–588.

[15] For a detailed example of job and curriculum analysis procedures used in the validation of an educational credential as a selection standard, see Robert J. Teare, Hubert S. Feild, Thomas P. Gauthier, *Job Analysis Procedures and Instruments,* vol. 2 in *Classification/Validation Processes for Social Services Positions* (Silver Springs, Md.: National Association of Social Workers, 1984); and Robert J. Teare, Bradford W. Sheafor, and Thomas P. Gauthier, *Curriculum Analysis Procedures and Instruments,* vol. 3 in *Classification/Validation Processes for Social Services Positions* (Silver Springs, Md.: National Association of Social Workers, 1984).

[16] Equal Employment Opportunity Commission et al., *Uniform Guidelines,* p. 38,303.

[17] Ibid., p. 38,295

[18] Ibid.

[19] Ibid., p. 38,302.

20 Ibid.

21 Robert M. Guion, *Recruiting, Selection, and Job Placement,* in Marvin D. Dunnette, ed., *Handbook of Industrial and Organizational Psychology* (Chicago: Rand McNally, 1974), p. 786.

22 Mary L. Tenopyr, "Content-Construct Confusion," *Personnel Psychology* 30 (1977): 47–54. See also, Robert M. Guion, "Content Validity—The Source of My Discontent," *Personnel Psychology* 1 (1977): 1–10; Robert M. Guion, "Content Validity: Three Years of Talk—What's the Action?" *Public Personnel Management* 6 (1977): 407–414; and Robert M. Guion, " 'Content Validity' in Moderation," *Personnel Psychology,* 31 (1978): 205–213.

23 American Psychological Association, *Principles for the Validation and Use of Personnel Selection Procedures.*

24 Robert M. Guion, *Personnel Testing* (New York: McGraw-Hill, 1965), p. 128.

25 One unique application of the construct validity model in personnel selection is the validation study of the federal government's Professional and Administrative Career Examination (PACE) as described in R. H. McKillip and Hilda Wing, "Application of a Construct Model in Assessment of Employment" in U.S. Office of Personnel Management and Educational Testing Service, *Construct Validity in Psychological Measurement: Proceedings of a Colloquium on Theory and Application in Education and Employment* (Princeton, N.J.: Educational Testing Service, 1980).

26 In some employment settings, an organization may not have as many applicants or employ as many persons as given in our example. Thus, empirical validity may not be technically feasible. Under such circumstances, other approaches to validity such as content validity, validity generalization, and synthetic validity may need to be considered.

27 Ghiselli, Campbell, and Zedeck, *Measurement Theory for the Behavioral Sciences,* p. 145.

28 Philippe Cattin, "Estimation of the Predictive Power of a Regression Model," *Journal of Applied Psychology* 65 (1980): 407–414.

29 Kevin R. Murphy, "Cost-Benefit Considerations in Choosing Among Cross-Validation Methods," *Personnel Psychology* 37 (1984): 15–22.

30 C. H. Lawshe and Michael J. Balma, *Principles of Personnel Testing* (New York: McGraw-Hill, 1966), p. 301.

31 Ibid., pp. 306–308.

32 Guion, *Personnel Testing,* pp. 141–144.

33 Robert L. Thorndike, *Personnel Selection* (New York: John Wiley, 1949), pp. 169–176.

34 Jerry S. Wiggins, *Personality and Prediction: Principles of Personality Assessment* (Reading, Mass.: Addison-Wesley, 1973).

35 Richard D. Arvey, *Fairness in Selecting Employees* (Reading, Mass.: Addison-Wesley, 1973).

36 H. C. Taylor and J. T. Russell, "The Relationship of Validity Coefficients to the Practical Effectiveness of Tests in Selection," *Journal of Applied Psychology* 23 (1939): 565–578.

37 Wayne F. Cascio, *Costing Human Resources: The Financial Impact of Behavior in Organizations* (Boston: Kent, 1982), p. 130.

38 James C. Naylor and L. C. Shine, "A Table for Determining the Increase in Mean Criterion Score Obtained by Using a Selection Device," *Journal of Industrial Psychology* 3 (1965): 33–42.

39 Lee J. Cronbach and Goldine C. Gleser, *Psychological Tests and Personnel Decisions* (Urbana, Ill.: University of Illinois Press, 1965).

40 As cited in Landy, *Psychology of Work Behavior,* pp. 214–217.

41 See, for example, Raymond Lee and J. M. Booth, "A Utility Analysis of a Weighted Application Blank Designed to Predict Turnover From Clerical Employees," *Journal of Applied Psychology* 59 (1974): 516–518; and Frank L. Schmidt, John E. Hunter, Robert C. McKenzie, and Tressie W. Muldrow, "Impact of Valid Selection Procedures on Work-Force Productivity," *Journal of Applied Psychology* 64 (1979): 609–626.

42 Cascio, *Costing Human Resources: The Financial Impact of Behavior in Organizations.*

43 Guion, *Personnel Testing,* p. 169.

44 Robert M. Guion, "Synthetic Validity in a Small Company: A Demonstration," *Personnel Psychology* 18 (1965): 49–63.

45 Landy, *Psychology of Work Behavior,* pp. 68–70.

[46] See, for example, Frank L. Schmidt, I. Gast-Rosenberg, and John E. Hunter, "Validity Generalization Results for Computer Programmers," *Journal of Applied Psychology* 65 (1980): 643–661; Frank L. Schmidt, John E. Hunter, and Kenneth Pearlman, "Task Differences as Moderators of Aptitude Test Validity in Selection: A Red Herring," *Journal of Applied Psychology* 66 (1981): 166–185; Frank L. Schmidt, John E. Hunter, Kenneth Pearlman, and G. S. Shane, "Further Tests of Schmidt-Hunter Bayesian Validity Generalization Procedure," *Personnel Psychology* 32 (1979): 257–281; N. S. Raju and Michael J. Burke, "Two New Procedures for Studying Validity Generalization," *Journal of Applied Psychology* 68 (1983): 382–395; Michael J. Burke, "Validity Generalization: A Review and Critique of the Correlation Model," *Personnel Psychology* 37 (1984): 93–116; Frank L. Schmidt and John E. Hunter, "A Within-Setting Empirical Test of the Situational Specificity Hypothesis in Personnel Selection," *Personnel Psychology* 37 (1984): 317–326; and Frank L. Schmidt, Benjamin P. Ocasio, Joseph M. Hillery, and John E. Hunter, "Further Within-Setting Empirical Tests of the Situational Specificity Hypothesis in Personnel Selection," *Personnel Psychology* 38 (1985): 509–524.

[47] For a study illustrating the classification of jobs in the context of validity generalization, see Edwin T. Cornelius, Frank L. Schmidt, and Theodore J. Carron, "Job Classification Approaches and the Implementation of Validity Generalization Results," *Personnel Psychology* 37 (1984): 247–260.

[48] See, for example, H. G. Osburn, J. C. Callender, J. M. Greener, and S. Ashworth, "Statistical Power of Tests of the Situational Specificity Hypothesis in Validity Generalization Studies: A Cautionary Note," *Journal of Applied Psychology* 68 (1983): 115–122; Jen A. Algera, Paul G. W. Jansen, Robert A. Roe, and Pieter Vijn, "Validity Generalization: Some Critical Remarks on the Schmidt-Hunter Procedure," *Journal of Occupational Psychology* 57 (1984): 197–210; Lawrence R. James, Robert G. Demaree, and Stanley A. Mulaik, *A Note on Validity Generalization Procedures*, Interim Technical Report, Office of Naval Research, Manpower R&D Program (Grant No. N00014-83-K-0480) (Arlington, Va.: Office of Naval Research, 1985); Schmitt et al., "Metaanalyses of Validity Studies Published Between 1964–1982 and the Investigation of Study Characteristics"; and Edward R. Kemery, Kevin W. Mossholder, and Lawrence Roth, "A Test of the Schmidt and Hunter Additive Model of Validity Generalization," paper presented at the Southeastern Industrial/Organizational Psychology Association, Atlanta, Ga., March 1985.

PART THREE

Job Analysis

in Human Resource

Selection

In selecting personnel to fill job vacancies, managers are ultimately faced with some important questions that must be addressed. These questions include: What tasks are new employees required to perform? What knowledge, skills, and abilities (that is, employee or job specifications) must new employees possess to perform these tasks effectively? If certain specifications are used, is it then possible to develop selection instruments such as tests or employment interviews that could be used in making selection decisions? For any job under study, what factors or measures exist that represent job success? These are but a few of the questions that confront managers involved in human resource selection. Answers are not always obvious and seldom easy. Yet, whatever the issue in human resource selection, there is one managerial tool that can and should be used first in addressing selection considerations — *job analysis*.

The purpose of this section is to provide an overview of the job analysis process in the context of human resource selection. Our objectives are four-fold:

1. To explore the role of job analysis
2. To describe various techniques used in collecting job information
3. To examine how job information can be used to identify employee

specifications (such as knowledge, skills, and abilities or KSAs) necessary for successful job performance

4. To examine how these specifications can be translated into the content of selection instruments such as tests, employment interviews, or application forms.

6

Preparing for

Job Analysis:

An Overview

Role of Job Analysis in Human Resource Selection

A Definition and Model

There are probably as many definitions of job analysis as there are writings on the topic. For our purposes though, when we refer to *job analysis,* we simply mean *a purposeful, systematic process for collecting information on the important, work-related aspects of a job.* Some possible types of work-related information to be collected might include:

1. Work activities — what a worker does; how, why, and when these activities are conducted

2. Tools and equipment used in performing work activities

3. Context of the work environment, such as work schedule or physical working conditions

4. Requirements of personnel performing the job, such as knowledge, skills, abilities, or other personal characteristics, like physical characteristics, interests, or personality[1]

The information obtained from a job analysis has been found to serve a wide variety of purposes.[2] For example, over 40 years ago Zerga identified more than 20 uses of job analysis data.[3] More recently job analysis data have been used in areas such as compensation, training, and performance appraisal among many others. Of particular interest here is the application to human resource selection.

Broadly speaking, job analysis data collected for selection applications generally result in either *work-oriented* or *worker-oriented* information. These two products, their subproducts, and their interrelationships are shown in Exhibit 6.1.

The first or work-oriented products involve defining a job in terms of work-related information (for example, task activities or worker functions). Subproducts of this information are criteria or employee performance measures such as performance appraisals or productivity assessments. In addition, from work-related information, inferences or judgments on the part of job analysts can be used to develop the second or worker-oriented products. These products involve identifying employee specifications (such as KSAs) that are necessary for successful performance on the job. These specifications permit an important subproduct. Once employee specifications have been identified, it is possible to develop predictors or selection instruments such as tests, application forms, and employment interviews that measure these specifications. Assuming that selection instruments as well as performance standards are derived from job analysis, it is expected that instruments used in selecting employees will be correlated with performance measures. As we saw in the previous chapter, a validation study tests this correlation. What is important here is the recognition that it is the job analysis process that impacts on the effectiveness of any human resource selection system. Where job analysis is incomplete, inaccurate, or simply not conducted, a selection system may be nothing more than a game of chance — a game that employer, employee, and job applicants alike may lose.

Growth in Job Analysis

As described by Jai Ghorpade and Thomas Atchinson, job analysis has had an interesting though, at times, erratic history. From the turn of the century through the 1940s, there was widespread enthusiasm for the use of job analysis. The management literature in the 1950s and 1960s did not devote as much attention to the field as previously, but practitioners were busy applying job analysis methods to problems of recruitment and placement.[4] For instance, in 1969 a national survey of 681 firms employing job analysis reported that over 90 percent used the information in recruiting and placing personnel.[5] There are not comparable data on current practices but the literature shows a significant increase in attention given to job analysis, beginning in the 1970s.[6] This attention has focused on the use of job analysis not only in the basic personnel areas of recruitment, placement, training, and compensation but in selection as well. At least three interrelated reasons account for this renewed interest. First, there has been the realization that jobs are not static entities; that is, the nature of jobs may change for any number of

Exhibit 6.1   Role of Job Analysis in Human Resource Selection

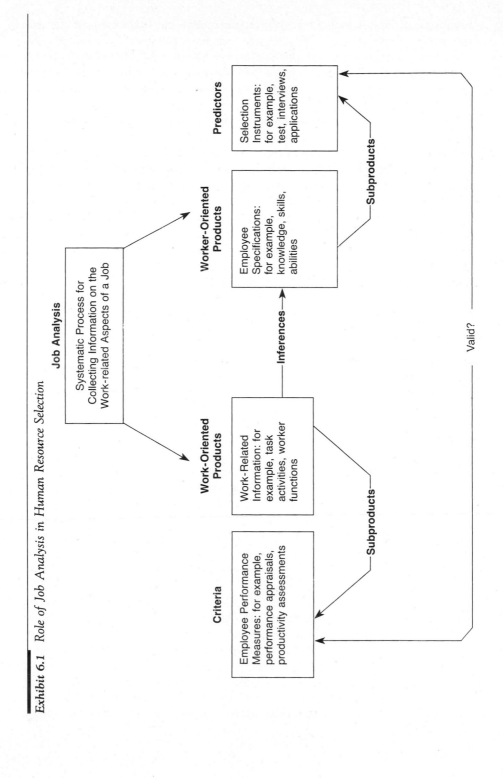

reasons, such as technological advancements, seasonal variations, or the initiatives of an incumbent.[7] Thus, as managers have recognized the importance of job information in human resource decision making, there has been an accompanying recognition of the need for up-to-date information on the jobs themselves. In addition to the need for current, accurate job data, two other factors have impacted on the role of job analysis in selection. Federal guidelines on employee selection procedures (such as the *Uniform Guidelines* mentioned in Chapter 2) have had a significant effect.[8] These guidelines have generally required that job analyses be performed as part of the development, application, and validation of selection devices. More will be said in the next section about these guidelines, but needless to say, they have elevated the importance of job analysis.

Similarly, the court cases involving discrimination in selection have underlined the significance of job analysis.[9] We will discuss selected cases in the section that follows. Generally speaking, rulings in various cases have held that job analysis must play an integral role in any research that attempts to show a correlation between job performance and a selection measure.

Legal Issues in Job Analysis

In recent years, job analysis has become a focal point in the legal context of human resource selection. The principal source for this development can be traced to the passage of Title VII of the 1964 Civil Rights Act. As we discussed in Chapter 2, Title VII makes it illegal for an organization to refuse to hire an individual or to discriminate against a person with respect to compensation, terms, conditions, or privileges of employment because of the person's race, sex, color, religion, or national origin. Since many Title VII cases have concerned the role of discrimination in selection for employment, job analysis has emerged as critical to the prosecution or defense of a discrimination case. Thus, job analysis and its associated methodologies have become intertwined with the law. Within this legal vein, two developments have amplified the importance of job analysis in selection research: (a) the adoption of the *Uniform Guidelines on Employee Selection Procedures* by the federal government and (b) litigation involving discrimination in hiring, arising under Title VII as well as the Fifth and Fourteenth Amendments to the Constitution.

Court Cases Involving Job Analysis   Although a number of cases involving job analysis have been heard in the courts, two early Supreme Court cases are particularly important. Perhaps the seminal one with respect to job analysis is *Griggs v. Duke Power Co.* which we discussed in Chapter 2.[10] Even though the term "job analysis" is not mentioned per se, *Griggs* gave the legal impetus to job analysis. The case implies that an important legal requirement in a selection device validation program is an analysis of the job for which the device is used.

As we have mentioned, in *Griggs*, Duke Power was employing a written test and a high school diploma as requirements for entry into a supervisory position. The Court noted that these selection standards were used "without meaningful study of their relationship to job-performance ability. Rather, a vice-president of the company testified, the requirements were instituted on the company's judgment that they generally would improve the overall quality of the work force."[11] Thus, the Court ruled that "What Congress has commanded is that any test used must measure the person *for the job* [emphasis added] and not the person in the abstract."[12] The implication behind the ruling in *Griggs* is that for employers to attempt to meet this job-relatedness standard, they must first examine the job. Measurement of the job is accomplished through job analysis.

Similarly, *Albemarle Paper Co. v. Moody*, another case we discussed, is especially important.[13] In *Albemarle*, the Court, for the first time, expressly criticized the lack of a job analysis in a validation study. It was noted by the Court that "no attempt was made to analyze the jobs in terms of the particular skills they might require."[14] As with *Griggs*, the Court again gave weight to the use of job analysis.

Albemarle is noteworthy for its support of job analysis. Like *Griggs*, its predecessor, *Albemarle* was a Supreme Court case. Plaintiffs as well as lower courts look for guidance from rulings of the Supreme Court. Thus, it can be expected that the insistence on a job analysis in selection cases will encourage other courts to look for the presence (or lack) of a job analysis.

The case is also significant for a second reason. The Court supported the EEOC *Guidelines on Employee Selection Procedures*,[15] which required the undertaking of a job analysis in a validation study. As will be seen in the next section, the Court's endorsement of these guidelines, as well as the subsequently issued *Uniform Guidelines*, has emphasized the role of job analysis in human resource selection.

There are numerous court cases which could be cited in addition to *Griggs* and *Albemarle*. On the whole, decisions and remedies in these cases emphasize the importance of job analysis. An examination of these cases would be helpful to isolating the standards used by the courts in evaluating job analysis in validation research. In this light, Duane Thompson and Toni Thompson reviewed 26 selected federal court cases to determine the criteria the courts used in assessing job analyses conducted in the development and validation of tests. Their review produced a set of job analysis characteristics, which they suggest are capable of withstanding legal scrutiny. Although these characteristics may vary depending upon issues such as type of job analysis, type of validation model, and purpose of the analysis, the standards serve as a useful guide for understanding the judicial view. The legal standards identified by Thompson and Thompson are as follows:

✳ **1.** Job analysis must be performed and must be for the job for which the selection instrument is to be utilized.

2. Analysis of the job should be in writing.

3. Job analyst(s) should describe in detail the procedures used.

4. Job data should be collected from a variety of current sources and by knowledgeable job analyst(s).

5. Sample size should be large and representative of the jobs for which the device will be used.

 * 6. Tasks, duties, and activities should be included in the analysis.

7. The most important tasks should be represented in the selection device.

8. Competency levels of job performance for entry-level jobs should be specified. *ex wpm*

9. Knowledge, skills, and abilities should be specified, particularly if a content validation model is followed.[16]

Federal Guidelines on Employee Selection   During the period from 1966 to 1978, various sets of federal regulations on employee selection were issued.[17] The Equal Employment Opportunity Commission (EEOC), the Office of Federal Contract Compliance (OFCC), the Civil Service Commission (currently the U.S. Office of Personnel Management), and the Department of Justice offered guidelines for employers to follow in their selection procedures. Although some employers may have treated these guidelines as nothing more than a "guide," the *Albemarle* case enhanced their role. As noted earlier, the Court gave deference to the EEOC guidelines, at least to the portion that discussed job analysis. The impact of the Court's opinion has been to make it mandatory for selection managers to be intimately familiar with their content.

Current federal regulations noted in the *Uniform Guidelines* supersede previous regulations and represent a joint agreement among the EEOC, Department of Justice, Department of Labor, and Civil Service Commission (now the U.S. Office of Personnel Management). Given the substantial weight accorded to the *Uniform Guidelines* in recent court cases, it can be expected that the courts will continue to give importance to job analysis.

Summary

Although it would be nice, it is simply impossible to specify one clear, suitable, standard means for meeting *all* the technical and legal considerations of a job analysis. Situations, problems, and technical issues are so varied that proper conduct of a job analysis is a complex, resource-consuming process. There is no one standard way. As Paul Sparks, former personnel research coordinator of Exxon, has stated, "I, for one, find it very difficult to find an agreed-upon professional standard in the area of job analysis. . . . We're due for a lot more research, a lot more litigation, and a lot more court decisions before we have a standard."[18]

Nevertheless, absence of an agreed upon standard should not be viewed

*if can't identify where, can't identify knowledge skills and abilities required.

as a basis for minimizing the legal role of job analysis. At the third Annual Conference on EEO Compliance/Human Resources Utilization, Donald Schwartz, EEOC personnel research psychologist, noted that, from a legal viewpoint, the government looks first to see if a job analysis has been undertaken in a validation study. He went on to say, "In my opinion, the absence of a job analysis is fatal to a validity study in a court challenge, and will continue to be fatal to a validity study regardless of what the professional standards say."[19] According to Schwartz, the legal requirements transcend the professional standards. The government as well as the courts look for adequacy in a job analysis. "The courts have since the earliest decisions in this area strongly emphasized the need for an adequate job analysis in support of the use of a test or other questioned procedure. . . . Job analyses which do not provide the necessary information do not support a claim of validity regardless of how much information they provide."[20]

So far, we have seen that job analysis plays both technical and legal roles in the development of a human resource selection system. The next section focuses on the implementation of job analysis in the context of selection.

Implementation of a Job Analysis

Implementation of a job analysis involves a sequence of activities and decision points. Even though these activities may vary depending upon their purpose, there are at least seven major decision points typically involved in job analysis for human resource selection purposes: (a) organizing for a job analysis, (b) choosing jobs to be studied, (c) reviewing the relevant literature, (d) selecting job agents, (e) collecting job information, (f) identifying job or employee specifications, and (g) incorporating employee specifications in selection devices. Successful job analysis research involves careful planning with respect to each of these tasks. In the remaining portions of this chapter, we will concentrate on the first *four* decision points of the job analysis process. Chapter 7 will focus on the fifth decision point, the methods of collecting job information. The final chapter in this section, Chapter 8, will deal with the last two decision points, that is, how job analysis results are used to identify employee specifications and how selection measures are developed from these specifications.

Organizing for a Job Analysis

We have already discussed some of the technical/legal issues that must be given consideration in conducting a job analysis. Now, we will turn our attention to the setting up of an administrative organization for coordinating the project. It is the project staff that will be responsible for seeing that the job analysis and associated activities are properly conducted.

Who should be responsible for these coordination efforts? The answer depends upon a host of factors including the scope of the work, its complexity, and the resources allocated to it. Usually, responsibility for job analysis rests with top management, the operating managers, and the personnel office.[21] Unless top management and line managers provide the necessary support, it will be difficult for the project to succeed.

Staffing the project raises other issues. Should one person or a number of individuals be involved? Such member(s) may come from an existing organizational unit or be employed on an ad hoc basis. Carrell and Kuzmits recommend the formation of a job analysis committee. Under a committee structure, individual representation would be from the major departments housing the jobs to be studied. Committee representation would permit members to discuss with their departments the nature of the process and to reassure employees who feel threatened.[22]

Whatever the organizational alignment, it is imperative for clear lines of authority to be established. Clarity of authority helps make possible coordination of many diverse activities. A single individual should be charged with responsibilities for coordination of the job analysis in addition to other activities such as selection device development or validation. Ideally, this individual would be familiar with job analysis and related validation activities. Realistically, the individual may not have the expertise. If such skills are not available within the organization, the core person should have the resources and authority for hiring an appropriate consultant.

The job analysis coordinator may be required to perform a wide array of duties. These would probably include the following:

1. Serve as a channel of communication to and from top management

2. Assess the technical capabilities of the internal staff

3. Recruit and transfer additional personnel to the project, such as clerical help (for editing, data coding, data entry), technical consultants, and data collectors

4. Make work assignments and monitor progress

5. Plan and schedule the job analysis and related activities

6. Design training and orientation sessions for staff

7. Supervise the selection of jobs and job agents

8. Prepare and revise job analysis materials

9. Supervise data analyses

10. Meet with and counsel employees to alleviate any perceived threats from job analysis (for example, layoffs, higher work standards, lower pay rates)[23]

The managing of a job analysis is not an easy assignment. It cannot be conducted by any "available" person. Some writers believe otherwise, but care should be exercised in assigning the responsibilities for a job analysis. Erich Prien succinctly summarizes this point:

Although job analysis is an essential feature of almost every activity engaged in by industrial-organizational psychologists, the subject is treated in textbooks in a manner which suggests that any fool can do it and thus it is a task which can be delegated to the lowest level technician. This is quite contradictory to the position taken by Otis (1953) in explicating and defending the practice, and is clearly at variance with the statements in the EEOC Selection Guidelines (however vague these statements may be) admonishing the researcher to do a *thorough* job analysis in test selection and in criterion development. Job analysis for these purposes is not accomplished by rummaging around in an organization; it is accomplished by applying highly systematic and precise methods.[24]

Choosing Jobs to be Studied

Once a job analysis staff has been assembled, the next issue to be addressed is the choice of job(s) on which an analysis will be made. The answer is not as obvious as it sounds. Most organizations conducting selection research are going to have limited resources that can be devoted to the project. Thus, an organization will be forced to choose among the many job possibilities on which analyses need to be made. A number of criteria might be employed for choosing the initial jobs for research. Some recommendations are listed below.

Representativeness of the Job   Based upon this standard, a job chosen as part of the study would be one that closely resembles other jobs within the organization. If we assume that correspondence between content of a selected job and a specific selection device is high, then it might be reasoned that other jobs resembling the job chosen for study might also correspond to the selection device. Therefore, validity generalization from one job to relevant others might be argued. It would seem that such a procedure would help to eliminate the time- and resource-consuming tasks of analyzing every job under consideration. This is not likely, however. Before such an inference can be made, it must be *documented* that jobs are indeed similar. Documentation is provided through job analysis. Given this requirement, it is difficult to conceive of significant benefits accruing to an organization relying *solely* on this criterion for choosing jobs.

Criticality of the Job   In some organizations, such as social or health services organizations, certain jobs may be so critical that the mental or physical well-being of the clients depends on them. They may be at greater risk due to an inappropriate selection standard than may other groups, for example, employees or job applicants. Therefore, those jobs posing possible physical or psychological harm to clients would seem to be a reasonable place to begin. If it can be assumed that the use of a device in selection decisions is not likely to harm eventual clients, one could claim this not to be a suitable criterion for choosing a job for study. Conversely, if it is thought that the use of such a standard could lead to negative impacts on clients, then the degree of client vulnerability that is characteristic of particular jobs would be a very relevant consideration.

Number of Applicants for the Job   From the perspective of employment discrimination, the number of applicants for a specific job is an important factor. If a selection device is not valid, the greatest impact would be on those jobs having the largest number of applicants. (Quite often, these are jobs with the greatest number of incumbents.) In order to protect an organization from this possibility, initial job analysis studies might be directed toward those jobs in which a discrimination charge is most likely. With this criterion, it is assumed that the greater the number of applicants for a specific job, the greater the probability of a discrimination charge by an aggrieved applicant.

Stability/Obsolescence of Job Content   As content (in terms of actual tasks or knowledge, skills, and abilities required for task performance) of jobs changes, it becomes necessary periodically to reexamine the job content. Therefore, another important criterion is the frequency of and extent to which job content is modified. Jobs that change often require more frequent checks on content. Conversely, jobs whose content remains stable over time do not require frequent checks once a thorough job analysis has been made.

Evidence of Adverse Impact in Selection   As we discussed in Chapter 2, adverse impact occurs when there is "a substantially different rate of selection in hiring . . . which works to the disadvantage of members of a race, sex, or ethnic group."[25] When adverse impact has taken place, the *Uniform Guidelines* specify that the employer must be able to demonstrate that the selection standard is related to job performance. To be in compliance, an organization would want to initiate a job analysis study for those jobs where adverse impact has occurred.

Entry-Level Jobs in an Organization   The *Uniform Guidelines* are directed principally toward entry-level jobs in any organization to which the guidelines apply.[26] Entry-level jobs are those positions in an organization that hirees enter having once passed the selection standards. The selection measures used for such jobs are of particular interest since it is those measures that determine who does and who does not get employed. Jobs requiring minimum performance on a selection device for entry by new employees would be the relevant ones for consideration.

Jobs Serving as Links to Higher-Level Jobs   Often, certain entry-level jobs serve as *gatekeepers* or *links* to other, higher-level jobs in an organization's career sequence. Thus, promotion to jobs providing more status, greater authority, or more pay may only occur when an individual has acquired experience in a specific job. When promotion rates from such linking jobs are low, these jobs become possible candidates for study.

Evidence of Performance Deficiencies Jobs characterized by performance deficiencies (such as low productivity, high turnover) call attention to the question of relevance (validity) of the selection devices used as qualifications for employment. Although the standards for job entry may not be the sole reason for inadequate performance, they certainly merit examination as to their validity. Organizations may want to select those jobs in which performance is inadequate because there is an implication that the selection standard may not be associated with job performance. Reexamination of the standard would begin by an analysis of the job.

There is not one, exclusive criterion that every organization should use in choosing specific jobs for job analysis. Organizational characteristics such as geographical location, size, resources, structure, policies, and practices will impinge upon the choices available. In practice, it will probably be found that several of the criteria described above will need to be applied simultaneously in choosing jobs for analysis. Depending upon the perspectives of the organization, however, different criteria may emerge. For example, from a legal point of view, the following types of jobs should be emphasized:

1. Jobs showing adverse impact in selection
2. Jobs serving as entry-level positions in an organization
3. Jobs having a large number of applicants

From the perspective of the client of special human services organizations, jobs that may affect the psychological or physical well-being of the client should be chosen. Finally, from the standpoint of management, the following options should be considered:

1. Jobs with performance deficiencies
2. Jobs whose content has changed
3. Jobs serving as links to higher-level positions

Obviously, these various criteria present the problem of where to begin. One must remember that the requirements of the particular organization will determine the options chosen. However, *at a minimum,* two types of jobs should always be considered first: (a) entry-level jobs and (b) jobs where adverse impact has occurred in hiring.

Caution should be exercised in the job choices made. In particular, careful attention should be given when using job titles to make the decision. Since titles may be associated with pay classifications that cluster jobs into a general pay class, they may mask task differences. For example, Thorton and Rosenfeld's analysis of the job of employment service interviewer revealed that a number of these people actually worked as claims examiners. Furthermore, they found 26 different jobs in an analysis of the job title "Police Sergeant."[27] Consultation with knowledgeable job experts (for example, experienced incumbents or supervisors) can help to clarify the jobs under consideration.

Reviewing the Relevant Literature

After a job has been selected for analysis, the next task is to conduct a review of job analysis literature for the job in question. The goal of the review should be to determine the data collection methods used by others, their analyses, problems, and results. A review of related literature can have the following benefits:

1. It can show how previous investigators have conducted their analyses and enable the researcher to evaluate various approaches for conducting the analysis.

2. It can serve to identify potential problems as well as associated methods and techniques for treating these problems should they develop.

3. It can help to locate additional sources of data not considered by the analyst.

4. It can serve as a means for comparing the results of the present job analysis with those of similar studies.[28]

A variety of sources of information are available. Initially, organization charts and existing job descriptions should be reviewed. Organization charts can show how a given job relates to other jobs in the company. Job descriptions, if they exist, serve as an orientation point for understanding major tasks and responsibilities of the job. Some caution should be taken in the acceptance of these descriptions, however. In many cases, they may not accurately or adequately capture the nature of a job. Preliminary interviews with informed incumbents or supervisors can be used as a check.

Other sources of materials in a literature review might include the *Dictionary of Occupational Titles,*[29] professional associations, labor unions and contracts, training and educational materials produced by the organization, professional publications (such as *Personnel Psychology, Public Personnel Management, Journal of Applied Psychology*), and previous job analyses or studies. Again, the purpose of this search is not to replace the proposed job analysis but to provide a frame of reference for comparing results with the proposed study. Knowledge gleaned from these sources should enhance the quality of job-related research and the development of selection measures.

The next two issues, selecting job agents and choosing a method for collecting job information, are really interrelated. Decisions made in one area necessarily affect those made in the other. However, in order to better clarify important aspects of each, these decision points will be discussed separately. In the remaining portion of this chapter, the emphasis will be on issues involved in choosing job agents. Chapter 7 will address the methods used in collecting job information.

Selecting Job Agents

Job information can be collected by a variety of means ranging from mechanical means, such as video-taping equipment, to human observers. Most often people serve as *job agents*. Job agents are *individuals who are responsible for collecting and providing information about jobs*. In general, there are three classes of agents that can be employed to collect job data: (a) job analysts, (b) job incumbents, and (c) job supervisors.[30] Each type has its own particular characteristics, advantages, and disadvantages. We will now focus our attention on unique aspects of each.

Job Analysts   Job analysts are individuals specially trained to systematically collect and analyze job information. Analysts generally have received formal training in one or more methods of job analysis, although, more often than not, they use interviews or observational methods to collect their data. Individuals serving as analysts may be employed within or from outside an organization requiring job analysis. When internal analysts are used, they frequently work as staff specialists out of personnel or industrial engineering offices. External analysts are typically private consultants. These individuals generally are hired under contract to analyze jobs for a specific purpose, for example, compensation, training, or selection.

The chief advantage when trained, capable analysts are used is that an organization is purchasing the services of skilled individuals; and, therefore, minimum orientation and time are needed for these individuals to perform their jobs. Because of their training, it might be expected (though little research is available) that resulting analyses would generally be more objective, valid, and reliable than comparable ones completed by less formally-prepared agents. If the number of jobs to be analyzed is small, consultants may provide useful, relatively economical data. However, when the number of jobs is large, the amount of time and associated expense required for good coverage may be prohibitive.

In addition to the number of jobs to be studied, there are other factors that should be considered in deciding whether to procure an analyst. Some of these include: (a) *the location of the jobs* — if widely dispersed, there will be greater expense in travel, time, and associated costs; (b) *the complexity of the jobs* — the less observable and the more diverse the tasks, the greater is the need for a skilled agent; and (c) *the receptiveness of the incumbents to external analysts* — if the incumbents feel threatened by external analysts (for example, they fear increased productivity standards, layoffs, or termination), the potential costs to the organization (such as lowered productivity) will be greater. This is not a comprehensive list but it provides a range of factors that should be evaluated in deciding whether to use job analysts.

Job analysts may be solicited from a variety of sources ranging from private consulting firms to university professors to branches of offices in state and federal governments. Certification of training (such as completion of specialized job analysis training programs) may be available from some analysts. However, training is no guarantee of quality. Examples of previous work, references from previous organizational clients, and acceptance of the analyst's work in a court case are some of the best screening tools for selecting job analysts.

Job Incumbents   The second type of agent is the job incumbent or employee. Generally speaking, employees working in a job should be in the best position to describe it. Furthermore, they can describe what is *actually* done rather than what *should be* done.

When using this type of agent, several issues have to be taken into consideration. First, employees may not be interested in reporting on their jobs. Emphasis on the importance of job analysis and use of incentives may be needed to gain the desired level of involvement. Second, employees are generally not prepared to participate in job analysis. Training may be required. Unless training is available, the project may be restricted to using only some of the easiest (not necessarily the most applicable) methods of collecting job data. An additional concern among some investigators is that employees may inflate their jobs.[31] If employees perceive it to be beneficial (such as having their jobs appear to be overly complex to improve their pay classification), they may overstate the exact nature of what they do.

Use of incumbents is not without its problems. Yet, there are some possible benefits. As noted earlier, employees are in the best position to provide complete, accurate data on their jobs. Usually large numbers of employees are available, thus providing multiple assessments of the same job. When a large number of jobs to be analyzed is involved, incumbents may be the most efficient option as a job data source.

Incumbents serving as job respondents should be selected carefully. Research on characteristics of good agents has not been plentiful, but some desirable traits can be hypothesized. The first requirement is that participation of an employee in job analysis should be voluntary. Where motivation and interest are low, quality of participation is likely to be low. Also, given the method of collecting job information (for example, interviews, questionnaires), employees should possess appropriate verbal and writing skills.

Incumbents should have been on their jobs a minimum of six months. This minimum standard may vary depending upon the nature of the job in question. The role of minimum job tenure is to insure that persons chosen will have been on their jobs long enough to give complete and accurate information about the job. Similarly, a maximum period of tenure may also be desirable. Since some job analysis methods require respondents to characterize tasks of newly-hired employees, workers with high seniority in a specific job may have difficulty with this requirement. Long-tenured employees may be unable to accurately recall what a job was like when they were hired. Then, too, tasks that were required when these employees were first employed may have changed. A maximum period of job tenure, like a minimum period, will vary from one job to the next. But avoiding workers with too short or too long periods of service can help to eliminate some potentially critical job analysis problems.

A final comment should be made about selecting a sample of incumbents. When jobs that have a small number of incumbents who meet our selection criteria are analyzed, it may be necessary to use all available persons. Conversely, when jobs have a large number of incumbents, a sample can be drawn. The specific sampling strategy may vary depending on the nature of the organization (for example, size, geographical dispersion) and type of job. In general, a form of stratified random sampling would be most appropriate. Under this sampling strategy, the sample is classified according to designated incumbent characteristics or strata (such as sex, race, tenure). Then, individuals are randomly drawn from these classifications. The idea behind the method is to choose a random sample of job agents that best represents the incumbent population being studied. Given the legal considerations involved in human resource selection, sampling strata based on sex and race should definitely be employed. Sampling based upon major individual difference variables, like sex and race, as well as other incumbent characteristics thought to be linked to quality of data obtained should be most defensible if a discrimination charge arises.

Sampling of incumbents will likely be necessary for most organizations when incumbents are used as data sources. However, some organizations have chosen to survey the entire population of employees in a job. For example, the U.S. Air Force has attempted to collect data from all incumbents in a job. Information is then deleted from individual raters if it does not approximate the average ratings of the group. With this type of analysis, the measure of job activity is the average of most, if not all, incumbents' judgments.[32]

Job Supervisors   Supervisors can also serve as job agents. Since they supervise incumbents performing the job under study, they should be in a position to provide objective data on jobs. Supervisory assessments assume, of course, that supervisors have worked closely with incumbents and have complete information about employees' jobs. Paul Sparks has suggested that supervisors know relatively well what employees do and should be able to make *relative* judgments about job activities. However, there appears to be a tendency for supervisors to characterize subordinates' work in terms of what *should be* done rather than what is *actually* done.[33]

Since only a few supervisors may be needed to supervise a number of jobs, supervisors will likely be widely dispersed. Thus, reliance on a large number of supervisors for job data may substantially increase project costs. Problems like inaccessibility have discouraged the use of supervisors in job analysis research. However, even where supervisors do not serve as the principal information source, they can serve as a means for cross-checking or verifying job data collected elsewhere.

Characteristics thought to be useful in choosing incumbents as job agents similarly apply to supervisors. Factors such as willingness to participate, possession of verbal and writing skills, and minimum and maximum tenure in a specific job should be important considerations.

Research on Job Agents   Attention has been given by researchers to various issues in job analysis. Unfortunately, little job agent research appears to have been directed toward problems such as the accuracy of agents, differences among agents in rating jobs, characteristics of effective agents, and the validity and reliability of job data produced by the various types of agents. Therefore, it is difficult to specify firm, consistent findings that can guide the selection of agents. Some limited data, however, are available.

Several investigations have been conducted for the purpose of comparing the responses of job incumbents with supervisors' responses in a job analysis. Lawshe and Meyer tested for differences between foremen and their supervisors in their perceptions of the foreman's job. Lawshe found large differences between managers and foremen regarding how foremen spent their time in various job functions.[34] Meyer reported relatively high disagreement between foremen and general foremen concerning the foreman's job responsibilities.[35] Similarly, disagreement between supervisors and subordinates was reported by O'Reilly over the level of skills and knowledge required to perform a job.[36]

In contrast to the above studies, Hazel, Madden, and Christal investigated supervisor-subordinate similarity in terms of ratings on general job duties versus specific tasks. Higher supervisor-subordinate agreement was noted for the ratings of general job duties than for specific tasks. Also, agreement for task performance was higher than for time spent on job tasks.[37]

Using a standardized job analysis questionnaire (the Position Analysis Questionnaire or PAQ), Smith and Hakel tested for differences among job incumbents, job analysts, job supervisors, and an independent group of college students in terms of their ability to use the PAQ to analyze a job. No practical differences were identified among the groups based on the reliability of the PAQ data. Supervisors and incumbents showed a tendency, however, to rate the PAQ questionnaire items higher than the job analysts.[38] In contrast, Cornelius, Denisi, and Blencoe have rebutted these findings. They concluded that Smith and Hakel had some methodological problems in the manner in which job similarity ratings among the raters were calculated. Their findings suggested that the Position Analysis Questionnaire measures unique rather than common knowledge about jobs.[39]

A series of investigations have been noted on the issue of possible differences between estimated versus actual time spent on different aspects of jobs. On the whole, moderate to high relationships have been listed between incumbents' estimated and actual time estimates of their job activities. Higher relationships between the time estimates have generally existed for demonstrable work activities rather than for more subjective activities such as planning.[40]

Wexley and Silverman sought to determine if the agent characteristic of managerial effectiveness was predictive of managers' responses to time spent in various work activities. They noted no differences between effective and ineffective managers.[41]

Finally, Boyles, Palmer, and Veres sought to test for racial differences in ratings of task statements collected as part of a job analysis of three job classes. Significant differences were found between black and white incumbents. Importantly, the task-rated differences were so large that they would have affected the content of a test based on the analysis.[42]

We might ask what these results tell us in terms of the differences among job agents in performing a job analysis and the reliability/validity of the data they collect. Definitive answers to these questions, which could specify how a manager should use a job agent, simply cannot be made. Our present research base on job agents' performance is not developed to the degree we would like. On the other hand, these results, as well as some recommendations from researchers in the field, can give us some *broad* guidelines to follow. As long as it is remembered that these are general suggestions, not answers, they may be useful to us in choosing and using job agents. Guidelines and conclusions that might be drawn include the following:

1. Job supervisors and incumbents will likely disagree on ratings of time spent in various job activities. The level of disagreement, however, may depend on the issue being rated, that is, general job duties versus specific job tasks. The more general the duties rated, the greater the agreement on time-spent ratings.[43]

2. Job supervisors should serve as agents when the importance of job tasks is being rated.[44]

3. Job incumbents should act as agents when the frequency of task performance or time spent on tasks is being judged.[45]

4. There is generally a high correlation between incumbents' estimated time spent with actual time spent on various aspects of jobs. The more specific the work activity rated, the higher the relationship.[46]

5. Use of a standardized job analysis questionnaire generally yields reliable ratings regardless of the type of job agent.[47]

6. Supervisors and incumbents versus job analysts may have a tendency to inflate ratings on a standardized job analysis questionnaire.[48]

7. From a legal perspective, the sample of job incumbents to be used as agents should be selected to represent the incumbent population in terms of sex and race as well as other characteristics (performance, job tenure) thought to be important.

In order to carry out our job analysis activities, a choice must be made as to the actual methods to be used. Our next chapter will review the major options to be considered when choosing among these methods.

References for Chapter 6

[1] Ernest J. McCormick, "Job and Task Analysis," in *Handbook of Industrial and Organizational Psychology,* ed. Marvin Dunnette (Chicago: Rand-McNally, 1976), pp. 652–653.

[2] Wayne Cascio, *Applied Psychology in Personnel Management* (Reston, Va.: Reston Publishing Co., 1978), p. 49.

[3] J. E. Zerga, "Job Analysis, A Resumé and Bibliography," *Journal of Applied Psychology* 27 (1943): 249–267.

[4] Jai Ghorpade and Thomas J. Atchinson, "The Concept of Job Analysis: A Review and Some Suggestions," *Public Personnel Management* 9 (June 1980): 134. For a review of the job analysis literature through 1970, see Erich P. Prien and William W. Ronan, "Job Analysis: A Review of Research Findings," *Personnel Psychology* 24 (1971): 371–396.

[5] Jean J. Jones and Thomas DeCotiis, "Job Analysis: National Survey Findings," *Personnel Journal* 48 (October 1969): 805–806.

[6] Thomas Rendero, "Consensus," *Personnel* 58 (January–February 1981): 4–12.

[7] Marvin D. Dunnette, *Personnel Selection and Placement* (Belmont, Calif.: Wadsworth, 1966).

[8] Donald W. Myers, "The Impact of a Selected Provision in the Federal Guidelines on Job Analysis and Training," *Personnel Administrator* 26 (July 1981): 41–45; D. P. Lacy, "EEO Implications of Job Analysis," *Employee Relations Law Journal* 4 (Spring 1979): 525–526.

[9] Duane E. Thompson and Toni A. Thompson, "Court Standards for Job Analysis in Test Validation," *Personnel Psychology* 35 (1982): 872–873; see also C. J. Berwitz, *The Job Analysis Approach to Affirmative Action* (New York: John Wiley, 1975).

[10] *Griggs v. Duke Power Co.,* 401 U.S. 424, 436 (1971).

[11] Ibid.

[12] Ibid.

Albemarle Paper Co. v. Moody, 422 U.S. 405 (1975).

[14] Ibid.

[15] Equal Employment Opportunity Commission, "Guidelines on Employee Selection Procedures," 35 Federal Register 12,333–12,336 (1970).

[16] Thompson and Thompson, "Court Standards for Job Analysis in Test Validation," pp. 872–873.

[17] Equal Employment Opportunity Commission, Civil Service Commission, Department of Labor, and Department of Justice, *Adoption of Four Agencies of Uniform Guidelines on Employee Selection Procedures,* 43 Federal Register 38,290–38,315 (Aug. 25, 1978), referred to in the text as the *Uniform Guidelines;* Equal Employment Opportunity Commission, Office of Personnel Management, Department of Treasury, *Adoption of Questions and Answers to Clarify and Provide a Common Interpretation of the Uniform Guidelines on Employee Selection Procedures,* 44 Federal Register 11,996–12,009 (1979); Equal Employment Opportunity Commission, *Guidelines on Employee Selection Procedures,* 41 Federal Register 51,984–51,986 (1976).

[18] Bureau of National Affairs, "Professional, Legal Requirements of Job Analysis Explored at Chicago Conference," *Daily Labor Report,* May 30, 1980, pp. A-1 to A-8.

[19] Ibid., p. A-5.

[20] Ibid. For additional perspectives on legal issues in job analysis, see Stephen E. Bemis, Ann Holt Belenky, and Dee Ann Soder, *Job Analysis: An Effective Management Tool* (Washington, D.C.: Bureau of National Affairs, 1983), pp. 126–138.

[21] Randall S. Schuler, *Personnel and Human Resources Management* (St. Paul: West Publishing Co., 1981), p. 96.

[22] M. R. Carrell and F. E. Kuzmits, *Personnel: Management of Human Resources* (Columbus, Ohio: Charles E. Merrill, 1982), pp. 75–76.

[23] Robert J. Teare and Hubert S. Feild, *The National Classification Validation Study: A Synthesis Report on the Analysis of Jobs* (Silver Spring, Md.: National Association of Social Workers, 1984), pp. 11–13.

[24] Erich P. Prien, "Development of a Clerical Position Description Questionnaire," *Personnel Psychology* 18 (1977): 167.

[25] Equal Employment Opportunity Commission et al., *Uniform Guidelines*, p. 38,307.

[26] Ibid., pp. 38,296–38,297.

[27] Richard F. Thorton and Michael Rosenfeld, *The Design and Evaluation of Job Analysis Procedures Conducted for the Purpose of Developing Content Valid Occupational Assessment Measures* (Princeton, N.J.: Center for Occupational and Professional Assessment, Educational Testing Service, 1980), p. 13.

[28] Ibid., p. 7.

[29] U.S. Department of Labor, Employment and Training Administration, *Dictionary of Occupational Titles*, 4th ed. (Washington, D.C.: U.S. Government Printing Office, 1977). For information on the reliability of job rating data provided by the *Dictionary of Occupational Titles*, see P. S. Cain and B. F. Green, "Reliability of Ratings Available From the *Dictionary of Occupational Titles*," *Journal of Applied Psychology* 68 (1983): 155–165.

[30] Ernest J. McCormick, "Job Information: Its Development and Applications," in *ASPA Handbook of Personnel and Industrial Relations*, ed. Dale Yoder and Herbert G. Heneman (Washington, D.C.: BNA Books, 1979), pp. 4–43. Sources of bias in job analysis have been studied by Richard D. Arvey, Greg A. Davis, Sherry L. McGowen, and Robert L. Dipboye, "Potential Sources of Bias in Job Analytic Processes," *Academy of Management Journal* 25 (1982): 621–629; Erich P. Prien and S. D. Saleh, "A Study of Bias in Job Analysis," *Journal of Industrial Psychology* 1 (1963): 113–117; L. W. Wiley and W. S. Jenkins, "Method of Measuring Bias in Raters Who Estimate Job Qualifications," *Journal of Industrial Psychology* 1 (1963): 16–22.

[31] Ernest J. McCormick, *Job Analysis* (New York: AMACON, 1979).

[32] In most applications, the mean is the preferred descriptive statistic for representing job analysis ratings.

[33] Paul Sparks, "Job Analysis," in *Personnel Management*, ed. K. Rowland and G. Ferris (Boston: Allyn and Bacon, 1981). See also Paul Sparks, *Job Analysis Under the New Uniform Guidelines* (Houston, Tex.: Personnel Research, Exxon Corporation, August 1979).

[34] C. H. Lawshe, *Psychology of Industrial Relations* (New York: McGraw-Hill, 1953).

[35] Herbert H. Meyer, "Comparison of Foreman and General Foreman Conceptions of the Foreman's Job Responsibility," *Personnel Psychology* 12 (1959): 445–452.

[36] A. P. O'Reilly, "Skill Requirements: Supervisor-Subordinate Conflict," *Personnel Psychology* 26 (1973): 75–80.

[37] J. T. Hazel, J. M. Madden, and R. E. Christal, "Agreement Between Worker-Supervisor Descriptions of the Worker's Job," *Journal of Industrial Psychology* 2 (1964): 71–79.

[38] Jack E. Smith and Milton D. Hakel, "Convergence Among Data Sources, Response Bias, and Reliability and Validity of a Structured Job Analysis Questionnaire," *Personnel Psychology* 32 (1979): 677–692.

[39] Edwin T. Cornelius, Angelo S. Denisi, and Allyn G. Blencoe, "Expert and Naive Raters Using the PAQ: Does it Matter?" *Personnel Psychology* 37 (1984): 453–464.

[40] S. J. Carrol and W. H. Taylor, "Validity of Estimates by Clerical Personnel of Job Time Proportions," *Journal of Applied Psychology* 53 (1969): 164–166; J. R. Hinrichs, "Communications Activity of Industrial Research Personnel," *Personnel Psychology* 17 (1964): 193–204.

[41] Kenneth N. Wexley and S. B. Silverman, "An Examination of Differences Between Managerial Effectiveness and Response Patterns of a Structured Job Analysis Questionnaire," *Journal of Applied Psychology* 63 (1978): 646–649.

[42] Wiley R. Boyles, Chester I. Palmer, and John G. Veres, "Bias in Content Valid Tests," paper presented at the annual conference of the International Personnel Management Association Assessment Council, Boston, July 1980.

[43] Lawshe, *Psychology of Industrial Relations*; Hazel, Madden, and Christal, "Agreement Between Worker-Supervisor Descriptions of the Worker's Job."

[44] R. E. Christal, *The United States Air Force Occupational Research Project* (Lackland Air Force Base, Tex.: Air Force Human Resources Laboratory, 1974).

[45] Ibid.

[46] Carrol and Taylor, "Validity of Estimates by Clerical Personnel of Job Time Proportions"; Hinrichs, "Communications Activity of Industrial Research Personnel."

[47] Smith and Hakel, "Convergence Among Data Sources, Response Bias, and Reliability and Validity of a Structured Job Analysis Questionnaire."

[48] Ibid.

7

Applying Job

Analysis Techniques

Collecting Job Information

Up to this point, we have discussed some of the issues involved in job analysis for human resource selection. In this chapter we are concerned with the various techniques available for collecting job information. A wide array of instruments (for example, questionnaires, worker diaries, interviews) may be used for capturing relevant job data. Our attention will be focused on those methods used most often for human resource selection applications.

Recall, earlier we said that *one* principal role of job analysis in human resource selection is to assess job content so that knowledge, skills, abilities (KSAs) and other requisite employee specifications can be identified. It is these employee specifications that we want to translate into selection measures, such as, tests, interviews, and the like. Assuming our selection measures are valid, they, in turn, may be used for selection decision-making purposes. From this Job Analysis→ Employee Specifications→ Selection Instrument Development process, we can see that there are several points where judgment or inferences must be made. Exhibit 7.1 summarizes these inferential leaps.

At the first inference point, data collected from a job analysis are used to infer KSAs and other relevant employee specifications. A second inference point is then reached concerning the content of selection measures that reflect these identified specifications. An important goal is to minimize the chance of error at each inference point. Our resulting specifications will be

Exhibit 7.1 *Points of Inference in the Job Analysis→Employee Specifications→Selection Instrument Development Process*

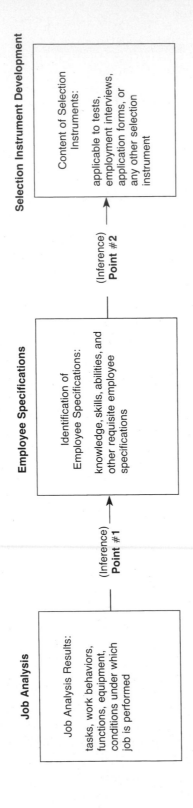

Job Analysis

Job Analysis Results:

tasks, work behaviors,
functions, equipment,
conditions under which
job is performed

(Inference)
Point #1

Employee Specifications

Identification of
Employee Specifications:

knowledge, skills, abilities, and
other requisite employee
specifications

(Inference)
Point #2

Selection Instrument Development

Content of Selection
Instruments:

applicable to tests,
employment interviews,
application forms, or
any other selection
instrument

useful only to the extent that our inferences are accurate and complete. If our inferences are wrong, our selection measures will be useless for predicting successful job performance.

Obviously, the process depends on the data derived initially from the job analysis. If these data are incomplete, inaccurate, or otherwise faulty, subsequent judgments based on these data will be incorrect. In the end, we will have an inappropriate, invalid, perhaps illegal selection device. The point is, we must be careful in our choice of methods for collecting job information.

A Categorization of Job Analysis Methods

Various systems have been used to classify methods for collecting job information. Dichotomies such as qualitative vs. quantitative, structured vs. unstructured, subjective vs. objective have been proposed for categorizing the various techniques. For our purposes, the distinction between *work-oriented* and *worker-oriented* methods seems most useful. As we will see in the next chapter, each of these types of methods has important implications for the ways in which employee specifications are derived from job analysis data.

Work-oriented job analysis deals with a description of the various work activities performed on a job. Emphasis is generally on what is accomplished by the worker, such as "codes data" or "records customer complaints."[1] The product of these methods is the description and characterization (in terms of ratings such as frequency, importance, and difficulty) of tasks or job duties. From these task descriptions, employee specifications are then inferred. The basis for all work-oriented job analysis techniques is the *task.*

Whereas work-oriented methods tend to focus on observable tasks and job activities, *worker-oriented analyses examine the attributes or behaviors required of the worker to perform a job.* The product of these methods is the importance of KSAs and other attributes required for effective job performance.[2]

Although we have suggested using work vs. worker orientation as a basis for classifying job analysis methods, the distinction is not always clear. Some techniques, such as the job analysis interview, can elicit both types of information. In addition, one approach is not necessarily better than the other. The decision of which to use will depend upon many factors, for example the purpose of the analysis, its cost, and the availability of trained personnel. Both forms are legally acceptable (assuming they are appropriately applied), so particular circumstances will determine which approach to use.

A Survey of Job Analysis Methods

We have divided our review of specific job analysis methods into two parts. The first part, presented in this chapter, covers the following three job analysis methods: (a) the job analysis interview, (b) the job analysis questionnaire, and (c) the Position Analysis Questionnaire (PAQ). The second part, found in the Appendix to this chapter, focuses on the following additional five techniques: (a) Comprehensive Occupational Data Analysis Program (CO-

DAP), (b) Guidelines Oriented Job Analysis (GOJA), (c) Iowa Merit Employment Systems (IMES), (d) Functional Job Analysis (FJA), and (e) Job Element Method (JEM).

This chapter will provide the reader with a basic description of three major forms of job analysis methods used in human resource selection applications. The reader interested in some other methods that are available, can refer to the Appendix for this information.

In both sections we describe each technique, its application, and its advantages and disadvantages. We do not advocate one particular technique to the exclusion of others. There are many methods available to the user; omission of a specific one should not be interpreted as a condemnation of it. We want to concentrate in this book on those methods that seem to be most popular in human resource selection practice. A total of eight methods are reviewed. With the exception of the job analysis interview and job analysis questionnaire, all represent specific job analysis systems and involve particular data collection/analysis procedures. As all of these systems depend on either a questionnaire or interview for collecting information, we begin with a description of these general methods (interviews and questionnaires) and then move to one specific method, the Position Analysis Questionnaire.

The Job Analysis Interview

Description

The interview is one of the most frequently used methods of job analysis, capable of meeting a wide array of purposes.[3] Essentially, a job analysis interview consists of a trained analyst asking questions of supervisors and incumbents about the duties and responsibilities; knowledge, skills, and abilities required; equipment; and/or conditions of employment for a job or class of jobs.

Job analysis data collected through interviews are typically obtained through group or individual interviews with incumbents or supervisors. A key assumption of the method is that participants are thoroughly familiar with the job being studied. Large groups of incumbents may be used when it is certain that all incumbents are performing the same major activities. Supervisory groups are usually employed in order to verify incumbent information and to provide information unavailable to employees in the job.

The interview can be applied to a variety of jobs ranging from those whose activities are basically physical in nature, such as a laborer's, to those whose activities are primarily mental, such as a manager's. Since incumbents are in the best position to be thoroughly familiar with their jobs, the interview makes it possible to identify activities that may go unobserved or occur over long time periods.

Certainly, there are numerous approaches that could be taken in phrasing and posing questions in an interview. No one method may be suitable for all cases. Exhibit 7.2 presents a sample job interview schedule that asks for

---

Exhibit 7.2 *An Example of a Typical Job Analysis Interview Schedule (Abbreviated) for Use with an Incumbent*

Name of Employee _____ Payroll Title _____
Job Analyst _____ Department _____

Important Job Tasks

1. Describe your job in terms of what you do.
2. How do you do it? Do you use special tools, equipment, or other sources of aid? If so, list the names of the principal tools, equipment, or sources of aid you use.
3. Of the major tasks in your job, how much time does it take to do each one? How often do you perform each task in a day, week, or month?

Knowledge, Skills, and Abilities Required

What does it take to perform each task in terms of the following:

1. Knowledge required

   a. What subject matter areas are covered by each task?
   b. What facts or principles must you have an acquaintance with or understand in these subject matter areas?
   c. Describe the level, degree, and breadth of knowledge required in these areas or subjects.

2. Skills required

   a. What activities must you perform with ease and precision?
   b. What are the manual skills that are required to operate machines, vehicles, equipment, or to use tools?

3. Abilities Required

   a. What is the nature and level of language ability, written or oral, required of you on the job? Are there complex oral or written ideas involved in performing the task, or simple instructional materials?
   b. What mathematical ability must you have?
   c. What reasoning or problem solving ability must you have?
   d. What instructions must you follow? Are they simple, detailed, involved, abstract?
   e. What interpersonal abilities are required? What supervisory or managing abilities are required?
   f. What physical abilities such as strength, coordination, visual acuity must you have?

Physical Activities

Describe the frequency and degree to which you are engaged in such activities as: pulling, pushing, throwing, carrying, kneeling, sitting, running, crawling, reaching, climbing.

Environmental Conditions

Describe the frequency and degree to which you will encounter working conditions such as these: cramped quarters, moving objects, vibration, inadequate ventilation.

Typical Work Incidents

Describe the frequency and degree to which you are doing the following:
a. Working in situations involving the interpretation of feelings, ideas, or facts in terms of personal viewpoint.
b. Influencing people in their opinions, attitudes, or judgments about ideas or things.
c. Working with people beyond giving and receiving instructions.

(continued)

Exhibit 7.2   (continued)

d. Performing repetitive work, or continuously performing the same work.
e. Performing under stress when confronted with emergency, critical, unusual, or dangerous situations; or in situations in which work speed and sustained attention are make-and-break aspects of the job.
f. Performing a variety of duties often changing from one task to another of a different nature without loss of efficiency or composure.
g. Working under hazardous conditions that may result in: violence, loss of bodily members, burns, bruises, cuts, impairment of senses, collapse, fractures, electric shock.

Records and Reports

What records or reports do you prepare as part of your job?

Source of Job Information

What is the principal source for instructions you receive on how to do your job? (For example, oral directions or written specifications.)

Supervisory Responsibility

1. How many employees are directly under your supervision?
2. Do you have full authority to assign work; correct and discipline; recommend pay increases, transfers, promotions, and discharge for these employees?

Other

Are there any additional elements about your job that would help me better understand what you do? If so, please describe them.

---

data in a wide variety of areas useful for characterizing a job. Again, the schedule is just one example of a means for systematically recording interview data.

An Example

An approach adopted by the U.S. Office of Personnel Management (formerly the U.S. Civil Service Commission) is one possibility when an interview is being used to collect job data.[4] The key initial step in characterizing a job with this interview procedure is the identification of critical job tasks. Once identified, each task is described in terms of factors such as knowledge, skills, and abilities required for task performance as well as environmental conditions surrounding task performance. Because of the importance of the task to the interview method, it may be helpful to review how job tasks are analyzed and structured with this method. After all, it is the task statement from which worker specifications are ultimately developed.

Task statements are written so that each shows:

1. What the worker does, by using a specific action verb which introduces the task statement

2. To whom or what he or she does it, by stating the object of the verb

3. What is produced, by expressing the expected output of the action

4. What materials, tools, procedures, or equipment are used[5]

Using these task characteristics, let's see how they are applied in an actual interview context to develop appropriate task statements.

Suppose, for example, an analyst is reviewing the job of welfare eligibility examiner. Assume further that background and supplementary data have been obtained from the incumbent. The interviewer asks the respondent to describe his or her job in terms of what is done, how, for what purpose, and using what equipment or tools. The interviewee then describes the job as follows:

> I interview applicants for food stamps — ask the applicants all the pertinent questions that will help to determine their eligibility. For example, are they working part time, receiving other assistance, etc.
>
> To carry out the job I have to interpret regulations, policies, and actually make decisions about eligibility. Some applicants are referred to other assistance units. Some applicants need detailed explanations of policies at a level they can understand, to avoid their reacting unpleasantly over a decision. They also get advice about their appeal rights from me. I visit homes to evaluate a client's circumstances and make determinations. I verify what the client has said on an application: household composition, shelter arrangements, income, etc. This helps me determine whether the food stamp costs have been correctly or incorrectly determined.
>
> At times, I work in outreach centers and homes of applicants to make determinations. I make personal appearances at high schools, colleges, and civic organizations to outline and explain the food stamp program.[6]

Following these comments, the analyst then uses the task statement criteria listed earlier to produce task statements representing important task activities. Table 7.1 summarizes the classification of content for one important task. Once classified, the content is rewritten to produce an easy-to-read, understandable statement. The goal of the rewriting process is to produce task statements that can be understood by persons unfamiliar with the job. For example, the task content classified in Table 7.1 could be rewritten as follows:

1. Asks client questions, listens, and records answers on standard eligibility form, using knowledge of interviewing techniques and eligibility criteria in order to gather information from which client's eligibility for food stamps can be determined.[7]

If the analyst follows through with the above process, six to twelve important task statements are typically identified. From the interview response given earlier, additional tasks might include the following:

Table 7.1   Classification of Interview Content to Develop a Task Statement

Performs What Action? (Verb)	To Whom or What? (Object of Verb)	To Produce What? (Expected Output)	Using What Tools, Equipment, Work Aids, Processes?
Asks Questions Listens Records Answers	To/of Applicant on Eligibility Form	In Order to Determine Eligibility	Eligibility Form Eligibility Criteria in Manual Interviewing Techniques

Source: U.S. Civil Service Commission, *Job Analysis: Developing and Documenting Data* (Washington, D.C.: Government Printing Office, 1973), p. 6.

2. Determines eligibility of applicant in order to complete client's application for food stamps using regulatory policies as a guide.

3. Decides upon and describes other agencies available for client to contact in order to assist and refer client to appropriate community resources using worker's knowledge of resources available and knowledge of client's needs.

4. Explains policies and regulations appropriate to applicant's case in order to inform applicants of their status with regard to agency's regulations and policies.

5. Evaluates information gained from home visit, interview, and observation in order to decide if home conditions are consistent with original application, using original application and agency's housing standards as guide.

6. Meets with, talks to, answers questions, and discusses with members of high schools, colleges, and civic organizations in order to outline and explain food stamp program using knowledge and experience of food stamp program.[8]

After the important job tasks have been stated, the analyst then characterizes each statement in terms of frequency of performance; knowledge, skills, and abilities required; physical activities required; environmental conditions; and other factors thought to be important to task performance. Questions such as those in the sample interview schedule can be used to make these determinations for each task. An illustration may help to clarify the task characterization process. For the moment, let's reexamine the second task identified in the study of welfare eligibility examiner. The task was stated as follows: "Determines eligibility of applicant in order to complete client's application for food stamps using regulatory policies as a guide." The description of the task using the interview schedule might be made as shown in Exhibit 7.3. This same process is then carried out for each task statement.

Exhibit 7.3   *Characterization of a Selected Job Task*
of the Job of Welfare Eligibility Examiner

Task 2:

Determines eligibility of applicant in order to complete client's application for food stamps using regulatory policies as a guide.

<u>Task Characterization</u>

Knowledge Required:

1. Knowledge of contents and meaning of items on standard application form
2. Knowledge of Social-Health Services food stamp regulatory policies
3. Knowledge of statutes relating to Social-Health Services food stamp program

Skills Required:

None

Abilities Required:

1. Ability to read and understand complex instructions such as regulatory policies
2. Ability to read and understand a variety of procedural instructions, written and oral, and convert these to proper actions
3. Ability to use simple arithmetic—addition and subtraction
4. Ability to translate requirements into language appropriate to laypersons

Physical Activities:

Sedentary

Environmental Conditions:

None

Typical Work Incidents:

Working with people beyond giving and receiving instructions

Interest Areas:

1. Communication of data
2. Business contact with people
3. Working for the presumed good of people

Source: U.S. Civil Service Commission, *Job Analysis: Developing and Documenting Data* (Washington, D.C.: Government Printing Office, 1973), pp. 13–14.

In the end, we should have a clearer picture of the demands, activities, and conditions of employment of the job being studied.

Guidelines for Use

At the conclusion of the interview, the analyst should attempt to verify the data collected. Verification may be obtained by reviewing the job analysis results with the immediate supervisor(s) of the incumbent(s) interviewed.

The success of the interview as a job analysis technique depends, to a large extent, upon the skill of the interviewer. A skilled interviewer may be able to tease out job information that may go undetected by other forms of analysis. To enhance the likelihood of success in using the technique, certain steps should be taken. Some suggestions offered by the *Handbook for Analyzing Jobs* for improving the chance of success in using the interview are as follows:

Opening the Interview

1. Put the worker at ease by learning his (or her) name in advance, introducing yourself, and discussing general and pleasant topics long enough to establish rapport. Be at ease.
2. Make the purpose of the interview clear by explaining why the interview was scheduled, what is expected to be accomplished, and how the worker's cooperation will help in the production of occupational analysis tools used for placement and counseling.
3. Encourage the worker to talk by always being courteous and showing a sincere interest in what he (or she) says.

Steering the Interview

1. Help the worker to think and talk according to the logical sequence of the duties performed. If duties are not performed in a regular order, ask the worker to describe the duties in a functional manner by taking the most important activity first, the second most important next, and so forth. Request the worker to describe the infrequent duties of his (or her) job, ones that are not part of his (or her) regular activities, such as the occasional setup of a machine, occasional repairs, or infrequent reports. . . .
2. Allow the worker sufficient time to answer each question and to formulate an answer. He (or she) should be asked only one question at a time.
3. Phrase questions carefully, so that the answers will be more than 'yes' or 'no'.
4. Leading questions should be avoided. . . .
5. Conduct the interview in plain, easily understood language. . . .
6. Control the interview with respect to the economic use of time and adherence to subject matter. For example, when the interviewee strays from the subject, a good technique for bringing him (or her) back to the point is to summarize the data collected up to that point.
7. The interview should be conducted patiently and with consideration for any nervousness or lack of ease on the part of the worker.

Closing the Interview

1. Summarize the information obtained from the worker, indicating the major duties performed and the details concerning each of the duties.
2. Close the interview on a friendly note.

Miscellaneous Do's and Don'ts for Interviews

1. Do not take issue with the worker's statements.
2. Do not show any partiality to grievances or conflicts concerning the employer-employee relations.
3. Do not show any interest in the wage classification of the job. . . .
4. Do not 'talk down' to the worker.
5. Do not permit yourself to be influenced by your personal likes and dislikes.
6. Be impersonal. Do not be critical or attempt to suggest any changes or improvements in organization or methods of work.
7. Talk to the worker only with permission of her or his supervisor.
8. Verify job data, especially technical or trade terminology, with foreman or department head.
9. Verify complete analysis with proper official.[9]

Limitations of the Job Analysis Interview

The interview is certainly one option for collecting job data. However, it has its limitations. When used as the principal data source in the context of selection, there is a question as to whether it will provide the detail and depth of information needed for developing worker specifications. If thorough documentation is not collected as these interviews are conducted, important legal requirements of job analysis information are likely to go unmet. The skill and procedures used by the individual analyst principally determine the utility of the interview.

In addition, there are other limitations. Unless group interviews can be conducted, the technique requires a great deal of time and may not be cost efficient if many jobs need to be studied. Depending upon the interviewee and the type of job being reviewed, an interviewer may literally be required to track through an entire job in specific detail. Such a process is not only expensive but may require a highly-skilled interviewer to identify the needed content.

Another major problem is that the technique may be plagued with distortion of information. Wayne Cascio has noted that if interviewees believe it to be beneficial (for example, leading to an increase in wages), they may exaggerate their activities and responsibilities to reflect a more complex job.[10] It can be quite difficult to identify distorted job information. Verification from the supervisor or other incumbents can be used as a check. But, comparisons across subjective data are difficult and expensive to make.

In general, a job analysis interview should not be relied upon as the sole or, in some cases, even the principal method when the analysis is being conducted for selection purposes. When employed as a supplementary source, however, interview data can be helpful. For example, interviews can be used to identify content for other job analysis methods, such as task analysis inventories, or for clarifying responses to other methods.

The Job Analysis Questionnaire

Description

The job analysis questionnaire has been proposed as a means for dealing with some of the problems of the job analysis interview (which suffers from lack of standardization of collected data and limited possibilities for coverage of large numbers of respondents). This analysis method consists of a standardized questionnaire listing job functions, tasks, activities, or incumbent characteristics that a respondent either checks or rates using a rating scale. There are many forms of job analysis questionnaires, but they tend to fall into one of two classes: (a) *prefabricated* or existing measures, or (b) *tailored* questionnaires developed for a specific job. Prefabricated questionnaires are constructed for use with a variety of jobs (for instance, McCormick, Jeanneret, and Mecham's *Position Analysis Questionnaire;*[11] Baehr, Lonergan, and Potkay's *Work Elements Inventory;*[12] Cunningham's *Occupation Analysis Inventory*[13]) or with a family of jobs (for example, Tornow and Pinto's *Management Position Description Questionnaire;*[14] Hemphill's *Executive Position Description Questionnaire;*[15] and Lawshe's *Clerical Task Inventory*[16]). Existing job analysis inventories consist of a preestablished set of items that respondents answer using a rating scale. In contrast, tailored measures are typically prepared by an organization (or its consultants) for application to a *specific* job. Like prefabricated instruments, these questionnaires also include tasks or other job elements to be checked or rated by a respondent. The important distinction between these two types of measures is the job orientation of the items to be judged. Prefabricated job analysis questionnaires consist of existing content suitable for many jobs; tailored questionnaires contain specifically developed items directed toward one or a small number of jobs. Since we will be discussing prefabricated measure (the PAQ) later in this chapter, we want to turn our attention now toward one particular type of tailored job analysis questionnaire. That type is the *task analysis inventory.*

The Task Analysis Inventory

A task analysis inventory is a questionnaire listing a large number of tasks (100 or more is not unusual) for which respondents make some form of judgment. Usually, these judgments are ratings given by respondents using a rating scale.

Because many different tasks may exist in any job, this type of job analysis questionnaire is typically directed toward only one job or a class of very similar jobs. Most often, the inventory is intended for use by incumbents. Nevertheless, supervisors and observers can use it assuming they are knowledgeable about the job being studied.

Historically, the method has been widely used in military settings, in particular, by the U.S. Air Force. Investigators such as Christal, Madden,

Morsh, and their associates at the Human Resources Laboratory at Lackland Air Force Base, Texas, are largely responsible for much of our knowledge about task inventories. Although the origin of task inventories may be traced to the military, their use for selection purposes by both public and private employers has grown substantially. One important reason for the increasing use of these inventories is that many employers have now adopted a content validation strategy for selection measures for which the inventories are particularly helpful.

The Nature of Task Inventories   Exhibit 7.4 presents a condensed version of a typical task analysis inventory. The inventory shown is one used to analyze various tasks associated with the job of personnel analyst. Since most inventories are similar to the one exhibited, we want to use it to point out two important characteristics: (a) the *phrasing of tasks* to be rated and (b) the use of a *rating scale* for judging the tasks. Most task inventories share these characteristics.

First, we see that the item being judged is a *task*. If we compare the

---

Exhibit 7.4   *A Condensed Example of a Task Analysis Inventory for the Job of Personnel Analyst*

Directions: We are interested in knowing more about your job. Below is listed a number of tasks you may perform on your job. Using the rating scales given below, rate each task as to (a) how *frequently* you perform it and (b) how *important* it is for newly-hired workers in a job like yours to be able to perform this task when they *first* begin work. Read each task and then place your rating in the two spaces to the right of each task.

Frequency of Performance	Importance for Newly-Hired
1 = Not Performed at All	1 = Not Performed at All
2 = Seldom	2 = Somewhat Important
3 = Occasionally	3 = Moderately Important
4 = Frequently	4 = Very Important
5 = Almost All of the Time	5 = Extremely Important

Task	Frequency of Performance	Importance for Newly-Hired
1. Prepare job descriptions for secretarial jobs.	[ ]	[ ]
2. Check file folders for disposition of health and dental records.	[ ]	[ ]
3. Initiate request for identification cards from terminated personnel.	[ ]	[ ]
4. Describe company policies to newly-hired employees.	[ ]	[ ]
5. Write computer programs in BASIC to analyze personnel absenteeism and turnover data.	[ ]	[ ]
.	.	.
.	.	.
.	.	.
105. Plan and develop training programs for newly-hired clerical personnel.	[ ]	[ ]

phrasing of the tasks shown in Exhibit 7.4 with those developed by the Office of Personnel Management interview procedure discussed earlier for the job of welfare eligibility examiner, we will find that the two sets of tasks differ. From our comparison, we see that the task statements developed previously appear to be more complex. Tasks that were identified under the interview procedure described what was done as well as the results of those actions. Work aids, materials, methods, and other requirements of a job incumbent were noted. In contrast, we find in our task inventory example that the tasks are not as fully developed. As Frank Sistrunk and Philip Smith have noted, most task statements are concerned with "what" gets done. Tasks, as listed in questionnaires, usually give no information on the situation surrounding the activity. On the other hand, tasks developed by other job analysis methods (for example, the Office of Personnel Management interview, Functional Job Analysis) usually provide information on "what," "how," and "why."[17]

Another important characteristic of any task inventory is the response scale used by the respondent to judge the given tasks. A response scale provides a continuum or range of options (most often consisting of five to seven steps) that a respondent can use to express his or her perceptions. Of the options provided, numerical codes are used to define some degree of a respondent's views. For example, frequency of task performance is an often used scale. One of several ways of assessing frequency of task performance on a response scale is as follows:

What is the frequency of task performance per week?

0 = Task not performed at all
1 = One time each week
2 = Two times each week
3 = Three times each week
4 = Four or more times each week

The above illustration is just one means of phrasing frequency of task performance. Many other forms are possible and could be used. Regardless of the scale, the objective of a response scale is to identify how job tasks are different or similar in terms of the judgments given.

Morsh and Archer have identified two general classes of rating scales used in task analysis inventories. The first class is referred to as *primary rating factors* and is used to describe an incumbent's involvement with each task. The second class, *secondary rating factors,* focuses principally on the task itself rather than incumbent involvement with each task.[18] Table 7.2 summarizes some examples of the primary and secondary task rating factors. When used in an inventory, each factor is associated with a response scale. The response scale provides the degree to which a task is perceived to possess a rated characteristic. Various scales from the primary and secondary factors can be used (such as frequency of task performance and task criticality) for evaluating the job tasks. The ones chosen for use will depend on any number of

Table 7.2   *Possible Factors for Use in Rating Job Tasks*

Primary Rating Factors (relates to incumbent's task involvement)	Secondary Rating Factors (relates to task itself)
1. Task performance (whether a task is or is not performed) 2. Frequency of task performance 3. Time spent on task (per unit of time) 4. Relative time spent on task (time spent relative to other tasks) 5. Task as part-of-job 6. Degree of discretion (in deciding how and when to do task)	1. Task complexity 2. Task criticality 3. Task importance 4. Difficulty of learning task 5. Method of learning task 6. Experience needed for task performance 7. Amount of special training needed 8. Task difficulty 9. Time necessary to learn task 10. Consequences of failure to perform task

Source: Based on J. E. Morsh and W. B. Archer, *Procedural Guide for Conducting Occupational Surveys in the United States Air Force* (PRL-TR-67-11, AD-664 036) (Lackland Air Force Base, Tex.: Personnel Research Laboratory, Aerospace Medical Division, 1967), pp. 18–20.

issues, such as number of tasks to be rated, time available, capabilities of incumbents (for example, educational level, reading ability), purpose of the analysis, and complexity of the job (the more complex, the more scales needed to adequately assess the job).

Development of Task Inventories   Because most task inventories are aimed toward a specific job, they may have to be developed by the user. This process is time-consuming and often expensive. Access to previous inventories or analyses of the job in question as well as use of technical experts in job analysis and questionnaire development are important determinants of the cost and success of the method. For those organizations committed to the development and administration of a task inventory, McCormick has summarized the major steps.[19] Similarly, Morsh and Archer have offered a series of guidelines to be followed in preparing task statements.[20] Only some of the major guidelines have been chosen to be presented in Table 7.3. Basically, development of a task inventory should be carried out in a sequential fashion such as that outlined. There is no one "best" way. However, suggestions like those noted increase the chances that the resulting questionnaire will meet the objectives for which it is intended.

Once developed the inventory is ready for application. In discussing various aspects of administering task inventories, Christal makes several useful suggestions. First, he recommends that respondents' names and other identifying information be collected. Several reasons for using identifying information are that it (a) helps insure high-quality information, (b) is necessary if follow-up studies are going to be conducted, and (c) is useful when combined with personnel file data (such as scores on selection measures,

Table 7.3   *Summary Guidelines for Developing Task Analysis Inventories*

Sequential Steps for Developing Content of Task Inventories	Guidelines for Writing Task Items
1. Technical manuals, previous job analyses, and other job-related reports are reviewed for possible item content.	**When task items are identified, they should:**
2. Technical job experts (consultants, selected incumbents/supervisors) prepare lists of tasks known to be performed.	1. Characterize activities not skills or knowledge.
	2. Have an identifiable beginning and ending.
3. Tasks identified are reviewed for duplication, edited, and incorporated into an initial version of the inventory. Tasks are developed subject to task-writing guidelines.	3. Represent activities performed by an individual worker; not activities performed by different individuals.
	4. Have an identifiable output or consequence.
4. First draft is prepared and submitted to a panel of experts (or incumbents and/ or supervisors) for review.	5. Avoid extremes in phrasing activities; statements should not be too broad or too specific.
5. Panel of reviewers adds, deletes, or modifies tasks for developing another draft of the inventory.	6. Be developed by full-time inventory writers (preferable); supervisors/ incumbents should serve as technical advisors.
6. Steps 4 and 5 are repeated, using the same or similar panel, until an acceptable draft has been developed.	**When items are written, they should:**
7. Task inventory is then tested on a sample of respondents to whom the final version will be given.	1. Mean the same thing to all respondents.
	2. Be stated so that the rating scale to be used makes sense.
8. Appropriate modifications are made as needed.	3. Be stated so that the incumbent is understood to be the subject of the statement. The pronoun "I" should be implied. For example "(I) number all card boxes."
9. Steps 7 and 8 are repeated until a final, acceptable version is developed.	4. Be stated so that the verb is in the present tense.
	5. Use terms that are specific, familiar, and unambiguous.

Sources: Based on Ernest J. McCormick, "Job Information: Its Development and Applications," *ASPA Handbook of Personnel and Industrial Relations,* ed. Dale Yoder and Herbert G. Heneman (Washington, D.C.: BNA Books, 1979), p. 4–66; J. E. Morsh and W. B. Archer, *Procedural Guide for Conducting Occupational Surveys in the United States Air Force* (PRL-TR-67-11, AD-664 036) (Lackland Air Force Base, Tex.: Personnel Research Laboratory, Aerospace Medical Division, 1967), pp. 8–11

demographic characteristics). Second, he advocates administration to large numbers of incumbents since data reliability is improved. Finally, optical scanning sheets are recommended to minimize time, cost, and errors in coding and data entry.[21]

Applications of Task Analysis in Selection   When we use a task analysis inventory, we are attempting to define the principal tasks or activities that account for incumbents' performance on a given job. Since most jobs which we are interested in studying may be reasonably complex, long lists of tasks and accompanying rating scales may be one of the principal sources we will use to make the definition. Once the data have been collected, subsequent statistical analyses of the ratings can be used to isolate the most important or most critical aspects of the job. One possible analysis is to use indices (means, standard deviations, frequencies) created from the ratings and decision rules applied to these indices to define important tasks. For instance, let's look at a simple example. Assume for a moment that we have given a comprehensive task analysis inventory to a large sample of bank clerks. Among other judgments, the clerks were asked to use a seven-point rating scale (1 = Of No Importance to 7 = Of Major Importance) to judge each task. Analyses of the data were conducted and descriptive information obtained. We will use two of the numerous tasks listed to illustrate our point. Below are two example tasks and some associated descriptive statistics:

Task Statement	*Mean*	*Standard Deviation*	*% Employees Performing Task*
9. Use basic arithmetic to add, subtract, divide, and multiply monetary figures with decimals.	6.74	0.68	99.2
67. Recommend to customers investment account options for investing savings.	1.21	1.56	8.9

In deciding which tasks should be classified as being important to the job, we may select some *minimum* statistical criteria that a task must meet to be considered critical. As a possibility, we could set the following (in this example, arbitrary) cut-off points:

1. A task must receive a mean rating of 4.00 or higher (the higher the mean, the more important the task).

2. A task rating must have a standard deviation of 1.00 or lower (the lower the standard deviation, the greater the degree of agreement among incumbents in their task ratings).

3. Most (75 percent or more) incumbents must perform the task.

Using these standards, we would choose Task 9 and omit Task 67. The task "Use basic arithmetic to add, subtract, divide, and multiply monetary figures with decimals" would be added to other tasks that meet our evaluation criteria. These tasks would be deemed the most important ones that compose the job. Inferences concerning the content of selection measures would be based on the pool of tasks derived from application of these criteria to the task ratings.

Whatever the analyses used, the most important tasks are the basis on which inferences regarding the content of our selection device rests. The major idea behind the application of task analysis inventories is to define important job content. That determination can serve as the source of statements about requisite worker specifications and development or selection of devices for choosing among job applicants. In addition, the defined job content can also serve as one basis for applying specific validation models such as content validity.

Advantages and Disadvantages of Task Analysis   Any job analysis technique will have its own unique assets and limitations; task analysis is no different. On the positive side, task inventories offer an efficient means for collecting data from large numbers of incumbents. Additionally, task inventories lend themselves to quantifying job analysis data. Quantitative data are invaluable in analyzing jobs and determining core job components.

Yet, Wayne Cascio has pointed out some important problems with these inventories. Development of task inventories can be time-consuming and expensive. Motivation problems often become significant when inventories are long or complex. Ambiguities and questions that arise during administration of the inventory may not be addressed; whereas in a method like the interview, problems can be resolved as they come up. As these difficulties become magnified, one can expect the respondents to become less cooperative, with a concomitant decline in the quality of data collected.[22]

Yes, there are problems with task inventories. But when properly developed, administered, and analyzed, they offer a viable option for collecting job information.

In comparison to job analysis interview and questionnaire methods that can be adapted to a variety of uses, a number of specialized job analysis systems are available. In general, these systems advocate particular procedures, analyses, or forms for collecting job information. Most often, these systems are copyrighted and are available only from commercial vendors, consulting firms, or the developers themselves. Special training in application of these various systems is sometimes required. As with job analysis materials, formal preparation in use of a particular technique is often available from vendors or special consultants.

Developments in many of these systems have made them particularly promising for human resource selection applications. The remainder of this chapter will concentrate on one of these popular job analysis systems: the Position Analysis Questionnaire or PAQ. The Appendix at the end of this chapter contains descriptions of five other specific job analysis systems.

The Position Analysis Questionnaire (PAQ)

Of all job analysis methods that we will review, perhaps none has the research base and breadth of application that does the Position Analysis Questionnaire or PAQ.[23] Roughly 20 years of research have established the PAQ as one of the leading "off-the-shelf" or prefabricated measures of jobs currently available. Primarily, the PAQ was developed to produce a means for analyzing a wide spectrum of jobs. Because the questionnaire is worker-oriented, that is, it focuses on generalized worker behaviors describing how a job is done, the PAQ can be used for virtually any job. Because of its prominence in the field of job analysis, we will look closely at the nature and use of this questionnaire.

Description

The PAQ is a standardized, structured job analysis questionnaire containing 194 items or *elements*. Of this total, 187 items concern work activities while the remaining seven relate to compensation issues. These elements are *not* task statements. Rather, they represent *general human behaviors involved in work*. An analyst must decide if each of the elements applies to the job under study. If it does, then a rating scale is used to indicate the degree to which that element applies to the job.

Items on the PAQ are organized into six basic divisions or sections. These divisions and a definition are as follows:

1. *Information Input* — Where and how an incumbent gets information needed to perform the job.

2. *Mental Processes* — The reasoning, decision making, planning, and information processing activities that are involved in performing the job.

3. *Work Output* — The physical activities, tools, and devices used by the worker to perform the job.

4. *Relationships with Other Persons* — The relationships with other people that are required in performing the job.

5. *Job Context* — The physical and social contexts where the work is performed.

6. *Other Characteristics* — The activities, conditions, and characteristics other than those described that are relevant to the job.[24]

An example of several PAQ elements dealing with *Work Output* activities is shown in Exhibit 7.5.

Rating scales are used in the PAQ for determining the extent to which the 194 elements are relevant to the job under study. Six different types of scales are used:

1. *Extent of Use* — Degree to which an element is used by the worker

2. *Amount of Time* — Proportion of time spent doing something

---

Exhibit 7.5   *An Example of Items from the Position Analysis Questionnaire (PAQ)*

---

3 WORK OUTPUT
3.1 Use of Devices and Equipment
3.1.1 Hand-held Tools or Instruments

Consider in this category those devices which are used to move or modify workpieces, materials, products, or objects. Do not consider measuring devices here.

Code Important to This Job (1)
N Does not apply
1 Very Minor
2 Low
3 Average
4 High
5 Extreme

Manually powered

50 _____ Precision tools/instruments (that is, tools or instruments powered by the user to perform very accurate or precise operations, for example, the use of engraver's tools, watchmaker's tools, surgical instruments, etc.)
51 _____ Nonprecision tools/instruments (tools or instruments powered by the user to perform operations not requiring great accuracy or precision, for example, hammers, wrenches, trowels, knives, scissors, chisels, putty knives, strainers, hand grease guns, etc. Do not include long-handled tools here.)
52 _____ Long-handled tools (hoes, rakes, shovels, picks, axes, brooms, mops, etc.)
53 _____ Handling devices/tools (tongs, ladles, dippers, forcepts, etc., used for moving or handling objects and materials; do not include here protective gear such as asbestos gloves, etc.)

Powered (manually controlled or directed devices using an energy source such as electricity, compressed air, fuel, hydraulic fluid, etc., in which the component part which accomplishes the modification is hand-held, such as dentist drills, welding equipment, etc., as well as devices small enough to be entirely hand-held)

54 _____ Precision tools/instruments (hand-held powered tools or instruments used to perform operations requiring great accuracy or precision, such as small dentist drills, or laboratory equipment used for especially accurate or fine work)
55 _____ Nonprecision tools/instruments (hand-held, energy-powered tools or instruments used to perform operations not requiring great accuracy or precision, for example, ordinary power saws, large sanders, clippers, hedge trimmers, etc., and related devices such as electric soldering irons, spray guns or nozzles, welding equipment, etc.)

Source: Ernest J. McCormick, P. R. Janneret, and Robert C. Mecham, *Position Analysis Questionnaire,* © 1969 by Purdue Research Foundation, West Lafayette, Ind. 47907. Reprinted with permission.

---

3. *Importance to This Job* — Importance of an activity specified by the item in performing the job
4. *Possibility of Occurrence* — Degree to which there is a possibility of physical hazards on the job
5. *Applicability* — Whether an item applies to the job or not
6. *Special Code* — Special rating scales used with a particular item on the PAQ[25]

On the whole, each of the rating scales consists of six categories. For example, the scale "Importance to This Job" is composed of the following rating points:

N = Does Not Apply
1 = Very Minor
2 = Low
3 = Average
4 = High
5 = Extreme

The scale, "Applicability" is a dichotomous one where the job analyst simply indicates N ("Does Not Apply") or 1 ("Does Apply").

The PAQ has served a variety of purposes. For the most part, the instrument has been used for (a) predicting aptitude requirements for jobs, (b) evaluating jobs and setting compensation rates, or (c) classifying jobs. Recently, the measure has been applied to other uses as well, such as grouping jobs into families, developing personnel evaluation systems, predicting stress associated with various jobs, and as an element in developing career planning systems.

Application

Actual application of the PAQ can be thought of as a four-step sequence of activities. Although the specific steps may vary somewhat from one administration to the next, the sequence to be described below explains most PAQ application activities.[26]

Selecting and Training Agents to Analyze Jobs   Various options are available for choosing agents to collect PAQ data. Either one or a combination of three groups of individuals are likely to be used from inside the organization to provide job information. These groups consist of (a) trained job analysts, (b) job incumbents, and (c) job supervisors. Job analysts will probably be the best prepared to use the PAQ. If job incumbents or supervisors are utilized, they should be individuals who know the job being studied (say, for example, six months or more job experience) and have high reading and verbal skills. (Interviewing *and* observational skills may also be required.) Most often, these incumbents are likely to be white-collar rather than operative or blue-collar personnel. Furthermore, when incumbents are being used as analysts, it is recommended that there be a group session with a discussion leader who can interpret the PAQ items in terms related to the job studied. Three to four incumbents plus the supervisor, working independently, are suggested for completing PAQs for a given job. The use of multiple analysts permits an examination of interanalyst job rating reliability, that is, the extent to which analysts agree in their analyses of a job.

Selecting Persons to Provide Job Information   Once the type of analyst has been chosen, individuals who will provide job information must be identified. These persons are usually incumbents who have sufficient experience to know the job. Supervisors can also be employed, assuming they have had relevant and recent experience on the job in question. Since persons chosen may be describing their jobs orally, they should be willing and able to express themselves verbally. Whatever the type of analyst used, great care should be exercised in the selection. The chosen individuals will literally determine the quality and value of the data obtained.

Analyzing the Jobs Selected   The PAQ can be completed by an analyst's observing the job or interviewing a selected incumbent or supervisor. It may also be completed by an incumbent or supervisor serving as a respondent. The particular method chosen (interview, observation, self-report question-naire) will depend to a large degree on the type of analyst selected for data collection.

Since the PAQ was developed to analyze a wide variety of jobs, some items will necessarily apply to some jobs and not to others. Thus, even though the questionnaire appears long, by design only one-third to one-half of the items will be answered for most jobs. Time requirements for PAQ completion may range from less than one hour for a trained analyst up to three hours for analyses involving interviews or group PAQ administration sessions.

Analyzing PAQ Data   Because empirical data are collected with the PAQ, a wide variety of analyses are available. These can range from simple tabula-tions to more complex analyses. For example, one analysis that is useful in human resource selection is to determine the basic nature of a job in terms of the dimensions of work activity measured by the PAQ. Several studies have found that the PAQ measures 32 specific and 13 overall dimensions of jobs.[27] Operational definitions of these dimensions are listed in Table 7.4. It is possible to score any job analyzed in terms of these dimensions. Once scored, a profile of job content can be created and used to characterize the job ana-lyzed. Thus, the PAQ makes it possible to depict a job quantitatively in terms of the job dimension scores. And, as we will discuss in Chapter 8, these dimension scores can then be employed to provide a direct estimation of worker aptitude requirements of jobs.

Whatever analyses are chosen, special arrangements for analysis will more than likely have to be made. These arrangements are made through PAQ Services, Inc. of Logan, Utah, a firm organized to distribute the PAQ and to conduct computer analyses and research on the method.

Advantages and Disadvantages

Wayne Cascio has noted two important problems with the PAQ. First, the reading level required by the instrument is that of a college graduate. There-fore, the questionnaire should not be used with analysts having reading skills

Table 7.4   *Operational Definitions of the Job Dimensions of the Position Analysis Questionnaire (PAQ)*

Specific Dimensions

Division 1: Information Input

1. Interpreting what is sensed
2. Using various sources of information
3. Watching devices/materials for information
4. Evaluating/judging what is sensed
5. Being aware of environmental conditions
6. Using various senses

Division 2: Mental Processes

7. Making decisions
8. Processing information

Division 3: Work Output

9. Using machines/tools/equipment
10. Performing activities requiring general body movements
11. Controlling machines/processes
12. Performing skilled/technical activities
13. Performing controlled manual/related activities
14. Using miscellaneous equipment/devices
15. Performing handling/related manual activities
16. General physical coordination

Division 4: Relationships With Other Persons

17. Communicating judgments/related information
18. Engaging in general personal contacts
19. Performing supervisory/coordination/related activities
20. Exchanging job-related information
21. Public/related personal contacts

Division 5: Job Context

22. Being in a stressful/unpleasant environment
23. Engaging in personally demanding situations
24. Being in hazardous job situations

Division 6: Other Job Characteristics

25. Working nontypical vs. day schedule
26. Working in businesslike situations
27. Wearing optional vs. specified apparel
28. Being paid on a variable vs. salary basis
29. Working on a regular vs. irregular schedule
30. Working under job-demanding circumstances
31. Performing structured vs. unstructured work
32. Being alert to changing conditions

Overall Dimensions

33. Having decision, communicating, and general responsibilities
34. Operating machines/equipment
35. Performing clerical/related activities
36. Performing technical/related activities
37. Performing service/related activities
38. Working regular day vs. other work schedules
39. Performing routine/repetitive activities
40. Being aware of work environment
41. Engaging in physical activities
42. Supervising/coordinating other personnel
43. Public/customer/related contacts
44. Working in an unpleasant/hazardous/demanding/environment
45. Unnamed

801 (752) 5698

Source: Ernest J. McCormick, Robert C. Mecham, and P. R. Jeanneret, *Position Analysis Questionnaire Technical Manual (System II)* (Logan, Utah: PAQ Services, Inc., 1977), pp. 7–9. Used with permission.

below the college level. Second, the PAQ assesses basic work behaviors rather than the specific tasks of a job. As a consequence, behavioral similarities in jobs may mask actual task differences. For instance, Cascio cites a study by Arvey and Begalla who found that a police officer's job profile is quite similar to a housewife's because of the trouble-shooting and emergency-handling orientation common to both jobs.[28]

Because the PAQ does not focus on task activities, there are some purposes of job analysis that cannot be adequately served by the PAQ alone. For instance, job descriptions may characterize a job in terms of the specific activities performed. Since the PAQ does not cover actual task activities, other methods of job analysis would be required in order to develop job descriptions.

These disadvantages are certainly limitations on the use of the PAQ. Yet, the method has some clear assets. The PAQ provides a standardized means for collecting quantitative job data across a wide spectrum of jobs. Standardization helps to insure that different jobs are assessed in a similar fashion. Because quantitative, standardized information is collected, comparisons across many jobs can be made.

The PAQ has also been found to provide reliable and valid job data. The method is one of the few we have that has extensive reliability and validity data reported. Finally, estimation of worker aptitude requirements in jobs can be obtained from the PAQ. This particular capability can help to suggest for study the employee specifications that are so necessary in establishing a viable human resource selection program.

Supplementary Methods for Collecting Job Information

The eight job analysis methods discussed in this chapter and its appendix offer a variety of ways for collecting and analyzing job information. In addition to these methods, several other procedures are also available for retrieving job analysis data. For the most part, these methods are merely supplementary ways for collecting job data. They are concerned with the analysis and use of job information. Nevertheless, some users may find them helpful in particular situations.

Technical conferences are one possibility. These conferences are simply group interview sessions, designed to identify the characteristics of a specific job, conducted between a job analyst and knowledgeable supervisors. *Worker diaries* are another option. Here, job incumbents record their daily job activities using some form of log or diary. The *critical incidents* approach involves the development of a series of statements, based upon direct observation or memory, describing incidents of good and poor job performance. Critical incidents can provide very valuable information about important components of the job. These components can serve as a basis for developing descriptive information about a job, such as the content of a task inventory.

Work participation can also be used to obtain job information in some limited contexts. With this procedure, the job analyst performs the job. Thus, first-hand information is obtained about what characteristics and tasks compose the job. Only relatively simple jobs typically lend themselves to application of the work participation method. Finally, for jobs comprised principally of physical activities, *direct observation* can be an appropriate method. This particular technique is usually used in conjunction with one or more of the other methods discussed in the chapter or the Appendix.

Collection of Job Information: A Comparison of Methods

In the context of human resource selection, the *Uniform Guidelines* state that all human resource selection techniques should be demonstrated to be job related. One of the critical components of this demonstration is a systematic review of information about the job for which a selection method is to be used. As far as a particular job analysis method is concerned, the *Uniform Guidelines* leave open to choice the specific techniques that may be applied. The *Uniform Guidelines* specify that "any method of job analysis may be used if it provides the information required for the specific validation strategy."[29] Although this guide appears to be a flexible one, a potential user may be in a quandary in deciding among the various analysis methods. Unfortunately, little empirical research is available on the superiority of one method over another. As Edwin Cornelius, Theodore Carron, and Marianne Collins conclude, only a small amount of research has been conducted that compares the utility of various approaches.[30] Since some of these studies may have important implications for those using job analysis in human resource selection, we want to review several of them briefly.

Edward Levine, Ronald Ash, and Nell Bennett have completed the most comprehensive comparative investigation to date on selected job analysis methods. Sixty-four public sector personnel specialists were asked to analyze four job classifications (Accountant 1, Accountant 2, Mental Health Worker, Mental Health Technician) using four methods of job analysis (critical incidents, task analysis, PAQ, Job Elements). In addition to conducting the actual job analyses, the participants were asked (a) to rate each job analysis method in terms of selected attitudinal criteria such as, difficulty of use, clarity of results, utility for content validation purposes, adequacy for developing performance measures, and (b) to develop a selection test or examination plan based upon the job analysis results. A number of important findings were reported. With respect to users' attitudes toward the methods, the PAQ was judged less favorably than the other methods. Much of the negative attitudes concerning the PAQ seemed to be due to its non-job-specific language and difficult reading level. Further, the critical incidents method was favored by study participants for providing relevant information for developing performance measures. Job Elements was viewed more favorably than other methods as being appropriate for highlighting specific job components and for establishing content validity. In actual conduct of job analyses, the PAQ was the least expensive while critical incidents was the most expensive method. On the other hand, the four methods did not differ substantially in terms of time and costs for developing selection test examination plans.[31]

In a related study, Levine, Bennett, and Ash surveyed 106 personnel specialists employed in state and local governments concerning their attitudes toward job analysis methods. Job Elements and task analysis were employed by more respondents and viewed more positively than critical incidents or the PAQ. However, none of the methods was thought to completely satisfy the requirements for job analysis information in selection.[32]

Levine, Ash, Hall, and Sistrunk sought to determine how job analysts viewed the practicality of a variety of job analysis methods. A questionnaire survey of 93 job analysts (respondents were about equally distributed across colleges and universities, state and local governments, private businesses, and private consulting firms) resulted in several important method differences. The PAQ consistently received the highest ratings in terms of standardization, off-the-shelf availability, and reliability, while critical incidents and the Job Elements Method were among the lowest rated. Additionally, the PAQ was judged to require the least amount of respondent time to complete.[33]

Finally, George Hollenbeck and Walter Borman compared the results of two job analysis methods for the job of stockbroker at a national brokerage firm. One of these methods consisted of a job-oriented task analysis questionnaire administered to 581 brokers. The other approach was the critical incidents method where 300 critical performance behaviors were collected from 26 representatively-selected managers of stockbrokers. Comparative examination of the two sets of job data showed some similarities. However, to a large extent, the results produced were different. These method discrepancies led Hollenbeck and Borman to conclude that different methods may be suitable for different selection purposes. For example, they suggested that a task inventory is probably most appropriate for defining the important elements of performance (sometimes referred to as the "performance domain") in a job. Once the performance domain is defined, selection tests can be developed to resemble important task statements from the inventory. If the content of the tests has been mapped from the content of the job, the task analysis approach could be useful in supporting the content validity of a test. They also suggested that critical incidents might be more useful for establishing the personal attributes (knowledge, skills, and abilities) that account for success or failure on the job. Thus, this method might be most useful for defining the content of measures to be used in selection.[34]

Potential Usefulness of Methods

Although some users may wonder which job analysis method is best for personnel selection purposes, the answer is not as straightforward as one would like. For one thing, our research base concerning the utility of various approaches is far from complete. Many of our judgments about job analysis methods rest more on opinion than on fact. Second, any overall assessment must account for a variety of considerations (such as cost and ease-of-use) in making an evaluation. Some methods may be appropriate in light of some criteria while others may have more utility given other considerations. Even though we may not make an overall assessment, we can evaluate, in a limited way, selected job analysis methods in terms of specific factors. We will offer such an appraisal here.

Gary Brumback, Tania Romashko, Clifford Hahn, and Edwin Fleishman have proposed a series of criteria that should be considered in judging the potential usefulness of methods for collecting job information.[35] We have taken most of their considerations plus an additional one suggested by Frank Sistrunk and Philip Smith (cost of applying a method)[36] and one of our own (ease of use in selection device development) and evaluated each of the methods reviewed in the chapter and its appendix. Our evaluations are summarized in Table 7.5 and are discussed below. Before reviewing our evaluations, a cautionary comment should be made. Our assessments are based principally on subjective judgments. As we have noted, little objective data are available for assessing many of these techniques; the ratings shown come from our own as well as others' opinions. So, in studying the table, you should be aware that different users may hold different views about these methods. Regardless of the ratings given, the criteria provide some critical considerations that should be reviewed by any user contemplating application of a specific technique.

1. Currently Operational: *Has the method been tested and refined so that it is now operational and ready for use?*   Each of the methods reviewed in this chapter and its appendix has been tested and can be adopted for use. However, the fact that these methods are available should not be interpreted to mean that they are equally suitable for every user or selection purpose.

2. Off-the-Shelf: *Is the methodological instrument involved ready-made or must it first be designed and constructed?*   Only one method, the PAQ, can be considered an off-the-shelf method ready for application without requiring further research activities. Methods such as GOJA, IMES, or FJA are, in part, ready for use, but additional developments are necessary. These developments consist of specifying the tasks or job elements required in a specific job. Existing rating scales are then applied to the identified tasks or elements. Methods like the task inventory require the development of task content as well as associated rating scales for characterizing these tasks. Although it may appear that off-the-shelf measures are preferable, some writers (for example, Brumback et al.) have suggested that methods involving the determination of specific task content are more appropriate for selection purposes than those having ready-made content.[37] Thus, in some situations, methods utilizing tailored measures *may* be more desirable than those incorporating preexisting measures.

Table 7.5 *Summary Evaluation of Eight Job Analysis Methods*

Evaluation Factor	Interview	Task Inventory	Comprehensive Occupational Data Analysis Program (CODAP)	Guidelines Oriented Job Analysis (GOJA)	Iowa Merit Employment Systems Approach (IMES)	Functional Job Analysis (FJA)	Position Analysis Questionnaire (PAQ)	Job Element Method (JEM)
Currently Operational?	Yes	Yes	Yes	Yes	Yes	Yes	Yes	Yes
Off-the-Shelf?	No	No	No	In Part	In Part	In Part	Yes	In Part
Occupational Versatility?	High	Moderate/High	Moderate/High	High	Moderate/High	High	High	High
Standardization?	No	Yes	Yes	No	No	No	Yes	No
User/Respondent Acceptability?	High	Moderate/High	Moderate/High	High	Moderate/High	High	Low/Moderate	Moderate/High
Amount of Required Job Analyst Training?	Moderate	Low	Low	Low/Moderate	Moderate/High	High	Moderate	Moderate/High
Sample Size?	Small	Large	Large	Moderate	Small	Small	Small	Small
Suitability for Content Validity?	Low	High	Moderate	High	High	Moderate	Low	Low
Suitability for Criterion-Related Validity?	Low/Moderate	High	High	High	High	High	High	High
Reliability?	Unknown	High	High	Unknown	Moderate/High	High	High	Unknown
Utility in Developing Selection Measures?	Low	High	High	High	Moderate/High	Moderate	High	Moderate/High
Cost?	Moderate/High	Moderate/High	Moderate	High	Moderate/High	Moderate/High	Moderate/High	Low/Moderate

Source: Based on, in part, Gary B. Brumback, Tania Romashko, Clifford P. Hahn, and Edwin A. Fleishman, *Model Procedures for Job Analysis, Test Development and Validation* (Washington, D.C.: American Institutes for Research, 1974), pp. 102–107.

3. Occupational Versatility: *To what extent can the method be applied to a wide variety of jobs?* On the whole, the various techniques can be applied to a wide variety of jobs. However, those that focus principally on tasks may be limited to jobs where it is easy to describe task content. For instance, in jobs such as managerial ones, it may be difficult to completely describe their content using typical task statements. In such jobs, some activities, such as planning, are not easily described by task statements. Therefore, task-based questionnaires may not be as occupationally versatile as methods like the PAQ that deal with broader worker functions.

4. Standardization: *Is the method capable of producing norms, that is, does it have the capability of comparing data collected from different sources at different times?* Many of the methods that use small groups of analysts in collecting job information do not have the capability of producing norms. Brumback et al., point out that methods like the Job Elements approach are generally weak on this factor because different panels of subject matter experts are likely to produce different lists of job elements.[38]

5. User/Respondent Acceptability: *To what extent is the method including the various aspects of its application acceptable to respondents and users of the method?* Most of the job analysis methods are at least minimally acceptable. However, it seems task-based methods create problems for some respondents because of their length. In order to complete many of the data collection devices used in these methods, respondents are sometimes required to spend rather lengthy, tedious periods of time completing the appropriate materials. Most respondents would prefer briefer, easier types of measures. As will be recalled, Levine, Ash, and Bennett's research showed the PAQ as receiving some of the most unfavorable ratings by users among the four methods studied.[39] Other investigators have drawn different conclusions.[40] Given its basic nature, the PAQ will probably elicit the greatest diversity of opinion of any of the methods reviewed.

6. Required Amount of Job Analyst Training: *How much training must a job analyst receive in order to adequately apply the method?* FJA appears to require the highest level of training. The reason is that FJA places a premium on the identification and correct preparation of task statements. In order to apply FJA correctly, training is mandatory not only in task development but in applying FJA rating scales to the specified tasks.

Methods like IMES and Job Elements can also require moderate levels of analyst preparation. Since these two methods employ a specific sequence of activities to be performed by an analyst, one should be totally familiar with the steps required for application. Also, these methods involve group application; thus, an analyst must also be prepared to direct group meetings and conduct group job analyses.

7. Sample Size: *How many respondents or sources of information are required to produce dependable job analysis data?*   More than any other technique, the PAQ involves the fewest number of respondents, typically as few as four. The Job Elements method is also efficient in this respect, requiring approximately six to eight participants. These methods contrast with ones such as the task inventory that may involve hundreds of respondents. The questions facing users of methods like the PAQ and Job Elements are how reliable are these few judges and how generalizable are the results. Unless careful choices are made in selecting job analysts to use such methods, statistical, and, possibly, legal challenges may be difficult to meet.

8. Suitability for Content Validity: *Will the method support the requirements for establishing content validity of a selection measure?*   In content validity, a selection measure is supported by showing that it representatively samples significant aspects of a relevant job. Since the PAQ and Job Elements procedures place such little emphasis on specific tasks completed on a job, we feel that these methods should not be used in content validation research. (Recent modifications have been offered by Primoff, Clark, and Caplan to the Job Elements procedure in order to make it more suitable for content validation research.[41] However, these changes may not be completely satisfactory.) Unless the job interview focuses specifically on task data, it alone should not be relied upon as well. As we saw in Chapter 5, content validation requires that specific information be collected about tasks on a job. The interview, PAQ, and Job Elements generally do not meet these requirements.

9. Suitability for Criterion-Related Validity: *Will the method support the requirements for establishing criterion-related validity of a selection measure?*   In criterion-related validity, a selection procedure is supported by establishing a statistical relationship between scores on a selection measure and measures of job performance. In general, most of the methods are useful in identifying content of selection measures and criteria of job performance that can be used in a criterion-related validation study. The lone exception may be the job analysis interview. Since many job analysis interviews tend to follow a format that may not produce information on specific tasks performed on a job, it is not likely that the interview will satisfy our needs in conducting a criterion-related validation study.

10. Reliability: *Will the method provide consistent, dependable results?*   Most of our methods can yield reliable job data. For some methods, such as the interview and GOJA, sufficient research has not been conducted to verify their ability to provide consistently reliable data. In contrast, IMES and the PAQ have established procedures for determining the extent to which analysts agree in their job assessments.

11. Utility in Developing Selection Measures: *How useful is a procedure in developing selection measures for a particular job?* Ideally, job analysis methods suggest content of selection devices, such as items or questions to be used in a test. The methods should permit specification of the explicit rationale for developing selection measures. In addition, acceptable job analysis methods should also serve as a source for ideas and content of criterion measures, such as rating scales, to be used in a validation study. Most of the methods can be used to meet these needs. Three of the methods (GOJA, IMES, JEM) have established procedures that systematically take an analyst through the analysis of a job to the development of selection measures. These specific procedures are likely to be most helpful in translating job content into job specifications and specifications into selection measures.

12. Cost: *What is the estimated cost of the method? (Cost includes cost of materials, necessary training, consulting assistance, salary of job analysts, and clerical support.)* In terms of dollar expenditures, the PAQ is probably the least expensive of all of the methods. Job Elements can also be relatively inexpensive; however, panels of job experts have to be convened at least on several occasions. Thus, indirect costs associated with taking key personnel from their jobs for extended periods must be considered. Task inventories can be rather expensive to develop, apply, and analyze. Because task inventories must be tailored to a job, costs will increase accordingly. Generally speaking, the more tailored the approach, the greater the associated costs.

Use of Multiple Job Analysis Methods

In this chapter and the Appendix, we have reviewed eight popular job analysis methods and have offered a series of evaluation criteria for determining how suitable each may be for human resource selection purposes. No one method will be completely appropriate for every selection situation. Specific methods will be better in some applications while other methods may be more appropriate in other situations.

For some users, a review of methods may show that one job analysis approach will not be sufficient in the context of human resource selection. Instead, multiple methods of job analysis may be needed. A survey by Edward Levine et al., of 93 experienced job analysts' attitudes toward using multiple job analysis methods showed support of a multiple-method approach. In their survey they found that of 93 respondents, 80 preferred a combination of methods, 9 preferred a single approach, and 4 were not sure.[42] In addition, Gary Brumback et al., note that job analysis is still a relatively imprecise endeavor, and the results of any one method should be corroborated by the results of another. Therefore, they recommend that whatever the job, whatever the measure, whatever the validation strategy to be used, a multi-methodological approach is preferable to reliance on a single method.

From their view, the costs involved in using multiple methods are more than offset by the advantages of their use. They conclude, "In this period of 'legislated employment,' the risk of having what may be an otherwise valid qualification requirement overturned is certainly not worth the modest cost of an independent verification of the job analysis results."[43] In general, we agree with their comments. Yet, we should also keep in mind that we may be faced with the problem of developing a means to reconcile any differences we may find in the results produced by two or more job analysis methods. If these differences cannot be reconciled, then the job analysis results may be open to both technical and legal challenges.

References for Chapter 7

[1] Ernest J. McCormick, "Job Information: Its Development and Applications," in *ASPA Handbook of Personnel and Industrial Relations,* ed. Dale Yoder and Herbert G. Heneman, (Washington, D.C.: BNA Books, 1979), p. 4–41.

[2] Ibid. For an analytic comparison of the phrasing of work- and worker-oriented questionnaire content, see J. C. Allen, "Multidimensional Analysis of Worker-Oriented and Job-Oriented Verbs," *Journal of Applied Psychology* 53 (1979): 73–79.

[3] Thomas Rendero, "Consensus," *Personnel* 58 (January–February 1981): 4–12.

[4] U.S. Civil Service Commission, *Job Analysis: Developing and Documenting Data* (Washington, D.C.: U.S. Civil Service Commission, Bureau of Intergovernmental Personnel Programs, 1973).

[5] Ibid., p. 5.

[6] Ibid., pp. 11–12.

[7] Ibid., p. 6.

[8] Ibid., p. 12.

[9] U.S. Department of Labor, U.S. Training and Employment Service, *Handbook for Analyzing Jobs* (Washington, D.C.: U.S. Government Printing Office, 1972), pp. 12–13.

[10] Wayne Cascio, *Applied Psychology in Personnel Management* (Reston, Va.: Reston Publishing Company, 1982), p. 59.

[11] Ernest J. McCormick, P. R. Jeanneret, and Robert C. Mecham, *Position Analysis Questionnaire* (West Lafayette, Ind.: Purdue University Bookstore, 1969).

[12] Melany Baehr, Wallace G. Lonergran, and Charles R. Potkay, *Work Elements Inventory* (Chicago, Ill.: Industrial Relations Center, The University of Chicago, 1967).

[13] J. W. Cunningham, R. R. Boese, R. W. Neeb, and J. J. Pass, "Systematically Derived Work Dimensions: Factor Analysis of the Occupation Analysis Inventory," *Journal of Applied Psychology* 68 (1983): 232–252.

[14] W. W. Tornow and Patrick R. Pinto, "The Development of a Managerial Taxonomy: A System for Describing, Classifying, and Evaluating Executive Positions," *Journal of Applied Psychology* 61 (1976): 410–418.

[15] J. K. Hemphill, *Dimensions of Executive Positions* (Columbus, Ohio: Bureau of Business Research, The Ohio State University, Research Monograph No. 89, 1980).

[16] C. H. Lawshe, *Individual's Job Questionnaire Checklist of Office Operations* (West Lafayette, Ind.: Purdue University Bookstore, 1955).

[17] Frank Sistrunk and Philip L. Smith, *Critiques of Job Analysis Methods,* vol. 2 (Washington, D.C.: Office of Criminal Justice Education and Training, Law Enforcement Assistance Administration, Grant Number 78-CD-AX-0003, 1980).

[18] J. E. Morsh and W. B. Archer, *Procedural Guide for Conducting Occupational Surveys in the United States Air Force* (PRL-TR-67-11, AD-664 036) (Lackland Air Force Base, Tex.: Personnel Research Laboratory, Aerospace Medical Division, 1967), pp. 18–20.

[19] McCormick, "Job Information: Its Development and Applications," pp. 4-66 to 4-67.

[20] Morsh and Archer, *Procedural Guide for Conducting Occupational Surveys in the United States Air Force*, pp. 8–11.

[21] R. E. Christal, *The United States Air Force Occupational Research Project* (Lackland Air Force Base, Tex.: Air Force Human Resources Laboratory, 1974), p. 50.

[22] Cascio, *Applied Psychology in Personnel Management*, p. 59. For a different view of using a task inventory-based system of job analysis labeled the "Work Performance Survey System (WPSS)," see Sidney Gael, *Job Analysis* (San Francisco: Jossey-Bass, 1983).

[23] Ernest J. McCormick, P. R. Jeanneret, and Robert C. Mecham, "A Study of Characteristics and Job Dimensions as Based on the Position Analysis Questionnaire (PAQ)," *Journal of Applied Psychology* 56 (1972): 347–368.

[24] Ibid., p. 349.

[25] PAQ Services, Inc., *Job Analysis Manual for the Position Analysis Questionnaire (PAQ)* (Logan, Utah: PAQ Services, Inc., 1977), pp. 2–3.

[26] Ibid., pp. 7–14.

[27] Ernest J. McCormick, Robert C. Mecham, and P. R. Jeanneret, *Technical Manual for the Position Analysis Questionnaire (PAQ) (System II)* (Logan, Utah: PAQ Services, Inc., 1977), pp. 7–9.

[28] Cascio, *Applied Psychology in Personnel Management*, p. 62.

[29] Equal Employment Opportunity Commission, Civil Service Commission, Department of Labor, and Department of Justice, *Adoption of Four Agencies of Uniform Guidelines on Employee Selection Procedures*, 43 Federal Register 38,300 (Aug. 25, 1978).

[30] Edwin T. Cornelius, Theodore J. Carron, and Marianne N. Collins, "Job Analysis Models and Job Classification," *Personnel Psychology* 32 (1979): 693–708.

[31] Edward L. Levine, Ronald A. Ash, and Nell Bennett, "Exploratory Comparative Study of Four Job Analysis Methods," *Journal of Applied Psychology* 65 (1980): 524–535.

[32] Edward L. Levine, Nell Bennett, and Ronald A. Ash, "Evaluation and Use of Four Job Analysis Methods for Personnel Selection," *Public Personnel Management* 8 (January–February 1979): 146–151.

[33] Edward L. Levine, Ronald A. Ash, Hardy L. Hall, and Frank Sistrunk, "Evaluation of Job Analysis Methods by Experienced Job Analysts," *Academy of Management Journal* 26 (1983): 339–347.

[34] George P. Hollenbeck and Walter C. Borman, "Two Analyses in Search of a Job: The Implications of Different Analysis Approaches," paper presented at the 84th annual convention of the American Psychological Association, Washington, D.C., August 1976.

[35] Gary B. Brumback, Tania Romashko, Clifford P. Hahn, and Edwin A. Fleishman, *Model Procedures for Job Analysis, Test Development and Validation* (Washington, D.C.: American Institutes for Research, 1974), pp. 102–108.

[36] Sistrunk and Smith, *Critiques of Job Analysis Methods*, pp. 16–17.

[37] Brumback et al., *Model Procedures for Job Analysis, Test Development and Validation*, p. 103.

[38] Ibid.

[39] Levine, Ash, and Bennett, "Exploratory Comparative Study of Four Job Analysis Methods," pp. 528–529.

[40] McCormick, Mecham, and Jeanneret, *Technical Manual for the Position Analysis Questionnaire (PAQ) (System II)*, pp. 3–4.

[41] Ernest S. Primoff, Cynthia L. Clark, and James R. Caplan, *How to Prepare and Conduct Job Element Examinations: Supplement* (Washington, D.C.: Office of Personnel Management, Office of Personnel Research and Development, 1982), p. 18.

[42] Levine et al., "Evaluation of Job Analysis Methods by Experienced Job Analysts," p. 9. For an application of a multi-methodological approach, see Ronald A. Ash, "Job Elements for Task Clusters: Arguments for Using Multi-Methodological Approaches to Job Analysis and a Demonstration of Their Utility," *Public Personnel Management* 11 (Spring 1982), pp. 80–90.

[43] Brumback et al., *Model Procedures for Job Analysis, Test Development and Validation*, p. 101.

7

Some Additional

Job Analysis

Techniques

We reviewed three job analysis techniques in Chapter 7. In this appendix we will study five additional methods that are useful for human resource selection applications. The purpose of this appendix is to provide the interested reader with a reference for additional job analysis systems that can be utilized to develop selection predictors or criteria. The methods we examine are as follows:

1. Comprehensive Occupational Data Analysis Program (CODAP)
2. Guidelines Oriented Job Analysis (GOJA)
3. Iowa Merit Employment System (IMES)
4. Functional Job Analysis (FJA)
5. Job Element Method (JEM)

Comprehensive Occupational Data Analysis Program (CODAP)

Description

The first of the five systems we will review is the *Comprehensive Occupational Data Analysis Program* (CODAP). CODAP was developed by Raymond Christal and his colleagues at the U.S. Air Force Human Resources Laboratory, Lackland Air Force Base, Texas.[1] Actually, CODAP was developed to be more of an approach to the statistical treatment of job analysis data than as a method of collecting such information. However, since it has been treated both as a means for collecting and for analyzing job data, we will offer a brief overview of the system.

Application

The vehicle for collecting job information under CODAP is a comprehensive task inventory. Two categories of information are collected: (a) *background data* and (b) job activity data expressed as *tasks*. Background data are those items answered by a job incumbent that describe the worker and his or her job environment. Items dealing with types of jobs previously held, training received, job satisfaction, sex of employee, or any other background or demographic data that might provide useful information to managers about "who" is on a job can be included. Task data generally include approximately 300 to 500 work-oriented task statements, clustered under major job duties, that are rated by incumbents. Task statements are constructed by incumbents, supervisors, or job experts and are phrased similarly to our earlier examples presented in our discussion of task analysis inventories in Chapter 7.

In completing a task inventory, incumbents are required to make a series of judgments. First, they are requested to indicate whether or not they perform each task shown. Next, they are asked to rate each task performed to indicate the relative amount of time spent in performing the task *relative to all other tasks performed*. A rating scale is used rather than estimates of time spent such as percentages. The scale employed is a seven-point measure consisting of the following scale points:

1 = Very Much Below Average
2 = Below Average
3 = Slightly Below Average
4 = About Average
5 = Slightly Above Average
6 = Above Average
7 = Very Much Above Average

If a task is not performed, the task is left blank.[2]

From these rating data, several computations are made. For each individual, ratings are summed across all tasks performed. Each task rating is then divided by that sum to provide a relative frequency of task performance. These same rating data are used to represent task performance in a variety of ways, such as the following examples:

1. Average percent of time spent by individual incumbents performing a task

2. Average percent of time spent by all incumbents performing a task

3. Cumulative sum of average percent of time spent by all incumbents performing a task

4. Percent of incumbents performing a task

Exhibit 7A.1 provides an example of these results for the job of journeyman medical laboratory specialist as described by CODAP and reported by Christal.[3] This example is but one of many possibilities that are available. The CODAP system provides more than 50 specific computer programs that can treat task data in practically any way desired. The power and capabilities of CODAP cannot be overstated. Over 20 years of work, hundreds of thousands of dollars, and thousands of in-service manhours have gone into producing CODAP computer listings that run more than 1,400 pages in length. Clearly, it is a premium system for analyzing task data.[4]

Exhibit 7A.1 *Example Task Description Developed From CODAP for the Job of Journeyman Medical Laboratory Specialist (N = 394)*

Duty	Task	Task Title	Percent of Members Performing	Average Percent Time Spent by Members Performing	Average Percent Time Spent by All Members	Cumulative Sum of Average Percent Time Spent by All Members
F	18	Collect blood specimens directly from patients	93.40	1.70	1.58	1.58
J	3	Perform blood count	89.09	1.56	1.39	2.97
J	17	Perform hematology procedures for differential cell counts	88.83	1.49	1.33	4.30
J	24	Perform hematology procedures for hematocrit tests	89.09	1.45	1.30	5.60
N	2	Examine urine specimens microscopically	88.07	1.43	1.26	6.86
J	5	Prepare blood smears	89.85	1.39	1.25	8.11
F	10	Prepare and process specimens	87.56	1.39	1.22	9.33
.	.	.	.	.	.	.
.	.	.	.	.	.	.
.	.	.	.	.	.	.
N	18	Perform urinalyses for urinary chlorides	35.03	0.54	0.19	90.03

Source: Based on Raymond E. Christal, *The United States Air Force Occupational Research Project* (Human Resources Laboratory, Occupational Research Division, Lackland Air Force Base, Tex., January 1974), pp. 61–64.

Christal has offered a number of suggestions that are useful in applying CODAP or any form of task inventory. These suggestions include:

1. Use full-time inventory writers to develop task lists and background questions.

2. Write specific task statements rather than broad task statements.

3. Include any background items which might answer questions asked by managers of the personnel system.

4. Collect worker name and identification information.

5. Administer inventories to large samples.

6. Collect data on optical scanning sheets.

7. Use a "relative time spent" scale as the primary rating factor and convert ratings into percent time estimates. . . .[5]

There appears to have been only one published account using CODAP in a nonmilitary setting in the context of human resource selection. Marvin Trattner employed the CODAP system in concurrent validity studies of the Professional and Administrative Career Examination (PACE) for three federal government jobs. CODAP was employed to develop the content of rating scales serving as criteria in the PACE exam validation studies. Prominent tasks identified by CODAP served as the basis for rating scale content.[6]

Advantages and Disadvantages

CODAP offers a very useful means for collecting and quantitatively analyzing task analysis information. The flexibility of CODAP's computer programs offers an investigator numerous possibilities for treating job analysis data. Many of these are very suitable for human resource selection purposes.

Years of research have been devoted by the military to the development and application of CODAP. An impressive number of studies testify to its usefulness. Validity and reliability studies have shown repeatedly that the system can produce useful, valuable results. However, with the exception of Trattner's study, CODAP has been applied almost exclusively to military work units. In addition, these reports have not been widely distributed outside of military settings. Thus, some questions remain as to its suitability in other types of job environments. Yet, even though generalizability *may* be a problem, there is no reason to expect inherent difficulties in the application of CODAP to other situations. With this caveat in mind, it is safe to say that CODAP offers some exciting possibilities for treating task data for selection purposes; possibilities that will likely be tapped in the near future. Where task inventories are used on a large-scale or continuous basis, the resources invested in obtaining and using CODAP are likely to pay significant dividends.

Guidelines Oriented Job Analysis (GOJA)

Description

Of those reviewed here, one of the newest job analysis systems is the *Guidelines Oriented Job Analysis* method (GOJA) developed by Richard Biddle and his associates.[7] The name is somewhat misleading, as GOJA is more than a job analysis method. It is designed to be a means for developing a job-related selection system based upon the content validity requirements of the 1978 *Uniform Guidelines*.[8]

   When implemented in its entirety, GOJA is a multistep process whose objective is to develop a selection plan where its content is reflective of the job being studied. For our purposes, however, we want to concentrate on some of the earliest steps in the process that deal with the identification and characterization of important job duties. We will see that development of job duties is one of the core elements of GOJA.

Application

The actual use of GOJA can be thought of as a step-by-step process carried out by a job incumbent. (Others could apply the method to a job, but it is intended for a knowledgeable incumbent.) A participant in GOJA receives a job analysis booklet that is to be completed systematically. The booklet instructs the incumbent and carries him or her through the process until relevant job content is identified. The steps leading to the development of that part of the product are briefly described below.[9]

1. Collecting Preliminary Job Data   Initially, an employee provides basic data on his or her job, such as job title, job tenure, company tenure, and immediate supervisor. In addition, information is obtained on the machines, tools, and equipment used on the job, number and types of people supervised, types of supervisory tasks performed, level of supervision received, and frequency of contacts with different groups of people.

2. Identifying Major Job Duties   Next, the "duties" actually performed by the incumbent are listed. Duties are defined by Biddle as a statement that "tells *what* is done, *how* and *why* it is done, and what products are obtained. It includes some examples to help explain the duty."[10] Probably in deference to terminology used in the *Uniform Guidelines*, Biddle chooses the term "duty" over that of "task" to refer to a fundamental job activity. However, a comparison of his definition of a duty with the definition of a task as discussed earlier in the Office of Personnel Management interview procedure in Chapter 7 suggests that the two meanings are similar. An example of a duty identified by Biddle is "Interview job applicants, recording interview procedure and results; conduct reference checks on final applicants and recommend final applicant to supervisor."[11]

3. Rating Frequency of Duty Performance   Once the associated duties have been developed, the incumbent is required to rate how often each duty is performed. The frequency ratings are made using the following rating scale:

D   = Daily
W   = Weekly
M   = Monthly
Q   = Quarterly
SA = Semiannually
A   = Annually

4. Rating Duty Importance   After all job duties have been rated, each individual completing GOJA for a job is requested to judge the importance of the duties. These ratings are made by using a two-step or dichotomous rating scale, where 1 = "Important" and 2 = "Critical." Critical duties are those duties in which major problems are perceived to result if they are performed poorly. Those duties that are not quite as critical to job performance are rated as "important." A sample listing of duties with accompanying frequency and importance ratings for the job of keypunch operator is shown in Exhibit 7A.2 With the exception of Duty 7, all duties are judged to be critical.

These various steps represent roughly one-half of the GOJA process applied to a specific job. However, these steps involving derivation and rating of job duties provide the foundation on which the other elements of GOJA are built. Like the procedures discussed thus far, GOJA also provides a basis for noting the most critical job content. The remaining portions of the process involve using the job content to determine the employee specifications on which a selection measure is developed.

Advantages and Disadvantages

One of the important assets of GOJA is the systematic process an analyst is taken through in analyzing a job. Documentation for the relevant decision points is also accumulated in its application. Given the legal significance of documentation in job analysis (particularly in content validation studies), the level of detailed documentation provided by GOJA is one prime advantage.

Like all methods requiring paper-and-pencil measures, GOJA has some limitations. Ability to express oneself in writing (for example, in specifying job duties), motivation of incumbents to participate, training (although not necessarily extensive) of incumbents in using the method are all relevant concerns with GOJA. Some of these concerns could develop into serious

---

Exhibit 7A.2 *An Example of Duty Specifications and Ratings for the Job of Keypunch Operator*

List Below the Typical Important or Critical Duties You Perform as Part of Your Job

Duties	How Often?	How Important?
1. Pick up source documents such as accounting reports and personnel records to be encoded.	D	2
2. Review documents before encoding to insure that all critical data such as priority, code, location, date, and user have been entered.	D	2
3. Return source document to user if an error is found, so error can be corrected.	W	2
4. Confirm that all departments have their week's work in by independently checking documents collected against work lists and making follow-up phone calls.	W	2
5. Sort and collate source documents by priority and type for encoding, checking with supervisor if there are questions.	D	2
6. Assign tape numbers on tape control log for the week's processing.	W	2
7. Neatly stack source documents and store on shelf until they are to be returned to user.	W	1

Note: D = Daily; W = Weekly; 1 = Important; 2 = Critical.

Source: Richard E. Biddle, *Brief GOJA: A Step-by-Step Job Analysis Instruction Booklet*, 5th ed. (Sacramento, Calif.: Biddle and Associates, Inc., April 21, 1978), p. 23. Reprinted by permission.

---

problems when large numbers of incumbents are involved, particularly when many have low levels of education or poor reading and writing skills. Finally, apparently little empirical research is available on the validity and reliability of the data produced. Until such information is developed, it is hard to objectively assess the overall utility of the method. (Of course, this same statement could be made about many job analysis methods. With the exception of a few techniques, empirical research studies on job analysis methods such as GOJA are limited in both quality and quantity.)

In sum, GOJA is one of the few methods available that systematically takes a user from content of the job to content of a selection plan. GOJA's thoroughness in application and documentation makes it an important method for consideration in collecting job data.

Iowa Merit Employment System (IMES)

Description

The *Iowa Merit Employment System* (IMES) is similar to GOJA in its objectives. It is a systematic, multistep process that is designed to lead to content valid selection devices such as tests.[12] Because the basic job analysis element is the task, it is a work-oriented procedure. The rationale behind IMES is to produce selection devices whose contents are derived from jobs for which they are to be used. In matching job and selection device content, a sequence of steps from job analysis through specification of knowledge, skills, and abilities (KSAs) is made. Our concern here is with the initial steps in the sequence, that is, job analysis.

Application

Job analysis under IMES is carried out through a series of activities. At the conclusion, a core group of tasks is identified that represents the performance domain of the job being analyzed. It is this domain that the selection measures are intended to assess.

As we indicated earlier, there are some important similarities and differences between GOJA and IMES. In terms of similarities, both IMES and GOJA were developed for users following a content validation model. The methods are aimed at a single job or class of jobs. Differences in the methods tend to involve the procedural steps taken in implementing the methods. For example, whereas GOJA typically involves the use of incumbents working alone or possibly in groups as analysts, IMES stresses the use of supervisors and incumbents working together in groups to identify relevant job content. In order to better understand the use of IMES, we will review the major steps taken in its application.

Job content information is collected through administration of a questionnaire called the "Job Analysis Questionnaire for Selection Device Content Validation."[13] The questionnaire is basically a workbook to be completed by individuals serving as job agents or informants. Specifics in the application of the method can vary from one situation to the next. But, there are three major phases common to most uses.[14]

1. Selecting Job Agents   The first step is the identification of individuals or agents who can serve as expert informants about the job or job classes being studied. Most often these individuals are a combination of incumbents and supervisors serving in the role of "subject matter experts" or SMEs.

Managers supervising persons in the job being studied are initially asked to nominate individuals who can serve as SMEs. Nominations can be made on any number of criteria, but minimum qualifications such as the following might be used: (a) the SME should work in one of the jobs or classes being studied; (b) a chosen individual should have a minimum of six months (or, perhaps, one year) of job experience; and (c) the SME should have demonstrated successful performance on the job. The objective is to choose approximately 12 individuals who can serve as SMEs.

2. Developing Job Tasks   Once the SMEs have been chosen, they are assembled into one group with a leader. It is the leader's role to facilitate the collection and analysis of job data from the group. After a brief orientation period, SMEs are asked to generate a listing of the tasks performed on the job. The goal is to be *exhaustive* in task development at this point.

Tasks that are developed are written subject to several criteria. Generally speaking, they are phrased quite like those in GOJA. Statements are composed to answer the following questions:

1. *What* is the action?
2. *To whom/what* is the action directed?
3. *Why* is the action being done?
4. *How* is the action done?[15]

The example below portrays an incorrect and corrected task statement under IMES.

> *Incorrect:* "*Assists with the inspection of construction projects.*"
> *Comment:* First, the *What* is ambiguous and gives no real information as to the action. Second, neither the *Why* nor the *How* questions have been answered.
>
>   *What*   *To Whom/What*
> *Corrected:* "Inspects/construction operations (erosion control, Portland cement concrete paving, asphaltic concrete paving, painting, fencing, sign placement)/in order to
>
>   *Why*
> insure compliance with construction specifications/by
>
>   *How*
> comparing visual observations with construction specifications and plans, and verbal instructions; with daily review by the supervisor."[16]

The actual editing of the job tasks according to the suggested format may be completed by the group leader or by the assembled SMEs. From the perspective of saving time, separate editing by the group leader is more advantageous.

3. Rating Job Tasks   After an acceptable pool of tasks has been created, task statements are distributed to approximately 60 additional SMEs organized into groups of 12. These five or six SME groups are then asked to judge each task according to factors such as (a) frequency of task performance, (b) time spent, (c) criticality/significance of error, (d) necessity of adequate task performance upon job entry, and (e) relationship of successful task performance to successful performance on the job. Following the rating of tasks, the SMEs are asked to review their ratings and then rank each task in terms of its importance relative to all other tasks. These resulting rating and ranking data are used for defining important job content.

Advantages and Disadvantages

For the most part, the problems and prospects of GOJA also characterize IMES. However, it should be noted that much of the success of IMES is dependent upon the skills of the group leader conducting the process. Considerable time and money may be required to locate and prepare people to conduct the job analysis session. Prior to embarking on an analysis of jobs using IMES, careful thought should be given to the selection of such analysts.

Functional Job Analysis (FJA)

Description

Over 35 years ago, Sidney Fine and his associates recognized that one of the problems in studying work is the impreciseness of language used in describing jobs. As a consequence, efforts were undertaken to begin work on a system for accurately defining and measuring workers' job activities. The system that emerged was labeled *Functional Job Analysis* (FJA). The method probably represents the most thorough procedure for applying a standardized, controlled language for describing and measuring what workers do.

Two types of information are obtained from FJA: (a) *what* gets done, that is, the procedures and processes engaged in by a worker as a task is performed and (b) *how* a task is performed in context of the physical, mental, and interpersonal involvement of the worker with the task.[17] These types of information are used to clarify both what a worker does and the results of those job behaviors.

Before describing some specifics of FJA, let's look at the method from a broad view. The key ingredient in analyzing a job is proper development of task statements. Once identified, these tasks are then rated by a job analyst using special sets of rating scales. The ratings provided serve as a basis for inferring worker specifications required for task performance.

When using FJA, judgments about jobs are based on at least two premises.[18]

1. *All jobs require workers to deal, in some degree, with People (clients, customers, coworkers, etc.), Data (information or ideas), and Things (machines or equipment).*
Thus, workers' job activities can be represented by task statements in relation to People, Data, and Things. Specific tasks require different levels of involvement with these three areas. For example, tasks characterized principally by relation to *Things* require a worker to draw upon physical resources (strength, coordination, etc.). When a task focuses on *Data*, the worker is required to use mental resources (knowledge, memory, etc.). When a task demands involvement with *People*, interpersonal resources (courtesy, empathy, tact, etc.) are needed.

2. The tasks a worker performs in relation to People, Data, and Things can be measured by rating scales.

Rating scales permit an analyst to describe empirically a task in terms of its relation to People, Data, Things, and other characteristics by using a standardized format and language. From these ratings, employee specifications are developed.

Application

FJA is applied by an analyst who systematically observes and/or interviews a worker about his or her job. The analyst's principal concern is with what a worker does in performing the job and *not* with what gets done. Take the job of bus driver for instance. As Sidney Fine and Wretha Wiley point out, FJA emphasizes what the bus driver does. That is, he/she performs a series of sequenced tasks in driving the bus and collecting fares. Emphasis is not given to what gets accomplished, that is, passengers being carried by a bus operated by a driver.[19]

As we suggested earlier, application of FJA involves a sequence of activities. The major phases are described below.

1. Identifying Job Tasks   The fundamental unit of work under study is the task. A task represents "a fundamental, stable work element consisting of a behavior and a result."[20]

Preparation of good task statements is the most critical step in applying FJA. Much time, care, effort, and expertise must be given to precisely wording a task statement to reflect a job activity. Such explicit task statements are needed to enhance the validity of inferences to be drawn about employee specifications. Thus, it is assumed that the more explicit and precise a task statement, the more accurate the inferences drawn about these specifications. Since the wording of a task statement is so crucial, we will review how these statements are constructed.

Based on information collected from observation of the job or interview with an incumbent, task statements are written so that they answer the following questions:

1. *Who* performs the task?
2. What *action* is performed?
3. What immediate *result* is accomplished?
4. What *tools*, equipment, or work aids are used?
5. What *instructions* (prescribed or discretionary) are followed.[21]

Table 7A.1 illustrates how a task statement may be decomposed and written to meet the above criteria. This same process is applied until a suitable list of task statements has been developed.

Table 7A.1 *An Example Task Statement Prepared Under Functional Job Analysis (FJA)*

Complete Task Statement: Asks client questions, listens to responses, and writes answers on standard intake form, exercising leeway as to sequence of questions, in order to record basic identifying information.

Criteria:	1. Who? (subject)	2. Performs what action?	3. To accomplish what?	4. With what tools?	5. Upon what instructions?
Guideline:	Subject of the statement is understood to be the "worker."	Use a specific action verb.	Purpose of the action performed should be stated so that its relation to objectives is clear and performance standards can be set.	Should identify the tangible instruments used by a worker in performing a task.	Should reflect the nature and source of instructions the worker receives in terms of that specified and that left to the worker's discretion.
Example:	No subject.	Asks client questions, *writes* answers, *listens* to responses.	To establish a client information system that enables workers to locate clients quickly and efficiently.	Forms, pens.	Prescribed: Following standard intake form. Discretionary: Exercising some leeway as to sequence of questions.

Source: Based on Sidney A. Fine and Wretha W. Wiley, *An Introduction to Functional Job Analysis* (Kalamazoo, Mich.: W. E. Upjohn Institute for Employment Research, 1971), pp. 10–12.

The next three phases of applying FJA are used to measure the complexity of the tasks defined in Step (1). To do so, task ratings are made using the following rating scales: (a) *Worker Functions Scales,* (b) *Scale of Worker Instructions,* and (c) *Scales of General Educational Development.*

2. Measuring Worker Functions   The *Worker Functions Scales* consist of separate ratings of People, Data, and Things. The scales themselves are too long to reproduce each one here, but the Data scale is shown in Exhibit 7A.3 to provide an illustration. The Data rating scale consists of six rating points or levels and eight functional areas (Comparing, Copying, Computing, etc.). The levels range from simple (Comparing) to complex (Synthesizing) functions. In applying the Data scale, for instance, a job analyst carefully reads a task statement. Definitions of each of the eight functions on the scale are studied, and the level is chosen that best describes the data orientation of the task statement. The level selected reflects the extent to which a worker is required to involve her- or himself with information, ideas, facts, and statistics in performing a task. Involvement may range from simple recognition through degrees of arranging, modifying, or even reconceptualizing data.[22] Although the specific content varies, the People and Things rating scales are similar in format and application.

The three Data, People, and Things scales provide two ways of assessing task requirements. These ways include (a) task *level* and (b) task *orientation.* Level shows the *relative complexity* of a task as compared to other tasks. In obtaining a score for level, an analyst studies a task and then selects the function on a scale that is most appropriate for the task examined. The numerical score for level is the number corresponding to the particular function chosen. For example, suppose an analyst is using the Data scale in evaluating a task. If *Compiling* (level = 3B) is chosen, the task involves a higher level of functioning than that required for *Copying* (level = 2) but a lower level of functioning than *Analyzing* data (level = 4).

The *Orientation* measure indicates the *relative involvement* of a worker with Data, People, and Things as a task is performed. The measure involves assigning a percentage (usually in units of 5 percent or 10 percent) to each of the three functions scored for a task. The sum of the three orientation scores equals 100 percent. The higher the percentage assigned to a function (that is, People, Data, Things), the greater the degree of emphasis of that function in the task rated.[23]

In summary, level and orientation measures represent the worker's mental, physical, and interpersonal involvement with a task. Level is determined by choosing three functions, one each from the Data, People, and Things scales. Orientation measures are derived by weighting (%) the three functions for each task to show the relative emphasis on the functions. Applications of level and orientation measures yield results similar to the following example task for the job of social worker.[24]

Exhibit 7A.3 Data Function Scale Used with Functional Job Analysis (FJA)

Level	Definition
	Comparing
1	Selects, sorts, or arranges data, people, or things, judging whether their readily observable functional, structural, or compositional characteristics are similar to or different from prescribed standards, e.g. checks oil level, tire pressure, worn cables; observes hand signal of worker indicating movement of load.
	Copying
2	Transcribes, enters, and/or posts data, following a schema or plan to assemble or make things and using a variety of work aids. Transfers information mentally from plans, diagrams, instructions, to workpiece or work site.
	Computing
3A	Performs arithmetic operations and makes reports and/or carries out a prescribed action in relation to them. Interprets mathematical data on plans, specifications, diagrams, or blueprints.
	Compiling
3B	Gathers, collates, or classifies information about data, people, or things, following a schema or system but using discretion in application.
	Analyzing
4	Examines and evaluates data (about things, data, or people) with reference to the criteria, standards, and/or requirements of a particular discipline, art, technique, or craft to determine interaction effects (consequences) and to consider alternatives.
	Innovating
5A	Modifies, alters, and/or adapts existing designs, procedures, or methods to meet unique specifications, unusual conditions, or specific standards of effectiveness within the overall framework of operating theories, principles, and/or organizational contexts.
	Coordinating
5B	Decides time, place, and sequence of operations of a process, system, or organization, and/or the need for revision of goals, policies (boundary conditions), or procedures on the basis of analysis of data and of performance review of pertinent objectives and requirements. Includes overseeing and/or executing decisions and/or reporting on events.
	Synthesizing
6	*Takes off in new directions* on the basis of personal intuitions, feelings, and ideas (with or without regard for tradition, experience, and existing parameters) *to conceive new approaches* to or statements of problems and the development of system, operational, or aesthetic "solutions" or "resolutions" of them, typically outside of existing theoretical, stylistic, or organizational context.

Note: The arabic numbers assigned to definitions represent the successive levels of this ordinal scale. The A, B, and C definitions are variations on the same level. There is no ordinal difference between A, B, and C definitions on a given level.

Source: Sidney A. Fine Associates, Washington, D.C., 1985. Used with permission.

Example Task: Asks client questions, listens to responses, and writes answers on standard intake form, exercising leeway as to sequence of questions, in order to record basic identifying information.

Area	Function	Level	Orientation (%)
Data	Copying	2	50
People	Exchanging Information	2	40
Things	Handling	1A	10

In this example, 50 percent of the worker's involvement in the task is at the *Copying* level (writing answers on a standard intake form). But the worker is also involved interpersonally with people (40 percent) by *Exchanging Information* (talking with people to obtain information). Also, the worker is required to use physical resources in *Handling* papers and pens (10 percent).

3. Measuring Worker Instructions   In addition to characterizing tasks in terms of Things, Data, and People, FJA also provides for measuring the degree of *prescription* and *discretion* in task performance. *Prescribed* aspects of tasks represent those areas in which the worker has no control over what is done. *Discretionary* components involve those aspects of tasks in which the worker must decide on the execution of tasks. In order to assess the degree of prescription/discretion, the *Scale of Worker Instructions* is used. It is similar in format and application to the *Worker Functions Scales,* where lower levels represent high task *prescription* and higher levels represent high task *discretion.* Where prescription is high, task performance requires little or no judgment; where discretion is high, mental effort is required in performing the task.[25]

The *Scale of Worker Instructions* is an eight-point rating scale. Examples of five rating levels are illustrated in Exhibit 7A.4.

4. Measuring Worker Qualifications   The final set of rating scales is specifically directed toward the problem of determining selected worker qualifications. The *Scales of General Education Development* (GED) serve as a means for determining basic educational skills needed to perform a task. Thus, the GED scales assess a specific task's demands on a worker's reasoning, mathematical, and language development. The following measures compose the GED scales:

1. *Reasoning Development Scale*—concerns the problem-solving and decision-making demands of a task.

2. *Mathematical Development Scale*—focuses on the mathematical operations ranging from counting to higher mathematics required by a task.

3. *Language Development Scale*—relates to the demands of a task to deal

Exhibit 7A.4 *Scale of Worker Instructions (Condensed) Used with Functional Job Analysis (FJA)*

Level	Definition
1	Inputs, outputs, tools, equipment, and procedures are all specified. Almost everything the worker needs to know is contained in the assignment. The worker is supposed to turn out a specified amount of work or a standard number of units per hour or day.
2	Inputs, outputs, tools, and equipment are all specified, but the worker has some leeway in the procedures and methods used to get the job done. Almost all the information needed is in the assignment instructions. Production is measured on a daily or weekly basis.
3	Inputs and outputs are specified, but the worker has considerable freedom as to procedures and timing, including the use of tools and/or equipment. The worker may have to refer to several standard sources for information (handbooks, catalogs, wall charts). Time to complete a particular product or service is specified, but this varies up to several hours.
· · ·	· · ·
7	There is some question as to what the need or problem really is or what directions should be pursued in dealing with it. In order to define the problem, to control and explore the behavior of the variables, and to formulate possible outputs and their performance characteristics, the worker must consult largely unspecified sources of information and devise investigations, surveys, or data analysis studies.
8	Information and/or direction comes to the worker in terms of needs (tactical, organizational, strategic, financial). Worker must call for staff reports and recommendations concerning methods of dealing with them. He/she coordinates both organizational and technical data in order to make decisions and determinations regarding courses of action (outputs) for major sections (divisions, groups) of the organization.

Source: Sidney A. Fine Associates, Washington, D.C., 1985. Used with permission.

with oral and written materials, covering from simple to complex sources of information.[26]

Exhibit 7A.5 summarizes three levels of each of the GED scales. Their application is identical to that discussed previously for other FJA ratings. Scores are obtained by choosing the level on a scale that best meets the task characteristics under review. The results of the GED scales, when coupled with results of other ratings, can provide the basic information needed for developing selected employee specifications.

Advantages and Disadvantages

Clearly, FJA represents a comprehensive quantitative procedure for analyzing jobs. The methods and standardized language that are employed help to insure a systematic approach to job analysis. Further, the rating scales em-

Exhibit 7A.5 *Reasoning, Mathematical, and Language Development Scales (Condensed) Used with Functional Job Analysis (FJA)*

Reasoning Development Scale

Level	Definition
1	• Have the common sense understanding to carry out simple one- or two-step instructions in the context of highly standardized situations. • Recognize unacceptable variations from the standard and take emergency action to reject inputs or stop operations.
2	• Have the common sense understanding to carry out detailed but uninvolved instructions where the work involves a *few* concrete/specific variables in or from standard/typical situations.
· · ·	· · ·
6	• Have knowledge of a field of study of the highest abstractive order (e.g., mathematics, physics, chemistry, logic, philosophy, art criticism). • Deal with nonverbal symbols in formulas, equations, or graphs. • Understand the most difficult classes of concepts. • Deal with a large number of variables and determine a specific course of action (e.g., research, production) on the basis of need.

Mathematical Development Scale

Level	Definition
1	• Counting to simple addition and subtraction; reading, copying, and/or recording of figures.
2	• Use arithmetic to add, subtract, multiply, and divide whole numbers. Reading scales and gauges as in powered equipment where readings and signals are indicative of conditions and actions to be taken.
· · ·	· · ·
5	• Have knowledge of advanced mathematical and statistical techniques such as differential and integral calculus, factor analysis, and probability determination. • Work with a wide variety of theoretical mathematical concepts. • Make original applications of mathematical procedures, as in empirical and differential equations.

Source: Sidney A. Fine Associates, Washington, D.C., 1985. Used with permission.

ployed with the method appear to provide reliable task analysis data.[27] On the other hand, FJA's assets have some associated costs. The method is laborious and time-consuming. Special training is mandatory in order to apply FJA effectively — training that can be expensive. Another possible weakness is that FJA places considerable reliance upon an analyst's abilities to accurately detect and comprehend task activities and then evaluate them. Unless multiple analysts, additional job analysis methods, or reviews of FJA results by supervisors are used, FJA data could, at times, be questionable.

Exhibit 7A.5 *(continued)*

Language Development Scale

Level	Definition
1	• Cannot read or write but can follow simple oral, *pointing-out* instructions. • Sign name and understand ordinary, routine agreements when explained, such as those relevant to leasing a house; employment (hours, wages, etc.); procuring a driver's license. • Read lists, addresses, safety warnings.
2	• Read short sentences, simple concrete vocabulary; words that avoid complex Latin derivations. • Converse with service personnel (waiters, ushers, cashiers). • Copy written records precisely without error. • Keep taxi driver's trip record or service maintenance record.
⋮	⋮
6	• Report, write, or edit articles for technical and scientific journals or journals of advanced literary criticism (e.g., *Journal of Educational Sociology, Science, Physical Review, Daedalus*).

Source: Sidney A. Fine Associates, Washington, D.C., 1985. Used with permission.

Job Element Method (JEM)

Description

Whereas many of the methods of job analysis we have examined began with identification of tasks or basic work functions, the *Job Element Method* (JEM) developed by Ernest Primoff has a different orientation.[28] Basically, it is a worker-oriented process designed to identify the characteristics of superior workers on a job. Supervisors and/or incumbents develop a list of these characteristics and then rate them in such a way that the characteristics essential to superior performers are delineated. These qualities are what Primoff calls *job elements*. Job elements include a wide variety of characteristics that describe superior performers on a job. These elements may consist of worker characteristics such as the following:

> A knowledge, such as knowledge of accounting principles; a skill, such as skill with woodworking tools; an ability, such as ability to manage a program; a willingness, such as willingness to do simple tasks repetitively; an interest, such as interest in learning new techniques; or a personal characteristic, such as reliability or dependability.[29]

Once identified, the elements are translated into more specific characteristics called subelements. Selection devices such as tests are then developed based upon these subelements.

In comparison to the other job analysis techniques we have discussed, the JEM approach differs in an important way. Rather than focusing on job tasks or worker functions per se, the JEM is aimed toward *directly* identifying those employee characteristics that should be assessed by selection measures. Thus, from this perspective, we view the JEM more as a means for developing worker specifications and their measures than strictly a means for collecting information about the important, work-related aspects of a job.

Application

The JEM involves several important phases that carry a user through the job element identification–selection device development process. The job element identification, or job analysis, side of the method involves several major steps.

1. Selecting a Panel of Raters   On the whole, success of the JEM depends upon judgments provided by a panel of experts. However, in contrast to some techniques, it does not use an independent group of analysts. The group or panel chosen typically consists of about six incumbents or supervisors working as raters or subject matter experts. Individuals used are those who know the requirements of a job and can recognize characteristics of superior performers.

2. Developing Job Elements   After a panel of experts has been assembled, the next step is to develop a comprehensive list of job elements and subelements. Panel members are told that they have been brought together to identify KSAs and personal characteristics that could be used to select superior workers on the job under study.

3. Rating the Elements and Subelements   The third phase of the JEM process involves each panel member independently rating the elements and subelements identified in the previous step. These ratings of suggested elements are made with respect to their usefulness in choosing superior employees for the job. Results of these ratings serve as criteria for choosing the content of selection measures.

4. Analyzing JEM Data   Once the ratings have been made, quantitative rating indices are computed for each of the elements and subelements. Decisions as to which elements and subelements should be included in the selection plan are based on the computed indices.

5. Allocating Subelements to Elements   The indices computed in the previous step are used to select the relevant subelements and elements describing superior performers. The next step in using JEM data is to classify the elements and subelements in order to describe important aspects of the job.

6. Developing Job Tasks From Subelements   The final step of the job analysis is a new addition to earlier applications of the JEM. Here, task statements are developed for each subelement. Ernest Primoff, Cynthia Clark, and James Caplan recommend the use of Fine's Functional Job Analysis (FJA) approach to develop and characterize task statements.[30]

Once all necessary task statements have been prepared, they are rated on the FJA scales we previously discussed. At the conclusion of these steps, we will have a list of important elements of the job, a list of the qualities for each element that can be measured by our selection system, and a specification of the tasks that link these worker qualities to requirements of the job. These data serve as the basis for developing selection measures.

Advantages and Disadvantages

When carried throughout the Job Analysis →Test Development →Test Validation process, the JEM offers a unique alternative for identifying important employee specifications and constructing measures for them. However, Gary Brumback and his associates have found that the method is "almost too unwieldy and unstructured . . . in the initial stage of soliciting preliminary job elements for subject matter experts."[31] In addition, Frank Sistrunk and Philip Smith point to logistical problems in simply assembling a panel of experts. They note that when using high-level personnel, the schedules of participants are not likely to mesh, making it difficult to organize panel members. Also, taking key members away from their jobs for the necessary amount of time may also create some organizational problems, particularly for small organizations.[32]

The JEM has also been criticized for ignoring the specification of job tasks. It has been alleged that the absence of task data makes it difficult to show that an element is job-related if it cannot be demonstrated that the element is necessary to do a specific task. As a result, the JEM may not be the best job analysis method to use for some types of validation studies (such as content validation). However, recent modifications in the JEM have attempted to address this criticism.[33]

The JEM has approximately a 25-year history; it has been widely used to develop examinations in various trades and labor occupations. With some of its newer modifications, it holds promise as another method for identifying employee specifications to be incorporated into selection measures.

References for the Appendix to Chapter 7

[1] R. E. Christal, *The United States Air Force Occupational Research Project* (Lackland Air Force Base, Tex.: Air Force Human Resources Laboratory, 1974), p. 50.

[2] Ibid., pp. 7–8.

[3] Ibid., pp. 61–64.

[4] Ibid., p. 9.

[5] Ibid., p. 50.

[6] Marvin H. Trattner, "Task Analysis in the Design of Three Concurrent Validity Studies of the Professional and Administrative Career Examination," *Personnel Psychology* 32 (1979): 109–119.

[7] Richard E. Biddle, *Guidelines Oriented Job Analysis* (Sacramento, Calif.: Biddle and Associates, Inc., September 9, 1982), p. 1.

[8] Ibid.

[9] Richard E. Biddle, *Brief GOJA: A Step-By-Step Job Analysis Instruction Booklet* (Sacramento, Calif.: Biddle and Associates, Inc., 1978).

[10] Ibid., p. 15.

[11] Ibid., p. 9.

[12] John W. Menne, William McCarthy, and Joy Menne, "A Systems Approach to the Content Validation of Employee Selection Procedures," *Public Personnel Management* 5 (November–December, 1976): 387–396.

[13] Iowa Merit Employment Department, *Job Analysis Questionnaire for Selection Device Development* (Des Moines, Iowa: Iowa Merit Employment Department, 1977).

[14] Menne, McCarthy, and Menne, "A Systems Approach to the Content Validation of Employee Selection Procedures."

[15] Iowa Merit Employment Department, *Job Analysis Guidelines* (Des Moines, Iowa: Iowa Merit Employment Department, 1974), p. 15.

[16] Ibid., p. 18.

[17] Sidney A. Fine and Wretha W. Wiley, *An Introduction to Functional Job Analysis: A Scaling of Selected Tasks From the Social Welfare Field* (Kalamazoo, Mich.: W. E. Upjohn Institute for Employment Research, 1977), pp. 9–10.

[18] Ibid., pp. 13–17.

[19] Ibid., p. 12.

[20] Howard C. Olson, Sidney A. Fine, David C. Myers, and Margaret C. Jennings, "The Use of Functional Job Analysis in Establishing Performance Standards for Heavy Equipment Operators," *Personnel Psychology* 34 (1981): 352.

[21] Fine and Wiley, *An Introduction to Functional Job Analysis*, pp. 10–12.

[22] Ibid., p. 15.

[23] Ibid., p. 16.

[24] Ibid., p. 17.

[25] Ibid., pp. 20–21.

[26] Ibid., pp. 27–30.

[27] Sidney A. Fine, A. M. Holt, and M. F. Hutchinson, *Functional Job Analysis: How to Standardize Task Statements* (Kalamazoo, Mich.: W. E. Upjohn Institute for Employment Research, 1974).

[28] Ernest S. Primoff, *How to Prepare and Conduct Job Element Examinations* (Washington, D.C.: Personnel Research and Development Center, U.S. Civil Service Commission, TS-75-1, 1975). See also Ernest S. Primoff, Cynthia L. Clark, and James R. Caplan, *How to Prepare and Conduct Job Element Examinations: Supplement* (Washington, D.C.: Office of Personnel Management, Office of Personnel Research and Development, 1982).

[29] Ibid., p. 2.

[30] Primoff, Clark, and Caplan, *How To Prepare and Conduct Job Element Examinations: Supplement*, pp. 5–6.

[31] Gary B. Brumback, Tania Romashko, Clifford P. Hahn, and Edwin A. Fleishman, *Model Procedures for Job Analysis, Test Development and Validation* (Washington, D.C.: American Institutes for Research, 1974), p. 19.

[32] Frank Sistrunk and Philip L. Smith, *Critiques of Job Analysis Methods* (Washington, D.C.: Office of Criminal Justice Education and Training, Law Enforcement Assistance Administration, vol. 2, Grant Number 78-CD-AX-0003, 1980).

[33] Primoff, Clark, and Caplan, *How to Prepare and Conduct Job Element Examinations: Supplement*.

8

Incorporating

Job Analysis Results

in Selection Measures

To this point, we have examined several aspects of job analysis. We have looked at the issues involved in preparing for a job analysis: organizing for a job analysis, choosing the jobs to be studied, reviewing the relevant literature, and selecting the job agents. Further, we have explored in some detail the actual application of job analysis in terms of collecting job information through various job analysis methods. But by this time you may be wondering how do we actually use our collected data for developing or choosing selection measures? Recall for a moment Exhibit 7.1, discussed in Chapter 7. In that figure, we showed that job analysis results are used to determine the relevant knowledge, skills, abilities (KSAs), or other employee specifications needed for effective performance on the job. Once identified, these specifications, in turn, serve as the basis for *constructing* (such as in developing questions for an employment interview schedule) or *choosing* (such as in selecting a previously-developed ability test) the needed selection measures. In this chapter we will study the last two elements of Exhibit 7.1, that is, (a) the determination of KSAs and other personal characteristics from job analysis data (identification of employee specifications) and (b) the incorporation of employee specifications in our selection instruments (determination of selection measure content). These two elements are the key steps in implementing job analysis results for human resource selection purposes.

Identification of Employee Specifications

In our earlier discussion of Exhibit 7.1, we noted that judgments or inferences on the part of job analysts play an important role in identifying employee specifications. However, the resulting specifications will be useful only to the extent that the inferences are accurate and complete. If the inferences are wrong, the selection measures will not be useful for predicting job performance. In addition, given current federal laws and executive orders, inappropriate selection measures may produce a situation that is ripe for charges of adverse impact against certain applicant groups or one where new employees are unqualified for the job for which they were employed. Both situations are unfair to employers and employees alike. The probability of situations such as these arising can be minimized by taking appropriate steps to insure, as much as possible, that the inferences are correct. Fortunately, several approaches have been developed for dealing with the problem of systematically inferring employee specifications from job analysis data. In this section, we will address the inference problem by describing a few of these methods.

We plan to review two different approaches to determining employee specifications from job analysis data. Each of these two approaches to inferring employee specifications offers a different perspective from the other. The first approach to be examined is derived from *task analysis* while the other is based on the *Position Analysis Questionnaire*. Both represent frequently used job analysis methods. As we have seen, task analysis inventory typically involves using a questionnaire composed of a large number of statements describing specific tasks or activities performed on a job. Respondents use rating scales (such as task importance or task frequency) to describe each task presented. Generally speaking, task analysis is specific to one job.

The Position Analysis Questionnaire, or PAQ, is the second job analysis method to be addressed. In Chapter 7, we noted that the PAQ is basically a standardized, commercially-available job analysis questionnaire that assesses general human behaviors involved in work. Rating scales are used to describe the extent to which any one of numerous behaviors characterize a specific job. Because the PAQ focuses on general human behaviors, it can be applied to a wide array of jobs.

These two approaches were chosen for specific reasons. The task analysis approach was picked because task data are oftentimes gathered and frequently recommended for developing employee specifications.[1] The PAQ was selected because it offers a unique means for deriving and measuring job attributes for use in selection.[2] It is representative of standardized questionnaires that use a predetermined set of items to study a variety of jobs. However, because of the prominence of the task analysis method in developing selection measures, most of our discussion will be centered on detailing this approach.

Before addressing these methods, we need to make a few general comments. First, as there are numerous job analysis methods other than those we have reviewed, there are also other job analysis/employee specifications approaches that could be offered. The two chosen represent a fairly diverse group of methods. Thus, they serve more as examples of the range of possible approaches than as final answers. Second, each one involves the use of judgment on the part of users. Even though judgment is involved, the approaches are designed to lead *systematically* from an analysis of the job to identification of employee specifications to determination of selection measure content. Finally, remember that whatever the approach, it is employed for two reasons: (a) to enhance the likelihood of choosing appropriate employee specifications and, in turn, valid selection instruments and (b) to meet certain legal requirements as mandated by the *Uniform Guidelines*. Depending upon the situation at hand, some approaches may be more appropriate than others.

Determination of Employee Specifications: Task Analysis Approach

The identification of KSAs and other employee specifications from the results of a task analysis generally follows similar procedures. Although there are unique aspects associated with any one employee specifications development method, most methods incorporate the following sequential steps:

1. Identifying and rating job tasks
2. Specifying KSAs necessary for successful job performance
3. Rating the importance of identified KSAs
4. Identifying other employee specifications necessary for job performance
5. Linking KSAs and other employee specifications to job tasks
6. Developing the content areas of selection measures

The goal of these six steps is the development of a systematic selection plan and content sources for constructing and/or choosing appropriate human resource selection instruments. We will now describe how each of these steps may be applied to accomplish this goal.

1. Identifying and Rating Job Tasks   Results from the application of a task analysis (or one or more of the work-oriented job analysis methods) serve as input to this step. Using data from a previous task analysis, for example, we attempt to isolate the most important tasks performed on a specific job. Where comprehensive task inventories are used, it is necessary to identify only those tasks most critical to the job. Typically, we would use job agents' ratings of the tasks to make this determination. In our earlier discussion of task analysis inventories, we described how tasks are frequently rated on a variety of rating scales, such as frequency of performance, criticality, and consequence of error, to name a few. As we saw in Chapter 7, we can employ these ratings to isolate a job's most important or most critical aspects. There, we saw that one possible tact is to use statistical indices (averages, standard deviations, frequencies) created from the rating scales and decision rules applied to these indices to define important tasks. For example, we may require that all important tasks receive a minimum average rating on one or more of our rating scales. Tasks whose average ratings exceed our cut-off score are then selected. Or, we may choose only those tasks rated in the upper quartile (top 25 percent) of all task ratings given. Any one or more of several criteria can be used. The important point is that a standard is employed so that it is possible to objectively justify the selection of important job tasks.

Whatever the analyses used, the "most important" tasks are the basis on which inferences regarding selection instrument content rests (Inference Point #2, Exhibit 7.1). The major idea behind the application of task analysis inventories is to define important job content. As illustrated in Exhibit 7.1, that determination serves as the source of statements about requisite employee specifications and development of selection instruments for choosing among job applicants.

When work-oriented methods like GOJA or IMES are used, it may not be necessary to choose a subset of important job tasks. Usually, such methods deal with significantly fewer tasks than those appearing on a task inventory. All tasks identified may represent important job duties; therefore, it may not be necessary to go through a task selection process.

2. Specifying KSAs Necessary for Successful Job Performance   Once critical job tasks have been identified, we are ready to specify the KSAs required for successful performance of these tasks. We cannot overemphasize the importance of producing accurate, complete KSA statements. As we will see, correct phrasing of the statements is *absolutely essential* to developing useful selection instruments. Several stages will be necessary in specifying these KSAs.

Selection of a KSA Rating Panel   The first stage is to select a panel of job experts who can identify important KSAs. Such a panel may be composed of those who participated in a job's prior analysis (Step 1) or formed from a new group of individuals. Listed below are several considerations that should be used in forming the KSA rating panel:[3]

1. *A panel of job experts (at least 10 to 20) is preferable over only one or two individuals.* Emphasis, however, should not be given exclusively to numbers of experts; we are more interested in the quality of their job knowledge and participation. If their assessments and inferences regarding KSAs are incorrect, resulting selection instruments will necessarily suffer.

2. *Characteristics we should seek in job agents (described earlier in Chapter 6) are also relevant in choosing the KSA rating panel.* These characteristics include: (a) participation should be voluntary, (b) incumbents should have performed adequately on the job in question, and (c) participants should have served on the job at least six months. In addition, women and minority group members should be represented on the panel.

Preparation of KSA Panelists   Whatever the data collection methodology, some form of orientation and training of KSA panelists will probably be needed. Panel members will likely require explanations as to what is meant by KSAs, why KSAs are important, and what their roles are to be in identifying and rating KSAs.

Collection of KSA data can take a variety of forms. Survey questionnaires completed independently by panelists can be used. Alternatively, group meetings of panel members can be convened, discussions held, and listings made of KSAs by panelists working independently within groups.

In specifying KSAs, panelists basically review the tasks identified from the job analysis and ask: "What knowledge, skills, or abilities are needed to perform each of these job tasks successfully?" Although the KSAs may not be written at the same level of specificity as task statements, several guides should be followed in their preparation. Again, the significance of the appropriate phrasing of the KSA statements is to facilitate making inferences concerning employee specifications for a job. Criteria that should be considered include the following:

1. *Panelists should have a clear understanding of what is meant by "knowledge," "skills," and "abilities."* Definitions of these terms can vary, but for our use the following definitions are appropriate:

Knowledge: A body of information, usually of a factual or procedural nature that makes for successful performance of a task.[4]

Skill: An individual's level of proficiency or competency in performing a specific task.[5]

Ability: A more general, enduring trait or capability an individual possesses at the time when he/she first begins to perform a task.[6]

Frequently, some analysts have difficulty in distinguishing between skills and abilities. For purposes of preparing KSA statements, it is not absolutely essential that a statement is correctly classified as a skill or an ability. In fact, some job analysis systems, such as GOJA, ignore the specification of abilities altogether and simply focus on knowledge and skills. What is important for us is the statement itself; the statement, not its classification, serves as the basis for inferring selection instrument content.

2. *Statements should be written so that they show the kind of knowledge, skill, or ability and the degree or level of each that is needed for successful task performance.* For example, in describing "typing skill," it should be specified if the typing skill requires typing tables of data composed of complex numbers within a specified time period, typing letters at a self-paced rate, or typing handwritten manuscripts at the rate of 40 words per minute.[7]

3. *Statements should be written at the highest level that is required for the job.* For example, if statistical skills involving the calculation of correlation coefficients are needed to perform a task, there is no need to list an ability

to count or a knowledge of basic mathematics as other KSAs. These would have been covered in the statistical skill statement.[8]

4. *Specific statements are preferable to broad, general ones that lack clarity as to what actual KSAs are required.* In preparing a statement it may be necessary to probe with job experts the exact nature, degree, breadth, and precision of a stated KSA. If, for instance, a statement such as "Knowledge of Mathematics" is offered, it may be necessary to ask "What kind?", "To what extent?", "To solve what types of problems?" Use of probing questions should permit the development of a more complete and useful statement of what specifications are needed to perform a job.

5. *Although it may be possible to prepare a long list of KSAs for many jobs, emphasis should be given to identifying those that determine "successful" performance on the job.*

6. *In preparing knowledge statements, adjective modifiers (for example, "thorough," "some") relative to the degree or extent of knowledge required should not be used.* Below are some examples of appropriate knowledge statements: "Knowledge of typing procedures for use on an IBM Datamaster word processor including setting margins, tabulating, automatic centering, making corrections, and storing files." "Knowledge of statistical principles, calculation on a programmable calculator, and interpretation of partial, simple, and multiple correlation coefficients."

7. *In preparing ability statements, adjective modifiers of level or extent of the ability required should not be used.* Vague adverbs implying some level of performance (for example, "rapidly," "effectively") should not be used to modify the action of the statement.[9] Ability statements should avoid confusing the action of the ability with the result of that action. For instance, look at this statement: "Ability to maintain accurate clerical accounting records." The result of the action "maintain accurate accounting records" is treated as the action itself. The statement would be better written like this: "Ability to log accounting transactions in order to maintain accurate and up-to-date accounting records."

After all KSAs have been suggested, it is quite possible some statements will require editing. Where editing is needed, the objective should be to specify important content in as much detail as possible and give examples where appropriate. Several illustrations of KSAs developed in previous job analysis studies follow:

Knowledge:
"Knowledge of building materials including the uses, storage, and preparation of materials such as aluminum siding, masonite, concrete block, and gypsum board."

"Knowledge of state workmen's compensation laws."

"Knowledge of the development, scoring, and application of employee performance appraisal techniques such as behaviorally-anchored rating scales, management-by-objectives, graphic rating scales, and mixed standard scales."

Skills:

"Skill in using a bank proof machine to process 50 checks per minute without error."

"Skill in writing BASIC computer programs to store, select, and sort demographic data (such as, age, sex, race) collected on job applicants."

"Skill in conducting a job analysis for content validation purposes that will meet the standards of the *Uniform Guidelines.*"

Abilities:

"Ability to testify as an expert witness in an employment discrimination suit."

"Ability to use basic arithmetic to calculate flow of current through an electrical circuit."

With respect to abilities, a special comment is needed. Rather than developing abilities tailored to a specific job, predetermined abilities can also be rated using the *Abilities Requirements Scales* (ARS) developed by Edwin Fleishman and his associates.[10] The ARS consists of rating scales designed to be used by an analyst in judging the extent to which each of 37 abilities is required to perform a job or task. Each ability is measured by a five- or seven-point rating scale, with example behaviors describing various ability levels. The abilities appraised cluster into four categories: (a) mental abilities, (b) physical abilities, (c) abilities that require some action to be taken when specific sensory cues are present, and (d) abilities having to do with perceived incoming sensory information.

At the present time, application of the scales for selection purposes is principally experimental. Further research is required prior to widespread adoption by practitioners. Nevertheless, the measures hold future promise as a means for systematically measuring abilities across a wide spectrum of jobs.

Care should be exercised as we derive and consider KSAs from defined job tasks because it is possible that a significant KSA may be overlooked. For instance, a KSA may under-lie several tasks but may not be detected unless examination is made of the less important tasks. For example, "Knowledge of Safety Procedures" may be an instance of such a KSA.[11]

3. Rating the Importance of Identified KSAs   For selection instruments to be useful, they should reflect the importance of different KSAs required for a specific job. That is, those KSAs that are most important for a job should account for more selection instrument content than less important ones. Determination of KSA importance is usually made by job experts giving ratings to the listed KSAs. Although KSAs can be judged on any number of factors, in general, there are three principal ways of viewing KSA importance to a job:

1. KSA importance in performing the job as a whole

2. KSA importance for job applicants to have when first hired

3. KSA importance in differentiating among applicants, that is, KSA importance in ranking candidates from good to poor as opposed to KSAs considered as indicators of who should and should not be employed[12]

Methods of Judging KSA Importance   The methods used in rating KSA importance are similar to those used in assessing the importance of job tasks. That is, some form of survey questionnaire consisting of a listing of KSA statements and relevant rating scales is used by respondents (KSA panel members) in judging KSA importance. Actual questionnaire formats including rating scales can vary from one application to the next. However, most rating scales employed resemble one or more of the following examples:

A. How important is this KSA for acceptable job performance?

    0. Of No Importance

    1. Moderately Important

    2. Very Important

    3. Critical

B. Must a newly-hired employee possess this KSA?

    1. Yes

    2. No

C. To what degree does this KSA distinguish between superior and adequate performance of newly-hired employees?

    0. Not At All

    1. Moderately

    2. Considerably

    3. To A Great Degree

David Lewin has cautioned that unless certain criteria are considered in choosing KSAs for selection measures, it is possible to obtain a distorted picture of the actual importance of employee specifications. Therefore, he has recommended that all KSAs be evaluated on at least the following criteria:

1. *The percentage of an applicant population that can be expected to have a sufficient amount of a KSA to successfully perform the job.* The smaller the percentage of the available labor pool possessing the KSA, the more

important it is to measure the KSA. However, if the KSA is learned on the job, it should not be assessed.

2. *The degree to which an employee with more of a KSA will be a better employee than one with less of the characteristic.* To the extent that more of a KSA is viewed as leading to better job performance, the more important is the KSA.

3. *The extent to which serious consequences could occur if a KSA is not examined.* If serious effects could occur, then more importance should be given.[13]

Example of KSA importance rating. In order to get a better appreciation of the nature and application of a questionnaire utilizing such scales, an example may be helpful. The U.S. Office of Personnel Management has developed an experimental method for obtaining job expert judgments on the importance of KSAs.[14] Basically, its application resembles the methods we have described earlier. That is, a survey questionnaire is distributed to a panel of experts who make judgments regarding identified KSAs. Application of the questionnaire is designed to enable an analyst to determine (a) the degree varying levels of KSAs among employees are related to differences in performance effectiveness, (b) those KSAs required when beginning a job, and (c) the extent to which it is practical for applicants in the labor pool to possess necessary KSAs.[15]

4. Identifying Other Employee Specifications Necessary for Job Performance   Other than KSAs, jobs may require that applicants possess certain personal specifications that are necessary for adequate performance. Such specifications typically include the following types: (a) physical requirements (b) licensure/certification requirements, or (c) other/miscellaneous requirements.[16]

Physical Requirements   Physical requirements are those qualifications workers must possess in order to physically perform their jobs. These requirements may involve a number of physical abilities requiring specific levels of hearing, seeing, speaking, or lifting, to name a few. For example, the ability to lift and carry a specific amount of weight might be set for firefighters. Or, minimum levels of corrected visual acuity could be used in choosing nuclear plant operators who must visually monitor dials and meters at a distance. Operative or physically demanding jobs are likely to require more physical abilities for adequate performance than are managerial positions. Thus, when setting employee specifications for operative positions, physical ability qualifications should routinely be considered.

The relevance of physical qualifications can be assessed in either of two ways: (a) listing and rating physical abilities required for a job or (b) rating a preestablished set of physical abilities. Where a listing and rating of physical abilities is concerned, the same methods described for generating and rating

KSAs can be used. Emphasis is placed on developing observable and measurable statements descriptive of physical job requirements. Examples of such statements include:

"See well enough to read a voltmeter dial from a distance of five feet."

"Be strong enough to carry a 180-pound dead weight down a 50-foot ladder."

"Hear well enough to carry on a telephone conversation without electronic amplification."

Once listed, these characteristics can be rated using appropriate scales like those utilized in judging KSAs. For example, ratings of physical abilities might be based on variables such as importance or criticality to performance. Analyses can then be made of the ratings to determine those physical abilities most important for a job. Selection measures comprising important physical abilities can next be developed or chosen.

Rather than developing a rating scale of physical requirements, existing measures, such as Edwin Fleishman's *Physical Abilities Analysis* (PAA) scales, can be employed. The PAA scales are designed to examine the extent to which a job requires various physical abilities to perform it.[17]

Use of the PAA scales consists of an analyst making ratings of a job on nine rating scales, one for each of nine physical abilities. Each rating scale has a set of definitions that include examples of tasks representing differing amounts of an ability. The scales are first applied by an analyst observing a job. Each scale is then studied and the job is rated by assigning the most descriptive scale point value to the job.

The PAA scales have been used in several different selection situations. For example, they have been used for identifying the physical requirements of jobs such as firefighter, sanitation worker, and police officer.[18] Importantly, the scales have been found to serve as a valuable foundation for determining which physical abilities are critical to a job. From such a foundation, a rationale is created for developing selection instruments for measuring these critical abilities.

Licensure/Certification Requirements   The next set of specifications that may be necessary for successful job performance are special licensure or certification requirements. If these requirements are critical in performing a job, then they are important specifications that should be used in selection. Examples of licensure/certification requirements are a driver's license, a teaching certificate, and a first-class FCC radiotelephone license. Since there may be a variety of such requirements, a particular questionnaire or form for determining these specifications is not provided. Instead, provision can be made on a survey questionnaire for a job analyst to list any important requirements. Like tasks and KSAs, these specifications can be rated on a scale to determine their importance in performing the job under study.

Other Necessary Requirements   It is possible for requirements other than KSAs, licenses, or certificates to be critical to a job. More than likely these requirements will be unique for a given job; but, if they are critical to job success, they should be evaluated. Examples of these "other" requirements might be ownership of specific tools, equipment, or a vehicle. Some jobs may also require a willingness on the part of an applicant/incumbent to work under unusual conditions of employment, such as, to relocate every six months, to work overtime, to work specific shifts, to travel five days out of seven. Again, these requirements can be listed and rated in terms of their significance to job performance.

5. Linking KSAs and Other Employee Specifications to Job Tasks   It is critical to a job analysis that a clear relationship between KSAs and other employee specifications be established with tasks performed on a job.[19] Therefore, provision must be made for showing that *each* identified KSA is tied to *at least* one task for which it is required. Tying KSAs and other specifications to job tasks is important for several reasons. First, KSA—job task link information may be needed in the legal defense of a selection procedure. The *Uniform Guidelines* state that a relation be shown between each identified KSA and a work behavior. By tying these specifications to job tasks, evidence can be provided on how these specifications are required on a job. Second, specifications can improve the efficiency and effectiveness of selection instruments. If unnecessary specifications are included in selection instruments, not only are these measures wasteful of resources, but they may not identify the most qualified job applicants. By linking KSAs with tasks, it is possible to check the appropriateness of selection specifications and associated selection instruments.

Methods of Establishing KSA—Job Task Links   Documentation of KSA—job task links can generally be accomplished in either of two ways: (a) by having job analysts list job tasks associated with each identified KSA or (b) by constructing a job task X KSA rating matrix and then having job analysts rate the degree to which a KSA is necessary to successfully perform each task.

Some job analysis methods, like GOJA, for instance, use a task-listing approach. An incumbent studies a knowledge or skill, reviews the stated job tasks, and then lists those duties that require each knowledge or skill. If a duty cannot be found to justify a particular knowledge or skill, then that specification is removed as an important consideration in developing selection instruments.

The second method of linking KSAs and job tasks consists of pairing every KSA with every task. Job analysts judge the link between the various task—KSA pairs. Table 8.1 shows a partial task X KSA rating matrix for selected tasks and KSAs for the job of personnel selection analyst. Only a portion of the tasks and KSAs are noted, but they serve to illustrate how the ratings are made. The numbers in the cells represent average ratings given by

Table 8.1   Mean Ratings of KSA Importance to Task Performance
for the Job of Personnel Selection Analyst

Knowledge, Skills, Abilities

Job Tasks	Knowledge of record-keeping procedures	Knowledge of psychometrics	Knowledge of applied statistics	Knowledge of test validation requirements	Knowledge of development of task inventories	Ability to give oral testimony in court hearings	· · ·	Skill in using computerized data analysis packages (e.g., SPSS)
1. Computes adverse impact statistics for selection measures	1.9	1.5	3.7	2.0	0.9	0.0		3.8
2. Constructs written tests for use in personnel selection	3.1	4.0	3.5	3.0	2.7	0.0	· · ·	1.7
3. Conducts job analyses on entry-level clerical jobs	3.3	3.0	2.9	3.7	3.9	0.0		2.1
4. Develops affirmative action plans and programs and monitors impact	2.4	1.2	0.7	1.2	0.8	1.0		1.3
⋮	⋮			⋮				⋮
N. Maintains job applicant applications and selection test records	3.8	0.0	0.5	0.3	0.0	0.0	· · ·	0.0

Note: The task and KSA statements have been abbreviated to conserve space.
    KSA – Task ratings were made using the following scale:
        How important is this KSA in performing this task?
            0 Not at all important
            1 Somewhat important
            2 Important
            3 Very important
            4 Extremely important

a group of panelists to the importance of KSAs. Greater importance of a
KSA is shown with higher mean ratings. As can be seen, some KSAs are
important for several tasks while others are critical to the performance of
only one.

Licensure/certification and other characteristics that may be treated as
employee specifications should also be tied to job tasks. When these specifications are used, they can be judged along with KSAs. However, in certain
situations, it may not be meaningful to tie a specification to a job task. In
those cases, reasons justifying their criticality should be listed. For example, if
it is specified that a suitable applicant for a radio technician job should hold
a first-class FCC radiotelephone license, it should be noted that this specification is required by federal law. The idea behind this documentation is to
provide evidence that the specification is indeed required to perform a job.

Whatever the method chosen (listing or rating), the linking of KSAs,
licensure/certification, and other specifications to job tasks is a critical step in
job analysis. This linking step should not be taken lightly. The data obtained
will ultimately help to justify the job analysis efforts and the content of
selection instruments.

6. Developing the Content Areas of Selection Measures   So far, in developing appropriate employee specifications, we have studied the tasks performed on a job, the KSAs and other specifications needed for job performance, and the relationships between these specifications and job tasks. Our
final step is to combine the task and KSA information in order to establish
employee specifications to be covered in the selection instruments. Once
established, selection instruments can be constructed or chosen to match
these specifications. More will be said about actually incorporating these
specifications in selection instruments in the last section of the chapter. For
now, however, attention will be given to the development of content areas of
the selection instruments. As we will see, these areas are derived from the
collected KSA information.

Important KSAs and Other Specifications   Table 8.2 presents a sample
form for recording relevant KSA information. The form has been completed
for the job we mentioned earlier, that is, personnel selection analyst. Basically, the completed sheet summarizes the relevant task and KSA information that have been collected about the job. This information will be used in
determining the content of the selection instruments. Let's see how each of
the sections was prepared.

Column 1, "KSAs and Other Employee Specifications," lists all KSAs
and other specifications identified by the panel of job experts. (The example
KSAs have been abbreviated.) Of those noted, the KSAs and specifications
most essential to successful job performance must be identified. The importance of these specifications was assessed by two ratings: (a) KSA importance
to successful job performance (where $0 =$ Of No Importance to $3 =$ Criti-

Table 8.2   *Summary of KSA Tabulations for Determining Content Areas of*
Selection Instruments for the Job of Personnel Selection Analyst

KSAs and Other Employee Specifications	KSA Importance Criteria		
	Mean Importance of KSA to Job Success:[a]	Percent Indicating a New Employee Should Possess This KSA[b]	Task Statement (Numbers) for which a KSA is Necessary[c]
1. Knowledge of record-keeping procedures	1.6	50%	2, 3, 4, N
2. Knowledge of psychometrics	3.0	100	2, 3
3. Knowledge of applied statistics	2.9	90	1, 2, 3
4. Knowledge of test validation requirements	3.0	100	1, 2, 3
5. Knowledge of development of task inventories	2.4	77	2, 3
6. Ability to give oral testimony in court hearings	1.1	30	None
.	.	.	.
.	.	.	.
.	.	.	.
N. Skill in using computerized data analysis packages (e.g., SPSS)	2.0	77	1, 3

Note: The KSA statements have been abbreviated.

[a]Important KSAs are those receiving a rating of 1.5 or higher.
0 = Of No Importance
1 = Moderately Important
2 = Very Important
3 = Critical

[b] KSAs that should be possessed by newly-hired employees are those chosen by 75% or more of the job analysts.
[c]The task statements are listed in Table 8.1.

cal) and (b) necessity for a newly-hired employee to possess (percent of job experts indicating Yes or No). Other types of rating scales could have been used. What is critical is that we collect the judgments of experts on KSA importance and the necessity for new employees to possess these KSAs. Columns 2 and 3 present these data.

KSA Necessity for Task Performance   Column 4 draws upon job task-KSA linking results like those shown earlier in Table 8.1. In Table 8.1, the job analysis panel's average ratings of KSA importance in performing each of the identified job tasks were presented. These ratings were based upon a five-point rating scale (where 0 = Not At All Important to 4 = Extremely Important). Now, suppose that any KSA with a 2.0 (= Important) or higher average rating for a particular task is judged as necessary for performance of that task. Column 4 in Table 8.2 summarizes those task statements (by number) for which each KSA noted in column 1 is important to task performance.

KSA Selections At the conclusion of the summary analysis, those KSAs that should be included in the selection instruments can be identified. These KSAs will represent the content areas of our human resource selection measures. Determination of these areas can be made by comparing the KSA ratings summarized on the rating form with preestablished rating criteria. For instance, in the example, the following rating criteria were used for defining important KSAs:

1. A KSA must receive a mean importance to job success rating of 1.5 or higher (see column 2 in Table 8.2).

2. The majority (75 percent or more) of job experts should agree that a KSA is necessary for a new employee to possess (see column 3).

3. A KSA must be linked with an *important* job task for it to be considered. Application of this criterion has two requirements: (a) determination of important job tasks and (b) determination of KSAs tied to those important tasks. As we have seen, important job tasks can be identified in many different ways, such as those we discussed in our review of task analysis in Chapter 7. Once important job tasks have been identified, another determination has to be made. Here, KSAs important to job success must be identified. Usually, these determinations are made through ratings. In our example, for instance, KSAs important to job success were identified by those having an average importance to job success rating of 1.5 or higher. In column 2 of Table 8.2, we can see six KSAs met this criterion (KSA numbers 1, 2, 3, 4, 5, and N). Only one KSA (number 6) did not. Column 4 of Table 8.2 shows that each of the KSAs receiving an importance rating of 1.5 or higher was judged as necessary in performing at least one important job task. The KSA "Ability to Give Oral Testimony in Court" was not viewed as important to job success or necessary to the performance of any single job task.

Content Areas of Selection Instruments Next, the KSAs that satisfy the rating criteria must be recorded. Content areas of the selection instruments are defined by those KSAs that meet *all* of the above criteria. That is, (a) if a KSA is rated as important, (b) if it is believed new employees should possess the KSA upon job entry, *and* (c) if the KSA is linked to performance of an important job task, then it should be represented in the contents of the selection instruments.

Table 8.3 summarizes the final tabulations of the KSAs being evaluated. A review of this table shows that of the seven KSAs rated, five meet all of the rating criteria. Therefore, these five KSAs should be employed in defining the content of selection instruments for the job of personnel selection analyst. Later, in the section of this chapter entitled "Incorporation of Employee Specifications in Selection Instruments," we will look at how we might take these results and translate them into selection measures such as tests, interviews, or application forms.

Table 8.3   *KSA Content Areas Identified for Measurement by Selection Instruments for the Job of Personnel Selection Analyst*

KSAs and other Employee Specifications	Selection Instrument Content Area Criteria			
	Is This KSA an Important One?	Is This KSA Necessary for Newly-Hired Employees to Possess?	Is This KSA Necessary for an Important Task?	Should This KSA Serve As Selection Content Area?[a]
1. Knowledge of record-keeping procedures	Yes	No	Yes	No
2. Knowledge of psychometrics	Yes	Yes	Yes	Yes
3. Knowledge of applied statistics	Yes	Yes	Yes	Yes
4. Knowledge of test validation requirements	Yes	Yes	Yes	Yes
5. Knowledge of development of task inventories	Yes	Yes	Yes	Yes
6. Ability to give oral testimony in court hearings	No	No	No	No
•	•	•	•	•
•	•	•	•	•
•	•	•	•	•
N. Skill in using computerized data analysis packages (e.g., SPSS)	Yes	Yes	Yes	Yes

Note: The KSA statements have been abbreviated.

[a]For a KSA to be chosen as a selection content area, each of the selection instrument content area criteria must be answered by a "Yes."

Determination of Employee Specifications: PAQ Approach

Whereas the task analysis approach uses a panel of job experts to infer employee specifications, the PAQ takes a different tack. Under the PAQ approach, computerized analyses of *existing* job aptitude data are used to identify attributes associated with PAQ job elements. Once a job's important elements have been identified, the associated attributes represent employee specifications.

Linking PAQ Job Elements–Job Attributes   In order to understand this method better, we need to refer to some previous research on job attributes assessed by the PAQ. Initially, a list of 76 human attributes (49 of an "aptitudinal" nature and 27 of an "interest" nature) thought to be most relevant in personnel selection was developed by McCormick and his colleagues.[20] Examples of these attributes are shown in Table 8.4. A sample of psychologists was asked to rate the relevance of each of these attributes to the job elements on the PAQ. (See Chapter 7 for a discussion of these elements.)

Table 8.4   *Selected Examples of PAQ Job Attributes*

Attributes of an Aptitude Nature	Attributes of an Interest or Temperament Nature
1. *Verbal Comprehension*—ability to understand the meaning of words and the ideas associated with them. 2. *Arithmetic Reasoning*—ability to reason abstractly using quantitative concepts and symbols. 3. *Perceptual Speed*—ability to make rapid discriminations of visual detail. 4. *Near Visual Acuity*—ability to perceive detail at normal reading distance. 5. *Manual Dexterity*—ability to manipulate things with the hands. 6. *Eye-Hand Coordination*—ability to coordinate hand movements with visual stimuli. 7. *Movement Detection*—ability to detect physical movement of objects and to judge their direction. 8. *Selective Attention*—ability to perform a task in the presence of distracting stimulation or under monotonous conditions without significant loss in efficiency.	1. *Working Alone*—working in physical isolation from others, although the activity may be integrated with that of others. 2. *Pressure of Time*—working in situations where time is a critical factor·for successful performance. 3. *Working Under Specific Instructions*—those that allow little or no room for independent action or judgment in working out job problems. 4. *Empathy*—seeing things from another person's point of view. 5. *Personal Risk*—risk of physical or mental illness or injury. 6. *Attainment of Set Standards*—attainment of set limits, tolerances, or standards. 7. *Scientific/Technical Activities*—using technical methods for investigating natural phenomena using scientific procedures. 8. *Influencing People*—influencing opinions, attitudes, or judgments about ideas or things.

Source: Based on Lloyd D. Marquardt and Ernest J. McCormick, *Component Analyses of the Attribute Data Based on the Position Analysis Questionnaire (PAQ)* (West Lafayette, Ind.: Occupational Research Center, Department of Psychological Sciences, Purdue University, 1973), pp. 34–38. Final report submitted to the Office of Naval Research, Arlington, Virginia.

From these ratings, a median rating for the relevance of each attribute for each PAQ job element was obtained. These job element–job attribute ratings permit some interesting descriptions. Once PAQ job elements can be identified for a job, the attribute ratings represent a profile of the attributes or specifications necessary for successfully performing the job. But how can these attribute ratings be used to develop specifications for any particular job? The answer to this question lies with the administration of the PAQ itself. After PAQ ratings of a job are obtained, important job elements are specified. And, once the elements characteristic of a job are known, it is simply a matter of identifying those attributes most relevant to performing these job elements. These identified attributes then serve as employee specifications to be used in hiring.

Example of PAQ–Job Attribute Links   Let's look at an example of some actual PAQ–job attribute results. Initially, the job of senior shipping and receiving clerk was analyzed by administration of the PAQ to five supervisors familiar with the job. Table 8.5 summarizes the results of the analyses of the PAQ data. This table shows some selected job attributes of an aptitudinal nature that were identified from the PAQ data as being important in performing the critical elements of the job in question. The identified attributes are listed in *descending* order of importance. Referring to the table, it can be seen that the two most important job attributes of an aptitude nature are:

1. *Depth Perception* — ability to estimate depth of distances or objects (or to judge their physical relationships in space)

2. *Mechanical Ability* — ability to determine the functional interrelationships of parts within a mechanical system

---

Table 8.5   *Job Attribute Ratings of an Aptitude Nature for the Job of Senior Shipping and Receiving Clerk*

Attribute Number	Job Attribute	Score[a]	Estimated Percentile
48	Depth Perception	1.33	78
76	Mechanical Ability	1.92	76
65	Rate of Arm Movement	1.12	75
71	Dynamic Strength	1.03	74
68	Speed of Limb Movement	.98	74
74	Explosive Strength	.59	73
61	Manual Dexterity	1.45	72
72	Static Strength	.88	72
62	Arm/Hand Positioning	1.48	71
45	Spatial Visualization	1.53	70
.	.	.	.
.	.	.	.
.	.	.	.
40	Selective Attention	3.16	19

Source: Based on analyses from PAQ Services Inc., Logan, Utah.

[a]Median attribute relevance rating; the higher the score, the more relevant the attribute to the job.

Beside each attribute is a percentile score. This score indicates the percentage of jobs (in the PAQ Services, Inc. data bank) scoring lower on a specific job attribute than the job under investigation. For example, 78 percent of the jobs for which PAQ data are available scored lower than the job of senior shipping and receiving clerk on the attribute "Depth Perception." It appears "Depth Perception" is an important attribute for employees to have in performing the shipping clerk job. These attribute data will be used for identifying employee specifications from which selection instruments will be developed. More will be said about the choice of selection methods shortly; but keep in mind, judgments about selection methods are *not* eliminated. Inferences must still be made in choosing measures of the attributes identified as relevant to the job.

Obviously, the PAQ approach to deriving employee specifications is much easier, briefer, and less expensive than the task analysis approach outlined earlier. The essential requirement is the collection of valid and reliable PAQ data on the job under study. However, before sole reliance is placed on the PAQ method for developing selection instruments at least *two* issues must be resolved. First, the utility of this approach for developing appropriate selection instruments needs further investigation prior to widespread adoption. Second, certain legal questions that may arise regarding the development of employee specifications for a specific job (relative to many other jobs) need to be answered. Irrespective of these issues, when a user decides to follow the approach, certain PAQ scoring arrangements must be made. As we mentioned earlier in our discussion of the PAQ, necessary analyses cannot be made by an individual user. These analyses must be coordinated through PAQ Services, Inc. of Logan, Utah.

Incorporation of Employee Specifications in Selection Instruments

Now that we know what is required to perform a job (the employee specifications), how do we know which job applicants possess these necessary requirements? These applicants are identified through administration of carefully chosen selection instruments, that is, instruments based on the specifications needed to perform a job. But, how do we translate these specifications into selection instruments? The answer to this question can be very technical and detailed. The development of assessment methods requires the use of specially trained individuals such as industrial psychologists or test development specialists. Yet people working in personnel and human resource management, like job analysts, can play an integral role in developing selection measures. The experience and information obtained during a job analysis is valuable for suggesting selection methods that reflect important KSAs and other employee specifications. To enhance the process of developing selection instruments, we need to look at several relevant considerations. It is the purpose of this section to indicate how identified KSAs can be incorporated into selection measures. As in the previous section, principal emphasis will be on a task-oriented approach to constructing selection instruments. Some attention will also be given to the role of the PAQ in choosing these measures.

Development of a Selection Plan: Task Analysis Approach

In choosing selection instruments, it must be decided which methods will be used to assess important KSAs and other specifications required for successful job performance. This process of specifying content areas to measure specific KSAs and other specifications and choosing selection instruments is referred to as *developing a selection plan*. We can view the development of a selection plan as consisting of the following important steps:

1. Determining the relative importance of employee specifications
2. Choosing selection methods to measure these employee specifications

Determining Relative Importance of Employee Specifications   Previously, employee specifications such as KSAs important to a job were identified. For most jobs, however, it is unlikely that all specifications will be equally critical to job success. Some specifications will be more important than others, and it is these specifications that should play a more dominant role in determining the content and use of selection instruments. Before choosing tests or other selection measures, the relative importance of employee specifications that they are intended to measure must be determined.

Relative importance of employee specifications can be defined in a number of ways. For example, job experts might be administered a survey questionnaire to make relative determinations of KSA importance.[21] The questionnaire might consist of a listing of important, previously identified KSAs. Respondents could be asked to assign a relative importance weight, from 0 to 100 percent, to each KSA so that the sum of weights totals 100 percent. The product of this process would be a relative weighting of the critical KSAs. Based upon the example job of personnel selection analyst, relative KSA importance weights might look as follows:

KSA	Mean Weight Assigned
1. Knowledge of psychometrics	25%
2. Knowledge of applied statistics	25%
3. Knowledge of test validation requirements	25%
4. Knowledge of development of task inventories	15%
. . .	.
. . .	.
. . .	.
N. Skill in using computerized data analysis packages (e.g., SPSS)	10%
Total Weight	100%

Shortly, we will see the role these importance weights will play in developing and choosing among human resource selection instruments.

Choosing Selection Methods to Measure Employee Specifications A wide variety of means are available for selecting personnel. The remaining chapters will discuss the nature and application of many of these methods. The choice of ways to assess relevant KSAs requires consideration of a number of factors. Inferences and judgments play an important role in deciding which means are best for measuring which specification. In considering the possible alternatives, a consultant, human resource manager, or any personnel decision-maker contemplating the choice of a selection measure should ask questions such as the following:[22]

1. *Have applicants previously demonstrated successful performance of the tasks of the job?* If so, evaluation of past performance, such as through a biographical data questionnaire may be appropriate.

2. *Can job applicants be observed performing the job or part of it? Is there a means for simulating a job in a test situation that is likely to require important behaviors as defined by the job? If so, is there a practical way of measuring performance?* Where demonstration of successful performance is possible and measurable, a work sample test might seriously be considered.

3. *Would a written test be best for examining worker requirements in terms of eliciting desired reactions and practical scoring?* If "yes," a written test should be proposed.

4. *Would an opportunity for applicants to express themselves orally through an interview cover job requirements that might go unassessed using other means?* In this case, a semi-structured, oral interview that can be objectively scored could be administered.

5. *Can the appraisal method produce reliable and valid data for evaluating applicants' possession of a KSA?* If not, the method should be dropped from consideration.

6. *Is it practical and within our resources to use a particular method for measuring a KSA?* If not, an alternative method may be considered.

John Campbell has illustrated how such a questioning approach might suggest alternative means for assessing the same KSA. For instance, suppose an ability such as "Ability to Relate Verbally to Persons of Varied Socioeconomic Levels" was found to be important for the job of social worker. Campbell notes that in studying this ability, several selection methods might be considered.

1. The applicant may have performed the same, or very similar, kinds of tasks in previous jobs. We could then try to find out how effective he or she was on that task in the past. . . .

2. If previous experience doesn't exist one might try to 'simulate' the task

in some fashion. For example, one might contrive a role playing situation and include as many of the real life dynamics as possible. . . .

3. Several steps further removed from a direct sample of job behavior is the response of the applicant to open-ended questions when interviewed by members of the target group. [The interview] could pose hypothetical situations and focus on the content of the answers; or minority group interviewers could play the role of a hostile minority group member to see how the applicant handled the hostility. . . .

4. Some paper-and-pencil predictor could be used which poses a number of hypothetical situations for the applicant. . . .

5. One could use some test like Rokeach's Dogmatism Scale in the belief that it had something to do with how people relate to the problem of minority group members.[23]

An Example Selection Plan for the Job of Personnel Selection Analyst
Table 8.6 shows a selection plan for the example job of personnel selection analyst. For illustrative purposes, it is assumed only five KSAs are critical to this job. At the top of our plan, a variety of selection methods that could be used for this or any other job have been listed. You may be unfamiliar with some of these techniques; however, for our present purposes, complete understanding is not critical. We will be dealing with many of these measures in subsequent chapters. What is important is understanding that we have chosen different methods to assess different KSAs. For purposes of illustration, we have purposely chosen a variety of methods to assess different KSAs. In practice, fewer methods would likely be used for any one job.

Now, let's study the example in more detail. With respect to the first two KSAs, "Knowledge of Psychometrics" and "Knowledge of Applied Statistics," we are dealing with specific bodies of information and knowledge in two related technical fields. Because we are interested in the extent to which applicants possess knowledge of these technical areas, a written, multiple-choice test is recommended. And, since the two content areas are judged to be equally important, half of the exam should concentrate on psychometric issues and the remainder should focus on applied statistics.

With respect to "Knowledge of Test Validation Requirements," we may be interested in applicants' knowledge and actual experiences with test validation matters. Three assessment methods are suggested. The application form could ask applicants for a list of previous experiences in test validation research. We may contact previous employers through reference checks to verify certain stated test validation capabilities. An oral interview could be used to let applicants describe in detail their experiences or, possibly, to respond to technical questions or situations concerning their knowledge of test validation research. Our selection method weights show that more emphasis should be placed on the interview than on the application form or reference check in appraising this KSA.

"Knowledge of Development of Task Inventories" could be assessed

Table 8.6   An Example Selection Plan for the Job of Personnel Selection Analyst

KSA	KSA Weight	Selection Method Weights									
		Application Form	Biographical Data Questionnaire	Reference Check	Personal Interview	Work Sample Test	Assessment Center	Written, Objective Test	Training and Experience Evaluation	Medical Examination	Other (specify)
1. Knowledge of psychometrics	25%							25%			
2. Knowledge of applied statistics	25							25			
3. Knowledge of test validation requirements	25	5%		5%	15%						
4. Knowledge of development of task inventories	15				10				5%		
N. Skill in using computerized data analysis packages (e.g., SPSS)	10	5				5%					
Total KSA Weight	100%	10%	0%	5%	25%	5%	0%	50%	5%	0%	0%

through a personal interview and a training and experience evaluation. In addition to questions about test validation, our selection interview should also incorporate questions involving applicants' knowledge about task inventories. Training and experience evaluations should also play a role in the objective judgment of applicants' experiences with task inventories.

Finally, applicants' "Skill in Using Computerized Data Analysis Packages" should be evaluated. Relative to other KSAs, this skill plays a less critical role in accounting for job success as a selection analyst. An application form could ask for information on formal training, experience, or self-rated expertise with data analysis packages. A work sample or performance test might be used as well. In a work sample test, an applicant would be given a typical research problem and asked to analyze it using these data analysis packages. Applicants would then be objectively scored on their skill in applying the packages to solve a realistic research problem.

In addition to suggesting alternative methods for appraising job-relevant KSAs, a selection plan has an additional value. That is, the weights assigned to a selection method for each KSA are useful in determining the relative emphasis on the content areas of the measures. For instance, think back to the job of personnel selection analyst. Let's say we decided we could use roughly 50 questions to appraise the five important KSAs identified for the job. If 50 items represent the total number of items we can use, how do we determine the number of items employed to measure each KSA and the number included in each selection measure? We make these decisions by referring to the selection plan. Using the weights in the plan, we can see that half of the 50 items should be included in a written, objective test. Of these 25 items, roughly 12 should be devoted to measuring "Knowledge of Psychometrics" and the remainder directed toward "Knowledge of Applied Statistics." In contrast, approximately 25 percent of the 50 items should be allocated to an oral interview. Seven of these should concentrate on applicants' "Knowledge of Test Validation Requirements" and five on their "Knowledge of Development of Task Inventories."

As you look at our proposed selection plan, you may notice an interesting result. Our job analysis appears to have produced a selection program whose contents seem to reflect the contents of the job. Selection measure/job content overlap is precisely what we want. The more we can insure a match between content of our selection methods and demands of the job, the more confident we can be of the value of our selection program. Of course, we would not stop with a job analysis as final evidence of selection method usefulness; job analysis is really the *first* step. Where feasible, we would want to plan validation research studies to examine empirically how well our proposed measures actually predict successful job performance.

Development of a Selection Plan: PAQ Approach

The PAQ approach offers a unique way of choosing paper-and-pencil tests to be used in human resource selection. While drawing upon a comprehensive analysis of a job by means of the PAQ, computerized statistical analyses are used to predict which tests may be most useful in selecting applicants for the job in question. The methods employed to identify the tests are complex and detailed. However, we can provide a general idea of what is done.

To convey the PAQ approach for developing selection instruments, we will focus briefly on some previous research involving the PAQ.[24] Essentially, multiple correlations were developed between PAQ job dimensions (predictors) and the following nine worker characteristics (criteria) as measured by the U.S. Employment Service's General Aptitude Test Battery (GATB):

1. General Intelligence
2. Verbal Aptitude

3. Numerical Aptitude

4. Spatial Aptitude   7. Motor Coordination

5. Form Perception   8. Finger Dexterity

6. Clerical Perception   9. Manual Dexterity

The objectives of these analyses were two-fold: (a) to determine how well the set of PAQ job dimensions predicted each of the nine aptitudes and (b) to develop prediction equations by which these aptitudes could be predicted from the PAQ job dimensions. On the whole, the job dimensions were strongly related to the aptitudes. Importantly, it was also possible to develop prediction equations for each GATB aptitude. Thus, for any new job, the PAQ could be applied, the job scored on the PAQ job dimensions, and the aptitudes important to job success identified. A user desiring selection measures for a job under study would choose measures of those aptitudes indicated as important for the job. Since the GATB tests are not available to private organizations, analyses similar to those outlined were conducted on several aptitudes as measured by selected, commercially available tests.[25] Results similar to the GATB tests were found. These results suggest that the PAQ might be valuable in isolating aptitudes important for human resource selection purposes.

Analyses of PAQ data to predict the best aptitudes for screening applicants for a job is an analysis option available only through PAQ Services, Inc. Their vast data bank of job information is used to identify these aptitudes. Once identified, those aptitudes suggested as important can be used as a basis for choosing (or developing) a test for use in selection. Using an actual analysis, let's return to the job of senior shipping and receiving clerk. After analyzing the job by means of the PAQ, computerized analyses are used to score the job on relevant PAQ job dimensions. From these data, a series of GATB aptitude predictions are then developed; actual results for the clerk's job are shown in Table 8.7. (We have presented only a portion of the most relevant information.)

In referring to the table, the "Mean Score" represents the predicted aptitude score of incumbents working as a clerk. For each of these nine aptitudes, the data have been statistically adjusted so that the average score is equal to 100; roughly 50 percent of the working population would obtain a score of 100 or less. In general, the higher the mean score, the more important the aptitude to job performance. Based upon these data, Manual Dexterity appears to be an important job aptitude.

"Predicted Validity Coefficient" in the table represents an estimate of the relationships between scores of these aptitudes and job performance. The higher the predicted validity coefficient, the more useful the measure in distinguishing among different individuals' levels of performance. Most of the predicted validity coefficients are low; however, Spatial Aptitude and Finger Dexterity seem most important relative to the other aptitudes considered.

"Use in Selection Score" is a specially created index that indicates whether the U.S. Employment Service would be likely to use a particular aptitude test. The higher the score, the more likely a test would be incorpo-

Table 8.7   *An Example of PAQ Analyses Used in Determining Aptitudes Important to Performance for the Job of Senior Shipping and Receiving Clerk*

General Aptitude Tests (GATB)	Mean Score	Predicted Validity Coefficient	Use in Selection Score	Cutting Score[a]
General Intelligence	95.1	.18	.33	82.2
Verbal Aptitude	96.0	.10	.21	80.3
Numerical Aptitude	95.6	.18	.24	78.7
Spatial Aptitude	96.5	.19	.47	79.3*
Form Perception	97.0	.08	−.36	82.9
Clerical Perception	98.3	.12	.34	83.0*
Motor Coordination	97.9	.15	.17	80.3
Finger Dexterity	91.2	.20	.21	73.3
Manual Dexterity	105.4	.16	.36	85.6*

Source: Based on analyses from PAQ Services, Inc., Logan, Utah.

[a]An * indicates an aptitude test that should be considered as a selection measure.

rated. Spatial Aptitude, Manual Dexterity, and Clerical Perception appear to have a good chance of being chosen.

Finally, the column "Cutting Score" shows two results: (a) the three aptitudes having the highest "Use in Selection Score" marked with an "*" and (b) estimates of employee scores one standard deviation below the mean. If the three passing or cut-off scores specified by the three tests had been used as the lowest scores for selecting applicants for the job of clerk, roughly one-third of the present employees would have been eliminated when they applied for employment. Thus, the "cutting score" gives a user some idea of the effect of possible passing/failing scores for the three tests that might be used.

After GATB aptitudes have been identified, commercially available tests can be sought or tests developed that assess these aptitudes. However, a note of caution should be given. The identified aptitudes should be treated as "hypotheses" of aptitudes thought to be important to performance on a job. Although the system may seem simple and straightforward, blind adoption of the results should be avoided and caution in their interpretation should be exercised. For instance, Gary Brumback and his associates reported that the PAQ GATB results were not helpful in identifying appropriate job aptitudes for the job of fireman.[26] On the other hand, the PAQ option to developing selection measures is an interesting one. At the least, the option probably offers direction to a user's search for appropriate selection measures.

References for Chapter 8

[1] Wayne Cascio, *Applied Psychology in Personnel Management* (Reston, Va.: Reston Publishing Company, 1982), p. 64.

[2] Edward L. Levine, Ronald A. Ash, and Nell Bennett, "Exploratory Comparative Study of Four Job Analysis Methods," *Journal of Applied Psychology* 65 (1980): 525.

[3] U.S. Civil Service Commission, *Job Analysis for Improved Job-Related Selection* (Washington, D.C.: U.S. Civil Service Commission, Bureau of Intergovernmental Personnel Programs, 1976), pp. 1–2.

[4] Equal Employment Opportunity Commission, Civil Service Commission, Department of Labor, and Department of Justice, *Adoption of Four Agencies of Uniform Guidelines on Employee Selection Procedures*, 43 Federal Register 38,307–38,308 (Aug. 25, 1978); Edwin A. Fleishman, "Evaluating Physical Abilities Required by Jobs," *Personnel Administrator* 24 (June 1979): 83.

[5] Ibid.

[6] Ibid. Also, Edwin A. Fleishman, "Evaluating Physical Abilities Required By Jobs," *The Personnel Administrator* 24 (1979): 82–87.

[7] Richard E. Biddle, *Brief GOJA: A Step-By-Step Job Analysis Instruction Booklet* (Sacramento, Calif.: Biddle and Associates, Inc., 1978), p. 27.

[8] Ibid., p. 28.

[9] Ibid.

[10] Edwin A. Fleishman, "Toward a Taxonomy of Human Performance," *American Psychologist* 30 (1975): 1,127–1,149. In addition, see Edwin A. Fleishman and Marilyn K. Quaintance, *Taxonomies of Human Performance: The Description of Human Tasks* (New York: Academic Press, 1984), pp. 344–349.

[11] David Lewin, "Cautions In Using Job Analysis Data for Test Planning," *Public Personnel Management* 5 (July–August 1976): 256.

[12] U.S. Civil Service Commission, *Job Analysis for Improved Job-Related Selection*, p. 23.

[13] Lewin, "Cautions in Using Job Analysis Data for Test Planning," p. 256.

[14] U.S. Civil Service Commission, *Job Analysis for Improved Job-Related Selection*, pp. 24–30.

[15] Ibid., p. 27.

[16] Ibid.

[17] Fleishman, "Evaluating Physical Abilities Required by Jobs," pp. 82–92.

[18] Ibid., p. 89. For a review of personnel selection studies involving physical abilities in physically-demanding jobs, see Michael A. Campion, "Personnel Selection for Physically Demanding Jobs: Review and Recommendations," *Personnel Psychology* 36 (1983): 527–550.

[19] U.S. Civil Service Commission, *Job Analysis for Improved Job-Related Selection*, p. 8; Equal Employment Opportunity Commission et al., *Uniform Guidelines*, p. 38,302.

[20] L. D. Marquardt and Ernest J. McCormick, *Attribute Ratings and Profiles of the Job Elements of the Position Analysis Questionnaire (PAQ)* (West Lafayette, Ind.: Occupational Research Center, Purdue University, 1972); R. C. Mecham and Ernest J. McCormick, *The Rated Attribute Requirements of Job Elements in the Position Analysis Questionnaire* (West Lafayette, Ind.: Occupational Research Center, Purdue University, 1969).

[21] Stephan J. Mussio and Mary K. Smith, *Content Validity: A Procedural Manual* (Chicago: International Personnel Management Association, 1973), pp. 24–27. For an alternative method of assessing KSAs, see Marvin D. Dunnette, Leatta M. Hough, and Rodney L. Rosse, "Task and Job Taxonomies as a Basis for Identifying Labor Supply Sources and Evaluating Employment Qualifications," *Human Resource Planning* 2 (1979): 37–51.

[22] U.S. Civil Service Commission, *Job Analysis for Improved Job-Related Selection*, pp. 10–11.

[23] John P. Campbell, "Comments on Content Validity: A Procedural Manual," unpublished report prepared for the Minneapolis Civil Service Commission as cited in Stephan J. Mussio and Mary K. Smith, *Content Validity: A Special Report* (Chicago: International Personnel Management Association, 1973), pp. 30–31.

[24] Ernest J. McCormick, Paul R. Jeanneret, and Robert C. Mecham, "A Study of Job Characteristics and Job Dimensions as Based on the Position Analysis Questionnaire (PAQ)," *Journal of Applied Psychology* 56 (1972): 347–368.

[25] Ernest J. McCormick, Angelo S. Denisi, and James B. Shaw, "Use of the Position Analysis Questionnaire for Establishing the Job Component Validity of Tests," *Journal of Applied Psychology*

64 (1979): 51–56. For an application of the PAQ in the context of personnel selection, see J. Sparrow, J. Patrick, P. Spurgeon, and F. Barwell, "The Use of Job Component Analysis and Related Aptitudes in Personnel Selection," *Journal of Occupational Psychology* 55 (1982): 157–164.

[26] Gary B. Brumback, Tania Romashko, Clifford P. Hahn, and Edwin A. Fleishman, *Model Procedures for Job Analysis, Test Development and Validation* (Washington, D.C.: American Institutes for Research, 1974), p. 17.

PART FOUR

Predictors of

Job Performance

Predicting future events is a common part of life. We have all tried to guess the winners of sporting events, who might ask us out, or what that someone-special may think of our latest goof-up. Some people, like fortune-tellers, meteorologists, economists, and selection specialists also make prediction a large part of their jobs. All use some limited amount of currently available information to make statements about future events. We really do not know which of these four is right the most often, but we are betting that this section will be of more value to selection specialists than to the other three.

The information that the selection specialist uses to predict future job performance can be obtained from several different types of devices: application forms, interviews, tests, work simulations, etc. Each of the six chapters of this section treats a major type of device in detail. Our viewpoint is that if selection devices are properly developed and used, the information about applicants that is used in predicting job performance improves. As this happens the success rate of prediction should also get better. For each of the chapters, the major objectives are to:

1. Describe the appropriate information about applicants that may be gathered by each type of selection instrument,

2. Point out the important measurement principles of each type of instrument, and

3. Present specific points about the proper development and use of each type of instrument

275

9

Application Forms
and Reference Checks

Application Forms

Nature and Role of Application Forms in Selection

When applicants apply for a job in an organization, they are usually asked to complete an *application form* or *blank*. Practically all organizations utilize employment applications as a method for collecting pre-employment information to assess applicants' likelihood of success with an organization.

An application form typically consists of a series of questions designed to provide information on the general suitability of applicants for jobs to which they are applying. Questions are usually asked regarding applicants' educational background, previous job experiences, and physical health, as well as other areas that may be useful in judging candidates' ability to perform a job. The form itself may be brief and general or long and detailed. Whatever its exact nature, its principal purpose is to serve as a pre-employment screen regarding the future job success of job applicants. As such, it serves as a means for (a) deciding if applicants meet the minimum requirements of a position and (b) assessing and comparing the relative strengths and weaknesses of individuals making application.

When taken at face value, an application form may appear to be rather innocuous; it may seem to offer no real threat to any particular group of individuals. However, when used as a basis for selecting among job applicants, these forms can provide information that unfairly discriminates against

277

some. For example, when application information that may be unrelated to a person's ability to perform a job (such as sex, race, age) is used to screen applicants, that application data can result in discriminatory selection practices.

Because application forms have been used to discriminate unfairly against protected groups, federal and state laws (such as Title VII of the 1964 Civil Rights Act and Fair Employment Practice statutes) have been passed to prevent discrimination by means of pre-employment inquiries. Further, the Equal Employment Opportunity Commission (EEOC) has adopted the view that application forms must conform to both the spirit and the letter of Title VII. The EEOC's *Guide to Pre-Employment Inquiries* specifies that:

> Employment application forms . . . have traditionally been instruments for eliminating, at an early stage, 'unsuited' or 'unqualified' persons from consideration for employment and often have been used in such a way as to restrict or deny employment opportunities for women and members of minority groups.[1]

Because of the widespread use of applications and the legal implications these forms hold for organizations, it is important that we look at some of the issues involved in the development and use of application forms.

Legal Implications of Application Forms

Some employers may think it desirable simply to obtain as much information as possible on the application form. With a lot of information available, it would seem easier to set up an initial screen for choosing among applicants. However, this "the more information, the better" mentality may create major problems for an employer. As we have said, federal and state laws affect the kinds of information that can be obtained on the application blank. Under these laws, it is generally assumed that *all* questions asked on an application form are used in making hiring decisions. Therefore, under a charge of discrimination, the burden of proof may be on the employer to demonstrate that *all* questions are indeed fair and not discriminatory.

The law, according to EEOC pre-employment guidelines, cautions against questions on the application form that (a) disproportionately screen out minority group members or members of one sex, (b) do not predict successful performance on the job, or (c) cannot be justified in terms of business necessity.[2] In judging the suitability of a potential item, an employer should thoroughly review each question. The rating criteria listed in Table 9.1 are useful for examining the appropriateness of application form questions.

An employer has the right to establish and use job-related information for identifying the individuals qualified for a job. With respect to an employment application, an organization is free to ask almost any question it regards

---

Table 9.1   *Questions to be Asked in Examining Appropriateness
of Application Form Items*

Yes	No	Question
[ ]	[ ]	1. Will answers to this question, if used in making a selection, have an adverse impact in screening out minorities and/or members of one sex (that is, disqualify a significantly larger percentage of members of one particular group than of others)
[ ]	[ ]	2. Is this information really needed to judge an applicant's competence or qualification for the job in question?
[ ]	[ ]	3. Does the question conflict with EEOC guidelines or recent court decisions?
[ ]	[ ]	4. Does the question conflict with the spirit and intent of the Civil Rights Act or other federal and state statutes?
[ ]	[ ]	5. Does the question constitute an invasion of privacy?
[ ]	[ ]	6. Is there information available that could be used to show that responses to a question are associated with success or failure on a specific job?

Source: Questions 1 and 2 were based on Equal Employment Opportunity Commission, *EEOC Guide to Pre-Employment Inquiries* (Washington, D.C.: Equal Employment Opportunity Commission, August 1981); questions 3 through 6 were based on E. C. Miller, "An EEO Examination of Employment Applications," *Personnel Administrator* 25 (March 1981): 68–69.

---

as important in selecting among job applicants. However, if a complainant can show adverse impact resulting from selection practices, then the burden of proof is on the employer to demonstrate that the information provided by the application questions is not used in a discriminatory manner that is prohibited by law. Most often a complainant will argue that application items result in (a) *adverse impact* or (b) *unequal treatment*. Under *adverse impact*, members of a protected minority group may respond differently to a question than members of a majority group. For example, in response to the item "Do you own your home," whites may respond "yes" in greater proportion than blacks. If persons responding "no" are screened out of employment consideration, then the question will have an adverse impact on minority applicants. Where *unequal treatment* is involved, different questions may be posed for different groups. For instance, it is unequal treatment if only women (not men) are asked "Do you have children under school age and, if so, what arrangements have you made concerning child care?"

In response, an employer has two basic options to show that application form items do not unfairly discriminate among applicants. An employer can either demonstrate (usually with statistics) that (a) the questions being challenged are predictive of job success or (b) the questions represent a bona fide occupational requirement. An item on an application form is justified as being a bona fide occupational requirement by showing "that it is necessary to the safe and efficient operation of the business, that it effectively carries out the purpose it is supposed to serve, and that there are no alternative policies or practices which would better or equally well serve the same purpose with less discriminatory impact."[3]

Selecting Application Form Content

For an organization to request information other than that necessary for initially judging applicants' qualifications to perform a job is to open itself to a discrimination charge. Thus, it is in the interest of an organization to carefully review the necessity of information requested on the application form.

What information is necessary? How does an organization decide what is in fact essential? Obviously, these are important questions; the answers depend on the job for which an application form is going to be used. Using job analysis methods like those discussed in Chapter 7, we can identify items that could be useful in screening applicants for a job. However, job analysis alone will not completely resolve which items should be included on an application form. Once we have identified the possible questions to appear on the form, each one should also be reviewed for its fairness and usefulness.

Using the rating criteria noted earlier in Table 9.1, employers should carefully review *all* items for their necessity and possible discriminatory impacts. For some questions under review (such as race), the answer may be obvious. For others, an appearance of discriminatory impact may not be so evident; yet, possible discriminatory effects may be present. Using principally the EEOC's *Guide to Pre-Employment Inquiries* as a basis, we will review some of the more frequently used content categories of application form items.[4] Although our review is not an exhaustive treatment of all possible types of items, it does provide some guides for consideration in preparing an application form to be used in selection.

Name   Questions about the national origin, ancestry, or descent of an applicant's name should be avoided. Specific inquiries into the previous name of an applicant where a name has been changed in court or by marriage or inquiries into the preferred title of an applicant such as Miss, Mrs., or Ms. should not be made.

Marital Status, Children, Child Care   Questions about marital status, pregnancy, and number and ages of children have been found to discriminate against women. It has also been found to be illegal to have different hiring policies for women and men with preschool children. Information on child care arrangements should not be asked solely of women.

Race   Items should not appear on the application form that request information concerning race. Similarly, items that could be construed as relating to an applicant's race (for example, hair and eye color) should not be asked unless they can be shown to be necessary requirements for the job.

Sex   As with questions related to race, questions involving an applicant's sex should also be avoided. These questions should only be used if shown to be a bona fide occupational requirement of the job.

Military Experience   Since minorities tend to have higher rates of undesirable discharges, general questions on an applicant's military service dates and type of discharge can prove to be discriminatory. However, questions that address specific skills or educational/training experiences acquired through military service that are relevant to the job may be posed.

Age   The Age Discrimination in Employment Act of 1967 prohibits discrimination in employment against people between the ages of 40 and 70. Any requirement or request that an applicant indicate his or her age (by directly stating, giving date of birth, or having to produce a birth certificate) will likely be viewed as deterring older applicants from applying for a job. Thus, questions related to the specific age of an applicant should be avoided. On the other hand, statements can be made that hiring is subject to verification of minimum legal age or that, if hired, the applicant must furnish proof of age.

Work Availability on Holidays/Weekends   Many employers feel it is important to know if an applicant is available for work on weekends or holidays. However, the EEOC notes that employers have an obligation to accommodate the religious preferences of applicants. Therefore, the EEOC has concluded that pre-employment inquiries focusing on an applicant's availability have an exclusionary effect on employment opportunities for some individuals holding certain religious beliefs. The EEOC states:

> Questions relating to availability for work on Friday evenings, Saturdays or holidays should not be asked unless the employer can show that the questions have not had an exclusionary effect on its. . . applicants who would need an accommodation for their religious practices, that the questions are otherwise justified, and that there are no alternative procedures which would have a lesser exclusionary effect.[5]

Height and Weight   Height or weight requirements are illegal if (a) they lead to a disproportionate number of minority members (such as Asian Americans) being screened out of a job, and (b) they are not related to job performance. In some cases where minimum height and weight requirements are used, higher proportions of American males will be hired since they tend to be larger on the average than women and some minority group members. Questions regarding height and weight should only be asked if an employer can demonstrate minimum height/weight requirements are necessary for successful job performance.

Friends/Relatives Working for Employer   Information on friends or relatives working for an employer is often requested of applicants. However, if this information suggests a preference for the friends and relatives of present employees and the makeup of the work force is such that hiring of relatives and friends would reduce employment opportunities for women or minorities, then the information would be illegal. For example, if the racial and sexual composition of a job for which applications are being taken is principally white males, then questions on the application concerning friends or relatives currently employed might be viewed as discriminatory. The supposition would be that the question would be used to "screen in" individuals similar to those currently employed, that is, white males.

Arrest/Conviction Records   Since some minority group members are arrested in higher proportion than their numbers in the population, the EEOC has ruled that arrest information has an unequal effect on the hiring of members of these groups. As a result, these minority group members have fewer employment opportunities and, therefore, arrest information is illegal. In developing an application form, an employer should omit any questions concerning arrest records.

Questions involving *conviction* records as opposed to arrest records have a different legal stance. An employer can give consideration to the relationship between an applicant's conviction for a crime and his or her suitability for a specific job. If conviction data are used, an employer should also collect and consider information on the number, recentness, and type of convictions of the applicant. The EEOC has also noted that if information on convictions is requested on the application form, the form should have a statement that a conviction record is not necessarily a bar to employment. Factors such as age, rehabilitation, and seriousness of the offense should also be taken into consideration in judging the applicant.

Citizenship   The EEOC *Guidelines on Discrimination Because of National Origin* specify that consideration of job applicants' citizenship may indicate discrimination on the basis of national origin.[6] The law protects both citizens and *noncitizens* in the United States from discrimination due to race, sex, color, religion, or national origin. Thus, questions concerning citizenship may raise the possibility of charges of discrimination due to national origin.

The categories described above provide a summary of some of the major issues involved in developing various types of application form items. As we have stated, it is the questions themselves that determine the usefulness and legality of the application form. Of critical importance is the phrasing of the items that make up the questions on the form. A miscast question can undermine the usefulness and legality of the form and leave the organization vulnerable to a lawsuit.

Using the research of a number of writers, we have summarized in Table 9.2 some acceptable and unacceptable example application form questions based upon some of the legal issues discussed earlier. In reviewing the table, several points should be kept in mind. First, an emphasis is placed on phrasing items to elicit information that is related to the specific job for which the application form is being used. Thus, as Ernest Miller suggests, simple rephrasing using appropriate job-related language can eliminate some "inappropriate" items. For example, a form could ask "Do you have any physical defects or impediments that might in any way hinder your ability to perform the job for which you have applied?" rather than "Do you have any physical defects?"[7] Second, an item that might be unacceptable in some situations could be acceptable in others. For example, an item may be usable if it can be shown that it provides information useful in predicting the success of a new employee on the job for which application is being made. Or, an item may provide information that represents a bona fide occupational requirement for a specific job. Further, the example items listed are not an exhaustive treatment of what should and should not be asked on the application form. The items shown are meant to be illustrative of what can be used. Thus, the examples serve as a guide to planning, developing, and using application forms.

Since laws exist that affect the content of application forms, it might be assumed that most current forms would comply with the law. However, several surveys suggest that numerous public and private employers still request information that could be viewed as inappropriate. (The term "inappropriate" does not mean that a question is illegal and cannot be asked. However, by their phrasing, the questions would be viewed by the courts in such a light as to make a user vulnerable to charges of discrimination if an investigation of unfair discrimination were conducted. Then, it would be up to each employer to justify the use of these questions.)

Burrington collected application forms from the state personnel office in each of the 50 states.[8] An analysis of the forms revealed that every form had at least one inappropriate inquiry; on the average, there were 7.7 such inquiries per application. Slightly less than half (42 percent) of the states had eight or more inappropriate items.

In a similar vein, Miller reviewed the applications of 151 randomly sampled Fortune 500 firms.[9] Only two used applications judged to be completely fair from an initial review. Almost 4 out of 10 firms' applications (38 percent) had more than 10 inappropriate inquiries. The following list shows four of the most frequent inappropriate questions and the percentage of firms where the most inappropriate inquiries occurred:

1. Have you ever been arrested for a misdemeanor or felony? Describe.	64.7%
2. Dates attended grammar school? High school?	61.4%
3. What was your grade point average? Class standing?	59.5%
4. In what extracurricular activities did you participate? Clubs? Sports?	45.8%

Table 9.2 *Examples of Acceptable and Unacceptable Questions Asked on Application Forms*

Subject of Question	Acceptable Questions	Unacceptable Questions	Comments
Name	"What is your name?" "Have you worked for this company under another name?" "Have you used a name (such as an assumed or nickname) the company would need to know to check your previous work and educational records? If so, please explain."	"What was your maiden name?"	Questions about an applicant's name that may indicate marital status or national origin should be avoided.
Age	"Are you between the ages of 18 and 70?" "Upon employment, all employees must submit legal proof of age. Can you furnish proof of age?"	"What is your date of birth?" "What is your age?" "Before being employed, you must show proof of your age."	The Age Discrimination in Employment Act of 1967 prohibits discrimination based on age of individuals from 40 to 70 years of age. A request for age-related data may discourage older workers from applying. Age data should only be collected when it can be shown to be a bona fide occupational requirement.
Race and Physical Characteristics	"After employment, a photograph must be submitted or taken of all employees. If employed, can you furnish a photograph?" "After employment, all employees are required to submit a physical description (eye, hair, and skin color; height and weight)."	"What is your race?" "What is your height and weight." "Would you please submit a photograph with your application for identification purposes?" "What is the color of your hair? Your eyes?"	Information relative to physical characteristics may be associated with sexual or racial group membership. Thus, unless such information can be shown to be related to job performance, the information may be treated as discriminatory.

(continued)

Table 9.2   *(continued)*

Subject of Question	Acceptable Questions	Unacceptable Questions	Comments
	"Do you read, speak, or write a foreign language?"	"What language do you commonly use?" "How did you acquire your ability to read, write, or speak a foreign language?"	
Religion	A statement may be made by the employer of the days, hours, and shifts worked.	"What is your religious faith?" "Does your religion keep you from working on weekends?"	Questions that determine applicants' availability have an exclusionary effect on some people's religious practices. Questions should only be used if they can be shown not to have an exclusionary effect and are justified by business necessity.
Sex, Marital Status, and Family	"If you are a minor, please list the name and address of a parent or guardian." "Please provide the name, address, and telephone number of someone who should be contacted in case of an emergency."	"What is your sex?" "Describe your current marital status." "List the number and ages of your children." "If you have children, please describe the provisions you have made for child care." "With whom do you reside?" "Do you have any dependents or relatives who should be contacted in case of an emergency?" "Do you prefer being referred to as Miss, Mrs., or Ms.?"	Direct *or* indirect questions about marital status, children, pregnancy, and childbearing plans frequently discriminate against women and may be a violation of Title VII.

(continued)

Table 9.2   (*continued*)

Subject of Question	Acceptable Questions	Unacceptable Questions	Comments
Physical Health	"Do you have any physical condition or handicap that may limit your ability to perform the job for which you are applying? If so, please describe." "Are you willing to take a physical exam if the nature of the job for which you are applying requires one?"	"Do you have any physical disabilities, defects, or handicaps?" "How would you describe your general physical health?" "When was your last physical exam?"	A blanket policy excluding the handicapped can be discriminatory. Where physical condition is a requirement for employment, employers should be able to document the business necessity for questions on the application form relating to physical condition.
Citizenship	"If you are offered and accept a job, can you submit proof of your legal right to work in the U.S.?" "Do you have the legal right to live and work in the U.S.?"	"Are you a citizen of the U.S.?" "Of what country are you a citizen?" "Please list your birthplace."	Consideration of an applicant's citizenship can constitute discrimination on the basis of national origin. The law protects all people, citizens *and* noncitizens in the U.S., from discrimination on the basis of sex, race, color, religion, or national origin.
Military Service	"Please list any specific educational or job experiences you may have acquired during military service that you believe would be useful on the job for which you are applying."	"Please list the dates and type of discharge you may have received from military service."	Minority service members have a higher percentage of undesirable military discharges. A policy of rejecting those with less than an honorable discharge may be discriminatory. This information may discourage minorities from applying for employment.

(*continued*)

Table 9.2   *(continued)*

Subject of Question	Acceptable Questions	Unacceptable Questions	Comments
Arrest and Conviction Records	"Have you ever been convicted of a felony, or, during the last two years, of a misdemeanor which resulted in imprisonment? If so, what was the felony or misdemeanor? (A conviction will not necessarily disqualify you from the job for which you are applying. A conviction will be judged on its own merits with respect to time, circumstances, and seriousness.)	"Have you ever been arrested?" "Have you ever been convicted of a criminal offense?"	Federal courts have held that a conviction for a felony or misdemeanor should not automatically exclude an applicant from employment. An employer can consider the relationship between a conviction and suitability for a job. When questions are used, there should be a statement that factors like age at time of offense, seriousness of violation, and rehabilitation will be considered.
Hobbies, Clubs, and Organizations	"Do you have any hobbies that are related to the job for which you are making application?" "Please list any clubs or organizations in which you are a member that relate to the job for which you are applying."	"Please list any hobbies you may have." "Please list all clubs or other organizations in which you are a member."	Applicant information on membership in clubs and organizations can be discriminatory. If membership is associated with the age, sex, race, or religion of the applicant, the data may be viewed as discriminatory. If questions on club/organizational memberships are asked, a statement should be added that applicants may omit those organizations associated with age, race, sex, or religion.

(continued)

Table 9.2 (continued)

Subject of Question	Acceptable Questions	Unacceptable Questions	Comments
Education	"Did you graduate from high school? College?" "While in school, did you participate in any activities or clubs which are related to the job for which you are applying?"	"When did you attend high school? College?" "In what extracurricular activities or clubs did you participate while in school?" "What was your grade point average? Your class standing?"	On the average, minority members tend to have lower levels of education than nonminority group members. Where educational requirements disqualify minority members at a higher rate than nonminority group members and it cannot be shown that the educational requirement is related to successful job performance, the courts have viewed educational requirements as discriminatory.
Credit Rating	None.	"Do you own your own car?" "Do you own or rent your residence?"	Use of credit rating questions tends to have a adverse impact on minority group applicants and has been found unlawful. Unless shown to be job-related, questions on car ownership, home ownership, length of residence, garnishment of wages, etc., may violate Title VII.

Source: Based on Bureau of National Affairs, BNA *Handbook: Personnel Management* (Washington, D.C.: Bureau of National Affairs, 1983), pp. 201:231–201:240. Clifford M. Koen, "The Pre-Employment Inquiry Guide," *Personnel Journal* 59 (1980): 825–829; Debra D. Burrington, "A Review of State Government Employment Application Forms for Suspect Inquiries," *Public Personnel Management* 11 (1982): 55–60; Equal Employment Opportunity Commission, *Guide to Pre-Employment Inquiries* (Washington, D.C.: Equal Employment Opportunity Commission, 1981); Ernest C. Miller, "An EEO Examination of Employment Applications," *Personnel Administrator* 25 (1981): 63–70; Richard S. Lowell and Jay A. Deloach, "Equal Employment Opportunity: Are You Overlooking the Application Form?" *Personnel* 59 (1982): 49–55; State of California, *Pre-Employment Inquiry Guidelines* (Sacramento, Calif.: Department of Fair Employment and Housing, 1982).

Research by Lowell and Deloach substantiates Miller's findings regarding the frequency of inappropriate questions on the application.[10] Their review of application forms from 50 large, well-known businesses showed 48 of the firms had at least one inappropriate item. The inappropriate items occurring in 25 percent or more of the forms reviewed tended to cluster into six categories: (a) military background, (b) education, (c) arrest records, (d) physical handicaps, (e) age, and (f) name.

The results of these research studies illustrate rather impressively that many organizations' existing application forms may not fully comply with current equal employment opportunity law. Resources need to be directed toward reviewing and, where needed, revising these forms to insure full compliance with the law while meeting an organization's selection needs.

Developing and Revising Application Forms

As we have seen, the questions asked on an application affect not only its effectiveness in selecting the best, most appropriate job applicants but may also result in a discrimination charge against the user or employer. Thus, it is imperative that employers carefully study the development and/or revision of their application forms. In making this review, there are several points or strategies that should be considered. These points include the following:

1. *Job analysis data should serve as one basis for choosing employment application questions.* Although job analysis data are commonly used in developing other selection devices such as tests, few users consider these data in constructing their application forms. Not only should these analyses produce useful items for the forms, but they should also serve as a basis for their legal justification.

2. *Every item proposed for inclusion should be reviewed using the item rating criteria listed in Table 9.1.* If a question (a) disqualifies a large percentage of members of protected groups, (b) appears not to be needed to judge an applicant's qualifications for a specific job, (c) has no evidence to show it is related to performance on the job, (d) could be viewed as an invasion of privacy, and/or (e) does not serve as a bona fide occupational requirement, then an employer should strongly consider excluding the question.[11]

3. *Because jobs are different, more than one application form will probably be needed.* At the extreme, there could be one application form for each job. More realistically, however, one form will likely be used to cover a class or family of jobs, that is, jobs that require similar types of knowledge, skills, abilities, or tasks. For example, different versions of application forms may be used for job classes such as clerical/office personnel, sales personnel, operative workers, and managers.

4. *Some jobs or classes of jobs may not require an in-depth applicant assessment by means of the application form. Therefore, if items are not needed or cannot be justified, then the questions should not be asked.* Only a brief form containing

essential data might be used. Ernest Miller points out that this brief form might contain information such as (a) name, (b) address, (c) telephone number, (d) work experience, (e) level of education and training received, (f) skills possessed, and (g) social security number.[12] In general, the higher the organizational level of a job or job class, the longer, more detailed the content of the application.

5. *Since application forms represent a selection device, they are subject to the Uniform Guidelines.* A study by the Bureau of National Affairs found that only about one out of ten of the firms surveyed had conducted validation studies of application items.[13] However, employers should conduct validation research studies to test the statistical relationships between application data and measures of job success. As with job analysis, validation studies help to insure that appropriate measures are used to predict job success, as well as to defend against a possible charge of unfair discrimination. We will have more to say about the validation of employment applications when we discuss weighted application blanks in the next chapter.

6. *The physical layout and format of the form should be thoroughly considered.* As a selection measure, the form should be reviewed for its attractiveness and ease of use by the applicant.

Because of various federal and state requirements, employers covered by these requirements need to collect and report demographic information (for example, sex, race, physical handicap) on their job applicants. Although it may appear efficient to simply collect the data on the application form, this strategy could lead to a discrimination charge. Descriptive data collected on a separate form or on a tear-off portion of the application form would be a more effective strategy. California's *Pre-Employment Inquiry Guidelines* provides an example for collecting and isolating demographic job applicant data from employment applications. The procedures mandated by the state are as follows:

1. The information must be set forth on a tear-off portion of the employment application or on a separate form.

2. The form should state the reason for requesting the information, how it is to be used, and that submitting the information is voluntary.

3. The form containing ethnic information shall be separated from the employment application as soon as that application is received by the employer and forwarded to the individual responsible for personnel research.

4. The forms shall be maintained in a separate file and the information shall not be made available to anyone involved in the hiring process.

5. The data shall be used to evaluate affirmative action recruitment efforts and to determine whether a protected class is adversely affected at any step in the selection process.

6. The data shall be kept to indicate final disposition on all job applicants.[14]

Whether employers follow procedures established by state laws or develop procedures on their own, they would be wise to adopt policies for handling demographic data on job applicants.

Accuracy of Application Form Data

Obviously, for application forms to be useful in selection, it is important that job applicants provide honest answers on the forms.[15] Some writers have argued that prospective employees may be more likely to respond honestly since their responses are given in their own handwriting. That is, they are personally accountable for their answers. On the other hand, an application form is a self-report selection measure. When people are competing for a job, self-report application data are susceptible to distortion; it is simply advantageous for an applicant to "look good." Falsification of application data can range from inflation of college grades to outright lies involving types of jobs held, companies worked for, or educational degrees earned.

A common distortion seen by many human resource managers involves reported college background. For applicants at some executive levels, misrepresentation of a specific degree such as the Master of Business Administration or MBA is a frequent practice. Walter Kiechel concludes that individuals who forge the MBA credential on their applications are typically individuals with little relevant job experience who completed their twenties just before the MBA became a highly-prized degree, and who do not believe they can compete against those who have the degree.[16]

How prevalent is the practice of giving fraudulent data on job applications? There are not many studies that have explored the problem in detail. However, some limited investigations have addressed the issue. A survey by Thorndike Deland Associates of 223 corporate human resource directors showed that roughly one-third believed falsifying employment or educational credentials was a common, growing problem.[17] The National Credential Verification Service of Minneapolis found that misrepresentation of academic and employment records occurred in almost one out of three of its investigations.[18]

Several empirical studies have identified the specific application items where distortion is most prevalent as well as their frequency of occurrence. Mosel and Cozan reported that accurate application data were found for job applicants applying for sales and office positions.[19] However, several studies have reported discrepancies in job application data. For instance, Weiss and Dawis compared application data provided by 91 physically-handicapped applicants with actual data. Of the 13 items studied, almost half (46 percent) of the items were distorted by over 20 percent of the applicants. These items and the prevalence of distortion by applicants were as follows: education (21 percent), pay on previous job (22 percent), job title of previous job (24 percent), length of employment (29 percent), age at disablement (33 percent), and receipt of assistance (55 percent).[20] In a similar study, Goldstein compared five application blank items with factual data for 111 persons applying for positions as nurse's aides. For the 111 previous employers, 15 percent indicated that an applicant had never worked for them. Also, there was a 25 percent disagreement for the item: "Reason(s) for leaving previous job." The two item categories for which discrepancies were greatest were duration of previous employment (57 percent) and previous salary earned (72 percent).[21]

If the data from these studies are applicable to other employment situations involving application forms, we can conclude that some distortion does take place. Most likely, distortion of these data is due to pressure on an applicant to obtain a desired job. Results also suggest applicants are most likely to distort those items believed to be related to whether a job offer will be made and the salary given. However, it should not be concluded that employment applications are worthless. Even though distortion is a problem, application forms can provide useful data for comparing and predicting the success of job applicants. Next, we will see how these data can be used for human resource selection purposes.

Using Application Forms in Human Resource Selection

An employment application represents only one means for evaluating job applicants' ability to perform a job. Certainly, other types of measures such as tests and interviews can also be used in conjunction with the application form. For the moment, however, we are concerned with *how* the application might be used in selection. Here, we want to briefly review several approaches for incorporating application data in hiring decisions.[22]

The alternatives for utilizing application data can range from those that are objective in their treatment of information to those that are more or less subjective. In addition, these approaches can be general or detailed. Although there is a wide variety of options available for handling application data, on the whole, the methods tend to fall into one of the following two categories: (a) weighted application blanks or (b) application checklists and evaluations.

Weighted Application Blanks   Under the weighted application blank or WAB approach, an empirical scoring key is used to score applicants on their answers to an application form. A research study is conducted to identify application items and to weight the responses that predict some aspect or measure of job success such as job tenure or productivity. Numerical scores are obtained for each applicant by summing the appropriate weights. The resulting scores are then used in making hiring decisions. We will discuss the development and use of weighted application blanks in more detail in the next chapter.

Application Form Checklists and Evaluations   There can be many varieties of application checklists and evaluations. Some are completed by the organization; others can be completed by the applicant. Regardless of who provides the data, a checklist or evaluation consists of a list of characteristics or qualifications identified (through a job analysis) as being important to the job for which applications are taken. They are particularly helpful in making a preliminary evaluation of applicants' work experience, training, or other qualifications needed to perform a job.

Once a checklist has been completed, either by an applicant or personnel specialist, it is reviewed to determine if an applicant possesses the minimum necessary qualifications. Applications meeting these minimum standards are then forwarded for further review or applicants are given additional screening, for example, a selection interview. For some jobs, such as unskilled operative jobs, selection decisions may be based solely upon the checklist itself.

Although there can be many types of application form checklists and evaluations, we will consider only two. Our first example might be suitable when only a brief check for very minimal qualifications is needed. The second example may be appropriate when a more thorough review of minimum qualifications is being made.

Brief Check   Exhibit 9.1 illustrates an example of a checklist to be completed by a company personnel specialist for applications submitted for the job of clerk/stenographer. The form is brief and simple, but it encourages the application reviewer to attend to those aspects of the application that are important for a successful clerk/stenographer. If an applicant meets each of the minimum qualifications listed, an employment decision may be made or additional testing offered. For example, if a candidate possesses the basic qualifications for the job, a filing or typing test might then be administered.

An application blank checklist like that in Exhibit 9.1 can be very helpful in making a quick, cursory screening of job applicants. In particular, it is useful in initial screening for those jobs in which large numbers of people are making application. When used in this context, the checklist can help to minimize unnecessary personnel selection costs by insuring that only suitable applicants receive further employment consideration. For example, if knowledge of how to use an IBM Datamaster word processor to prepare letters and reports is a necessary requirement for successfully performing the job of clerk/stenographer, we might have on our checklist "Used an IBM Datamaster word processor to type letters and reports." An applicant must have at least this much relevant job experience, in addition to meeting other minimum qualifications, before being asked to complete another selection measure such as a filing test. It is important to emphasize that the minimum qualifications listed on any pre-employment checklist should meet the criteria for establishing employee specifications that we discussed earlier in Chapters 7 and 8.

Training and Experience Forms   Another form of application evaluation involves the training and experience evaluation (sometimes referred to as "T&E" ratings). Training and experience evaluations may be part of the

---

Exhibit 9.1   *Application Form Checklist for Reviewing Applications
Submitted for the Job of Clerk/Stenographer*

Name of Applicant: _____

Directions: Before beginning to complete this form, review the minimum qualifications for the
job of Clerk/Stenographer listed below. Then, study each application form submitted for the
job. After reviewing each application, indicate if the applicant possesses each minimum qualification. If an applicant meets the necessary requirements, check "Yes"; if not, then check "No."
When there are job openings, applicants meeting all minimum qualifications will be invited in
for additional consideration. After completing the checklist, please attach it to the application
form and return the application to the personnel file.

		Minimum Qualifications
Yes	No	
☐	☐	1. Maintained a filing system of letters, reports, documents, etc.
☐	☐	2. Used an IBM Datamaster word processor to type letters and reports.
☐	☐	3. Used a dictaphone in transcribing correspondence.

application form itself or a separate questionnaire.[23] At any rate, a form is
usually completed by applicants on which they describe their training, work
experience, and educational credentials. This form is then evaluated by a
prospective employer. These evaluations may be particularly useful when it is
important to determine if applicants have sufficient training and experience
to perform specific tasks on the job for which they are applying. There are a
number of different approaches these self-evaluations can take. Wayne
Porter, Edward Levine, and Abram Flory have provided an excellent review
of the major methods.[24] In general, most have in common the following
characteristics: (a) a listing of important job tasks or job content areas, (b) a
means for applicants to indicate their training or experience with these tasks
or content areas, and (c) a basis for scoring applicants' training and experience.

Exhibit 9.2 presents an example of a training and experience evaluation
form for the job of personnel research analyst. Based upon a previous job
analysis, tasks critical to the job were identified. We have listed only a few of
the more critical ones. For each of the important job tasks, applicants are
asked to indicate their specific work experiences and/or training received.
With regard to work experience, for example, applicants might be asked to
list dates of employment, previous employers, previous job titles, and supervisory responsibilities. Applicants might also be asked to describe their educational background, specialized training, or specific skills acquired that
might have prepared them to perform each of these tasks.

One of the products of the job analysis is to determine what experience,
education, and training are relevant for successful task performance.[25] For
instance, for the task "Computed and monitored applicant flow statistics for

Exhibit 9.2 *An Example Training and Experience Evaluation Form for the Job of Personnel Research Analyst*

> Directions: Listed below are some important job tasks performed by a Personnel Research Analyst. Read each of the tasks. If you have had experience or training in performing a task, check the box marked "Yes." If you have not, then check the box marked "No." For the task(s) marked "Yes," please describe your experience and training. All of your responses are subject to review and verification.

Have you had
experience or training
with this task?   *Task*

Yes   No
☐   ☐   1. Computed and monitored applicant flow statistics for nonexempt job applicants using computerized statistical packages (for example, SPSS, SAS).

Experience   *Training*

Employer: _____ Title: _____   Formal coursework and location: _____
Dates of employment: From _____ To ___
Describe your experience with this task: ___   Training programs attended and location: __

_____

_____   On-the-job training: _____

☐   ☐   2. Designed and conducted test validation studies for entry-level jobs.

.
.
.   .
                                                             .
                                                             .

☐   ☐   3. Supervised research assistants in collecting data for human resource studies.

.
.
.   .
                                                             .
                                                             .

☐   ☐   4. Trained personnel assistants in the use of personnel tests (for example, typing, basic math and verbal tests) for entry-level jobs.

.
.
.   .
                                                             .
                                                             .

(continued)

Exhibit 9.2   (continued)

Yes   No
☐   ☐

> 5. Made oral presentations to line and/or upper-level
>   managers on the results of personnel research studies.

Experience	*Training*
Employer: _____ Title: _____	Formal coursework and location: _____
Dates of employment: From _____ To _____	_____
Describe your experience with this task: ___	Training programs attended and location: ___
_____	_____
_____	On-the-job training: _____
_____	_____

_____

nonexempt job applicants using computerized statistical packages (for example, SPSS or SAS)," we may require the completion of a college-level introductory psychological statistics course and training in the use of SPSS, SAS, or equivalent computerized statistical packages. The reviewer of the application would simply study the applicants' experience, education, and training descriptions to determine if the minimum standards have been met. Each task would be reviewed in a similar manner, that is, comparing applicant descriptors with job task qualifications. These comparisons would be recorded using a summary form like that in Exhibit 9.3. Individuals who meet or exceed these minimum qualifications would be recommended for further consideration.

Training and experience evaluations can be a helpful tool in evaluating employment applications. Like any selection method, however, training and experience ratings have their strengths and weaknesses. The utility of any good application evaluation system will depend upon a thorough job analysis. Langdale and Weitz have shown the importance of job analysis data when evaluating application blanks. They found that when little job information was provided to application form reviewers, the degree of agreement among reviewers' assessments of applicants was likely to be low.[26] Seemingly, lack of job information contributes to greater reliance on non-job-related information such as applicants' sex, race, age.[27] Reliance on non-job-related factors leads to reviewers' use of their own personal biases in evaluating application forms; hence, the result is low agreement among reviewers.

Only through a job analysis can a user be assured that application evaluations are being made on application data that are appropriate for use in selection. In addition, job analysis data will be useful in determining the validity of the evaluations themselves. As with all measures used in human resource selection, we need to determine if our application form ratings are useful in identifying successful workers. Finally, since training and experience evaluations involve self-report data, some form of verification of the data,

Exhibit 9.3   *An Example Rating Form for Use in Evaluating Training and*
Experience of Applicants for the Job of Personnel Research Analyst

> Directions: Read the minimum qualifications required to perform the job of Personnel Research Analyst. Then, compare these qualifications to the applicant's training and experience evaluations. If an applicant's qualifications meet or exceed the requirements for the job, check "Meets Requirements." If not, check "Does Not Meet Requirements."

Name of Applicant _____

Task	Minimum Qualifications	Applicant Rating
1. Computes and monitors applicant flow statistics for nonexempt job applicants using computerized statistical packages (for example, SPSS, SAS).	1. Had college-level introductory psychological statistics course; formal coursework, training, or on-the-job training in use of SPSS, SAS, or equivalent statistical packages.	☐ Meets Requirements ☐ Does Not Meet Requirements
2. Designs and conducts test validation studies for entry-level jobs.	2. Was responsible for conducting empirical validation studies of selection tests. Is knowledgeable of the content of the *Uniform Guidelines*.	☐ Meets Requirements ☐ Does Not Meet Requirements
3. Supervises research assistants in collecting data for personnel selection studies.	3. Directed or was primarily responsible for the work of others involving the collection of empirical data.	☐ Meets Requirements ☐ Does Not Meet Requirements
4. Trains personnel assistants in the use of personnel tests (for example, typing, basic math and verbal tests) for entry-level jobs.	4. Had college-level course in testing and test administration.	☐ Meets Requirements ☐ Does Not Meet Requirements
5. Make oral presentations to line and/or upper-level managers on the results of personnel research studies.	5. Made formal oral presentations of 15 to 30 minutes' duration involving the presentation of quantitative data and results to nontechnical audience.	☐ Meets Requirements ☐ Does Not Meet Requirements

Based upon the information shown, the applicant:
☐ Meets Requirements
☐ Does Not Meet Requirements for the job of Personnel Research Analyst.

Notes: _____   Rater: _____
_____
_____   Date: _____
_____
_____

particularly data from applicants who are going to be offered a job, should be made.

Reference Checks

The Role of Reference Checks in Selection

Another technique that is sometimes used to select among job applicants is the checking of applicants' *references or recommendations.* This method involves *an employer's collecting information about prospective job applicants from people who have had contact with the applicants.* Information collected is used for the following purposes: (a) to *verify* information given by job applicants on other selection measures (such as, application forms, employment interviews, or biographical data questionnaires) and (b) to serve as a basis for *predicting* job success of job applicants.[28] We saw in our earlier review of the accuracy of application form data that distortion can be a very real problem. Inaccurate information on self-reported prior employment, education, and acquired job skills have been given by job applicants to enhance their employability. Therefore, one principal purpose of a reference check is to verify what applicants have stated. When used in this manner, the method is only useful when it fails to confirm previous selection measure information given by applicants. Thus, *reference checking serves more as a basis for negative selection, that is, detection of the unqualified, rather than identification of the qualified.*[29]

The second purpose of the reference check is to serve as a predictor of job success. Like application form data, a reference check used in this way assumes that past performance is a good predictor of future performance. Where an application form may summarize what applicants say they did, a reference check is meant to assess how well others say the applicants did. It is presumed that information provided by others can be used to forecast how applicants will perform on the job in question.

Reference checking is a common practice among many employers. Several surveys have documented that over 95 percent of the firms sampled engage in checking references.[30] When information is collected, a significant number of organizations use the data for prediction rather than just for verification purposes. For example, Beason and Belt's survey of 250 public and private organizations showed that over one-half utilized the method to obtain additional information about an applicant.[31] A more recent survey by the Bureau of National Affairs reported that 52 percent of 421 firms using reference checks employed the procedure to pass or fail job applicants.[32]

Types of Reference Information Collected

Generally speaking, four types of information are solicited through reference checks: (a) employment and educational background data, (b) appraisal of an applicant's character and personality, (c) estimates of an applicant's job performance abilities, and (d) willingness of the reference to rehire an applicant.[33] Of these, information relative to the applicants' employment background and educational background is, by far, the most frequently requested.[34]

Methods of Collecting Reference Data

Reference information is usually collected in one of three ways: (a) in person, (b) by mail, or (c) by telephone.

In-Person Contacts   In-person checks involve personal contact with a reference giver. Most often, these contacts are part of background investigations and concern jobs where an incumbent is a potential security or financial risk.

There is some indication that in-person contacts may uncover information not captured by written methods. Research by Goheen and Mosel showed that sensitive applicant characteristics, such as alcoholism and inadequate job performance, were revealed by in-person contacts that were not reported in a written questionnaire. In general, the investigators found little agreement between the two methods in the assessment of applicant characteristics.[35] However, because collecting reference information by means of in-person contacts is expensive and time consuming, it is not frequently used in most industrial selection programs. Therefore, we will turn our attention to mail and telephone checks.

Mail Checks   Reference checks requested through the mail involve a written questionnaire or letter. With a questionnaire, references are usually asked to rate an applicant on a variety of traits or characteristics. When used in this manner, reference checks resemble traditional employee job performance ratings. Raters provide judgments of individual characteristics using some form of graduated rating scale. Space may also be provided for comments as well. Exhibit 9.4 presents one example of a typical reference questionnaire.

Reference checks collected through the mail can be a systematic, efficient means for collecting reference data. However, one of the biggest problems associated with mail questionnaires is their low return rate by reference givers. Mosel and Goheen reported a 56 percent return rate for over 4,700 reference questionnaires for 12 skilled occupations and a 64 percent return rate for over 16,000 questionnaires for 22 professional and semi-professional occupations.[36] One exception to these low return rates is in a study by Nash and Carroll. They reported receiving 85 percent of the reference check questionnaires mailed to previous employers of 147 clerical job applicants.[37]

Another form of mail check is the letter of reference or recommendation. In this case, references write a letter evaluating a job applicant. Reference givers may be asked to address specific questions about an applicant or simply told to express any comments of their choice. Although there do not appear

Exhibit 9.4 *Example of a Mail Questionnaire Reference Check*

Sales Applicant Reference Check

> We are in the process of considering James Ridley Parrish (SS Number: 123-45-6789) for a sales position in our firm. In considering him/her, it would be helpful if we could review your appraisal of his/her previous work with you. For your information, we have enclosed a statement signed by him/her authorizing us to contact you for information on his/her previous work experience with you. We would certainly appreciate it if you would provide us with your candid opinions of his/her employment. If you have any questions or comments you would care to make, please feel free to contact us at the number listed in the attached cover letter. At any rate, thank you for your consideration of our requests for the information requested below. As you answer the questions, please keep in mind that they should be answered in terms of your knowledge of his/her previous work with you.

1. When was he/she employed with your firm? From _____ 19____ to _____ 19____.

2. Was he/she under your direct supervision? ☐ Yes ☐ No

3. If not, what was your working relationship with him/her? _____
   _____.

4. How long have you had an opportunity to observe his/her job performance? _____
   _____.

5. What was his/her last job title with your firm? _____.

6. Did he/she supervise any employees? ☐ Yes ☐ No. If so, how many? _____.

7. What was his/her last gross income? _____ per year.

8. Why did he/she leave your company? _____.

> Below are a series of questions that deal with how he/she might perform in the job for which we are considering him/her. Read the question and then use the rating scale to indicate how you think he/she would perform based upon your previous knowledge of his/her work.

9. For him/her to perform best, how closely should he/she be supervised?
   ☐ needs no supervision
   ☐ needs infrequent supervision
   ☐ needs close, frequent supervision

10. How well does he/she react to working with details?
    ☐ gets easily frustrated
    ☐ can handle work that involves some details but works better without them
    ☐ details in a job pose no problem at all

11. How well do you think he/she can handle complaints from customers?
    ☐ would generally refuse to help resolve a customer complaint
    ☐ would help resolve a complaint only if a customer insisted
    ☐ would feel the customer is right and do everything possible to resolve a complaint

(continued)

Exhibit 9.4 *(continued)*

12. In what type of sales job do you think he/she would be best?
    ☐ handling sales of walk-in customers
    ☐ traveling to customer locations out-of-town to make sales

13. With respect to his/her work habits, check *all* of the characteristics below that describe his/her *best* work situation:
    ☐ works best on a regular schedule
    ☐ works best under pressure
    ☐ works best only when "in the mood"
    ☐ works best when there is a regular series of steps to follow for solving a problem

14. If you have any additional comments, please make them on the back of this form.

Your Name: _____
Your Title: _____
Address: _____
        _____
          City   State   Zip

Company: _____
Telephone: _____

Thank you so much for your time and help. The information you provided will be very useful as we review all application materials.

---

to be comparative data on the frequency of use, letters of reference are prob-ably restricted to high-skill or upper-level managerial jobs. When properly completed by a knowledgeable reference, letters may provide greater depth of information on an applicant than that obtained on a rating scale. However, since letters of recommendation usually come from writers suggested by a job applicant, negative comments are seldom given.

Several investigations of the letter of reference have implied that the method may offer some predictive utility about an applicant. These studies suggest that even if only positive comments are given, it may still be possible to obtain some indication of the writer's true feelings.

Peres and Garcia compiled a list of 170 adjectives used in 625 letters of recommendation submitted for applicants of engineering jobs. Two hundred supervisors were asked to review the list of adjectives and to rate how well each one described their best and worst engineers. Analyses showed that there were five basic categories of adjectives used in the letters. These catego-ries included adjectives dealing with applicants' (a) mental ability, (b) urban-ity, (c) vigor, (d) dependability, and (e) cooperation. Adjectives dealing with mental ability were most related to job performance while adjectives dealing with cooperation and urbanity were least related to performance. Thus, the researchers concluded that when reference givers do not believe an applicant is really qualified for a job, about the best they can say is that "Joe is a pretty nice guy." A seemingly positive letter of reference may actually be "damning with faint praise."[38]

Research by Mehrabian[39] and Wiens, Jackson, Manaugh, and Matarazzo[40] suggest that the number of words in a letter of reference may be a better indicator of a reference giver's attitude toward the person written about than the content itself. This body of research shows that a long letter is more indicative of a positive attitude than a short letter. Mehrabian's work suggests that this finding may be useful in those situations where social constraints may inhibit a reference giver from expressing a negative attitude toward the person written about.

Even though there may be some positive aspects to letters of reference, there are some important disadvantages associated with them. Some of these disadvantages include the following:

1. Writers have the difficult task of organizing the letter.

2. Letter quality will depend upon the effort expended by the writers and their ability to express their thoughts.

3. The same information will not be obtained on each applicant.

4. Areas or issues important to an organization may be omitted.

5. Scoring of the letter is subjective and based upon the reader's interpretation.[41]

Telephone Checks   Pyron's survey of personnel managers in 60 firms showed that telephone contacts were used more frequently than written reference checks obtained through the mail. A number of advantages attributed to the method probably account for its disproportionate use. These assets include the following:

1. Reference givers can be questioned and ambiguous comments clarified.

2. Information may be given orally that would not be given in writing.

3. The reference checking process can be speeded up.

4. It is easier to insure that reference comments are being given by the person named rather than a clerk or secretary.

5. The way oral comments are given (for example, voice inflections, pauses) may be revealing of what a person really thinks.

6. A telephone reference check can yield a better reference return rate.

7. Personal nature of the telephone check contributes to greater responsiveness of the reference giver.[42]

In conducting the check, prepared questions may be asked or questions may be developed and posed by the reference taker during the interview. If an unstructured approach is used over the telephone, the utility of the data collected will be highly dependent upon the skill and training of the telephone interviewer. Table 9.3 lists some questions frequently asked during a telephone reference check.

**Table 9.3   *Some Example Questions Frequently Asked
in a Telephone Reference Check***

1. Would you rehire the job applicant?
2. Why did the applicant leave your firm?
3. How long did the applicant work for your firm?
4. What is your general overall evaluation of the applicant?
5. What was the applicant's absenteeism record?
6. Does the applicant work well with others?
7. What were the applicant's responsibilities in order of importance?
8. What were the applicant's principal strengths, outstanding successes, and significant failures in his/her job activities?
9. How would you compare the applicant's performance to the performance of others with similar responsibilities?
10. How would you describe the applicant's success in training, developing, and motivating subordinates?
11. What does the applicant need to do for continued professional growth and development?

Source: Questions 1 through 7 were based on H. C. Pyron, "The Use and Misuse of Previous Employer References in Hiring," *Management of Personnel Quarterly* 9 (1970): 15–22; and questions 8 through 11 were based on Peter A. Rabinowitz, "Reference Auditing: An Essential Management Tool," *Personnel Administrator* 24 (1979): 37.

Note: The above questions are those that have frequently been used to collect information on job applicants. These questions are *not* being recommended. In general, any question may be asked, but we want to be sure that the information collected is related to the job for which the applicant is being considered before using the information in selection decision making.

Usefulness of Reference Data

We have studied several aspects of the reference check including its role in selection as well as various approaches to collecting reference data. The next question is how valuable are these data in predicting the success of job applicants? Although there are not many empirical studies that have examined the effectiveness of the method, we will present the limited results that are available on the type of reference giver and the reliability and validity of reference data.

Reference Giver   One essential element to having useful data is the reference giver. Unless the giver provides reliable and valid data on applicants, the information will not be helpful to selection decision making. For these data to be useful, individuals serving as references must meet four conditions: (a) they must have had a chance to observe the applicant in relevant situations, (b) they must be competent to make the evaluations requested, (c) they must want to give frank and honest assessments, and (d) they must be able to express themselves so that their comments are understood as intended.[43]

Many different types of individuals, such as friends, relatives, college professors, teachers, immediate supervisors, co-workers, subordinates, and personnel managers can serve as references. Because these individuals are likely to differ in areas such as opportunity to observe the applicant, freedom from bias, and knowledge of the applicant, we would expect differences in the quality of their reference information. Several studies have evaluated the comparative value of information obtained from various groups. Mosel and Goheen examined the validity and leniency of ratings given by different reference groups. For 795 reference questionnaires collected on 400 employees in five jobs, they found supervisors and acquaintances provided reference data predictive of subsequent job performance, while personnel officers, co-workers, and relatives did not. In terms of rating leniency (that is, giving higher ratings than may be deserved) for 3,000 reference questionnaires on applicants for seven federal government jobs, friends and previous subordinates were most lenient while previous employers were least.[44]

Surveys of employers' opinions of the value of reference data given by specific reference groups have yielded similar results. Dudley and French's survey of commercial banks indicated that former employers' comments were most valuable.[45] Pyron explored which specific groups associated with the previous employer were most helpful. The past immediate supervisor as opposed to the personnel department of the previous organization was viewed as most beneficial.[46]

Reliability and Validity of Reference Data   In spite of the widespread use of reference checks, there is surprisingly little research evidence regarding their effectiveness in predicting applicants' subsequent job performance. Of the ten or so studies currently available, their findings generally show that the relationships between reference ratings and measures of employee success (performance ratings and turnover) are low to moderate at best.[47] Other predictors such as biographical data and ability tests generally fare far better in predicting job success than do reference checks. Several factors apparently have some bearing on the utility of references in predicting job success. Conclusions regarding the impact of some of these factors include:

1. References are likely to be more useful in predicting employee success when completed by an applicant's previous immediate supervisor.[48]

2. Prediction is enhanced when (a) the reference giver on the previous job has had adequate time to observe the applicant, (b) the applicant is the same sex, race, and nationality as the supervisor on the previous job, and (c) the old and new jobs are similar in content.[49]

You may wonder why reference checks do not perform better than they do in predicting applicants' subsequent performance. There are several possible explanations. First, the criteria or success measures with which reference checks have been statistically correlated have generally suffered from low reliability. As we saw in Chapters 4 and 5, when a criterion is characterized by unreliable information, we should not expect reference data to predict it statistically. Many of the criteria utilized in studies of the utility of reference data have been subject to poor reliability. Supervisory ratings have frequently served as criteria; and these are notorious for their subjectivity and, sometimes, low reliability.

Another explanation for the apparent low value of reference measures is the narrow or restricted range of scores characteristic of many reference reports. Quite often, the scores tend to be high with little negative information being given on an applicant. If all applicants generally receive the same high reference scores, then it is unreasonable to expect a reference check to predict how applicants will perform on a subsequent job. If we used only positive information, we would predict that all applicants would succeed. Yet, we know that differences in job success will exist.

A third factor accounting for low validity of reference data is the problem of applicants' preselection of who will evaluate them.[50] Since applicants recognize that references may have a bearing on their employability, they are most likely to choose those who will have something positive to say about them. As we have noted, leniency is the rule rather than the exception. Preselection of references by applicants only exacerbates the restriction of range and inflation problems.

Other factors that we have already listed may also contribute to the effectiveness problem. Reference givers may not have had sufficient opportunity to observe the applicant on a job; they may not be competent; they may distort their ratings to help the applicant; and they may not be able to adequately communicate their evaluations.

Legal Issues in Using Reference Checks

As with any human resource selection measure in use, there are important legal implications that an employer should consider when applying reference checks. So far, there has not been a significant amount of litigation involving reference checks. At the time of our review, we found only two relatively recent cases that specifically involved issues surrounding the use of reference checks in personnel selection.

In *Equal Employment Opportunity Commission v. National Academy of Sciences,* a job applicant was refused employment on the basis of a poor reference by her previous supervisor. It was argued by the plaintiff that the reference check excluded a disproportionate number of blacks and was not related to performance on the job. Evidence presented by the defense led the court to conclude that there was no adverse impact and that the reference check (through presentation of a validation study) was job-related.[51] In *Rutherford v. American Bank of Commerce,* an individual brought a charge against her former employer because, in a letter of recommendation, the employer mentioned she had brought a sex discrimination charge against the firm. She was able to demonstrate that she could not obtain later employment because of the letter of recommendation. The court ruled on her behalf, saying that the employer illegally retaliated against her because she exercised her rights under Title VII.[52]

These two cases illustrate four important points:

1. It is necessary to determine if a reference check is discriminatory against protected groups.

2. The ability of a reference to predict performance on the job should be substantiated with a validation study.

3. If, in fact, a reference check is discriminatory, the user may be found liable.

4. A previous employer may be held liable for information provided on a reference check that is submitted to another employer and used for human resource selection purposes.

Because of the *Uniform Guidelines,* which affect many public and private organizations, the Fair Credit Reporting Act and the Privacy Act, which impact on federal employers, and some statutes included under state labor codes, there is a growing concern among employers about the legal implications of using reference checks in selection. Pyron describes a situation that could confront an employer using a reference check to screen applicants. He states, for instance, suppose an employer obtains letters of reference from previous supervisors who describe an applicant as a "trouble maker" and "real rebel." Using this information, the employer rejects the applicant. The applicant demands to know why; and, in response, the employer presents information obtained from the letters of reference. Pyron asks, "In short, the question is this: the two letters have, in a very real way, kept him from getting employment. Is he not entitled to sue the two supervisors for defamation of character? Might not he even be able to sue you, because you have, by your action agreed with the judgment of the two supervisors?"[53]

The point in Pyron's example is that there is a tendency among some reference givers to go beyond necessity in describing people. Potential employers must recognize the signals of defamation and discount such reference data.

Because of the threat in a situation such as that described by Pyron, some commentators have made the following recommendations to organizations using reference information:

1. Not to use subjective information (such as requesting ratings of individual traits like "honesty," "dependability")

2. To obtain applicants' written consent to contact references

3. To ask only for specific, job-related information about applicants

Companies providing reference data on previous employees should:

1. Not blacklist employees

2. Not give information over the telephone

3. Document all information that is released

4. Provide only specific, objective information

5. Obtain written consent from the employee prior to providing reference information

6. Not answer a question involving an opinion of whether a previous employee would be rehired.[54]

L. A. Wangler states that many businesses, afraid of being accused of misrepresenting facts of employment, will only verify the dates of employment and the last position held in the firm. Requests that require opinions or beliefs, such as trait ratings of a previous employee, are being ignored. Wangler recommends that "it would probably be best not to respond to the rating part of the inquiry, since ratings are quite subjective."[55] It is apparent that the application of reference checks will be quite different in the future. We will have to give careful attention to the development of reference checking systems and the use of reference data for selection purposes.

Recommended Steps From legal and practical perspectives, employers wanting to use reference checks should undertake several steps. *First, reference data are most properly used when the data involve job-related concerns.* Thus, requested data should address the knowledge, skills, abilities (KSAs), or any other characteristics of the applicant that are necessary for successful job performance. How do we identify what KSAs or other characteristics are critical? As we discussed in earlier chapters, we make the determination from an analysis of the job for which we are selecting employees. If questions or ratings are restricted to those that can be demonstrated as being related to the job, then there should be no difficulties.

Second, because we are tailoring the content of our reference check to the content of a specific job, we will likely need more than one general form for the various positions in an organization. At the least, we will need a reference form for each cluster or family of jobs that require similar KSAs. Multiple forms obviously add multiple costs and additional work. But, if we are going to obtain useful, legal selection data and if we choose to use reference checks, multiple forms will probably be a necessity.[56]

Third, reference checks are subject to the Uniform Guidelines. Thus, as for any selection measure, we will need to monitor the fairness and validity of the reference check. If our reference checking system unfairly discriminates against protected groups or is not related to job success, we should change or eliminate our system. To do otherwise is not only legally foolish but jeopardizes our ability to choose competent employees.

Fourth, an objective rather than a subjective reference checking system is less likely to be open to charges of discrimination. Objective methods are more amenable to the development of scoring procedures and reliability and validity analyses. These methods consist of those that focus on behaviors and have a specific scoring system. Objective approaches also help to insure that the same information is obtained systematically on all applicants and that the information is used in the same manner. We should be sure that the information that qualifies or disqualifies one, qualifies or disqualifies all. Written recommendations (such as a letter of reference) followed by a brief review often lead to subjective impressions and hunches that may not be valid.[57] If we are going to use these measures in our selection program, subjective impressions and judgments are woefully inadequate.

Fifth, applicants should be asked to give written permission to contact their references. When actually contacting references, information should also be collected on how long that person has known an applicant and the position the person holds. This information can be useful for verifying responses or, if necessary, legally proving that the person contacted is in a position to provide the assessments being requested.

Sixth, reference takers collecting information by telephone or in person should be trained in how to interview reference givers. Preparation will be necessary in how to formulate questions and record responses systematically. Here again, an objective approach to information collection will improve the quality of data ultimately collected.

Finally, a caveat on the use of negative information. Negative information received during a reference check frequently serves as a basis for rejecting an applicant. Caution is certainly advised in using *any* negative data as a basis for excluding applicants. *Before negative information is employed, we should (a) verify its accuracy with other sources, and (b) be sure that disqualification on the basis of the information will distinguish between those who will fail or succeed on the job.* In addition, the same information should be used in the same way for all applicants.

As you read the literature on reference data, it is interesting to note an apparent pattern. Practitioner-oriented journals tend to view reference checks as playing an important role in human resource selection. Apparently, the belief is that reference checks provide information not given by other measures. In contrast, articles in research-oriented journals generally regard reference checks as a relatively minor selection tool. Research studies that have investigated the utility of selection devices have typically concluded that references are not especially useful.[58] Although reference reports may not be as useful as other measures in predicting employee job success, they may be the only basis for detecting some information that would indicate unsatisfactory job performance. In this role, reference data will serve as a basis for identifying a relatively small portion of applicants who should not be considered further for a job. However, it may not be efficient to incorporate reference checks in selecting applicants for every job in an organization. The decision of whether to employ reference checks will vary across organizations and jobs. But we would suggest that the higher the responsibility level associated with a specific job, the more strongly a reference check might be desirable.

References for Chapter 9

[1] Equal Employment Opportunity Commission, *Guide to Pre-Employment Inquiries* (Washington, D.C.: Equal Employment Opportunity Commission, August 1981), p. 1.

[2] Ibid.

[3] Ibid.

[4] Ibid. For some examples of application forms, see *BNA Handbook: Personnel Management, 1983* (Washington, D.C.: Bureau of National Affairs, 1983), pp. 201:906–201:927.

[5] Ibid., p. 5.

[6] Equal Employment Opportunity Commission, *Guidelines on Discrimination Because of National Origin*, 29 Code of Federal Regulations.

[7] Ernest C. Miller, "An EEO Examination of Employment Applications," *Personnel Administrator* 25 (March 1981): 63–70.

[8] Debra D. Burrington, "A Review of State Government Employment Application Forms for Suspect Inquiries," *Public Personnel Management* II (1982): 55–60.

[9] Miller, "An EEO Examination of Employment Applications," pp. 63–70.

[10] Richard S. Lowell and Jay A. Deloach, "Equal Employment Opportunity: Are You Overlooking the Application Form?" *Personnel* 59 (1982): 49–55.

[11] Miller, "An EEO Examination of Employment Applications," p. 66.

[12] Ibid.

[13] Bureau of National Affairs, *Selection Procedures and Personnel Records*, Personnel Policies Forum Survey No. 114 (Washington, D.C.: The Bureau of National Affairs, September 1976).

[14] Department of Fair Employment and Housing, State of California, *Pre-Employment Inquiry Guidelines* (Sacramento, Calif.: Department of Fair Employment and Housing, May 1982).

[15] Wayne R. Porter and Edward L. Levine, "Improving Applicants' Performance in the Completion of Applications," *Public Personnel Management* 3 (1974): 314–317. For guidelines to applicants completing an application form, see Wayne R. Porter, "The Job-Winning Application" (Tempe, Ariz.: Personnel Service Organization, 1976).

[16] Walter Kiechel, "Lies on the Resumé," *Fortune* 106 (August 23, 1982): 221–222, 224.

[17] Ibid., p. 221.

[18] Ibid.

[19] J. N. Mosel and L. W. Cozan, "The Accuracy of Application Blank Work Histories," *Journal of Applied Psychology* 36 (1952): 365–369.

[20] David J. Weiss and Rene V. Dawis, "An Objective Validation of Factual Interview Data," *Journal of Applied Psychology* 44 (1960): 381–385.

[21] Irwin L. Goldstein, "The Application Blank: How Honest Are the Responses?" *Journal of Applied Psychology* 65 (1974): 491–494.

[22] Edward L. Levine and Abram Flory, "Evaluation of Job Applications: A Conceptual Framework," *Public Personnel Management* 4 (1975): 36–42.

[23] J. L. Stone, "Using a Questionnaire with an Employment Application," *Public Personnel Management* 2 (1973): 99–101.

[24] Wayne L. Porter, Edward L. Levine, and Abram Flory, *Training and Experience Evaluation* (Tempe, Ariz.: Personnel Services Organization, 1976). In general, T&E ratings should only be used as *rough* screening devices for jobs where previous experience and training are necessary. For information on the validity, reliability, and scoring time required for four T&E evaluation methods, see Ronald A. Ash and Edward L. Levine, "Job Applicant Training and Work Experience Evaluation: An Empirical Comparison of Four Methods," *Journal of Applied Psychology* 70 (1985): 572–576.

[25] Frank A. Malinowski, "Job Selection Using Task Analysis," *Personnel Journal* (April 1981): 288–291.

[26] John A. Langdale and Joseph Weitz, "Estimating the Influence of Job Information on Interviewer Agreement," *Journal of Applied Psychology* 57 (1973): 23–27.

[27] Y. Wiener and M. L. Schneiderman, "Use of Job Information as a Criterion in Employment Decisions of Interviewers," *Journal of Applied Psychology* 59 (1974): 699–704.

[28] A. N. Nash and S. J. Carroll, "A Hard Look at the Reference Check — Its Modest Worth Can Be Improved," *Business Horizons* 13 (1970): 43–49.

[29] Richard A. Lilenthal, *The Use of Reference Checks for Selection* (Washington, D.C.: U.S. Office of Personnel Management, May 1980), p. 1.

[30] Ibid.

[31] G. Beason and J. A. Belt, "Verifying Applicants' Backgrounds," *Personnel Journal* 55 (1976): 345–348.

[32] Bureau of National Affairs, *ASPA-BNA Survey No. 45 — Employee Selection Procedures* (Washington, D.C.: The Bureau of National Affairs, May 5, 1983), p. 7.

[33] Wayne F. Cascio, *Applied Psychology in Personnel Management* (Reston, Va.: Reston Publishing Company, 1982), p. 190.

[34] Edward L. Levine and S. M. Rudolph, *Reference Checking for Personnel Selection: The State of the Art* (Berea, Ohio: American Society for Personnel Administration, 1977).

[35] H. W. Goheen and J. N. Mosel, "The Validity of the Employment Recommendation Questionnaire: II. Comparison with Field Investigations," *Personnel Psychology* 12 (1959): 297–301.

[36] J. N Mosel and H. W. Goheen, "The Validity of the Employment Recommendation Questionnaire in Personnel Selection: I. Skilled Trades," *Personnel Psychology* 11 (1958): 481–490.

[37] Nash and Carroll, "A Hard Look at the Reference Check — Its Modest Worth Can Be Improved," pp. 43–49.

[38] S. H. Peres and J. R. Garcia, "Validity and Dimensions of Descriptive Adjectives Used in Reference Letters for Engineering Applicants," *Personnel Psychology* 15 (1962): 279–286.

[39] A. Mehrabian, "Communication Length as an Index of Communicator Attitude," *Psychological Reports* 17 (1965): 519–522.

[40] A. N. Wiens, R. H. Jackson, T. S. Manaugh, and J. D. Matarazzo, "Communication Length as an Index of Communicator Attitude: A Replication," *Journal of Applied Psychology* 53 (1969): 264–266.

[41] Lilenthal, *The Use of Reference Checks for Selection*, p. 3. Cf. Stephen B. Knouse, "The Letter of Recommendation: Specificity and Favorability of Information," *Personnel Psychology* 36 (1983): 331–342.

[42] H. C. Pyron, "The Use and Misuse of Previous Employer References in Hiring," *Management of Personnel Quarterly* 9 (1970): 15–22; Lilenthal, *The Use of Reference Checks for Selection*, p. 2.

[43] Milton Blum and James Naylor, *Industrial Psychology: Its Theoretical and Social Foundations* (New York: Harper and Row, 1968), p. 168.

[44] J. N. Mosel and H. W. Goheen, "The Employment Recommendation Questionnaire: III. Validity of Different Types of References," *Personnel Psychology* 12 (1959): 469–477.

[45] D. Dudley and W. French, "Personnel Reference Checking by Banks: Practice and Face Validity," *Business Review* (April 1964): 50–58.

[46] Pyron, "The Use and Misuse of Previous Employer References," pp. 15–22.

[47] For examples of these studies, see Mosel and Goheen, "The Validity of the Employment Recommendations Questionnaire in Personnel Selection: I. Skilled Trades," pp. 481–490; Goheen and Mosel, "The Validity of the Employment Recommendation Questionnaire: II. Comparison with Field Investigations"; Mosel and Goheen, "The Employment Recommendations Questionnaire: III. Validity of Different Types of References"; R. C. Browning, "Validity of Reference Ratings from Previous Employers," *Personnel Psychology* 21 (1968): 389–393; Peres and Garcia, "Validity and Dimensions of Descriptive Adjectives Used in Reference Letters for Engineering Applicants," pp. 279–286.

[48] Mosel and Goheen, "The Employment Recommendation Questionnaire: III. Validity of Different Types of References"; Pyron, "The Use and Misuse of Previous Employer References," pp. 389–393.

[49] S. J. Carroll and A. N. Nash, "Effectiveness of a Forced-Choice Reference Check," *Personnel Administration* 35 (1972): 42–46.

[50] Paul M. Muchinsky, "The Use of Reference Reports in Personnel Selection: A Review and Evaluation," *Journal of Occupational Psychology* 52 (1979): 287–297.

[51] *Equal Employment Opportunity Commission v. National Academy of Sciences*, 12 FEP 1690 (1976).

[52] *Rutherford v. American Bank of Commerce*, 12 FEP 1184 (1976).

[53] Pyron, "The Use and Misuse of Previous Employer References," p. 18.

[54] John D. Rice, "Privacy Legislation: Its Effect on Pre-Employment Reference Checking," *Personnel Administrator* 23 (1978): 46–51.

[55] L. A. Wangler, "The Employee Reference Request: A Road to Misdemeanor?" *Personnel Administrator* 18 (1973): 47.

[56] Lilenthal, *The Use of Reference Checks for Selection*, p. 6.

[57] Cascio, *Applied Psychology in Personnel Management*, p. 191.

[58] Example practitioner articles that tend to view reference checks as making a positive contribution to human resource selection include the following: Bruce D. Wonder and Kenneth S. Keleman, "Increasing the Value of Reference Checking," *Personnel Administrator* 29 (1984): 98–103; Peter A. Rabinowitz, "Reference Auditing: An Essential Management Tool," *Personnel Administrator* 24 (1979): 34–38; Carol Sewell, "Pre-Employment Investigations: The Key to Security in Hiring," *Personnel Journal* 60 (1981): 376–379; Harry David, "The Art of Checking References," *Nation's Business* 69 (1981): 82–85. In contrast, for research publications that have a less favorable view of reference checks see: J. D. Baxter, B. Brock, P. C. Hill, and R. M. Rozelle, "Letters of Recommendation: A Question of Value," *Journal of Applied Psychology* 66 (1981): 296–301; Muchinsky, "The Use of Reference Reports in Personnel Selection," pp. 287–297.

10

Weighted

Application Blanks

and

Biographical Data

Weighted Application Blanks

The Need for Systematic Scoring of Application Forms

As we have seen, application forms can provide much useful information about job applicants. Even though this information might be helpful in making selection decisions, a key issue facing any application reviewer is in deciding *what* application data are most beneficial in choosing successful job applicants. Where clear guides are not provided, selection decisions focusing on application information may be based on the personal biases, prejudices, and whims of each application reviewer. For example, in considering applicants for first-line supervisory jobs, some managers believe only applicants possessing a high school diploma should be hired. Others may not hold this view. But, in fact, is a minimum level of education mandatory for successful performance as a supervisor? Unless relationships between application data and job success are known, application information may be of limited help to managers involved in selection decisions. However, empirical scoring and statistical analyses performed on application data can be very helpful in isolating those specific factors predictive of job success. These analyses, in turn, can lead to a better understanding of application information and standardization in its use.

The Nature of the Weighted Application Blank

The *weighted application blank,* or *WAB* as it is sometimes called, is actually a technique for *scoring* application forms rather than a different personnel assessment tool. The procedure serves as a means for determining if individual items on an application form (such as previous job experience or years of education) distinguish between successful and unsuccessful employees. Once identified, items related to employee job success are then weighted to reflect their degree of importance in explaining the relationship. Applicants for a specific job are scored on the items on the form, and predictions are made of their probable job success. Total scores for all applicants are determined by summing the respective weights for the relevant application blank items. In this sense, the total score for a WAB is like that of any personnel selection test. The score represents a measure of how well an applicant performs on items found to be predictive of job success. Cut-off or passing scores can then be set for comparison with total WAB scores in order to maximize the number of applicants who are predicted to be successful on the job.

The idea of the WAB has a long history. William Owens has traced the concept of a scorable application to an address made by Col. Thomas L. Peters of the Washington Life Insurance Company of Atlanta to the 1894 Chicago Underwriters' meeting.[1] Peters noted in his speech that one way to improve selection of life insurance agents was "for managers to require all applicants to answer a list of standardized questions, such as the following: Present residence? Residences during the previous ten years? . . . Dependent or not dependent for support on own daily exertions? Amount of unencumbered real estate? Occupation during previous ten years? Previous experience in life insurance selling?"[2]

Although occasional articles on application of WABs still appear in the professional literature, most attention was directed to the technique in the 1950s and 1960s. (George England lists over 100 studies on the WAB appearing during this period.)[3] In general, many of these studies found WABs to be very appropriate in selection. A number were particularly successful in predicting job tenure criteria for clerical[4] and sales[5] jobs. However, these are not the only types of jobs and measures of employee success for which WABs have been successful. WABs have also been successfully developed for jobs ranging from telephone operator[6] to production supervisor[7] to research scientist.[8] Further, other applications suggest that WABs can serve as a basis for reducing various personnel costs such as those associated with turnover. For instance, Raymond Lee and Jerome Booth reported that use of a WAB in selecting clerical personnel for a county government resulted in a potential savings of about $250,000 over a 25-month period.[9]

George England notes that WABs may be particularly valuable in employment situations having the following characteristics:

1. Jobs in which a large number of employees are performing similar activities

2. Jobs in which adequate personnel records are available on individual employees

3. Jobs that require long and costly training programs

4. Jobs in which the turnover rate is high

5. Jobs in which there is a large number of applicants relative to position openings

6. Jobs in which it is expensive to bring in applicants to the organization for interviewing and testing[10]

Because of the potential applicability of the method to a variety of jobs, we will summarize the major steps involved in applying the technique. The steps outlined are adapted from England's thorough treatment of the development of WABs. Interested readers are encouraged to review his monograph, *Development and Use of Weighted Application Blanks.*[11]

The Development of Weighted Application Blanks

At this point, we assume that an application form has been made up. Ideally, the items appearing on the application were developed from an analysis of the job. We further assume that the items have been screened for possible discriminatory impacts against protected groups (see Chapter 9). The objective now is to develop a scoring procedure for the application that will permit the prediction of job success. The eight steps that are typically involved in the development and application of a WAB are briefly described below.

1. Choosing the Criterion   Perhaps, the most critical step in the process is the choice of a measure of employee success or a criterion. It is this measure that a WAB is developed to predict; subsequent hiring decisions are based on this measure. If measurement of the criterion is poor, then selection decisions based on a system designed to predict from the measure will also be poor. Thus, success of the entire development process will depend on the adequacy and accuracy of the criterion measure.

There are many different types of criteria that can be employed. These might include criteria such as the following: (a) job tenure, (b) absenteeism, (c) training program success, (d) rate of salary increase, (e) supervisory ratings, or (f) job performance.

Criteria involving *behavioral* measures of performance such as job tenure, absenteeism, tardiness, compensation history, and job output are likely to provide more reliable data than subjective measures such as ratings. However, care should be taken to be sure that these behavioral measures provide reliable and meaningful assessments. In many cases, the most readily available criterion may not be the most useful.

Job tenure measures appear to be particularly amenable to prediction with WABs. As we noted earlier, most previously published studies have employed tenure as a criterion.

2. Identifying Criterion Groups   Once a criterion has been chosen, it is necessary to form two criterion groupings of employees. A minimum of 75 employees is assigned to each group, one representing a *high* criterion group (successful or desirable employees) and one representing a *low* criterion group (unsuccessful or undesirable employees).

For example, suppose we were attempting to develop a weighted application to predict job tenure of salesclerks at a large department store located in a large city. Through some preliminary research, we find that clerks who stay with the store six months or less are considered short-tenure employees while those who stay 12 months or more are considered long-term employees. After reviewing our employment files for the last 18 months, we identified 150 *short*-tenure and 150 *long*-tenure employees. Next, we need to further split each of our two criterion groups into *weighting* and *holdout* groups. Our groups should be formed such that a ratio of two employees are in each weighting group for every one employee in each holdout group. Thus, in the case of our present example, the product of this step will be a weighting and holdout group for our long-tenure clerks and a weighting and holdout group for our short-tenure clerks. Each of the two weighting groups will consist of approximately 100 employees, and the two holdout groups will be composed of about 50 employees. Exhibit 10.1 summarizes the formation of our groups.

Weighting groups serve as a basis for developing weights for application form items that differentiate between short- and long-tenure employees. Holdout groups are used to determine if the weights derived will hold up when applied to a sample of employees *not* included in the original development of the weights.

3. Selecting Application Blank Items   The items that will be used in developing the WAB will depend upon the content and number of items on the application form itself. Based on our earlier discussion, the specific content of the form should be derived from a thorough analysis of the job for which a WAB is being developed.

England recommends that as many items as possible be used in initial analyses since many will not differentiate among our successful and unsuccessful employee groups. Thus, the objective of this step is to propose items or variables derived from the actual application form that might be predictive of employee success. Many different types of items have been used in previous WAB studies. A number have been found to be predictive of various criteria such as tenure, absenteeism, and performance; some example items: (a) size of hometown, (b) number of times moved in recent years, (c) length of residence at previous address, (d) years of education, (e) courses taken and preferred during high school, (f) type of previous jobs, (g) number of previous jobs, (h) tenure on previous jobs, (i) distance of residence from company, (j) source of reference to company, (k) reason for leaving last job, (l) length of time before available for employment, and (m) can current employer be con-

Exhibit 10.1 *Example of Use of Weighting and Holdout Groups in Developing a Weighted Application Blank (WAB) to Predict Job Tenure of Salesclerks*

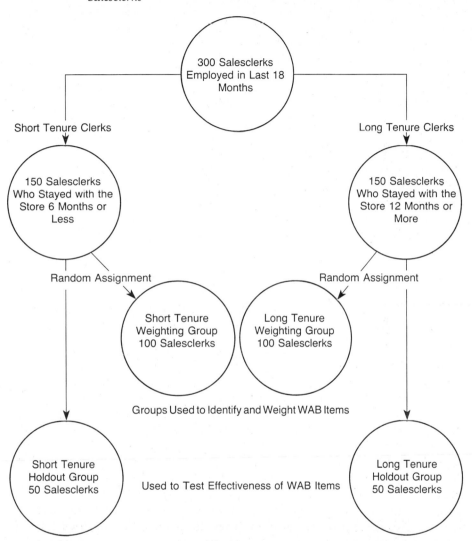

tacted. Many other examples could be cited. One point should be kept in mind when items are being proposed. The simplest and most apparent form of an item on the application may not be the most useful. It may be possible to develop several potential items from one question appearing on an application. For instance, if a question asks about individuals' previous jobs within a specified period, we may be able to develop items on the *number* as well as the *type* of jobs held. All forms of items should be included in the study.

4. Specifying Item Response Categories   For an application blank item to be useful in prediction, we have to know if certain responses are related to specific outcomes on our criterion of employee success. In order to test for any possible item response-criterion relationship, response categories must first be created for each of the WAB items. These categories serve as a way of scoring applicants' responses to our application blank items. For example, on an application blank for a life insurance salesperson, a question may ask "On how much life insurance do you personally pay premiums for yourself?" In order to score the item, we may create response categories to measure the applicants' answers. For example, categories such as the following might be used to classify their answers:

A. None or less than $1,000   D. $50,001 to $75,000

B. $1,000 to $25,000   E. $75,001 to $100,000

C. $25,001 to $50,000   F. More than $100,000

Response categories must be created for every item being examined as a possible predictor of the criterion. Next, we will see how these categories are used.

5. Determining Item Weights   For an application blank item to be beneficial in predicting employee success, individuals in successful and unsuccessful weighting groups should differ in their responses to the item. Furthermore, the greater the response differences between the two groups, the more important an item is in predicting the criterion. Thus, items should be given weights to reflect the degree of relationship with the criterion of employee success. These weights, in turn, will reflect an item's importance when future job applicants' WAB scores are determined.

To better understand this notion of weighting, let's return to our example of selecting salesclerks for a large department store. Recall in Step 2 we formed two weighting groups: a short-term group consisting of 100 employees (who worked 6 months or less and quit) and a long-term group composed of 100 employees (who worked 12 months or more). Among a number of items derived on the basis of a job analysis and appearing on the salesclerk application, there are two example items we want to review for their usefulness in predicting salesclerk turnover. These items are: "What is your level of education?" and "How many years experience do you have in customer sales in a department store?" In Exhibit 10.2, we show the frequencies of the employees' answers to the response categories we developed for the two items. From examining the pattern of responses in the high- and low-tenure groups (see Columns 1 and 2), we can see what appears to be a relationship between the employees' responses to the questions and their tenure on the job. Specifically, high-tenure employees appear to have a high school diploma or equivalent and have experience in customer sales. To reflect these relationships, it is necessary to develop weights for scoring new salesclerk applicants'

responses to the application questions. Column 3 shows the percent differences in response categories between our high- and low-tenure weighting
groups. The greater the positive difference, the more weight a category is
given in scoring. Columns 4 and 5 represent weights that are derived from
tables presented by England.[12] Notice the assigned weights in Column 5.
These assigned weights represent scores for actual item responses to be
summed when determining a total WAB score for future applicants. Hence,
if applicants indicate they have a high school diploma or equivalent, they
would receive 2 points. Applicants having less *or* more than a high school
diploma or equivalent would receive 0 points. These item points would be
combined with all other item responses found to be predictive of salesclerk
job tenure (such as "More than 2 years experience as a salesclerk"). Based
upon these analyses, we would predict that the higher the total WAB score,
the more likely an applicant would stay with the store for 12 or more
months. However, before using these scoring weights, we must test their
ability to predict tenure by applying them to an independent group of employees, that is, our holdout groups.

Exhibit 10.2 *The Development of Scoring Weights for*
Two Application Blank Items

	% Responding[a]				
	(1)	(2)	(3)	(4)	(5)
	High	Low		Net	Assigned
Application Blank Item	Tenure	Tenure	(1)−(2)[b]	Weight[c]	Weight[c]
Level of education:					
A. Less than high school diploma	5	5	0	0	0
B. High school diploma or GED	85	15	70	27	2
C. Some college	5	20	−15	−5	0
D. College diploma	5	60	−55	−17	0
Customer sales experience:					
A. None	3	70	−67	−25	0
B. 1 to 2 years	60	20	40	10	2
C. More than 2 years	37	10	27	6	1

[a]Based on 100 employees in each high- and low-tenure weighting group.

[b]Column 1 minus Column 2.

[c]Derived from tables presented in George W. England, *Development and Use of Weighted Application Blanks* (Minneapolis: Industrial Relations Center, University of Minnesota, 1971), pp. 27–28.

6. Applying Weights to Holdout Groups   Edward Cureton, among others, has argued that distorted results can be obtained when the usefulness of a test is evaluated for the same groups on whom the test was developed.[13] Similarly, George England states that it can be misleading to develop item weights for a WAB that differentiate between successful and unsuccessful groups and then evaluate the weights on these *same* groups.[14] Application of WAB analyses are not recommended unless the weights can be evaluated on groups different from those used to develop the scoring weights. It is essential that we check our scoring weights on a new applicant sample. This process of checking our weights is referred to as cross-validation.

One means for cross-validating these weights is to try out the weights on new applicants. This option is somewhat analogous to our predictive validation strategy discussed in Chapter 5. That is, new applicants complete the application form as well as other selection measures. Applicants are evaluated on the usual selection measures, but they are not scored using the WAB procedures. After a period of time for employees to have exhibited either job success or failure, we go back and score their initial applications using our weighting scheme. If the weighting system is useful, we should find that successful employees have significantly higher WAB scores than unsuccessful ones. If so, we can conclude that our WAB has value as a selection device. This evaluation strategy can be a good one to adopt; its main drawback, however, is the time one must wait to test the WAB.

Fortunately, we have another option. Recall that in Step 2 we created two holdout groups: a short-tenure group made up of 50 clerks (who worked six months or less and quit) and a long-tenure group made up of 50 clerks (who worked 12 months or more). These groups were held out from our initial development of the WAB scoring weights. Since we have designations of successful and unsuccessful clerks (that is, short and long tenure), our holdout groups can serve as a basis for trying out our scoring system. Thus, our next step is simply to score individuals in both holdout groups on responses to the application form that were found to discriminate between our short- and long-tenure weighting groups.

7. Evaluating Holdout Groups' WAB Scores   At this point, all members of the holdout groups have received total WAB scores. A total WAB score is the sum of the assigned weights developed for those application form questions that differentiated among our initial weighting groups.

In order to see how well our scoring system separates our short- and long-tenure holdout groups, we can plot their total WAB scores. Example plots for the two holdout groups are shown in Exhibit 10.3. Total scores are shown on the bottom axis of each graph; each dot represents the total WAB score for one person.

By looking at the two graphs, we can see that scores for our high-tenure group are skewed toward high WAB total scores. Conversely, the low-tenure group is principally composed of lower WAB scores. These distributions

Exhibit 10.3 *Distributions of Total WAB Scores for High- and*
Low-Tenure Holdout Groups

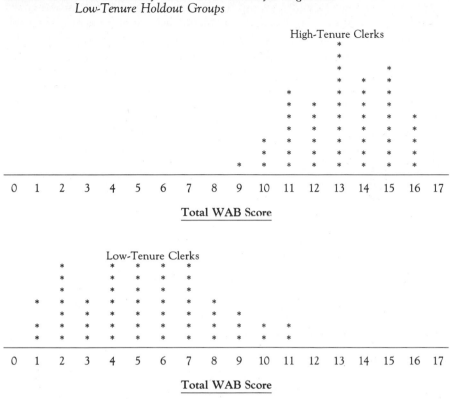

help us test our expectation: if the WAB is successful, high-tenure employees should have higher WAB scores than low-tenure employees. Our plots tend to confirm this expectation.

8. Setting Cut-Off Scores for Selection   In order to use the WAB in practical selection applications, we need to know what minimum or cut-off score should be used in selection decisions. The cut-off WAB score represents the point above which an applicant is hired or moved forward for further selection processing and below which an applicant is not. Our objective is to obtain a score that will optimally classify our holdout group members in the correct group (low versus high tenure). England provides computational details for deriving our optimum cutting score, but we can visually obtain a close approximation by inspecting our plots in Exhibit 10.3.[15] As you study the plots, draw a vertical line at the point where the overlap of the tails of the two distributions is the least. In Exhibit 10.3, that point occurs at a score of 10. Thus, 10 is the WAB cut-off score that appears to optimally separate our two tenure groups. Notice that if we set a cut-off score higher than 10, say 12, we would reject all low-tenure job applicants; however, we would also reject some applicants who would have high tenure on the job. Similarly, a score set lower than 10, say 9, would accept all high-tenure job applicants but would raise the number of low-tenure applicants chosen. Ideally, the cut-off score we should use is that which rejects the maximum number of unsuccessful applicants and accepts the maximum number of successful ones. However, in applying cut-off scores, we cannot always employ the optimal score. External factors, such as labor market supply and demand will affect our score settings. For example, when few applicants relative to job openings are available, we may have to lower our cut-off score to obtain the desired number of new employees. On the other hand, when we have a large number of applicants available, we can be more selective and, thus, set a higher cut-off score.

Using WABs in Human Resource Selection

Weighted application blanks can be used in at least two basic ways. They can be employed as (a) a preliminary screening device or (b) as part of a battery of selection measures (including tests, interviews, etc.). As an initial screening tool, a WAB might be employed in those situations in which it is very expensive to further test or interview applicants or in which there is a very large number of applicants relative to positions available.[16] Applicants would first complete a WAB and, if successful, would then complete additional selection measures. Such a selection strategy could save considerable selection costs associated with test administration or recruitment (such as company visits by prospective employees). Application of the WAB would serve to trim the applicant pool to those for whom further investment of recruitment and selection resources would likely be beneficial.

A second strategy for utilizing a WAB is as an additional tool in a series of selection measures.[17] Rather than complete and successfully pass a WAB before taking other measures, applicants may take the entire battery of measures. However, before adopting a WAB as part of a selection battery, one might ask whether a WAB is likely to improve prediction over other measures in the selection battery. England is careful to point out that WABs are typically developed on employee groups who were already hired using other selection measures. Nevertheless, since WABs frequently enhance the prediction of job success over that of other selection measures, it would appear that WABs can contribute something unique to the prediction of employee success. Thus, for some applications, WABs may prove to be a worthwhile addition to a group of selection measures.

Assets of a WAB   There are several benefits that a WAB has over traditional selection measures such as tests. First, it is not likely to be perceived as threatening to applicants. People applying for a job generally expect to fill out an application form for employment. Since there would appear to be no right or wrong answers, application forms may seem rather innocuous to an applicant. Second, if application information is something we are going to collect, WAB information is valuable if for no other reason than we do not have to pay for it.[18] Tests, interviews, and the like can have high direct costs associated with their administration and scoring. When a measure requires a one-to-one relationship with an administrator, such as in a selection interview, direct costs can be quite high. Direct costs associated with a WAB are likely to be considerably lower. Finally, a WAB may assess important applicant characteristics that are not measured by tests or other selection measures. For example, in a classic study of the prediction of taxicab driver performance, Viteles found that a WAB significantly distinguished successful from unsuccessful drivers. But, what is most impressive about the WAB that was used is that seven application blank items significantly improved prediction over the company's selection tests of mental alertness and accident susceptibility. When cross-validated on 188 new drivers, the WAB would have rejected 60 percent of the poorest drivers but only 22 percent of the best; these results were obtained *after* use of the tests in driver selection.[19] Thus, the WAB apparently was measuring important driver characteristics not measured by the tests.

Concerns in Using WABs   At first glance, it is easy to be impressed by the potential applicability of WABs to various selection situations. However, as with any technique, there are concerns that a potential user would be wise to consider prior to adoption. Some of these concerns have to do with the assumptions of the method while others are similar to guidelines for use. Nevertheless, these are important considerations and should not be taken lightly. Below are listed some of the issues to be evaluated when designing and implementing a WAB within a selection program:

1. *No single WAB will apply to all jobs in a given organization or the same job in different organizations.* Every selection situation presents unique characteristics and thus necessitates that WABs be developed specifically for that situation. Users should carefully review claims that a WAB can be developed for a wide cross section of jobs. WABs should be tailored to the situation for which they are intended.

2. *When a WAB is developed, one assumption is that applicants who will be scored do not differ from the employees on whom the WAB was developed.* To the extent that applicant groups differ from employee groups on whom the WAB was developed (for example, in terms of race, sex, or other demographic characteristics, as well as life histories), scoring keys may not be useful in predicting applicant job success. In this sense, a WAB scoring key may produce an invalid selection measure.

3. *The measure of employee success (criterion) used in developing a WAB may change in importance over time.*[20] Therefore, if a new or different criterion

emerges as important for prediction in selection, new WAB development procedures will need to be initiated.

4. *Over time, the utility of a WAB in predicting employee success may diminish.* For example, Dunnette, Kirchner, Erickson, and Banas[21] as well as Wernimont[22] found that the ability of a WAB to predict clerical employees' job tenure fell quite drastically within a five-year period. When a useful measure in selection is found, it is quite natural not to want to tamper with success. The tendency of some personnel administrators is simply to continue to use the measure. This strategy could be a serious mistake with a WAB. Once developed and implemented, its usefulness in prediction should be reevaluated through cross-validation on new samples of employees hired in subsequent years. Reevaluation should occur every one to two years.

    There are exceptions to this general concern of WAB decay over time. Brown reported that the utility of a WAB held up for over a 38-year period despite labor market, economic, and job changes. Two principal reasons were the confidentiality of the scoring key and the large number of people on whom the system was developed.[23]

5. *Certain items on a WAB may violate state fair employment practice statutes or federal laws.* Although older WAB studies have found demographic characteristics of employees (such as age, sex, marital status, height, and weight) related to various employee success measures, many of these types of application blank items now violate several states' fair employment practice statutes. Users should be certain that items scored on a WAB do not violate these statutes or laws.

6. *Organizational changes can affect the applicability of a WAB.* Roach conducted a cross-validation study of a WAB over time to determine if changes in various organizational factors might affect the predictive power of a WAB. He found that changes in labor market conditions, increases in salary schedules, decentralization of the user company, and changes in personnel policies lowered the predictive power of the blank.[24] Since most organizations are likely to change in ways similar to those studied by Roach, periodic monitoring of WABs is again recommended.

Legal Considerations in Using WABs   Like tests and other selection measures, WABs are subject to the *Uniform Guidelines*. Users would be well-advised to consider the legal implications of developing and using weighted application blanks in selection. It may be apparent from our description of the development of WABs, that the method is basically an empirical procedure. Thus, it is possible that application blank items that are weighted may bear no obvious or rational relationship to the job under study even though there may be a statistical relationship to employee success. Larry Pace and Lyle Schoenfeldt argue that a purely statistical relationship of application blank items to job success may not be a legally satisfactory explanation for using weights of non-job-related items in a discriminatory manner.[25] As a case in point, they reviewed the application of a WAB by Rosenbaum designed to predict employee theft.[26] Using procedures like those we have outlined, Rosenbaum found seven items to be predictive of employee theft in a mass merchandising company. These items included: weight of 150 pounds or more, Detroit address, two or more previous jobs, does not wear eyeglasses, application carelessly prepared, at present address less than 13 years, and weight of less than 130 pounds. Pace and Schoenfeldt state that WAB procedures that weight items concerning sex, race, religion, or national origin, or items that correlate with sex, race, religion, or national origin are potentially illegal if a protected group is adversely affected in employment. That is, if members of a minority group are hired less frequently than members of majority groups and if these decisions are based on items related to sex, race, or religion, then a WAB raises questions of illegality. As an example, they point out that Rosenbaum found applicants with Detroit addresses were more likely to have been caught stealing. They argue that since blacks may be more likely to live within the inner city, a location of residence item may adversely affect black applicants. (In contrast, Wayne Cascio presents an interesting application of how a WAB was developed to meet legal requirements. He found that a legally fair WAB could be developed and be useful in predicting the job tenure of minority and nonminority female clerks.[27]) Pace and Schoenfeldt recommend that job analysis be integrated into the development of weighted application blanks. We noted in the previous chapter that by tying application blank content to requisite job characteristics and demands, less potentially discriminatory and more rationally, legally defensible items can be developed. Unfortunately, many previous developers of application forms and users of WABs have not done this. As we specified earlier, we recommend that developers of applications and users of the WAB methodology begin with a thorough job analysis. The job analysis methods we have discussed can be helpful in developing both the application form and the criteria the form is designed to predict.

Although numerous studies have documented the benefits in selection, the WAB is not much used. For example, a recent survey by the Bureau of National Affairs of 437 companies' selection practices revealed that only 11 percent used a WAB in choosing new employees.[28] What reasons may explain this measure's limited use? The answer, quite likely, can be found in the following list:

1. Lack of familiarity with the technique
2. Belief that a WAB is not useful in selection or will not improve prediction over other measures
3. Fear that use of the technique will open the company to charges of discrimination

We hope that this chapter will help to acquaint potential users with the possible benefits of weighted application blanks. We have seen that a WAB can be a useful selection tool; numerous studies have shown that it can be especially beneficial in selecting sales, clerical, and secretarial workers. Further, there is some limited evidence to suggest that WABs may assess important characteristics of applicants not addressed by other selection devices.

Fear that use of a WAB may lead to charges of discrimination is not misguided. Although a WAB appears to hold promise for use in human resource selection, the blind adoption of empirical procedures performed on questions haphazardly thrown together and called a "job application form" may lead to more problems than benefits. Sometimes WAB analyses identify items that empirically predict employee success but rationally are hard to explain. Should these items create adverse impact against protected groups, users may have a difficult time defending their legality.

We think that WABs can play a beneficial role in human resource selection. However, we strongly recommend that any user contemplating installation of a WAB begin with a thorough analysis of the job in question. As we prescribed earlier in Chapter 9, the actual questions on the application form should be based on a job analysis. If the content of the application form can be tied to the results of a thorough job analysis, then the presence of items that are weighted, scored, and used in selection can be justified. Justification can be made both rationally *and* empirically.

Biographical Data

What Are Biographical Data?

A Definition   Previous experience with scored or weighted application blanks has provided compelling evidence that these measures have been valuable for predicting several important aspects of job behavior. However, because application blanks tend to be short, nonsystematic in their coverage, and ad hoc in their content, many selection psychologists have felt that prediction and understanding of important job behaviors could be enhanced by a deeper study of applicants and their backgrounds. William Owens has recounted the history of the development and use of biographical data in selection, and there is no need to retrace his comments here. It is sufficient to note that the origins of the use of biographical data in selection settings today can be traced to several sources: (a) the successful experiences of selection researchers with weighted application blanks in the 1940s and 1950s, (b) the successful application of biographical data in identifying military officer talent during World War II, and (c) the writings and research of advocates of biographical data such as Edwin Henry of Standard Oil (New Jersey) and William Owens of the University of Georgia.[29]

Although opinions differ as to exactly what should be called biographical data, this information generally comprises those questions asked of applicants concerning their personal backgrounds and life experiences. The questions themselves are commonly presented in a multiple-choice format and ask applicants to characterize themselves in terms of "demographic, experiential, or attitudinal variables presumed or demonstrated to be related to personality structure, personal adjustment, or success in social, educational, or occupational pursuits."[30] Thus, items may concern facts (such as, "what is your age?") but may also involve "attitudes, feelings, and value judgments resulting from experience."[31] Various labels have been given to biographical data such as "autobiographical data," "personal or life history information," or "background data." We will use the term "biodata"; whatever the name used, all refer to the same concept.

As is evident from our definition, a biodata questionnaire (frequently referred to as a "Biographical Information Blank" or BIB) can cover a variety of topics such as educational experiences, hobbies, family relations, use of leisure time, personal health, and early work experiences, to name only a few. Whereas the WAB generally focuses on limited, factual, verifiable information involving educational background, training, work experience, and the like, a BIB, in contrast, may range over a broader spectrum of an individual's background, experiences, interests, attitudes, and values. Thus, many of the items on a BIB may be more subjective than those on a WAB and may not be as easily verified, if at all. In terms of length, a BIB will typically be much longer than a WAB. For example, it is not unusual to find a BIB with a hundred items or more. A WAB, on the other hand, may involve only 10 to 15 items.

Types of Biodata Items   We have taken some time to explore the general nature of biodata as a selection measure, now we will examine some biodata item content. We can classify biodata item content into two groups: (a) the first based on the type of response options offered to a respondent (*response* type) and (b) the second based on the specific behavioral content of the item (*behavior* type).

Response type classification was developed by William Owens and refers to the kind of response scale a respondent is asked to use in answering biodata items.[32] Table 10.1 classifies some example biodata items into seven categories of response type.

The type of rating scale employed on a biodata questionnaire can significantly affect the subsequent scoring and analysis of the items. Most preferable (and probably the most common item format in biodata questionnaires) is a biodata item having an underlying continuum and requiring a single choice (see category 2 in Table 10.1). The continuum, single-choice form of item is most amenable to various kinds of statistical analyses; the other item types require special steps for scoring and analyses. At times, however, when constructing biodata questionnaires, it is not possible to put all items in the continuum, single-choice format; it may make more sense to use something different. In these instances, the other biodata item formats should be em-

---

Table 10.1   *Classification of Biographical Data Items By Response Type*

1. Yes-No Response:

Are you satisfied with your life?
a. Yes
b. No

2. Continuum, Single-Choice Response:

About how many fiction books have you
read in the past year?
a. None
b. 1 or 2
c. 3 or 4
d. 5 or 6
e. More than 6

3. Noncontinuum, Single-Choice Response:

What was your marital status when you
graduated from college?
a. Married
b. Single
c. Divorced
d. Separated
e. Widowed

4. Noncontinuum, Multiple-Choice Response:

Check each of the following activities
you had participated in by the time you
were 18.
a. Shot a rifle
b. Driven a car
c. Worked on a full-time job
d. Traveled alone over 500 miles from
   home
e. Repaired an electrical appliance

5. Continuum, Plus Escape Option:

When you were a teenager, how often
did your father help you with your
schoolwork?
a. Very Often
b. Often
c. Sometimes
d. Seldom
e. Never
f. Father was not at home

6. Noncontinuum, Plus Escape Option:

In what branch of the military did you
serve?
a. Army
b. Air Force
c. Navy
d. Marines
e. Never served in the military

7. Common Stem, Multiple Continuum:

In the last 5 years, how much have you
enjoyed each of the following? (Use the
continuum 1 to 4 shown below.)
a. Reading
b. Watching TV
c. Working on your job
d. Traveling
e. Outdoor recreation
   (1) Very much
   (2) Some
   (3) Very little
   (4) Not at all

Source: Based on William A. Owens, "Background Data" in *Handbook of Industrial and Organizational Psychology*, ed. Marvin Dunnette (Chicago: Rand-McNally, 1976), p. 613.

---

ployed. Scoring (through dummy variable coding and the treating of each item option as a separate variable) and statistical provisions can be made to handle these variations.

Table 10.2 presents another taxonomy of biodata items. This particular classification system, developed by James Asher, categorizes example biodata items in terms of behaviors to be judged by respondents.[33] By using this system, life history items can be classified along one or more of the following dimensions: (a) verifiable-unverifiable, (b) historical-futuristic, (c) actual behavior-hypothetical behavior, (d) memory-conjecture, (e) factual-interpretive, (f) specific-general, (g) response-response tendency, and (h) external

---

Table 10.2 *Classification of Biographical Data Items by Content*

1. Verifiable:	**Unverifiable:**
Do you own a home?	How much did you enjoy high school?
2. Historical:	**Futuristic:**
How many jobs have you held in the past five years?	What job would you like to hold five years from now?
3. Actual Behavior:	**Hypothetical Behavior:**
Did you ever repair a broken radio so that it later worked?	If you had your choice, what job would you like to hold now?
4. Memory:	**Conjecture:**
How would you describe your life at home while growing up?	If you were to go through college again, what would you choose as a major?
5. Factual:	**Interpretive:**
How many hours do you spend at work in a typical week?	If you could choose your supervisor, which characteristic would you want him or her to have?
6. Specific:	**General:**
While growing up, did you collect coins?	While growing up, what activities did you enjoy most?
7. Response:	**Response Tendency:**
Which of the following illnesses have you had?	When you have a problem on your job, to whom do you turn for assistance?
8. External Event:	**Internal Event:**
When you were a teenager, how much time did your father spend with you?	Which best describes your feelings when you last worked with a computer?

Source: Based on James J. Asher, "The Biographical Item: Can it be Improved?" *Personnel Psychology* 25 (1972): 252; and Wayne F. Cascio, *Applied Psychology in Personnel Management* (Reston, Va.: Reston Publishing Co., 1982), p. 195.

event-internal event. These categories are not mutually exclusive because it is possible for any single item to be characterized by more than one dimension. At any rate, the items listed provide some typical examples of what appears in a biodata questionnaire.

Advantages of Biodata Biodata can provide some unique advantages to the assessment of job applicants. These assets certainly argue for its consideration and inclusion in our battery of selection devices. Owens has summarized some of these advantages as follows:

1. Biodata can serve as another means for collecting some of the information obtained in the selection interview with the advantages that an applicant is asked each question in the same way, and the answers are amenable to empirical scoring.

2. At least for verifiable information, the responses provided on a BIB tend to be very reliable and accurate.

3. Biodata items make it possible to achieve understanding of what makes for an effective employee rather than just simple prediction of employee success. By studying the content of items related to measures of employee success, a great deal can be determined about what types of individuals stay on a job, are high producers, or are promoted through an organization. This information may be useful to personnel policy makers as well as selection managers.

4. Application of usual empirical scoring procedures generally insures that only job-related questions are posed on a BIB. Although the procedures will not satisfy all legal requirements concerning fairness and avoidance of adverse impact, they provide an initial, important step toward meeting these needs.

5. Biodata has generally been shown to be as good of a selection measure as other methods; in many cases, the evidence suggests that biodata may be among the best in terms of prediction of job success.

6. Biodata items can serve as both predictors and criterion measures of employee behavior. Thus, it is possible to assess an important employee behavior with one item serving as a criterion and then examine correlations of other biodata items with the item criterion.[34]

Assumptions of Biodata   In using biographical data as a selection tool, we make several key assumptions. These assumptions are important since they influence the quality and utility of the data we use in selection decision making. Therefore, when asking applicants to describe their past behaviors and their feelings about these behaviors, we assume the following:

1. *With the context reasonably constant, the best predictor of job applicants' future behaviors is what they have done in the past.*[35] This assumption is really a basic axiom of psychological measurement, and the available evidence generally supports the assumption. For example, numerous studies have shown that the best predictor of college grade point average is high school grade point average. Sometimes only a few items of past behavior can be a predictor of important job behaviors. Cureton, for instance, reported that the *single* item, "Did you ever build a model airplane that flew," contained in a BIB administered to prospective pilots during World War II, was almost as good a predictor of success in flight training as the *entire* Air Force test battery.[36] Apparently, individuals' previous work with airplanes reflected their interest and abilities to work with aircraft in the future. Similarly, Hoiberg and Pugh found that just four biodata items collected on a sample of almost 8,000 women and men could predict performance effectiveness in seven naval occupations.[37] Empirical evidence collected by William Owens and Edwin Henry generally verify that biographical data serve as an outstanding predictor of criteria representing future employee behaviors.[38]

2. The systematic measurement of applicants' behaviors will provide an indirect measure of their motivational characteristics. These characteristics may be extremely difficult to measure with other forms of selection devices.[39] Owens has persuasively argued that an assessment system based upon biodata can serve as a basis for not only predicting but describing individuals. Such data can provide great amounts of information about individuals without requiring great amounts of time from them.[40]

3. Individuals will be less defensive in describing their previous behaviors than in discussing their motivations for these behaviors.[41] Where behaviors are public and have occurred, individuals may be less hesitant to report on these behaviors rather than *why* these behaviors have taken place.

The Development of a Biodata Questionnaire

So far, we have defined biodata, examined some typical kinds of items appearing in a questionnaire, and looked at some of its assets and assumptions. It may seem to you that a biodata questionnaire merely consists of a lot of questions about job applicants' life histories. In part, that impression is true. We will probably use a questionnaire that is made up of a number of items. But, there is a great deal more time, effort, and resources that must be expended in deciding precisely what questions will be asked. It is the questionnaire content that will determine in a large way the effectiveness of biodata as a selection measure. Since there is not likely to be a commercially available, off-the-shelf biodata questionnaire suitable for the numerous selection situations we may encounter, we will probably have to have our questionnaire tailor-made. Whether a questionnaire is developed by a user or by a consultant, users should be aware of the necessary steps to produce such a selection device. Thus, at this point, we will review one procedure for developing a biodata questionnaire.

Steps in Construction There are four general steps involved in the development of a BIB. In practice, these steps apply to the development of almost any selection measure. Nevertheless, we will summarize their application in constructing a BIB to be used in selection. The steps are discussed below.

1. Selecting a Job Our starting point is the choice of a job for which we plan to use a BIB in selection. Biographical data questionnaires have been utilized in a wide variety of occupational settings. These applications have included jobs such as life insurance agents, executives, pharmaceutical scientists, and managers at various organizational levels. From these titles, you can see that biodata questionnaires have been applied to jobs that are relatively high in responsibility. A BIB is not restricted to such jobs; it can be applied to lower-level jobs as well. However, because of the resource investment required to develop a BIB adequately, for some jobs there may not be a high enough return on investment to warrant development of the measure. For some lower-level jobs, a weighted application blank alone may suffice. That decision will differ from one selection situation to the next. Nevertheless, a potential user will first have to decide if a BIB is worthwhile for the job under consideration.

2. Analyzing the Job   Once we have identified the job, our next concern is with conducting a thorough analysis of the job (See Chapters 6, 7, and 8). Whatever approach we adopt, we need to identify two principal products: (a) information on and measures of employee success (that is, criteria) and (b) information on job tasks and the KSAs needed to perform these tasks successfully. Our goal is to use the job information to help us infer the attributes required for employee success.

The development of life history items to predict employee attributes identified through a comprehensive job analysis is consistent with the suggestions of Larry Pace and Lyle Schoenfeldt.[42] Job analysis results will serve as the rational basis for BIB development.

3. Forming Hypotheses of Life History Experiences   After we have inferred those attributes believed to be important for job success, we want to develop life history items that will reflect those attributes. Thus, at this point, we develop hypotheses regarding the life history experiences that will measure these important job attributes. If our hypotheses are correct, we should be able to identify life history items that could be used to predict success on the job.

Research by William Williams underscores the importance of forming hypotheses or a rationale for including specific items in a BIB.[43] He developed a 98-item BIB designed to predict reenlistment in the Air Force Reserve Officers' Training Corps. During development of the measure, he formed specific hypotheses for including 35 items; no specific hypotheses were given for the remaining 63 questions. Following administration, he found that 46 percent of the hypothesized items predicted reenlistment whereas only 13 percent of the nonhypothesized items served as a predictor. Thus, Owens recommends, "although one may include some items because they have priorly demonstrated validity in reasonably similar circumstances, biodata items are much more likely to validate if they are knowledgeably beamed at a specific target."[44]

The formation of hypotheses for developing life history items is critical to the successful application of biographical data. Here, we want to draw upon a research study completed by John Miner to illustrate the role of hypothesis formation in developing a biodata questionnaire.[45] Although Miner's research dealt with the construction of a scoring procedure for applicant file data, his rationale illustrates the role of hypotheses in BIB development.

Miner was interested in determining if applicant life history (developed from applicants' resumés, application forms, psychological evaluation reports, reference letters) could be used to predict the success of management consultants in an international management consulting practice. An analysis of the consultants' jobs showed that they usually worked on project teams in large business organizations. Their principal contact was with top management. In general, the consultants tended to develop as generalists with their work being in the area of financial affairs rather than human or material resources.

Further analysis of the consultants' role within the firm suggested two hypotheses for explaining consultant success. First, it was hypothesized that an applicant's life history of outstanding accomplishments was a predictor. This rationale could be characterized as the "pattern of previous success" hypothesis. Second, it was thought that successful consultants to business management come from those backgrounds that provide exposure to corporate top management culture. Individuals having such exposure were felt to possess greater interpersonal effectiveness in dealing with top executives. This second hypothesis regarding the link between life history data and consulting success might be termed the "top management culture" hypothesis.

Once hypotheses for consulting success had been formulated, specific life history experiences indicative of these hypotheses could be developed. Reviews of pertinent literature and research within the firm led Miner to propose a rationale for developing specific life history indicators. For instance, it was hypothesized that applicants with fathers who had high levels of education and held positions in top management would be more likely to have been exposed to top management culture. An applicants' previous business experience, use of a company officer as a reference, and undergraduate and graduate education at a prestigious college were all suggested as being indicative of exposure to top management. Similarly, military experience in the Navy or Air Force (in contrast to the Army with its lower intellectual standards and its tendency to attract lower socioeconomic personnel) were also proposed as valuable indicators.

Based on the hypotheses developed for the study, 15 life history items were prepared. Applicants' scores on these items were then related to three measures of management consulting success: performance ratings, compensation changes, and job tenure. Analyses showed that life history data were useful, and the following nine items were predictive of consultant success: (a) extent of prior business experience, (b) type of prior business experience, (c) branch of military service, (d) type of military service, (e) type of secondary schooling, (f) type of college graduated from, (g) graduate education, (h) extent of father's education, and (i) father's highest occupational attainment.

As you can tell, Miner's biographical data were limited in both number (15 items) and type (factual). His items were restricted principally because he was confined to existing application file data. Had he chosen to develop a BIB rather than use file information, other types of items would probably have been relevant. Nevertheless, his process is a useful example of the role of hypothesis formulation in the development of life history items.

4. Developing Biodata Items After hypothesizing the life history experiences that may predict our identified criteria, we select or construct biodata items to reflect these experiences. Thus, our hypotheses guide the selection or development of specific life history items to appear on the BIB. As we have noted, the items can be selected from previous biodata research studies or originally developed. Available publications can serve as sources of items. For example, J.R. Glennon, Lewis Albright, and William Owens have prepared a compendium of life history items.[46] Their catalog consists of over 500 biodata items classified into the following categories: (a) habits and attitudes, (b) health, (c) human relations, (d) money, (e) parental home, childhood, teens, (f) personal attributes, (g) present home, spouse, and children, (h) recreation, hobbies, and interests, (i) school and education, (j) self-impressions, (k) values, opinions, and preferences, and (l) work. Items from the catalog can be selected if it appears that they may be useful in measuring the hypothesized life experiences thought to be predictive of success. In addition, research articles on biodata can also be reviewed for possible biodata item content. The *Journal of Applied Psychology* and *Personnel Psychology* are the two literature sources that have published the most on applications of biographical data. Bibliographies of biographical data research can also be a valuable source of references with potentially useful items.[47]

This four-step approach can enhance the effectiveness of biodata as a predictor as well as our understanding of how and why biodata works. And as Wayne Cascio specifies, it is likely the only legally defensible approach to employing biodata in human resource selection.[48]

Phrasing of Biodata Items   An excellent review of research studies investigating various aspects of writing biodata items has been provided by Owens.[49] These investigations have important implications for the validity and reliability of biodata questionnaires. We will not review those studies per se, but we do want to summarize some item-writing guides distilled from the research. These guidelines should be followed as biodata items are actually formatted into a BIB. Guidelines for preparing BIB items include the following:

1. Biodata items should principally deal with past behavior.

2. Items dealing with family relationships are usually viewed as offensive.

3. Brevity of items is desirable.

4. Numbers should be used to define a biodata item's options or alternatives.

5. All possible response options or an "escape" option should be given.

6. Item options should carry a neutral or pleasant connotation.

7. Items dealing with past and present behaviors and with opinions, attitudes, and values are generally acceptable.

Scoring a BIB   After a BIB has been developed and administered, we can score applicants who complete the questionnaire. These scores, in turn, can be used with a variety of statistical procedures to predict an applicant's probable job success. But, how are these scores determined? Although a number of BIB scoring procedures have been developed, the various approaches tend to fall into one of two categories: (a) the calculation of a *single,* total score for BIB items that is predictive of employee success[50] or (b) the development of *multiple* scores for dimensions or groups of related items appearing on a biodata inventory.[51]

The first approach (sometimes referred to as "empirical keying") to scoring a BIB is like that discussed for a weighted application blank. That is, each item on a BIB is analyzed to determine its relation with some measure of job success, such as job tenure or turnover. Items related to the criterion are identified and weights assigned to the item alternatives to reflect the strength of their relationship. Scores are obtained for individuals by summing the weights corresponding to their responses. Once the keys are cross-validated, they can be used like any of our other selection measures.

The empirical scoring key approach has been both popular and useful. It enjoyed the most attention by biodata researchers from the early 1950s through the 1960s and is still employed today. As far as selection research is concerned, empirical keying probably represents the most common method of scoring a BIB. However, the method has many of the problems associated with the weighted application blank. For one, the scoring of a BIB is basically limited to predictions for a specific pool of applicants and for a specific job success measure. Because of this specificity, the scoring key may not be applicable to another job, organization, or for a criterion different from the one for which the key was developed. In addition, because the total score is often composed of such a wide assortment of BIB items, there is some uncertainty as to what the score really means. Although a BIB score might enhance our ability to predict employee success for a specific job, it may contribute very little to our understanding of *why* employees are successful.

A second approach (sometimes referred to as "homogeneous keying") to biodata scoring involves the development of clusters or groups of related items appearing on a biodata questionnaire. Statistical procedures such as factor analysis are used to identify and group related items into dimensions of life history experience. The results of these procedures are a number of biodata dimensions or factors measured by the life history questionnaire.

Exhibit 10.4 presents as an example one biodata factor that was identified in a study by one of the authors of biodata correlates of managerial careers in a large textile firm.[52] As you look at the items shown, it appears that most deal with people's feelings about school and their academic performance. Thus, based on a common theme represented in the items, the name "Positive Academic Attitude" was assigned by the investigators to this biodata dimension. Rather than one overall biodata score, scores can be obtained on each of the identified BIB factors or dimensions. For example, on the factor in Exhibit 10.4, respondents' answers were added to obtain a total "Positive Academic Attitude" score. Persons scoring high on the factor

Exhibit 10.4 *Example of the Biographical Data Factor "Positive Academic Attitude"*

Factor Name	Item Number	Biodata Item Stem
Positive Academic Attitude	29.	Did you generally expect to do well in school?
	32.	What was your approximate standing in your high school class?
	33.	Compared with your classmates in school, how hard did you try to excel?
	34.	Up to the time you left school, how did you feel about school?
	95.	When you were still in high school, what were the standards you set for yourself with regard to your studies?

Source: Hubert S. Feild and William F. Giles, *Career Planning at West Point Pepperell, Inc.* Final report submitted to West Point Pepperell, Inc., West Point, Ga., August 1978.

Note: The biographical data factor "Positive Academic Attitude" was identified through the use of a statistical technique called "factor analysis." This technique can serve as a means for reducing a large number of questionnaire items to a smaller set of dimensions composed of items having similar themes. By focusing on the interrelations among biodata questionnaire items, factor analysis enables us to determine the dimensions or categories of life history experiences measured by a biodata questionnaire. We can then describe and score people according to these underlying biodata dimensions. In the present example, we are illustrating only one of many possible biodata factors. Only the item stems are presented, the response options are not shown.

were characterized as follows: always expected to do well in school, in the upper 10 percent of their high school class, tried to excel much harder than other students, liked school very much; and set very high standards for themselves.

A study by Morrison, Owens, Glennon, and Albright illustrates how dimensions of biodata can be used to predict and understand significant aspects of employee job performance.[53] One of the purposes of their research was to examine how dimensions of life history were related to industrial research scientists' job performance. They factor analyzed 75 biodata items and three criteria (creativity ratings, overall job performance ratings, and number of patent disclosures) collected on 418 petroleum research scientists. The five biodata dimensions identified and a brief description of individuals with high scores follows:

1. Favorable Self-Perception
   In the top 5 percent of performance in their occupation
   Could be a highly successful supervisor if given the chance
   Work at faster pace than most people
   Desire to work independently

2. Inquisitive Professional Orientation
   Completed Ph.D.

Belong to one or more professional organizations
Devote much time to reading of many kinds
Have high salary aspirations

3. Utilitarian Drive
Desire extrinsic rewards from business and society
Prefer urban dwelling
Feel free to express self and perceive themselves as influencing others
Do not desire to work independently

4. Tolerance for Ambiguity
Desire to have many work activities
Are not single
Have solicited funds for charity
Have friends with various political views

5. General Adjustment
Feel that school material was adequately presented
Came from happy homes
Express their opinions readily; feel that they are effective in doing so

An examination of the association of the five factors with the three criteria revealed some interesting findings. *Different* biodata factors were associated with *different* types of performance on the job. For example, scientists who received high ratings on overall job performance tended to be those with high scores on the BIB factors of Favorable Self-Perception, Utilitarian Drive, and General Adjustment. Conversely, scientists with many patent awards had an opposite life history profile. They scored high on Inquisitive Professional Orientation and Tolerance for Ambiguity. Among others, these results suggest that different types of life experiences (that is, biodata factors) might be used to predict different types and levels of job performance (criteria). Thus, by weighting some BIB factors more than others in selection decisions, we could contribute to subsequent performance in our organization. For instance, in the current example, if greater weight were given to hiring applicants high in Inquisitive Professional Orientation and Tolerance for Ambiguity, we would expect higher performance in number of patents awarded than if other factors such as General Adjustment were emphasized.

As popularized by William Owens and Lyle Schoenfeldt, the scoring of biodata questionnaires by identifying life history dimensions appears to be the contemporary trend.[54] Their research program supports the idea that prediction as well as greater understanding of the relation between life history and employee job success can be enhanced by scoring biodata in terms of dimensions.

The Validity of Biodata in Human Resource Selection

A number of major reviews of human resource selection studies have been conducted with the purpose of examining the validity of biographical data in prediction. Edwin Ghiselli's classic review of the validity of various types of occupational aptitude tests revealed that when averaged over a number of occupations, biographical data was the most successful predictor of job proficiency and success in job training.[55] Asher's reanalysis of reviews of test validation studies confirmed the predictive power of biodata. His comparisons of life history data with tests such as finger dexterity, personality, motor ability, mechanical aptitude, intelligence, and interest clearly showed biodata to be superior in predicting job proficiency.[56]

However, there have been some reports that are not as supportive of biographical data as Ghiselli's and Asher's. Korman's review of predictors of managerial performance concluded that the predictive utility of biographical data was lower than that for other measures. Also, he noted that biodata appeared to have less predictive power for managers at higher organizational levels than for others.[57] Schwab and Oliver reviewed Schuh's analysis of 21 biodata studies and pointed out that many of the studies reporting positive results with biodata did not incorporate cross-validation as part of their procedures. Thus, they argued that some of these studies may have capitalized on chance findings. Further, they suggested that biodata reports published in the professional literature are biased since journals typically only publish articles with significant results.[58] Because negative findings are not readily available, it would be very difficult to ascertain the true validity of biodata.

In spite of Korman and Schwab and Oliver's criticisms, other comprehensive reviews by Asher and Sciarrino,[59] Owens,[60] Owens and Henry,[61] and Reilly and Chao[62] generally conclude that biographical data is a useful tool in human resource selection. A few summary comments from these studies amplifies this conclusion. Edwin Henry, for example, found that "with very few exceptions it [biodata] has been found to be the best single predictor of future behavior where the predicted behavior is of a total or complex nature."[63] Likewise, William Owens reported that "one of the unmixed and conspicuous virtues of scored autobiographical data has been its clear and recognized tendency to be an outstanding predictor of a broad spectrum of external criteria."[64] Finally, Wayne Cascio adds that "compelling evidence exists that when appropriate procedures are followed, the accuracy of biographical data as a predictor of future behavior is superior to any known alternatives."[65] Given the overwhelmingly positive results, biodata should at least be considered for adoption in any selection program.

Why Is Biodata a Good Predictor?   If we accept that biodata is a good predictor of important work behaviors, we might also ask: Why does it work? There are at least four plausible explanations. First, a BIB is representative of an individual's life history while other predictors, such as a selection interview, may only provide a caricature.[66] For example, in an unsystematic selection interview, individuals may provide a broad sketch of themselves, while in a BIB a more systematic, comprehensive, and accurate picture may be obtained. Second, when empirical scoring keys are used, the very nature of their development insures that only relevant items are used to predict measures of job success.[67] In developing keys, only items that relate to job success and are cross-validated are included. Thus, the final key should be a valid predictor of the criterion. Third, biographical data may work because of the one-to-one correspondence between content of a BIB and the criterion being predicted.[68] Biographical data may contain all of the important elements of consequence to the criterion. As James Asher points out, tests generally assume that job success is determined by traits, aptitudes, abilities, or intelligence. Thus, when tests are developed, they are constructed to measure those characteristics thought to be related to job performance. Rather than use the indirect approach of tests, biodata generally attempts to measure aspects of the criterion directly. For example, high school grade point average predicts college grade point average better than aptitude tests.[69] Finally, the evidence is very persuasive that past behavior is a predictor of future behavior. Apparently, people's behavior over time is reasonably consistent. If we can accurately assess important life history experiences, then future behavior can be predicted.

Legality of Biodata Our earlier comments on legal issues involved in weighted application blanks also apply to the use of biographical data. Items can be included in a BIB if it can be shown (a) that they are job related and (b) do not unfairly discriminate against protected groups of job applicants. Unfair discrimination might be established if it can be shown that a biodata item, total score on a BIB, or a score on a BIB dimension affects a group disproportionately. For example, Laurence Siegel and Irving Lane describe a situation where BIB item weights scored equally for black and white applicants would have resulted in discrimination.[70] It was discovered that the BIB item: "How were you referred for a job with us?" required different weights for minority and nonminority applicants. A positive weight was assigned to a response from nonminority applicants indicating referral by one of the organization's present employees. Conversely, the item had no relationship with job performance for minority applicants because the company employed few minority group members who might make a referral. If all applicants regardless of their race had been scored on the item, then the item would have had a discriminatory impact on minority applicants.

Once a case has been established against an employer (that is, a prima facie case of discrimination), a user of a BIB must provide evidence of validity and fairness of the BIB item, total, or dimension score. If these requirements can be met, then the BIB is acceptable.

It is impossible to answer in the abstract and with complete certainty whether biodata are discriminatory or not. Previous research on the matter is far from conclusive. William Owens finds from his review that "all in all, the available evidence would seem to suggest that the major dimensions of biodata response are quite stable across cultures, age, race, and sex groups."[71] On the other hand, Richard Reilly and Georgia Chao summarize some studies reporting race and sex differences in biodata scoring keys.[72] Perhaps, the best advice that can be offered is that a user of a BIB should always check for validity and fairness. Some BIB items involving topics such as education and socioeconomic background may very well be associated with applicant sex or race. So, appropriate care should be taken. Validity and fairness should not be taken for granted.

Accuracy of Biodata   As with the application form, for biodata to be useful in selection, the information collected by means of a BIB should be accurate. Proponents claim that a unique asset of biodata is its accuracy because it is subject to verification. Our earlier review of application data accuracy is probably relevant. We saw that research by Goldstein[73] and Weiss and Dawis[74] revealed distortion of application data by unskilled job applicants. In contrast, Mosel and Cozan found that applicants for sales and office positions provided accurate application data.[75]

These studies provide some evidence on the accuracy of verifiable data collected by an application form. But, what about data collected by a BIB? Only one study was found that provides any evidence on the issue; however, it was conducted under research rather than employment conditions. Cascio administered a 184-item BIB to currently employed police officers. Of 17 historical and verifiable BIB items, he found only two with substantial discrepancy: age when first married (32 percent discrepancy) and number of full-time jobs held prior to present employment (50 percent discrepancy).[76] But, even if we assume that verifiable data collected by a BIB are generally accurate, we simply do not know if accuracy characterizes those BIB items not so easily verifiable such as attitudes, interests, preferences, or opinions.

Another point relevant to this issue is whether job applicants may be able to fake their responses to a BIB to enhance their chances of being hired. Again, only one study is relevant. Schrader and Osburn examined how well college students could fake their answers to an empirically-keyed BIB. Without going into the details of their research, results showed that students could indeed complete a BIB in such a way as to optimize their chances of being employed.[77]

Criticisms of Biodata   So, where does this leave us? It seems that applicants are likely to provide generally accurate answers to BIB items that are verifiable. They *may* also give accurate responses to items that cannot be verified. However, *if* applicants want to distort their responses to a BIB to enhance their employability, they may be able to do so. To what extent distortion actually occurs in such cases, we do not know.

We can see that biographical data offer outstanding potential as a predictor in our selection program. But, as with all measures, there are pitfalls that any user would be wise to consider.[78] One criticism that has been made is that biographical data are deterministic in nature. That is, people who do not have the "correct" life history background will be excluded from a job; and there is little they can do about their past. Regardless of individual effort or intervening circumstances, an applicant cannot change those life experiences that may be considered indicative of job success. Like all selection measures, biodata are an indicator of behavior. We should be sensitive to the fact that people may be excluded who have not had the opportunity to obtain the "right" life history experiences. Of course, we should have the same sensitivity for all of our selection measures.

A second criticism is that use of life history data in prediction is nothing more than "dustbowl empiricism; it may work, but who knows why?" If we choose to use biodata or any measure for that matter, we should be careful to understand how our scored life histories are related to job success. William Ennis raises this question: "Docs it make sense (assuming validity for such items) to give a job candidate minus or plus values on a background questionnaire simply because he had few (or many) books in his home as a child or had no father (or mother) in the home, even though other factors point to good potential?"[79] Sometimes selection managers in their desire to apply objective standards in selection can be seduced by the attractiveness of a number assigned to a job applicant. However, a blind approach to scoring and using biodata, without understanding what that score represents and how it rationally relates to the job, can lead to unintentional biases against some job applicants. Travers reports one instance where blind empirical scoring of a BIB led to such biases.[80] A study was conducted to identify life history predictors of the success of research scientists as administrators. The criterion to be predicted by the biodata was the scientists' job performance ratings. Biodata variables that were positively related with success were those of (a) having a rural background and (b) coming from a family of skilled craftsmen. Characteristics negatively correlated with success were (a) having a large city background and (b) coming from a retail-merchant family. Clearly, these characteristics were immutable, but the findings did not make sense rationally. Further research revealed the explanation. It was discovered that many of the urban-reared scientists were Jewish, and the performance evaluations used to define job success had an anti-Semitic cast. That is, the criterion to be predicted by the biodata measure being developed was found to be discriminatory. Blind application of the apparently valid scoring system would simply have perpetuated the bias. If we use biodata, we should always ask: "Do these results make sense?" Our job analysis results and the formation of rational hypotheses in selecting the content of our biographical inventories can help us in answering this question.

The "deterministic flavor" and "dustbowl empiricism" criticisms of biodata have some merit. However, recent work by Owens,[81] Schoenfeldt,[82] and their colleagues,[83] in their derivation of a developmental-integrative model based on biodata to predict behavior, has helped to dispel some of the criticisms. Their research has clarified our thinking with regard to understanding what biodata measures and how it can be used. To date, many of the studies employing the developmental-integrative model are promising. Future research will help to further clarify the meaning of biodata and its effectiveness as a human resource selection measure. In the meantime, biodata should continue to be considered a viable selection alternative.

References for Chapter 10

[1] William A. Owens, "Background Data," in *Handbook of Industrial and Organizational Psychology,* ed. Marvin Dunnette (Chicago: Rand-McNally, 1976), pp. 609–644.

[2] L. W. Ferguson, "The Development of Industrial Psychology," in *Industrial Psychology,* ed. B. H. Gilmer (New York: McGraw-Hill, 1961), pp. 18–37.

[3] George W. England, *Development and Use of Weighted Application Blanks* (Minneapolis: Industrial Relations Center, University of Minnesota, 1971), pp. 53–63.

[4] William D. Buel, "Voluntary Female Clerical Turnover, the Concurrent and Predictive Validity of a Weighted Application Blank," *Journal of Applied Psychology* 48 (1964): 180–182.

[5] J. N. Mosel, "Prediction of Department Store Sales Performance from Personal Data," *Journal of Applied Psychology* 36 (1952): 8–10.

[6] A. Friedman and Ernest J. McCormick, "A Study of Personal Data as Predictors of the Job Behavior of Telephone Operators," in *Proceedings of the Indiana Academy of Science* 62 (1952): 283–294.

[7] H. C. Lockwood and S. O. Parsons, "Relationship of Personal History Information to the Performance of Production Supervisors," *Engineering Industrial Psychology* 2 (1960): 20–26.

[8] Lewis E. Albright, W. J. Smith, J. R. Glennon, and William A. Owens, "The Prediction of Research Competence and Creativity from Personal History," *Journal of Applied Psychology* 45 (1961): 59–62.

[9] Raymond Lee and Jerome M. Booth, "A Utility Analysis of a Weighted Application Blank Designed to Predict Turnover for Clerical Employees," *Journal of Applied Psychology* 59 (1974): 516–518.

[10] England, *Development and Use of Weighted Application Blanks,* pp. 4, 40.

[11] Ibid.

[12] Ibid., pp. 27–28.

[13] Edward E. Cureton, "Validity, Reliability, and Baloney," *Educational and Psychological Measurement* 10 (1950): 94–96.

[14] England, *Development and Use of Weighted Application Blanks,* p. 30.

[15] Ibid., p. 36.

[16] Ibid., p. 40.

[17] Ibid., p. 42.

[18] Roger Bellows, *Psychology of Personnel in Business and Industry* (New York: Prentice-Hall, 1961).

[19] Morris Viteles, *Industrial Psychology* (New York: W.W. Norton, 1932).

[20] England, *Development and Use of Weighted Application Blanks,* p. 43.

[21] Marvin D. Dunnette, W. K. Kirchner, J. Erickson, and Paul Banas, "Predicting Turnover Among Female Office Workers," *Personnel Administrator* 23 (1960): 45–50.

[22] Paul Wernimont, "Re-evaluation of a Weighted Application Blank for Office Personnel," *Journal of Applied Psychology* 46 (1962): 417–419.

[23] Steven H. Brown, "Long-Term Validity of a Personal History Item Scoring Procedure," *Journal of Applied Psychology* 63 (1978): 673–676.

[24] Darrell E. Roach, "Double Cross-Validation of a Weighted Application Blank Over Time," *Journal of Applied Psychology* 55 (1971): 157–160.

[25] Larry A. Pace and Lyle F. Schoenfeldt, "Legal Concerns in the Use of Weighted Applications," *Personnel Psychology* 30 (1977): 159–166.

[26] R. W. Rosenbaum, "Predictability of Employee Theft Using Weighted Application Blanks," *Journal of Applied Psychology* 61 (1976): 94–98.

[27] Wayne F. Cascio, "Turnover, Biographical Data, and Fair Employment Practice," *Journal of Applied Psychology* 61 (1976): 576–580.

[28] Bureau of National Affairs, *ASPA-BNA Survey No. 45 — Employee Selection Procedures* (Washington, D.C.: The Bureau of National Affairs, May 5, 1983).

[29] Owens, "Background Data," pp. 609–644.

[30] Ibid., pp. 612–613.

[31] Ibid.

[32] Ibid., p. 613.

[33] James J. Asher, "The Biographical Item: Can it be Improved?" *Personnel Psychology* 25 (1972): 252.

[34] Owens, "Background Data," pp. 611–612.

[35] William A. Owens, "Toward One Discipline of Scientific Psychology," *American Psychologist* 23 (1968): 782–785.

[36] Edward E. Cureton, "Comment," in Edwin R. Henry, *Research Conference on the Use of Autobiographical Data as Psychological Predictors* (Greensboro, N.C.: The Richardson Foundation, 1965), p. 13.

[37] A. Hoiberg and W. M. Pugh, "Predicting Navy Effectiveness: Expectations, Motivation, Personality, Aptitude, and Background Variables," *Personnel Psychology* 31 (1978): 841–852.

[38] William A. Owens and Edwin R. Henry, *Biographical Data in Industrial Psychology: A Review and Evaluation* (Greensboro, N.C.: The Richardson Foundation, 1966).

[39] Abraham K. Korman, *Industrial and Organizational Psychology* (New York: Prentice-Hall, 1971), p. 239.

[40] William A. Owens, "A Quasi-Actuarial Basis for Individual Assessment," *American Psychologist* 26 (1971): 992–999.

[41] Korman, *Industrial and Organizational Psychology*, p. 239.

[42] Pace and Schoenfeldt, "Legal Concerns in the Use of Weighted Applications," pp. 159–166.

[43] W. E. Williams, "Life History Antecedents of Volunteers versus Nonvolunteers for an AFROTC Program." Paper presented at the Midwestern Psychological Association, Chicago, 1961.

[44] Owens, "Background Data," p. 613.

[45] John B. Miner, "Success in Management Consulting and the Concept of Eliteness Motivation," *Academy of Management Journal* 14 (1971): 367–378. An example of the development of a content valid biodata questionnaire designed for predicting test performance of electrician job applicants can be in found in Ronald D. Pannone, "Predicting Test Performance: A Content Valid Approach to Screening Applicants," *Personnel Psychology* 37 (1984): 507–514.

[46] J. R. Glennon, L. E. Albright, and William A. Owens, *A Catalog of Life History Items* (Greensboro, N.C.: The Richardson Foundation, 1966). See also Owens and Henry, *Biographical Data in Industrial Psychology*.

[47] W. M. Brodie, W. A. Owens, and M. F. Britt, *Annotated Bibliography on Biographical Data* (Greensboro, N.C.: The Richardson Foundation, 1968). See also Owens and Henry, *Biographical Data in Industrial Psychology*.

[48] Wayne F. Cascio, *Applied Psychology in Personnel Management* (Reston, Va.: Reston Publishing Company, 1982), p. 196.

[49] Owens, "Background Data," pp. 614–615. For a somewhat different approach to the collection of important life history accomplishments from professional job applicants, see L. M. Hough, "Development and Evaluation of the 'Accomplishment Record' Method of Selecting and Promoting Professionals," *Journal of Applied Psychology* 69 (1984): 135–146 and Leatta M. Hough, Margaret A. Keyes, and Marvin D. Dunnette, "An Evaluation of Three 'Alternative' Selection Procedures," *Personnel Psychology* 36 (1983): 261–276.

[50] See, for example, Sam C. Webb, "The Comparative Validity of Two Biographical Inventory Keys," *Journal of Applied Psychology* 44 (1960): 177–183; Raymond E. Christal and Robert A. Bottenberg, *Procedure for Keying Self-Report Test Items* (Lackland Air Force Base, Tex.: Personnel Research Laboratory, 1964); William H. Clark and Bruce L. Margolis, "A Revised Procedure for the Analysis of Biographical Information," *Educational and Psychological Measurement* 31 (1971): 461–464.

[51] See, for example, William A. Owens and Lyle F. Schoenfeldt, "Toward a Classification of Persons," *Journal of Applied Psychology Monograph* (1979): 569–607; Michael T. Matteson, "An

Alternative Approach to Using Biographical Data for Predicting Job Success," *Journal of Occupational Psychology* 51 (1978): 155–162; Michael T. Matteson, "A FORTRAN Program Series for Generating Relatively Independent and Homogeneous Keys for Scoring Biographical Inventories," *Educational and Psychological Measurement* 30 (1970): 137–139; Terry W. Mitchell and Richard A. Klimoski, "Is it Rational to be Empirical? A Test of Methods for Scoring Biographical Data," *Journal of Applied Psychology* 67 (1982): 411–418.

[52] Hubert S. Feild and William F. Giles, *Career Planning at West Point Pepperell: A Strategy for Matching People with Jobs* (Auburn, Ala.: Auburn Technical Assistance Center, 1980).

[53] Robert F. Morrison, William A. Owens, J. R. Glennon, and Lewis E. Albright, "Factored Life History Antecedents of Industrial Research Performance," *Journal of Applied Psychology* 46 (1962): 281–284.

[54] Owens and Schoenfeldt, "Toward a Classification of Persons," pp. 569–607.

[55] Edwin E. Ghiselli, *The Validity of Occupational Aptitude Tests* (New York: John Wiley, 1966).

[56] Asher, "The Biographical Item: Can it be Improved?" pp. 251–269.

[57] Abraham K. Korman, "The Prediction of Managerial Performance," *Personnel Psychology* 21 (1968): 295–322.

[58] Donald P. Schwab and Richard L. Oliver, "Predicting Tenure with Biographical Data: Exhuming Buried Evidence," *Personnel Psychology* 27 (1974): 125–128.

[59] James J. Asher and J. A. Sciarrino, "Realistic Work Sample Tests: A Review," *Personnel Psychology* 27 (1974): 519–533.

[60] Owens, "Background Data," p. 617.

[61] Owens and Henry, *Biographical Data in Industrial Psychology*.

[62] Richard Reilly and Georgia Chao, "Validity and Fairness of Some Alternative Employee Selection Procedures," *Personnel Psychology* 35 (1982): 1–62.

[63] Edwin R. Henry, "Conference on the Use of Biographical Data in Psychology," *American Psychologist* 21 (1966): 248.

[64] Owens, "Background Data," p. 617.

[65] Wayne F. Cascio, "Turnover, Biographical Data, and Fair Employment Practice," p. 576.

[66] Asher, "The Biographical Item: Can it be Improved?" p. 258.

[67] Pace and Schoenfeldt, "Legal Concerns in the Use of Weighted Applications," p. 160.

[68] Asher, "The Biographical Item: Can it be Improved?" pp. 259–260.

[69] Ibid.

[70] Laurence Siegel and Irving Lane, *Personnel and Organizational Psychology* (Homewood, Ill.: Irwin, 1969).

[71] Owens, "Background Data," p. 620.

[72] Reilly and Chao, "Validity and Fairness of Some Alternative Employee Selection Procedures," pp. 1–62.

[73] Irwin L. Goldstein, "The Application Blank: How Honest Are the Responses?" *Journal of Applied Psychology* 55 (1971): 491–492.

[74] David J. Weiss and Rene V. Dawis, "An Objective Validation of Factual Interview Data," *Journal of Applied Psychology* 40 (1960): 381–385.

[75] J. N. Mosel and L. W. Cozan, "The Accuracy of Application Blank Work Histories," *Journal of Applied Psychology* 36 (1952): 365–369.

[76] Wayne F. Cascio, "Accuracy of Verifiable Biographical Information Blank Responses," *Journal of Applied Psychology* 60 (1975): 767–769.

[77] Alec D. Schrader and H. G. Osburn, "Biodata Faking: Effects of Induced Subtlety and Position Specificity," *Personnel Psychology* 30 (1977): 395–404. Cf. C. D. Anderson, J. L. Warner, and C. C. Spencer, "Inflation Bias in Self-Assessment Examinations: Implications for Valid Employee Selection," *Journal of Applied Psychology* 69 (1984): 574–580.

[78] Benjamin Schneider, *Staffing Organizations* (Pacific Palisades, Calif.: Goodyear Publishing Co., 1976), p. 204; Ernest McCormick and Daniel Ilgen, *Industrial Psychology*, 7th ed. (Englewood Cliffs, N.J.: Prentice-Hall, 1980), p. 188.

[79] William H. Ennis, "Use of Nontest Variables in the Government Employment Setting." Paper

presented as part of a symposium, *Use of Nontest Variables in Admission, Selection, and Classification Operations,* American Psychological Association, Miami Beach, September 8, 1970, pp. 11–12.

[80] R. M. Travers, "Rational Hypotheses in the Construction of Tests," *Educational and Psychological Measurement* 11 (1951): 128–137.

[81] For a review of studies incorporating the developmental-integrative model, see Owens, "Background Data," pp. 609–644.

[82] Lyle F. Schoenfeldt, "Utilization of Manpower: Development and Evaluation of an Assessment-Classification Model for Matching Individuals with Jobs," *Journal of Applied Psychology* 59 (1974): 583–595.

[83] For example, see Donald R. Brush and William A. Owens, "Implementation and Evaluation of an Assessment Classification Model for Manpower Utilization," *Personnel Psychology* 32 (1979): 369–383; A. G. Niener and William A. Owens, "Relationships Between Two Sets of Biodata with Seven Years Separation," *Journal of Applied Psychology* 67 (1982): 146–150; Kermit R. Davis, "A Longitudinal Analysis of Biographical Subgroups Using Owens' Developmental-Integrative Model," *Personnel Psychology* 37 (1984): 1–14.

11

The Selection

Interview

A recent survey of members of the American Society for Personnel Administration (ASPA) about employee selection procedures found that the selection interview was one of the most often used assessment devices for all classes of jobs from unskilled to executive.[1] This finding was consistent with previous surveys that have indicated the longstanding popularity of the interview for selection.

As most students and personnel specialists know, however, despite its widespread popularity many questions have been raised by researchers and practitioners alike about the general usefulness of this device. Both groups have recognized the interview's limitations and also some widely practiced misuses. This recognition has in turn prompted a steady stream of "interview guides" purported to improve the accuracy of the interview. Perhaps like all cases of recommendations developed by a variety of "experts," these interview guides do not always agree in their specifics. Most discuss the need for training interviewers and providing ample opportunity for the interviewee to talk rather than having the interviewer dominate the conversation; however, there is a diversity of opinion regarding such items as the amount of structure to be imposed on the interview, the nature of questions to be asked, and the attention to be given to nonverbal cues from the interviewee. For example, one author has suggested that a few moments of silence by the interviewer after an interviewee's response is an effective technique. This is based on the assumption that the unsatisfactory applicant will begin talking after a few seconds of silence while the satisfactory one will patiently wait for the next question. Another recommendation focuses on the hand movements of the applicant, with the most critical being the fingers of both hands raised and touching in a steeple fashion. This gesture indicates, the writer claims, that the applicant feels superior and, therefore, would make an undesirable employee. Many such recommendations are made with little or no systematic study.

We assume that the selection interview will continue to be widely used and that the user will continue to be inundated with a plethora of recommendations for its use. In this chapter we summarize what is currently known about the selection interview, and we stress the results of studies of factors that affect an interviewer's decisions about the interviewee. We conclude with a series of procedures that have been demonstrated through research to improve the interview. We hope to provide sufficient information so that the reader will be able to formulate the appropriate use of this important selection device and be better able to evaluate the recommendations of interview guides.

Uses of the Interview in Selection

There have been many reasons offered for the use of the interview in selection. Generally these reasons fall into three main categories: (a) the interview provides an opportunity for the organization to sell itself to good candidates; (b) the interview is an efficient and practical method for measuring a number of different KSAs (knowledge, skills, and abilities) of an applicant; and (c) the decision about the acceptability of the applicant is made by a member of the organization who should be able to judge the match of the applicant and the job. We will discuss each of these reasons in the next sections.

Selling the Applicant on the Job

Difficulty in Providing Job Information   In almost all employment situations the applicant will have questions about the conditions of employment. For entry-level positions these questions may be as simple as working hours, rate of pay, and shift responsibilities. For managerial and technically complex positions, questions could also include work aspects such as the amount of discretion in decision making, the control over organizational resources, and the factors used in the evaluation of job performance. The selection interview has frequently been the vehicle used for answering these questions because it allows for a give-and-take between the two parties, with the clarification of misunderstandings. The interview is thus valued as a public relations tool; it gives a personal touch to all job applications and improves the organization's image in both the labor and consumer markets.

While the interview can be used for these purposes, some limiting factors should be noted. Both personal anecdotes and communication research studies provide many examples of oral information between two individuals subsequently being recalled differently by the two. While not all aspects of working conditions can be placed in written form, there is good reason for a written job description to be given to applicants that would convey a good deal of the information often transmitted in the interview. Obviously the level of detail would differ according to the job, but the advantage would be a permanent statement that could easily be referred to by the applicant after the interview has been concluded. A part of the time allocated for the interview could be saved and used for more direct selection purposes, and misunderstandings would be avoided.

Development of Inappropriate Attitudes   The public relations value of the interview is not an automatic benefit, either. Many applicants, after waiting for appointments, have felt more negatively than positively about organizations that summarily dismiss them after a brief interview or inform them that there are no suitable openings at present and that the application will be held for a period of time. Related to this is the finding that perceived interviewer personality, the manner of delivery of the interviewer, and the adequacy of information provided influenced the interviewee's evaluation of the interviewer, the company, and the likelihood of job acceptance.[2] In some cases the interviewees' negative reaction to the interviewer led to a negative impression of the organization itself.

Even more uncertain is the value of the interview for selling the applicant on the job and the organization. The common thought has been that it is beneficial to the organization to present the most favorable impression possible to the applicant. In this way many more applicants should be available and, theoretically, the company has a better chance of hiring quality employees. But as we discussed in Chapter 1, recent study of the Realistic Job Preview (RJP) has led to a reexamination of such selling as a viable strategy in recruitment and selection.[3] Frequently, because of such selling attempts, job candidates develop unrealistically inflated expectations about the organization they join. The period of time after entry into the organization can be characterized by the defeat of these expectations and the increase in dissatisfaction. This dissatisfaction in turn can lead to a number of undesirable organizational consequences including increased job turnover.

As explained previously, the RJP has been used as an alternative strategy to such recruiting. A wide variety of methods for presenting the RJP have been used: booklet, film, videotape, oral presentation, job visit, and work sample simulation. Although not enough testing has been done to identify which of these methods is the best, the present indication is that oral presentations (such as the interview) seem to be ineffective.[4] Techniques that are superior present a more direct view of the job than does a verbal description. This use of the interview, therefore, would seem to be very limited.

Our overall conclusion is that it is not appropriate to use a significant portion of the selection interview for attracting applicants, providing detailed employment information, and improving the company's image in the labor market. Spending a major proportion of the interview on these activities, especially in brief 30- to 40-minute initial interviews, appears to be an unwise use of time. Much of this type of information can be presented to the applicant in more effective ways. In addition the time can be more usefully devoted to the gathering of information about those applicant KSAs for which the interview is appropriate.

Measuring Applicant KSAs

Difficulty of Too Many KSAs   This issue is concerned with the number and type of applicant characteristics that the interview attempts to measure. During the early 1970s there was a general decrease in the use of scored ability and performance selection tests in favor of unscored interviews. In part this was attributable to a misconception regarding the EEOC's review of selection programs. Early selection discrimination cases revolved around the use of written mental and special ability tests, with the conclusion that these must be validated before they could be used for selection. It was not until somewhat later that it was expressly clear to many that the selection interview was viewed as a selection test and must also be validated before use. In the interim period, however, the interview was used to assess a wide variety of applicant characteristics. One problem in using the interview in such a way is that often, especially in brief preliminary sessions, the amount of time in the interview is not great enough to gather an adequate amount of information about a wide variety of characteristics. The result is superficial data which are of limited value. Another problem is that by substituting the interview for other assessment devices that more efficiently measure particular applicant characteristics, a human resource specialist may be collecting less accurate, more expensive data than is necessary.

Most of the major studies that have reviewed the use of the interview have come to the same conclusions. For example Lynn Ulrich and Don Trumbo state that "the interviewer is all too frequently asked to do the impossible because of limitations on the time, information, or both, available to him. . . . When the interviewer's task was limited to rating a single trait, acceptable validity was achieved."[5] They further point out that even when the interviewer concentrates on only a few characteristics, there are some that are not profitably addressed. For example, they contend that all too often a conclusion about the applicant's mental ability, arrived at during a 30-minute interview, may be less efficient and accurate than one based on the administration of a 10-minute test which would leave the interviewer time to assess those areas in which his/her judgment was more useful.

Appropriate KSAs   The question, therefore, is which specific characteristics are best assessed in the interview? Here the major reviews are in general agreement. There are two main types of characteristics: *personal relations,* such as sociability and verbal fluency; and *good citizenship* such as dependability, conscientiousness, stability, and career motivation.[6] Furthermore, it appears that the interview is better suited to measure these characteristics than are other assessment methods. Personal relations in this sense usually means characteristics important for successful personal interaction in short-term or initial meetings. The interview, by its very nature, is an example of such a situation and therefore should be an accurate indicator of ability in these areas. The good citizenship characteristics are often evaluated after discussion of work habits, tasks completed, and work environments. Such discussions usually require clarification or elaboration of statements made by the respondent. The interview, because of its interactive nature, is suitable for such probing by the interviewer.

A third characteristic, *job knowledge,* has also been evaluated in interviews. There are some guidelines as to when an interview would usefully assess this characteristic. If there is to be a large number of job knowledge questions and especially if the answers are fairly short and routine, a written test would be preferable. Such a test would usually be less expensive to administer and score, would provide a permanent record, and would often be a more familiar format for the applicant. If interview questions refer to actual behaviors such as diagnosis of defects, operation of equipment, and manipulation of data or information, job simulation instruments usually would be more appropriate. One condition that would argue for the use of job knowledge questions in the interview is when the applicant has serious reading or writing deficiencies that would impede selection evaluation but not job performance. The interviewer would be able to determine if the question is understood and to clarify unclear or poorly worded responses. Another condition would be selection situations for jobs that require the verbalization of technical information and work procedures, for example advisory or consulting jobs in which most of the requests for service are oral. In such situations the interview approximates a job simulation selection device.

Selection Evaluation by An Organization Member

Theoretically, one advantage of the interview over other selection instruments is that the data gatherer and interpreter is a human being who understands the job and the organization. The interviewer can vary questions or methods as the situation demands, thereby obtaining more appropriate information from each applicant. Other instruments do not have such adaptable characteristics. It seems probable that given these characteristics the match between applicant and position requirements could effectively be made.

Unfortunately, the overwhelming sense of the evidence does not support such assumptions. As early as 1915, Walter D. Scott, a pioneer in industrial psychology and personnel administration, examined the selection interview. In one study of six personnel managers who each interviewed 36 applicants for a sales position and ranked all applicants as to suitability, he found very little agreement among the rankings of the six. In another study he compared results of one selection interview with those of a follow-up interview of the same applicants. Again little agreement was found.[7] Other major studies of the interview have not only confirmed these findings of unreliability in decisions but have pointed out other deficiencies as well. Table 11.1 summarizes the major findings of several of these studies.

As can be easily deduced from these findings, the interview, when left in its unaltered forms, is not a very useful device for selection purposes. In fact, the most that can be said for its use is that an interviewer usually evaluates an interviewee in the same manner at different times. This reliability in selection decisions for an interviewer is, undoubtedly, important in the operation of a selection program. However, many other important requirements are routinely violated in the selection interview. The most serious problem is the lack of validity. In other words, decisions about applicants that result from the selection interview are usually not related to their subsequent performance on the job.

Inappropriate Interviewer Behavior   The other findings listed in Table 11.1 at least partially explain this lack of validity in the use of the interview. It seems logical that if the interviewer dominates the conversation and spends much of the allotted time on topics that are not directly related to job behaviors and necessary KSAs, the predictive accuracy of the interviewer's evaluation of the applicant would be impaired. In such cases there usually are insufficient relevant data about the applicant to make an accurate judgment. Such deficiencies are often addressed in interview guides with recommendations that stress the need for both open-ended questions to gather more information and also job-relevant questions to increase the usefulness of the responses.

Table 11.1   *Common Deficiencies in the Selection Interview*

1. Much time is spent on non-job-related topics while many appropriate job-related topics are overlooked.
2. Unfavorable information, whether job-related or not, influences interviewer's decisions more than favorable information.
3. The interviewer frequently talks more than the interviewee.
4. The interviewer tends to evaluate the acceptability of the applicant early in the interview.
5. Different interviewers interviewing for the same job gather different information from applicants.
6. While a single interviewer may reliably evaluate applicants, a group of interviewers are often not reliable in their evaluation of the same applicant.
7. The selection interview generally has low validity.

The common finding that an evaluation of the candidate is made early in the interview seems to contradict the purpose of the interview. The interviewer should be gathering information about the applicant during the complete interview. The evaluation of the applicant would, logically, be the most accurate when all the gathered information is reviewed and the evaluation is deduced from the data. In many cases the process is just the opposite. The evaluation is made very early in the interview, frequently in the first four minutes, on the basis of very little verbal information. The remaining portion of the interview is spent in gathering data to support the early decision.[8] Almost as puzzling is the strong influence of unfavorable information, job-related or not, on interviewee evaluation. If the objective of the interview is the systematic comparison of applicant KSAs against a standard that is important for job performance, such exaggerated weighting of unfavorable data would seem to be dysfunctional, especially when such data are not clearly job-related.

We think these findings clearly indicate that the supposed advantage of having a person who is familiar with the organization and the job judge the match between the applicant and the job usually is not demonstrated. In fact, this process may be inferior to alternative assessment methods. It is impractical, however, to recommend that the interview be dropped from selection programs; its use has become too ingrained. Fortunately, these findings of deficiencies in the interview decision-making process have prompted an extensive study of factors that influence interviewers' decisions. It has been demonstrated that evidence gathered from these studies can provide guidelines for interviewers to use in order to increase the accuracy of their decisions. The next section will summarize some of these studies.

Interviewer Decision Making

As we have said, the clear implication of research on the interview is that interviewers frequently use other types of information than job-relevant data to evaluate interviewees. The questions then become what kind of information is used and how is it used. Although we do not have the complete answer, recent studies have identified some of the important factors.

Physical Characteristics   The physical attractiveness of the applicant has often been related to the interviewer's overall evaluation, with more attractive candidates being evaluated higher than less attractive ones. This has been observed even in highly structured interviews and in interviews given by trained interviewers.[9] Attractiveness, as one would expect, is not the same to all interviewers. Job, race, and dress are some of the important considerations.

It has also been found that the personal liking of the interviewer for the applicant is positively related to the interviewer's evaluation.[10] This has occurred even in situations in which the interviewer did not previously know the interviewee, was not scheduled to work personally with the interviewee in the future, and firmly believed that his/her personal feelings did not influence the assessment. As with physical attractiveness, the factors influencing "liking" do not seem to be consistent for all interviewers but appear to be specific to each situation.

Nonverbal Behaviors   An area that has received much recent attention has been the relationship of the applicants' nonverbal characteristics to the interviewers' decisions. While there has not been unanimous agreement, most studies have concluded that nonverbal cues are in fact related to evaluations. A variety of cues have been studied but the ones investigated the most often are eye contact, head movement, smiling, hand movement, and general body posture (rigidity versus movement). It appears that moderately high but not extreme levels of these cues are related to favorable interview decisions. These decisions have included overall judgments of appropriateness for employment, salary recommendations, and specific ratings of such characteristics as assertiveness, motivation, self-confidence, enthusiasm, and sociability. In many of these studies the interviewee has been trained to demonstrate various levels of these cues. One can conclude, therefore, that these nonverbal cues do indeed affect the interviewer's decision. Further, these studies lend support to the idea that an interviewee can manipulate the outcome of the interview through learned behaviors.

Negative Information   The relatively larger weight given to negative information over positive information in the interviewer's decision has also been demonstrated, even for experienced interviewers.[11] For example, in one study unfavorable ratings on only one of several characteristics resulted in the rejection of the applicant in over 90 percent of the cases.[12] Related work has found that interviewers could usually specify why a rejected applicant was not likely to be a good employee but could not clearly articulate reasons why acceptable applicants would be satisfactory, indicating a clearer use of negative data.[13] In some cases it is not definite what the source of these negative judgments is. There is some evidence that impressionistic information rather than actual facts gathered in the interview are related to these judgments. Such decision making would clearly be at odds with the stated purpose of the interview but consistent with the evidence that physical attractiveness, liking, and nonverbal cues affect the decision. This would also be compatible with the findings that evaluations are frequently made in the opening minutes of the interview and are consistently held throughout the interview. In such cases it would be likely that impressions rather than facts would be more important if only because of the limited time available to gather factual data. Finally, it has been shown that the average number of factual questions an interviewer was able to answer correctly immediately after an interview was only 50 percent, a further indication that facts are not the main determinant of ratings.[14]

Previous Applicants   In instances in which an interviewer conducts a series of interviews, each with a different applicant, there is evidence that at least part of the rating is due to the quality of the applicants preceding the one being rated. This is referred to as the "contrast effect" in interview ratings. If an average applicant is preceded by highly qualified individuals, his/her rating is lower than average. If the preceding applicants are poorly qualified, then the rating is higher than average. Finally, the previously mentioned findings of low reliability among interviewers in their evaluations has been linked to the different weighting of information by each interviewer in reaching a final evaluation. What is surprising, however, is evidence that the actual weighting of information (determined from statistical analyses) is greatly different from the intended weighting described by an interviewer, indicating that in some cases interviewers are not aware of their manner of forming judgments.[15]

What does all this mean? One clear conclusion is that *there are many factors only marginally related to job activities that influence an interviewer's evaluation, even if the interviewer is experienced.* One might argue that some of these, for example appearance, liking, and nonverbal behavior, are important personal characteristics that affect interaction with others. Since most jobs require some personal interaction, these cues are important for at least those aspects of job performance. One problem with such an argument is that these characteristics can be learned by interviewees specifically for the interview and may not be representative of their behavior in other situations. Secondly, the lack of agreement in evaluating such applicant characteristics as appearance and liking limit the usefulness of these factors. How could an interviewer be certain as to whether or not the company members who would be working with the applicant would judge the applicant favorably or unfavorably?

It is possible that the influence of these extraneous factors is partially caused by the misuse of the interview. We mentioned previously that the interview has proven useful for gathering only limited types of information. Many interview situations exceed these limits and ask the interviewer to judge applicant characteristics that are not appropriately measured in an interview. In such situations the interviewer would be forced to rely on a variety of factors to make such decisions.

A second conclusion is that *an interviewer may be unaware of the factors and the weighting of the factors used in reaching a judgment about an applicant.* In addition to the work already cited, factors such as pressure from the organization have been shown to influence evaluations. One might argue that the role that the interviewer sees him-/herself playing in the selection process affects decision making. If the interview is seen as a screening-out process that is intended to eliminate a large number of applicants in order to quickly reduce the pool to a manageable number, then any deficiency, perceived or real, job-related or not, is useful in making decisions. On the other hand, if the interview is a screening-in process whose function is to identify candidates who could possibly perform well, the emphasis would change. Assets would be viewed more critically than deficiencies.

Explanations of Interviewer Decision Making

A major purpose in identifying the various factors that affect interviewer decision making is the hope that a clearer understanding of these factors will provide direction for improving the interview as a selection device. It has been surmised that the observed deficiencies in reliability and validity are a function of differences in the information used and the decision rules employed by interviewers. As more study is completed, however, it is becoming evident that there are numerous specific factors that may enter into the decision-making process. It would be unwieldy, if not impossible, to identify each of these and determine its effect. Instead recent attention has been given to forming models that are used to identify broad classes of factors and describe how these classes influence the interview decision-making process. These models should be useful for both practitioners and researchers. Practitioners can use the models to become aware of the diversity of elements that affect the interview and take steps to minimize negative effects. Researchers can use the models to organize current findings and direct further study.

While the work in developing these models is relatively recent, some useful products have merged. Two models that are similar are one developed by Neil Schmitt and another developed by George Dreher and Paul Sackett.[16] We will describe Dreher and Sackett's (Exhibit 11.1) because it goes into more detail in identifying cause-effect relationships.

The Dreher-Sackett model specifies the information that is important in the interview process, generally how this information affects the behavior of both the interviewer and the interviewee, and how both information and behavior lead to a final hiring decision. An important characteristic of the model is the numbered linkages between the various parts. These linkages indicate factors that have important influences in the interview process.

Pre-interview Factors

The first two linkages specify two factors that can affect the interviewer's expectations about the applicant even before the interview takes place. One is the actual characteristics of the applicant that is known from such sources as application forms, previous test data, letters of reference, comments of previous supervisors, etc. The second is the attitudes or stereotypes that the interviewer holds about various groups of people. For example, beliefs that women are responsible, men are aggressive, and people with several job changes are disloyal are held to have direct effects on the expectations about particular applicants.

Exhibit 11.1 Dreher and Sackett's Model of Interviewer Information
Seeking, Receipt, and Processing

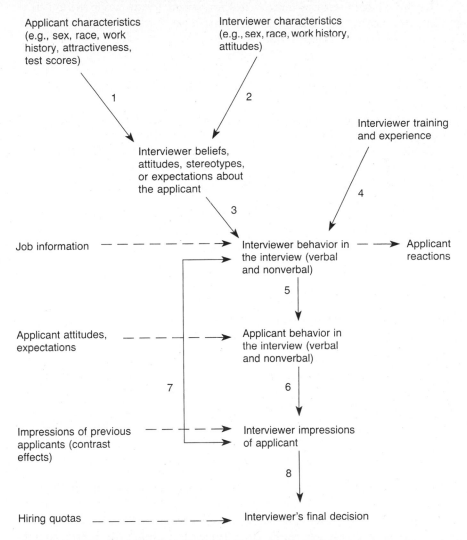

Source: George Dreher and Paul Sackett, *Perspectives on Employee Staffing and Selection* (Homewood, Ill: Richard D. Irwin, Inc., 1983), p. 324. Reprinted with permission.

The importance of these prior expectations is that they influence the behavior of the interviewer toward the applicant during the interview (linkage three). This influence is in contrast to the common view that the interviewer begins each interview in a neutral state and reacts only to the information presented and the behavior of the applicant in the interview. This is a very important consideration for it means that general notions made with very little, if any, direct knowledge about the individual applicant can indirectly affect the information obtained and ultimately the evaluation of the applicant.

The model does not postulate that impressions formed by pre-interview data are necessarily incorrect or always detrimental to the evaluation of a candidate. At present there is not enough evidence to even hazard an estimate of the frequency of formation of incorrect impressions. However, the logic is that in most cases these impressions are formed by generalizing from a very small amount of information. Evidence from other work in the behavioral sciences indicates that such a process is not accurate often enough for making judgments about individuals such as those that characterize the selection process. For example, let us assume it to be accurate that, in general, individuals with three prior job changes have a higher probability of leaving the organization within the first year. An interviewer may use this assumption when reviewing the application material of candidates to form impressions of a specific individual's acceptability. However, in most cases there is a cross-over pattern for each group; many individuals with prior job changes will stay longer than a year, and many individuals without prior job changes will leave within a year. Therefore the pre-interview impression, even if generally correct, is very limited when it comes to evaluating one particular individual. Obviously it is worthless if it is an inaccurate conclusion about a group.

Another point is that if these pre-interview impressions are usually highly related to the final evaluation of the applicant, then the interview largely becomes a redundant selection device. This would be true whether the decision about the applicant is valid or invalid; it merely argues that the interview process does not substantially alter the evaluation of the applicant and, therefore, becomes superfluous to the selection program. It is for reasons very similar to these that it is sometimes recommended that the interviewer not use previously gathered data either before or during the interview.[17] A major concern is to keep the interview as an independent assessment device rather than as an extension of those previously used.

We have emphasized the importance of pre-interview impressions on the interviewer's behavior during the interview because of the supporting evidence. Dreher and Sackett's model, however, points out that there are other factors that affect the interviewer's behavior as well: the interviewer's training and experience (linkage four) and information about the particular job being considered. Both of these factors can reduce the effects of pre-interview impressions on interviewer behavior. We will discuss training in more detail later on in this chapter.

Ongoing Interview Factors

The fifth linkage in the model holds that the interviewer's behavior in the interview is a strong determinant of the applicant's. This recognizes the fact that the interviewer is in control of the interview and that his/her conduct and the structure of the interview can significantly influence the applicant.

The model also states that the applicant's attitudes and expectations contribute to his/her behavior during the interview. At most times, however, the applicant is responding to the interviewer rather than controlling the interview. This usually constrains the actions and the information that he/she provides.

Linkages six and seven describe other interactions between the applicant and the interviewer. The applicant's verbal and nonverbal behaviors provide the data for the interviewer to form impressions and judgments about him/her. As our previous discussion has indicated, other factors, such as contrast effects (impressions from previous candidates), also influence the interviewer's impressions. There is evidence that these impressions are formed continually throughout the interview, not only at the end. Consequently, they affect the subsequent behavior of the interviewer toward the interviewee in much the same fashion as the pre-interview impressions did. There is no evidence, however, as to which of the two is the stronger in determining interviewer behavior.

The eighth linkage indicates that the impressions formed by the interviewer influence the overall evaluation of the applicant. The importance here is that the emphasis is on the impressions of the interviewer and not the characteristics of the applicant. For all the reasons previously discussed, the same applicant can be evaluated quite differently by independent interviewers because of the differences in their impressions. In fact, this is what is demonstrated by the low reliability frequently found among interviewers.

We have treated this model of the interview in some detail because we feel that an understanding of the complete process of the interview is essential to its appropriate use as a selection instrument. It also provides a framework for viewing the various attempts that have been developed to improve the interview.

Attempts to Improve the Interview

As was mentioned earlier in the chapter, the deficiencies of the selection interview in terms of reliability and validity have been documented since the early part of the century. For almost as long a period of time, human resource specialists have attempted to improve these deficiencies. The most frequent efforts have been in the training of interviewers, the structuring of questions, and the developing of scoring formats for evaluating applicants.

Training

Up until the recent development of models of the total interview process, such as the one we have just discussed, the interview was thought of primarily in terms of the interaction between interviewer and interviewee. The factors and linkages that occur before the face-to-face exchange were not considered in any depth. Therefore, almost all of the attempts to train interviewers to be better at what they did focused on improving either the interpersonal skills of the interviewer or his/her ability to evaluate applicants with a minimum of interference from extraneous factors that occurred during the interview.

Early work determined that the interview was often hindered by numerous errors committed by the interviewer, errors such as the following:

1. Excessive talking by interviewers which limited the amount of job-related information obtained from interviewees

2. Inconsistency in questioning resulting in different types of information gathered from each applicant

3. Overconfidence and a sense of infallibility in his/her evaluation ability that encouraged hasty decisions

4. Decision style errors in which the interviewer had a tendency to rate many applicants the same, either all superior (leniency) or all average (central tendency) or all poor (stringency)

5. Inability to put the interviewee at ease during the interview, making it very difficult to gather spontaneous or follow-up information

6. Allowing one or two either good or bad characteristics to influence the evaluations of all other characteristics (halo effect)

7. Stereotyping the applicant and allowing personal bias to influence the evaluation of the applicant

8. Being influenced by the nonverbal behavior of the applicant

9. Asking a number of questions that were either unrelated or only slightly related to performance on the job

The Semi-Structured Interview   A great many training programs have been developed to overcome these and similar deficiencies. Obviously it would be impossible to summarize the characteristics of all of them. There have, however, been recurrent themes which we will discuss. One major theme is the development of semi-structured interviews. In order to limit talkative and verbally wandering interviewers, limits have often been imposed on the questions used. Interviews can be classified according to the percentage of questions that are determined before the interview begins: unstructured interviews have virtually no predetermined questions; structured interviews have almost all predetermined questions (making the interview similar to an oral questionnaire); semi-structured interviews have basic questions that are predetermined but allow for the addition of others to probe or expand information.

There are many arguments for using a semi-structured rather than an unstructured interview. In an unstructured interview the interviewer can ask any question that he/she wishes. The logic of the questions is up to the interviewer. From our knowledge about interviewing models, we can immediately point out the potential problems of such a strategy. In essence the extraneous factors that affect an interviewer's decisions are given free rein.

Research has supported this notion—many of the problems of the selection interview have been identified in unstructured situations. Unfortunately this type of interview is still commonly used.

The semi-structured interview is based on key topics that should be job related. For example, persistence in completing unstructured tasks may be important for the job under consideration. The semi-structured interview provides questions to gather information about such persistence, such as "Have you ever worked on a project in which it was not clear what exactly should be done or how the project should be completed?" These questions are asked of all applicants. Probing questions, which are not predetermined, are asked by the interviewer until enough information is obtained about the topic. These probe questions, of course, depend on the nature of the conversation between the interviewer and the applicant.

The main advantage of such a semi-structured interview is that information about the same topics is collected from all applicants. This makes the comparison of applicants easier. In an unstructured interview usually this does not happen and comparison among applicants is subject to impressions and guesses. Additionally, information about all major job topics is more assured. Studies have frequently indicated that the reliability of interviewers' evaluations is increased by using the semi-structured interview. Other deficiencies such as the interviewer's dominating the conversation can also be controlled.

The Interview Process   A second theme in interview training programs addresses how to successfully conduct the interaction process itself. The central issues are usually:

1. Creating an open-communication atmosphere

2. Delivering questions consistently

3. Maintaining control of the interview

4. Developing good speech behavior

5. Learning listening skills

6. Taking appropriate notes

7. Keeping the conversation flowing and avoiding leading or intimidating the interviewee

8. Interpreting, ignoring, or controlling the nonverbal cues of the interview

One purpose of this work is to create an interview situation in which the interviewee feels relaxed and comfortable. Logically this should make it easier for the interviewee to think of difficult to remember information and provide complete answers about the topics asked. Another purpose is to minimize what may be called administrative errors that can occur in the interview. These are such events as misunderstanding what was said, not correctly remembering information provided, tipping off the applicant as to the "best" answers to a question, and using time foolishly so as not to cover all topics. The general effect of such training is to increase the amount of information obtained in the interview and to insure its accuracy.

Decision-Making Methods   A third theme has been instruction in decision-making methods. One frequently used technique is to explain and demonstrate the most common rating errors: contrast effects, halo, leniency, and central tendency. Practice is then given in recognizing how these errors may influence the interviewer's own decision making. Other techniques have attempted to model the way information is weighted by the interviewer in reaching final, overall judgments about applicants. Frequently models are also built that weight the same information more appropriately, and the interviewer is trained to imitate this model. Such programs frequently focus on interviewee appearance and mannerisms, and interviewer stereotypes and biases as causes of inappropriate weighting. The major point of training in decision making is that learning the nature of such errors will result in minimizing the distortion caused by these errors in actual interviews. The formation of interview teams or panels is also frequently recommended for the purpose of cancelling the bias of any individual interviewer.

Systematic Scoring   A fourth theme advocates systematic scoring of the interview. It is almost universally recognized that the intuitive evaluation of an applicant by an interviewer, still very common in interviewing, is to be avoided if carefully determined evaluations are desirable. Formal evaluation forms usually contain a number of defined applicant characteristics, all preferably related to job performance, a separate rating scale for each characteristic, space for recording specific notes or observations regarding that characteristic, and a rating of the overall acceptability of the applicant.

Results of Training   How much improvement have these changes made in the use of the interview? The results have generally been encouraging but have not meant that all problems have been corrected. For the most part the various training programs have reduced some of the more common rater errors: contrast, halo, leniency, and stringency. There is also evidence that training programs such as the five-day University of Houston Interviewing Institute can produce significant changes in the actual interviewing behaviors of participants.[18] This institute uses presentations, demonstrations, exercises, and videotaped practice to improve the skills of professional interviewers. After training, participants have demonstrated large improvements in questioning techniques, interview structure, interviewing supportiveness, techniques of rapport, active listening skills, and attention to relevant materials. Finally, structuring of the interview questions and systematic scoring has generally improved the reliability of evaluations among sets of interviewers.

Interview Panels

The limiting finding has been that the validity of the interview has not increased as much as would be hoped. One tactic that has shown consistent improvements in validity has been the use of interview panels.[19] A variety of studies have demonstrated significant validities when two or more interviewers have been used simultaneously in the selection of police officers, civil service employees, and various groups of manufacturing employees. It appears that the discussion and the comparison of impressions that characterize interview panels reduce the effect of irrelevant impressions and focus the evaluation more on job-relevant factors.

Discrimination and the Interview

Because of its long history of low validity for selection and its widespread use, the interview often poses a potentially serious legal problem for organizations. Recalling material in Chapter 2, an organization would be in a vulnerable position in a question of discrimination if two conditions occurred: (a) decisions of the selection interview led, or assisted in leading, to a pattern of adverse impact; and (b) the interview could not be demonstrated to be valid in a normally accepted manner.

Court Cases

Table 11.2, which is part of Richard Arvey's thorough treatment of unfair discrimination in the selection interview, contains a summary of the major cases.[20] As was discussed in Chapter 2, the *Uniform Guidelines* specify that any device that is used to select applicants must adhere to the standards presented. These standards were applied by the courts in these decisions.

In both *Stamps v. Detroit Edison* and *U.S. v. Hazelwood School District*[21] the court noted that adverse impact had occurred and that the interview was a subjective process that unnecessarily contributed to this impact. The interviewers had not been given specific job-related questions to follow nor had they been instructed in either the proper weights to apply to specific pieces of information or the decision rules for evaluating the applicant as acceptable or unacceptable. In *Weiner v. County of Oakland* the issues of the preceding two cases were partially addressed by the organization in that the interview was scored in a systematic fashion.[22] However, the questions asked in the interview were specifically reviewed by the court once adverse impact had been determined. The court ruled that questions such as whether Mrs. Weiner could work with aggressive, young men, whether her husband approved of her working, and whether her family would be burdened if she altered her normal household chores were not sufficiently job-related to warrant their use in the interview. A similar court decision was reached in *King v. New Hampshire Department of Resources and Economic Development* in which ques-

Table 11.2   *Legal Cases Treating the Selection Interview*

Case	Comments
Stamps v. Detroit Edison (1973)	All interviewers were white Interviewers made subjective judgments about applicant's personality No structured or written interview format No objective criteria for employment decisions
U.S. v. Hazelwood School District (1976)	All school principals (interviewers) were white Principals could freely weight subjective factors No uniformity in applying selection criteria
Weiner v. County of Oakland (1976)	All interviewers were male Interview questions suggested bias against women Selection decision rule not clearly specified
King v. New Hampshire Department of Resources and Economic Development (1977)	Interview questions suggested bias against women and were not job-related No rigid eligibility criteria for employee selection
Hester v. Southern Railway (1974)	No adverse impact demonstrated in selection results Interview was subjective with no formal standards or procedures
Bannerman v. Department of Youth Authority (1977)	No adverse impact demonstrated in selection results Interview had no structured format
Harless v. Duck (1977)	Adverse impact relative to women Structured questionnaire Questions based on job analysis Relationship between interview performance and training Interview upheld

Source: Richard Arvey, "Unfair Discrimination in the Employment Interview: Legal and Psychological Aspects," *Psychological Bulletin* 86 (1979): 736–765.

tions that asked about work experience in building and construction and the previous use of specific tools were held not to be job-related to the position under consideration, that of state meter patrol officer.[23]

Two cases that were not decided against the organization were *Hester v. Southern Railway* and *Bannerman v. Department of Youth Authority*.[24] In both cases the court did not find clear evidence of adverse impact. One case in which the interview was successfully defended even though adverse impact was demonstrated was *Harless v. Duck*.[25] In this case involving the selection of police officers, the department used an interview board to gather responses to approximately 30 questions. These questions tapped such KSAs as the applicant's communication skills, decision-making and problem-solving skills, and reactions to stress situations. The court accepted the defendant's arguments that the interview was valid in that the questions were based on dimensions identified through job analysis and that interview performance was related to performance in training at the police academy.

Some Common Practices

In addition to these court cases, there have been many recent research studies about discrimination in the selection interview that are worth noting. Several have pointed out that race is an important dimension in the behavior of both interviewers and interviewees. These studies have not been in total agreement as to differences that take place; but, in general, black interviewees have been found to produce less verbal information and to demonstrate less nonverbal body movement than whites. Various differences have also been demonstrated in the amount of verbal information that can be obtained by white and black interviewers from interviewees of both colors. What is interesting is that despite these differences there is very little evidence in recent studies that indicates adverse impact between blacks and whites is a common problem with the interview.[26] That is, there is little evidence that disproportionate numbers of blacks are evaluated poorly in the selection interview. Apparently the recent attention to the possibility of discrimination occurring against blacks, especially with many interviewers being white, has made interviewers extremely conscious of this potential problem and has thus influenced their decision making.

Comparisons of the evaluation of males versus females, however, have produced a different pattern of results. Studies have consistently found that females are given lower evaluations than males even when candidates have similar or identical characteristics.[27] These differences seem to be particularly pronounced in interviews for jobs that are frequently thought of as being "male" jobs. These are jobs that have traditionally been held only by males, that have heavy physical demands, that require socializing after work hours, or that have hazardous components. This pattern of different evaluations has been less pronounced or negligible for jobs in areas that are regarded as feminine or neuter, even when the position is managerial. Such areas are personal care, education and training, staff positions requiring the review of incoming data and/or the preparation of reports, and public relations. The conclusion seems to be that women, while given equal consideration for many managerial and professional positions, are frequently at a disadvantage for many jobs that have requirements different from regular office work. On the surface, it does not seem that many of these jobs actually have requirements that would disproportionately disqualify female applicants. Given the evidence from these studies, it would seem logical to carefully review the results of interviews for "male" jobs.

Recommendations for Interview Use

As we have said, the interview is one of the most popular and easily used selection instruments. There is evidence that with careful construction and implementation it can contribute to the selection program. Using the research findings we have discussed in this chapter, we will now look at some factors that we feel should be considered when the interview is used as part of the selection program. These factors are summarized in Table 11.3.

Narrow the Scope of the Interview

We believe that one of the major weaknesses in the use of the interview is that it is often used to accomplish too many purposes. It frequently happens that the interview is used simultaneously as a public relations vehicle to project an image of the organization, as a recruitment vehicle to convey job description and organization information to potential applicants, and as a selection vehicle to evaluate the job-related KSAs of the applicants. The interview is essentially a verbal process. It is used in a variety of other human resource functions as well: performance appraisal, training, disciplinary hearings, etc. However, no one recommends that it be used simultaneously for all of these functions. Of course, all of these personnel functions do not usually occur at the same time for an employer, whereas recruitment, selection, and projecting a good public image do. However, we ought not to confuse time similarity with function similarity. Just because these three functions are compressed into a short period at the beginning of the human resource management cycle does not mean that they should be addressed at the same time. The purposes of and the data for public relations, recruitment, and selection are simply not the same.

There is evidence that the interview can be combined with other techniques to accomplish the purposes of selection, recruitment, and public relations. We think that these personnel functions should be systematically reviewed. If it is decided that the interview, as a process, should be used in any one or in any combination of these functions, then each separate interview

---

Table 11.3   *Recommendations for Interview Use*

1. Restrict the use of the interview to the most job-relevant KSAs.
2. Limit the use of pre-interview data about applicants.
3. Adopt a semi-structured format by predetermining major questions to be asked.
4. Use job-related questions.
5. Use multiple questions for each KSA.
6. Develop a formal scoring format that allows for the evaluation of each KSA separately.
7. Use multiple interviewers simultaneously whenever possible.
8. Train interviewers in the process of the selection interview.

process ought to be planned according to the models for effective use that have been developed for that function. In this way the selection interview becomes focused, and is not a multiple-purpose, hybrid activity. This should substantially increase its usefulness.

There is a second way in which the interview suffers from a multiple-purpose use. It frequently occurs when the assessment of applicant characteristics is the only function served by the interview. Earlier in this chapter we noted that it is the conclusion of several writers that often too many KSAs are evaluated in the interview. Most selection specialists have fairly clear-cut expectations as to the specific information that is appropriately yielded by particular assessment devices: application forms provide general information about job activities and educational programs; knowledge tests provide estimates of how much information an applicant possesses on specific topics; performance tests allow the applicant to demonstrate competency in certain skills such as typing, auto repair, etc. Such a clear connection is not drawn for the interview. Rather, in practice, the interview is frequently used as a general evaluation device to measure job knowledge, leadership ability, personality, motivation, professional deportment, etc. This is a lot to expect from one assessment device, especially if it is only 30 to 60 minutes long. No other assessment instrument is used to make evaluations in such diverse areas.

It has been recommended that the scope of the interview be limited to a much narrower band of applicant characteristics: *job knowledge, sociability* and *related interpersonal abilities,* and *to a lesser extent corporate citizenship* (work habits, dependability, compliance, cooperation, adaptability, etc).

This use is closely related to material that was presented in Chapter 8. In that chapter we described how to proceed from task statements to the identification of KSAs, to the specification of appropriate assessment devices to measure these KSAs. Let us use the information presented in Table 11.4 to demonstrate the appropriate use of the interview in a selection program. Through the procedures previously described, we have completed a job analysis of the job of maintenance foreman based upon task statements. From these task statements the KSAs listed in Table 11.4 have been derived. The remainder of the table presents the appropriate use of various selection instruments for the measurement of the KSAs by presenting the percentage of the selection program that should be devoted to each of the selection instruments.

Our judgment is that only three of these KSAs are appropriate for assessment in the interview, and that the interview should comprise 40 percent of the selection program to measure these adequately. "Verbal ability to give work instructions to laborers regarding construction and repair" is best demonstrated through a verbal exchange process like the interview. Measurement of the "ability to schedule work crews for specific tasks" would frequently entail the exchange of information about specific characteristics of tasks and also an explanation of the reasoning used in making specific assign-

Table 11.4   *Selection Plan for the Job of Maintenance Foreman*

Job: Maintenance Foreman	KSA Importance	Selection Instruments					
		Application Form	Biodata Form	Interview	Performance Test	Personality Inventory	Ability Test
KSA							
Knowledge of construction principles of small buildings	15%	3%					12%
Knowledge of building systems: heating, electrical, plumbing	15	3					12
Knowledge of inventory control methods	15	3					12
Skill in performing basic carpentry, plumbing, electrical wiring operations	5				5%		
Ability to diagnose defects in building and building systems	10				10		
Verbal ability to give work instructions to laborers regarding construction and repair	20			20%			
Ability to schedule work crews for specific tasks	5			5			
Ability to simultaneously direct multiple work crews and work projects	15			15			
	100%	9%	0%	40%	15%	0%	36%

ments. Such an exchange is more appropriate for an interview than for a written test. The "ability to simultaneously direct multiple work crews and work projects" is, perhaps, the most difficult of the KSAs to measure accurately. Ideally, we would use a simulation that creates several situations and evaluates the applicant's responses. However, to be accurate, the simulation should be carried out for an extended period of time. This would not usually be feasible. Our approach, therefore, would be to view this ability as a work habit, a facet of corporate citizenship, and use the interview to determine information about the applicant's behavior in similar, previous situations.

We thus conclude that of the eight KSAs to be measured in this selection program, only these three should be measured by the interview. As Table 11.4 indicates, three other KSAs are tapped by a combination of the application form and ability tests. The remaining two KSAs are best measured by performance tests.

Limit Use of Pre-Interview Data

Perhaps the most common sequence of steps in selection programs is that the applicant completes an application form or provides a resumé and then participates in the employment interview. In most cases the interviewer has access to this information and uses it, at least initially, to formulate questions and direct conversation during the interview.

As we have mentioned previously in the chapter, there is a question as to whether or not this pre-interview information is of real benefit to the interviewer. Many argue that pre-interview data is essential to good interviewing. It provides basic information about previous work and educational experience that can be developed in the interview. Some interview guides even recommend that interviewers develop hypotheses about the type of KSAs possessed by a specific applicant based on application information and then use the interview to test these hypotheses.

Recent work, however, that has closely studied this issue has not totally supported these proposed advantages of using pre-interview data and has found some detrimental effects. We have already presented the model developed by Dreher and Sackett that emphasizes that pre-interview information is used to develop assessments of applicants before the interview is conducted. These assessments affect the interview process itself and can serve as sources of error in the evaluation of applicants. For example, in one study, Dipboye, Fontelle, and Garner carefully compared the interviewing methods and decision-making results of one group of interviewers who had application material prior to the interview with those of another group of interviewers who did not have such information.[28] They found that interviewers with this information asked more questions and gathered more nonapplication form information than did the interviewers who did not have the pre-interview data. However, this had no advantage in terms of the quality of the interviewers' decisions. In fact, the interviewers using application information demonstrated less accuracy in estimating personal characteristics of applicants and also less reliability in the ratings of both applicant performance in the interview and goodness of fit to the job than did interviewers who did not use pre-interview data. Overall, then, there appears to be both advantages and disadvantages in the use of pre-interview data.

There have not been enough studies done to draw a firm conclusion about the use of such data in the selection interview. Our recommendation is therefore based on a combination of research and common sense. An important point would seem to be the completeness of the pre-interview data that is available to the interviewer. If it is a personnel file, as may be the case in selection among applicants already in the organization, such data may provide relatively extensive and useful information about the applicant's ability to perform certain tasks. This could definitely be helpful to the interviewer for developing probing questions. The problem may come when very sketchy information is obtained, for example only job titles or education degrees or brief verbal statements. As we know, there is a common inclination for the interviewer to weave this information together to form an impression of the applicant. Impressions formed on such little data could easily be inaccurate.

Assuming that the interview focuses on a limited number of KSAs, our recommendation is to exercise some screening of pre-interview data. Two types of information seem to be useful for interviewers to have. The first is *relatively complete data about any of the KSAs to be covered in the interview.* This could save time or allow for more detailed questioning. The other type would be the *incomplete or contradictory statements presented on the application blank or other similar instruments:* such items as employment gaps, overlapping full-time positions, a nonregular career movement pattern, etc. This kind of irregularity could be clarified in the interview.

There is enough evidence to indicate that access to data not directly relevant to the purposes of the interview only contributes to deficiencies in the interviewers' decisions. Therefore, these other data, e.g., ability test scores, letters of reference, brief reactions of others, etc., should be withheld until after the interview is completed.

The Semi-Structured Format

One of the most consistent recommendations made by those who have written about ways to improve the use of the interview in selection has been to impose structure on the verbal exchange between the parties. This is done by providing the interviewer with a set of questions that must be asked of all interviewees. The amount of interview structure is a function of the proportion of the total questions asked that is constituted by this predetermined set.

In this format *a set of questions should be formulated for each KSA* identified as appropriate for the interview. Referring to the previous example of the maintenance foreman job, this would mean a set of questions concerning each KSA: "verbal ability to give instructions," "ability to schedule work crews," and "ability to simultaneously direct multiple work crews." These questions must be asked of each applicant. However, the interviewers are also permitted to go beyond these questions as they feel necessary, either to clarify a given response, to seek other important details, or to pursue a closely related area.

The logic behind imposing this structure is to build consistency in the interview regarding essential information. This means insuring that the interviewer consistently gathers information about each of the appropriate KSAs from each applicant. Structuring the interview helps to develop this consistency either across a set of interviewers or with one interviewer who is examining a set of applicants and must choose among them. The major benefit of this consistency in questioning is that it makes comparison among applicants much easier. If done properly, the human resource specialist would have information from each applicant on the same KSAs. This would facilitate the identification of those applicants most suitable for the job.

Use Job-Related Questions

Having an appropriate semi-structured format for the interview is only of limited value if the predetermined set of questions provides information that is only marginally related to job performance. Therefore, another concern in the interview is to insure that the questions used are job related, that is, gather information useful in measuring the appropriate KSAs identified for each job.

The issue of what kind of interview question best achieves these objectives is one of the most perplexing problems for selection specialists. There has been little systematic study about the content or the type of question that provides the most useful information about applicants. The following statements, therefore, are primarily our opinions about this subject.

Questions of Job Knowledge   Logically, questions are useful if the applicant's responses provide direct information about how well the KSA of interest is possessed by the applicant. For example, let us refer once again to one of the KSAs listed in Table 11.4 for the maintenance foreman, "verbal ability to give work instructions to laborers regarding construction and repair." One type of question that is often used to measure such a KSA is to ask about previous work experience. Such questions as the following are examples:

> "Have you ever given direction to work crews?"
>
> "If so, for what kind of assignments were these given?"
>
> "Have you had any difficulties in giving directions?"
>
> "How long have you directed work crews?"

Such questions are indirect indications of the KSA. Answers do not reflect the respondent's verbal ability directly but, at most, only whether or not he or she states the activity under question has been demonstrated. There would be little data in the responses given to these questions that would allow the interviewer to evaluate accurately how much verbal ability in giving instructions the applicant currently possesses.

A more useful question would be to ask the applicant to actually give instructions to the interviewer, or to a fictitious work crew, as to how to perform some task that is representative of work assignments that were identified through the job analysis. In this case a question might be, "What instructions would you give a work crew that was about to string 220v electric cable in a laboratory building under construction?" The resulting answer provides direct evidence of the applicant's ability to provide instructions. Strengths and weaknesses both can be identified by the interviewer. No assumption is made that previous performance of a related action is in itself indicative of a high level of ability. In addition, it is difficult for the applicant to fake or distort his or her response. This is in contrast to questions that ask only descriptions of previous experience. An applicant can exaggerate or describe many false instances because there is little opportunity for the interviewer to verify the answer. Finally, the direct demonstration of verbal ability to give instructions that is required by such a question reduces the value of the job experience type of question; and one is able to omit it from the interview. It makes little difference what the previous activities of the applicant were if, in fact, the verbal ability itself can be evaluated.

We stated previously that there are three primary KSAs that can effectively be measured in the interview: (a) sociability and initial interpersonal interaction, (b) job knowledge or ability, and (c) corporate citizenship. Developing questions that directly tap job knowledge or ability is the easiest case to formulate, as the previous example illustrates. It is considerably more difficult to develop appropriate questions in the other two areas.

Questions of Social Interaction   The measurement of KSAs related to sociability and initial interpersonal interaction seem to be especially dependent on how they are stated. For example, an office receptionist position usually requires short-term, nonrecurring interaction with individuals. The worker attributes necessary for such behavior would be appropriate for evaluation through an interview. However, if these worker attributes are specified in terms of general personality characteristics such as "poise," "friendliness," "pleasantness," or "professional bearing," assessment becomes more difficult because of the ambiguity of these terms.

A better tactic would be to try to phrase the relevant worker attributes in terms of abilities or skills. For example, the receptionist's position may require "the ability to provide preliminary information to angry customers about the resolution of product defects" or "the ability to query customers regarding the exact nature of complaints in order to route them to appropriate personnel." Phrased in this manner, it is easier to develop questions that require the demonstration of these skills and abilities.

Questions of Work Behaviors   The group of KSAs identified as corporate citizenship is, perhaps, the most difficult to assess accurately in applicants. It might include work habits such as persistence in completing assignments, ability to work on multiple tasks simultaneously, and ability to plan future actions. Frequently these are referred to under the very general term of "motivation." Another set of attributes included in this category are "helping co-workers with job-related problems, accepting orders without a fuss, tolerating temporary impositions without a complaint, and making timely and constructive statements about the work unit."[29]

One method frequently used in the attempt to measure these attributes is to ask the applicant in various ways whether he or she has worked or is willing to work in circumstances requiring these habits. The limitation with this type of question is that the information is virtually unverifiable and subject to distortion by the respondent who wishes to portray generally favorable characteristics. Most job applicants, especially experienced ones, know that almost all organizations desire employees who cooperate with other workers, can plan ahead, accept orders, and tolerate impositions. It is in the self-interest of the applicant to portray him- or herself as having demonstrated, or being willing to demonstrate, these characteristics.

A strategy that is increasingly being used to at least partially avoid this situation is to question the applicant in detail about participation in activities that are similar to those of the job under consideration. David Grove has described such an interview used by the Procter & Gamble Company for entry-level selection.[30] This interview is aimed at forming judgments of the applicant in terms of five factors that are important for effectiveness in beginning production work in P&G plants: stamina and agility, willingness to work hard, working well with others, learning the work, and initiative. The applicant is asked to write answers to "experience items" on a special form. These experience items ask the applicant to describe several relevant experiences which may have occurred in either a work or nonwork setting for each of the five factors. For example, one experience item for assessing the factor "working well with others" may be "Describe a situation in which you had to work closely with a small group of others to complete a project." Responses to these experience items are then probed in each of two separate interviews. (A recent book, *Behavior Description Interviewing* by Janz, Hellervik, and Gilmore discusses this type of question in detail."[31])

The interviews are conducted separately by a member of the plant employment group and a line manager. Each independently rates the applicant on a seven-point scale for each of the five factors. The interviewers are trained in four-to-six-hour sessions on how to conduct such interviews. In conducting the interview, an evidence organizer is used. This is a worksheet with a section for each of the five factors. Each section contains several questions and reminders which guide interviewers as they seek evidence about the applicant. The organizer provides structure for gathering, categorizing, and documenting descriptive evidence. Statistical analyses indicate high reliability between the two interviewers and some preliminary evidence of the validity of the ratings of the applicant in terms of subsequent supervisors' ratings.

We have developed a list of questions that could be used in a selection interview for the job of maintenance foreman that we mentioned previously. These questions, presented in Table 11.5, are intended to gather information about the three KSAs to be measured with the interview and to demonstrate many of the ideas explained in this section. The number of questions used for each KSA was determined from the data presented in Table 11.4.

Table 11.5   *Selection Interview Questions for the Job of Maintenance Foreman*

KSA #1: Verbal ability to give work instructions to laborers regarding construction and repair.

1. What instructions would you give a work crew that was about to string a 220v electric cable in a laboratory building under construction?
2. Two laborers, with limited experience, ask about the procedures for tuckpointing and restoring a damaged brick wall. What instructions would you give them regarding what equipment they should use and how they should operate it?
3. You assign a group of four to inspect the flat, tar-and-gravel roofs on four buildings. They are also to make minor repairs and describe major repairs to you for future action. What instructions do you give them? (You can assume that each one knows how to operate any necessary equipment.)
4. You will use eight summer employees to do the repainting of the third floor hall, ten private offices, and two public restrooms. What instructions do you give them both about general work and specific painting procedures?

KSA #2: Ability to schedule work crews for specific tasks.

1. You need to send a work crew to the far part of the industrial park to inspect and (if necessary) repair a 40' × 10' brick wall and to prepare a 40' × 60' flower bed. It is Monday morning. Rain is expected Tuesday afternoon. How many people do you assign to which tasks? How long should each task take?
2. You are in charge of a work crew of 12. Included in this are four experienced carpenters and two electricians. These six are also permitted to do other jobs. You are to finish a 100' × 200' area that will have five separate offices and a general meeting room. Tell me the first five tasks that you would assign your crew and how many people you would put on each task? How long should each task take?

KSA #3: Ability to simultaneously direct multiple work crews and work projects.

1. Go back to the situation in the previous question. Tell me which tasks you would try to complete in the first two days. Which sequence of tasks would you schedule? How would your work crews know when to start a new task?
2. Describe a specific experience in the past few years in which you had at least five people reporting to you that were performing different parts of a bigger project. This could either be in work, school, community activities, or the military.
3. Describe a specific experience in the past few years in which you and a group of others were working under a tight deadline on a project that had several parts. This could either be in work, school, community activities, or the military.

Multiple Questions for Each KSA

A basic psychological measurement principle that we discussed in Chapter 4 was that an *assessment device should contain several items or parts that gather data about the same variable in order for the assessment device to be a useful instrument.* The reason is, to a certain extent, that both reliability and validity of measurement are generally related to the number of items on the measuring device. In selection this means that, all else being equal, the more items that an assessment device possesses that measure the same KSA, the greater is its reliability and validity.

As we have already seen, the principle of multiple items is used in both biodata and training-and-experience forms. In later chapters we will show how special ability tests (e.g., mathematical knowledge, verbal reasoning, etc.), performance tests (e.g., typing, carpentry, welding, etc.), and simulations (e.g., assessment centers) all are developed with multiple measures of each KSA.

The interview should be developed and used in the same manner. As we have already mentioned, interviews, in attempting to measure corporate citizenship attributes of applicants, often request the interviewee to describe several examples of specified work situations. The same principle should be incorporated into the measurement of each KSA that is specified as being appropriate for the interview.

Returning once more to our example of the maintenance foreman in Table 11.5, the use of this principle of multiple questions would mean that applicants would be asked to respond to four questions to provide examples of instructions given to work crews, to two questions to measure ability to schedule work crews for specific tasks, and three questions to measure the ability to simultaneously direct multiple work crews and work projects. There is no rule for the exact number of questions to be asked. This is primarily a function of two factors: the information developed from the job analysis and the time available for each applicant. Concerning the information developed from the job analysis, it is necessary to consider first the relative importance of the KSAs to be measured in the interview. In our previous example in Table 11.4, "verbal ability to give work instructions" had the highest weight [20], followed by "ability to coordinate and direct multiple work crews" [15], and "ability to schedule work crews" [5]. As was explained in Chapter 8, this would mean that roughly one-half of the interview questions gathering data about KSAs should be on work instructions, three-eighths on directing work crews, and one-eighth on scheduling. The second consideration is the diversity of the tasks that relate to each KSA to be assessed in the interview. If the maintenance foreman must give instructions about many different types of tasks, then it may take more questions to have a representative sample than if there are very similar tasks.

The total amount of time available for the interview is, in some cases, beyond the control of the interviewer, for example in on-campus interviews or in many job-fair situations. In these cases an estimate should be made before the interview as to the number of questions possible based on the total time allocated for the interview and the estimated length of time required to answer each question.

The Formal Scoring Format

After the initial discrimination cases concerning selection practices were heard in the courts, many organizations discontinued the use of scored ability tests in selection and relied heavily on the use of unscored interviews. The rationale behind this strategy was that these court cases ruled against organizations that could not offer statistical evidence of job relatedness using the scores that were generated by these selection instruments. It was hoped that if formal scores were not developed in the use of the selection device, the organization would not be under the same burden of proof nor would the data be present to be used as evidence against the organization. Hence, it became more common for organizations to use selection interviews that did not require any systematic, quantitative ratings but rather depended on a global evaluation of the acceptability of the applicant made by the interviewer.

Such use of the interview was not new at that time nor is it unknown at the present time. It does present a much easier and often quicker evaluation than does a system that requires data gathering and quantitative analysis. However, the study of the interview has consistently concluded that an interview format that does provide a formal, defined scoring system is superior in many ways to a format that relies on global judgment. This is in terms of legal defensibility, reliability and validity of judgment by the interviewer, and acceptance by the interviewee.

Based upon a variety of material, it is easy to understand such findings. We have made the point that measurement is the essence of a selection program. Without measurement of the KSAs of applicants, any comparison of these applicants becomes too complex to be done accurately. It is simply not possible for a selection specialist to retain all relevant information, weigh it appropriately, and use it to compare a number of individuals — at least in a consistent and effective manner. The issue, therefore, becomes not whether to score the interview but rather how best to score it.

The most commonly used systems require the interviewer to rate the interviewee on a series of interval measurement scales. The number of rating points on such scales varies but usually consists of between four and seven scale points. These scale points have a number at each point that is used to reflect various amounts of the applicant characteristics being judged. These scale points also usually have either a set of adjectives describing differences among them, e.g., not acceptable, marginal, minimal, good, superior, etc., or a brief definition for each scale point, e.g., instructions given were not understandable, instructions given were understandable but mainly incorrect, instructions were understandable and generally correct, etc.

A second aspect of scoring concerns the dimensions to be scored. Tables 11.6 and 11.7 contain examples of two types of rating forms that have been used in interviews for a position such as maintenance foreman. The first type (Table 11.6) is general, personal characteristics and the second type (Table 11.7) is of KSAs identified through job analysis. Not surprisingly, we favor the second type as being more useful.

The first table shows a set of general attributes that are commonly thought to be characteristic of good employees — especially supervisors and managers. The problem is that it is very difficult for interviewers to use the scales consistently and accurately. Also it is very difficult to translate these scales into questions that can be asked in an interview. To avoid these problems, it seems best to rate the applicant directly on the KSAs for which the interview was intended and for which the questions were designed. If the question is developed in the manner previously described, the information provided by the applicant should quite easily be used to make judgments about these dimensions.

There are other points to make. The first is that it is logical to use only scales that measure the KSAs to be assessed in the interview. Adding other scales about job-related KSAs measured by other selection instruments is not useful. Secondly, the rating form should provide space for comments about the applicant's performance on the KSA being rated. These comments are usually examples or summaries of the responses provided by the applicant to the questions that were designed to assess the KSA. The purpose of the comments is to provide both documentation to support the rating, if it is questioned in the future, and more information that can be used to compare a series of applicants. Table 11.7 is an example of a completed form with such comments.

The final point to be made is that an overall scale that serves for a general or global evaluation of the applicant generally should not be provided. The logic is that the KSAs have been identified as separate characteristics. Combining the information for several of these into a general judgment usually forces the interviewer to make a very difficult decision by forcing different characteristics together into one. Moreover, the overall rating loses much meaning. A rating of "4" or "above average" on a general scale can be obtained by various combinations of answers to the interview questions. Therefore, it becomes more difficult to compare applicants correctly using the overall ratings. A study by Landy supports this conclusion. In evaluating the validity of an interview for police officers, Landy established the validity of *individual* interview factors in relationship to supervisor ratings. However, *no validity was determined for the ratings of the applicants' overall suitability* for the position.[32]

Use An Interview Panel

The point has been made in previous sections of this chapter that the most consistent finding regarding improving the validity of the interview is to have

Table 11.6   *An Example of Interview Rating Scales Using Personal Characteristics*

Personal Characteristics	Low	Below Average	Average	Above Average	Superior
1. Cooperation—will applicant get along with others and work as a member of team?	1	2	3	4	5
2. Need for achievement—are the goals of this applicant consistent with company opportunities?	1	2	3	4	5
3. Work experience—does work history indicate ability to learn and work consistently?	1	2	3	4	5
4. Judgment—will individual exercise good judgment in getting job done?	1	2	3	4	5
5. Manner and appearance—will others react positively to this individual?	1	2	3	4	5
6. Overall acceptability—considering everything in the interview, the individual's overall probability of performing well.	1	2	3	4	5

Table 11.7   *An Example of Interview Rating Scales Using KSAs*

Job Analysis KSAs	Unsatisfactory	Minimal	Average	Good	Superior
1. Verbal ability to give instructions.	1	2	③	4	5

Comments: Generally accurate instructions given. However, instructions lacked specificity as to worker assignment and standard of performance.

2. Ability to coordinate and direct multiple crews and projects.	1	2	③	4	5

Comments: Previous situations indicate difficulty in setting priorities among tasks. Also poor evaluation of adequacy of completed tasks.

3. Ability to schedule work crews.	1	2	3	4	⑤

Comments: Responses correctly estimated appropriate crew size and length of time needed to complete project.

interview panels. An interview panel is different from having multiple inter-viewers. An interview panel meets with the applicant and *all interviewers participate simultaneously in the interview.* The actual conduct of the interview requires the interviewers (most often two interviewers) to coordinate their questioning before the actual interview. This coordination includes the or-dering of major questions, deciding who is to ask different sets of questions, allocating time for each set, and identifying areas of special importance. On the other hand, using multiple interviewers means that more than one inter-viewer will interview the same applicant but that each interviewer conducts a separate interview. Any coordination among these interviewers is usually only concerning the time schedule of the interviews and the topics to be covered.

The demonstrated superiority of the interview panel apparently comes from the interaction among panel numbers in evaluating the applicant on the KSAs to be rated. Usually a discussion is conducted among panel members on each scale. This discussion frequently allows the interviewers to sharpen the definition of the scale, to exchange observations and recollections about the applicant's responses, and to share opinions about ratings. This is possi-ble because all the interviewers have heard and observed the same behaviors of the applicant and have a common base of information to discuss.

In multiple interviews, the interviewers have different behaviors, unob-served by others, to use in their ratings. This apparently reduces the benefi-cial effects of discussing the applicant after the series of interviews is com-plete.

Training the Interviewer

Another point that has been previously made but is important to reiterate is the value of training the interviewer. It is commonly agreed that the focal skills of an interviewer are the abilities to: (a) accurately receive information, (b) critically evaluate the information received, and (c) regulate his/her own behavior in delivering questions.[33] Most training programs focus on at least one of these areas, many address all three. While it is not within the scope of this book to present the specific features of such training programs, the following characteristics have frequently been included in successful pro-grams.

Receiving Information   In training interviewers to receive information ac-curately, instruction has concentrated on factors that influence hearing what the respondent has said, observing the applicant's behavior, and remember-ing the information received. In accomplishing this, programs frequently ad-dress such topics as taking notes, reducing the anxiety of the interviewee, establishing rapport with the interviewer, taking measures to reduce fatigue and loss of interest by the interviewer, and minimizing the effect of inter-viewer expectations on perceiving what the applicant says.

In addition, many training programs have recently focused on the non-verbal behavior of the applicant. There seems to be more difference of opinion about this topic, however, than about the others. While there is general agreement that nonverbal behavior can greatly affect the actions and judgment of the interviewer, the difference of opinion is whether this is a positive or negative factor. Some training programs, in essence, treat nonverbal behavior as a source of error in interviewer decision making that is unrelated to any future job performance by the applicant. Therefore, the interviewer is instructed on methods of reducing the effect of such cues. On the other hand, there are training programs that treat nonverbal behavior as an indicant of the applicant's attitude and personality and as useful information to the interviewer for evaluating the capability of the individual. Even among these programs, there are differences as to which behaviors are regarded as important for the interviewer. A critical issue, for which there is little data, is whether the nonverbal behavior of applicants, especially inexperienced ones, is specific to the interview situation or whether it is indicative of long-term job behavior.

Evaluation of Information   Training interviewers in the critical evaluation of information obtained from the interviewee usually focuses on improving the decision-making process of the interview by pointing out common decision errors and methods of overcoming these errors. For example, one workshop training program included videotapes of a simulation of job candidates being appraised by a manager. The trainees used a rating scale to estimate how they thought the manager would evaluate the applicant and how they themselves would assess him or her.[34] Group discussion followed as to the reasons for each trainee's rating of both the manager's evaluation and his/her own evaluation. Four exercises were used that concentrated on the halo effect, the similar-to-me effect, the contrast effect, and the first impressions error. In another program trainees received short descriptions of the halo, leniency, and central tendency errors as well as examples of these errors.[35] The materials were discussed and the trainees were given specific statements as to how to minimize these errors. For example, to minimize halo, instruction was given to evaluate each applicant on each dimension separately, regardless of the ratings given to that candidate on the other dimensions. As described previously in the chapter, other training programs have been directed toward identifying how interviewers weigh various pieces of information about the applicant in making judgments.

Interviewing Behavior   As mentioned previously, The Interviewing Institute of the Department of Psychology at the University of Houston offers a five-day program that addresses skills related to regulating behavior in the delivery of questions. The program is 40 hours in length and consists of videotaped practice interviews on the first, third, and fourth days. Each interview lasts up to 30 minutes. Training sessions address topics of questioning techniques and interview structure. Three group playback sessions of the videotapes are also conducted in which three interviewers review the video-tape of their interviews with a member of the Institute's staff, whose duty it is to critique each interviewer's performance.

As an overall summary, it seems that the critical components of training are to identify the specific behavioral objectives to be addressed in the training program, to provide the trainees with opportunities to demonstrate and review their skills, and to have a method of evaluating the trainees' demonstrated behavior and offering suggestions for change. As a final point Raymond Gordon observes that although practice and analysis can quickly improve performance skills, these skills deteriorate over time through disuse or lack of critical self-analysis.[36] This implies that interviewers should attend training sessions on a regular basis to maintain the necessary skills.

References for Chapter 11

[1] The Bureau of National Affairs, *ASPA-BNA Survey No. 45 — Employee Selection Procedures* (Washington, D.C.: The Bureau of National Affairs, May 5, 1983), p. 2.

[2] Neil Schmitt and Bryan Coyle, "Applicant Decisions in the Employment Interview," *Journal of Applied Psychology* 61 (1976): 184–192.

[3] Paula Popovich and John Wanous, "The Realistic Job Preview as a Persuasive Communication," *Academy of Management Review* 7 (1982): 570–578.

[4] Bernard Dugoni and Daniel Ilgen, "Realistic Job Previews and the Adjustment of New Employees," *Academy of Management Journal* 24 (1981): 579–591.

[5] Lynn Ulrich and Don Trumbo, "The Selection Interview Since 1949," *Psychological Bulletin* 63 (1965): 100–116.

[6] Neal Schmitt, "Social and Situational Determinants of Interview Decisions: Implications for the Employment Interview," *Personnel Psychology* 29 (1976): 79–101.

[7] Eugene Mayfield, "The Selection Interview — A Re-evaluation of Published Research," *Personnel Psychology* 17 (1964): 239–260.

[8] Richard Carlson, Paul Thayer, Eugene Mayfield, and Donald Peterson, "Research on the Selection Interview," *Personnel Journal* 50 (1971): 268–275.

[9] Faye Hargrove and Robert Gatewood, "The Moderating Effects of Training and Structure on Selection Interview Decisions," Southern Management Association Meeting, New Orleans, La., November 1985.

[10] Andrew Keenan, "Some Relationships between Interviewers' Personal Feeling about Candidates and Their General Evaluation of Them," *Journal of Occupational Psychology* 50 (1977): 275–283.

[11] Patricia Rowe, "Individual Differences in Selection Decisions," *Journal of Applied Psychology* 47 (1963): 305–307.

[12] B. Bolster and B. Springbett, "The Reaction of Interviewers to Favorable and Unfavorable Information," *Journal of Applied Psychology* 45 (1961): 97–103.

[13] Thomas Hollman, "Employment Interviewers' Errors in Processing Positive and Negative Information," *Journal of Applied Psychology* 56 (1972): 130–134.

[14] Richard E. Carlson, "Selection Interview Decisions: The Effect of Interviewer Experience, Relative Quota Situations, and Applicant Sample on Interviewer Decisions," *Personnel Psychology* 20 (1967): 259–280.

[15] Enzo Valenzi and I. R. Andrews, "Individual Differences in the Decision Process of Employment Interviewers," *Journal of Applied Psychology* 58 (1973): 49–53.

[16] Neil Schmitt, "Social and Situational Determinants of Interview Decisions," p. 93; George Dreher and Paul Sackett, *Perspectives on Employee Staffing and Selection* (Homewood, Ill.: Richard D. Irwin, 1983), p. 324.

[17] John Drake, *Interviewing for Managers* (New York: AMACOM, 1982), p. 85.

[18] George Howard and Patrick Dailey, "Response-Shift Bias: A Source of Contamination of Self-Report Measures," *Journal of Applied Psychology* 64 (1979): 144–150.

[19] Richard Arvey and James Campion, "The Employment Interview: A Summary and Review of Recent Research," *Personnel Psychology* 35 (1982): 281–322.

[20] Richard Arvey, "Unfair Discrimination in the Employment Interview: Legal and Psychological Aspects," *Psychological Bulletin* 86 (1979): 736–765.

[21] *Stamps v. Detroit Edison Co.,* 6 FEP 612 (1973); *United States v. Hazelwood School District,* 11 E.P.D. 10,854 (1976).

[22] *Weiner v. County of Oakland,* 14 FEP 380 (1976).

[23] *King v. New Hampshire Department of Resources and Economic Development,* 15 FEP 669 (1977).

[24] *Hester v. Southern Railway Company,* 8 FEP 646 (1974); *Bannerman v. Department of Youth Authority,* 17 FEP 820 (1977).

[25] *Harless v. Duck,* 14 FEP 1,616 (1977).

[26] Richard Arvey, "Unfair Discrimination in the Employment Interview," p. 756.

[27] James Haetner, "Race, Age, Sex, and Competence as Factors in Employer Selection of the Disadvantaged," *Journal of Applied Psychology* 62 (1977): 199–202.

[28] Robert L. Dipboye, Gail A. Fontelle, and Kathleen Garner, "Effects of Previewing the Application on Interview Process and Outcomes," *Journal of Applied Psychology* 69 (1984): 118–128.

[29] Thomas S. Bateman and Dennis W. Organ, "Job Satisfaction and the Good Soldier: The Relationship Between Affect and Employee 'Citizenship'," *Academy of Management Journal* 26 (1983): 587–595.

[30] David Grove, "A Behavioral Consistency Approach to Decision Making in Employment Selection," *Personnel Psychology* 34 (1981): 55–64.

[31] Tom Janz, Lowell Hellervik, and David C. Gilmore, *Behavior Description Interviewing* (Boston: Allyn and Bacon, Inc., 1986).

[32] Frank Landy, "The Validity of the Interview in Police Officer Selection," *Journal of Applied Psychology* 61 (1976): 193–198.

[33] Raymond L. Gordon, *Interviewing: Strategy, Techniques, and Tactics,* 3d ed. (Homewood, Ill.: Dorsey Press, 1980), p. 480.

[34] Gary Latham, Kenneth Wexley, and Elliott Pursell, "Training Managers to Minimize Rating Errors in Observation of Behavior," *Journal of Applied Psychology* 60 (1975): 550–555.

[35] Robert Vance, Kenneth Kuhnert, James Farr, "Interview Judgements: Using External Criteria to Compare Behavioral and Graphic Scale Ratings," *Organizational Behavior and Human Performance* 22 (1978): 279–294.

[36] Gorden, *Interviewing,* p. 486.

12

Ability Tests

History of Ability Tests in Selection

The history of the use of ability tests in selection is almost as old as the fields of industrial psychology and personnel management. Par Lahy described his work in 1908 of developing tests for use in the selection of street car operators for the Paris Transportation Society.[1] Among the abilities he measured in applicants were reaction time, speed and distance estimating, and choosing correct driving behavior in reaction to street incidents. All of these tests were administered in a laboratory, using specially designed equipment, and given to each applicant individually. The following nine years saw this type of ability test used in selection for other jobs such as telegraph and telephone operators, chauffeurs, typists, and stenographers.

World War I, with its need for rapid mobilization of military manpower, became a major impetus in the development of other tests used in selection. In 1917 the five-man Psychology Committee of the National Research Council was formed and chaired by Robert Yerkes. The group decided that the development and use of tests was the greatest contribution that psychology could offer to military efficiency. The immediate objectives of this committee were to develop tests quickly that could be simultaneously administered to a large number of military recruits and that would provide scores that could be used to reject recruits who were thought to be unfit for military service.

The first test developed by this group was a mental ability or intelligence test. The Committee required that this test correlate with existing individually administered tests of intelligence, have objective scoring methods, be rapidly scored, have alternate forms to discourage coaching, require a minimum of writing that was necessary in making responses, and be economical in the use of time.[2] These same requirements have characterized industrial ability tests ever since. The result of the Committee's work was the famous (at least among test specialists) Army Alpha. Five forms were developed, each containing 212 items and taking about 28 minutes to administer. Approximately 1,250,000 men were tested in 35 examining units located across the United States.

The conspicuous size of this program generated interest in the development of other ability tests for use in vocational counseling and industrial selection. The next two decades saw the development of mechanical, motor, clerical, and spatial relations ability tests among others. World War II provided another boost to test development as all three U.S. military organizations had extensive psychological testing programs. The main emphasis at this time was on the development of tests to assist in placing recruits in the most appropriate job. Remember that by this time the military had tremendously increased both the technical complexity and the diversity of its jobs. The resultant tests were used extensively by industrial organizations after the war, partially because many jobs in these organizations were similar to military jobs and also because a large number of war veterans became suddenly available as applicants and efficient selection devices were needed.

The growing use of ability tests halted abruptly in the late 1960s and 1970s mainly because of EEO laws and the Supreme Court decisions that specifically addressed a few of the most popular of these tests (see Chapter 2). A recent Bureau of National Affairs survey indicated that only 20 percent of a national sample of organizations regularly administer these types of tests in selection.[3]

In this chapter we will discuss the nature of the major types of ability tests that have been used in selection and describe a few representative tests in some detail to show what these tests actually measure. We will also discuss their usefulness in present day selection. Much recent work has been done that indicates that these tests, when used appropriately, are valid selection measures and can cut costs significantly when used in employment decision making.

Definition of Ability Test

As a first step we need to discuss briefly what we mean when we use the term "ability test." In this chapter we discuss devices that measure mental, mechanical, and clerical abilities, and sensory capacities. Except for the sensory capacity tests, in industrial settings ability tests are almost always paper-and-pencil tests administered in a standardized manner to applicants. In addition they are developed to be given to several applicants at the same time. Tests of sensory capacity, as the name implies, measure physical abilities such as vision, hearing, strength, etc. Usually special equipment is required for these measurements.

The devices we are calling ability tests are often referred to as *aptitude* or *achievement* tests. Achievement tests are intended to measure the effects of a relatively standardized learning experience such as a course in English grammar, business math, or computer programming. The purpose of the test is to determine the amount of learning achieved by an individual as a result of this experience. The emphasis is on what the individual can do at the present time. On the other hand, aptitude tests are intended to reflect the accumulation of learning from a number of diversified and nonstandardized living experiences.[4] In addition, they are intended to be useful for predicting the fully developed ability of the individual at some future time. In the context of selection, this usually means the time after job training or the time after the applicant is hired for the job.

In reality, such distinctions are somewhat arbitrary. The recent development of brief adult education seminars has provided formal, specific education programs in many areas thought to be measured by aptitude tests. Examples include topics such as mechanics, electronics, and clerical tasks. Also, achievement tests are often used to predict some future behavior. Tests of such areas as mathematics, English grammar, and statistical analysis are frequently used for admission into training programs or placement on special technical tasks. Moreover, it should be understood that all tests measure what a person has learned up to that point in time. Tests measure what the individual currently knows or can do based on what he/she has already learned. No test can truly measure "innate capacity" to learn.[5] This is because all tests measure some type of current behavior, e.g., writing of answers, verbal responses, or actions in simulated situations. Psychologists agree that such behavior inevitably reflects a large degree of previous learning. Therefore, tests cannot be pure measures of "innate" or unlearned capacity. Also, all tests may be useful in predicting future behavior if, as is commonly assumed, past behavior is an indication of future behavior. Individuals who have learned topics in the past can be expected to continue such learning in the future. For these reasons, terms such as "aptitude" and "achievement" are being replaced by the term "ability." These tests are more appropriately differentiated by the nature of the abilities they measure (e.g., mechanical, mental, clerical, etc.) and the breadth of topics covered (specific, general). We will now take a look at some of the major types of ability tests that have been used in selection.

Mental Ability Tests

Mental ability tests were at the center of many of the early, critical Supreme Court decisions regarding the discriminatory effect of the use of tests in selection. One of the reasons this happened was that mental ability tests became commonly used for many different types and levels of jobs in the years after World War II. Given their extensive use, it was not surprising that those tests were included in early selection cases. As has been mentioned previously, after the initial Supreme Court decisions, the use of mental ability tests in selection dropped drastically. Personnel managers were reluctant to risk using tests that had already been implicated in adverse impact situations. However, recent work in selection has indicated that mental ability tests can be related to job performance for a number of jobs. Because of their wide use in selection and the fact that many of the principles that govern the appropriate use of ability tests in general have been developed for mental ability tests, we will spend more time discussing mental ability tests than we will other types of ability tests.

History

To fully understand the use of mental ability tests in selection, it is important to know something of the history of their development. What is generally thought to be the first work on mental ability or intelligence tests, as we currently know them, was done by the French psychologists Alfred Binet and Theodore Simon in the years 1905 to 1911. They attempted to develop a test that would identify mentally retarded children in the French school system who should be assigned to special education classes. Most of the items that made up the test were developed through consultation with teachers in the school system. A number of tests were developed because Binet and Simon sought to develop age scales for each year between three and adulthood. An age scale contained those curriculum items that were appropriate for instruction at each academic grade level. A child's mental age was based on correct answers to the various grade level scales. For example, if a child correctly answered the items for the first grade and incorrectly answered the items on the second grade scale, the child's mental age would be estimated at six years (average age of first grade students). Mentally retarded students were identified as those whose calculated mental age was substantially below their chronological age.[6] Binet and Simon's test items included material such as indicating omissions in a drawing, copying written sentences, drawing figures from memory, repeating a series of numbers, composing a sentence containing three given words, giving differences between pairs of abstract terms, and interpreting given facts.[7] This mental ability test was designed to be administered by a trained professional to one individual at a time. In 1916 this test was modified for use in the United States and published as the Stanford-Binet. It is modified periodically and is still extensively used today.

The first group-administered mental ability test to have widespread use in industry was the *Otis Self-Administering Test of Mental Ability*. This test took approximately 30 minutes to complete and consisted of written, multiple-choice questions that measured such abilities as numerical fluency, verbal comprehension, general reasoning, and spatial orientation. The Otis served as the model for the development of several other mental ability tests that have been used in human resource selection.[8]

What Is Measured

There are two points that become obvious from this brief description of the early mental ability tests that are important for understanding this type of test. The first is the close association between the content of these tests and academic material. The first mental ability test was developed using formal education materials. Many other tests have closely followed the same strategy. Moreover, mental ability tests have commonly been validated using educational achievement as a criterion measure. Early studies correlated scores on a mental ability test with such measures as amount of education completed, degrees obtained, or, occasionally, grade point average.[9] The rationale was that mental ability should be related to success in school. Robert Guion has commented that it seems acceptable to equate this type of test with scholastic aptitude, meaning that an adequate definition of what is measured by these tests is the ability to learn in formal education and training situations.[10]

The second point is that mental ability tests actually measure several distinct abilities. A list of the abilities most commonly measured in mental ability tests is contained in Table 12.1. As we can see, the main abilities included are some form of verbal, mathematical, memory, and reasoning abilities. This clearly indicates that mental ability tests can actually differ greatly from one to another in what is measured. All of the topics in Table 12.1 are mental abilities. However, they obviously are not the same ability. Therefore, logically, depending on the specific nature of the tests used, the same individual could score differently on each of a series of mental ability tests. What this means to the personnel specialist is that *all mental ability tests are not interchangeable just because they have similar names or are described as being mental ability or intelligence tests.*

Moreover, a variety of scores can be obtained from tests called mental ability tests. General mental ability tests measure several of these abilities and combine scores on all items into one total score that is, theoretically, indicative of general mental ability. Other tests provide separate scores on each of the tested abilities and then report a general ability total score. A third type of test concentrates on one or more separate abilities and does not combine scores into a general ability measure. We will now discuss two of the more famous and widely used mental ability tests in order to illustrate the concepts we have discussed.

The Wonderlic Personnel Test

The Wonderlic Personnel Test (WPT) was first developed in 1938 and is still widely used. It was also the mental ability test used by the Duke Power Company that was questioned by Griggs in the landmark EEO selection case.

Table 12.1 *Abilities Measured by Various Mental Ability Tests*

Memory Span	Figural Classification
Numerical Fluency	Spatial Orientation
Verbal Comprehension	Visualization
Conceptual Classification	Conceptual Correlates
Semantic Relations	Ordering
General Reasoning	Figural Identification
Conceptual Foresight	Logical Evaluation

The WPT is a 12-minute, multiple-choice, group test that consists of 50 items. The items covered include areas of vocabulary, "common sense" reasoning, formal syllogisms, arithmetic reasoning and computation, analogies, perceptual skill, spatial relations, number series, scrambled sentences, and knowledge of proverbs. Table 12.2 contains items that are similar to those used in the WPT to illustrate the kinds of items contained in this test. They are not part of the test itself. Statistical analysis has found that the primary factor measured by the test is verbal comprehension, with deduction and numerical fluency being the next two factors in order of importance.[11]

Over the years, nine different forms of the WPT have been developed and published. The forms are said by the publisher to be "equal and similar to a very high degree."[12] However, the forms are not perfectly equal and an individual's score can vary depending on which of the forms is taken. For this reason a conversion table is provided to test users that indicates how many

---

Table 12.2 *Example Items Similar to Items on the Wonderlic Personnel Test*

1. Which of the following months has 30 days?
   (a) February   *(b) June   (c) August   (d) December
2. Of these four things, three are alike in some way. Which is not?
   (a) jade   (b) live leaves on a tree   *(c) iron   (d) grass
3. If 4 boys each bought 4 packs of baseball cards and each pack contained 8 cards, how many cards do they have?
   (a) 16   (b) 32   (c) 64   *(d) 128
4. Alone is the opposite of:
   (a) happy   *(b) together   (c) single   (d) joyful
5. Which is the next number in this series:
   1, 4, 16, 4, 16, 64, 16, 64, 256,
   (a) 4   (b) 16   *(c) 64   (d) 1024
6. Twilight is to dawn as autumn is to:
   (a) winter   *(b) spring   (c) hot   (d) cold
7. If Nat can outrun Dane by 2 feet in every 5 yards of a race, how much ahead will Nat be at 45 yards?
   (a) 5 yards   *(b) 6 yards   (c) 10 feet   (d) 90 feet
8. The two words relevant and immaterial mean:
   (a) the same   *(b) the opposite   (c) neither same nor opposite

---

*Correct response.

---

score points should be added or subtracted to equate scores on all possible pairs of forms. This conversion is usually necessary because it is recommended that organizations alternate the use of two or more forms of the tests to maintain the security of the items. This adjustment is of three points at the maximum. All forms of the test are easily scored by counting the number of correct answers out of the total of 50 items. No attempt is made to convert this score to an I.Q. score, even though the WPT is a test of general mental ability. On all forms the 50 items are arranged in order of ascending difficulty. These items range from quite easy to fairly difficult with the average difficulty being at a level at which approximately 60 percent of the test takers would answer the item correctly.

One very appealing feature of the test is the extensive set of norm scores that has been developed through its long use. The test publisher provides tables indicating the distribution of scores by education level of applicants, position applied for, region of the country, sex, age, and racial grouping. In addition, parallel form reliability among the forms is given and ranges from .82 to .94. During the almost 50 years of its use, many selection programs have been described in various journals that have used the WPT as a predictor device. Unfortunately, these studies have not been systematically accumulated to summarize this possibly useful information. It is known, however, that the WPT correlates highly with number of years of education, even when this correlation is computed within various age groups.

The Wechsler Adult Intelligence Scale

The Wechsler Adult Intelligence Scale (WAIS) is generally recognized as being the most complete and best developed of the several measures of adult mental ability. This test, which has been available in various forms since 1939, is given individually and requires a specially trained individual to administer and score it. For this reason it is considered to be too expensive for widespread use except in those cases of managerial and professional selection where the cost of error would exceed the cost of administration.

The WAIS consists of eleven subtests. Six subtests are grouped into a verbal scale and five into a performance scale. Three subtests of each scale are presented below, together with general scoring procedures.[13]

Verbal Subtests

1. *Comprehension*—fourteen questions in order of ascending difficulty, requiring more detailed answers. Measures practical knowledge, social judgment, and ability to organize information. Questions are presented until examinee fails four in a row. Responses are scored 2, 1 or 0.

2. *Arithmetic*—fourteen arithmetic word problems presented in order of increasing difficulty. Measures elementary knowledge of arithmetic, together with the ability to concentrate and reason quantitatively. Successive problems are presented until the examinee fails four consecutive items.

3. *Similarities* — thirteen items of the type "In what way are A and B alike?" This subtest is designed to measure logical or abstract thinking — the ability to categorize and generalize. The items, in order of ascending difficulty, are presented until the examinee fails four in a row. Responses are scored 2, 1, or 0.

Performance Subtests

1. *Digit Symbol* — the examinee is directed to fill in each of 90 boxes with the appropriate coded symbol for the number that appears above the box. Testing begins with a 10-item practice series, after which the examinee is given 90 seconds to fill in the 90 blank boxes with the correct symbol copied from a key listed above. The test was designed to measure attentiveness and persistence in a simple perceptual motor task.

2. *Picture Arrangement* — eight items that require the examinee to arrange a series of small pictures into a sensible story. The test measures ordering or sequencing ability, as well as social planning, humor, and ability to anticipate.

3. *Object Assembly* — four cardboard picture puzzles presented to the examinee in a prearranged format, with directions to put the pieces together to make something. The test was designed to measure thinking, work habits, attention, persistence, and the ability to visualize a final form from its parts.

Each of the subtests is scored separately and a profile from these scores is identified. This allows the trained administrator to be able to identify relative strengths and weaknesses for an individual among these special abilities. These subtest scores are also combined into three additional scores: verbal, performance, and full scale. These three scores are reported in terms of I.Q. scores, which can be interpreted in reference to fairly extensive norm groups distributed over seven separate age levels between 16 and 64 years. Split-half reliabilities for the verbal, performance, and full scale scores are .96, .94, and .97 respectively. Reliabilities for the special ability subtests are somewhat lower, as might be expected because of their shorter length, and range from .64 to .96.

Over the years much work has been done to determine more precisely which abilities are measured by the WAIS. The scales correlate highly and, in some cases, do not appear to be measuring independent abilities. One extensive study found three major group factors. One was *verbal comprehension*, composed mainly of the vocabulary, information, comprehension, and similarities subtests. A *perceptual organization* factor was found chiefly in the performance scales of block design and object assembly. The third major factor, *memory*, was found primarily in the verbal scales of digit span and arithmetic. These three factors were also highly correlated indicating the presence of a general mental ability factor running through the whole test.

Some studies have been done on the validity of the WAIS. These include mean I.Q. differences among various educational and occupational groups. In general, the higher the level of education or job, the higher the measured average WAIS I.Q. Persons in white-collar jobs averaged higher in verbal than in performance I.Q. Skilled workers demonstrated the opposite pattern. Correlation in the .40s and .50s have been found between verbal I.Q. and college grades. Correlation of grades with full-scale scores was at approximately this same level, with correlations with the performance measures at a much lower level.

General Comments About Mental Ability Tests

As is obvious from the preceding sections, mental ability tests and those that have been called intelligence, or I.Q., tests are the same type of tests. We think that because of widespread misconceptions about the terms "intelligence" and "I.Q.," selection specialists can more appropriately conceptualize these tests as mental ability. The term "mental ability" makes explicit that these tests measure various cognitive abilities of the applicant. These cognitive abilities can most directly be identified by the general factors that compose the test or, in some cases, from the content of the items themselves. These cognitive abilities should really be thought of in the same manner as the abilities we have discussed in other parts of this book, abilities that primarily indicate the individual's level of mental manipulation of words, figures, numbers, symbols, and logical order.

Following from this, it is fairly easy to understand the strong relationship between mental ability test scores and academic performance. Formal education primarily stresses cognitive exercises and memorization of facts, and these are the components that make up a large part of most mental ability tests. Also, many mental ability tests have been validated against educational achievement because it is sensible to think that those with the greatest mental ability will progress farther and do better in school situations than those with lesser ability. It is for these reasons that it has been said that these tests measure basic academic ability. This, however, does not mean that mental ability is only useful for academic selection. There are many jobs in organizations that demand the use of the same abilities, such as managerial, technical, and some clerical jobs to name a few. We will develop this later in the chapter when we discuss the validity of ability tests.

Mechanical Ability Tests

There is not a strict definition of the construct of mechanical ability, even though it is a term that has long been used by testing specialists. For the most part mechanical ability refers to characteristics that tend to make for success in work with machines and equipment.[14] One of the earliest tests of this type was the *Stenquist Mechanical Assembly Test* (SMAT), developed in 1923. It consisted of a long, narrow box with ten compartments. Each compartment had a simple mechanical apparatus (e.g., mousetrap, push button, etc.) that had to be assembled by the test taker. Stenquist also developed two picture tests that were designed to measure the same abilities. The SMAT thus demonstrated the two testing methods that have been generally used in mechanical ability tests, performance and written problems. Early tests like the SMAT and the *Minnesota Mechanical Assembly Test* (1930) emphasized actual mechanical assembly or manipulation. However, the cost and time involved in administering and scoring such tests with large numbers of individuals can quickly become prohibitive. Therefore, the group-administered, paper-and-pencil tests that attempted to present problems of mechanical work through pictures and statements were developed. Over the last 30 years the use of paper-and-pencil tests has greatly exceeded the use of performance tests.

Attempts have been made to determine more precisely the abilities measured in mechanical ability tests. As with mental ability tests, this varies from test to test; but, in general, the main factors are spatial visualization, perceptual speed and accuracy, and mechanical information.[15] Mechanical ability tests can also be thought of as measuring general or specific abilities. We will discuss two of the most frequently used general ability tests, the *Bennett Mechanical Comprehension Test* (BMCT) and the *MacQuarrie Test for Mechanical Ability*. These tests have been utilized for a large number of different jobs. Specific ability tests have been developed and used for jobs such as carpenter, engine lathe operator, welder, electrician, etc. These tests use many of the same testing principles as the general ability tests but narrow the content of the questions to the particulars of the job of interest.

Bennett Mechanical Comprehension Test

There have been six different forms of this paper-and-pencil test plus a Spanish language edition. The first three forms that were developed were AA, BB, and CC. Each had 60 items and was designed to have a different level of difficulty and, therefore, applicability. Form AA was the easiest and was designed for essentially untrained and inexperienced groups. Form CC was the most difficult and was designed for use with engineering students. Items on all forms are of general mechanical situations common to shop and garage activities. Form W-1 was developed expressly for testing women and drew its items primarily from situations in the kitchen and sewing room. As the reader can guess, these tests were developed during the 1940s and reflect some of the cultural differences between the sexes that were more common then than now. The two new forms, S and T, were developed in 1969 and are parallel forms of 68 items each. For the most part these forms use many questions from the previous forms AA, BB, and W-1, with approximately 11 new items added.

The items of the BMCT contain objects which are almost universally familiar in American culture: airplanes, carts, steps, pulleys, seesaws, gears, etc. The questions measure the respondent's ability to perceive and understand the relationship of physical forces and mechanical elements in practical situations. While requiring some familiarity with these common tools and objects, the questions purportedly assume no more technical knowledge than can be acquired through everyday experience in an industrial society such as ours. Partially supporting this assumption is evidence that formal training in physics only slightly increases test scores. Items are pictures with a brief accompanying question. For example, a sample item is a picture of two men carrying a weighted object hanging down from a plank and it asks, "Which man carries more weight?" Each figure has a letter below its base. Because the object is closer to one man than to the other, the correct answer is the letter of the closer man. Another item has two pictures of the same room of a house. In one picture the room contains several pieces of furniture, carpeting, and objects on the wall. In the other picture the room contains only a minimum of objects and no carpeting. The question is, "Which room has more of an echo?" Given some basic knowledge or experience, the question can be answered by logical analysis of the problem rather than the mastery of detailed and specific facts.

The tests have no time limit and usually 30 minutes is ample for most individuals to complete the items. A score is the number of items answered correctly. The manuals for the various forms give percentile norms for various groups of industrial applicants, industrial employees, and students. Reported reliabilities are in the .80s. Studies have correlated scores on the older forms of the BMCT with scores on other ability tests to further understand the abilities being measured. Results indicate a moderate correlation with both verbal and mathematical mental ability tests and tests of spatial visualization. The relationship to verbal ability and spatial visualization can partially be a function of the test as it is a written test with pictures as items.

The MacQuarrie Test for Mechanical Ability

The *MacQuarrie* is a paper-and-pencil group test that requires about 30 minutes to administer. The seven subtests are called: tracing, tapping, dotting, copying, location, blocks, and pursuit. Examples of items similar to items on three of these subtests are contained in Exhibit 12.1. The tracing test requires the test taker to draw a line through small openings in a series of vertical lines. The tapping test requires making pencil dots inside of figures as rapidly as possible. The dotting test requires placing one dot in each of a series of small squares spaced irregularly. The copying test requires the copying of series of simple designs. In the location test the test taker locates points drawn on a large scale and transposes them onto an area drawn on a smaller scale. The blocks test requires spatial visualization by asking how many blocks in a pile touch a given block. The pursuit test requires following a line in a maze using only the eye.

Reported reliabilities for these subtests range from .72 to .90. Norms based upon scores of 1,000 males and 1,000 females 16 years and over are given. Additional norms are supplied for school-age children of 14 to 16. Not

Exhibit 12.1 *Items Similar to Items of the MacQuarrie Test for Mechanical Ability*

Tracing: draw a continuous line through each space without touching the lines.

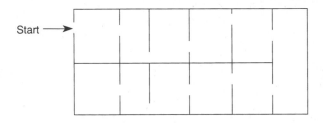

Tapping: put three dots in each triangle as quickly as you can.

Dotting: put one dot in each square as quickly as you can.

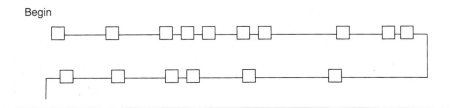

surprisingly, this test appears to measure manipulative ability involving finger and hand dexterity, visual acuity, muscle control, and spatial relationship among figures, rather than the understanding of mechanical or physical principles as does the BMCT. However, correlations of .40 to .48 have consistently been found between the MacQuarrie and the BMCT.[16] Also the subtests of copying, location, pursuit, and blocks have been found to correlate in the .30s and .40s with the Otis mental ability test, presumably indicating the ability to learn mechanical principles.[17]

Clerical Ability

Traditionally, clerical jobs have been thought of as those similar to bookkeeping, typing, filing, and record-keeping positions. Early job analyses of these types of jobs indicated that they consist of extensive checking or copying of words and numbers and the movement and placement of objects such as office equipment, files, and reports. It was therefore thought that clerical jobs required perceptual speed and accuracy and also manual dexterity. However, research has not supported the importance of manual dexterity. One conclusion has been that the degree of manual dexterity necessary to perform these jobs is so low that almost all individuals qualified in other abilities possess enough of this to perform adequately. Therefore, clerical ability tests have predominantly measured perceptual speed and accuracy in processing verbal and numerical data.

The Minnesota Clerical Test

Developed in 1933, the *Minnesota Clerical Test* (MCT) is generally regarded as the prototype of clerical ability tests and has been the most widely used of these tests for much of its existence. The test is a brief, easily administered, and easily scored instrument. It has two separately timed and scored subtests: number checking and name checking. In each subtest there are 200 items. Each item consists of a pair of numbers or names. The respondent is to compare the pair and place a check on a line between the two entries of the pair if these two entries are identical. If the two entries are different, no mark is placed on the line. Table 12.3 contains items similar to those used in both of these subtests. The entries in the numbers subtest range from 3 through 12 digits; the entries in the names subtest range from 7 through 16 letters. The tests are timed separately at 8 minutes for numbers and 7 minutes for names. The score is the number right minus the number wrong, and scores are determined for each subtest separately as well as for the total score of both.

Although the two subtests are related, they do measure separate abilities. The names subtest has been found to be correlated with speed of reading, spelling, and group measures of intelligence. The numbers subtest has been related to the verification of arithmetic computations.[18] Scores on the subtests are only slightly related to either education level or experience in cleri-

---

Table 12.3 *Example Items Similar to Items on the Minnesota Clerical Test*

Name Comparison

Dink Huseman	_____	Dick Huseman
Jennifer Gatewood	_____	Jenipher Gotwood
Versailles	_____✓_____	Versailles
B. Springsteen	_____	B. Springstein
Nat the Jock	_____	Matt the Jock

Number Comparison

84644	_____	84464
179854	_____	176845
123457	_____	12457
987342	_____✓_____	987342
88776659954	_____	8876659954

cal positions. Reliability has been estimated as .90 for parallel forms and .85 for test-retest. Norm group scores are provided for various job groups for each sex.

Sensory Abilities

The first measurements of individual differences were taken on sensory and motor characteristics. The Englishman Sir Francis Galton opened an Anthropometric Laboratory in London in 1884 and gathered data on 17 variables from 9,337 individuals. Some of these measures were of height, weight, arm span, keeness of sight, discrimination of color, and breathing capacity. In analyzing these data, Galton reported two surprising discoveries. One was that blind individuals, contrary to popular belief, had no greater tactile or auditory sensitivity than sighted people. The second was that scientists as a group had much poorer visual imagery than nonscientists.[19] The American psychologist James McKeen Cattell, who worked with Galton, developed an intelligence test in the 1890s that consisted mainly of sensory and motor tests. Among these tests were measurements of:

1. Pressure from a squeeze of the hand

2. Movement of the hand from rest through 50 cm.

3. The distance on the skin by which two points must be separated in order to be felt as two points

4. Amount of pressure causing pain

5. The least noticeable difference in weight

6. Reaction time to a sound

7. Reaction time to see and name a color

8. Accuracy of the bisection of a 50-cm. line

9. Judgment of ten seconds of time

10. Number of letters repeated on hearing once

As we now know, such tests were not accurate measures of intelligence. At that time, however, mental ability and sensory ability to receive and process information were thought to be closely related.

Even though not indicative of intelligence, the testing of sensory abilities has continued and has been useful for treating learning and behavioral deficiencies. Sensory testing in selection has been focused on sight and hearing and has been related to quantity and quality of output, spoilage and waste of materials, job turnover, and accidents.[20] We will review the major aspects of both vision and hearing testing.

Vision

Visual sensitivity includes several separate functions. For industrial work the most important are color discrimination, near acuity at reading (13 to 16 inches), far acuity (usually measured at 20 feet), depth perception, and muscular balance of the eyes (phoria). The most commonly thought of measure of vision is the Snellen Chart which contains rows of letters of gradually decreasing size. This is designed to measure only far acuity. Accuracy in reading the letters of this chart has been found to be affected by many factors in a normal employment testing situation: amount of illumination, distance from chest, position of examinee's head, etc. For this reason more accurate and complete visual measures are taken by using specially designed instruments such as the Ortho-Rater, the AO Sight Screener, and the Keystone Telebinocular. These instruments provide measures of near and far acuity, depth perception, lateral and vertical phorias, and color discrimination. These data have been used to develop visual requirements for groups of similar jobs.

Hearing

The most important aspect of hearing for selection is auditory acuity, the faintest sound that the individual can just barely hear. The most reliable measurement of this involves electronic audiometers. In using these, one ear is tested at a time with the subject receiving the sound through a headphone pressed against the ear. The examiner increases the decibel level of the transmitted sound until the subject indicates that sound has been heard. This sound threshold is then remeasured by starting with a clearly audible sound and decreasing the decibel level until the subject reports no hearing. At each sound wave frequency, the subject's hearing loss in decibels can be determined from the audiometer dial. This dial has been calibrated at "normal hearing" for the population. Normal hearing levels have been determined through testing a large, representative sample of people.

Variations on this testing procedure have been developed for specific employment situations. One modification has used the human voice pronouncing numbers, words, or sentences instead of a pure tone for testing. This provides a better measure of the individual's ability to understand spoken conversation. The level is above that to barely hear sound. Other modifications in testing have included the use of constant or varied background noise and varying the background from noise to spoken conversation.

Honesty Testing

A major concern of many businesses is the cost of employee theft which has been estimated in the millions of dollars. Consequently, various testing programs have been developed to assist in identifying the honesty of applicants and employees. These tests are not ability tests of the same nature as the other types we have discussed. They are included in this chapter, however, because of their widespread use and the fact that they use testing methodologies similar to those of ability testing. There are two major types of such tests: the polygraph and paper-and-pencil tests. A major limitation of any method of honesty testing is the criteria used to determine the validity of the test — such as, admission of guilt or being caught in a dishonest act. Such criteria are not honesty but rather obvious or clumsy dishonesty. Therefore, it is not clear what is actually being measured by these tests. For this and other reasons that will be obvious in the next pages, we wish to make clear that *we are not endorsing such tests for selection* but present them because of their current use.

Polygraph Testing

Physiological measures are the relevant data collected in polygraph tests and, therefore, polygraph tests are somewhat similar to vision and hearing tests. The most common field polygraph examination uses readings of three types of physiological data. One set of readings, the electrodermal channel, displays changes in palmar skin resistance or galvanic skin response. The second set, the "cardio" channel, records changes in upper arm volume associated with the cardiac cycle. From this channel it is possible to determine heart rate and some changes in pulse volume. The third channel is connected pneumatically or electrically to an expandable belt around the respondent's chest and records respiration. The purpose of these sets of data is to provide information to the polygraph specialist about the respondent's physiological reactions during questioning. The assumption is that lying can be detected by the specialist through detection of changes in the subject's physiological response pattern.

Procedures   In most polygraph examinations, the specialist conducts a pretest discussion with the respondent that covers all the questions to be used in the test. The purpose is to make sure that the respondent understands the wording and the meaning of the questions and can answer them with a simple yes or no. After this is completed the polygraph is attached to the respondent and the actual interview is conducted. The list of questions is then gone over again and usually repeated once or twice to obtain more reliable data. There are usually three types of questions used in the examination. One type is the irrelevant, nonemotional question, such as "Are you six feet tall?" A second type is the emotional control question. Such questions are designed to elicit an emotional reaction, preferably of guilt. Questions such as "Did you ever lie to escape punishment?" are frequently asked. The third type is specifically about the behavior of interest. In employment selection this almost always concerns stealing of company resources. To detect lying, the polygrapher looks for evidence of autonomic disturbance associated with the answers to the last type of question.[21] When the subject is lying, there should be a disturbance that is more intense and persistent than that associated with the other two types of questions. Most polygraph examiners make an overall judgment of lying based both upon the polygraph information and other data, such as the demeanor of the respondent, the examiner's knowledge of the evidence, the respondent's prior history, etc.[22]

Limitations   One of the difficulties with such testing, however, is that other respondent reactions besides guilt can trigger an emotional response. Specifically, responses can be affected by the respondent's lability, the autonomic arousal threshold that differs from individual to individual. Respondents with high lability are more likely to have physiological reactions that may be interpreted as lying behavior than are respondents with low lability. Similar differences have been noted in respondents regarding their fear of the consequences of being found guilty and their confidence in the validity of the polygraph procedure.

Another difficulty is that there are a variety of countermeasures that respondents can use to avoid detection. Any physical activity that affects physiological responses is a potential problem for interpretation of polygraph readings. Such movements as tensing muscles, biting the tongue, flexing the toes, and shifting one's position can affect physiological response.[23] In general, polygraph examiners are watchful for these movements. The use of drugs to obscure physiological reaction differences is more difficult to detect unless a urinalysis is conducted. Experience with polygraphs and biofeedback training also have had demonstrated effects on polygraph results.

The major drawback in using the polygraph in employment testing is the frequency of the false positive. The false positive is the identification of an individual as lying who is, in fact, not lying. The frequency of the false positive depends upon both the validity of the test and the base rate of the lying behavior in the population. To illustrate the possible magnitude of false-positive identification we will make the following assumptions: (a) that the accuracy of the polygraph is 90 percent (commonly regarded as a high estimate), and (b) that the rate of lying about company stealing is 5 percent of the working population. If 1,000 polygraph tests are conducted, we would expect that 50 of the respondents would be lying and that 45 (90 percent) of these would be detected. The serious problem concerns the remaining 950 respondents. Assuming the 90 percent accuracy rate, 95 of these (950 × .10) would be inaccurately identified as lying about their actions. Therefore, a total of 140 individuals would be identified as lying, 68 percent of which would be false positives. The consequence of such examinations is that those singled out as lying are denied employment or, if they are present employees, are commonly terminated from employment. It can be easily seen from this example that unless a polygraph test has perfect validity, a large number of false-positive identifications can occur when the device is used to test for a behavior that has a low incidence in the general population. Given the limitations in validity mentioned previously, it is feasible to suppose that the actual frequency of false positives is much greater than this example would indicate. Mainly for this reason well over 20 states have prohibited the use of the polygraph in specific employment decisions.

Paper-and-Pencil Honesty Tests

Because in most instances these state prohibitions have expressly been written in terms of the polygraph, paper-and-pencil tests have recently been developed to accomplish the same purposes as polygraph testing but to do this legally. Paul Sackett and Michael Harris have done a comprehensive review of these tests.[24] Much of the following is taken from their work. Most of these honesty tests question the respondent's attitudes toward theft and other defalcations. Statements similar to the following are used which require "yes" or "no" answers.

> Should a person be fired if caught stealing more than $10?
>
> Most of your friends have stolen something in their life.
>
> The courts are too easy on law breakers.
>
> An employer who doesn't pay well should expect to have things stolen.

Other types of questions ask respondents about the frequency of theft in society (What percentage of people take more than $5 per week from their employer?), personal ruminations about theft (Have you ever thought about taking some money from any place where you worked?), perceived ease of theft (How easy is it to steal and not be caught?), and assessment of one's own honesty (In comparison to others, how honest are you?).

Only one of ten popularly used tests has another type of item. That one is composed of 37 standard personality test items that statistically differentiate responses of employees fired for theft from responses of presumably honest employees. The other nine tests range from 40 to 158 items with most having at least 100 items. Some of these tests contain drug or alcohol abuse scales also.

Sackett and Harris studied the reliability and validity of these tests by reviewing a series of studies. These studies were grouped as shown below:

1. Comparing honesty test scores with polygrapher judgments and admissions of guilt given during polygraph testing

2. Correlating honesty test scores with being discharged for theft or the number of work days where a cash shortage was found. These measures were gathered after testing.

3. Correlating honesty test scores with admissions of theft or dishonest actions. These data were collected anonymously.

4. Comparing storewide shrinkage or loss rates from before and after testing was begun

5. Contrasting test scores between a dishonest group (e.g., convicts) and others representing the general population

A major limitation of all these studies is the nature of the criteria used. In essence, test scores are related to admission of guilt or having been caught in a dishonest act. As we said previously, such a criterion is *not* a measure of honesty but more accurately only a limited measure of dishonesty. It is not really feasible to presume that all those who do not admit guilt or have not been caught are honest. It is not possible to estimate the size of this distortion.

However, there is a positive side. High reliabilities were consistently reported (most of .90 or greater). In addition the validity estimates for all five types of studies were consistently positive and generally comparable in magnitude to those of ability tests. Despite these findings Sackett and Harris did not generally endorse the use of these tests mainly because of the serious methodological limitations of most of the studies reviewed, especially with the criteria measures used. They also noted the problem of false positives that we discussed regarding polygraphs, and the serious consequences such false positives could have on the careers of present employees. The authors tentatively conclude that it is only feasible to use these honesty tests discretely with outside applicants.

The Validity of Ability Tests

Now that we have a better idea of what ability tests measure and how they are constructed, let us turn our attention to their actual use in selection. One advantage of having as long a history as ability tests do is that there is a large number of selection programs that have used this type of test. There have also been a number of studies that have attempted to synthesize the results of these selection programs. In this section we will discuss the findings of two of the most extensive of these studies.

The Validity of Occupational Aptitude Tests

In 1966 Edwin E. Ghiselli authored a book entitled "The Validity of Occupational Aptitude Tests," which summarized the use of the tests we have described from 1920 through the early 1960s.[25] In 1973 he updated this work and included studies through 1971.[26] These summaries present much useful information to selection managers and should be read in their entirety. His major findings are as follows.

Types of Tests and Jobs   Ghiselli first grouped both the different tests and the different jobs in these studies. The following groups of tests were formed:

1. *Tests of intellectual abilities* — similar to the Wonderlic Personnel Test

2. *Tests of spatial and mechanical abilities* — similar to the Bennett Mechanical Comprehension Test and the copying and location subtests of the MacQuarrie Mechanical Ability Tests

3. *Tests of perceptual accuracy* — similar to the Minnesota Clerical Test and the pursuit subtest of the MacQuarrie Mechanical Ability Tests

4. *Tests of motor abilities* — similar to the tracing, tapping, and dotting subtests of the MacQuarrie Mechanical Ability Tests

5. *Personality traits* — similar to tests that we will describe in Chapter 13.

(For this reason we will postpone discussion of this type of tests.)

He also formed the following groups of jobs:

1. Managerial occupations

2. Clerical occupations

3. Sales occupations

4. Protective occupations (e.g., policemen, firemen)

5. Service occupations (e.g., waiters, hospital attendants)

6. Vehicle occupations

7. Trades and crafts

8. Industrial occupations (e.g., machine tenders, gross manual workers, bench workers)

The studies that Ghiselli reviewed were all empirical validity studies. He also categorized these studies according to the criterion measure used: trainability or work performance.

    The major results of this work are summarized in Table 12.4. The next few paragraphs will discuss this information. The first thing to know is that the entries in Table 12.4 are mean validity coefficients for all the studies fitting a particular cell. These average correlations between predictors and criteria should be thought of as *underestimates* of the true validity because the various statistical artifacts that lower the validity coefficient in such studies were not corrected.

Validity of Tests   The most important finding for us is that for each of the job types there is at least one, and usually more, ability test that is significantly related to job performance. This, of course, means that there exists extensive empirical support for the use of ability tests in selection. For several of the job types, e.g., clerical occupations, protective occupations, and trades and crafts, the numerical value of these validity coefficients is high, especially keeping in mind that these are underestimates of true validity. Ghiselli also comments that, for the most part, the data are of single tests correlated separately with a criterion measure. He indicates that validity would probably be higher if combinations of the tests had been used.

    The only exception to this finding of generally valid ability tests is in sales occupations for which validity coefficients are noticeably lower than for other jobs. However, in some ways the coefficients for sales occupations reported in Table 12.4 do not give a complete description. Ghiselli's longer report forms separate job classes within each of the occupational groups

Table 12.4   *Validity Coefficients for Occupations*

Occupations	Training	Performance
Managerial Occupations		
Intellectual abilities	.30	.27
Spatial and mechanical abilities	.28	.22
Perceptual accuracy	.23	.25
Motor abilities	.02	.14
Clerical Occupations		
Intellectual abilities	.47	.28
Spatial and mechanical abilities	.34	.17
Perceptual accuracy	.40	.29
Motor abilities	.14	.16
Sales Occupations[a]		
Intellectual abilities	—	.19
Spatial and mechanical abilities	—	.18
Perceptual accuracy	—	.04
Motor abilities	—	.12
Protective Occupations		
Intellectual abilities	.42	.22
Spatial and mechanical abilities	.35	.18
Perceptual accuracy	.30	.21
Motor abilities	—	.14
Service Occupations		
Intellectual abilities	.42	.27
Spatial and mechanical abilities	.31	.13
Perceptual accuracy	.25	.10
Motor abilities	.21	.15
Vehicle Occupations		
Intellectual abilities	.18	.16
Spatial and mechanical abilities	.31	.20
Perceptual accuracy	.09	.17
Motor abilities	.31	.25
Trades and Crafts		
Intellectual abilities	.41	.25
Spatial and mechanical abilities	.41	.23
Perceptual accuracy	.35	.24
Motor abilities	.20	.19
Industrial Occupations		
Intellectual abilities	.38	.20
Spatial and mechanical abilities	.40	.20
Perceptual accuracy	.20	.20
Motor abilities	.28	.22

Source: Edwin E. Ghiselli, "The Validity of Aptitude Tests in Personnel Selection," *Personnel Psychology* 26 (1973): 461–467. Reprinted with permission.

[a]No data on training are available.

reported in this table. The sales occupation was broken down into salesmen and salesclerks. For salesmen the validity coefficients were: intellectual abilities .33, spatial and mechanical abilities .20, perceptual accuracy .23, and motor abilities .16. These coefficients are similar to those of other occupations. It is the job of salesclerk that shows very low validity coefficients and, when these data are combined with that of salesmen, lowers the figures for the occupation in general. No explanation is given for these findings for salesclerks. One possible reason may be that these jobs require minimal levels of abilities. This is one of very few jobs for which personality inventories were valid predictors of job performance (average validity = .35).

The second noticeable finding is that in all occupations these ability tests do a better job of correlating with training criteria than job performance. Partially this may be because of the administrative differences in these two measures. Training measures are usually made upon completion of the training program with consistently administered measuring devices. Job performance measures are made over different time periods, are not consistently administered, and, as we maintained in Chapter 1, are affected by factors other than the employee's effort. Second, we have already discussed that some of these various ability tests correlate with mental ability tests which, in turn, reflect academic abilities. To the extent that training programs are formal, education-type situations, high correlations between ability tests and training measures would be expected. Third, this pattern of validity coefficients outlines a useful human resource management strategy. This would be to develop an effective training program for jobs, one that clearly teaches the necessary KSAs for job performance. The first objective of the selection program would then be to identify those applicants who could successfully complete such a program. This strategy would therefore, be the two steps of selecting individuals with the appropriate abilities and then systematically developing these abilities with an effective training program.

Without correcting Ghiselli's findings for the many statistical artifacts that can affect correlation coefficients, it is not possible to discuss which type of ability test is the best predictor. However, the apparent general usefulness of mental ability tests in all occupations, except possibly vehicle occupations, is demonstrated when either job or training performance is the criterion measure. To a lesser extent, tests of spatial and mechanical abilities and perceptual accuracy are generally related to performance across several occupations. Tests of motor abilities appear to have the most restricted usefulness.

Validity Generalization Studies

We have discussed validity generalization previously in Chapter 5. Without going over the details of this concept, we will discuss the implications of the work for our question about the use of ability tests in selection. For many years selection specialists had noted that validity coefficients for the same combination of selection instruments and criteria measures differed greatly for studies in different organizations. This was even true when the jobs for which the selection program was designed were very similar. Selection specialists explained these differences in terms of undetermined organizational factors that affect the correlation between selection instruments and criteria. The standard recommendation was that it was necessary to conduct a validation study for each selection program that was developed. This was the only way to be sure that validity could be demonstrated and that these undetermined organizational factors did not have a large, adverse effect on the validity correlations.

Importance in Selection   The validity generalization studies conducted by Frank Schmidt and John Hunter have *totally disagreed* with these previous conclusions and have suggested a much different use for ability tests in selection. Schmidt and Hunter's point is that the differences in validity coefficients for the same selection instruments for similar jobs is not a function of unknown organizational factors. Rather these differences are due to methodological deficiencies in the validation studies themselves. If it were possible to correct these deficiencies, the differences among these validity coefficients would really be close to zero. One of the major methodological deficiencies is the size of the sample of workers on which the validity study was done. It had commonly been thought that a group of 30 workers was adequate. Schmidt, Hunter, and Urry demonstrated, however, that even with a sample of 68 workers, a truly valid selection test will show a statistically significant correlation coefficient in only about 50 percent of validity studies.[27] This means that much of the previously found differences in validity coefficients from organization to organization could be explained in terms of these differences in the size of the samples for which the study was done. Moreover, there are ways of statistically correcting the coefficients to correct for these differences. It is also possible to identify the other methodological factors that affect validity coefficients and to make adjustments for some of them. This is the work that is discussed in Chapter 5.

Impact on Selection Steps   For our present purpose the significant finding is that once these corrections have been made many of the observed differences in validity coefficients are reduced. If the validity coefficients from study to study are very similar, this means that organizational factors have little effect on these coefficients. Schmidt and Hunter argue, therefore, that *it is not necessary to conduct a validation study for each selection program*. If enough prior data are available to perform a validity generalization study for the particular job-selection instrument combination of interest and if this study produces the results we have described, then the selection specialist can use the selection instrument that has *already* demonstrated validity. The essential

Table 12.5   *Estimated Validities from Validity Generalization Studies*

Job	Ability	Estimated Average Validity Coefficient
First line supervisor[a]	General mental ability	.64
	Mechanical ability	.48
	Spatial ability	.43
Mechanical Repairman[a]	Mechanical ability	.78
Bench Worker[a]	Finger dexterity	.39
General Clerk[a]	General mental ability	.67
Computer Programmer[b]	Number series	.43
	Figure analogy	.46
	Arithmetic reasoning	.57
Operator (petroleum industry)[c]	Mechanical ability	.33
	General mental ability	.26
	Chemical comprehension	.30
Maintenance (petroleum industry)[c]	Mechanical ability	.33
	General mental ability	.30
	Chemical comprehension	.25

[a]Source: Frank Schmidt, John Hunter, Kenneth Pearlman, and Guy Shane, "Further Tests of the Schmidt-Hunter Bayesian Validity Generalization Procedure," *Personnel Psychology* 93 (1972): 257–281.

[b]Source: Frank Schmidt, Ilene Gast-Rosenbery, and John Hunter, "Validity Generalization for Computer Programmers," *Journal of Applied Psychology* 65 (1980): 643–661.

[c]Source: Frank Schmidt, John Hunter, and James Caplan, "Validity Generalization Results for Two Job Groups in the Petroleum Industry," *Journal of Applied Psychology* 66 (1981): 261–273.

requirement is to demonstrate through job analysis that the job being considered is closely similar to the jobs in the validity generalization study.

Many of the existing validity generalization studies have used the ability tests we have discussed in this chapter because there have been many validity studies conducted with them. As an illustration, Table 12.5 contains some of the types of ability tests that have been studied and the estimated average validity coefficients. As is obvious from this table, a *number of ability tests have proven to be valid* when examined across a series of selection programs. Many of the validity coefficients are, in fact, very high. The logic of validity generalization would argue for the use of these tests in selection programs.

Ability Tests and Discrimination

As was mentioned previously, the widespread use of ability tests that characterized selection programs since the 1920s has diminished considerably since the early 1970s. Partially, this is the direct result of the court rulings in the early EEO selection cases. Ability tests were specifically singled out and found to be discriminatory. In the preceding section we pointed out that the extensive validity data that have accumulated about ability tests were analyzed to study their effectiveness in selection programs. Similarly these data were used to study more fully the issue of disciminatory effects of ability tests in selection. In this section, we will summarize this work.

Differential Validity

Differential validity is the term used to describe the hypothesis that employment tests are less valid for minority group members than nonminority. The situation is one in which the validities for the same selection test in the two groups is statistically significant but unequal. For example, the test may be significantly more valid for whites than for blacks. In many ways this term is related to the issue of test bias that has often been addressed regarding ability tests.

Most explanations of test bias include hypotheses of differential validity. This argument is generally that the actual content of ability tests (especially mental ability tests) is based on the content of white middle class culture and, therefore, does not mean the same thing to other groups as it does to whites. Nonwhite middle class respondents must use terms and symbols that are unfamiliar; and, in essence, this unfamiliarity reduces the score achieved on the test. The test scores will not have the same meaning for whites and nonwhites nor will the pattern of validity coefficients with other measures, such as job performance, school grades, etc., be the same for the two groups. This different pattern of validity coefficients is differential validity. Taken a step further, the presence of differential validity would imply that selection managers should develop separate selection programs for each applicant group for each job. This would be necessary to control the differences in terms and symbols of selection tests among the various cultures.

To examine differential validity more closely, recent studies have analyzed data collected from several selection programs simultaneously. It has been a consistent conclusion of these studies that *differential validity does not exist*. Those few selection programs in which differential validity has been observed have been characterized by methodological limitations that seem to account for the observed differences. For example, one investigation examined 31 studies in which 583 validity coefficients were reported.[28] These studies were also scored on methodological characteristics such as sample size, use of criterion measures that were identified as being for research purposes only, and use of a predictor chosen for its theoretical relationship to the criterion measures. For the most part, differential validity was only observed in those studies with several methodological limitations. For the methodologically sound studies, no differences in validity coefficients between black and white groups were observed.

Another study used 781 pairs of validity coefficients. The pairs were made up of the correlation between the same predictor variable (commonly an ability test) and criterion variable for both a white and a black group of workers.[29] These correlations ranged from approximately $-.37$ to $+.55$. Exhibit 12.2 is part of this study and shows the result of graphing these pairs of validity coefficients. As can be seen, the two curves, one composed of validity coefficients for black workers and one of corresponding validity coefficients for white workers, look almost identical. This means that these tests acted in the same manner for both blacks and whites. The major conclusion of the study was that differential validity was not demonstrated and that tests that ordered whites successfully with respect to some given job criterion *also* ordered blacks equally successfully.

Adverse Impact

Another way of studying the discriminatory effect of ability tests was undertaken by Richard Reilly and Georgia Chao.[30] They categorized selection procedures into the following groups:

Exhibit 12.2 *Graph of 781 Pairs of Validity Coefficients*

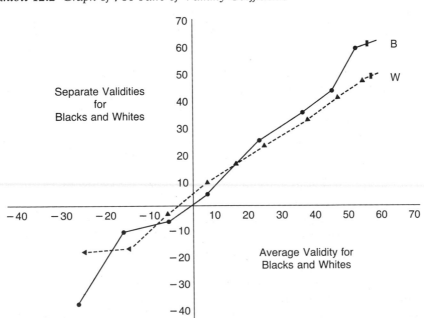

Source: John Hunter, Frank Schmidt, and Rhonda Hunter, "Differential Validity of Employment Tests by Race: a Comprehensive Review and Analysis," *Psychological Bulletin* 85 (1979): pp 721-735. Copyright 1979 by the American Psychological Association. Reprinted by permission.

1. Conventional tests (primarily ability tests)
2. Biographical information
3. Interviews
4. Peer evaluations (ratings given by fellow trainees, workers, etc.)
5. Self-assessments
6. Reference checks
7. Academic performance measures (GPA or class work)
8. Expert judgment (evaluations usually provided by consultants)
9. Projective techniques (personality measures)

Work sample tests and assessment centers were not reviewed in this work. Data were accumulated for each of these groups concerning validity, adverse impact, and feasibility of use in selection. The primary purpose of the study was to compare conventional tests with the other eight methods. The results of this comparison are contained in Table 12.6. As is shown, none of the other methods is superior and only biographical data and peer evaluations are comparable to conventional tests in terms of validity.

If we compare the adverse impact of biographical data and peer evaluations with conventional tests, we reach the following conclusions. The adverse impact of biographical data, as was discussed in Chapter 10, is somewhat dependent upon the nature of the items used. If items reflect marital status, region of residence, educational degrees, etc., then differences in response patterns between nonminority and minority respondents might be heightened. Because biographical data forms are empirically validated and usually lack conceptual relationships to job activities, such differences may be questionable. However, several selection programs have developed biographical data forms that have avoided such items and the demonstration of adverse impact of race. It is common, however, that these forms do demonstrate differences in male-female response patterns. In most cases this necessitates performing separate empirical validation procedures for the two groups. The result is different scoring keys for males and females but not demonstrable adverse impact in terms of final scores achieved by applicants. If constructed properly, biographical data forms need not result in adverse impact and are, thus, equal to conventional tests.

The same result was not thought to be the case for peer evaluations. There were no direct studies of the adverse impact of this selection method, partially because it is logistically difficult to implement and is seldom used. The authors thought, however, that racial adverse impact would occur in its use. Presumably, nonminority members would rate nonminority peers higher than minority peers and the opposite pattern would occur for minority members. Such patterns would be consistent with racial differences found in supervisory ratings and could be an extension of the friendship bias noted in several studies.

Table 12.6   *Comparison of Eight Selection Methods with Conventional Tests*

| | Selection Methods | | | | | | | |
	Biographical Data	Interview	Peer Evaluation	Self-Assessment	Reference Checks	Academic Performance	Expert Judgment	Projective Techniques
Validity	Equal	Less	Equal	Less	Less	Less	Less	Less
Adverse Impact	Equal	More	Presumed to Be More	Equal	Equal	Presumed to Be More	Unknown	Equal
Feasibility	Equal	Equal	Less	Less	Less	Less	Less	Less

Source: Richard Reilly and Georgia Chao, "Validity and Fairness of Some Alternative Employee Selection Procedures," *Personnel Psychology* 35 (1982): 1–62.

None of the other selection methods was judged to have less adverse impact than conventional tests, with interviews and academic performance thought generally to demonstrate a greater amount. The remaining methods were approximately equal to conventional tests in adverse impact but were generally less desirable because of lower validity.

The third characteristic, feasibility, included various factors of development and implementation such as ease of gathering and scoring data, cost of doing so, and demonstrated reliability of the device. Only biographical data and the interview were thought to be as feasible as conventional tests. All other methods had distinct and large limitations, especially in terms of actually collecting data. For example, peer evaluation, reference checks, and expert judgment would all require contacting and questioning third parties. Of the two methods thought equally feasible, the interview was criticized for its typical lack of validity and its demonstrated adverse impact, especially against women as we mentioned in Chapter 11.

Reilly and Chao's conclusions were that it is not apparent that any of the other selection methods would demonstrate *less adverse impact than tests.* Coupled with the fact that most were also less valid and more difficult or costly to administer, the urging of the *Uniform Guidelines* to employers to seek alternatives to conventional tests does not seem clear. Only biographical data forms appear to be an acceptable alternative and it is not certain that less adverse impact would result.

Conclusions

How should we interpret the findings of these various studies in light of the specific statements of discriminatory effect in the EEO court decisions? One thing to remember is that the court decisions and the studies summarized here have two different bases of analysis. The court decisions have focused on selection programs in one specific organization. The studies summarized in this section have tried to accumulate data across many organizations. Even though ability tests have been demonstrably valid in many situations, it does not mean that ability tests will be valid no matter how they are used in all organizations. As a general rule, the organizations that were found guilty of discrimination in the use of ability tests in selection had taken only superficial steps in the development of their selection programs. More complete development procedures might have yielded different results.

Second, the analyses reviewed in this section were completed after many of the court decisions regarding the discriminatory use of ability tests were handed down. It is fair to assume that both plaintiffs and defendants were using the traditional viewpoint of the necessity of demonstrating validity for a selection device for the job in the organization under question. As we have said previously, the results of recent validity generalization studies radically change this perspective. Not only does the concept of validity generalization shift the chief concern to an accumulation of validity results, but it argues that studies within a single organization may not be interpretable. This would especially be true if the study were limited by small sample size, restriction of range, or some of the other statistical artifacts that were mentioned. Aspects of validity generalization were an issue in one court case and were supported.[31] Also in light of these recent findings about ability tests, both the EEOC and the U.S. Commission on Civil Rights are planning reviews of federal regulations and the discriminatory effect of employment tests.[32]

The general conclusion for us is that ability tests have proven to be valid selection devices for a number of years in a number of different jobs. A close look at the validity of these tests indicates that when properly used, differences between nonminority and minority groups are minimized when the relationship of scores to job criteria measures is taken into account. Moreover, few alternative selection methods can match ability tests in terms of overall validity, lack of adverse impact, and feasibility of use. Thus, the markedly diminished use of these tests in recent years seems to be unfounded.

Using Ability Tests in Selection

At the beginning of this chapter there were brief descriptions of a few tests that are representative of ability tests. These tests were included because of their extensive use in selection over several years. However, it should be made clear that there is a large number of other ability tests that are available to personnel specialists that have not been described in this chapter. For example, the volume *Tests in Print III* contains descriptions of 2,672 different tests which are placed into 17 subject categories.[33] A large number of these are some type of ability test. In addition, there are ability tests that have been developed by many management consultants that are also available.

The sheer number of these tests creates a difficult situation for personnel specialists. What is needed is a means of evaluating an ability test in order to assess its potential usefulness. Obviously the best method of doing this would be to become very familiar with the principles of psychological test construction and measurement. We have already presented some, but not nearly all, of these principles in Chapters 3 to 5, which were devoted to the role of measurement in selection. We will now apply the concepts of these chapters to this problem of assessing the potential usefulness of available ability tests.

Our primary assumption is that a useful ability test should have developmental information available to users. One part of such information should be work done to estimate the reliability of the test. As has been discussed previously, reliability is the essential characteristic of a selection test. High reliability is an indication that the test would be expected to yield consistent scores for applicants and that uncontrolled factors that might affect the score of an applicant are minimized. Therefore, information about the method of estimating reliability, the size of the sample used to collect these data, and the magnitude of the reliability estimate should all be fully presented to users. These next paragraphs discuss the importance of these data about reliability for test users.

Review Reliability Data

As we know, each of the four major ways of estimating reliability is appropriate for specific circumstances and inappropriate for others. For example, test-retest reliability calculated with a very short intervening period of time, such as a few hours or even a few days, may be an inflated estimate because of expected memory factors among the respondents. So it is necessary for the test user to determine if the appropriate method of estimating reliability was employed and if this method was carried out correctly. It is generally thought that the use of larger samples (200+) yields better estimates of reliability than do smaller samples. Occasionally samples of 30 to 50 respondents have been used in reliability studies. We discussed the limitations of small sample correlation estimates when we discussed validity generalization. Essentially the same limitations exist when reliability is calculated.

It is also desirable for the sample to be similar to the individuals for whom the personnel specialist intends to use the test. Perhaps the most common way of judging similarity is on the basis of demographic characteristics such as race, sex, average age, average education level, and occupational background. One can argue that these are not the most accurate indicants of similarity because similarity between two groups actually means that the test is interpreted and answered in the same fashion by the two groups. However, collecting such data would require work far beyond that normally done in test development. Information about demographic characteristics allows the user to at least note major differences and form hypotheses about the meaning of such differences. For example, if the reliability of a test of English grammar and writing has been estimated using a sample of college students and the applicant pool in the selection situation is mainly high school students, the reliability may not be the same for the two groups. If the test is of moderate difficulty for the college students, it may be very difficult for individuals with less formal training in reading and writing tasks. Difficult tests often have low reliability because respondents frequently guess in making their responses and such guesses are really sources of error of measurement. Therefore, the stated reliability of the test may not be accurate for the applicant pool. The same argument can be applied to many craft or mechanical ability tests that have used experienced workers rather than inexperienced ones in reliability estimates.

We have indicated that a reliability estimate of .85 is commonly thought to be necessary for selection use. This is because selection involves making a decision for each applicant as to whether to extend a job offer or not. This decision is based on the scores of the selection tests used. If the test is not highly reliable, the large standard error of measurement accompanying a test score would make choosing among applicants very uncertain. For example, using the standard error of measurement information contained in Chapter 4, we would estimate that the range of true scores for a test with an estimated reliability of .60 and a standard deviation of 15 is $\pm$ 9.5 points with a 68 percent confidence level. If an applicant scores an 80 on this test, the true score realistically could be anywhere between 70 and 90. With such a large range, identifying meaningful differences among applicants is very difficult. However, if the same test has a reliability of .90, then the standard error becomes $\pm$ 4.7 points with the same confidence level. The range of probable true scores becomes much smaller, and the test results are easier for the selection specialist to use.

Review Validity Data

The second major kind of information that should be made available to test users is validity data accumulated during test development and use. Two kinds of validity data are desirable. One kind is data that aid in determining that the ability test measures what it is said to measure. Frequently this kind of information is reported in terms of statistical analyses of the scores. Two of the most common types of analyses are correlational analyses of the scores of the test with other psychological measures and factor analyses of the items of the test or of the test with other tests. We have mentioned examples of such correlational analyses when we discussed mental ability tests. To know that scores on mental ability tests are correlated with various measures of educational achievement greatly improves our understanding of what these tests measure. In some cases correlations with other tests are conducted. For example, we noted that the *Bennett Mechanical Comprehension Test* was correlated with verbal ability and spatial visualization tests. This indicates that the test measures more than mechanical concepts.

Factor analysis is a technique for analyzing the interrelationships among several tests or a set of test items. For example, if 20 test items have been given to 400 individuals, the first step is to correlate each item with every other item. Further statistical manipulations attempt to identify small groups of items that are highly correlated with one another and minimally correlated with other groups of items. Each group of items is called a factor and is named by the common psychological characteristic measured. For example, on this 20-item test, one group of ten basic arithmetic problems might be identified as being one factor and ten vocabulary questions might be identified as a second factor. This test can then be said to measure arithmetic ability and vocabulary. The ability that is measured is identified from the common content of the items that make up the factor. The importance of this type of information is that the personnel specialist can examine the correspondence between the factors that are identified and the abilities that are to be tested in the selection program. It is necessary that the test, in fact, match the abilities identified from the job analysis.

The second type of validity information that can be provided is the correlation of the test scores with some measure of training or job proficiency. This is the classic test validity to which we have frequently referred. Demonstration of validity for jobs similar to the one of interest to the test specialist is, obviously, the most desirable data.

Our opinion is that at least this information about reliability and validity of the ability test must be available to the user. Other test construction data such as norm group scores, difficulty levels of items, and homogeneity or heterogeneity of the tests can also be useful. However, such data are usually of secondary importance to basic reliability and validity information. If reliability and validity data are not provided or are inappropriately calculated, the personnel specialist should be wary of using the ability test. It is not a difficult task physically to construct a purported ability test. Most intelligent individuals, with a few friends and a long weekend, could write fifty multiple-choice test items that were intended to measure any of several abilities, e.g., mathematics, English, logical reasoning, or given enough reference books, some technical areas like computer programming, football analysis, and carpentry. The trick is to make sure that the test is what it is intended to be. The only way that a human resource specialist who is considering using an ability test can tell this is by examining the reliability and validity information. No amount of verbal assurance provided by the test seller can substitute for such information. After all, the test seller has a vested interest in describing the test in favorable terms.

We have compiled a brief list of some ability tests that have demonstrated necessary test construction data. The names of these tests, grouped according to the ability which each is designed to measure, and their publishers are presented in Table 12.7. This list should not be interpreted as a complete list of useful ability tests. Rather, it provides a preliminary grouping of such tests.

Our last comment on the use of ability tests is a theme that has conspicuously run throughout the chapter. Well-developed ability tests have *consistently demonstrated their usefulness in selection.* Generally ability tests are efficient and fairly inexpensive selection devices. The secret is to match the test to the ability that is desired to be measured. Frequently an ability test is the only feasible way of measuring the characteristics of applicants. Recent trends in avoiding the use of ability tests and relying excessively on other selection devices, especially interviews, may not be a wise choice. As we have discussed, there is a growing body of studies supporting both the validity and the minimization of adverse impact with the use of ability tests. Also, if the trends in the early work in validity generalization continues, the use of ability tests for selection for many jobs will be greatly simplified. These trends would allow for the relatively easy improvement of selection programs.

Table 12.7   *List of Selected Ability Tests and Publishers*

Ability	Publisher
Differential Aptitude Tests	The Psychological Corporation Cleveland, Ohio
Wonderlic Personnel Test	E. F. Wonderlic Personnel Tests, Inc. Northfield, Illinois
SRA Short Tests of Educational Ability	Science Research Associates Chicago, Illinois

Reading Ability

Iowa Silent Reading Tests	Science Research Associates
Industrial Reading Test	The Psychological Corporation
Basic Reading Rate Scale	University of Minnesota Press Minneapolis, Minnesota
Minnesota Speed Reading Test for College Students	University of Minnesota Press

Mathematical Ability

California Achievement Tests: Mathematics	McGraw-Hill Publishing Co. New York City, New York
Sequential Tests of Educational Progress Mathematics Series II	Educational Testing Service Princeton, New Jersey
Doppelt Mathematics Reasoning Test	The Psychological Corporation

Mechanical Ability

MacQuarrie Mechanical Ability Test	McGraw-Hill Publishing Co.
Bennett Mechanical Comprehension Test	The Psychological Corporation
Revised Minnesota Paper Form Board Test	The Psychological Corporation
SRA Mechanical Aptitudes	Science Research Associates
Primary Mechanical Ability Tests	Steven, Thurew and Associates, Inc. Chicago, Illinois
Mechanical Familiarity Test	Educators-Employers Test and Services Association Cincinnati, Ohio

Clerical Ability

Minnesota Clerical Test	The Psychological Corporation
Short Tests of Clerical Ability	Science Research Associates

continued

Table 12.7 *continued*

Motor Ability

Crawford Small Parts Dexterity Test	The Psychological Corporation
Manual Accuracy and Speed Test	Lafayette Instrument Company Lafayette, Indiana
Leavell Hand Eye Coordination Test	Keystan View Davenport, Iowa
AO Sight Screener	American Optical Corporation Buffalo, New York
Ortho-Rater	Bausch and Lomb, Inc. Rochester, New York
Test for Color-Blindness	Graham-Field New Hyde Park, New York
Minnesota Rate of Manipulation Test	American Guidance Service Circle Pines, Minnesota

Skilled Crafts

Purdue Trade Tests	University Bookstore West Lafayette, Indiana
Ohio Construction Electricity Achievement Test	Vocational Instructional Materials Laboratory Columbus, Ohio
Short Occupational Knowledge Test	Science Research Associates

Computer Programming

Computer Programmer Aptitude Battery	Science Research Associates
Programmer Aptitude/Competence Test System	Haverly Systems, Inc. Danville, New Jersey

References for Chapter 12

[1] Par Lahy, "La selection psycho-physiologique des machinistes de la société des transports en common de la région parisienne," *L'Année Psychologique* 25 (1924): 106–72.

[2] Philip DuBois, *A History of Psychological Testing* (Boston: Allyn and Bacon, Inc., 1970).

[3] Bureau of National Affairs. *ASPA-BNA Survey No. 45 — Employee Selection Procedures* (Washington, D.C.: The Bureau of National Affairs, May 5, 1983).

[4] Anne Anastasi, *Psychological Testing*, 5th ed. (London: Macmillan and Co., 1982), p. 393.

[5] Ibid., p. 394.

[6] Lewis Aiken, *Psychological Testing and Assessment*, 3d ed. (Boston: Allyn and Bacon, Inc., 1979), p. 107.

[7] Ibid., pp. 108–109.

[8] Anastasi, *Psychological Testing*, p. 387.

[9] Donald E. Super and John O. Crites, *Appraising Vocational Fitness*, rev. ed. (New York: Harper and Row, 1962), pp. 87–88.

[10] Robert Guion, *Personnel Testing* (New York: McGraw Hill, 1965), p. 234.

[11] Ibid., p. 221.

[12] John Foley, "Review of the Wonderlic Personnel Test," *The Seventh Mental Measurements Yearbook*, ed. Oscar K. Boros (Highland Park, N. J.: The Gryphon Press, 1972), pp. 401–403.

[13] Aiken, *Psychological Testing and Assessment*, pp. 114–115.

[14] Donald E. Super and John O. Crites, *Appraising Vocational Fitness*, rev. ed. (New York: Harper and Row, 1962), p. 219.

[15] Ibid., pp. 220–221.

[16] Ibid., p. 262.

[17] Ibid., p. 261; John Kinzer, "Review of MacQuarrie Test for Mechanical Ability," *The Third Mental Measurements Yearbook*, ed. Oscar K. Buros (New Brunswick, N.J.: Rutgers University Press, 1949), p. 661.

[18] R. B. Selover, "Review of the Minnesota Clerical Test," *The Third Mental Measurements Yearbook*, ed. Oscar K. Buros (New Brunswick, N.J.: Rutgers University Press, 1949), pp. 635–636.

[19] Dubois, *A History of Psychological Testing*, p. 13.

[20] Joseph Tiffin and Ernest McCormick, *Industrial Psychology*, 5th ed. (Englewood Cliffs, N.J.: Prentice-Hall, 1965), pp. 174–183.

[21] David Z. Lykken, "Psychology and the Lie Detector Industry," *American Psychologist* 29 (1974): 725–739.

[22] Ibid.

[23] Leonard Saye, Denise Dougherty, and Theodore Cross, "The Validity of Polygraph Testing," *American Psychologist* 40 (1985): 355–66.

[24] Paul Sackett and Michael Harris, "Honesty Testing for Personnel Selection: A Review and Critique," *Personnel Psychology* 37 (1984): 221–246.

[25] Edwin E. Ghiselli, *The Validity of Occupational Aptitude Tests* (New York: John Wiley & Sons, 1966).

[26] Edwin E. Ghiselli, "The Validity of Aptitude Tests in Personnel Selection," *Personnel Psychology* 26 (1973): 461–477.

[27] Frank Schmidt, John Hunter, and Vernon Urry, "Statistical Power in Criterion-Related Validity Studies," *Journal of Applied Psychology* 61 (1976): 473–485.

[28] Virginia Boehm, "Differential Validity: A Methodological Artifact?" *Journal of Applied Psychology* 62 (1977): 146–154.

[29] John Hunter, Frank Schmidt, and Ronda Hunter, "Differential Validity of Employment Tests by Race: A Comprehensive Review and Analysis," *Psychological Bulletin* 85 (1979): 721–735.

[30] Richard Reilly and Georgia Chao, "Validity and Fairness of Some Alternative Employee Selection Procedures," *Personnel Psychology* 35 (1982): 1–62.

[31] *Pegues v. Mississippi State Employment Service* (N. D. Miss.) 22 FEP Case 392, 488 F. Supp. 239.

[32] Colleen Cordes, "Review May Relax Job Testing Rules," *APA Monitor* 16 (1985): p. 1.

[33] James V. Mitchel, ed., *Tests in Print III* (Lincoln, Neb.: The University of Nebraska Press, 1983).

13

Personality

Assessment

The use of personality information in human resource selection is one of the most complex and apparently contradictory topics in the assessment of applicants. On the one hand, many selection programs in organizations utilize data about personality as an important part of the evaluation of applicants.[1] Frequently this evaluation takes the form of either scores from professional tests or judgments about the applicant's motivation, attitude, or capability to be a "team member." The importance of such qualities in workers seems intuitively apparent. On the other hand, the documented usefulness of such personality information in making *accurate* selection decisions is extremely limited. The evidence is so limited, in fact, that many writers have concluded that personality test results are, in general, invalid predictors of job performance.[2]

The discrepancy between apparent usefulness and documented usefulness is serious for those participating in selection programs. Obviously data on personal characteristics of applicants that relate to work performance should be included in selection. However if these data are not valid, they are dysfunctional to the purpose of the selection program. This chapter will address itself primarily to this discrepancy. We will discuss what is meant by personality and why its determination may be useful in human resource selection. We will also treat the major problems and methods of attempting to measure personality in selection. In doing this we will make use of material from both business and psychology. Finally, as in other chapters, we will present some guidelines as to the appropriate use of personality data in selection programs.

Definition and Use of Personality in Selection

In popular usage, personality is often equated with social skill. It is thought of as the ability to elicit positive reactions from others in one's typical dealings with them. Psychologists who professionally study personality have a slightly different concept. Although there is not one standard definition of the term *personality*, most formal definitions agree that personality refers to *the unique organization of characteristics that define an individual and determine that person's pattern of interaction with the environment.*[3] The term *characteristics* is usually interpreted to include thoughts, feelings, and behaviors which are combined distinctly in each individual.[4] These characteristics are regarded as interrelated and explanatory of the individual's adaptation to various aspects of his or her life. The environment includes both human and nonhuman (organizations, governments, physical property, etc.) elements. We can see, then, that personality involves much more than social skill; in fact many believe that no other area of psychology encompasses as broad a topic as does personality.[5]

Arguments For Use in Selection

Personality would seem, therefore, to be of critical importance to selection. If we were to review job analysis information, especially for jobs above entry-level positions, we would find many occasions when the personality characteristics of the worker seem to be essential for job performance. For example, many jobs require the incumbent to interact with others. Some, such as receptionist, salesperson, and customer service representative, emphasize short-term, nonrepetitive interaction with people. Others — supervisor, consultant, teacher — emphasize long-term, repetitive interaction. Other jobs — air-traffic controller, law enforcement officer, high school principal — require individuals to cope with the stress of hazardous conditions and demands from parties with conflicting interests. Still other jobs — assembly line worker, machine operator, quality inspector — require constant attention to a small number of repetitive, structured job tasks; and there is another group, with an opposite emphasis, such as research and marketing positions, that calls for persistence in exploring alternate paths to relatively nonspecific goals like a "better cleaner" or an "interesting display."

In addition to these anecdotal observations, there are studies that attempt to identify distinct personality characteristics for various jobs. One such study found that there were consistent patterns of agreement among 132 professional employment interviewers on the degree to which 20 personality characteristics were descriptive of a typical person in each of 15 occupations, including carpenter, orchestral librarian, and purchasing agent.[6] Another study found that professional interviewers' judgments of the suitability of applicants for specific jobs could largely be explained by a congruence between the personality of the applicants and perceived personality requirements of the jobs.[7] Two researchers, Glen Grimsley and Helton Jarrett, have concluded that there are testable personality differences between more and less successful managers. These differences are in the characteristics of drive, energy, social adjustment, self-confidence, social aggressiveness, and emotional stability.[8] Similarly, a longitudinal study of managers at AT&T found personality differences between those managers who had been promoted to middle management positions and those who remained at lower managerial levels during an eight-year period. Among these differences were that the more successful had become more work oriented whereas the less successful became more involved in their families and in their religious, recreational, and social activities.[9]

Evidence Against Use in Selection

Given these findings, we should expect to find evidence that personality data are valid for selection. However, this has not often proven to be the case. In the mid-1960s several individuals reviewed the use of personality data in selection. The following comments by Robert Guion and Richard Gottier are typical of the conclusions of this work:

> It cannot be said that any of the conventional personality measures have demonstrated really general usefulness as selection tools in employment practice. . . . The number of tests resulting in acceptable statements of validity is greater than might be expected by pure chance — but not much. The best that can be said is that in *some* situations, for *some* purposes, *some* personality measures can offer helpful predictions.[10]

One of their observations was that there was a tendency for tailored personality measures that were carefully and competently developed for a specific situation to be more successful for prediction than a standard personality measure with a standard system of scoring.

Studies conducted in more recent years have generally agreed with these earlier conclusions. For those working in selection these contradictory findings present a dilemma. There is evidence indicating that personality characteristics are associated with successful job performance. Representative personality characteristics of incumbents can even be identified for different occupations. However, the studies of the effectiveness of personality data for selection seemingly offer little encouragement for the use of personality information. We do not yet have an answer to this dilemma; however, a broader understanding of how personality affects behavior and how personality is measured should be of help in developing strategies for the use of personality measures in selection. The next sections will discuss these topics.

Personality Traits

The use of personality data in selection requires the labeling, classifying, and measuring of individuals according to some set of personality characteristics. Over the years there have been numerous approaches to these tasks using such individual characteristics as body size, handwriting, shape of head, etc., as a basis. At present the scientific study of personality generally uses the concept of *trait* as the key feature of personality assessment. A trait is a continuous dimension on which individual differences may be arranged quantitatively in terms of the amount of the characteristic the individual has.[11] Sociability, independence, and need for achievement are all examples of traits. Individuals have been found to have large differences in the degree to which they demonstrate such traits.

The concept of traits begins with the common observation that individuals differ by quite a bit in their reactions to the same situation. There are many examples of this in organizations. One individual enjoys the routine and structure of an assembly line job while another is quite unhappy about the same task features. Similarly, one person is very verbal and argumentative in a committee meeting while another is reticent. The concept of trait is used to explain these different reactions to the same situation. In these cases individuals are thought to have different amounts of traits that could be referred to as need for structure and social aggressiveness, respectively. Traits are also used to explain the consistency of one individual's behavior over a variety of situations. It has been observed that an individual who is socially aggressive in a committee meeting acts similarly in other group interaction sessions, frequently in both business and nonbusiness occasions. From this brief description, we can understand that traits are frequently regarded by some psychologists and many nonpsychologists as the cause of a person's reactions to situations.[12] The essence of traits has been conceptualized in many ways, for example, as biophysical (Gordon Allport) and as mental structure (Raymond B. Cattell). There is not a general agreement on this issue.

Identifying Important Traits   The use of personality in human resource selection requires the steps of identifying important traits and then determining their differences among applicants. Table 13.1 presents some jobs and matching personality traits that have been used in selection. There are, however, many problems in completing these steps, most of which arc identical to those with which personality psychologists in general have been concerned. The first difficulty is that of isolating the most important personality traits for behavior. In the English language alone there are over 18,000 trait terms.[13] Personality psychologists have tried to reduce this to a manageable number in a variety of ways. One method has been to follow a particular personality theory of individual behavior. Over the years various models of personality have been developed. Most do not agree on the particular traits

---

Table 13.1   *Personality Traits for A Sample of Jobs Studied in Selection*

Job	Personality Trait
Executive	Cooperativeness
Foreman	Succor, nurturance, endurance
Engineer	Tolerance, social presence, intellectual efficiency
Sales	Order, dominance, friendliness, thoughtfulness
Secretary	General activity, emotional stability
Electronic technician	Aggression, deference, order
Computer programmer	Original thinking
Insurance agent	Original thinking, personal relations
Newspaper writer	Ascendancy

---

identified. However, each has focused on a relatively small number of traits and has used these to explain behavior. Those who use a particular personality theory or model frequently limit their work to those traits also.

Another major method of reducing the number of traits has been through systematic statistical analyses. These analyses usually include content analysis to reduce synonyms among trait names and correlational analyses to identify groups of traits that are thought of similarly. Raymond B. Cattell used this method to produce a list of 16 traits. Unfortunately for those working in selection, this approach has not been well developed for organizational behavior. David McClelland has developed one of the few models linking personality and work performance.[14] He identifies needs for achievement, power, and affiliation as being essential personality traits for job behavior. The previously discussed studies that identify the general matching of personality traits to particular occupations and linking traits to successful performance may be important starts for such models. Similarly, only limited work has been done to identify statistically the most commonly used or thought of personality traits for work performance. Such efforts include the job analysis systems of the Position Analysis Questionnaire (PAQ) and Threshold Traits Analysis (TTA). The extent of use of even these limited attempts to isolate the most critical personality traits in selection is, of course, unknown. It is our estimate, however, that such use is limited. It is more common for those involved in selection to use their own particular models of personality to guide their decisions.

Central vs. Surface Traits   The second problem in using traits for selection is very much related to this issue of overabundance of traits. This is the question of which traits are related to many aspects of behavior and which are related to only a few. The significance here is that it would be more efficient to have selection decisions made using those traits that are important for multiple work performance behaviors. Personality psychologists have addressed this issue also. Allport makes a distinction among *cardinal, central,* and *secondary* traits.[15] Cardinal traits are the most generalized and seem to organize a person's whole life. Less pervasive but still quite generalized are central traits, and Allport thought that many people are broadly influenced by central traits. Finally, more specific, narrow traits were called secondary traits or "attitudes." These were thought to have very limited effect on behavior. Cattell distinguished between *surface* traits and *source* traits.[16] Surface traits are clusters of responses that are related. Source traits are the underlying, more generalized, traits that are the cause of the surface traits. Table 13.2 lists some of the surface and source traits identified by Cattell. Another psychologist, Hans Eysenck, has studied the two dimensions of *introversion-extroversion* and *emotional stability-instability* as two primary traits.[17] These two traits have also been identified as basic in several other works.[18]

In general, trait psychologists agree that there are differences in the degree to which traits are related to different behaviors. It would seem logical to assume, therefore, that not all traits would be of equal value in selection decisions. Differences in central or basic traits would seem to be more generally related to work performance differences. Differences in surface or limited traits would seem to have less generalizability to work behaviors. Unfortunately, this distinction has not been properly utilized in selection. A review of many of the specific personality traits utilized in selection programs indicates that several of these are very similar to those traits listed by Cattell as surface traits. It would not be surprising, therefore, to find only limited validity for these traits.

Table 13.2   *Representative Surface and Source Traits Identified by Raymond Cattell*

Surface Traits

Integrity	—	Dishonesty
Reliability	—	Changeability
Determination	—	Evasiveness
Emotional maturity	—	Self-centeredness
Thoughtfulness	—	Foolishness
Friendliness	—	Hostility
Adaptability	—	Rigidity
Boldness	—	Apathy
Independence	—	Dependence
Sociability	—	Aloofness

Source Traits

Intelligence, general mental capacity	—	Mental Deficiency
Emotionally mature, stable character	—	Demoralized, general emotionality
Frustration tolerance	—	Infantile emotionality
Dominance	—	Submissiveness
Positive character integration	—	Immature, dependent character
Rigidity, toughness, poise	—	Anxious emotionality
Trained, socialized, cultured mind	—	Boorishness

Interaction of Personality Traits and Situations

As we have described, an underlying assumption regarding traits is that they are stable characteristics and that traits are related to an individual's actions in various situations. However, when psychologists began to study this assumption more closely, they soon realized that individuals tended to show considerable variability in their behavior even across seemingly similar conditions. To be sure, behavior is not random; but the consistency was less than many trait psychologists believed. Some of the studies of the consistency of trait behavior across different situations is represented by the early work of Hugh Hartshorne and Mark May. Investigating the honesty and deception of children in varied conditions, these researchers concluded that children's behavior was less a function of any internalized predisposition to be honest (trait) and more a function of the particular situation.[19] Many other studies have agreed with these findings.[20] Other studies, however, have supported the notion of consistent trait responses over time in the same or very similar situations. For example, some individuals do respond to criticism from a work superior in much the same manner at different periods in their jobs; other individuals demonstrate very similar behavior over time at parties with their friends. Such consistency is taken as support for the concept of traits predictably guiding behavior.

Powerful and Weak Situations Psychologists lately have turned their attention to the interactions of traits and situations. The reasoning is that neither can be offered as the major determiner of behavior in all cases; rather they interact with each other, exerting a different influence on behavior depending on the circumstances. Following this reasoning, one line of recent work has labeled situations as either *powerful* or *weak*. Situations are powerful to the degree that they lead individuals to interpret particular events in the same way, create uniform expectancies regarding the most appropriate behavior, provide adequate incentives for the performance of that behavior, and require skills that everyone possesses roughly to the same extent. Peter Herriot has discussed the selection interview in this fashion noting that roles of both the interviewer and interviewee are frequently well known and individuals often behave very similarly in these situations.[21] A weak situation is one with opposite characteristics: it is not uniformly interpreted, does not generate uniform expectations concerning desired behavior, does not offer sufficient incentives for one type of behavior, and is one in which a variety of skills may produce acceptable behavior. Some sales situations could be classified as weak because of the differences in the expectations and knowledge of customers and differences in the characteristics of products or services.

The general conclusion is that in strong situations individual behavior is more attributable to the known situational roles than to individual traits. In our example, knowing that the interview is for an entry-level managerial position in a large financial institution may better explain an interviewee's behavior than inferences about his/her responsibility, level-headedness, or other traits. Herriot points out that many of the differences in the behavior of interviewees can be explained in terms of inconsistency in perceptions of the proper role rather than trait differences. In weak situations, on the other hand, traits would seem to be important explanations of behavior. In these situations if individuals are uncertain as to appropriate behavior, the individual is assumed to interpret the situation and act in accordance with his/her own personality traits. In our sales example, there are noticeable behavioral differences among sales personnel in friendliness, aggressiveness, and persistence, and these differences could be thought of as related to different levels of these traits.

Situation Type and Selection   These concepts have major implications for the use of personality in selection. The first is that for a strong situation-type job, personality may not be an important dimension for selection purposes. Perhaps concentration on identifying the abilities necessary to perform the job may be more advantageous. Second, personality assessment drawn from strong situations would not seem to yield accurate personality information about the applicant. We have mentioned the interview as an example. Initial screening and campus recruitment interviews seem to be especially characteristic of this. Most often these interviews are very short, highly structured interactions about which the interviewees have been well coached from classes, articles, and friends. Accordingly, applicant behavior should be more a function of learning what behavior and responses are appropriate in these sessions than a function of the personality traits of an applicant. We will make the inference, therefore, that personality characteristics are more important for weak situation selection devices and job assignments than for strong.

One way that has been used to identify situations as strong or weak has been to ask a number of individuals to rate the appropriateness of a variety of behaviors for a specific situation.[22] If one or a very small number of behaviors are rated as appropriate, this would constitute a strong situation. The rating of many behaviors as appropriate would indicate a weak situation. Such a strategy could presumably be used in organizational situations to identify strong and weak job performance situations. Related work has attempted to characterize the appropriate personality traits for a situation.[23] In one method children were exposed to a controlled situation in which each had a chance to delay taking an immediate, smaller reward in order to obtain a preferred reward later. The researchers measured how long each child waited and also asked parents to judge their child on various personality traits. These judgments were used to make a personality profile of the traits of the ideally performing child in this situation. Again such a methodology would seem feasible in organizations by obtaining personality judgments of superiors and/or co-workers of the more successful workers in a specific job.

To some extent the AT&T study previously discussed did this by comparing personality traits of successful and less successful managers.

Conclusions   We have introduced much information from the field of personality psychology and have drawn implications from this work to the use of personality in organizations. We have done this because, as was mentioned at the beginning of this chapter, although personality would seem to be important in selection programs, the overwhelming sense of the evidence is that personality data have not proved to be generally valid selection standards. Recent work in personality offers some suggestions as to why this may be the case. First is the observation that traits vary greatly in the extent to which they influence behavior. A seemingly small number of central traits have strong influence on behavior. A larger number of traits have limited or superficial influence. The other major observation is that the circumstances of some situations apparently have a greater influence on individual behavior than do traits. These two observations offer a partial explanation for the lack of positive findings in the use of personality data for selection and also some implications for improvement.

Personality Measurement Methods

We stated in Chapter 1 that accurate measurement of many human characteristics important for selection is a difficult task because we are trying to quantify intangible constructs through the use of inferred data. This is especially true in the measurement of personality. To fully understand the use of personality in selection, it is necessary to understand the nature and characteristics of these measurement methods. The three most commonly used methods in selection are inventories, judgment of interviewers, and behavioral observation. We will discuss each of these separately.

Inventories in Personality Measurement

This technique is composed of those devices that use the written responses of an individual as the information for determining personality. There are literally hundreds of such measures, all differing substantially in their characteristics. Many can be found in the test sources that were mentioned in Chapter 3, for example Buros' *Mental Measurements Yearbook*. Some of these are designed to measure abnormal personality traits while others measure normal traits; some devices measure several personality dimensions while others measure only one. It would obviously be impossible to discuss each one of these devices. Instead, we will discuss only a few to illustrate the major characteristics of such devices. There are two major types of inventories that we will discuss, self-report questionnaires and projective techniques.

Self-Report Questionnaires   These instruments consist of a series of usually brief questions asking the respondent to use a multiple-choice answer
format to indicate personal information about thoughts, emotions, and past
experiences. Typical questions are "I am happy" or "I enjoy going to small
parties" or "I think good things happen to those that work hard." The
respondent is frequently given only three response categories: agree, unde-
cided, or disagree. These questionnaires assume that a correspondence exists
between what a person says about himself/herself and what is actually true.
Moreover, the assumption is also made that the individual is aware of his/
her thoughts, emotions, etc., and is willing to openly share them.

The first such questionnaire was developed during World War I as a
screening device for Army recruits. It was designed to identify soldiers who
would have a high likelihood of not adjusting to wartime stress. Because of
the large number of recruits processed, it was not possible to administer a
psychiatric interview to each one. Instead the *Woodworth Personal Data Sheet*
was developed. Woodworth listed the kinds of symptoms psychiatrists
would probably ask about in interviews and condensed them into a paper-
and-pencil questionnaire of more than one hundred items. Example questions are "Do you wet your bed at night?" and "Do you daydream frequently?" Those who gave many "yes" answers were scheduled for individual
interviews. The questionnaire proved useful as a low-cost, limited selection
device.

Minnesota Multiphasic Personality Inventory   Prompted by the apparent
successful use of the *Personal Data Sheet,* other similar personality inventories
were developed. One inventory that has been used frequently in selection
and which also was produced through extensive developmental activities is
the *Minnesota Multiphasic Personality Inventory* (MMPI). This was published in
the early 1940s to assist clinicians in classifying mental patients into types of
psychological abnormality.[24] The inventory contains ten clinical or personality scales and four "validity" scales, which permit the examiner to judge the
credibility of the responses. Table 13.3 presents the names of these fourteen
scales. As is readily apparent, the names of the clinical scales are not trait
names normally used in describing personality dimensions in employment
situations. Lately, many clinicians have ceased to use the scale names and
instead use a standard number to identify each scale.

The MMPI consists of 550 printed statements developed through a review of textbooks and other social and personal questionnaires. The items
used are similar to these:

> I am fearful of going crazy.
>
> I am good at meeting other people.
>
> Sometimes I think I may kill myself.
>
> I am shy.
>
> Sometimes evil spirits control my actions.

Table 13.3   *Minnesota Multiphasic Personality Inventory Scales*

Clinical Scales	Validity Scales
Hypochondriasis	Question Scale
Depression	Lie Scale
Hysteria	F Scale
Psychopathic Deviate	K Scale
Masculinity-Femininity	
Paranoia	
Psychasthenia	
Schizophrenia	
Hypomania	
Social Introversion	

Respondents are to select among three alternatives: "true," "false," or "cannot say." The development of each of the ten scales from among these 550 items is what distinguished the MMPI from other questionnaires. To use the *Depression* scale as an illustration, 50 hospitalized patients of psychiatric institutions were identified who were generally sad in mood, had feelings of worthlessness, entertained suicidal thoughts, and frequently exhibited slowness of thought and action. These 50 individuals completed all items and their responses were compared to those of 1,500 normal (not hospitalized) individuals. Those 60 items that the two groups answered significantly differently then formed the Depression scale. For example, if for an item like "My sleep is easily disturbed" a large number of the 50 hospitalized respondents answered "true" while a large number of the normals answered "false," the item would be included in the Depression scale. Raw scores for respondents on the Depression scale are then calculated by reviewing the respondents' answers to these 60 items. One raw score point is given for each item that is answered with the same alternative as chosen by the large number of hospitalized patients. Higher scores, therefore, indicate a response pattern similar to that of diagnosed depressive patients and preliminarily identifies the respondent as also being depressive.

Complete scoring of the MMPI is done by comparing the score of an individual on each scale to the score distribution of the group of normals for each scale. Typically, scores higher than that of 98 percent of the normal population are taken as a possible sign of abnormality. Complete interpretation of responses is done by using the respondent's score profile across all ten clinical scales. Because of the simple language of the questions and limited response format, administration of the MMPI is fairly easy and it can even be given in groups. Scoring and interpretation is facilitated by a number of published manuals.

California Psychological Inventory   Another inventory used in selection is the *California Psychological Inventory* (CPI) which in many ways is similar to the MMPI.[25] The CPI has 480 items which require answers of "true" or "false." Almost half of these questions come directly from the MMPI. Unlike the MMPI, however, the intent of the CPI is to measure normal personality traits rather than abnormal ones. Eighteen scale scores are developed, fifteen of which are clinical scales; the remaining scales are used to assess the general credibility of the responses. Table 13.4 lists the scales. As is apparent, these personality scales are ones more frequently used in organizational studies and would seem to be highly relevant for performance on many jobs.

Many of the scales of the CPI were developed in a manner similar to that of the MMPI; however, none of the comparison groups used were hospitalized patients but rather different groups of normal individuals. For example, for the *Dominance* scale peer ratings of members of fraternities and sororities as to the most dominant individuals among them served to identify the criterion group for the scale. Differences in responses to individual items between this group and a sample of non-nominated individuals defined the items on the scale. In the development of the CPI this reference sample of normals was designed to be representative of the general U.S. population, as it consisted of 13,000 men and women with a wide range of ages, socioeconomic levels, and geographic regions of residence.

Limitations of Self-Report Questionnaires   As was mentioned the MMPI and the CPI are only two of a very large number of self-report inventories that are possible to use in selection. Many of them, like the *Edward's Personal Preference Schedule, Cattell's Sixteen Personality Factor Test*, the *California F Scale*, the *Thurstone Temperament Schedule*, and the *Guilford-Zimmerman Temperament Survey*, are also products of extensive pre-testing and developmental work, although of a different nature from that of the MMPI and the CPI. Many other personality questionnaires lack such preparation and overstate their ability to measure personality characteristics. The glaring limitation of

Table 13.4   *California Psychological Inventory Scales*

Clinical Scales	Validity Scales
Dominance	Sense of well-being
Capacity for status	Good impression
Sociability	Commonality
Social presence	
Self-acceptance	
Responsibility	
Socialization	
Self-control	
Tolerance	
Achievement via conformance	
Achievement via independence	
Intellectual efficiency	
Psychological mindedness	
Flexibility	
Femininity	

many such instruments is that they lack any developmental or measurement information. At the very least data should be provided on the reliability of the test, the group that serves as the norm or reference group to enable interpretation of any particular score, and the basis or evidence supporting the selection of the items on the scale(s). Obviously if such information is either lacking or not appropriate for the intended use of the test in the organization, one should be very skeptical of the usefulness of the instrument despite its publicity brochures.

There are also other limitations in the use of self-report questionnaires, even those that are carefully developed, that affect their usefulness in selection. One of these is the modest correlation (usually of .20 to .30) frequently found between self-report questionnaire scores and other behavior indicative of the same trait.[26] In light of our discussion of "strong" and "weak" situations, this might not be a surprising finding, but it does indicate the difficulty of using these measures to predict future job behavior. If the correspondence between trait scale scores and situational behavior measures of the same trait is low, then the correspondence of trait scale scores with job behavior that is only partially dependent on that trait would most likely be even lower. Partially, this can be attributed to the nature of the questions and answers used on these questionnaires. The questions require the respondent to generalize across many behaviors and to make interpretations of their generalized behavior. For example, the question "I am quite shy" makes it necessary for the respondent to draw one conclusion about his/her behavior in a variety of social situations. In addition, it must then be decided whether this conclusion corresponds in the respondent's mind with the undefined term "shy." Given such ambiguity in responding to scale items, it is not unexpected that the correlation between these answers and behavior in specific situations would be low.

Another issue is that of "faking good." Many studies have demonstrated that respondents have been able to change their scale profiles on personality questionnaires after "fake good" instructions.[27] For example, respondents were able to change their responses to closely approximate those profiles indicative of military officers. The obvious implication for selection is that applicants may be able to distort their answers on these types of tests to reflect what they feel are "good" personality traits from the organization's viewpoint. Many applicants have been told by professional recruiters, interview trainers, or job search booklets that organizations generally favor individuals who are social, aggressive, decisive, responsible, and goal directed. Given the nature of questions and answers on these types of questionnaires, it is possible to respond selectively to questions such as "I enjoy meeting new people" or "I generally stick with something until I finish it" to reflect these favored characteristics.

Projective Techniques   These devices are similar to self-report questionnaires in that they require verbal responses which are scored to obtain measures of personality characteristics. However, they differ noticeably on several other important aspects. In contrast to the structure of both the questions and the answers of self-report questionnaires, projective techniques are intentionally ambiguous. For example, the respondent is presented with a series of inkblots or pictures and asked to make up a story about each one. Instructions are usually kept brief and vague. Another frequently used technique is to present the respondent with a series of sentence stems such as "My father . . . ," or "My favorite . . . ," and ask the respondent to complete each sentence. In both types the respondent is encouraged to say whatever he or she wishes. The inkblots, pictures, or sentence stems are purposefully chosen to be open to a wide variety of reasonable answers.

The assumption underlying projective techniques is that they allow the respondent to expose central ways of "organizing experience and structuring life" as meanings are imposed on a stimulus having "relatively little structure and cultural patterning."[28] In this sense these devices might be classified as "weak situations" in which individual differences in personality strongly account for the differences in responses among people. These techniques are called "projective" because, given the ambiguity of the items, the respondent must project his/her interpretation and organization on them. This interpretation and organization is an extension of the personality of the individual. The proposed advantage of these devices for obtaining clear data on personality is that the respondent is not supposed to realize the possible interpretation of the information provided. This encourages the respondent to make public information that he or she might otherwise not provide. For example, a subject might interpret a picture of two interacting people as a violent argument which will lead to one individual physically assaulting the other. According to the theory of projective techniques, the aggression expressed in this story is more a function of the aggressive impulses of the individual than the context of the picture, because the picture was chosen to be deliberately ambiguous. It would then be hypothesized, given additional data, that the respondent is an angry person with a predisposition to experience his world as peopled by hostile individuals.[29]

Rorschach Inkblot Technique   One of the most popular of the projective techniques is the *Rorschach Inkblot Technique* which was developed in 1921 by Hermann Rorschach to provide a way of scoring perceptual responses to inkblots. The Rorschach test consists of ten cards (8″ × 10¾″) that each have a bilaterally symmetrical inkblot. The inkblots are standardized for all test sets used presently but were originally formed by Rorschach by dropping ink on paper which was then folded in half. After using various blots for a ten-year period, he identified the ten currently in use because of their ability to prompt a variety of responses among individuals. Five of the cards have only black and shades of grey. Two others have small areas of bright red added to the black and grey, while the remaining three have a spectrum of pastel colors. All cards have a white background.

There are a variety of ways of administering the Rorschach, but one of the most frequently used is the Klopfer system which has four parts.[30] During the *performance proper* phase, the respondent is given the ten inkblots and instructed to examine each separately and to communicate what he or she sees. The person giving the test records the comments, interacting as little as possible with the respondent. The second phase, *inquiry,* is designed to discover how the respondent arrived at the recorded perceptions for each card. To do this the examiner asks questions about the images identified on each inkblot. For example, the examiner might ask "What is it on the card that makes it seem smooth?" or "Tell me how the groundhogs got to the top of the tree." These two phases are always completed; the other two are optional. One optional phase is the *analogy period* which is used to clarify ambiguities in responses by probing the possible use of some information given for other inkblots to the one under consideration. For example, if the respondent indicated on the first card that an owl flew to the top of the tree to escape attack, the examiner might inquire whether the bear seen on top of a hill in another inkblot also was avoiding attack. The last phase is called *testing the limits* and is used especially in cases in which the respondent has provided very few responses. In this phase the examiner becomes directive and asks if certain popular images are seen by the respondent. Follow-up inquiry is also used.

Given the nature of the information obtained, the scoring and interpretation of results is complex and often differs among examiners. The details of scoring are beyond the scope of this text, so we will limit our description. Responses are evaluated on the basis of location (how much of the inkblot is used), determinants (quality of the blot related to response, e.g., color), content (human, animal, and abstract), form level (tying together various parts of the inkblot), and popularity-originality (responses reflective of those most commonly given). Data collected from these categories have been used to assess intelligence, creative potential, spontaneity, degree of mood fluctuation, depression, euphoria, anxiety, passivity, introversion, assertiveness, reaction to emotional stress, and control of emotional impulses, as well as to diagnose neurotic and psychotic illnesses.[31]

Thematic Apperception Test (TAT)   The TAT is another commonly used projective technique but differs from the Rorschach in some notable features. The most important of these is that instead of inkblots the respondent is asked to tell a story about each of nineteen cards that depict one or more human beings in a variety of ambiguous situations. A twentieth card—a totally white, blank card—is also frequently used. It is assumed that the content of the individual's stories about these cards will reveal unconscious desires, inner tendencies, attitudes, and conflicts. The cards are administered individually in two one-hour sessions. As with the Rorschach, the TAT can be scored in a variety of ways, all of which are complex systems. The most popular is Henry Murray's system which analyzes several aspects of the stories, including the following: *the hero* (the leading character in each story), *the needs of the hero* (such as achievement, order, and aggression), *press* (the pressures operating on the hero), and *themes* (the interplay between needs and press and resolution of conflict).[32]

David McClelland has developed a variation of the TAT which also has been used extensively.[33] In this system six cards, similar to those of the original TAT set, are administered. The respondent sees a card for no more than 20 seconds and then is asked to write a story that includes information on what is happening, who the people are, what led up to the situation, what is wanted, and what will happen. McClelland has developed a scoring system that evaluates the content of the stories for three distinct needs: *power* (concern about getting or maintaining control of the means of influencing others), *achievement* (concern about a standard of excellence, long-term goal, or a unique accomplishment), and *affiliation* (concern with emotional relationships). Much work has been done by McClelland and his associates to study the job behavior of managers with various amounts of these three needs or motives. For example, it has been concluded that managers high in affiliation alone are seen as ineffective, probably because they fear disrupting relationships by forthrightness and confrontation.[34] Success as a manager is dependent on the manner of fulfilling all three needs.

Miner Sentence Completion Scale (MSCS)   The MSCS was developed by John Miner specifically for the assessment of motives that are characteristically manifested at work and in the managerial role.[35] The respondent is presented with 40 items or sentences and asked to complete each. Only 35 of the items are scored to form measures on seven different motivation scales. Table 13.5 contains these scales and some similar items. Many of the specific items of this instrument refer to situations which are either outside the work environment entirely or are not specifically related to the managerial job. This is done to minimize the ability of respondents to distort their responses to present a particular image of themselves. Each of the seven scales has been developed to measure a particular managerial motive. *Authority Figures* provides a measure of the subject's capacity to meet role requirements in the area of relationships with his superior. *Competitive Games* and *Competitive Situations* both focus on occupational or work-related competition. The *Assertive Role* generally reflects confidence in one's ability to perform well and a wish to participate in activities. *Imposing Wishes* refers to controlling or directing the behavior of others. The *Standing Out from the Group* scale uses items in which an individual is highly visible and serves to measure the desire to assume a somewhat deviant position as compared with subordinates. The last scale, *Routine Administrative Functions,* is used as an indicant of the desire to meet job requirements related to day-to-day administrative work.

A complete scoring guide has been developed. Using this, each individual response is scored as positive, neutral, or negative according to whether or not the response is a positive or negative emotion in association with the content of the item. In addition various overall scores can be obtained, one

---

Table 13.5   *Scales and Example Items from the Miner Sentence Completion Scale*

Scale	Example Items
Authority Figures	My family doctor . . . Policemen . . .
Competitive Games	Playing golf . . . When playing cards, I . . .
Competitive Situations	Running for political office . . . Final examinations . . .
Assertive Role	Shooting a rifle . . . Wearing a necktie . . .
Imposing Wishes	Punishing children . . . When one of my men asks me for advice . . .
Standing Out from the Group	Presenting a report at a staff meeting . . . Making introductions . . .
Routine Administrative Functions	Dictating letters . . . Decisions . . .

Source: John B. Miner, *Studies in Management Education* (New York: Springer Publishing Company, Inc., 1965).

---

of which compares the respondent's answers to those of a normative sample of 160 individuals. Work with the MSCS has generally focused on describing managerial motivation and success within large, bureaucratic organizations.

Limitations of Projective Techniques   On the surface it would seem that projective techniques could provide more beneficial information than self-report questionnaires in assessing personality. One would expect that defined role responses would not be as evident as in the questionnaires and that responses would be more reflective of personality characteristics of the respondent than of learned situational roles. This is, in fact, the basic assumption of projective techniques. However, various issues have arisen concerning the scoring and use of the information obtained from projective instruments that have limited their general usefulness in selection. The following points are addressed to these techniques in general.

The first issue is the consistency of an individual's responses at two different times. In all other selection devices it is assumed that the characteristic demonstrated by the respondent is reliably measured. The quantitative scores derived from projective tests, however, often have low reliabilities.[36] There is a question as to the proper measurement of reliability and if, in fact, this is a useful concept for these techniques. It has been thought that observed changes in test responses over time reflect real changes in the individual, since many of the characteristics measured, like emotion and mood, change over time. The problem this causes for personnel selection decisions is significant. Usually the applicant only completes an assessment device once. The information obtained is then generalized to descriptions of the applicant. Even if changes in response patterns are indicative of real changes in the individual, the selection specialist can have little confidence in the usefulness of such personality data in predicting long-term job performance. This problem could partially be due to the measurement of surface personality dimensions rather than those thought of as source or central dimensions.

The second issue in the use of projective techniques is the impact of the total number of responses given on the score of an individual. This is not a major issue for some devices, such as the MSCS, that limit responses to a relatively constant number for all subjects. However, for those instruments that encourage free response, there is evidence that the scores of personality characteristics are related to the volume of information given.[37] The problem here is that the number of responses given may not be a function of personality but rather specific skills such as verbal or test-taking skills. If this is the case, the accuracy of the personality data would be reduced as would be its usefulness in selection.

A third major concern is the scoring of the information provided. In this, the proposed benefit of projective instruments becomes a liability. The quantity and complexity of the responses make scoring, even using a designated scoring manual, very difficult. This is a greater problem for those instruments that encourage free response and less of a problem for those that limit response. The result is that at times the same answers have not been scored and interpreted identically.[38] Such findings cloud the usefulness of the resulting personality scores for selection because it would appear that the scoring of the information is indicative of the examiner's particular scoring system and judgment as well as the individual's responses. This adds error to the scores as far as personnel specialists are concerned because they want the scores to be reflective of the applicant only since the selection decision is to be made about this individual. One tactic that has been used by psychologists to reduce this problem is to give more than one projective device. Each device is scored and the total information is reviewed in developing the description of the respondent. The accuracy of the description is strengthened by looking at the correspondence between the various test results.

A fourth concern is that few personnel specialists are trained in administering, scoring, and interpreting data from projective tests. This means that consultants must be hired to administer and score these tests. At times such consultants are not familiar with the job under consideration and evaluate the candidate in comparison to a general profile of a good worker. In many cases this profile is based only on the opinion of the consultant. However, given the complexity of projective test data and the unfamiliarity of the personnel specialist with scoring, it is difficult to find an alternative route. As a result, the personality description is often accepted by the specialist but actually is of little value.

A fifth concern is that an ever increasing amount of literature is being published about the most common scoring systems for many projective tests. This information is easily available to applicants through college and public libraries. Projective tests are most often used in managerial selection. It is possible that members of this generally sophisticated and intelligent applicant pool can read such information and deliberately distort their responses accordingly.

The Interview in Personality Measurement

We have already discussed the selection interview as a device to predict productivity through the assessment of applicant characteristics. We will not repeat that information. However, it is known that the interview also serves as a primary device for estimating personality characteristics of applicants. In this use the emphasis is on determining whether an applicant is the type of person who can be expected to fit in and get along in a particular firm. This is probably the most widespread use of the interview.[39] Something about the process of personally judging applicants produces a strong feeling of accuracy, even when accuracy is not present. It is common for the interview to serve as a major source of information when decisions are made as to whether an applicant will adjust well to work demands, be an irritant to a future supervisor, or be happy in the general atmosphere of the organization.

As was the case in the use of the interview to predict job performance, there is little evidence to generally demonstrate the usefulness of the interview in making these personality judgments. However, because of its widespread use in this manner, we do not intend to argue for its discontinuation. Instead we will briefly discuss some of the major aspects of this use of the interview in the hopes of pointing out major limitations. We will also make some recommendations about appropriate usage.

When personality is assessed in an interview situation the interviewer is actually the measuring device. The interviewer collects, organizes, and interprets data. Very few organizations, however, either provide instructions or train interviewers in the process of making personality judgments. It is important to know how this process is performed by the interviewer because then one could evaluate and refine the activity. Recently, psychologists and personnel managers have studied this personality assessment process extensively and have come up with several important findings.

Linking Traits to Individuals One important finding is that interviewers tend to overemphasize personality traits in making causal attributions about behavior. For example, an interviewer wishes to know why an applicant has changed employment twice in five years. In this situation interviewers generally assign personality causes to the behavior of others rather than situational causes — the job moves would more likely be attributed to the "restlessness" of the person rather than to any factors of the work situation. This can occur even after discussion of the topic between the interviewer and the interviewee. Such an attribution contrasts to the analysis of our own behavior in which the conditions of a situation are more often held to be the determinants of our action than are personality traits.[40]

Second, researchers have found that individuals tend to interpret even the simplest behaviors as signs of underlying traits and motives; and they easily attribute elaborate intentions to behavioral sequences, rapidly going from acts to hypothesized personality characteristics.[41] The obvious problem with such attribution is that, as we discussed earlier in this chapter, behavior is the product of the interaction of individual traits and situational factors. To assume that traits are the primary facet of observed behavior and to infer traits of an applicant from extremely limited information is very uncertain. Some psychologists have thought that a more useful way of judging the personality of another would be to view their actions in the same fashion that we view our own actions. As noted previously, it is more frequent to view situational factors as influential for our own behaviors. As psychologists describe it, we tend to view ourselves as a package of underlying values and strategies that are brought into behavior by particular circumstances while we view others as a package of personality traits that prompt behavior. It may be more useful in making judgments about the personality of others to take into account the situational characteristics of actions.

Related to this is the finding that we also tend to rely upon a few central traits in forming our impressions of others. That is, certain pieces of information are given greater weight than other information; and we commonly use these weighted data to organize our impressions. For example, it has been found that if the trait of "warmth" is attributed to an individual, he or she will also be assigned the traits of being generous, good natured, happy, sociable, and wise. On the other hand, if the individual is thought of as being "cold," the traits of being ungenerous, unhappy, irritable, and humorless are quickly assigned. Other characteristics such as being polite or blunt do not have such an effect on the personality impression formed.[42] There appears to be three kinds of these central traits: *evaluations* (like warmth), in which we organize trait judgments around a good-bad dimension; *potency*, in which we use a strong-weak dimension; and *activity*, in which we use an energetic-lazy dimension. In essence this implies that in an interview situation once one or more of these central trait dimensions is attributed by the interviewer to the interviewee a number of other traits are assigned to the individual. More than likely these additional traits will be uniformly positive or negative depending on the nature of the judged central trait. The difficulty with this process, however, is that traits are not usually so highly interrelated. It is possible for a person to be warm but not necessarily generous or wise. To the extent that the association of secondary traits to a central trait is made without actually basing the secondary trait on information of its own, the probability of incorrect judgments about the personality of another is increased.

A third factor in the formation of impressions of others is the sequencing of observations. For example, if we learn that a person is sociable and later that he or she is also dominant, our impression is quite different than if the order is reversed. First impressions are especially important and given extra weight in the total image that is formed. Psychologists refer to this as the "primacy effect."[43] Once an interviewer has formed this initial impression, there is a strong tendency to retain this impression even in light of contradictory information; the interviewer often discounts this contradictory information in favor of information that supports the original impression. Obviously, the effect of this is that the full value of all the information is not used in making judgments of others. An initial impression could have other effects also because, as we discussed in Chapter 11, there is evidence to indicate that what an interviewer expects about the applicant may affect the whole interview process. This was illustrated in one study with interviewers. In this study some interviewers were led to believe that they were interviewing either an introvert or an extrovert. Actually, they were assigned interviewees by chance alone. During the recorded interviews the interviewers seemed to have influenced the interviewed person to act in ways that conformed to the initial impression. That is, the interviewees who were thought to be extroverts soon began to act that way, displaying more poise, energy, and confidence. Conversely, the interviewees who were thought to be introverted began to act that way.[44]

Much of this discussion is part of what is referred to as *implicit personality theories,* which is the perceiver's idea about what traits go together and how these traits can be identified. The interviewer's implicit personality theory prompts very efficient judging and categorizing of individuals. In many instances the process is based on accurate information and produces useful information. In many other cases, however, the process acts in the opposite manner for many of the reasons we have discussed. In these cases the resulting personality assessment may indeed be comfortable and seem accurate to the interviewer but, in fact, be distorted because of the stages of impression formation.

Questions Used to Measure Personality   Often the inaccuracies in forming impressions of personality through an interview are compounded by the questions asked by the interviewer. Many of the most popular questions asked in interviews almost resemble projective techniques of personality assessment. Table 13.6 contains several such questions. They are very open-ended, nonstructured questions that can be answered with a wide variety of responses.

Because there are not obvious right or wrong answers to these questions, the responses given, theoretically, are prompted by the interviewee's own personality and should serve as accurate indicators of it. However, there seem to be two problems with these types of questions that would severely limit their usefulness. The first is the large number of interview preparation programs that have recently been developed. Private companies, universities, and

---

Table 13.6   *Questions Frequently Used in Selection Interviews*
                to Judge Personality

What are your future vocational plans?

How do you feel about your family?

How much money do you hope to earn at age 30? 35?

What do you think determines a person's progress in a good company?

Tell me about your home life during the time you were growing up.

Tell me a story.

Can you take instructions without feeling upset?

Are you primarily interested in making money or do you feel that service to your fellow
    human beings is a satisfactory accomplishment?

What is your major weakness?

What is your major strength?

Will you fight to get ahead?

---

social service agencies all regularly conduct interview training sessions for a variety of audiences. In addition, many books and newspaper articles have been published to advise individuals on appropriate actions and answers in interviews. Whether advice given from these sources is accurate or not is almost irrelevant to the intended use of these questions. If the interviewee's response is prompted by learned behavior from these various programs, then the response is no longer determined by the personality of the respondent. The response may indicate nothing more than what is developed in an interview training program. Moreover, the impression formed by the interviewer on the basis of the interviewee's responses could mainly be a function of the chance agreement between the interview training course and the implicit personality theory of the interviewer. Actually, very little information about the interviewee could be obtained.

Compounding this is the fact that for questions of this type there is very little other information that can be gathered to either support or contradict the statement of the interviewee. For example, in response to the question "What are your future vocational plans," an applicant may describe a steady progression through an organization, stressing increased skill development and responsibility in areas compatible with his/her abilities. In reality, the person wishes to start his/her own small business and feels that the management experience to be gained from two years with a large company would be valuable training. There is no feasible way for the interviewer to develop much other information to relate to this response; and, therefore, any assessment of traits of motivation or compatibility with the organization would be incorrect.

The Appropriate Use of the Interview   Saying all this, what statements can we make about the use of the interview in personality assessment? Many experts who have studied the selection interview have concluded that it is a potentially appropriate way for assessing interpersonal skills and motivation.[45] Unfortunately, we know much more about what can go wrong in an interview than we do about insuring accuracy. However, we can comment on a number of factors that should improve the usefulness of the interview.

Corresponding to the conclusion that the interview is useful for the assessment of interpersonal skills and motivation is the recommendation that the scope of the assessment be limited. Instead of attempting to develop a complete personality description, it would be more feasible to specifically identify social interaction patterns and motivation patterns (such as attention to detail, meeting difficult objectives, etc.) based on job analysis information. This would limit the number of personality characteristics that must be judged and more carefully identify ones that are to be assessed. For example, attention to detail may be an important personal characteristic for many clerical or computer system jobs within organizations. The interviewer should, therefore, attempt to find information about this trait rather than attempt a more complete personality description that would include traits such as ambition, aggressiveness, and sociability that may seem desirable but are not directly related to job activities.

The obvious problem, however, is how to successfully accomplish even this limited objective. From our discussion it should be clear that there is no certain way to obtain accurate personality assessment data from interviews. However, one tactic that might serve to minimize errors is to concentrate on previous behaviors that would seem to be dependent on the same personality trait. In this case, questions and discussion could be addressed to previous instances in which the interviewee demonstrated behaviors requiring attention to detail. It is not necessary that these be employment activities. Possibilities might include hobbies and academic behaviors as well as employment. It is hoped that information could be obtained about the nature of the behavior or activity, length of time involved, situational determinants of behavior (weak or strong situation), and whether one or multiple instances can be cited. In interviews the interviewer is the measuring device. One hopes that by limiting the scope of the decisions that the interviewer must make and also by maximizing the correspondence of the information gathered to the type of assessment that must be made, errors in personality assessment will be reduced.

Another suggestion is that an interviewer examine the judgments he or she has made about an applicant to reevaluate the basis for the judgment. We have discussed the various factors of forming impressions of others and the role of one's "implicit personality theory." Many of these factors are not conscious parts of the process and, therefore, not easily manageable by the interviewer. A review of the possible workings of these factors in the final impression may place the judgment in a better perspective. An interview panel might facilitate such a review.

Behavioral Assessment in Personality Measurement

The third major method of personality assessment is behavioral assessment. In this technique the emphasis is on trained individuals using judgments about the actual behavior of others to estimate personality characteristics. If we go back to our original definition of personality as the unique organization of characteristics that defines an individual and determines that person's pattern of interaction with the environment, the information gathered in this manner would seem to be very compatible with this definition. Behavior is the interaction of the individual with the environment and, logically, should serve as a direct indicator of personality. This is in contrast to self-report inventories that focus on limited written indicants of behavior, and interviews that, while capturing some behavior of the interviewee, primarily focus on verbal descriptions of behavior.

The classic studies of Hartshorne and May used behaviors to assess such traits as honesty, truthfulness, self-control, and persistence in children.[46] For example, in assessing honesty with money, children were given boxes of coins which had been secretly identified so that the experimenters could later determine which child had a particular box. Since the children were unaware of this arrangement, their honesty in handling money could be determined without their knowledge, using their behaviors as data. In another case children were given an impossible task to perform and then asked to report their own scores.

Methods of Behavioral Assessment   In human resource selection such techniques have been referred to as situational, work sample, or simulation problems and have been used to assess job-related KSAs as well as personality characteristics. Chapter 14 addresses these types of instruments and goes into detail on the nature, construction, scoring, and interpretation of these techniques. Therefore, we will limit our comments at this point to the use of behavior tests to measure personality without going into detail in describing these devices.

There are two basic methods that have been used to gather such data for selection. In one of these, the personnel specialist develops structured situations which are similar to important job situations. These situations require the interaction of a small number of individuals whose places are filled by job applicants. Trained company members observe, record, and interpret what goes on among these groups of applicants and use these data to make judgments about personality characteristics. One such method that will be described further in Chapter 14 is the Leaderless Group Discussion (LGD). In this situation applicants usually interact in groups of six. The group is presented with an organizational problem that frequently requires the division of scarce resources, for example, money for raises. Each member is given the information to play a certain role. Usually this calls for the applicant to be an advocate for a particular department or subordinate and prompts the applicant to attempt to persuade the other group members to agree with his/her point of view. Trained judges view the interaction of the applicants and rate them on a variety of traits such as persuasiveness, persistence, stress maintenance, and conflict management.

The second behavioral method is used when existing organizational members are being considered for other positions in the company. In one application, the supervisors of these people are trained and asked to record and interpret certain behaviors thought to be closely related to actions of the job being considered. In another application, the *critical incident technique,* the supervisor systematically records extremely good or poor instances of work performance or, in some cases, a particular personality trait, like persuasiveness. To do this the supervisor must make a detailed description of the incident that occurred, including behaviors and circumstances. These written incidents are then used as the data for forming impressions of the individual. Both methods have had reported success within organizations and if performed correctly would appear to be superior to other methods of personality assessment in terms of the nature of the information produced.[47]

Limitations of Behavioral Assessment   There are three potential limitations in behavioral assessment that must be addressed to improve its accuracy. The first is the situation(s) in which the individuals are placed. The essential characteristic of these situations is that they be representative of situations of the job being considered. We have observed previously that behavior is a product of the interaction of traits and situations and concluded that behavior is prompted by different mixes of these two. It is necessary that the selection situation(s) and the job situation(s) be closely related so that we can generalize from the judgments of personality characteristics. For example, stressful demands are part of many jobs and an individual's reaction to stress is important to successful performance. However, all stressful job aspects are not the same; and an individual's reactions to different types of stress is not necessarily the same. If a particular middle management job is characterized by stress attributable to several conflicting project demands, all with short time deadlines, it is not justifiable to develop a selection situation in which the applicant faces stress caused by an antagonistic interviewer or an embarrassing social situation.

The second limitation that must be addressed is that the behavior to be recorded or rated should be defined as clearly as possible. Being "persuasive" or "sociable" are complex sets of behavior that can be confused or misinterpreted. If persuasiveness is to be defined as getting another to change his/her own verbal or physical behavior through any means other than force, then this definition should be communicated to the judges. Examples should also be provided of specific actions that demonstrate various levels of persuasiveness.

The third limitation is the training of the judges. Those evaluating the actions of applicants in these behavior situations are subject to the same problems of impression formation as are interviewers. To limit these distortions judges should be extensively trained in observation techniques and should practice making judgments about personality characteristics. In addition, in many cases multiple judges are used and the personality assessment is a product of the judgment of them all. More detail about each of these points will be presented in Chapter 14 in the discussion of assessment centers.

Factors in the Appropriate Use of Personality Data

We started this chapter with a discussion about the apparent contradiction in using personality data in selection programs. There is ample evidence that personality should be a worker characteristic that is related to performance in many jobs. This type of data conceivably should be as useful in selection decisions as data about applicant KSAs which have been stressed in other chapters. The evidence, however, does not support this conclusion. The demonstrated usefulness of personality data in selection programs is at best inconsistent. A possible explanation of this dilemma is that the methods of personality assessment in selection have usually been inadequate. To many working in selection, this would seem more probable than the conclusion that personality data are simply not related to job performance. The major focus of the chapter, therefore, has been on the definition and measurement methods of personality assessment. Much of the information has been drawn from psychology because personality psychologists have studied these topics in much more depth than have personnel specialists. Of major importance for our purposes is the application of some of the findings of personality specialists to the field of human resource selection. At this point there are no certain directives that can be made to insure the accurate collection and use of personality data. However, given the material available, it is possible to draw some conclusions that should be useful to selection managers.

Personality Traits in Terms of Job Behaviors

As we have seen, personality is a complex concept. It has been observed that there are several thousand separate personality traits that have been identified. A large amount of work has been devoted to reducing this number of traits to a smaller, more manageable number. These attempts, however, have not identified the same set of traits; and there is no consensus as to which are the most appropriate to use in assessing individuals. One implication of this for selection specialists is that general objectives such as ''a manager that fits in well with our team" or "a salesperson who has a good personality" or "a clerical staff member who works well with others" are almost useless. With such broad objectives there is little direction as to what in particular should be assessed. With many personality traits possible, it would be unlikely to have agreement among different selection specialists as to what particular personality traits are being evaluated. Even if only one specialist is involved, there is little assurance that the personality characteristics evaluated are, in fact, the most appropriate ones.

There seem to be two workable methods of identifying personality traits for selection. One is the use of information obtained from job analysis as a source. As has been discussed in previous chapters, a complete job analysis will provide information about job tasks, interaction patterns, working conditions, and equipment used. From these data a personnel specialist should be able to infer personality traits that correspond to work performance. In many ways this would be the same process as the determination of KSAs from job analysis data that also has been previously discussed. It would also be useful to identify the specific tasks or features of the job that lead to these inferences. This would illustrate and add some precision to the personality traits identified.

A second method would be gathering information from job incumbents or supervisors as to personality traits necessary for the job. One way to do this is to use already developed questionnaires. The *Threshold Traits Analysis* system which uses 33 different traits is one example. Included among these 33 are concentration, adaptability, and control.[48] Another way would be to have a personnel specialist direct a conference discussion that identified personality characteristics necessary for a specific job. These methods should generate job-based information as necessary background for selection decisions. The Job Element Method described in the appendix of Chapter 7 is one example.

Basing the identification of personality traits for selection on such job analysis data could also serve another important purpose. Given all that has been said about personality measurement, it should be apparent that the use of personality data could leave a company vulnerable in a discriminiation charge. Such charges, under law, are initiated by applicants who feel that they have been inappropriately treated in selection. Using personality traits carefully identified by job analysis could be beneficial to the company in two ways. First, the traits measured could appear to have "face validity" to the applicant, that is, appear to be reasonable for the job being considered. This "face validity" may reduce the inclination of the applicant to initiate a charge. Second, and perhaps more important, being able to justify the personality traits through the evidence of job analysis is absolutely *essential* to being able to defend the selection program in the face of a charge. It will not assure that the use of personality will be defended; but without such data, any successful defense would be highly unlikely.

Importance of Situational Factors

Much of the recent work in personality psychology has studied the relationship of personality traits to behavior. It is clear from this work that the assumption commonly made that personality traits are the major determinants of behavior is not accurate. In selection situations this assumption frequently is manifested in the process of inferring the personality traits of an applicant from observed or described behavior. There is a much greater tendency to make such inferences about others than there is about ourselves. For example, it is common when finding out that an individual has been fired from a previous job to attribute negative characteristics such as laziness, aggression, or unpleasantness to the individual. In interview situations, body movements have often been related to personality dimensions such as confidence, poise, and ambition. Psychologists have pointed out, however, that such inferences are usually not accurate. The nature of the situation in which the behavior takes place is of critical importance. In "weak" situations behavior can more clearly be attributed to individual personality traits; in "strong" situations such an attribution is not so appropriate.

In selection, the nature of the situation can be of importance in two ways. The first is the situation in which the data are collected. If this situation can be regarded as strong, the conclusion would be that the behavior is more related to learned role behaviors than to personality traits. This would certainly limit the accuracy of the personality judgments made in such circumstances. We have already discussed the structured interview as one possible example of this. Other possible examples are brief social engagements, such as luncheons or dinners, or behaviors described in resumés. These selection situations are often discussed and extensively written about for the general public in the media. It is not too difficult for an individual to learn expected or socially desirable responses for each of these instances. What is not known, however, is whether the behavior or responses in these situations will generalize to job situations. This is the inherent problem in assessing poise, confidence, ambition, etc., from such well-known selection situations.

The second way the concept of "strong" and "weak" situations may be of importance in selection is in identifying those jobs in which the personality characteristics of workers are related to performance. A first reaction commonly is that personality is an important basis of performance for all jobs. However, this may not be true. For highly structured jobs, jobs with specific control and feedback systems, and jobs with highly detailed, formalized training programs, the personality of the job incumbent may be of much less importance than the KSAs necessary to do the activities. These may be termed as strong job situations in which roles, activities, and output are well known and measured. We might reasonably conclude that in such cases job performance is closely related to the learning of the proper role and activities and to developing the KSAs necessary to perform them. Work situations with opposite characteristics, on the other hand, would be prime candidates for the inclusion of personality assessment in selection.

Related to these conclusions is the hypothesis that perhaps the wrong job performance measures have been used to judge the validity of personality data in selection. Rather than be related to general measures of work performance, personality characteristics may be more closely related to specific work factors over which the employee has wide control: absenteeism, lateness, turnover, adaptability to change in work methods, willingness to exert extra effort in critical situations, etc. Such behaviors have been referred to as "corporate citizenship" by some. Although such relationships have not been extensively studied, absenteeism and tenure have been found to be related to personality.[49]

Appropriate Measuring Device

Reviewing the studies of the validity of personality measures in selection, one might conclude that there seems to be almost an inverse relationship between the ease of use of the measuring device and the usefulness of the resulting data. Robert Guion's comments that carefully developed, tailor-made measuring devices have proven better than standardized, pre-developed measures reflect this same observation.

Multiple-choice, standardized questionnaires are used frequently and have a number of positive characteristics. They are relatively easy to administer and score, can be completed in a relatively brief time period, and, if well-constructed, provide reliability estimates and scoring and interpretation guidelines. They do have limitations, however. In many cases the instruments were developed for clinical use and the personality traits measured do not correspond well to traits related to job performance. Another issue is the possible distortion of responses by an applicant in order to present a socially acceptable image to the organization. This, of course, does not happen in all cases; but it is difficult to distinguish either those in which distortion is occurring or the extent of the distortion. A third issue is the use of instruments of this type that are not well developed or tested. There are hundreds of inventories available to personnel specialists. Many have seemingly appropriate titles and are vigorously promoted. However, if basic evidence cannot be presented of the reliability and validity of measurement, the common problems in the use of such instruments are compounded. Reflecting Guion's comments, most successful uses of multiple-choice inventories have been in situations in which these instruments have been modified to be appropriate to the work situation. These modifications have included using only selected trait scales that match information obtained from job analysis and even developing and validating new scales based on combinations of items from various scales of the original instrument.

Projective techniques provide a wealth of information about the respondent. It also seems evident that they minimize the problems of distortion of responses. However, the large amount of information frequently creates problems in scoring and interpretation. The most appropriate use of these techniques appears to necessitate the use of specially trained test administrators and evaluators and the merging of results of the inventory with data collected from other sources to cross-check conclusions that are made about personality characteristics. This, in essence, parallels the use of projective techniques in clinical assessment situations. Limitations of such use are in the time and expense involved in such an analysis. A common strategy is to reserve such use for selection of upper-level positions in the organization.

The interview is also an easily used vehicle for making personality judgments. Everyone, perhaps especially interviewers, acts as a "psychologist" in his/her activities and forms judgments about others. Recent study by personality psychologists, however, indicates that in most cases this common judgmental process about others is more efficient than accurate. That is, information about others is organized and processed quickly. We are usually not left in an uncertain situation about how we feel about another individual. However, the relationship between our feelings and the person's suitability for a given job frequently does not correspond. Suggestions to improve the accuracy of the use of the interview in making personality judgments have mainly focused on more precise definitions of traits of interest, limiting the number and nature of the traits assessed, and basing judgments on more extensive and verifiable data. However, how much interviewer judgments can actually be improved by using these principles is not clear.

Although behavioral assessment situations have not been extensively used because of large developmental and administrative costs, they appear to have great promise. This is because data generated from an individual interacting with others are closer to the actual personality behavior of interest than are the data generated by other personality measurement techniques. Recently there has been an increase in the use of behavioral assessment in both private and public institutions. In these cases, usefulness of the data seems contingent on the correspondence of the testing situation to job activities and the adequacy of the training in the judges of the testing situation.

References for Chapter 13

[1] Edwin B. Flippo, *Personnel Management*, 5th ed. (New York: McGraw-Hill, 1980), p. 137.

[2] Michael R. Carrell and Frank E. Kuzmits, *Personnel: Management of Human Resources* (Columbus, Ohio: Charles E. Merrill Publishing Co., 1982), p. 217.

[3] Gordon W. Allport, *Pattern and Growth in Personality* (New York: Holt, Rinehart & Winston, 1961), p. 19.

[4] Mark Sherman, *Personality: Inquiry and Application* (New York: Pergamon Press, 1979), p. 1.

[5] Walter Mischel, *Introduction to Personality*, 3d ed. (New York: CBS College Publishing, 1981), p. 2.

[6] Douglas N. Jackson, Andrew C. Peacock, and Ronald R. Holden, "Professional Interviewers' Trait Inferential Structures for Diverse Occupational Groups," *Organizational Behavior and Human Performance* 29 (1982): 1–20.

[7] Douglas N. Jackson, Andrew C. Peacock, and Joelle P. Smith, "Impressions of Personality in the Employment Interview," *Journal of Personality and Social Psychology* 39 (1980): 294–307.

[8] Glen Grimsley and Hilton Jarrett, "The Relation of Past Managerial Achievement to Test Measures Obtained in the Employment Situation: Methodology and Results—II," *Personnel Psychology* 28 (1975): 215–231.

[9] Douglas W. Bray, Richard J. Campbell, and Donald L. Grant, *Formative Years in Business* (Huntington, N.Y.: Robert E. Krieger Publishing Co., 1979), p. 179.

[10] Robert M. Guion and Richard F. Gottier, "Validity of Personality Measures in Personnel Selection," *Personnel Psychology* 18 (1966): 135–164.

[11] Mischel, *Introduction to Personality*, p. 18.

[12] Ibid., p. 19.

[13] Richard I. Lanyon and Leonard D. Goodstein, *Personality Assessment*, 2d ed. (New York: John Wiley & Sons, 1982), p. 28.

[14] David C. McClelland, *The Achieving Society* (Princeton, N.J.: D. Van Nostrand Co., Inc., 1961), p. 267.

[15] Allport, *Pattern and Growth in Personality*, p. 365.

[16] Raymond B. Cattell, *The Scientific Analysis of Personality* (Baltimore: Penguin Books, 1965), p. 67.

[17] Hans Eysenck, "The Effects of Psychotherapy: An Evaluation," *Handbook of Abnormal Psychology: An Experimental Approach*, ed. H. J. Eysenck (New York: Basic Books, 1961), pp. 697–725.

[18] Mischel, *Introduction to Personality*, p. 26.

[19] Hugh Hartshorne and Mark May, *Studies in the Nature of Character* (New York: Macmillan, 1928), p. 384.

[20] Lanyon and Goodstein, *Personality Assessment*, p. 30.

[21] Peter Herriot, "Towards an Attributional Theory of the Selection Interview," *Journal of Occupational Psychology* 54 (1981): 165–173.

[22] Richard H. Price and Dennis L. Bouffard, "Behavioral Appropriateness and Situational Constraint as Dimensions of Social Behavior," *Journal of Personality and Social Psychology* 30 (1974): 579–586.

[23] Daryl J. Bem and David C. Funder, "Predicting More of the People More of the Time: Assessing the Personality of Situations," *Psychology Review* 85 (1978): 485–501.

[24] Starke R. Hathaway and J. Charnely McKinley, *Manual for the Minnesota Multiphasic Personality Inventory* (Minneapolis: University of Minnesota Press, 1943).

[25] Harrison G. Gough, *California Psychological Inventory* (Palo Alto, Calif.: Consulting Psychologists Press, 1956).

[26] Mischel, *Introduction to Personality*, p. 170.

[27] Lanyon and Goodstein, *Personality Assessment*, p. 30.

[28] Mark Sherman, *Personality: Inquiry and Application* (New York: Pergamon Press, 1979), p. 205.

[29] Ibid., p. 206.

[30] Bruno Klopfer, Mary Ainsworth, Walter Klopfer, and Robert Holt, *Developments in the Rorschach Technique*, vol. 1 (Yonkers-on-Hudson: World Book Company, 1954).

[31] Benjamin Kleinmuntz, *Personality and Psychological Assessment* (New York: St. Martin's Press, 1982), p. 276.

[32] Henry A. Murray, *Thematic Apperception Test* (Cambridge, Mass.: Harvard University Press, 1943).

[33] McClelland, *The Achieving Society*, p. 40.

[34] David Kolb and Richard Boyatzis, "On the Dynamics of the Helping Relationship," *Journal of Applied Behavior Science* 6 (1970): 267–290.

[35] John B. Miner, *Motivation to Manage: A Ten-Year Update on the "Studies in Management Education" Research* (Atlanta, Ga.: Organizational Measurement Systems Press, 1977), p. 6.

[36] Lanyon and Goodstein, *Personality Assessment*, p. 144.

[37] Ibid., p. 145.

[38] Sherman, *Personality: Inquiry and Application*, p. 213.

[39] John B. Miner, "The Interview as a Selection Technique," *Contemporary Problems in Personnel,* rev. ed. W.C. Hamner and F.L. Schmidt (Chicago: St. Clair Press, 1977), pp. 44–50.

[40] Mischel, *Introduction to Personality,* p. 490.

[41] Ibid.

[42] Solomon E. Asch, "Forming Impressions of Personality," *Journal of Abnormal and Social Psychology* 41 (1946): 258–290.

[43] Harold H. Kelley, "Attribution Theory in Social Psychology," *Nebraska Symposium on Motivation,* ed. D. Levine (Lincoln, Nebr.: University of Nebraska Press, 1967), pp. 192–238.

[44] Melvin Snyder and William Swann, "Behavior Confirmation in Social Interaction: From Social Perception to Social Reality," *Journal of Experimental Social Psychology* 14 (1978): 148–162.

[45] David J. Schneider, "Implicit Personality Theory: A Review," *Psychological Bulletin* 80 (1973): 294–309; Lynn Ulrich and Don Trumbo, "The Selection Interview Since 1949," *Psychological Bulletin* 63 (1965): 100–116.

[46] Hartshorne and May, *Studies in the Nature of Character,* pp. 49ff.

[47] Bray, Campbell, and Grant, *Formative Years in Business,* p. 177; John C. Flanagan, "The Critical Incident Technique," *Psychological Bulletin* 51 (1954): 327–358.

[48] Felix M. Lopez, Gerald Kesslman, and Felix E. Lopez, "An Empirical Test of a Trait-Oriented Job Analysis Technique," *Personnel Psychology* 34 (1981): 479–502.

[49] Donald P. Schwab and Gary L. Packard, "Response Distortion on the Gordon Personal Inventory and the Gordon Personal Profile in a Selection Context: Some Implications for Predicting Employee Tenure," *Journal of Applied Psychology* 58 (1973): 372–374; James F. Gavin, "Predicting Performance and Attendance Criteria," *Personnel Journal* 52 (1973): 213–217.

14

Performance Tests

and Assessment

Centers

Performance Tests

This chapter will describe those selection devices that assess applicants primarily by presenting testing situations that closely resemble actual parts of the job being considered. In their most common form these devices are referred to as *performance tests* because they require the applicant to complete some activity, either motor or verbal, under structured testing conditions. As such, performance tests are different in orientation from previously discussed selection devices that primarily measure applicants on characteristics that are presumed to be related to job behavior instead of on the job behavior itself.

Differences from Other Selection Devices

One such difference is that it is commonly assumed that performance tests provide direct evidence of the applicant's ability and skill to work on the job while other selection devices provide indirect evidence. In well-constructed performance tests the activities presented to the applicant are representative of job tasks, equipment, etc., actually used on the job. In completing these activities the applicant, therefore, does a representative part of the job for which he or she is being evaluated.

If we consider the other types of selection devices we have discussed, we realize that these collect primarily either verbal descriptions of activities or verbal indicants of job knowledge. Application and biodata forms concentrate on written descriptions of previous educational or vocational experi-

451

ences. Interviews are oral exchanges that are also primarily descriptions of work and educational experiences or oral demonstrations of job knowledge. Ability tests are primarily written indicants of knowledge; and personality inventories are most often written descriptions of behavior.

In most selection situations the specialist must take this verbal information and make an inference as to its meaning in terms of the applicant's future job performance. As we have stated previously, there often are limitations to these verbal data that hinder this inference. One is that these data are subject to willful distortion or faking by the applicant. The possibility for such distortion varies — it is the greatest in the description of past experience that is difficult to verify and it is least in the demonstration of job knowledge. The second limitation is that the carryover from verbal description to job performance is not always complete. Most of us can cite personal examples in which we know the correct way of doing something, like hitting a backhand shot in tennis, tuning the motor of a car, or organizing our work and study habits more efficiently, but yet do not translate that knowledge well into actual behavior. A parallel situation often exists in selection. To the extent that these two limitations occur in the collection of data from applicants, the accuracy of the selection decision becomes more tenuous.

Presumably, with performance tests the probability of both of these limitations is greatly reduced. In most cases applicant descriptions of what to do, what equipment to use, etc., are minimized. Instead the applicant acts in the work situation. These actions and their results are what are important. The only time written or oral information is produced is when the actual job activity consists of written or oral components. Some examples would be the preparation of a written press release or the answering of questions posed by an assembled group of consumers.

A second difference between performance tests and other selection instruments is in the identification of the KSAs measured by the device. As we have frequently pointed out in other chapters, the order of steps in the development of a selection program is first to perform a detailed job analysis, next to specify the worker KSAs that are necessary for job performance, and then to develop or choose assessment devices that best tap the specific KSAs.

In using performance tests, however, the focal point is not as much on producing instruments that validly measure a specific KSA as it is on ensuring that the work sample test is clearly representative of important job activities. In many cases KSAs are not formally identified. The assumption is that if the work sample test is very close to the job activities, then those who do well on the work sample will also do well on the job.

A frequently used performance test is a good illustration of this point. It is common in selection for a secretarial position to have an applicant complete a typing test. In the most useful situations, the applicant is asked to type a document that is representative of or actually part of the work demands for the position. For one position this document might be insurance forms, for another it might be technical reports of chemical experiments. At any rate, the applicant's typed document is reviewed for accuracy. It is generally held that those applicants that complete the document with few errors will also perform the typing demands of the position well.

An alternative strategy would be first to determine worker KSAs that are essential for typing, such as visual acuity, eye-hand coordination, and finger dexterity. Then tests could be developed that would measure these KSAs, such as an eye chart and a puzzle assembly problem. We can easily see that this latter strategy seems unwise because it has more steps, requires more inferences, and therefore more chances for error. A selection manager could be mistaken in the KSAs identified or in the assessment device chosen to measure a KSA. It seems more efficient and accurate simply to use the typing test.

Limitations

Looked at in this way a logical reaction might be, "If performance tests are so sensible and efficient, shouldn't they be used in all selection situations?" In fact such instruments have been used extensively, especially for clerical and skilled manual labor positions. Recently performance tests have been used extensively in the form of assessment centers for managerial and professional selection. However, there are a number of factors that limit their use in selection programs. For one, much care must be taken in the construction of work sample tests to ensure their representativeness of job activities. For many complex and multiple demand jobs this is a difficult task. We are all familiar with selection devices that may be intended as work samples but really are not. One example is the attempt by an interviewer to create a stressful situation during the interview by asking many questions rapidly, not allowing much time for the applicant's response, or acting in a cold, aloof manner. Even if the job of interest can be regarded as one of high work demands that may produce stress, the situation staged in the interview most often is not representative of those demands. Very few jobs consist of semi-hostile individuals rapidly questioning the job holder. The behavior of the applicant in such an interview situation is not readily generalizable to the job and should not be used as a direct indicator of actual job behavior.

Another factor in the use of performance tests is that these devices commonly assume that the applicants already have the knowledge, ability, and skill to perform the job behavior. The purpose of selection is to identify those applicants who are the most proficient in these job activities. Such an idea is best suited for jobs with tasks that are very similar to jobs in other organizations or tasks that can be taught in formal education programs. In other words, the most appropriate tasks are those that do not depend on specialized knowledge, skill, or ability to use company products, personnel, materials, customers, etc. Performance tests, for the most part, assume that the called for job behavior has previously been learned and is in the repertoire of the applicant. To the extent that this assumption is not accurate and the performance tests would require specialized training by the company, the tests must be modified to provide instruction about equipment, materials, etc., before the testing can be performed.

A third factor limiting the use of performance tests is the cost involved. Ordinarily, performance tests are much more expensive than other selection devices if many applicants are involved. Some examples of costs are: equipment and materials used only for selection, the time and facilities needed for individual or small group administration of the selection instruments, the staff time spent in detailed identification of representative tasks during job analysis, and the development of test instruction, testing situation, and scoring procedures. Some of these costs can be reduced, however, if the number of applicants is low. If the performance test is to be used infrequently, then existing equipment may be usable and no special facilities needed.

In the sections of this chapter that follow, we will discuss in more detail the rationale underlying the use of performance tests, describe examples of successful tests, and present the important steps in their development for selection programs. Finally, we will describe the development and use of assessment centers for managerial selection. As we have indicated previously, these may be regarded as performance tests that are used by many organizations for this difficult selection problem.

Consistency of Behavior

Paul Wernimont and John Campbell have made the most direct statement of the principles of performance tests as selection devices.[1] Their major point is that the selection process benefits in those cases in which "behavioral consistency" is the major thrust of the selection program. Their viewpoint is that the prediction of job behavior should be the purpose of selection. To clarify their point, Wernimont and Campbell categorize all the selection devices that could be used to predict job behavior into either *signs* or *samples.*

Signs are selection tests that are used as indicators of an individual's predisposition to behave in certain ways. To the extent that these signs are different in their characteristics from the job behaviors that are being predicted, their ability to relate directly to these job behaviors is limited. *Samples,* on the other hand, are those selection tests that gather information about behaviors that are consistent with the job behavior being predicted. To the extent that these samples are similar in their characteristics to the job behaviors, their ability to predict job behavior is increased.

There are two major types of instruments that are regarded as samples. One type is instruments that gather information about an applicant's work experience and educational history to determine if any of the relevant job behavior has been required of the applicant or has been demonstrated by him or her in the past. If so, rating methods are then developed to judge the frequency of these behaviors, the applicant's success in performing them, and the similarity of their content to the job situation addressed in the selection program. The result is a rating of the probability of relevant behavior being demonstrated by the applicant on the job. The whole process should be systematic and founded on behavior. Wernimont and Campbell do not discuss specific selection devices to do this. However, if the reader considers our previous chapters, these ideas were part of discussions on the appropriate design of training and experience evaluations, biodata forms, interviews, and the gathering of behavioral descriptions in personality assessment. In each of these cases, an emphasis was placed on the gathering of several descriptions of behavior closely related to job activities.

The second type of sample selection instrument discussed by Wernimont and Campbell is work-sample tests and simulation exercises. Such devices are in essence what we have called performance tests and require the applicant to complete a set of actions that demonstrate whether or not the job behavior of interest can be completed by him or her. It is this second type of sample that we will discuss in this chapter.

Examples of Performance Tests

Work sample tests are tailor-made to match the important activities of the job being considered and have been classified as either motor or verbal.[2] The term *motor* is used if the test requires the physical manipulation of things, for example operating a machine, installing a piece of equipment, or making a product. The term *verbal* is used if the problem situation is primarily language or people oriented, for example, simulating an interrogation, editing a manuscript for grammatical errors, or explaining a decision in how to train subordinates.

Examples of various performance tests and the jobs for which they were used is presented in Table 14.1. As is evident from this table, there have been a wide variety of tests used, even for the same job. Traditionally, motor performance tests have been most often used for selection of skilled craftsmen, technicians, and clerical staff. These jobs usually have a large component of equipment and tool usage and, therefore, are appropriate for such tests. However, such jobs often utilize a diversity of equipment which means that one performance test would not be appropriate for all positions. Several tests, each directed to a specific set of job tasks, have been used in selection programs for any given job. This has been especially true for the skilled craft positions such as mechanic, electrician, and machine operator.

Motor Tests The following two examples are illustrations of motor performance tests. David Robinson has described their use in a selection program for the position of construction superintendent.[3]

> *Construction Error Recognition Test*—A major responsibility of this position is the construction of buildings according to the construction documents. Through interviewing several construction experts, a list of 25 common and expensive construction errors was generated. Then

Table 14.1   *Examples of Work Sample Tests Used in Selection*

Test (Motor)	Job
Lathe Drill press Tool dexterity Screw board test Packaging	Machine operator
Shorthand Stenographic Typing	Clerical worker
Blueprint reading Tool indentification Installing belts Repair of gear box Installing a motor Vehicle repair	Mechanic
Tracing trouble in a complex circuit Inspection of electronic defects Electronics test	Electronics technician

Test (Verbal)	Job
Report of recommendations for problem solution Small business manufacturing game Judgment and decision-making test Supervisory judgment about training, safety, performance evaluation	Manager or supervisor
Processing of mathematical data and evaluating hypotheses Basic information in chemistry Mathematical formulation and science judgment	Engineer or scientist
Oral fact finding Role playing of customer contacts Writing business letters Oral directions	Communication specialist

an 8′ by 12′ shed was constructed which incorporated these errors. For example: a window was installed upside down so that the "weep joint" was at the top, which would prevent moisture that might collect inside the window frame from draining out; four corners of plywood subflooring were joined at one point, which created a weak joint; and "sway braces" were not attached to join floor and ceiling plates. Applicants were given unlimited time to examine the building inside and out, and to list the errors on a pad of paper. Applicants were given one point for each error identified.

Blueprint Reading Test—An architect was retained to identify common architectural errors in blueprints and to incorporate these errors in the drawings of buildings which had actually been executed by the company. Applicants were asked to review the blueprints and to mark the location of the errors with a felt tipped pen on copies of the drawings. The test was scored by counting the number of correct markings.

Verbal Tests   Verbal performance tests have become more extensively used as selection programs that focus on managers, staff specialists, engineers, scientists, and similar professionals have increased. These jobs frequently require the use of spoken or written messages or interpersonal interaction to complete tasks. It is these components that are simulated in verbal performance tests. The diversity of test types that characterized the motor tests also holds true for the sample of verbal tests listed in Table 14.1.

The following two examples are illustrations of verbal performance tests. The first was also reported by David Robinson and was used in the selection of a construction superintendent.

> *Scrambled Subcontractor Test* — In the construction business, interruption of the critical construction path can be extremely costly. The most important factor in staying on the critical path is that subcontractors appear in the right order to do their work. Knowledge of the proper order of subcontractor appearance is a prerequisite to staying on this path. In order to test this knowledge, applicants were given a list of 30 subcontractors (e.g., roofing, framing, plumbing, fencing) and were asked to list them according to order of appearance on the job site. The order of appearance given by the applicant was compared with the order of appearance agreed upon by the company managers. The applicants were given the opportunity to discuss their rationale for particular orders. Minor deviations from the managers' solution were accepted.

The second example is of a reading test developed for packers of explosive materials that was reported by Robert Gatewood and Lyle Schoenfeldt.[4]

> *Reading Test for Chemical Packagers* — Reading and understanding written material was critical to the job of chemical packager because often explosive chemicals were involved. Through job analysis it was determined that 50 percent of the material read dealt with safety procedures, 30 percent with work procedures, 15 percent with daily operations, and the remaining 5 percent with miscellaneous, company material. These four areas were referred to as content categories of reading material. A reading test was developed that used the actual materials read on the job. In this test the applicant read a short passage drawn from work documents. The content of these passages appeared in the same proportions as did the content categories of the

job materials. After each passage were a few true-false and multiple-choice items that asked about the behavior called for on the job. Answers were scored based on their conformity to the information contained in the passage that had been presented.

Development of Performance Tests

Even though performance tests vary considerably in the jobs for which they are used and the problem situations they present to applicants, they all should be similar in terms of the steps taken by personnel specialists in their development. These steps are listed in Table 14.2 and have been identified as essential to the construction of performance tests that are both legally defensible and useful in selecting capable applicants.[5] This section will present the details of these steps.

Job Analysis   The material presented in Chapters 6 through 8 of this book on the methods and procedures of job analysis is relevant in developing a performance test. Special care must be taken in describing job tasks to provide enough detail to clearly identify material and equipment used (motor), or the nature of interpersonal discussion and interaction (verbal) so that this information may serve as a basis for the performance test. To maximize the likelihood that the statement of the job tasks is accurate, one should obtain information from multiple independent sources, that is, several job incumbents and supervisors. One issue in doing this is the proficiency level of the workers and supervisors who are involved. It would seem necessary to rely heavily on information supplied by individuals who perform the job well. If the information in the job analysis is to be used in designing and scoring the performance test, accurate information about the correct method of performance is necessary.

Identification of Job Tasks   The judging of job tasks according to frequency, importance, time required, level of difficulty, and/or consequence of

---

Table 14.2   *Steps in the Development of Performance Tests*

- Job analysis

- Identification of tasks to be tested

- Development of testing procedures

- Scoring

- Training of judges

- Tryout of test before general use

---

error is also quite important. The results of such evaluation should contribute significantly to identifying the content of a performance test. The test should be addressed to those tasks that have a strong bearing on job performance. Usually task ratings provide such information. Special attention must be paid to tasks that are seasonal or not often repeated. Such tasks may be critical and have major consequence if not performed correctly. For this reason it is usually recommended that multiple ratings be obtained.

Development of Testing Procedures   Once the tasks that will serve as the basis for the performance test have been identified, another important judgment must be made as to whether an applicant can realistically be expected to perform the task or not. As we have mentioned previously, in most cases it is usually assumed that the applicant can do the task, and it is directly incorporated into the performance test. In fewer cases the job task has some idiosyncratic features and cannot be done except by experienced workers. In such cases modifications must be made in the test situation. One modification is to provide the applicant with instructions about the operation of equipment, features of special materials used, or background information about company policy before the test is given. This modification is obviously workable only in those cases in which the amount of information necessary to perform the job task is relatively simple and easy to learn. In those cases in which this preliminary information is complex or difficult, the performance test is modified to measure the ability to develop the skill to perform the task. In those cases the test is usually made to consist of the preliminary steps of the task or of the motor or verbal processes that are fundamental to learning the task.

Screening Tasks   Even after the most appropriate job tasks to be included in the performance test have been identified, further study of these must be made to make the most efficient use of testing time. The most important considerations in this study are the following:

1. The total time required to perform the task must be reasonable. It is expensive to administer performance tests, and the cost increases as the length of the task to be completed in the test increases.

2. Tasks that a large majority of applicants can do provide little help in discriminating among good and poor applicants.

3. If two tasks are approximately equally appropriate to include in the performance test, but one task uses less expensive materials, equipment, or facilities, usually this one is chosen.

4. Tasks should also be judged on the nature of the material that would be scored in a test. All else being equal, tasks that have standardized operations or products or have easily defined verbal or interaction components are more appropriate in performance tests than tasks not so

characterized. It is usually far easier and less expensive to both develop and score the test for these types of tasks.

Standard Administration   As with other selection tests, it is important that the performance test be consistently administered to all applicants and that its scoring be consistent among all evaluations. To accomplish these objectives, attention must be paid to several points in the construction of the performance test. For one, the problem presented in the tasks of the performance test should normally be representative of the job in terms of difficulty and complexity. For example, in the performance tests that we previously described, it would not have been appropriate to include a very rarely occurring defect in the *Construction Error Recognition Test*, or only the most difficult reading passages in the *Reading Test for Chemical Packagers*. Similarly, a typing test that presents easier material than is normally included in on-the-job typing assignments is usually less useful than it might be. The reason is that the testing of only very easy or very difficult material usually results in less discrimination among applicants. With very easy material almost all applicants pass and with very difficult material only very few are successful. If the purpose of using the performance test is to identify finer differences among applicants, the difficulty level of the performance test tasks should be more representative of the difficulty level of the tasks of the job.

Standardization of testing conditions requires that a set of instructions be developed that informs the applicant of the nature of the task, what is expected of him or her, and the materials and equipment to be used. Also, the same or identical conditions for testing should be provided each applicant. To the extent possible, information should be provided on what actions, products, or outcomes will be scored.

Independent Test Sections   In developing the task problem of the performance test, another important consideration to keep in mind is the independence of various parts of the test. All else being equal, it is preferable *not* to have the applicant's performance on one part of the test be closely tied to a previous part of the test. For example, the *Construction Error Recognition Test* was designed so that each error that was demonstrated could be recognized even if other errors were not recognized by the applicant. By having the 25 errors independent of one another, one obtains a larger sample of the behavior of the applicant. If, on the other hand, the test was developed so that the identification of one or two errors would disclose the other errors, there is a greater probability of obtaining a distorted measurement of the applicant's performance. If the applicant does not recognize the one or two central errors, he or she has no opportunity to correctly identify the remaining errors; if he or she does identify the central errors, then the rest become apparent. This actually makes the test only a one or two item test for such applicants.

This problem is most likely when the performance test is a sequence of steps in a job process like sewing a garment or constructing a small piece of apparatus. In either case an error in measuring the materials to be used would adversely affect the remaining steps. The applicant may be able to perform these remaining steps well and, in fact, does acceptably given the starting materials. However, most scoring systems judge the accuracy of the behavior or product and do not make allowances for faulty starting materials. To avoid this problem, some tests have been designed to provide a new set of acceptable materials for each phase of the job process. For example, if the first phase of a small-apparatus-construction performance test is measuring and cutting the necessary pieces, the applicant stops after this phase. The pieces are taken to be scored by the judges, and the applicant is provided with a set of acceptable pieces to use in the next phase of the construction task.

Eliminating Contaminating Factors   Another important feature to keep in mind in the development of a performance test is to ensure that apparatus, jargon, or other testing elements that have only a minor influence on job performance do not interfere with or limit the test performance of some applicants who are not familiar with these elements. For example, in a performance test for a personnel specialist, some numerical data may be provided from a company attitude survey. The applicant is asked to make some preliminary data analyses and use these results to answer a few specific, management questions about the employees' attitudes about company procedures. The data analyses are to be performed on a personal computer. A serious problem could occur if an applicant does not know how to operate the computer that is provided for the performance test. The central concept of the test is to measure the ability to choose and interpret the appropriate statistical analyses for the management questions that are asked. The skill to operate a personal computer is of almost no importance. For those who are unable to operate this particular piece of equipment efficiently, however, the equipment becomes a major component of the test. In cases such as this, it is appropriate to either provide a variety of apparatuses, to train the applicant in the use of the apparatus before the performance test begins, or to provide an operator of the apparatus to carry out the requests of the applicant. From previous remarks it should be apparent that modifications such as these are not necessary if the operation of a particular apparatus is essential to the job task and not easily learned. In such a case, the apparatus becomes an essential part of the performance test.

Frequency of Test Problem   A final point to be addressed in test construction is the number of times an applicant will be asked to perform a job activity during a performance test. The trade-off is between the time and cost of test administration and scoring, and the increased reliability of having multiple demonstrations of the task by the applicant. The general guideline is to have the applicant repeat the task several times within cost limitations.

For example, many skilled craft positions, e.g., typing, sewing, maintenance, machine operation, etc., have short-cycle tasks. An applicant can provide several products within a relatively brief period of time by repeating the cycle of tasks. In such cases, it is desirable to design several repetitions of the task into the performance test. This would be especially true if a high degree of precision or accuracy is necessary in the product. In these cases, a larger data sample would be more useful for assessing the applicant's performance level. Obviously, if the task of the performance test is very long or costly to stage, a very limited number of trials should be scheduled.

Scoring   The scoring of the performance test must be clearly defined because the decisions facing the scorer are often very difficult. In many cases a judgment must be made as to the acceptability of task performance when multiple factors are present. Scoring generally is a function of comparing the test task performance of the applicant to a standard defined by the organization as being satisfactory. Table 14.3 provides examples of several factors that have been used primarily in scoring *motor* performance tests. In this type of test, the *task process* and/or the *task product* is scored. The task process is the actions or observable behaviors that are demonstrated by the applicant in doing the task. The task product is the result of the task process. In motor performance tests, products are usually physical objects such as a typed document, a piece of sewn clothing, or a set of joined pieces of wood or other building materials. In general, a process is scored when there are clearly a small number of ways to do the job and these ways invariably lead to an acceptable product. The operation of machinery in a continuous job process would be an example. A product is scored in those situations in which a large number of different behaviors can lead to an acceptable product.

Standards   A number of separate standards can be scored for both process and product categories. Quality is, of course, important in almost all jobs. However, it assumes increased importance for those tasks in which time or cost to complete the task is secondary to the correctness of the task effort. Tailoring, inspection, and equipment repair are examples. Quantity is most importantly scored for those performance tests in which amount produced within a given time period is within the control of the worker and means cost savings to the organization. The review of payments made by customers is an example. Cost becomes important as a scorable standard when expensive materials are involved in constructing a product and waste should be minimized. An example would be tasks like the repair of a research apparatus in which there are several options available which vary greatly in their expense.

The remaining two standards, learning time and safety, are used much less frequently than the previous standards. Learning time is a logical measure for tasks which are characterized by having a variety of novel demands placed on the incumbent. Jobs such as the technical repair of a variety of sophisticated, electronic equipment would be an example. In many cases the

Table 14.3 *Criteria Used in Scoring Motor Performance Tests*

Standard	Process Criteria	Product Criteria
Quality	Accuracy	Conformance to specifications
	Error rate	Dimensions or other measurements
	Choice of tools and/or materials	Spacing
		Position
	Efficiency of steps taken	Strength
		Suitability for use
		General appearance
Quantity	Time to complete	Quantity of output
Learning time	Number of steps for which guidance is needed	Improvement in meeting quantity standards
		Improvement in meeting quality standards
Cost	Amount of material used	Number of rejects
Safety	Handling of tools	Safety of completed product
	Accident rate	

Source: Lynnette B. Plumlee, *A Short Guide to the Development of Performance Tests* (Washington, D.C.: Personnel Research and Development Center, U. S. Civil Service Commission, Professional Series 75-1, January 1975).

task of repair requires the worker to use new methods of diagnosis and correction. Safety is obviously an important dimension to score when physical injury can be caused by incorrect process or product. In many cases more than one of these standards are used in scoring; for example, quantity and quality are often used together. Also process and product can both be scored in the same performance test.

Process dimensions used in scoring can be identified by using excellent workers presently on the job. Both demonstration and descriptions of task steps given by these workers have been used. Most organizations have defined the physical dimensions or properties of satisfactory products. This information is often used in scoring product dimensions of motor performance tests. For example, the diameter of rolled wire, the strength of welds, and the location of buttons sewn on a blouse are all such standards.

Rules In the actual scoring of the motor performance test, the assignment of numbers to the applicant's test performance must have defined rules. Most often, especially if there are several repetitions or separately scored parts of the performance test, a simple "0, 1 rule" is used. Performance meeting standard is scored "1" and performance that does not is scored "0." Total score for the test is obtained by summing across all parts of the test. For example, if ten repetitions of making a weld are required, an applicant's score could range from 0 to 10. Another scoring option is to use scales, for example 1 to 5. The highest number on the scale is assigned if the performance meets the desired level and other numbers are assigned to less acceptable performance, in descending order of acceptability. In doing this, however, it is necessary to determine how much of a deviation from the desired level each number on the scale represents.

If many different standards are scored in the performance test, e.g., quality of the products, quantity produced, and cost of the work process, a rule must be stated to allow for the combining of these separate scores into one total score. In defining this rule, weights are assigned to each different standard scored. These weights can be determined by statistical analysis, by using cost of correction of error data compiled by the company, or judgments of relative importance of the factors by experts. For example, suppose that on each of the previously mentioned three scoring standards the highest possible score is 10, and we have determined by one of these methods that quality is four times as important as cost and quantity is twice as important as cost. An applicant's raw score on the quality standard is multiplied by 4, the raw score on quantity is multiplied by 2, and the raw score on the cost factor is left unchanged. These three adjusted scores are then added together to obtain the total score for the performance test. In those cases in which evidence cannot be determined that argues for differentially weighting the standards, each standard should remain unweighted and unadjusted scores summed for a total.

The scoring of verbal performance tests is different from that of motor performance tests. The general principle is essentially the same — the verbal performance of the applicant is compared against a standard that has been deemed satisfactory by the organization. However, in verbal performance tests frequently there is no important product that results nor is there a definite set of actions that must be used. The use of words and concepts, and the interaction among individuals cannot be as precisely defined as standards of motor performance tests. In many cases the scoring of verbal performance tests depends on the extensive training of judges. We will discuss such scoring methods later in the chapter in the discussion of assessment centers which have a large component of verbal performance tests.

The Training of Judges   For motor performance tests, if scoring standards and rules have been well defined, training raters in how to judge applicant performance is relatively straight forward. Videotapes of applicant task behaviors have been used to train raters to make judgments about process dimensions.[6] Whether videotapes or live demonstrations are used in training, the rater is given an explanation and a description of appropriate job process behaviors including the sequence of the behaviors. Emphasis is then placed on demonstrations of appropriate and inappropriate behavior. Videotapes seemingly have an advantage in this phase because they can be used frequently, stopped at critical moments, and replayed to demonstrate specific points. Logically, it is important to present numerous inappropriate behaviors during this training to familiarize the rater with these before actual testing begins.

Training raters to evaluate product dimensions is usually conducted by using multiple examples of actual products. The raters are instructed in the definition of the scoring dimensions and how to make measurements. Frequently, special tools such as gauges, micrometers, and electronic equipment are used in doing this. In this training, raters are required to make measurements of each product dimension and the resulting numbers are compared to predetermined, accurate measurements. If the numerical values generated by the rater match the accurate measurements, the rater is able to correctly measure the scored product dimensions. If the two sets of numbers do not match, the rater should receive more training. In addition to being able to obtain the correct measurements, raters must be trained in using the scale and assigning a score to the measured product dimension. In doing this, the rater is instructed in the decision rules of scoring, which we have discussed previously, and asked to use these rules to score several products that vary on the product dimensions. Usually these products have been scored by experts. The scores of the rater are compared with those of the experts to determine accuracy.

Reliability of measurement is important in developing a scoring system and training raters in its use. By using some measure of interrater reliability, discussed in Chapter 4, high agreement among raters in their measurement and scoring should be demonstrated. If raters do not demonstrate reliability in their judgments after training, either more training is necessary, the scoring system must be changed, or the raters replaced.

The Test Tryout   The final step in the development of a performance test is the tryout of the test before it is actually used for selection. It is good practice to have a fairly large sample of individuals, approximately 80 to 100 if one follows present guidelines, complete the test and have multiple raters (approximately 5 to 10) score these tests. In this way both the test and the rater training can be evaluated.

Representative Sample   A critical variable in the selection of individuals to complete the performance test in the tryout is to identify those that are representative of the applicant group for which the test will be used. At times this may require contacting and paying individuals, such as students, who are affiliated with the same sources as typical applicants. Present workers on the job for which the performance test is intended are other potential individuals for the tryout. It is necessary to judge, however, if the test performance of these employees is representative of the applicant group or whether it has been significantly changed by actual job experience. The raters used in the tryout should also be representative of those within the organization who will serve in this capacity. It is beneficial to have individuals who were not involved in the development of the performance test itself among these raters.

Data Analysis   Statistical analysis of the data resulting from the tryout is used to evaluate the test and the training of raters. Essentially, most analyses are directed toward obtaining data to answer the following kinds of questions:[7]

1. Should some test tasks be eliminated as serving no useful purpose because all applicants can perform them satisfactorily?

2. Is practice time necessary before the actual test begins? If so, how much is necessary?

3. Do different raters agree on the scores assigned?

4. Are applicants consistent in their performance on the test? (This may require applicants to repeat the performance test at two different times).

5. Are the obtained scores sufficient to identify satisfactory process and/or product performance or are critical dimensions omitted?

6. Are the obtained score dimensions successful in obtaining differences in performance among the applicant group?

7. Do an appropriate number of applicants meet the desired standards on the scoring dimensions, or is the test extremely difficult or easy?

The results of the analyses indicate whether or not changes must be made in the test or rating process. When deficiencies in the performance test are minimal, the test is ready for use in the selection program.

An Example of Developmental Steps

James Campion's description of the development of a motor performance test used in the selection of maintenance mechanics is presented in Table 14.4.[8] This description illustrates many of the points of our discussion. The development began with an extensive job analysis, including the identification of a list of task statements by a group of experts who had direct knowledge of the maintenance mechanic job. This group of experts also provided a second list and descriptions of job-related tasks that previous applicants for this job had been able to perform successfully. This second list was not of those job tasks that all previous applicants had mastered but rather of tasks that a significant proportion of applicants could perform. As is described, these two lists were combined with attention being given to the tasks common to both lists. These common tasks were those that were both part of the job and also within the repertoire of job applicants. As has been discussed, a common assumption about performance tasks is that they are tasks that have

---

Table 14.4   *Development of Motor Performance Test for Maintenance Mechanics*

The development of the work sample measure required a thorough examination of the job. This information was obtained from several technical conferences with a group of job experts. These job experts were an industrial engineer, who was an assistant to the plant maintenance superintendent, and three foremen, who were responsible for supervising the work of the maintenance mechanics. These conferences progressed through several stages, each of which was designed to achieve a specific objective.

Stage 1. In the first stage the experts were requested to list all possible tasks that maintenance mechanics were required to perform in the company; and for each task they were asked to indicate frequency of performance and to evaluate its relative importance to the job.

Stage 2. In the second stage these experts, plus a member of the personnel department, were requested to provide another task listing based upon the previous work experiences of their maintenance mechanic applicants. All five members who participated in this conference were responsible for screening applicants for maintenance mechanic work.

Stage 3. In the third stage the objective was to delineate the crucial dimensions of work behavior for maintenance mechanics. First, the group experts listed the major dimensions of work behavior that they felt discriminated between effective and ineffective performance on the job. Second, each expert independently generated behavioral incidents to illustrate performance on each dimension. Following this, the experts pooled their information, discussed differences, and decided that there were two critical dimensions of work behavior for maintenance mechanics: use of tools and accuracy of work.

Stage 4. In the next stage tasks were selected as possible work sample measures. It was important that the tasks selected were representative of the tasks performed by the maintenance mechanics in the plant, but they could not be unique to this plant. They also had to make them appropriate for the job applicants. These two requirements were satisfied by considering as possible job sample measures only those tasks which were common to the lists obtained in Stages 1 and 2. In addition, each job sample task had to meet two other requirements. Each task had to provide a situation where the opportunities were maximal for the examinee to exhibit behaviors relevant to use of tools and accuracy of work. Also, the behaviors elicited by the job sample tasks had to be the kind that a test administrator could reliably record.

Based on the above criteria, four tasks were selected: installing pulleys and belts, disassembling and repairing a gearbox, installing and aligning a motor, and pressing a bushing into a sprocket and reaming it to fit a shaft.

Stage 5. In the final stage these four tasks were broken down into the steps logically required to complete them. Each step was then analyzed in detail, in order to determine the various approaches a job applicant might follow. The recordable behaviors associated with these approaches were specified and weights assigned to them based on their correctness as judged by the job experts. This resulted in a list of possible behaviors associated with each step in task performance, with every behavior assigned a weight for scoring purposes. Thus, the recording form was in a checklist format which required that the test administrator simply describe rather than evaluate the job applicant's behavior. The applicant's responses were later evaluated by adding the weights associated with the behaviors marked on the checklist.

Test instructions were written for the examiner to read. A set of tools and materials were selected that maximized the opportunity for the unqualified examinee to respond inappropriately. The tools and materials, the manner in which they were displayed, and the time given examinees to study them were standardized. All testing was done in the same test administration room, with only the examiner and examinee present. Four hours were allotted for test administration.

Example items and their corresponding weights are as follows:

	Scoring Weights
INSTALLING PULLEYS AND BELTS	
1. Checks key before installing against:	
_____ shaft	2
_____ pulley	2
_____ neither	0

continued

Table 14.4   *continued*

DISASSEMBLING AND REPAIRING A GEAR BOX

10. Removes old bearing with:

_____ press and driver	3
_____ bearing puller	2
_____ gear puller	1
_____ other	0

INSTALLING AND ALIGNING A MOTOR

1. Measures radial misalignment with:

_____ dial indicator	10
_____ straight edge	3
_____ feel	1
_____ visual or other	0

PRESSING A BUSHING INTO SPROCKET AND REAMING TO FIT A SHAFT

4. Checks internal diameter of bushing against shaft diameter:

_____ visually	1
_____ hole gauge and micrometers	3
_____ Vernier calipers	2
_____ scale	1
_____ does not check	0

Source: James E. Campion, "Work Sampling for Personnel Selection," *Journal of Applied Psychology* 56 (1972): 40–44. Copyright 1972 by the American Psychological Association. Reprinted by permission of the author.

previously been learned. Identification of tasks common to these two lists helped maximize the probability that the tasks making up the maintenance mechanic performance test met this assumption.

Additionally, the experts identified two major work activities that differentiated good and poor job performance: use of tools and accuracy of work. The motor performance test was therefore of tasks that were representative of these two activities and within the repertoire of applicants. These tasks were installing pulleys and belts, disassembling and repairing a gearbox, installing and aligning a motor, and pressing a bushing into a sprocket and reaming it to fit a shaft. In turn, each of these tasks was analyzed in great detail and a scoring system based primarily on task process was determined. A distinct feature of this scoring system was that the experts attempted to identify all possible task behaviors that an applicant might demonstrate in carrying out the performance test. Each separate behavior was evaluated and weighted and placed on a list. The rater, therefore, had only to observe the behaviors of the applicant and check them on this list. The applicant's score was determined by adding the weights previously assigned to the checked behaviors. In this way, the difficulty facing the rater during the actual administration of the performance test was minimized. The rater could concentrate on observing and recording the behavior of the applicant and did not have the additional burden of simultaneously evaluating and scoring these behaviors. Campion reported that this performance test was efficient to administer and significantly related to job performance.

The Effectiveness of Performance Tests

Evaluations of the results of using performance tests in selection programs have almost universally been positive and have identified several benefits in this use. Not surprisingly, primary interest has been focused on the demonstrated validity of these selection tests. James Asher and James Sciarrino did an extensive review of the validities of eight different types of selection tests.[9] When a measure of job performance was used as the measure to determine validity, the motor performance tests were found to be the second best selection test, behind biographical data. Verbal performance tests ranked fourth. When a measure of success in training was used to determine validity, the pattern was reversed with verbal performance tests being superior to motor tests. These authors concluded that both types of performance tests consistently demonstrated validity with motor tests being a better predictor of job performance than job training and the opposite being true of verbal performance tests. This indicates that the use of each type of performance test is affected by the measure of success that is important.

In a few cases, performance tests have been directly compared for validity with other types of tests for the same job. One study examined both a verbal performance test and an intelligence test in relationship to success in a police training program.[10] Data were collected from three different samples of cadets. The verbal performance test was found to be valid in all three cases, while the intelligence test was valid for only one sample. Moreover, when prediction of success in training was analyzed, it was determined that the work sample test gave adequate prediction and the additional information obtained from the intelligence test did not improve this predictability. Another study compared a motor performance test for maintenance mechanics with a battery of paper-and-pencil tests. Included in this battery were both mechanical comprehension and intelligence tests. All tests were evaluated against supervisors' ratings of work performance. The differences between the two types of tests were large as all of the motor performance tests were found to be valid and none of the paper-and-pencil tests were. These findings of the validity of performance tests reflect our previous comments about the effectiveness of sample over sign tests.

Adverse Impact   In addition to validity, adverse impact of performance tests on minority applicants has also been examined. As we discussed in Chapter 2, adverse impact refers to the disproportionate rejection rate of one demographic group in comparison with other demographic groups. One study by a group of researchers at Michigan State University compared the scores of minority and majority applicants on both written and performance tests for positions as metal trade apprentices.[11] A difference in scores between the two groups was identified for only one of three performance tests but for all five of the written tests. One conclusion was that the adverse impact of the performance test was less than one-half that of the written tests.

A related study by Wayne Cascio and Niel Phillips did a comprehensive study on the selection rates of minority and nonminority groups using performance tests for a series of city government positions.[12] Comparisons were made among white, black, and Latin applicants for 21 tests, 11 of which were motor performance and 10 of which were verbal performance, used for selection in 21 jobs. No difference in selection rates was found for any of the jobs. When comparisons were made of test scores only for the three groups, in order to study possible differences attributable only to the test, significant differences were found in 3 of the 21 tests. Each racial group scored significantly higher on one of the tests—there was no pattern of nonminority applicants outscoring minority applicants. Other analyses found that no sex or race bias occurred among raters in scoring the performance of different applicant groups.

Other Aspects   These last two studies also found other positive results of using performance tests. One desirable condition in selection is to have applicants accept the instruments as having "face validity"—being appropriate for selection. The Michigan State study analyzed the attitudes of the applicants about different selection tests. Large percentages of both nonminority and minority applicants judged the performance test as "about right" in difficulty. Cascio and Phillips reported that during the first 17 months that performance tests were used no complaints about their appropriateness were lodged. This was in contrast to the previous complaint rate of 10 to 20 percent of all applicants when other types of tests were used.

Cascio and Phillips concluded that performance tests also serve as realistic job previews and can lead to the benefits that we discussed in Chapter 1 as sometimes accompanying them. They cite as an example the test for sewer pumping station operator. During an initial one-hour instruction period a sewer mechanic explained and demonstrated (as if he were the applicant's supervisor) procedures for the general maintenance of sewer pipes and equipment, for example how to clean filters, grease fittings, and read a pressure chart. The test was given during the second hour, when each applicant was required to repeat the demonstration as if he or she were on the job. Follow-up interviews revealed that those who qualified for and accepted the job had an accurate idea of the job demands. For all jobs combined, the turnover rate before the use of performance tests was approximately 40 percent. During the 9 to 26 months after performance testing was started this rate dropped to less than 3 percent. It was estimated that this had saved the city $336,199 in costs.

At the risk of stating the obvious, it is findings such as these that have led prominent selection researchers to highly recommend performance tests as selection devices. It is in this sense that Cascio and Phillips entitled their study, "Performance Testing: A Rose Among Thorns?"

Assessment Centers

The definition of an Assessment Center (AC) that was developed by the Task Force on Assessment Center Standards is: an assessment center consists of a standardized evaluation of behavior based on multiple inputs. Multiple trained observers and techniques are used. Judgments about behavior are made, in part, from specially developed assessment simulations. These judgments are pooled by the assessors at an evaluation meeting during which assessment data are reported and discussed and the assessors agree on the evaluation of the dimension and any overall evaluation that is made.[13]

In more familiar terms, an AC is a procedure for measuring KSAs in groups of individuals (usually 12 to 24) that uses a series of devices, many of which are verbal performance tests. The KSAs are patterns of behavior that are demonstrated when the applicant completes the performance tests. The devices in an AC, often called *exercises,* are designed so that the participants have several opportunities to demonstrate each of the patterns of behavior being evaluated. The evaluators, referred to as *assessors,* are specially trained in the observing and recording of behavior of participants in the exercises. This information is used when the assessors meet as a group to share their observations of each participant and also to develop a consensus evaluation of each.

ACs have been used for both selection and career development. In selection, the emphasis is on identifying those participants that demonstrate the behavior thought necessary to perform in the position being considered. When used for career development, the emphasis is on determining those behaviors which each participant does well and those in which each is deficient. The latter are subsequently included in training programs to correct the deficiency. For our purposes, we will concentrate on the ACs used for selection. The next sections will discuss in some detail the topics that we have briefly introduced.

The History of Assessment Centers

ACs were first linked to the testing of leadership and managerial abilities in military assessment programs.[14] German psychologists were heavily involved in the selection and training programs that were part of the military buildup of the 1930s. The dominant philosophy in the selection of young officers was that the total personality of candidates must be assessed rather than several specific traits. To measure personality, an emphasis was placed on the observation of the behavior of officer candidates in staged, but natural, military situations. For example, *positive will* was demonstrated by a habit of voluntary response to the command of the superior officer and *determination* was demonstrated by the creation of ways to achieve a goal. Some methods of assessing these characteristics were for the officer candidate to carry out a series of assignments over a demanding obstacle course or to be placed in charge of a group of soldiers and assigned a group task.

In addition to these "situational" tests, some standard paper-and-pencil tests of intelligence and special abilities were also administered. Assessment procedures lasted for two or three days and evaluations of the officer candidates were performed by a group of five officers, including the command officers, psychologists, and physicians.

During World War II the British War Office Selection Boards implemented a similar program for officer selection. The concept is attributed to a British military attaché who had been stationed in Berlin and who had observed the German selection program. Under the assessment program that finally evolved, three or four days of procedures were used which consisted of individual psychological tests, interviewing devices, and group exercises.[15] Candidates were usually processed in groups of eight. One of the most interesting of the group exercises was one in which the eight-man group was presented with either a verbal or a motor performance problem that required cooperation to solve. None of the participants was placed in charge of the group, however. Judges, in teams of four or five, watched the group and met to develop consensus evaluations of specific leadership characteristics of each officer candidate.

In the United States a similar program was developed by the Office of Strategic Services. However, instead of concentrating on officer selection only, the program assessed candidates for a variety of jobs: intelligence agents, secretaries, office workers, and saboteurs, among others. As in the other programs, both group exercises and individual paper-and-pencil tests were used and evaluations were made by a group of raters. The program was initiated and staffed by a number of industrial psychologists and, perhaps for this reason, was greatly concerned with the measurement issues of developing, scoring, and interpreting the diverse instruments used.

Assessment Centers in Industry

Drawing heavily upon the testing and evaluation principles of these military programs, the Management Progress Study of AT&T marked the beginning of the use of the assessment center for industrial organizations.[16] The Management Progress Study was begun in 1956 to study the career development of men hired for managerial purposes. According to Douglas Bray, who designed the study, the general questions that prompted the study were:

> What significant changes take place in men as their lives develop in a business career?
>
> Conversely, are there changes we might expect or desire that do not occur?

What are the causes of these changes or stabilities? More particularly, what are the effects of company climate, policies, and procedures?

How accurately can progress in management be predicted? What are the important indicators and how are they best measured?

The study was to provide information to be used in directing the career development of managers at AT&T.

One major focus of the study was to identify a list of personal attributes of managers that were initially thought to be related to successful career progress. In all, 25 characteristics (e.g., communication skill, goal flexibility, self-objectivity, etc.) were identified by using information drawn from research literature, industrial psychologists specializing in management career patterns, and senior executives at AT&T. The design of the study was to periodically measure these characteristics in 274 new managers over several years and to relate these data to progress through the levels of management. During this time none of the data were made available to anyone but the researchers.

Obviously, the immediate problem for those conducting the study was to develop devices to measure the 25 characteristics of interest. It was in this area that the military officer assessment programs were utilized. It was decided that it would be necessary to examine each manager thoroughly at each testing period to obtain useful data. To do this a 3½-day assessment center was devised. Managers were brought together in groups of 12 and several methods of measuring personal characteristics were administered. These included tests of general mental ability, personality and attitude questionnaires, interviews, several group problems, an individual administrative exercise, and projective tests of personality.

It is not within the scope of this book to discuss in detail the results of the study. However, as a summary, the reports published over the years have provided much useful information about managerial careers. More importantly for us, the assessment information obtained from the various exercises was shown to be related to subsequent movement through managerial levels. This, of course, prompted much attention in the use of these types of exercises and the whole concept of assessment centers for managerial selection. The use of multiple-day, multiple-exercise testing programs quickly grew. Although there were variations among these programs, there was much similarity in the types of assessment devices used. These usually paralleled those used in the AT&T study. The next section will discuss each of these types of exercises, mainly emphasizing the individual and group performance tests that were used.

Assessment Center Exercises

Dimensions The development of an AC starts with a job analysis that identifies clusters of job activities that make up the important parts of the manager's job. Each cluster should be specific, observable, and consist of job tasks that can be logically related. These job clusters are referred to as *dimensions* and it is these that are measured by the assessment center devices. Table 14.5 provides a list and brief definitions of nine dimensions that are commonly used in ACs. It is important to note that these dimensions are defined in terms of actual activities on the job. The definitions in Table 14.5 give brief summaries of the kinds of activities included. In actual use, the definitions are more detailed. For example, the dimension of *Tolerance for Stress* is often described in terms of the actions taken to meet specific multiple demands (e.g., from subordinates, superiors, outside pressure groups, etc.) and the specific multiple roles (e.g., negotiator, public relations specialist, performance evaluator, etc.) that characterize the job under study. These behaviors described for each dimension serve as the basis for the development of assessment devices to measure the dimension. It is easy to understand why

Table 14.5   *Behavioral Dimensions Frequently Measured in Assessment Centers*

Dimension	Definition
Oral Communication	Effective expression in individual or group situations (includes gestures and nonverbal communications)
Planning and Organizing	Establishing a course of action for self and/or others to accomplish a specific goal; planning proper assignments of personnel and appropriate allocation of resources
Delegation	Utilizing subordinates effectively; allocating decision making and other responsibilities to the appropriate subordinates
Control	Establishing procedures to monitor and/or regulate processes, tasks, or activities of subordinates and job activities and responsibilities; taking action to monitor the results of delegated assignments or projects
Decisiveness	Readiness to make decisions, render judgments, take action, or commit oneself
Initiative	Active attempts to influence events to achieve goals; self-starting rather than passive acceptance. Taking action to achieve goals beyond those called for; originating action
Tolerance for Stress	Stability of performance under pressure and/or opposition
Adaptability	Maintaining effectiveness in varying environments, with various tasks, responsibilities, or people
Tenacity	Staying with a position or plan of action until the desired objective is achieved or is no longer reasonably attainable

Source: George Thornton III and William Byham, *Assessment Centers and Managerial Performance* (New York: Academic Press, 1982).

ACs have relied heavily on performance tests as a primary measurement device; it is usually straightforward to translate these job activities into test activities. Because of the nature of managerial work, these performance tests are usually what we have called verbal performance tests.

In looking through the list of dimensions in Table 14.5, you probably have noticed that many of them have the same title as personality dimensions we discussed in Chapter 13. This should not be surprising. Remember that personality describes the interaction of an individual with his or her environment. Interaction is usually described in terms of activities. When AC dimensions identify either clusters of job activities completed with other organization members or activities to meet organization demands, these dimensions clearly approach the notion of personality dimensions. You might also remember that in Chapter 13 we pointed out that measurement of personality characteristics with paper-and-pencil tests is tenuous because written descriptions of behavior do not always correspond to actual behavior. We went on to say that a useful measurement strategy would be to collect actual behavioral data in job situations. In essence ACs, by using performance tests, attempt to do this. It is not surprising, therefore, that there is a close similarity between personality dimensions and the behavioral dimensions of assessment centers.

Traditional Assessment Devices Following the example of the AT&T assessment center, various paper-and-pencil tests and interviews have frequently been used, many of them being the types of tests we discussed in previous chapters. Because this chapter centers on performance tests, we will only generalize about the use of these traditional types of tests in ACs.

Intelligence or mental ability tests have been used not only in ACs but in several other managerial selection programs. Although results have varied somewhat depending on the specific test used, generally scores on these tests have been related to a variety of measures of managerial success and are usefully included in an AC. Personality tests, both objective and projective, have not been as successful and are commonly being omitted from recent ACs. As we have previously mentioned, the measurement limitations of these tests are great and more useful information about the candidate's behavior is supplied from the performance test.

The interview is also employed quite often in ACs; in many ways it is similar to the selection interview we recommended using in Chapter 11. Commonly referred to as the *Background Interview*, the emphasis of the AC interview is to gather information from the candidate about job activities that represent the behavioral dimensions being evaluated in the AC. The interviewer is to gather as much information as possible about these dimensions but not to evaluate the candidate's ability to perform the job. This is quite different from the usual selection interview. Many of the recommendations made in Chapter 11 for the use of the interview are incorporated in the AC Background Interview: each interview is structured and focuses on previous job behaviors, relatively few behavioral dimensions are utilized and multiple questions are prepared to tap each dimension, interviewers are trained to record relevant job actions for each behavioral dimension, and a formal scoring system is used to evaluate each candidate on each behavioral dimension. Used in this fashion, the interview has been shown to be very effective in contributing to the information generated from other AC devices to arrive at a final evaluation of a candidate.

Performance Tests   It is the use of performance tests, sometimes referred to as *simulation tests*, that distinguishes ACs from other selection programs. We will describe the most frequently used of these devices.

In-Basket   This is a paper-and-pencil test that is designed to replicate administrative tasks of the job under consideration. The name of the test is taken from the "in- and out-baskets" that are on some managers' desks and are used to hold organizational memos coming to and going from the managers.

The content of the administrative issues contained in the set of memos that make up the In-Basket should be obtained from job analysis information and should be representative of the actual administrative tasks of the position. Examples of typical In-Basket items are presented in Table 14.6. The In-Basket is completed individually and usually takes two to three hours. The candidate is seated at a desk in a private area on which is found the written material of the In-Basket. Usually no oral directions are given by the AC staff nor is there any interaction between AC staff and the candidate while the test is being taken.

The In-Basket has an introductory document that describes the situation in which the candidate finds himself or herself. This situation is some variation of the theme that the candidate has recently been placed in a position because of the sudden resignation, injury, or death of the previous incumbent. A number of memos, describing a variety of problems, have accumulated and must be addressed. Unfortunately, the candidate is also informed that he or she has made previous plans that cannot be changed that require leaving the company for the next several days. The candidate must, therefore, indicate what action should be taken about the issues in the memos by leaving written memos in the out-basket before departing. No other office members can be contacted. In addition to the memos, the candidate is provided with background information about the unit he or she is now managing through organization charts, mission statements, and company policy statements.

The memos themselves are presented on different types and sizes of paper and are both typed and handwritten to add realism. The candidate is to read the memos and to write his or her recommendation as to what action should be taken and which personnel should be involved. A standard time period is given each candidate. After the candidate has completed the test, he

Table 14.6   In-Basket Memos

TO: Management Employees

FROM: J. Bowditch, Corporate Accounting

RE: Budget Review

As you know, we are near the end of our fiscal year. At this time all managers should compare actual expenditures against the budget. Also estimate projected expenditures until year's end and report any variance. If we all work together, AMER Division can continue its fine record of operating within budget.

TO: R. Perloff

FROM: J. Ledvinka, Marketing

For the third time this year your Texas sales manager, L. Schoenfeldt, missed our regional sales meeting. He says he is training for the Waco-Dallas marathon and has your permission to miss meetings. Is this true? If it is, I hope the race is all downhill like his career in this company.

TO: E. Perloff

FROM: V. Gulbinas-Scarpello

This is to remind you that during the week of January 6–10, Jim Lahiff and Bob Finn will be attending a time-management seminar which they badly need. If I can remember, that week was busy last year because we got in all of the sales records for AMEX TRICARB sold over the holidays. Should I worry about this?

---

or she often is interviewed by one of the AC staff and asked to explain the overall philosophy used in addressing the memos and the reasoning behind the specific recommendations made for each administrative problem.

The written and oral information is used by the AC staff to evaluate decision-making behavioral dimensions, such as planning and organizing, ability to delegate, decisiveness, independence, and initiative.

Leaderless Group Discussion (LGD)   The In-Basket and the LGD together are probably the two most often-used performance tests in ACs. The LGD is designed to represent those managerial attributes that require the interaction of small groups of individuals to solve a problem successfully. In the LGD, participants are tested in groups of six. These six are seated around a conference table usually placed in the middle of a room. AC assessors are seated along the walls of the room to observe and record the behavior of the LGD participants.

The LGD has its name because no one member of the LGD is designated as the official leader or supervisor of the group. The meeting is one of equals faced with a common problem. This problem could emphasize either cooperation or competition among the six participants. A problem describing an employment situation in which the organization must issue a statement in response to charges of discrimination in hiring or lack of control of environmental pollutants would be an example of an emphasis on cooperative actions. Competitive problems are usually characterized by a small amount of some organizational resource (e.g., money for raises, new equipment, a one-time fund for capital investment, etc.), that is not large enough to satisfy the wishes of all LGD members. In both cases the group is provided with a written description of the issue together with relevant supporting material. The group is then usually charged with producing a written report that specifies the action to be taken by the company. In most cases 1½ to 2 hours is the maximum time allotted.

In addition to being classified as cooperative or competitive, the LGD problem can have either defined or undefined roles. Defined roles occur when each group member is given specific information, unknown to the others, that both describes his or her position in the company and provides additional information about the department or the individuals that the LGD participant is supposed to be representing. This information is to be used by the participant as he or she sees fit to influence the actions of the group. Unassigned roles are obviously those in which such information is not provided to each participant. Assigned roles are most commonly used in competitive LGD problems. Each member's role information is used to argue that the scarce resource should be allocated for that participant's purposes. Table 14.7 contains examples of a general problem and two assigned roles that could be used in such LGD situations. The LGD is used to measure behavioral dimensions such as oral communication, tolerance for stress, adaptability, resilience, energy, leadership, and persuasiveness.

Case Analysis   In case analysis exercises each participant is provided with a long description of an organizational problem which changes according to the job being considered in the AC. For a higher level position, the case frequently describes the history of certain events in a company, with relevant financial data, marketing strategy, and organizational structure. Frequently industry data concerning new products, consumer trends, and technology are introduced. The case focuses on a dilemma that the participant is asked to resolve. In doing so, specific recommendations must be given, supporting data presented, and any changes in company strategy detailed.

The content of the case is varied to be appropriate for the position being considered. For middle-management jobs the major issue frequently revolves around the design and implementation of operational plans or systems, for example, management information systems or job process systems. For first-level management, the focus often is either on the resolution of subordinate conflicts, subordinate nonconformity with policies, or reevaluation of specific work methods. After the candidate has been given time to read and analyze

Table 14.7   *Leaderless Group Discussion Problem*

Problem: Because of an unexpected resignation, your department has $5,000 available to use as one-time bonuses for department personnel. Your group is to submit a written recommendation as to how this money should be allocated.

Assigned
   Role #1:   Archie Carroll, Administrative Coordinator

Your assistant, Hugh Watson, has performed excellently in the last eight months. On his own time he has taken two mini-courses on office automation equipment to become familiar with differences among products that you are considering buying. His recommendations were valuable in saving $1,700 in the purchase of two electronic mail processing units. His other work is also impressive. He is currently receiving only $1,200 a year more than a senior secretary, even though you assign him much more responsibility.

Assigned
   Role #2:   John Hatfield, MIS Coordinator

Jamie Cox has been with the company for 18 months, coming directly from college. In the last six months he has made significant contributions to the development of an improved inventory control system. He not only wrote the programs but also led the training of the users of the system. At the most recent staff meeting, four people commented on how much time they have saved in scheduling because of the accuracy of the system. Recently Jamie has been offered a position with Auburn, Inc. at a $5,000/yr. increase. Because of several personal reasons, he has indicated that he would prefer to remain with you if the pay difference could be reduced.

the case, he or she may be asked to prepare a written report, make an oral presentation to AC staff members, or discuss the case with other participants. The primary dimensions usually evaluated are oral and written communication, planning and organizing, control, decisiveness, resilience, and analysis.

The Training of Assessors

As has been discussed previously, the scoring of the verbal performance tests that characterize ACs is usually more difficult than the scoring of motor performance tests. Therefore, for an AC to be useful as a selection device, the training of the staff members, referred to as assessors, who have the responsibility of observing and evaluating the behavior of the participants, is crucial. As has been pointed out, the focus of ACs is on the behavioral dimensions. The exercises are designed to require the participants to provide behaviors relative to these dimensions. Each dimension must be measured by more than one exercise. Also each exercise usually measures more than one dimension. The major duty of an assessor is to record the behavior of a participant in an exercise and use the data to rate the participant on each behavioral dimension appropriate for the exercise. For example, if the LGD is designed to measure the dimensions of oral communication, adaptability, and persuasiveness, the assessor must use his or her observations of the actions of a participant in the LGD problem to rate the participant on these dimensions. Usually the rating is done on a five-point scale.

In most cases, there are one-half as many assessors in an AC as there are participants. These assessors are also usually managers within the organization who are in positions one level above the position of interest for the AC. In this way it is assumed that the assessors are very familiar with the job and the behaviors required in the job. After recording and judging the participants' behavior in the AC, and after all exercises have been completed, the whole group of assessors comes together to discuss their observations. The ratings and data gathered by each assessor are used to develop group or consensus judgments of each participant on each behavioral dimension. These consensus ratings are then used to develop an overall rating of the acceptability of each candidate for the position of interest. The major difficulty in having managers within the organization perform these activities is that, even though they are very knowledgeable about the job behavior, they are usually unskilled in systematically observing behaviors representative of each dimension and then using the behavior to develop ratings. It is to develop these skills that assessor training programs are developed. If assessors are not adequately trained in these observation and rating methods, the value of the AC evaluation is lessened.

William Byham has written an excellent, detailed description of the training of assessors.[17] Much of the material in the following paragraphs is drawn from his ideas. Essentially this training is to develop the six key abilities listed in Table 14.8. We will describe some methods for doing this.

Understanding the Behavioral Dimensions   As has been mentioned, one fundamental part of an AC is the determination of which behavioral dimensions of the job are to be evaluated. These should be dimensions that are

---

Table 14.8   *Abilities To Be Developed In Training Assessors*

- Understanding the behavioral dimensions

- Observing the behavior of participants

- Categorizing participant behavior as to appropriate behavioral dimensions

- Judging the quality of participant behavior

- Determining the rating of participants on each behavioral dimension across the exercises

- Determining the overall evaluation of participants across all behavioral dimensions

---

representative and important to the job. The first step in training assessors is, therefore, to have them become thoroughly familiar with the dimensions. Frequently this is done by providing assessors with a clear and detailed definition of each. Time is then spent discussing each dimension within the group. The major goal is to insure that all assessors have a common understanding of the dimensions. Frequently dimensions such as adaptability, decisiveness, tolerance for stress, etc., have different meanings for different individuals.

An example of a definition that could be used for an AC focused on first-line supervisors is the following:

> *Tolerance for Stress* — stability of performance under pressure and/or opposition. At times behavior is directed toward individuals who are angry or hostile because of a work situation. A first-line supervisor finds himself/herself in a stressful situation because of two main factors: multiple demands on the work unit which must be completed at approximately the same deadline, and the joint roles he/she must play as a representative of management to nonmanagement employees and also the representative of nonmanagement employees to management.

Observing the Behavior of Participants   After the assessors have become familiar with the dimensions to be used in the AC, the next step is to train them to observe and record behavior. The initial tendency of most managers when they first become assessors is immediately to make evaluative judgments about the performance of participants in the AC exercises. For example, when observing a LGD problem, a common reaction is to make the judgment that a participant can or cannot handle stress. However, such immediate judgments are dysfunctional to the purpose of the AC. An AC, you will remember, is to provide multiple exercises or opportunities for participants to demonstrate behaviors that exemplify the dimensions under study.

These demonstrated behaviors of a participant are the crucial information collected in the AC. When the assessors come together after the exercises have been completed, they discuss the behavior of a participant and then form ratings. For this reason if assessors make judgments about the behavior of the participant rather than record the actual behavior, the purpose of the group meeting of assessors is limited.

This step in training, therefore, is designed to overcome the tendency of assessors to form immediate judgments and instead to focus on recording the behavior of the participant. Commonly this step has two parts. One part explains to the assessors in detail the differences between recording behavior and making judgments by providing examples of each. Often a list of statements is prepared about each of the dimensions and the assessor is asked to indicate whether the statement reflects behavior or judgment. The following provides an example:

Dimension: Tolerance for Stress

Indicate whether each of the following is a statement of a participant's behavior or a statement of an assessor's judgment.

Participant Behavior	Assessor Judgment	
	✓	Resolved the conflict quietly
✓		Listened to the explanations of both parties as to how the conflict started
✓		Offered some tentative suggestions as to changes that could be made
	✓	Broke down when the argument heated up

After the meaning of the term *behavior* is clear, the second step of training
presents examples of participants' behavior in the exercises for the assessors
to practice recording behaviors. These examples can be taken from either live
exercises or videotaped exercises. The advantage of a videotaped exercise is
that it can be stopped at specific points or parts can be replayed for discussion.

Categorizing Participant Behavior   The next phase of training merges the
first two steps. In this phase the assessor learns to record the behavior of the
participant under the proper dimension. The purpose of this is to insure that
assessors are consistent in recording participant behaviors that are examples
of the dimensions. This consistency is also essential to the reliability and
validity of the ratings.

For the most part, training in this phase centers around both descriptions and discussions of the behavior representative of each dimension and
also demonstrations of these behaviors. In terms of descriptions, assessors
are provided with material that briefly defines each dimension and also presents a list of behaviors that are representative of both high and low levels of
the dimension. Such a list may take the following form:

Tolerance for Stress — stability of performance under pressure and/or
opposition.

Examples:
When engaging the two arguing parties, participant soon began
screaming at the two.
Suggested that the two arguing parties walk with him or her to an
unoccupied conference room.

Asked the individuals observing the arguing parties to return to work stations.

Physically grabbed nearest arguing party and pulled him or her from the area.

A list of the representative behaviors is prepared for each dimension and is reviewed in group discussion among the assessors. Other example behaviors are also frequently generated during this time. In some cases the assessors are then provided with a list of recorded behaviors that have been drawn from previous ACs and are asked to indicate which dimension is identified by the described behavior. The correct answers are reviewed by the group and differences of opinion discussed. The last part of training for this step has the assessors observe either a live set of exercises or a videotaped set and record the behaviors that demonstrate each dimension. A group discussion of the records is also conducted.

Judging the Quality of Participant Behavior This portion of training attempts to develop consistency among assessors in the use of rating scales to evaluate the behavior of participants on the dimensions. In most ACs each dimension is rated using the following six-point scale:

5 — a great deal of the dimension was shown (excellent)

4 — quite a lot of the dimension was shown

3 — a moderate amount of the dimension was shown (average)

2 — only a small amount of the dimension was shown

1 — very little was shown or this dimension was not shown at all (poor)

0 — no opportunity existed for this dimension to be shown.

The major problem in using a scale such as this is to develop a common frame of reference among assessors such that each will assign the same scale point to the same observed behaviors. This is a problem common to the use of rating scales in other personal activities (e.g., performance appraisal, scoring interviews, assessing training needs, etc.). Training in ACs revolves around providing examples of behavior that are representative of scale points for each dimension. Frequently these example behaviors are drawn from other ACs.

In doing this the group of assessors is presented with either written descriptions or videotapes of examples of behaviors and asked to rate this set of behaviors on all appropriate dimensions. After each assessor has completed the ratings, a discussion follows that brings out any differences in ratings. This discussion is intended to identify common definitions of each scale point. It is usually the case that when practicing managers are used as assessors, this phase of the training is completed quite easily. Often such managers have a common viewpoint as to what constitutes extremely good or extremely poor behaviors on the dimension. For example, most assessors agree that physically grabbing a person that is confronting the participant is an unsatisfactory demonstration of tolerance for stress. More difficulty arises in arriving at a consensus for the middle scale points. Even in this case, however, a common understanding is reached fairly quickly, owing greatly to the common work experiences of the assessors.

Determining Dimension and Overall Evaluation Ratings   We will combine the discussion of the last two stages of assessor training. The training in each of these stages is similar in that it involves the use of rating scales and it draws heavily on the training discussed in the previous stage.

After participant behaviors for any one AC exercise are described appropriately on the dimensions, the next task is to combine the data on the same dimension across two or more exercises. For example, say that planning and organization are gathered on three different exercises. Assessors must learn to combine these data into *one overall dimension rating.* Training again is primarily based both on group discussions to form a common frame of reference and several examples that serve as trials. Differences in ratings are fully discussed. Such factors as consistency of demonstrated behavior across exercises, how good each exercise is at bringing out a variety of behaviors, and the strength and duration of behaviors become relevant in forming overall dimension ratings.

The last training step is how to use the final dimension ratings to form the *overall rating* of the participant to perform the job. Job analysis information is critical for this. From the job analysis, it can be determined which dimensions are the most critical or the most frequently used in the job. The dimensions are then weighted more heavily than other dimensions in producing the overall rating of acceptability. As a means of training for these last two steps, assessor groups are often required to complete a mock assessment of a small group of candidates under the observation of experienced assessors.

The Effectiveness of Assessment Centers

Validity   As we have discussed, the major purpose of ACs is to evaluate the potential of individuals for management positions. In many organizations the overall assessment of each AC participant is placed in corporate files, and/or summarized for the participant's current immediate supervisor, and communicated directly to the participant. When these participants are then considered for higher level positions, this information is frequently made available together with other data. Such practice, however, presents a problem in evaluating the validity of ACs in predicting managerial success. If the AC evaluations are made known, it is impossible to determine how much effect

these evaluations had on the selection decision. This issue is sometimes referred to as the "Crown Prince Syndrome." If the AC evaluation does affect
the selection decision, then the rating creates a self-fulfilling prophecy.

There have been a few studies, most of them at AT&T, that have
avoided this problem by not releasing the results of the AC to anyone, even
the participants themselves. In general these studies have been supportive of
the AC's accuracy in predicting the career advancement of individuals. The
most famous of such studies is the AT&T Management Progress Study we
discussed previously. In this case the AC was used to predict the advancement of each participant into middle-level management within 10 years.
Eight years after the study had begun it was shown that a significantly high
percentage of those individuals who had been predicted to move into middle
management had in fact done so as compared to the percentage of those who
had been predicted not to move that far but who, in fact, had. When the
sample was categorized into college graduates and noncollege graduates and
each sample analyzed separately, the same patterns of significant differences
were identified.

Other studies that also have investigated AC results have reported similar favorable findings. For example, a study of 47 IBM participants found a
significant correlation between AC ratings and the level of management attained by each participant eight years later.[18] Another study at AT&T focused on identifying successful salesmen rather than managers.[19] An AC was
set up to simulate tasks representative of AT&T communications consultants and 78 men completed the exercise. Six months later, after these 78
participants had been placed in a sales position, their actual sales behavior
was evaluated by a field-review team. Again, there was strong agreement
between the AC evaluation and these ratings of sales behavior. Other studies
have also reported significant relationships between AC evaluations and
other variables such as salary level and various measures of overall job performance.

Adverse Impact   Another positive feature of ACs is their generally favorable support by the courts and the EEOC in alleged discrimination cases. For
example, in the much publicized sex discrimination case against AT&T, ACs
were identified as a method to use in changing AT&T's promotion policies.[20]
The essence of the discrimination charge was the adverse treatment of females in promotion through management ranks. Under the agreement between AT&T and the EEOC, ACs were extensively used to identify those
females who were most likely to be successful in higher management positions.

There have also been a few discrimination cases that have directly evaluated the use of ACs in selection. In *Berry v. City of Omaha*, ACs were used in
selection for the position of Deputy Police Chief. The main issue was
whether the three different assessor groups that evaluated candidates used
different standards in evaluating participants.[21] After reviewing descriptions

of the development of the AC and data analysis regarding reliability among assessors, the court upheld the use of the AC. In another case, *The Richmond Black Police Officers Association v. the City of Richmond,* the use of an AC for selection for supervisory positions in both the police and the fire departments was upheld. Of interest in this case was that a combination of written tests and the AC was used in selection. Evidence indicating that the paper-and-pencil tests were discriminatory was presented. However, final selection decisions were based on both sets of devices and these final decisions were not discriminatory.[22] In this case the nondiscriminatory features of the AC compensated for the discriminatory characteristics of the written tests.

One study of the performance of white females and black females in an AC did find differences in the assessors' judgments between the two groups in favor of the white females.[23] Further investigation indicated, however, that there were also differences between the two groups in job performance rated by supervisors. The white group was rated significantly higher than the black group. In addition, there was no significant difference in the correlation between AC evaluations and job performance ratings for the two groups. The conclusion, therefore, was that even though the black females performed less well in the AC, no discrimination was evidenced because these differences were also reflected in subsequent job performance.

Criticism of ACs   These findings of the general validity of ACs and their lack of adverse impact does not mean that their use is without some criticism. Generally such criticism has taken two forms. The first is that an AC is very expensive to develop and maintain and, if selection among applicants is its only use, there might be alternative methods that are much less expensive. John Hinrichs raised such an issue when he compared the correlation of AC evaluations with management level attained with the correlation of ratings obtained only from evaluations of personnel files with a job success measure.[24] Both correlations were statistically significant but not different from one another. If the same accuracy of prediction is possible, it would be more sensible to use the least expensive method.

Following similar reasoning, Donald Brush and Lyle Schoenfeldt have described an integrated appraisal system to generate information comparable to that yielded by assessment centers.[25] Their approach consists of the following parts: job analysis to establish the critical tasks and abilities of each managerial position, training line managers in assessing behavior of subordinates on critical dimensions identified in the job analysis, and systematic procedures for obtaining and evaluating the assessment data supplied by these line managers. Brush and Schoenfeldt explain that dimensions closely related to the behavioral dimensions measured in assessment centers can be constructed and that such actual job performance tasks as management presentations, completion of reports, unit productivity, and quality of employee performance reviews can be substituted for assessment center exercises. One advantage of this is to eliminate the coaching of participants before they attend the assessment center by colleagues who have previously completed the assessment process. Their conclusion is that it is possible to use data currently available in organizations to yield comparable selection data that is content valid at a lower cost than assessment centers.

The second area of criticism focuses on the reliability of assessors' dimension ratings of participants across the various situational tests. There is some evidence that assessors' ratings of the same dimension across multiple exercises in an AC do not correlate highly.[26] Other data indicate that in some performance tests within an AC, different groups of assessors do not strongly agree on their ratings of the same participants. Also participants do not always receive the same ratings when they complete two similar forms of the same performance exercise.[27] Such criticisms need more investigation but could certainly have major implications for the training of assessors and the kinds of dimensions used in ACs.

References for Chapter 14

[1] Paul Wernimont and John Campbell, "Sign, Samples, and Criteria," *Journal of Applied Psychology* 52 (1968): 372–376.

[2] James Asher and James Sciarrino, "Realistic Work Sample Tests: A Review," *Personnel Psychology* 27 (1974): 519–533.

[3] David Robinson, "Content-oriented Personnel Selection in a Small Business Setting," *Personnel Psychology* 34 (1981): 77–87.

[4] Robert Gatewood and Lyle F. Schoenfeldt, "Content Validity and EEOC: A Useful Alternative for Selection," *Personnel Journal* 56 (1977): 520–528.

[5] Lynnette B. Plumlee, *A Short Guide to the Development of Performance Tests* (Washington, D.C.: Personnel Research and Development Center, U.S. Civil Service Commission, Professional Series 75-1, January 1975).

[6] Joseph L. Boyd and Benjamin Shimberg, *Handbook of Performance Testing* (Princeton, N.J.: Educational Testing Service, 1971), p. 24.

[7] Plumlee, *A Short Guide to the Development of Performance Tests*, p. 27.

[8] James E. Campion, "Work Sampling for Personnel Selection," *Journal of Applied Psychology* 56 (1972): 40–44.

[9] Asher and Sciarrino, "Realistic Work Sample Tests: A Review," pp. 519–533.

[10] Michael F. Gordon and Lawrence S. Kleiman, "The Prediction of Trainability Using a Work Sample Test and an Aptitude Test: A Direct Comparison." *Personnel Psychology* 29 (1976): 243–253.

[11] Frank Schmidt, Alan Greenthol, John Hunter, John Berner, and Felicia Seaton, "Job Sample vs. Paper-and-pencil Trade and Technical Tests: Adverse Impact and Examiner Attitudes," *Personnel Psychology* 30 (1977): 187–197.

[12] Wayne Cascio and Niel Phillips, "Performance Testing: A Rose Among Thorns?" *Personnel Psychology* 32 (1979): 751–766.

[13] Task Force on Assessment Center Standards, "Standards and Ethical Considerations for Assessment Center Operations," *The Personnel Administrator* 25 (1980): 35–38.

[14] George C. Thornton, III and William C. Byham, *Assessment Centers and Managerial Performance* (New York: Academic Press, 1982), p. 23.

[15] Ibid., p. 28.

[16] Douglas W. Bray, Richard J. Campbell, and Donald L. Grant, *Formative Years in Business: A Long-term AT&T Study of Managerial Lives* (Huntington, N.Y.: Robert E. Kriegor Publishing Company, 1979), p. 6.

[17] William C. Byham, "Assessor Selection and Training," *Applying the Assessment Center Method*, ed. J.L. Moses and W. C. Byham (New York: Pergamon Press, 1977), pp. 89–126.

[18] John R. Hinrichs, "An Eight-Year Follow-up of a Management Assessment Center," *Journal of Applied Psychology* 63 (1978): 596–601.

[19] Douglas W. Bray and Richard J. Campbell, "Selection of Salesmen by Means of an Assessment Center," *Journal of Applied Psychology* 52 (1968): 36–41.

[20] "Landmark AT&T-EEOC Consent Agreement Increases Assessment Center Usage," *Assessment & Development* 1 (1973): 1–2.

[21] *Berry v. City of Omaha*, 14 FEP 391 (1977).

[22] Thornton and Byham, *Assessment Centers and Managerial Performance*, p. 383.

[23] James R. Hock and Douglas W. Bray, "Management Assessment Center Evaluation and Subsequent Job Performance of White and Black Females," *Personnel Psychology* 29 (1976): 13–30.

[24] Hinrichs, "An Eight-Year Follow-up of a Management Assessment Center," pp. 596–601.

[25] Donald H. Brush and Lyle F. Schoenfeldt, "Identifying Managerial Potential: An Alternative to Assessment Centers," *Personnel* 26 (1980): 68–76.

[26] Paul R. Sackett and George F. Dreher, "Constructs and Assessment Center Dimensions: Some Troubling Empirical Findings," *Journal of Applied Psychology* 67 (1982): 401–410.

[27] Harry W. Hennessey, Jr. and Robert D. Gatewood, "An Experimental Investigation of the Reliability of Assessors' Judgments in Leaderless Group Discussion Problems," paper presented at the Academy of Management Annual Meeting, Boston, Mass., 1984.

PART FIVE

Criteria Measures

As has been stated more times in this book than any of us would wish to count, the ultimate test of appropriateness of a selection program is how well those selected perform on the job. As Hugo Munsterberg, the German-born psychologist who did much early work in selection, might say, "Toll" (awesome). Just as selection instruments should be properly constructed to obtain the most useful information about applicants, job performance measures should be carefully developed to obtain accurate data. If this is not done, the adequacy of the selection program may be criticized inappropriately. The program itself could be suitable, with the data used to evaluate the job performance of those selected being flawed. This chapter is intended to:

1. Describe the various measures that may be used to determine job performance
2. Discuss the appropriate use of each type of measure
3. Detail the important characteristics of whatever measure is used

15

Measurement of

Worker Performance

One fact that should be apparent by now is that the results of empirical validation studies are crucially important for understanding several of the major topics in selection. For example, these results have provided the most complete way of learning about the proper use of many selection instruments, such as semi-structured vs. unstructured interviews, scored vs. unscored application information, and behavioral vs. written personality measures. Validation results have also been used for analyzing socio-political topics that have national interest, such as differential validity and validity generalization.

Parallel to this is the importance of this type of information for selection programs in individual firms. As we pointed out many pages ago in Chapter 1, validation is the most direct way of determining if the selection program works the way it should for the organization. It answers the question, "Is there a relationship between performance on the selection instruments and performance on the job?" Also validation is one of the more effective ways of defending a firm's selection program against charges of illegal discrimination. We can see, then, that validation has uses for both selection researchers and practitioners.

In previous chapters we discussed two of the major parts of validation work: (a) the statistical procedures necessary to conduct validity studies (Chapter 5), and (b) the methods of developing predictor measures (Chapters 9 to 14). In this chapter we turn our attention to the third part of validation, the criteria measures. These are the instruments used to measure the job performance of individual workers. The adequacy of criteria measures is as important to validation work as is the adequacy of predictor measures, even though much more work has gone into the study of predictors. The purpose of this chapter is to present several topics that are necessary to understand for the development of sound criteria: the strengths and limitations of the major types of performance data, the essential characteristics of any measure that is used, and the EEO implications for these measures.

Types of Job Performance Measures

There are a number of different types of job performance measures that can be used singly or in combination as a criterion measure. We will present an overview of each of these major types and discuss its use in selection. For a more detailed treatment of each type, recent books such as *The Measurement of Work Performance Methods, Theory, and Application* by Frank Landy and James Farr, *Increasing Productivity Through Performance Appraisal* by Gary Latham and Kenneth Wexley, and *Performance Appraisal: Assessing Human Behavior at Work* by John Bernardin and Richard Beatty are excellent sources.[1]

One way of presenting the various types of job performance measures is to group them according to the nature of the data gathered. This forms the following four categories:

1. Production data—quality, quantity of output, etc.

2. Personnel data—lateness, absenteeism, turnover, etc.

3. Training proficiency—a specially developed test or simulation of training information or activities

4. Judgmental data—supervisors' opinions of subordinates' performance, etc.

Each of these four categories may be further subdivided, as will be seen in the following discussion.

Production Data

This category consists of the results of work. The data comprise things that can be counted, seen, and compared directly from one worker to another. Other terms that have been used to describe these data are *output, objective,* and *nonjudgmental performance measures.* Such measures are usually based upon the specific nature of the job tasks, and quite different measures have been used for the same job title. The variety of measures that can be used is actually so great that it is not possible to summarize them in any representative manner. Instead, Table 15.1 contains a list of job titles and some of the various production criteria measures that have been used for each title. It is

Table 15.1   *Production Criteria Measures for Various Jobs*

Job Title	Production Measure Quantity	Quality
Key punch operator	Number of columns punched per hour	Number of errors per hour
Skilled machine operator	Number of units produced per week	Number of defects
	Weight of output per week	Weight of scrap
Salesperson	Dollar volume of sales	Number of cancelled orders
	Number of orders	Number of returns
Manager	Profit of unit	Number of grievances filed by subordinates

apparent from this table that data about both quantity and quality of production have been used. Quantity is usually expressed in terms of the number of units produced within a specified time period. Quality is, in a way, indirectly measured by the number of defects, errors, or mistakes identified either per number of units or amount of time.

Many consider the use of production data as the most desirable type of measure for a number of reasons. First, such data are often easy to gather because they are collected routinely for business operations such as production, planning, and budgeting. Also, the importance of such measures is thought to be obvious. Production data are the direct result of job actions. They are the objectives of the work process. Finally, these data are thought to be unchallengeable and easily accepted by workers. Production output can be seen and counted, and, therefore, no argument can be made about its measurement.

Our opinion is that such enthusiasm about production data as criteria measures is not entirely justified. None of these four major categories of work measurement data is without limitation. Each is appropriate in some circumstances and inappropriate in others. We will discuss some of the limitations in the use of production data to illustrate this point.

Consider first the argument of the ease of gathering the data through commonly used business operations. Frequently such operations are concerned with the records of total work units as opposed to individuals. For example, budgeting usually compares a departmental unit's actual production and cost to a projection of these variables. Production planning frequently is concerned with the optimum movement of goods through various stages of the manufacturing process. In neither case is attention paid to the individual worker, especially if he or she frequently moves to different work stations. To gather accurate, individual data is not always possible, even with much added effort.

The assumption that production data are countable and, therefore, indisputable, is also tenuous. As Table 15.1 indicates, there are numerous measures that are used for sales performance. All seem to be straightforward measures that would be acceptable to those concerned. However, the literature and the practice of sales management contradict such a notion. There is a consensus in sales work that sales performance is closely related to the characteristics of the territory that is worked. Such items as population, store density, socio-economic status of customers, number of competitors, amount of advertising, etc., are all relevant characteristics.

Various modifications of sales records have been suggested to control for these differences in territory. One of the most popular is to calculate monthly sales as a percentage of a quota set for the territory.[2] Quotas are usually determined by the sales manager. However, this assumes that the judgment of the sales manager is accurate and acceptable to all. Another adjustment is to divide sales volume by years that the salesperson is in the territory.[3] The rationale is that as a salesperson learns the territory, sales should increase rather than merely staying level. This simplified judgment may not be acceptable to all.

Similar issues have been raised regarding the production data of managers. Several studies, especially those of assessment centers, have used rate or level of promotion or salary increase as job performance measures. The assumption is that high performance by a manager will result in promotion and salary increase. Such an assumption probably is not totally accurate because labor market availability, job tenure, and area of specialization are all known to affect compensation and promotion.

The major point of all this is to say that production measures have frequently been used in validation studies and are desirable mainly because of their direct relationship to job activities. However, these measures are often limited either by lack of availability or by variations in the work situation. While the former may prevent measurement entirely, the latter frequently complicates validation work. Most correction factors require that a manager make a judgment about how to adjust the raw data to minimize the effect of these differences in work situations. Different correction factors can vary considerably in their effects on measurements of performance. In these cases, the objectivity of the data and its direct relationship to job activities may be questionable.

Personnel Data

Absenteeism, turnover, grievances, and accidents are the variables that are grouped into the second type of performance data, personnel data. These variables are similar in many ways to production data. They are usually collected as part of other personnel data files, almost always on an individual basis. In addition, they are reflective of important aspects of work behavior — attendance, after all, seems to be a prerequisite for performance. Finally, the data for these variables are countable and seemingly objective.

The drawbacks of these variables are their limited applicability across jobs and the many variations of measures that have been applied to them. Limited applicability means that these measures have been used as criteria measures mainly for lower-level jobs in which attendance at specific times is critical to performance. Assembly jobs on manufacturing lines, clerical positions, and some retail sales clerk positions are all examples. However, it is thought that, in general, personnel data are less meaningful for professional, managerial, and technical jobs in which performance is not clearly linked to time.

The difficulty with variations in the measures that have been used for these concepts is that these variations do not always agree in the results generated. We will discuss the variations that have been used for each major variable to explain this difficulty more fully.

Absenteeism   The most frequently used measures of absenteeism have been:

1. Number of separate instances
2. Total number of days absent
3. Number of short absences (one or two days)
4. Blue Mondays (occurrence of a one-day absence on a Monday)[4]

A major concern in these measures has been the distinction between voluntary and involuntary absences. Involuntary absences are usually thought of as those due to severe illness, jury duty, union activities, death in the immediate family, and vacation. Voluntary absences are all other absences. Presumably the distinction is made to differentiate between absences that workers have control over and others that they do not. A high frequency of the former indicates conscious restriction of output. The latter, while not desirable, may only reflect unfortunate circumstances that affect a worker.

We can see how this distinction is reflected in the four measures identified above. Counting the number of short absences or the number of Mondays missed is clearly an attempt to measure voluntary absences. The assumption is that a majority of each type of absence is taken by the employee to avoid work. The number of separate instances of absenteeism, logically, reflects the same idea. Presumably, undesirable workers are absent more times than desirable ones. Therefore, only frequency of instances are recorded. The number of days missed each time is irrelevant in this measure as is the reason for absence. The measure of the total number of days absent makes a different assumption. Time off is undesirable for whatever reason. Moreover, if one assumes that illness is evenly distributed in the population of workers, much of the difference among individuals is a function of voluntary absences.

Even without spending a great deal of effort in examining these various assumptions, it is obvious that each categorizes and counts items differently.

One could take the same set of personnel employee data records and construct widely different sets of criteria measures by using all four of the previous definitions. Another problem in the use of any of the four is the length of the time period to use for measurement. In most organizations, absenteeism is controlled within specified limits. Most employees realize that flagrant or repeated absenteeism, especially within a short time period, would prompt a reaction from the organization. Therefore, it has tentatively been concluded that absence data should be accumulated over at least one year to be useful.[5]

These points emphasize that the use of absenteeism as a performance measure requires judgmental assumptions by the user. The most difficult aspect is to define a measurement process that corresponds to the concept of interest. This means that the personnel specialist must first decide if total absences or only voluntary absences are intended as the criterion. As we have seen, this decision leads to a choice among several similar, but not identical, measures. The specialist must then decide which measure best suits the circumstances of the selection situation. Choosing an acceptable time period for data collection is a little easier but not without problems. The one-year recommendation is based on partial data and recognizes that other periods may be used depending on employment circumstances.

Turnover　　This is a measure of permanent separation from the organization. We have mentioned that turnover is a frequently used criterion in validation studies of weighted application blanks. In general, its use in selection is very similar to the use of absence data. A primary question is whether to separate turnover data into voluntary/involuntary categories or use the data without such a distinction. Voluntary usually means resignation despite the opportunity for continued employment; involuntary means termination by the organization for any of several reasons. Frequently it is desirable in validation work that turnover be applied to those who left without any pressure from the organization. Roughly speaking, stability of employment is the behavior sought. However, measures of this concept can quickly become complicated. If the company has dismissed employees because of an economic downturn, these terminations should not be counted as voluntary.

It is not always clear how to classify the remaining cases of separation. Some workers are allowed to resign rather than be terminated. On paper these would look like voluntary turnover even though they are not. Similarly, at the perceived threat of dismissal for either financial or performance reasons, some employees may seek other jobs and resign from the company. These, too, appear to be voluntary, yet this behavior was prompted by the organization's actions and might not have occurred otherwise.

As with absences, another issue is the time period for which data should be accumulated. The most acceptable strategy is to use a constant time period for all workers, for example the first 12 months of employment. The other option is to collect data for a 12-month calendar interval (e.g., 1986) for a group of workers, ignoring differences as to when each joined the company.

This second strategy is generally unacceptable because it is known that the probability of resigning decreases with increasing tenure. This would distort the data collected under the second strategy. We used a one-year time period in this example because that is the interval that has been used most often in validation programs. Other time periods could be equally acceptable, depending on employment circumstances such as length and cost of training.

Grievances   A grievance is an employee's complaint against some aspect of management behavior or personnel administration. These have been used as criteria measures for supervisor and management selection. Theoretically, a large number of grievances would indicate poor treatment of subordinates and/or inferior management decision making. Grievance systems exist almost always as part of a union-management contract. In these agreements the steps and procedures for filing a grievance are outlined.

When grievances are used as job performance measures, the assumption must be made that the tendency to file a grievance is equal among all work groups and that the working conditions related to grievances are also equal for all work groups. In reality, neither assumption is likely to be true. For example, working conditions vary dramatically within the same organization. Safety hazards, amount of overtime, job pressure, and ambiguity of task objectives are just a few conditions that could be correlated with grievances. Also, individuals and work groups can differ in their willingness to file grievances and engage in open confrontation. In fact, one study has found that the number of grievances is at least as much a function of the union steward's personality as they are an indication of management performance.[6] As was true in the use of turnover, it may be best to limit the use of grievances to a constant time period during a supervisor's career, job, or assignment to a new work group. For example, the first year may be used. Using a calendar year, in which the sample of managers would be at different points in their work experience, could introduce error into the measurement.

Accidents   Accidents are usually measured either in terms of injury to the worker or damage to the equipment being used (e.g., car, truck, etc.). In either case some threshold of damage must be exceeded before the incident is classified as an accident. For personal injury, usually a medical determination of damage that prevents working on the job for some period of time is required. In the case of equipment damage, frequently some dollar amount of repair (e.g., $100) must be exceeded before the incident is recorded. The assumption is made that the worker's carelessness precipitated the accident.

Even more than in the use of other personnel data, such assumptions are probably not valid. Jobs differ in inherent hazards, equipment differs in its operating condition, and employees differ in the amount of safety training they have received. There is no easy way of removing these factors from accident rates. The only way to overcome them is to equalize their occurrence within the sample. For example, a group of long-distance truck drivers may be measured usefully on accidents if they receive a standardized training program, drive approximately the same schedules and locations, and operate equally maintained trucks. If such conditions cannot be used, accident rates are questionable as criteria measures. This is underscored by the studies that have failed to find accident-proneness as a stable worker characteristic and have concluded that a large proportion of accidents are situationally determined.

Training Proficiency

Arguments for Its Use A seldom used but very desirable criterion measure is training proficiency, that is, a measure of employees' performance immediately after completing a training program. We pointed out in our discussion of ability tests in Chapter 12 that over the 50+ years in Edwin Ghishelli's study, training proficiency criteria had been used for each of the occupational groups studied.[7] If the reader remembers, Ghishelli found that training proficiency demonstrated higher validities than did the various other criteria of job performance. In addition, our discussion of the legal issues of selection in Chapter 2 mentioned that in at least two court rulings, *Spurlock v. United Airlines* and *Washington v. Davis*, the acceptable use of training measures as criteria was directly pointed out. In addition, the EEOC *Uniform Guidelines* explicitly state that the use of training proficiency is permissible. Despite these points, the reported use of these measures in recent validation studies has been infrequent.

There are strong arguments for the use of training measures that can explain Ghishelli's very positive findings. Essentially these arguments point out the increased control that the selection specialist has in the measurement process and the resulting reduction in error of measurement. This would be expected to increase the magnitude of the validity coefficient.

The first of these arguments focuses on the amount of standardization possible in this form of criterion measurement. The most common sequence of events in using training proficiency is to select the employees, place them in a training program, and at the end of training, but before job assignment, administer some measure(s) of mastery of training. In such a sequence it is possible to first design a formal training program that is consistent for all employees, even if they are at different physical locations. Companies commonly develop instruction booklets, films, exercises, etc., that are sent to several cities. In addition, the training instructors can be trained in the sequencing of topics and specific instructional methodologies. Perhaps most important, standardized measures of proficiency can be developed and used. All of these factors would reduce measurement errors that would adversely affect validity coefficients.

A second argument is that validity coefficients between predictors and

training measures are oftentimes clearer indicators of the relationship between KSAs and work level than are validity coefficients using other criteria
measures. To explain this let us start with a point we made in Chapter 1. In
discussing the inherent limitations in developing and evaluating selection
programs, the statement was made that usually the adequacy of selection is
judged in terms of the level of actual job performance achieved. However, the
management literature is filled with organizational factors other than worker
KSAs that affect work performance. This means that performance levels
could possibly be influenced by these other factors even though the selection
program itself is basically sound. In measurement terms this means that the
validity coefficient between selection devices and job performance measures
could be artificially lowered by these factors. This is, in fact, the finding of
Ghishelli's studies that we presented in Chapter 12, that validity coefficients
using job performance as criteria measures were lower, often greatly lower,
than coefficients using training proficiency. One explanation of these findings
is that there is less opportunity for other organizational factors to operate
when training proficiency is used because of the brief time that has elapsed.
The training proficiency measure, therefore, is influenced more by the workers' KSAs and less by the organizational factors. This is clearly a desirable
state of affairs for attempts to validate selection programs.

Measures   There are three basic measures that can be used in quantifying
training proficiency. All assume that the training program is representative of
the job itself. This may seem to be a superfluous statement. However, it is
common to find training programs that are really orientation sessions covering general company issues, not job activities, or are improperly designed to
teach the main features of the job. The first of these three measures is the
judgment made by the training instructor about the trainees. This could be
judgments about parts of the training and/or a judgment of overall proficiency. In either case this method is prone to the common drawbacks of
decision making. These drawbacks and appropriate corrections will be discussed in the next section, *Judgmental Data*.

The second method is the development of a paper-and-pencil test. To do
this correctly, basic test construction principles should be followed. We will
not elaborate on these principles but the following issues are important.
There should be a match between the extent of topic coverage in training and
the number of questions asked about this topic on the test. It would make
little sense, for example, to have five of fifty questions asked about how to
operate a wine processing machine if one-half the training program was devoted to this. Also, standardized administration and scoring procedures must
be developed and utilized, as they reduce errors in the measurement process.

The third measurement method is to develop a performance test. This is
exactly the same kind of device we described in Chapter 14. This may be
confusing because in that chapter we presented performance tests as predictors. Now we introduce them as criteria measures. To clarify this, it may help

to remember that the central characteristic of a performance test is that it replicates the major tasks of the job. However, performance tests cannot be used in all selection situations, especially if the assumption cannot be made that the applicants already possess the KSAs necessary to attempt the task. In those instances in which performance tests may not be appropriate as selection devices, they could be appropriate as training proficiency measures. The training program is designed to be representative of the job activities. Performance tests are similarly designed. Therefore, a performance test should be appropriate as a measure of adequacy of training.

Sidney Gael, Donald Grant, and Richard Ritchie have described two selection programs validated at AT&T that used performance tests in this fashion.[8] One selection program for telephone operators used ten specially developed ability tests as predictors. The criterion, administered upon the completion of a formal training program, was a one-hour job simulation. In this simulation trainers acting as customers initiated calls at a steady pace in the same way for each operator-trainee. Each operator activity that was to be performed for each call was listed on the evaluation form. Supervisors directly observed and assessed the effectiveness of trainees in processing each call during the simulation. The second selection program used ten different paper-and-pencil tests of mental ability and perceptual speed and accuracy as predictors for clerical jobs. In this case the criterion was an extensive two-day simulation that was given by a specially trained administrator. This simulation consisted of eight separate exercises. Five were timed clerical activities — filing, classifying, posting, checking, and coding. The remaining three were untimed tests covering plant repair service, punched card fundamentals, and toll fundamentals.

Judgmental Data

In the fourth type of criterion measure, judgmental data, an individual familiar with the work of another is required to provide a measurement of this work. For selection, this measurement is usually obtained by using a scale with numerical values. In almost all cases the individual doing the evaluation is the immediate supervisor of the worker being evaluated. The evaluation is based on the opinion or judgment of this supervisor, hence the term *judgmental* data.

Because of this reliance on opinion, there is a general skepticism on the part of personnel specialists and managers about the use of such data. Many of the deficiencies in decision making that we described in the use of the unstructured interview have also been observed with judgmental performance data. However, as with the selection interview, much effort has been devoted to correcting these deficiencies. In reality, the use of judgmental data is unavoidable in modern business. Many jobs such as managerial, service, professional, and staff jobs are no longer of the type that produces tangible, easily counted products on a regular basis for which the use of production data would be appropriate. In most cases neither personnel nor training performance data are relevant or available. Almost by default judgmental data are increasingly being used for work measurement. In addition to availability, there are other arguments for the use of this type of criteria data. The information is supplied by supervisors who should know first-hand the work and the work circumstances; and after initial development, the use of the judgment scales should be relatively easy.

The Problem of Bias   The strong distrust in the use of these measures centers on the problem of intentional or inadvertent bias by the supervisor in making the judgment. Intentional bias is very difficult, if not impossible, to accurately detect, especially if it is done selectively. The general feeling among selection specialists, however, is that it is not a widespread problem. As is explained later in the chapter, when criteria data are collected for validation these data are not used for any other purpose. This creates circumstances in which there can be little profit for intentional distortion in ratings. It is thought that this minimizes the problem.

Inadvertent bias in responses is a more frequently found problem. Commonly called *rater error*, this bias most frequently is described in one of the following four ways: halo, leniency, severity, and central tendency. *Halo* is rating the subordinate equally on different performance scales because of a general impression of the worker. Specific attention is not paid to each individual scale used. *Leniency* or *severity* occurs when a disproportionate number of workers receive either high or low ratings respectively. This bias is commonly attributed to distortion in the supervisor's viewpoint of what constitutes acceptable behavior. *Central tendency* occurs when a large number of subordinates receive ratings in the middle of the scale. Neither very good nor very poor performance is rated often enough. The effect of all these forms of bias on validation work is usually to lower the calculated correlation. Generally, bias lowers the range of scores on the criteria measures which mathematically lowers the magnitude of the validity coefficient.

There have been several major tactics developed to reduce the frequency of bias in judgmental data. We will group these into four major topics and briefly summarize the recommendations for each.

Job Behavior vs. Personal Characteristics   To collect judgmental data, the most common method is to ask the supervisor to evaluate the subordinates on various topics called *dimensions*. These dimensions generally fall into two types: personal characteristics or job behaviors. Examples of each, contained in Exhibit 15.1, were taken from forms used for managerial positions in a drug manufacturing company. Research evidence indicates that the use of personal characteristic dimensions aggravates the problem of bias.[9] This is because the supervisor is asked to judge personality traits of subordinates. These are difficult to assess for trained psychologists and almost impossible

Exhibit 15.1 Examples of Dimensions Used in Judgmental Data

		Low	Average			High
Personal Characteristics Dimensions						
Initiative	a self-starter, looks for something to do, does not wait for instruction for each task	1	2	3	4	5
Cooperation	interacts well with others, is an accepted member of the work group	1	2	3	4	5
Attitude	willingness in all activities, is enthusiastic and concerned about the company	1	2	3	4	5
Judgment	makes sound decisions based upon information available, is not impulsive	1	2	3	4	5
Job Behavior Dimensions						
Design of management information systems to meet the information-processing needs of users		1	2	3	4	5
Implementation and maintenance of user systems		1	2	3	4	5
Training of end users in system operation		1	2	3	4	5

for untrained managers. In addition, little guidance is given in the definition of these traits or which work behaviors are indicative of these traits. The job behavior dimensions, on the other hand, are phrased directly in terms of job activities and are more easily understandable and directly related to the job. For this reason they are recommended for use in selection.

Scale Construction Principles   A "scale" is the measuring device used in judgmental data gathering. It consists of a dimension plus the numerical values used for rating performance. We can consider each statement in Exhibit 15.1 to be a separate scale. Much research has gone into identifying the proper way of constructing these scales for selection. The use of job behavior for dimensions is one part of these findings. Another part has focused on the appropriate number of scale points (numerical values) to use. The general recommendation is to use an odd number of points and to have no more than seven. Most often only five-point scales are used; they have been shown statistically to be similar to longer scales.[10] The reasoning is that this provides enough scale points for the supervisor to be able to discriminate among different levels of performance but not too many to overburden the decision-making capability.

Another feature of scale construction is the use of anchors, or definitions, that accompany scale points. Exhibit 15.2 contains the most frequently used types: a) adjectives that generally describe various levels of performance and b) brief descriptions of job behaviors that can be considered to be appropriate for that scale point. Both have been used in validation. For effective application, simple adjectives require thorough training of supervisors in their use in decision making. For job behaviors, extensive developmental work must be done to identify appropriate scale values.

Training to Avoid Rater Bias   A third approach is to attack the problem of rater bias directly by developing training programs that identify various types of bias and provide methods of overcoming them. Gary Latham, Kenneth Wexley, and Elliott Pursell designed such a program around the use of videotapes.[11] This program consisted of five videotaped interactions in which a manager was to rate another person. At the end of each videotape, each individual in the training program was asked to give ratings for the following two questions: (a) How would you rate the person? and (b) How do you think the manager rated this person? Each of the five videotapes demonstrated a different form of rating error. A discussion followed each videotape in which the particular rating error was pointed out and various solutions were developed to minimize this error. Evaluation of the program six months later found that the managers made no rating error in evaluating another set of videotapes.

Systematic Data Collection   Incomplete data is an additional source of bias about the job performance of subordinates. Such incompleteness forces the manager to base judgments on partially formed impressions. One example, known as the *primacy effect,* describes situations in which judgments are based on events that occurred during the first part of the evaluation period. The term *recency effect* is used when the judgments are based on events that occurred in the latter part of the period. To avoid this source of bias, managers have been taught to systematically record behavior during the complete period of evaluation. Usually this entails making written notes at fixed intervals describing the actual work behavior of each subordinate. These notes are not summary evaluations of the goodness or badness of the behavior but, rather, nonevaluative descriptions. Often these notes are also shared with the subordinate. At the time of the appraisal, the manager reviews the file and bases his or her judgment on the total job descriptions gathered over the complete time period of evaluation.

Types of Judgmental Instruments   There are many different instruments that have been used to collect judgmental criteria data. The most commonly used have been graphic rating scales and behavioral rating scales.

Graphic Rating Scales   Graphic rating scales were first developed in 1922 and have been extensively used ever since. There are many variations; Exhibit 15.2 presents some of the more popularly used scales. The scales in Exhibit 15.1 are other examples. As can be seen in Exhibit 15.2, graphic rating scales differ greatly in the type of scale that is used. In this exhibit, scale *a* allows for checking any point on the line. This check is translated into a score by measuring the length from the left end of the scale to the mark. Scales *b, c,* and *d* are designed to limit some of the ambiguity that can arise from using scale *a.* Scale *b* also allows a mark to be placed anywhere on the

Exhibit 15.2 *Examples of Graphic Rating Scales*

Job Dimension		Alternative Scales				

Completion of Marketing Reports
thoroughness of data sources used, completeness of statistical analysis, and clarity of recommendations

(a) _____ ✓ _____
  Low   High

(b) 1   2   3   4 ✓ 5
  Low   High

(c) unacceptable   poor   average   good   superior
        ☐   ☐   ☐   ☑   ☐

(d) poor   average   above average   excellent
      ____ 1   ____ 3   ✓ 5   ____ 7
      ____ 2   ____ 4   ____ 6   ____ 8

(e)   1   2   3   ✓ 4   5

Reports are not satisfactory.	Reports contain several errors.	Reports are generally acceptable with few errors.	Reports are thorough and complete.	Reports use well thought out analysis and are carefully reasoned.

scale, but defines various scale points with numbers and also uses adjectives placed at the extreme ends of the scale. Scales *c* and *d* restrict the possible judgments to a fixed number with each point being described by a number and/or an adjective. Scale *e* is generally thought to be superior because scale points are described in terms of job descriptions which have previously been linked to these places on the scale. The rater records his or her judgment by marking the point that comes closest to describing the behavior of the individual being judged on this aspect of work.

Behavior Rating Scales   This form of judgment scale uses the concept we mentioned previously of defining scale points in terms of job behaviors instead of adjectives. An example of such a scale is presented in Exhibit 15.3 for judging the classroom teaching of a college professor. The major difficulty in developing such a scale is to identify appropriate job behaviors that could be used as scale points and then to determine the appropriate numerical value for each behavior. It is *not* appropriate to merely write statements of behaviors that are hypothesized to be at certain scale values. It is not necessary that these behaviors be scaled at whole numbers along the dimension, either.

The development of such scales (commonly referred to as BARS or BES)

Exhibit 15.3 *Example of a Behavioral Rating Scale for College Professors*

**Dimension: Classroom Teaching Performance—The Presentation of
Course Material during Class Sessions**

5.00—Professor can be expected to vary syllabus of class to fit students' background. Emphasis would be placed on projects and discussion rather than lecture. Grading is based on quality of projects and tests.

4.00—Professor can be expected to meet all classes, to add to lecture with current materials, to answer course material thoroughly, and present a variety of testing methods.

3.00—Professor can be expected to meet all classes, to deliver organized lectures with appropriate standardized testing devices.

2.00—Professor can be expected to meet almost all classes and to closely repeat text, paying little attention to outside material or student questions.

1.00—Professor can be expected to hold classes irregularly. Also can be expected to present "true life" examples frequently which have little relationship to course material.

---

is usually an involved process requiring several participants. In one method four different groups of experts are used to: (a) identify and define the major dimensions to be judged, (b) generate examples of job behaviors for each dimension, (c) allocate the behaviors reliably to the appropriate dimension, and (d) determine the appropriate scale value of each of the behaviors to be associated with each dimension.

Concluding Comments on Judgmental Scales   All of these types of scales have been used in validation studies. To maximize the effectiveness of their use, the principles that were presented in this section should be kept in mind. First, the use of job-related scales rather than personal characteristics is recommended. The role of selection is to identify individuals who will perform well on the job, not to identify those with desirable personality characteristics. Therefore, job-related dimensions are the only acceptable kind.

Second, the use of either of the two forms of scales requires the extensive training of those who are to use it. Training should probably be more detailed in the use of graphic rating scales than with behavioral scales. This is because the scale points in graphic scales, which are defined by numbers and/ or adjectives, are more difficult for raters to use than are the scale points in the other type. Training must include developing in the raters a sense of the scale points for each dimension.

Finally, the history of selection argues that the dimensions used be fairly broad statements of performance or job behaviors.[12] We hope the following example will help to clarify what is meant by this statement. Directors of management information systems have multiple, diverse activities. If we were validating a set of selection instruments for this job, we would probably use some form of judgmental data as part of the criteria measures. Suppose that one performance dimension is the design and implementation of computer systems for various groups within the company. This behavior is actually made up of several, more specific, job behaviors, e.g., the discussion of user information needs, the development of a report describing the nature of the recommended system, the design of a detailed hardware plan, the development of software packages, and the training of users in software packages. It is better to determine one rating that is a measure of the general performance dimension than it is to treat each of these separate, behavioral dimensions as a criterion measure. This is because selection measures have less ability to correlate with specific, narrow job dimensions than to correlate with broad, encompassing dimensions. For this reason, criterion data should be collected by asking the supervisor to make one judgment of the overall job dimension or, if he or she is asked to rate the more specific dimensions, they should all be combined into one single score.

Characteristics of Selection Criteria Measures

As we have mentioned, it is possible to use each of the performance measurement devices that we have presented in validation. It is the role of the selection specialist to choose those measures that are the most appropriate for the selection program under consideration. Partially this choice depends on how the strengths and limitations of each device match the work situation under which the validation must be carried out. In addition, this choice is dependent upon the extent to which the criterion measure possesses the characteristics that we shall discuss in this section. Possession of these characteristics helps insure that the criterion has the information that is necessary to conduct validation. We have briefly mentioned a few of these characteristics in Chapter 3. In the following section we will discuss these more completely.

Individualization

Selection programs are designed to support the decision of whether or not to extend an offer of employment to each applicant. As we have described these programs, the applicant completes various selection instruments, each of which is designed to measure specific KSAs. In validation these measures of KSAs are gathered for each member of a group and correlated with corresponding measures of job performance. The logic of this is that the job performance measure must also be a measure of the individual. If we are attempting to determine if high scores on the selection instruments are indicative of high scores on job performance, it would be dysfunctional to have the job performance be representative of anyone except the individual. This may seem to be obvious but there are many work situations that create job performance outputs that violate this principle. For example, team or group tasks are becoming increasingly popular. Even traditional manufacturing operations have formed groups of 10 to 12 workers who are assigned all operations necessary for completion of the product. Workers are interchangeable and move unsystematically from work station to work station. It would not be appropriate to use the number of articles produced as a criterion measure for selection. Such a number would not measure the distinct performance of an individual and, therefore, should not be correlated with individual selection instrument scores.

Controllability

The logic of selection also indicates that measuring the KSAs of applicants is important because these KSAs affect job performance. Those workers who possess more of the desirable KSAs should perform better. This can only be tested if the work performance measure is a reflection of the employee's use of these KSAs. In other words, the measure of job performance should allow for differences in KSAs to be reflected in performance.

Again there are many frequently used measures of job performance that do not have this characteristic. For example, it has been common that branch managers' performance for financial service institutions is evaluated partially on the basis of profits generated by the branch. Offhand this seems accurate because profits are of central importance to financial institutions, and branch managers are commonly assumed to be the chief executive of the unit and in charge of operations. On closer inspection, oftentimes this assumption does not hold up. Interest rates for deposits are set by the highest level of management. Loans are also often controlled by standard policy. Loans over a certain amount must be approved by others and guidelines concerning loan evaluation are used for smaller loans. Furthermore, other items such as size and salary of staff are dictated by company headquarters. Therefore, many of the factors that greatly affect the profits of the branch are not influenced by the branch manager. To use profits as a criterion measure in selection would be an error in such a situation. Logically, differences in the KSAs of various branch managers may be reflected in other performance aspects such as completeness and timeliness of reports. The branch manager's use of KSAs can make a difference in the reports, therefore, reports are controllable by the branch manager. The use of KSAs does not make a difference in profits — profits are not controllable by the manager.

There are other easily thought of examples. Job scheduling and quality of materials frequently affect production output of workers, even though neither may be controlled by the worker. Repair records of maintenance workers in plants are often evaluated in terms of time spent on service visits and frequency of return calls. In many instances these factors are more attributable to the performance of the operators of the machinery than they are to the maintenance worker who repairs the machine.

The complexity and sophistication of current work arrangements often make it impossible to obtain measures that are totally controllable by workers. It is the responsibility of personnel specialists, in such instances, to carefully evaluate the options and choose those that best reflect this characteristic.

Relevance

Selection is designed to contribute to the productivity of the organization. Individuals are employed primarily to perform well on the critical or important parts of a job. It is these parts, therefore, that should be included in job performance measures. Sometimes it is easy to overlook this principle because other job performance aspects are easy to obtain. For example, promptness and attendance are, at times, easily obtained records. However, as we mentioned previously, in many jobs such attendance is not a critical dimension of performance. This is commonly the case for managers and professionals in an organization in which little attention is paid to coming and going or the use of company time for doctor visits, etc. Such events are irrelevant as long as "the work gets done." Our point is that this may also be true of other jobs for which attendance records are carefully kept. Therefore, these records are not appropriate criteria measures.

The primary method of judging the relevance of a criterion measure is job analysis. Job analysis should identify the important, critical, or frequently performed job activities. The question of relevance is whether the job performance measure corresponds to this information.

Measurability

Given the nature of validation, this is one of the more obvious characteristics. It is not possible to perform an empirical validation study unless behavior on both the selection and the job performance instruments is quantified. This quantification is how we have defined measurement (see Chapter 3). As we discussed in the previous section, the source of this measurement can be production output units, an individual's judgment, training examinations, work sample tests, attendance records, etc.

The most frequently experienced difficulty in meeting this measurement characteristic is determining how to quantify a job behavior dimension. For example, a regional sales manager may be in charge of advertising for the region. Ultimately the purpose of advertising is to increase sales. However, this end may not be achieved for a long period of time. The problem is what should be measured in place of sales that will measure the effectiveness of the advertising. In many cases some associated measure is obtained. For example, a judgment is made about the quality of the advertising campaign based on its correspondence to accepted standards of advertising. The judgment becomes the job performance measure.

Reliability

Chapter 4 discussed in detail the importance of reliability in measurement. Frequently, personnel specialists are greatly concerned with the reliability of selection instruments but pay less attention to the reliability of job performance measures. This is unfortunate because unreliability in these measures can negatively affect validation coefficients also. As has been noted, the unreliability of supervisors' judgments of subordinates has been of great concern to selection specialists.

Unreliability in other measures is not thought of as commonly but does exist and must be corrected. Monthly sales volume for many jobs, such as furniture or clothing representatives, fluctuates with seasonal buying patterns. In these cases it is necessary to accumulate sales data for a longer period of time than a month to compensate for these seasonal fluctuations. As has been mentioned, a major difficulty in using absenteeism as a criterion variable has been unreliability in some forms of its measurement. This has been especially true if total days absent is used as a measure. One severe illness could distort the data. For this reason various alternative measures have been designed.

Differentiation

It is conceptually useless and statistically difficult to validate a selection program in cases in which there is little, if any, difference in performance levels of workers. If every worker performs at the same level, the amount of KSAs of workers is apparently irrelevant — the difference in KSAs makes no difference in performance levels. This lack of difference can be caused by two factors: (a) standardization in output due to work process, or (b) inappropriate use of the measurement device. Output for machine paced manufacturing is an example of the former. If an assembly line is set to move at a certain speed continuously, all workers should produce the same volume. The latter case is often demonstrated in supervisors' judgments of subordinates. At one time the military experienced severe problems with its appraisal forms. Theoretically, 100 scale points were to be used for rating with a score of 70 being designated as average performance. In practice, however, the great majority of personnel were rated between 90 and 100 to insure their chances for promotion. The same problem has been repeated in other situations in which a supervisor feels that all the subordinates are exceptionally good workers.

A problem for selection specialists is determining whether such supervisory judgments reflect actual similarity in performance or misuse of the rating instrument. After all, it is possible that members of a work group, especially one that is experienced and well trained, could all perform at the same level. In most cases the decision is made that the appraisal form is being used incorrectly and a training program is implemented for its users to encourage the spread of ratings in future measurement.

Practicality

This characteristic refers to the cost and logistics of gathering data. In those rare circumstances in which these factors are not constraints, this can be ignored. In most cases, however, time and money become major issues. For example, most companies that operate direct sales operations feel that both sales volume and customer service are important performance dimensions. The problem is that to collect customer service data accurately, many time-consuming and costly steps must be carried out. A representative sample of customers for each salesperson would have to be compiled. Then each must be contacted and questioned, using a standardized interview, about the behaviors of the salesperson and the customer's reaction to the services rendered. Obviously, this is not a feasible operation in most cases. Instead, less time-consuming and costly measures are used. For example, often the number of complaints made by customers is used. To do this, however, the logical assumption must be made that the probability of customer complaints is the same for all sales personnel and the frequency of complaints is directly related to the frequency of poor customer service. If such an assumption cannot be made, then this measure is not useful as a job performance measure.

No Contamination

Criterion contamination occurs when the applicants' scores on the selection instruments are used to make employment decisions about these individuals, and these employment decisions, in turn, have a bearing on criterion scores. One of the best examples has occurred in the use of assessment centers. Most often ACs are used for internal selection for higher level management jobs. For this example let us assume an AC for lower level managers that is designed to determine their suitability for higher management positions. The lower level managers complete the AC and receive formal feedback from the assessors.

In many cases the assessment ratings and descriptions are also given to the superiors of those who have completed the AC and are also placed in central personnel files. Contamination occurs when these assessment center data are used to make decisions about whom among the group should be promoted, and then promotion is used as the criterion variable. Obviously such an action would artificially increase the validity coefficient. These events would constitute a self-fulfilling prophecy: individuals would be promoted because they scored well at the AC, and the AC scores would be validated against promotion records of individuals. Such similar contamination could occur when scores on selection devices are used for placement of employees into desirable sales territories or "fast-track" positions.

Specificity for Selection

Selection specialists generally prefer to use job performance data in validation that is specifically collected for selection program development rather than data collected primarily for one of the other P/HRM purposes. Frank Landy and James Farr discuss this as the difference between the administrative and the research use of performance data within organizations.[13] They clearly point out that there are basic differences between the two uses. For our purposes the major difference is that validation is impersonal. The emphasis is on using quantitative performance and predictor scores of unknown individuals. The administrative uses of performance data, in contrast, frequently emphasize the individual on whom the measurement is taken. Especially when judgmental methods are used, this sometimes means that other factors affect the measure. For example, when performance measures are used for salary increases, supervisors may consider such factors as the worker's experience, market demand, potential career, and personal relationships when making the evaluation.

Concluding Comments

After this discussion of characteristics, the question that undoubtedly arises in the reader's inquiring mind is "What happens if these characteristics are violated?" Without going into a long explanation, *the general conclusion is that major violations of these characteristics can artificially lower the correlation coefficient and reduce the probability of demonstrating empirical validity.* This is because such violations would introduce unsystematic errors into the measures. We have previously said that the effect of unsystematic error usually is to lower both reliability and validity. We use the word "artificially" because the lowering is due to extraneous factors that could be controlled. In other words, the validity coefficient provides an indication of the relationship between predictor and criterion. It should be low if no relationship exists and high if such a relationship is present. Under the circumstances we have mentioned, however, the relationship could still be high in reality but the validity coefficient low because of the presence of unsystematic error. The low correlation would not be representative of the actual relationship between predictor and criterion.

Single vs. Multiple Criteria

One of the most perplexing issues for selection specialists involved in validation is how to decide on the number of measures of job performance to use. This issue is commonly referred to as the choice between single or multiple criteria. In validation the use of a single measure of job performance translates into viewing it as total or global performance. This single measure is thought to be indicative of all relevant job performance. The measure could be either of two forms. One form consists of a single aspect of performance. For example, for sales personnel a measure of dollar sales volume frequently has been used. For computer key punchers, the measure has been the number of entries made. The second form consists of two or more measures that are algebraically combined to yield one overall measure. For example, a district sales manager's rating of quality of customer service may be combined in some manner with the sales volume figures to arrive at one total composite of job performance for sales personnel.

The argument for using a single performance measure in validation is partially based on the fact that validation procedures become more straightforward with one criterion. The predictor(s) is correlated with this one measure in the manner described in Chapter 5. In most instances, only one correlation coefficient would be tested to determine significance. This makes the interpretation of the findings and the judgment about the adequacy of the selection program relatively simple.

The argument for the use of multiple criteria measures is made on the basis of research findings and logic. Essentially this argument starts with the fact that job analysis studies identify multiple tasks within jobs. Multiple tasks are indicative of the multiple aspects of job performance. Also, review studies, specifically of job performance, have concluded that a global measures of performance is not valid even for simple, entry-level jobs.[14] For example, in manufacturing jobs, both days present and lack of defective assembly items are, at the minimum, thought to be important. Even in typing and stenography the argument can be made for the importance of both speed and accuracy as performance measures.

When to Use Each

Wayne Cascio has presented the most straightforward solution to the dilemma and the following reflects his writings.[15] Cascio makes the distinction between using job performance measures to assist in managerial decision making or to serve research purposes. A validation study can be used for either purpose. In most cases a validity study is done to identify a set of selection devices that assist in managerial decision making. That is, the applicants' scores on the selection devices are used in making decisions about to whom to extend job offers. In these cases a composite criterion would generally be used. Managers are essentially interested in selecting individuals who, all things considered, perform well in an overall manner. The use of the composite criterion reflects this thinking.

In a few cases a validity study is done for research purposes. For example, we may wish to study the relationship of specific mental abilities (e.g., mathematical reasoning, spatial visualization, etc.) to different parts of a research engineering job (e.g., development of research plans, preparation of technical reports, etc.). In such a case, the major emphasis is on linking a specific mental ability to each subpart of the job. Such information could later be used in selection, training, and career development work. It would, therefore, be appropriate to use multiple criteria and to validate the mental ability tests against each separate measure of job performance.

Forming the Single Measure

If a composite measure is desired, the immediate problem is how to combine the different measures into one. Essentially there are three methods of doing this.

Dollar Criterion The first, which Cascio points out is the logical basis of combining, is to develop a composite that represents economic worth to the organization. This entails expressing the various job performance measures that we have discussed as a monetary amount that represents the value of worker performance to the organization. Logically, this is in agreement with the concept of using validation data to assist managerial decision making. Put simply, a main management concern with selection is to improve the economic position of the firm by means of the more able workers employed through using a valid selection program. Expressing job performance in dollars would be a direct reflection of this thinking.

This line of reasoning was first expressed over 30 years ago by Hubert Brogden and Erwin Taylor, who developed the dollar-criterion.[16] It has been only recently, however, that refinements have been made in how practically to estimate the monetary worth of job performance. These refinements are part of the general topic of *utility analysis*. Without going through a detailed description of this topic, there are three major methods of determining this dollar value of job performance. One method has job experts estimate the monetary value of various levels of job performance.[17] A second method assumes this dollar value to be a direct function of yearly salary.[18] The third method also uses employee salary but partitions this among a job's principal activities so that each activity is assigned a proportion of that salary in accord with the job analysis results.[19]

Factor Analysis The second method of combining separate criteria measures into one composite relies upon statistical correlational analysis. In one approach all individual criteria measures are correlated with one another. The intercorrelation matrix is factor analyzed which, statistically, combines these separate measures into clusters or factors. Ideally, a majority of the separate measures would be combined into one factor that would then serve as the composite performance measure. The factor analysis procedure also provides weights that could apply to each specific measure in forming the composite.

Expert Judgment A third method uses judgments of job experts to form the composite. Essentially the problem for these judges is to identify the relative weights of the specific performance aspects. For example, let us assume that the job of laboratory technician has five components that we wish to combine. The role of the job experts is to specify the numerical value that each component should be multiplied by to derive the overall performance score. This weighting should be reflective of the importance of each of the five components to overall performance. If all five components are regarded as being equally important, then all five parts carry a weight of "1" and are directly added. If the five components are thought to be unequal in importance, there are two different procedures that are often used to determine the appropriate weights. Under the first procedure, each judge is given 100 points and asked to divide these up among the five parts. The weight for each part is the average number of points assigned to it by the judges. The second procedure asks each judge to assign a value of 1.0 to the most unimportant part. The number assigned to each of the other four is to represent how many times more important each part is to this least important one. The weight is again the average of these values. Both procedures assume reliability among the judges in terms of both the ordering of the five parts and the relative importance among them. This means that if the judges do not closely agree as to which components are unimportant and which are very important, the computed averages are conceptually meaningless and ought not to be used.

Work Measurement and EEO Issues

The precise effect of EEO principles on work measurement is not as clear as it is for other areas of selection. Partially this is because only a small part of the *Uniform Guidelines* explicitly treats work measurement, and it really does not fully discuss the necessary features of such systems. Similarly, while there have been a number of court cases that have addressed work measurement, there have been very few cases in which it has been the major issue in the case. Moreover, the major proportion of even this sketchy treatment has focused on judgmental data, not the complete topic of work measurement. For these reasons it is difficult to state specifically what action personnel specialists should take to minimize the chances of having a court disagree with the nature of a performance evaluation system.

To provide an understanding of what is known about this topic, this section will indicate those parts of the *Uniform Guidelines* that pertain to performance measurement, summarize the results of relevant court decisions, and present some recommendations regarding necessary features of work measurement systems. As other authors have put it, these recommendations ought to be treated as "a set of hypotheses regarding the legal ramifications" rather than a strict set of guidelines.[20]

Uniform Guidelines

Three sections of the *Uniform Guidelines* have the most direct statements about work measurement. Of these Section 2.B is the most often cited. Its purpose is to make clear that any procedure that contributes to any employment decision is covered by the *Uniform Guidelines*. This is addressed by the statement, "These guidelines apply to tests and other selection procedures which are used as a basis for any employment decision." To the extent that work measurement data are used in validation, or for any other purpose in selection, they are covered. Some interpret this section to mean that all procedures used in these employment decisions are to be generally labeled as "tests" and subject to all the statements of the *Uniform Guidelines* directed at tests.

The second statement, Section 14.B.(3) (see Table 15.2), serves several purposes. For one, it makes explicit that three of the four types of data we have discussed are permissible: production data, personnel data, and training proficiency. More detail is provided about training proficiency than the others. It is pointed out that the relevance of the training to actual important dimensions of job performance must be demonstrated and that various measures of training proficiency may be used including instructor evaluations, performance samples, and paper-and-pencil tests. The statement is also made that these three types of criteria measures may be used without a previous job analysis if "the user can show the importance of the criteria to the particular employment context." Presumably this is done by pointing out the direct relationship of these criteria measures to the purpose of the job. Other issues in section 14 refer to some of the points we made in the previous section of this chapter, "Characteristics of Selection Criteria Measures." These include preventing contamination and insuring relevance. A statement is also made that it is permissible to develop one, overall measure of job performance. We have discussed appropriate methods of doing this in the previous section of this chapter.

Table 15.2   From the Uniform Guidelines *Pertaining to Work Measurement*

Section 14.B.(3).

(3) Criterion measures. Proper safeguards should be taken to insure that scores on selection procedures do not enter into any judgments of employee adequacy that are to be used as criterion measures. Whatever criteria are used should represent important or critical work behavior(s) or work outcomes. Certain criteria may be used without a full job analysis if the user can show the importance of the criteria to the particular employment context. These criteria include but are not limited to production rate, error rate, tardiness, absenteeism, and length of service. A standardized rating of overall work performance may be used where a study of the job shows that it is an appropriate criterion. Where performance in training is used as a criterion, success in training should be properly measured and the relevance of the training should be shown either through a comparison of the content of the training program with the critical or important work behavior(s) of the job(s), or through a demonstration of the relationship between measures of performance in training and measures of job performance. Measures of relative success in training include but are not limited to instructor evaluation, performance samples, or tests. Criterion measures consisting of paper and pencil tests will be closely reviewed for job relevance.

Source: *Adoption of Four Agencies of Uniform Guidelines on Employee Selection Procedures*, 43 Federal Register 38, 290–38, 315 (Aug. 25, 1978).

A third section, 15.B.(5), makes clear that the data used to identify and develop the criterion measure(s) of validation must be made explicit. This is done by the statement, "The bases for the selection of the criterion measures should be provided. . . ." This includes the description of the criterion and how the measure was developed and collected. Explicit statements are also made recognizing the fourth type of work measurement data, judgmental data. When this type is used, both the forms used to collect the judgments and the explicit instructions given to the judges must be provided.

Court Decisions

A comprehensive review of court decisions about judgmental performance measures was done by Hubert Feild and William Holley that examined 66 cases heard between 1966 and 1980.[21] All of the cases focused on judgmental rather than other measures. From statements in the *Uniform Guidelines* and our previous remarks, it is understandable that EEO regulatory agencies would be far more concerned with the discriminatory effects of this type of performance measure than any of the other three. Presumably, court state-ments about judgmental data would also be applicable to the other types.

Feild and Holley reviewed 66 cases and classified each on the 13 appraisal system characteristics shown in Table 15.3. They also divided the cases into those that were decided in favor of the plaintiff (31 cases) and those decided in favor of the defendant (35 cases). The purpose of the study was to deter-

Table 15.3   *Characteristics of Judgmental Appraisal Systems Related to Court Decisions*

Appraisal System Characteristic	N	Number of Legal Cases with Decisions for		Statistically Significant
		Plaintiff	Defendant	
Purpose of the appraisal system?	61			No
Promotion		18	15	
Other (layoffs, transfers, discharges)		10	18	
Job analysis used to develop appraisal system?	17			Yes
Yes		0	3	
No		11	3	
Type of appraisal system used?	48			Yes
Trait-oriented		17	8	
Behavior-oriented		7	16	
Presented validity information on appraisal system?	65			No
Yes		10	10	
No		21	24	

continued

Table 15.3 *continued*

Appraisal System Characteristic	N	Number of Legal Cases with Decisions for		Statistically Significant
		Plaintiff	Defendant	
Presented reliability information on appraisal system?	58			No
Yes		3	3	
No		28	24	
Frequency that appraisals were conducted?	19			No
Mean		3.75	3.45	
SD		.71	.93	
Number of evaluators used?	32			No
Mean		1.56	2.00	
SD		1.37	1.75	
Evaluators given formal training in appraising performance?	15			No
Yes		0	1	
No		11	3	
Evaluators given specific written instructions?	27			Yes
Yes		1	11	
No		14	1	
Appraisal results reviewed with employees?	12			Yes
Yes		2	7	
No		3	0	
Basis for employment discrimination charge?	55			No
Race		19	21	
Sex		8	7	
Type of organization (defendant)?	65			Yes
Industrial		14	4	
Nonindustrial		17	30	
Geographical location of organization (defendant)?	66			No
Inside the Southeast		13	8	
Outside the Southeast		19	26	

Source: Hubert Feild and William Holley, "The Relationship of Performance Appraisal System Characteristics to Verdicts in Selected Employment Discrimination Cases," *Academy of Management Journal* 25 (1982): 397. Reprinted with permission from the authors.

mine how these appraisal characteristics might be related to the court decisions. As Table 15.3 indicates, 5 of the 13 characteristics were found to have a statistically significant relationship with these decisions.

These five characteristics seem to provide useful information about critical features of performance systems in discrimination cases. The most strongly related characteristic was the type of organization of the defendant. Court decisions usually went with the plaintiff in cases involving manufacturing companies and went against the plaintiff in cases within service industries, many of which were educational systems. This pattern is not explainable in terms of EEO directives, but it does reflect a viewpoint possible within the regulatory model.

The remaining characteristics provide information to form recommendations about necessary features of work measurement systems. The second characteristic was a concept explicitly mentioned in the *Uniform Guidelines*, the presence of specific written instructions given to raters describing the system of evaluation. As you might guess, the overwhelming majority of cases with specific instructions were decided in favor of the defendant; and the opposite pattern was found in those cases without such instruction. This is an expected result and also conforms with general principles about the professional development of judgmental data systems. This is also true of the remaining three critical characteristics. The plaintiff was generally upheld in cases involving trait or personal characteristic dimensions while the company was upheld when behavior-oriented dimensions were used. Similarly, the use of job analysis to establish the dimension upon which judgments were made and the practice of sharing the results of the appraisal with the workers were also related to decisions made in favor of the defendant. The lack of job analysis and lack of sharing of information favored the plaintiff. Again, these practices are part of standard, professional evaluation practices. Based on these cases it would seem essential to base work measurement systems on job analysis, to use job behaviors as dimensions, to provide specific instructions on the use of the system, and to communicate the results to all employees.

References for Chapter 15

[1] Frank J. Landy and James L. Farr, *The Measurement of Work Performance Methods, Theory, and Applications* (New York: Academic Press, 1983); Gary P. Latham and Kenneth N. Wexley, *Increasing Productivity Through Performance Appraisal* (Reading, Mass.: Addison-Wesley Publishing Co., 1981); H. John Bernardin and Richard W. Beatty, *Performance Appraisal: Assessing Human Behavior at Work* (Boston: West Publishing Co., 1984).

[2] William W. Ronan and Erich P. Prien, *Perspectives on the Measurement of Human Performance* (New York: Appleton-Century-Crofts, 1971), p. 73.

[3] Ibid., p. 94.

[4] Landy and Farr, *The Measurement of Work Performance Methods, Theory, and Applications*, p. 30.

[5] Ibid., p. 33.

[6] Dan R. Dalton and William D. Todor, "Manifest Needs of Stewards: Propensity to File a Grievance," *Journal of Applied Psychology* 64 (1979): 654–659.

[7] Edwin E. Ghishelli, *The Validity of Occupational Aptitude Tests* (New York: John Wiley & Sons, 1966).

[8] Sidney Gael, Donald L. Grant, and Richard J. Ritchie, "Employment Test Validation for Minority and Nonminority Telephone Operators," *Journal of Applied Psychology* 60 (1975): 411–419; Sidney Gael, Donald L. Grant, and Richard J. Ritchie, "Employment Test Validation for Minority and Nonminority Clerks with Work Sample Criteria," *Journal of Applied Psychology* 60 (1975): 420–426.

[9] Bernardin and Beatty, *Performance Appraisal: Assessing Human Behavior at Work*, pp. 64–65.

[10] Landy and Farr, *The Measurement of Work Performance Methods, Theory, and Applications*, p. 83.

[11] Gary P. Latham, Kenneth N. Wexley, and Elliott Pursell, "Training Managers to Minimize Rating Errors in the Observation of Behavior," *Journal of Applied Psychology* 60 (1975): 550–555.

[12] Neil Schmidt and Benjamin Schneider, "Current Issues in Personnel Selection," *Research in Personnel and Human Resources Management*, vol. 1 (JAI Press, 1983), p. 93.

[13] Landy and Farr, *The Measurement of Work Performance Methods, Theory, and Applications*, pp. 191–207.

[14] Wayne F. Cascio, *Applied Psychology in Personnel Management*, 2d ed. (Reston, Va.: Reston Publishing Co., 1982), pp. 116–118.

[15] Ibid., p. 109.

[16] Hubert E. Brogden and Erwin K. Taylor, "The Dollar Criterion—Applying the Cost Accounting Concept to Criterion Construction," *Personnel Psychology* 3 (1950): 133–154.

[17] Frank L. Schmidt, John E. Hunter, Robert C. McKenzie, and Tressie W. Muldrow, "Impact of Valid Selection Procedures on Work-Force Productivity," *Journal of Applied Psychology* 64 (1979): 609–626.

[18] Frank L. Schmidt, John E. Hunter, and Kenneth Pearlman, "Assessing the Economic Impact of Personnel Programs on Workforce Productivity," *Personnel Psychology* 35 (1982): 333–348.

[19] Wayne F. Cascio, *Costing Human Resources: The Financial Impact of Behavior in Organizations* (Boston: Kent Publishing, 1982), p. 163.

[20] Bernardin and Beatty, *Performance Appraisal: Assessing Human Behavior at Work*, p. 43.

[21] Hubert S. Feild and William H. Holley, "The Relationship of Performance Appraisal System Characteristics to Verdicts in Selected Employment Discrimination Cases," *Academy of Management Journal* 25 (1982): 392–406. Also see Hubert S. Feild and Diane Thompson, "A Study of Court Decisions in Cases Involving Performance Appraisal Systems," *The Daily Labor Report*, December 26, 1984, pp. E1–E5.

PART SIX

Summary

This is it! We now bring this book to a quick and painless conclusion. This summary presents a series of questions that selection managers should find useful in developing or evaluating a selection program. These questions are categorized according to chapters in the text and refer to material found in that chapter. We suppose that for this reason, creative instructors using this as a text may be able to find some test/discussion items here also.

16

The Human Resource Selection Audit

This final chapter provides a summary of the preceding chapters of the book. However, as you will see, the chapter is presented somewhat differently from the summary chapters of most books. Basically, it consists of a series of questions developed to highlight many of the important issues previously discussed. These questions are listed on the following pages. Because these questions can be used by a selection manager to study an organization's selection program, we have titled the chapter "The Human Resource Selection Audit." In evaluating an existing selection program or in implementing a new one, we strongly suggest that each of these questions be reviewed, contemplated, and answered, preferably in writing. Only when addressed in this manner can a selection manager have the confidence that a selection program is performing or will perform in the manner for which it is intended.

An Overview of Selection (Chapter 1):

1. Are the developmental steps that are necessary to selection programs specified in detail in terms of actions and personnel involved?

2. Has the interaction of the selection program and the corresponding training program been reviewed?

3. Has the interaction of the selection program and the corresponding recruiting program been reviewed?

Legal Issues in Selection (Chapter 2):

1. Are recruiting practices designed to contact and encourage the various groups that constitute at least 2 percent of applicants in the labor market?

2. Have records been kept, or are there plans to keep records, for tabulating the selection ratios for all demographic groups that constitute 2 percent of the labor market?

3. Are there similar records for the handicapped, Vietnam-era veterans, and applicants in the 40-years-and-older groups?

4. Are the selection ratios of these various groups within the "4/5ths" rule of thumb?

5. If the selection ratios are not within the "four-fifths rule," are there appropriate data to justify these results (see questions in *Validity of Selection Measures,* Chapter 5)?

6. Do selection instruments measure KSAs quickly learned on the job? If so, consider omitting these.

7. Do selection instruments measure KSAs required for high-level jobs but not for entry-level? If so, does job progression data support such use?

8. Are there data to support the decision rules that define the use of cut-off selection scores?

9. Are all selection instruments administered using standardized, professional procedures?

10. Are various demographic groups represented in the pool of selection test administrators?

Human Resource Measurement in Selection (Chapter 3):

1. In locating existing selection measures, has a comprehensive search of secondary sources been undertaken?

2. Have systematic steps been undertaken in developing selection measures?

3. Have each of the selection measures been checked against the criteria to consider in choosing selection measures (see Exhibit 3.3)?

Reliability of Selection Measures (Chapter 4):

1. Are reliability data available on all predictors, criteria, and other variables?

2. Is it important to know how stable scores on a measure are over time?

3. If so, which is likely to be more applicable, parallel forms or test-retest reliability?

4. Is it important to know the extent to which parts of a measure are measuring the same construct?

5. Is the reliability coefficient high enough to warrant confidence in a selection measure?

Validity of Selection Measures (Chapter 5):

1. What are the inferences to be made from scores on a selection measure?

2. Why is a particular validity strategy chosen?

3. Have validity studies been conducted on all predictors and criteria?

4. Under content validation:

    a. Have the tasks essential to performance of a job been identified?

    b. Have the KSAs necessary to perform these tasks been identified?

    c. Have the contents of selection measures been developed so that they are representative of the KSAs identified as critical to job success?

    d. Why is a criterion-related validity strategy not feasible?

5. Under criterion-related validity:

    a. Is it possible to obtain a relevant, reliable, uncontaminated measure of job performance?

    b. Is the job reasonably stable and not undergoing change?

    c. Can an adequate, representative sample of respondents be obtained? Is this sample representative of job applicants in terms of age, sex, race, or other relevant characteristics?

    d. Are validity coefficients high enough to warrant the use of the selection measures?

6. In conducting a validity study, has a job analysis been conducted for all predictors and criteria being studied?

Preparing for Job Analysis: An Overview (Chapter 6):

1. Has an "appropriate" person (in terms of knowledge and ability to conduct/coordinate a job analysis project) been identified to coordinate a job analysis study?

2. Have appropriate authority, responsibility, and necessary resources (financial, space, clerical, data analysis, professional staff) been committed to the job analysis project?

3. Does the job analysis have the support of top management? Have this support and the purposes of the study been communicated to relevant operating managers?

4. Why was a particular job as opposed to another job chosen for analysis?

5. Has the relevant literature been reviewed for information about the job(s) in question?

6. What job agents or individuals will be responsible for collecting and providing information about jobs in the study?

7. Are these job agents properly trained for completing the analysis?

8. If job incumbents are used as agents, are they representative (in terms of sex, race, tenure, level of job performance) of the job incumbent population?

Applying Job Analysis Techniques (Chapter 7):

1. In choosing a particular job analysis technique:
   a. Is the method operational and ready for use?
   b. Is the measurement instrument involved ready-made or must it be constructed?
   c. Can the method be applied to a wide variety of jobs?
   d. Will the method be acceptable to respondents and users?
   e. How much training must a job analyst receive in order to apply the method adequately?
   f. How many respondents or sources of information are required to provide job analysis data?
   g. Will the method support the requirements for establishing the content-or criterion-related validity of a measure?
   h. Will the method provide consistent, dependable job data?
   i. Is the method useful in *developing* selection measures?
   j. What is the cost (including materials, training, consulting assistance, clerical support, data analysis) of the method?

2. For the job analysis itself, will it be:
   a. In writing?
   b. Completed by competent job analysts?
   c. Representative of the jobs under study?

3. What specific unit of analysis (task, duty, work element, function) is needed from the job analysis?

4. How does the job analysis assess the unit of analysis in terms of relative frequency, criticality, importance, complexity, or consequences of error?

Incorporating Job Analysis Results in Selection Measures (Chapter 8):

1. Are job task data available?

2. If so, have KSAs critical to performance of important job tasks been identified? Are they correctly stated? Are KSAs linked to job tasks?

3. Has the relative importance of these KSAs been ascertained?

4. Have these important KSAs been used in developing the content of a selection measure or in choosing an existing measure?

Application Forms and Reference Checks (Chapter 9):

1. Is all information appearing on the application form related to a person's ability to perform the job for which the form is used?

2. Can application form items be justified in terms of business necessity?

3. Do items on the application form screen out a disproportionate number of minority group members or members of one sex?

4. Has the content of application forms been based upon job analysis?

5. Has *every* item on the application been judged for its suitability?

6. Have reliability and validity studies been made of reference checks?

7. Are reference data provided by someone who has had adequate opportunity to observe the applicant?

8. Are subjective traits of applicants assessed on the application form?

9. Have applicants' written consent been obtained prior to contacting their references?

10. Is the reference form designed for a specific job for which it will be used?

11. Have reference takers been trained in how to solicit reference information?

12. Before negative information is used, has its accuracy been verified? Will applicant disqualification on the basis of negative information distinguish between those who will fail and those who will succeed on the job?

Weighted Application Blanks and Biographical Data (Chapter 10):

1. Does the job for which a weighted application blank is being considered have a large number of employees?

2. Are adequate personnel records available on these employees?

3. Have a large number of employees on a job been hired in a relatively short time period (two years or less)?

4. Is a suitable criterion available?

5. Has the validity of the weighted application blank been checked at least every two to three years?

6. Do any items on the weighted application blank violate fair employment practice statutes or federal laws?

7. Have any organizational changes affected the applicability of the weighted application blank?

8. Is the criterion on which the weighted application blank was constructed still important in selecting employees?

9. Is the weighted application blank being used for only one job or jobs with very similar activities?

10. Have scoring keys for the weighted application blank been cross-validated?

11. Has a thorough analysis of the job for which biographical data will be used been conducted? Have hypotheses regarding the development of biographical data items been formed and based on this analysis?

12. Has the literature been searched for biographical data items that may be predictive of important criteria for a job?

13. Have all proposed biographical data items been written, edited, and reviewed for proper phrasing, fairness, and scoring?

14. If an empirical scoring key is used in scoring a biographical data questionnaire, has the key been cross-validated?

15. Do any biographical data items or scoring keys have any discriminatory effects on groups of job applicants?

16. Does the content of biographical data items appear to "make sense" when used in selecting employees for a job?

The Selection Interview (Chapter 11):

1. Is the time of the selection interview primarily allocated to obtaining information about the applicant's characteristics rather than providing information about the organization to the applicant?

2. Is the selection interview intended to measure a small number of appropriate KSAs?

3. Is the selection interview designed to gather information from the applicant independently of other selection instruments?

4. Is a semi-structured questioning format used to insure consistency of information across all applicants?

5. Are all questions that are used to judge the acceptability of the applicant clearly related to job activities?

6. Are multiple questions used to gather data about each of the KSAs of interest to obtain more complete information?

7. Is there a formal, defined system for scoring the applicant's responses to interview questions?

8. Are interviewers trained in both the process and the scoring of interviews?

9. Is it possible to use an interview panel?

Ability Tests (Chapter 12):

1. Is the content of the ability test to be used clearly linked to the KSAs and job activities identified through job analysis?

2. Has a search been conducted to review validity studies of selection programs using the ability test for closely related jobs?

3. Do the supporting materials for the ability test explain test development procedures and descriptions of the measurement of the reliability and validity of the test?

4. Is there evidence of use of the test on groups of individuals similar to potential applicants for the job under consideration?

5. Are there data comparing the performance of appropriate demographic groups on the test?

6. Is the ability test to be administered and scored under standardized conditions?

7. If paper-and-pencil honesty tests are to be used, are there explicit procedures for evaluating and processing applicants that especially address false positives?

Personality Assessment (Chapter 13):

1. Have the personality traits to be evaluated been identified through job analysis and attention to the content of job tasks rather than through general impressions of the job or "what kind of person" fits the job?

2. Are specially trained individuals involved in the administration, scoring, and interpretation of the assessment results?

3. Is the personality assessment device specifically designed or adapted for the job under consideration or is it an "off-the-shelf" instrument?

4. Are multiple personality assessment devices being used when possible?

5. Are the personality traits being assessed related to broad patterns of job behavior rather than narrow patterns?

6. Are the personality traits of interest accountable for behavior in work situations or is role learning a more important factor than traits?

7. Are the personality traits to be measured specifically defined?

8. Have the questions and the scoring procedures to be used been carefully linked to the definition of the trait?

9. Is it possible to directly collect data on behaviors rather than use indirect measures such as the applicant's description of behavior?

10. Has the evidence about the use of the personality assessment instrument in similar selection programs been reviewed?

11. Has the evidence of reliability and validity of the assessment device been reviewed?

12. Does the administration of the personality measuring device take into account the limitations that accompany the use of this type of device?

13. If the validity of the personality instrument is to be determined, are the criteria measures suitable in the sense of being made up of behaviors or actions influenced by the incumbent's personality?

Performance Tests (Chapter 14):

1. Does the job analysis information clearly identify appropriate job tasks (e.g., important or frequently performed) to serve as a basis for testing?

2. Can it be assumed that most applicants will have the necessary KSAs to complete the task without extensive prior training?

3. If prior training is necessary, are standardized instructions provided before the performance test is administered?

4. Has the cost of developing and using a performance test been calculated?

5. Is there a suitable physical location (e.g., free from nonjob interruptions, a replica of the actual work setting, etc.) available for testing?

6. Is the time available to perform the test activities suitable?

7. Have standardized instructions and testing procedures been identified?

8. Have appropriate standards (e.g., behavior vs. results) been identified for scoring?

9. Have scoring procedures and rules been explicitly stated?

10. Are various parts of the performance test that are scored independent of one another?

11. Are the equipment and materials used for the performance test representative of those used in the job task?

12. Has the number of task repetitions or the total time of performance been determined?

13. Have scorers been trained in scoring procedures?

14. Has the performance test been tried out before testing applicants?

Assessment Centers (Chapter 14):

1. Has a job analysis been completed to identify the job behaviors that serve as the basis of situational exercises?

2. Have behavioral dimensions been identified and defined?

3. Have multiple measures been designed for the measurement of each behavioral dimension?

4. Have appropriate situational tests been developed?

5. Have appropriate traditional instruments been identified to be used with situational tests?

6. Have assessors been trained in behavioral observation, recording, and evaluation?

7. Have scoring procedures and rules been specified?

8. Has the interrater reliability of assessors been determined?

Measurement of Worker Performance (Chapter 15):

1. Have the various job performance dimensions been identified through job analysis?

2. For each job performance dimension, has the appropriate type of performance measure been identified: production, personnel, training proficiency, or judgmental?

3. Have the limitations that frequently accompany the use of each type of performance measure been taken into account and methods developed to minimize them?

4. Have the job performance measures to be used been evaluated to determine if they possess the requisite characteristics (e.g., individualization, controllability, relevance, etc.)?

5. Have those who are to gather or record performance measures been trained and given specific instructions about the measurement process?

6. Have workers been informed as to what data are being collected as performance measures?

7. Has a method been identified to combine multiple measures into one composite measure, if necessary?

Name Index

Aiken, Lewis, 111, 417, 418
Ainsworth, Mary, 449
Albright, Lewis, 334, 336, 342, 343
Alexander, Ralph, 125, 166
Allport, Gordon, 422, 448, 449
Anastasi, Anne, 117, 126, 166, 417
Andrews, I.R., 381
Archer, W.B., 204, 205
Armstrong, J. Scott, 22
Arvey, Richard, 167, 214, 381, 382
Asch, Solomon E., 450
Ash, Ronald A., 216, 219, 273
Asher, James, 328, 338, 339, 343, 344, 487
Atchinson, Thomas, 172, 188

Backer, T.E., 86
Balma, Michael, 83, 85, 86, 167
Banas, Paul, 324
Barrett, Gerald, 125, 166
Bateman, Thomas S., 382
Beason, G., 298, 310
Beatty, Richard, 492
Bellows, Roger, 342
Belt, J.A., 298, 310
Bem, Daryl J., 449

Bennett, Nell, 216, 219
Bernardin, John, 492
Berner, John, 487
Biddle, Richard E., 245, 273
Bigalla, 214
Binet, Alfred, 386
Blencoe, Allyn G., 186, 189
Blum, Milton, 117, 310
Bolster, B., 381
Booth, Jerome, 314, 342
Borman, Walter, 216
Bouffard, Dennis L., 449
Boyatis, Richard, 449
Boyd, Joseph L., 487
Boyles, Wiley R., 187, 189
Bray, Douglas W., 449, 450, 487, 488
Britt, M.F., 343
Brodie, W.M., 343
Brogden, Hubert, 513
Brown, Steven H., 324, 342
Brumback, Gary, 217, 221, 245, 272, 274
Brush, Donald, 486, 488
Buel, William D., 342
Buros, Oscar K., 85
Burrington, Debra D., 283, 309
Byham, William C., 487, 488

Campbell, John P., 22, 166, 167, 267, 273, 454, 455, 487, 488
Campbell, Richard J., 449, 450
Campion, James, 466, 487
Caplan, James, 244, 245
Carlson, Richard E., 381
Carrell, Michael R., 178, 188, 448
Carroll, Stephen J., 189, 190, 299, 310, 311
Cascio, Wayne, 85, 86, 117, 161, 167, 188, 201, 208, 212, 214, 272, 310, 311, 325, 334, 338, 342, 344, 470, 487, 512, 513, 519
Cattell, James McKeen, 396, 449
Cattell, Raymond, 422, 423, 424
Cattin, Phillipe, 150, 167
Chao, Georgia, 338, 339, 344, 408, 411, 418
Christal, Raymond E., 186, 189, 190, 202, 205, 225, 244
Chun, Ki-Taek, 86
Clark, Cynthia, 244, 245
Cobb, Sidney, 86
Comrey, A.L., 86
Cordes, Colleen, 418
Cornelius, Edwin T., 186, 189
Coyle, Bryan, 381
Cozan, L.W., 291, 309, 340, 344
Cranny, C.J., 127, 166
Crites, John O., 417, 418
Cross, Theodore, 418
Cureton, Edward, 320, 330, 342, 343

Dailey, Patrick, 382
Dalton, Dan R., 518
Dawis, Rene V., 291, 309, 340, 344
DeCotiis, Thomas, 188
Deloach, Jay A., 289, 309
Denisi, Angelo S., 186, 189, 273
Dick, Walter, 117
Dipboye, Robert L., 369, 382
Dougherty, Denise, 418
Drake, John, 382
Dreher, George, 356, 369, 488
DuBois, Philip, 417, 418
Dudley, D., 304, 310
Dugoni, Bernard, 381
Dunnette, Marvin D., 188, 324, 342

England, George, 314, 315, 316, 320, 322, 342
Ennis, William H., 341, 344

Erickson, J., 324
Eysenck, Hans, 449

Faley, Robert H., 166
Farr, James, 382, 492, 511, 518
Feild, Hubert, 189, 344, 516, 519
Ferguson, L.W., 342
Fine, Sidney A., 245
Fleishman, Edwin, 217, 245
Flippo, Edwin B., 448
Flory, Abram, 294, 309
Foley, John, 417
Fontelle, Gail A., 369, 382
French, Wendal, 304, 310
Freyd, M., 22
Friedman, A., 342
Funder, David C., 449

Gail, Sidney, 500
Garcia, J.R., 301, 310
Garner, Kathleen, 369, 382
Gatewood, Robert D., 381, 457, 487, 488
Ghiselli, Edwin, 22, 85, 166, 167, 337, 338, 401, 402, 404, 498, 519
Ghorpade, Jai, 172, 188
Giles, William F., 344
Gilmore, David C., 373, 382
Glaser, E.M., 86
Glennon, J.R., 334, 336, 342, 343
Gleser, Goldine C., 117
Goheen, H.W., 299, 304, 310
Goldstein, Irwin L., 292, 309, 340, 344
Goodstein, Leonard D., 449
Gordon, Michael F., 487
Gordon, Raymond, 381, 382
Gother, Richard, 421
Gottier, Richard F., 449
Gough, Harrison G., 449
Grant, Donald L., 449, 450, 487, 500, 519
Greenthol, Alan, 487
Grimsley, Glen, 421, 449
Grove, David, 373, 382
Guion, Robert, 13, 14, 21, 22, 85, 100, 117, 127, 151, 162, 166, 167, 387, 418, 421, 447, 449

Haetner, James, 382
Hahn, Clifford, 217, 245, 274
Hakel, Milton D., 186, 189
Hargrove, Faye, 381
Harris, Michael, 400, 418

Hartshorne, Hugh, 425, 444, 449, 450
Hathaway, Starke R., 449
Hazel, J.T., 186, 189
Hellervik, Lowell, 373, 382
Hennessey, Harry W., 488
Henry, Edwin, 326, 330, 338, 343, 344
Herriot, Peter, 425, 449
Hinrichs, John R., 488
Hock, James R., 488
Hoiberg, A., 330, 343
Holden, Ronald R., 448
Hollenbeck, George, 216
Holley, William, 516, 519
Hollman, Thomas, 381
Holt, Robert, 449
Holt, Thaddeus, 48
Howard, George, 382
Hunter, John, 161, 164, 405, 418, 487, 519
Hunter, Ronda, 418

Ilgen, Daniel, 381

Jackson, Douglas N., 448, 449
Jackson, R.H., 302, 310
Janz, Tom, 373, 382
Jarrett, Hilton, 421, 449
Jeanneret, Paul R., 273
Jennings, Margaret C., 245
Jones, Jean J., 188

Katzell, Raymond A., 22
Keenan, Andrew, 381
Kelly, Harold H., 450
Kelly, T., 117
Kerlinger, Fred N., 85
Kiechel, Walter, 309
Kirchner, W.K., 324
Kleiman, Larry S., 166, 487
Kleinmutz, Benjamin, 449
Klopfer, Bruno, 449
Klopfer, Walter, 449
Kolb, David, 449
Korman, Abraham K., 338, 343, 344
Kotter, John P., 21
Kuhnert, Kenneth, 382
Kuzmits, Frank E., 21, 178, 188, 448

Lahy, Par, 383, 417
Landy, Frank, 85, 166, 167, 377, 382, 492, 511, 518, 519

Lane, Irving, 339, 344
Langdale, John A., 296, 310
Lanyon, Richard L., 449
Latham, Gary, 382, 492, 519
Lawshe, Charles, 83, 85, 86, 166, 167, 186, 188, 189
Ledvinka, James, 24, 26, 48
Lee, Raymond, 314, 342
Levine, Edward, 216, 219, 221, 273, 294, 309, 310
Lewin, David, 254, 273
Lilenthal, Richard A., 310, 311
Lockwood, H.C., 342
Lopez, Felix E., 450
Lopez, Felix M., 450
Lowell, Richard S., 289, 309
Lykken, David Z., 418

McCarthy, William, 245
McClelland, David, 423, 434, 449
McCormick, Ernest J., 188, 189, 205, 263, 273, 342, 418
McCulloch, Kenneth J., 48
McKenzie, Robert C., 519
McKinley, J. Charnely, 449
Madden, J.M., 186, 189, 202
Malinowski, Frank A., 310
Manaugh, T.S., 302, 310
Marquardt, L.D., 273
Matarazzo, J.D., 302, 310
May, Mark, 425, 442, 449, 450
Mayfield, Eugene, 381
Mecham, Robert C., 273
Mehrabran, A., 302, 310
Menne, John W., 245
Menne, Joy, 245
Meyer, Herbert H., 186, 189
Milk, Leslie B., 48
Miller, Ernest, 283, 290, 309
Miner, John, 332, 333, 343, 434, 449, 450
Mischel, Walter, 448, 449, 450
Mitchell, James V., 85, 418
Morrison, Robert F., 336, 344
Morsh, J.E., 203, 204, 205
Mosel, J.N., 22, 291, 299, 304, 309, 310, 340, 342, 344
Muchinsky, Paul M., 311
Muldrow, Tressie W., 519
Murphy, Kevin, 150, 167
Murray, Henry A., 449
Mussio, Stephan J., 273
Myers, David C., 245
Myers, Donald W., 188

Nash, A.N., 299, 310, 311
Naylor, James C., 117, 167, 310
Nunnally, Jum, 52, 85, 111, 117

Oliver, Richard, 338, 344
Olson, Howard C., 245
O'Reilly, A.P., 186, 189
Organ, Dennis W., 382
Osburn, H.G., 340, 344
Owens, William, 314, 326, 327, 329, 330, 332, 334, 336, 337, 338, 339, 341, 343, 344

Pace, Larry, 324, 325, 332, 342, 343, 344
Packard, Gary L., 450
Palmer, Chester I., 187, 189
Parsons, S.O., 342
Peacock, Andrew C., 448, 449
Pearlman, Kenneth, 519
Peres, S.H., 301, 310
Perlson, Michael R., 166
Peterson, Donald, 381
Phillip, James, 125, 166
Phillips, Niel, 470, 487
Plumlee, Lynette B., 487
Popovich, Paula, 381
Porter, Wayne, 294, 309
Price, Richard H., 449
Prien, Erich, 178, 189, 518
Primoff, Ernest, 244, 245
Pugh, W.M., 330, 343
Pursell, Elliott, 382, 519
Pyron, H.C., 302, 304, 306, 310, 311, 344

Reilly, Richard, 338, 339, 344, 408, 411, 418
Rendero, Thomas, 188
Rice, John D., 311
Ricks, James H., 86
Ritchie, Richard, 500, 519
Roach, Darrell E., 342
Robinson, David, 455, 457, 487
Romashko, Tania, 217, 245, 274
Ronan, William W., 518
Rorschach, Hermann, 432
Rosenbaum, R.W., 325, 342
Rosenfeld, Michael, 181, 189
Rowe, Patricia, 381
Russell, J.T., 161, 167

Sackett, Paul, 356, 369, 400, 418, 488
Saye, Leonard, 418
Schmidt, Frank, 21, 161, 164, 405, 487, 519
Schmitt, Neil, 356, 381
Schneider, Benjamin, 344
Schneider, David J., 450
Schneiderman, M.L., 310
Schoenfeldt, Barbara, 166
Schoenfeldt, Lyle, 116, 324, 325, 332, 337, 341, 342, 343, 344, 345, 457, 486, 487, 488
Schrader, Alec D., 340, 344
Schuler, Randall S., 21, 188
Schwab, Donald P., 338, 348, 450
Schwartz, Donald, 177
Sciarrino, James A., 338, 344, 487
Scott, Walter D., 352
Seashore, Harold G., 86
Seaton, Felicia, 487
Selover, R.B., 418
Shaw, James B., 273
Sherman, Mark, 448, 449, 450
Shimberg, Benjamin, 487
Shine, L.C., 167
Siegal, Laurence, 339, 344
Silverman, S.B., 187, 189
Simon, Theodore, 386
Sistrunk, Frank, 204, 216, 245
Smith, Jack E., 186, 189
Smith, Joelle P., 449
Smith, Mary K., 273
Smith, Philip, 204, 245
Snyder, Melvin, 450
Sparks, Paul, 186, 189
Springbett, B., 381
Stone, J.L., 309
Super, Donald E., 417, 418
Swann, William, 450

Taylor, Edwin, 161, 513, 519
Taylor, H.C., 167
Taylor, W.H., 189
Teare, Robert J., 189
Tenopyr, Mary L., 167
Thayer, Paul, 381
Thompson, Duane, 175, 188
Thompson, Toni, 175, 188
Thorndike, Robert, 86, 156, 157
Thornton, George C., 487, 488
Thornton, Richard F., 181, 189
Tiffin, Joseph, 418

Todor, William D., 518
Trattner, Marvin H., 245
Travers, R.M., 341, 345
Trumbo, Don, 85, 350, 381

Ulrich, Lynn, 350, 381
Urry, Vernon, 405, 418

Valenzi, Enzo, 381
Vance, Robert, 382
Veres, John G., 187, 189
Viteles, Morris, 342

Wangler, L.A., 307, 311
Wanous, John, 9, 21, 381
Weiss, David J., 291, 309, 340, 344

Weitz, Joseph, 296, 310
Wernimont, Paul, 324, 342, 454, 455, 487
Wesman, Alexander, 110, 117
Wexley, Kenneth N., 187, 189, 382, 492, 519
Wiener, Y., 310
Wiens, A.N., 302, 310
Wiggins, Jerry S., 167
Williams, William E., 332, 343
Womer, Frank, 112, 117

Yerkes, Robert, 383

Zedeck, Sheldon, 22, 166, 167
Zerga, J.E., 188

Subject Index

Ability, 251
Ability Tests,
  definition of, 384–385
  and discrimination, 407–412
  lists of selected tests & publishers,
    416–417
  recommendations for use,
    412–415
  validity of, 401–404
Adverse Impact,
  and ability tests, 407–412
  and application blanks, 278–280
  and assessment centers, 485–486
  and biographical data forms,
    339–340
  definition of, 31
  and the interview, 363–365
  and performance tests, 469–470
Age Discrimination in Employment
    Act of 1967, 281
Age Discrimination in Employment
    Act of 1974, 27, 29
Albemarle Paper Company v. Moody
    (1975), 40–41, 175
Application Forms,
  accuracy of data, 291–292
  checklist for, 292–293
  development of, 289–291
  examples of legally acceptable/
    unacceptable questions,
    284–288
  legal implications of, 278–280
  nature of, 277–278
  revision of, 289–291
  selecting content of, 280–289
  use in Human Resource Selection,
    292–298
Assessment Centers,
  adverse impact of, 485–486
  assessment devices used,
    475–479
  definition of, 471
  dimensions of, 473–475
  effectiveness of, 484–487
  history of, 471–473
  limitations of, 486–487
  training of assessors, 479–484
  validity of, 484–485

*Bannerman v. Department of Youth
    Authority,* 364
Base Rate, 159–161

Behavioral Assessment,
  and Personality Measurement,
    424–444
Behavioral Consistency, 454–455
Bennett Mechanical Comprehension
    Test, 392–393
Biographical Data,
  accuracy of, 340
  advantages of, 329–330
  assumptions of, 330–331
  criticisms of, 340–342
  definition of, 326–327
  legality of, 339–340
  types of items, 327–329
Biographical Data Questionnaire,
  development of, 331–334
  validity of, 337–342

Civil Rights Act of 1964, Title VII,
    26–27
Clerical Ability Tests,
  Minnesota Clerical Test, 395–396
Comprehensive Occupational Data
    Analysis Program (CODAP),
    225–228
Concurrent Validity, 121–126
Connecticut v. Teal (1982), 43–44,
    45
Construct Validity, 139–140
Content Validity,
  strategies of, 128–137
  and the Uniform Guidelines, 137
  versus criterion related validation,
    137–138
Correlation, 140–143
Criteria Variables, 53, 65–67,
    492–506
Criterion Contamination, 156–157,
    510
Criterion Related Validity,
  strategies of, 121–128
  versus content validation, 137–138
Cronbach's Coefficient Alpha, 106
Cross Validation, 149–150

Differential Validity, 407–408
Discrimination,
  forms of, 30–32
  measurement of, 32–34
Dreher-Sackett Model of Interviewer,
  Information Seeking, Receipt, and
    Processing, 356

EEOC v. Detroit Edison (1975),
    42–43, 45
EEOC v. National Academy of
    Sciences, 350
Empirical Validation, 14
Employee Specifications,
    determination of, PAQ Approach,
        263–265
    determination of, task analysis
        approach, 249–262
    determining relative importance of,
        266–267
    identification of, 248–249
    incorporation into selection
        instruments, 265–272
    licensure/certification, 256–257
    physical requirements, 255–256
    selection methods to measure,
        267–268
Equal Employment Opportunity
    (EEO),
    laws and executive orders of,
        26–29
    regulatory model of, 24–26
Equal Employment Opportunity
    Commission (EEOC),
    Guidelines on Discrimination Due
        to National Origin, 282
    Guide to Pre-Employment
        Inquiries, 278–279, 280, 288
Equivalent Forms of Reliability
    Estimates, 100–102
Error Score, 92, 94
Executive Order 11246, 27–28
Expectancy Charts, 150–151
Expectancy Tables, 150–151
Experience and Training Forms,
    293–298

Four-Fifths Rule, 32
Functional Job Analysis (FJA),
    234–242

Griggs v. Duke Power Company, 38,
    45, 174
Guidelines Oriented Job Analysis
    (GOJA), 229–231

Harless v. Duck, 364
Hester v. Southern Railway, 364
Honesty Testing,
    paper-and-pencil honesty tests,
        400–401
    polygraphs, 398–399

In-Basket, 476–477
Intentional Prejudice, 30
Internal Consistency Reliability
    Estimates, 102–103
Interval Scale of Measurement,
    60–62
Interview,
    appropriate KSA's, 367
    attempts to improve, 359–363
    common deficiencies in, 352
    court cases, 363–365
    formal scoring format, 376–377
    inappropriate information, 353–356
    interviewer decision making,
        356–359
    and job analysis methods,
        194–201
    job related questions, 371–374
    recommendations for use,
        366–381
    scoring of, 362, 378
    semi-structured format, 370
    sex stereotypes, 365
    training in the process of, 361–362
    use of interview panels, 363,
        377–389
    use of pre-interview data, 369
    uses in selection, 348–353
Interview Panels, 363, 377–379
Iowa Merit Employment System
    (IMES), 231–234

Job Agents, 183–188
Job Analysis,
    court cases involving, 174–177
    criteria for choosing jobs, 179–182
    defined, 11, 130, 171–172
    implementation of, 177–187
    legal issues in, 174
    organizing for, 177–179
    role in Human Resource Selection,
        171–177
Job Analysis Interview,
    definition of, 196–199
    guidelines for use, 199–201
    limitations of, 201
Job Analysis Methods,
    categorization of, 193–194
    comparison of, 215–222
    Comprehensive Occupational Data
        Analysis Program, 225–228
    Functional Job Analysis, 234–242
    Guidelines Oriented Job Analysis,
        229–231

Iowa Merit Employment System,
231–234
Job Element Method, 242–244
Position Analysis Questionnaire,
209–214
Task Analysis Inventory, 202–208
Job Analysis Questionnaire,
description of, 202
task analysis inventory, 202–208
Job Element Method (JEM), 242–244
Job Performance Measures,
associated court cases, 516–518
types of, 492–506
and Uniform Guidelines, 514–516
Judgemental Data Performance
Measures, 500–506

*King v. New Hampshire Department
of Resources and Economic
Development,* 363–364
Knowledge, 251
KSA's,
definition of, 251
identification of, for selection
program, 261–263
linking to job tasks, 257–259
methods of rating importance of,
253–255
specification of, 250
statements, the writing of, 251–252
use of a rating panel, 250–253
Kuder-Richardson Reliability
Estimates, 105–106

Labor Market Analysis, 33
Leaderless Group Discussion,
477–478
Linear Regression, 144–149

MacQuarrie Test for Mechanical
Ability, 393–394
Measurement,
defined, 18, 51–52
errors of, 89–94
nature of, 51
scales of, 55–63
standard error of, 114–115
Mechanical Ability Tests,
Bennett Mechanical
Comprehension Test, 392–393
definition of, 391–392
MacQuarrie Test for Mechanical
Ability, 393–394

Minnesota Mechanical Assembly
Test, 392
Stenquist Mechanical Assembly
Test, 391
Mental Ability Tests,
abilities measured by, 388
history of, 386–387
nature of questions, 387
Otis Self-Administering Test, 386
Wechsler Adult Intelligence Scale,
389–391
Wonderlic Personnel Test,
387–389
Minnesota Clerical Test, 395–396
Minnesota Mechanical Assembly
Test, 392
Multiple vs. Single Criteria, 511–514

Nominal Scale of Measurement, 58
Norms, 81–82

Ordinal Scale of Measurement,
58–60
Otis Self-Administering Test of
Mental Ability, 386

Parallel Forms of Reliability
Estimates, 100–102
Percentiles, 82–85
Performance Tests,
adverse impact of, 469–470
applicants reactions to, 470
and consistency of behavior,
454–455
differences from other selection
devices, 451–453
limitations of, 453–454
motor tests, 455–457
scoring of, 462–464
steps in developments of, 458–466
training of judges, 464–465
validity of, 469
verbal tests, 457–458
Personality,
definition of, 420
methods of measurement,
427–437
use in selection, 420–421, 444–448
Personality Inventories, 427–430
Personality Measurement,
and Behavioral Assessment,
442–444

Personality Measurement, (Continued)
  California Psychological Inventory,
    429–430
    and the Interview, 437–442
  Miner Sentence Completion Scale,
    434–435
  Minnesota Multiphasic Personality
    Inventory, 428–429
  Rorschach Inkblot Technique,
    432–433
  Thematic Apperception Test,
    433–434
Personality Traits,
  central vs. surface, 423
  definition of, 422
  interaction with situations,
    425–427
  and job behaviors, 444–445
  and situational factors, 446–447
*Personnel Administrator of
    Massachusetts v. Feeney
    (1979)*, 44, 45
Personnel Data Performance
    Measures, 494–498
Position Analysis Questionnaire,
  advantages of, 212–214
  application of, 211–212
  description of, 209–211
  disadvantages of, 212–214
  job dimensions of, 213
Prediction Equation, 144–149
Predictive Validity, 126–128
Predictor Variables, 53, 64–65
Production Data Performance
    Measures, 492–494

Ratio Scale of Measurement, 62–63
Realistic Job Preview, 349
Recruitment, 7–9
  and selection, 5
Reference Checks,
  legal issues of, 305–309
  methods of collecting data,
    299–303
  reliability of data, 304–305
  role of, in selection, 298
  steps for use of, 307–309
  types of information collected,
    298–299
  and Uniform Guidelines, 306–309
  validity of data, 304–305
Rehabilitation Act of 1973, 27, 28–29
Reliability,
  definition of, 89

  methods of estimating, 94–106
  and validation, 120–121
Reliability Coefficients,
  acceptable level of, 110–111
  definition of, 107–108
  evaluation of, 116–117
  interpretation of, 107
*The Richmond Black Police Officers
    Association v. the City of
    Richmond*, 486
*Rutherford v. American Bank of
    Commerce*, 305

Selection Criteria Measures,
    506–511
Selection Measures,
  construction of new, 73–74
  criteria for evaluating, 67–68
  development of content areas, 259
  interpreting scores on, 81–85
  sources for locating old, 70–73
  steps in developing, 74–81
  types of, 64
  utility of, 161
Selection Plan,
  development of, PAQ approach,
    270–272
  development of, task analysis
    approach, 266–270
Selection Ratio, 158–159
Semi-Structured Interview, 360–361,
    370
Sensory Ability Tests, 396–397
Single vs. Multiple Criteria, 511–514
Skill, 251
Split-half Reliability Estimates,
    103–105
Spurlock v. United Airlines, 43, 45
Stamps v. Detroit Edison, 363, 364
Standard Deviation Rule, 32
Standard Error of Measurement,
    114–115
Standard Scores, 82–85
Stenquist Mechanical Assembly
    Test, 391
Synthetic Validity, 162–164

Task Analysis,
  advantages of, 208
  disadvantages of, 208
  guidelines for developing, in
    selection, 206–208

Task Analysis Approach to Determining Employee Specifications, 249–262
Task Analysis Inventory, description of, 202–208
development of, 205–206
phrasing of tasks, 203–204
rating scales, 203–206
Task Statements, 196
Test-Retest Reliability Estimates, 96–100
Training and Experience Forms, 293–298
Training of Interviewers, 359–360, 379–381
Training Proficiency Performance Data, 498–500
True Score, 91

Unequal Treatment, 31
Uniform Guidelines on Employee Selection Procedures (1978),
and content validation, 137
description of, 35–38
and job performance measures, 514–516
and reference checks, 306–309
United States v. Georgia Power (1973), 39–40, 45
United States v. Hazelwood School District, 363, 364

Utility of Selection Measures, 161

Validation Procedures, 14
strategies of, 121–140
Validity,
definition of, 119–120
and reliability, 120–121
Validity Coefficients,
computing of, 140–143
factors affecting size of, 151–158
minimum value of, 158–161
restrictions of range of, 153–156
use in prediction, 144
Validity Generalization, 164–165, 404–406
Vietnam Era Veteran's Readjustment Act of 1974, 27, 29

Washington v. Davis (1975), 41–42, 45
Wechsler Adult Intelligence Scale, 389–391
Weighted Application Blanks,
definition of, 292
development of, 315–322
legal considerations of, 324–326
nature of, 314–315
use in Human Resource Selection, 322–326
Weiner v. County of Oakland, 363, 364
Wonderlic Personnel Test, 387–389